Population Health
INFORMATICS

Driving Evidence-Based Solutions into Practice

Edited by

Ashish Joshi, PhD, MBBS, MPH

Associate Dean of Students
Associate Professor
Graduate School of Public Health and Health Policy
The City University of New York
New York, New York

Lorna Thorpe, PhD, MPH

Professor
Department of Population Health
New York University School of Medicine
New York, New York

Levi Waldron, PhD, MSS

Assistant Professor
Graduate School of Public Health and Health Policy
The City University of New York
New York, New York

JONES & BARTLETT
LEARNING

W9-DDQ-549

Handwritten annotations:

③ Econ assess
check — ④ Emergency
⑤ telemed
⑥

① Aid monitork
② pH admn tools
 besign
 chatroom

⑥ monte
 cerlo

no code
↓
excel
↓
monte cerlo
↓
dashboard
↓
web

⑦ LAW?

Brother
mFC
— L2720
DW

voice chutt
 no code
need
jevescript?

630 823 2000
scottishplumber
.com

World Headquarters
Jones & Bartlett Learning
5 Wall Street
Burlington, MA 01803
978-443-5000
info@jblearning.com
www.jblearning.com

Jones & Bartlett Learning books and products are available through most bookstores and online booksellers. To contact Jones & Bartlett Learning directly, call 800-832-0034, fax 978-443-8000, or visit our website, www.jblearning.com.

Substantial discounts on bulk quantities of Jones & Bartlett Learning publications are available to corporations, professional associations, and other qualified organizations. For details and specific discount information, contact the special sales department at Jones & Bartlett Learning via the above contact information or send an email to specialsales@jblearning.com.

Production Credits

VP, Executive Publisher: David D. Cella
Publisher: Michael Brown
Associate Editor: Danielle Bessette
Senior Production Editor: Amanda Clerkin
Production Editor: Vanessa Richards
Senior Marketing Manager: Sophie Fleck Teague
Manufacturing and Inventory Control Supervisor: Amy Bacus
Composition: codeMantra U.S. LLC
Cover Design: Theresa Manley
Rights & Media Specialist: Merideth Tumasz
Media Development Editor: Shannon Sheehan
Cover Image (Title Page, Part Opener, Chapter Opener): © VLADGRIN/Shutterstock
Printing and Binding: Edwards Brothers Malloy
Cover Printing: Edwards Brothers Malloy

Library of Congress Cataloging-in-Publication Data

Names: Joshi, Ashish, 1975- editor. | Thorpe, Lorna, 1967- editor. | Waldron, Levi, 1973- editor.
Title: Population health informatics : driving evidence-based solutions into practice / Edited by Ashish Joshi, Lorna Thorpe, Levi Waldron.
Description: Burlington, Massachusetts : Jones & Bartlett Learning, [2019] | Includes bibliographical references and index.
Identifiers: LCCN 2017011759 | ISBN 9781284103960
Subjects: | MESH: Public Health Informatics | Medical Informatics Applications | Demography
Classification: LCC R858 | NLM WA 26.5 | DDC 610.285—dc23
LC record available at https://lccn.loc.gov/2017011759

6048
Printed in the United States of America
21 20 19 18 17   10 9 8 7 6 5 4 3 2 1

Contents

Foreword

I n the past two decades, informatics as a terminology has been widely disseminated. Within the health sciences context, medical informatics and bioinformatics have played an important role in advancing the health services domain
as well as in discovering biological associations and informing new treatment
discoveries. Population health informatics is a newer emerging science that promises to influence global health dynamics in a unique and significant way. This
text elucidates the underpinnings of this terminology, and explains its unique
parameters and singularly effective applications both from descriptive and inter-
ventional dimensions. The readership of this text will gain new insights and will
be able to use newly acquired knowledge in both theoretical and applied context.
Knowledge gained through this text will inform large data users, health scientists
and researchers, health administrators, and policymakers, as well as economists and
modelers. Many of the challenges associated with population health informatics
relate to difficulties in assembling data, combining data sources, identifying innovative approaches to data analysis, and finally, extracting the most relevant and pertinent information toward predicting and resolving emergent and prevalent health
problems. Many of these challenges are addressed and demystified in this text, in a
way that is accessible to students, researchers, and practitioners in the field.

Ayman El-Mohandes, MD, MBBCh, MPH
Dean, The City University of New York
Graduate School of Public Health and Health Policy
New York, New York

Acknowledgments

This book would not have been possible without the wholehearted support and participation of several individuals. First, we would like to thank the Dean of the CUNY Graduate School of Public Health and Health Policy, Dr. Ayman El-Mohandes, for his motivation and invaluable support and commitment to helping us bring this book to its completion.

We would also like to thank Chioma Amadi, Research Associate and a doctoral student of Epidemiology of CUNY Graduate School of Public Health and Health Policy, for her valuable assistance in writing a chapter and reviewing the content of the book. Further, we would like to thank Princy Bhardwaj, MPH, Environmental and Occupational Health Sciences, and Rinzin Wangmo, MPH, Health Policy and Management, who provided assistance in reviewing the references included in the book and gave us valuable insight about their level of understanding of the content of the book.

In addition, we acknowledge the extraordinary competence of our Executive Editor, Michael Brown, and Associate Editor, Danielle Bessette, at Jones & Bartlett Learning, who guided us through the publication stages and provided valuable advice. Our Senior Production Editor, Amanda Clerkin, and her colleagues adeptly dealt with a number of challenges to make this book look better than it would have otherwise.

Finally, we would also like to acknowledge the chapter contributors who played a very significant role in making this book possible. Despite their hectic work commitments, they shared their expertise by writing the chapters, responding to inquiries, and modifying the draft chapters as suggested. We are very thankful to these esteemed contributors who come from various areas of population health informatics.

Contributors

Chioma Amadi, MPH
Research Associate, Doctoral Student
in Epidemiology
CUNY Graduate School of Public
Health and Health Policy
New York, New York

Luk Arbuckle, BSc, MSc
Research Manager
Children's Hospital of Eastern
Ontario Research Institute
Ottawa, Ontario, Canada

Ann Cavoukian, PhD
Executive Director
Privacy and Big Data Institute,
Ryerson University
Toronto, Ontario, Canada

Michelle Chibba, MA
Strategic Privacy/Policy Advisor
Privacy and Big Data Institute,
Ryerson University
Toronto, Ontario, Canada

Brian E. Dixon, PhD, MPA, FIMMS
Associate Professor
Richard M. Fairbanks School of
Public Health Researcher
Center for Biomedical Informatics,
Regenstrief Institute
Indianapolis, Indiana

Khaled El Emam, PhD
Professor
Department of Pediatrics, Faculty of
Medicine, University of Ottawa
Ottawa, Ontario, Canada

Hadi Kharrazi, MD, PhD
Research Director
Center for Population Health IT
Johns Hopkins Bloomberg School of
Public Health
Baltimore, Maryland

Harold P. Lehmann, MD, PhD
Associate Professor
Johns Hopkins Bloomberg School of
Public Health
Baltimore, Maryland

Edward Mensah, PhD
Associate Professor
Health Policy and Administration,
School of Public Health
University of Illinois at Chicago
Chicago, Illinois

Katharine H. McVeigh, PhD, MPH
Director of Research
Division of Family and Child Health,
NYC Department of Health and
Mental Hygiene
Queens, New York

Saurabh Rahurkar, BDS, DrPH
Postdoctoral Public Health Informatics
Fellow
Center for Biomedical Informatics,
Regenstrief Institute
Indianapolis, Indiana

About the Editors

Ashish Joshi, PhD, MBBS, MPH
Associate Dean and Associate Professor
CUNY Graduate School of Public Health and Health Policy and the CUNY Institute
for Implementation Science in Population Health

Ashish Joshi is an Associate Dean of the CUNY Graduate School of Public Health and Health Policy and an Associate Professor at CUNY Institute for Implementation Science in Population Health. Dr. Joshi's combined training in medicine, public health, and informatics provides a unique combination to utilize innovative technology-enabled interventions at the intersection of clinical care and population health. Dr. Joshi's journey has been that of an academician, applied researcher, administrator, innovator, and entrepreneur to implement sustainable, multi-sector, accessible, affordable, reimbursable, and tailored (SMAART) technology solutions to address the population health challenges of the 21st century. His research interest focuses on the design, development, implementation, and evaluation of contextually relevant informatics interventions to enhance population health outcomes. Dr. Joshi utilizes the principles of social cognitive theory, human-centered design, and information processing theory to develop culturally relevant health technology solutions that can be adapted to different settings, audiences, and health conditions. Dr. Joshi has done several population health informatics projects in various countries including the United States, Nigeria, India, Brazil, and Haiti. His research related to mobile and Internet-enabled interventions, population-based surveillance, consumer health informatics, and health dashboards has been widely funded by several national and international agencies.

Lorna Thorpe, PhD, MPH
Professor and Director of Epidemiology
NYU School of Medicine, Department of Population Health

Lorna Thorpe is Professor of Epidemiology and Director of the Epidemiology Division at the NYU School of Medicine in the Department of Population Health. Her current research focuses on improving modern forms of public health surveillance, as well as the intersection between epidemiology and policy, mostly with respect to chronic disease prevention and management. Dr. Thorpe is on the Board of Directors for the American College of Epidemiology, has served on Institute of Medicine committees, and has been an advisor to the Centers for Disease Control and Prevention (CDC) on population health surveillance issues. Prior to joining academia, Dr. Thorpe spent 8 years at the New York City Department of Health and Mental Hygiene, serving as Deputy Commissioner of Epidemiology for much of that time. Dr. Thorpe began her applied research career as a CDC Epidemic Intelligence Service Officer in international tuberculosis control. Dr. Thorpe completed her PhD in epidemiology at the University of Illinois at Chicago, her MPH at University of Michigan, and her BA at Johns Hopkins University. She has lived and worked in Asia (China, Indonesia) and published widely on both chronic and infectious disease topics.

Levi Waldron, PhD, MSS
Assistant Professor
CUNY Graduate School of Public Health and Health Policy and the CUNY Institute for Implementation Science in Population Health

Levi Waldron completed his education at the University of British Columbia (BSc), University of Waterloo (MSS), and University of Toronto (PhD). After doing post-docs at the Ontario Cancer Institute and Harvard School of Public Health, he took a faculty position in biostatistics at CUNY. He is a technical advisor to the Bioconductor open-source project for computational biology, and was a Fulbright scholar to Italy where he taught applied statistics for high-throughput biology. He continues to pursue interests in high-dimensional data analysis, particularly the development of databases and methods for integrating genomics data into cancer and microbiome research.

Introduction

The rapid growth in digital data due to the increased usage of mobile phones and wearable sensors has created an urgent need to develop new, innovative tools and technologies that can make data meaningful. Population health informatics is an emerging field that aims to utilize technology to put into practice evidence-based solutions to improve population health outcomes across diverse settings. The goal of this book is to present a practical, step-by-step approach on how to implement evidence-based, data-driven informatics solutions to enhance population health. We aim to engage students and professionals across various disciplines who are interested in using technology as a medium to reduce health disparities and improve healthcare access and delivery in diverse settings.

The book is broadly divided into four parts:

Part 1: Overview of Population Health Informatics
Part 2: Setting the Stage for Population Health Informatics
Part 3: Specialized Population Health Informatics Applications
Part 4: Other Population Health Informatics Topical Areas

Part 1 begins by describing the need for population health informatics (Chapter 1) and then discusses the workforce's needs, competencies, and the various training programs (Chapter 2). Part 2 discusses differences among data, information, and knowledge (Chapter 3); health information exchange and related interoperability (Chapter 4); informatics-enabled population health surveillance (Chapter 5); statistical issues (Chapter 6); and opportunities and challenges related to big data due to the rapid increase in data volume, velocity, and variety (Chapter 7). Chapter 7 also examines the role of cloud computing and population health visual analytics to facilitate population health data storage, data analysis, and data visualization in a meaningful format. Part 3 describes the specialized population health informatics applications such as design, development, and system evaluation (Chapter 8); electronic health records and telehealth applications (Chapter 9); personal health records (Chapter 10); and the opportunities, challenges, and applications related to mobile health interventions (Chapter 11). Lastly, Part 4 discusses other key population health informatics topics related to the economic value of informatics applications in population health (Chapter 12); issues related to privacy, confidentiality, security, and ethics (Chapter 13); and the role of innovations and sustainability in population health technologies (Chapter 14).

We hope that the information and resources provided in this textbook help readers to better understand the utilization of information and communication technology–enabled interventions and innovations in the United States and beyond. The book fulfills a key component of the new Association of Schools and Programs of Public Health recommendations for "Critical Components for the Core of a 21st Century MPH Degree." The book also equips a new generation of the workforce with the expertise necessary to make data meaningful and to design, develop, and evaluate accessible and affordable technology-enabled solutions to effectively address the population health challenges of the 21st century.

Ashish Joshi, PhD, MBBS, MPH
Lorna Thorpe, PhD, MPH
Levi Waldron, PhD, MSS

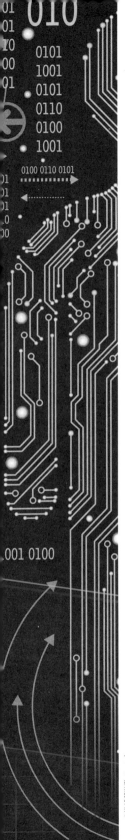

PART 1

Overview of Population Health Informatics

© VLADGRIN/Shutterstock

CHAPTER 1

Emerging Need for Population Health Informatics

Ashish Joshi

KEY TERMS

Affordable Care Act (ACA)
American Recovery and Reinvestment Act
of 2009 (ARRA)
Cognitive fit theory
Electronic health records (EHRs)
Geographic information systems (GISs)

Health information technology
Population health
Population health informatics (PopHI)
Public health informatics (PHI)
Social determinants of health

LEARNING OBJECTIVES

- Describe the growth of the Internet and social media in the 21st century.
- Define population health and its determinants.
- Distinguish between population and public health informatics.
- Assess the importance of social determinants of health data.
- Examine the intersection of technology and health care.
- List the challenges and opportunities related to population health informatics solutions.
- List the factors to consider in the adoption and implementation of population health informatics solutions.

QUESTIONS FOR THOUGHT

- What is the significance of social determinants of health to enhance population health outcomes?
- What opportunities does the growing usage of the Internet, mobile media, and social media have on health?
- How can stakeholders and consumers address the challenges related to implementation of population health informatics solutions in diverse settings?
- What opportunities do population health informatics solutions provide to improve population health outcomes?

CHAPTER OUTLINE

▶ I. Population Health and Its Determinants

D rivers of health outside the traditional medical care include social, behavioral, and environmental determinants and need to be addressed to improve health and diminish health disparities. The section below highlights the significance of these factors in the improvement of population health outcomes.

Defining Population Health

Population health describes the health needs of a defined group's entire life span (Evans, Barer, & Marmor, 1994). Population health is a linking thread to help understand the determinants of health of populations (Evans et al., 1994). Social, economic, and physical environments; personal health practices; individual capacity; and coping skills all influence health status indicators. In turn, the health status indicators measure population health (Kindig & Stoddart, 2003). Population health is also considered as a summary measure that includes mortality and health-related quality of life (Field & Gold, 1998) (TABLE 1.1).

Public health services are typically provided by government agencies and include the core public health functions of health assessment, assurance, and policy setting. Several differences exist among the various aspects of Population health and public health, as shown here. Population health

TABLE 1.1 Overview of the Definitions of Population Health

Definition of Population Health	Source
Exploring reasons about some populations being healthier than others	Young, T. K. (2005). *Population health: Concepts and methods.* New York, NY: Oxford University Press.
Improve health and reduce health inequalities of diverse populations	Health Canada. (1998). *Taking action on population health.* Ottawa, Ontario: Health Canada.
Paradigm for understanding why some populations have better health outcomes than others	Young, T. K. (1998). *Population health: Concepts and methods.* New York, NY: Oxford University Press.
Focuses on factors that influence the health of populations over the life course, variations in their patterns of occurrence resulting in actions, and policies to improve health and well-being of populations	Dunn, J. R., & Hayes, M. V. (1999). Toward a lexicon of population health. *Canadian Journal of Public Health, 90,* S7.
Highlight[s the] role of social and economic forces in combination with biological and environmental factors that shape the health of entire populations	Kreuter, M., & Lezin, N. (2001). *Improving everyone's quality of life: A primer on population health.* Atlanta, GA: Group Health Community Foundation.
Health outcomes of a group of individuals, including the distribution of such outcomes within the group	Kindig, D., & Stoddart, G. (2003). What is population health? *American Journal of Public Health, 93*(3), 380–383.
Improve[s] the health of populations as one element in the Institute for Healthcare Improvement's (IHI) Triple Aim	Berwick, D. M., Nolan, T. W., & Whittington, J. (2008). The triple aim: Care, health, and cost. *Health Affairs, 27*(3), 759–769.
Approach that fosters decision making by policymakers, allowing them to assess the implications of non-health-related policies	Bostic, R. W., Thornton, R. L., Rudd, E. C., & Sternthal, M. J. (2012). Health in all policies: The role of the US Department of Housing and Urban Development and present and future challenges. *Health Affairs, 31*(9), 2130–2137.

- Is less associated with health departments at the government level (Stoto, 2013)
- Includes the healthcare delivery system and is seen as separate from governmental public health (Stoto, 2013)
- Is more than the sum of its individual parts (Stoto, 2013)
- Includes a broader array of the determinants of health than is typical in public health (Stiefel & Nolan, 2012)
- Has outcomes that go beyond state and local public health agencies and healthcare delivery systems (Ayana, 2016)

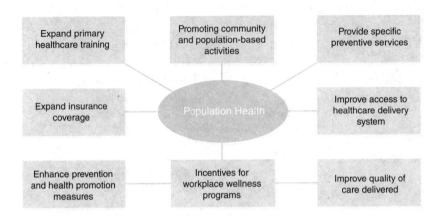

FIGURE 1.1 The Affordable Care Act

Data from Affordable Care Act. (2011). *Federal Sentencing Reporter, 23*(3).

The Affordable Care Act (ACA) addresses population health in several ways (ACA, 2011; see FIGURE 1.1). The ACA defined the affordable care organization (ACO), which includes clinicians, hospitals, and other healthcare organizations. They share mutual responsibility for the population of patients with the goal of improving health outcomes and reducing health costs and inefficiencies. A critical change is required by key stakeholders at the cultural, operational, and financial levels to improve population health. Collaboration among a variety of stakeholders (patients, providers, health plans, employers, government, the private sector, and the local community) is a vital component of the population health approach to strengthen care delivery and improve the well-being of individuals and families.

Determinants of Population Health

Multiple determinants, including educational, social, behavioral, and environmental factors, influence population health outcomes (Kindig & Stoddart, 2003; see FIGURE 1.2). Improving population health requires partners across many sectors including public health, healthcare organizations, community organizations, and businesses (Drummond & Stoddart, 1995). Population health data help organizations to do the following (Parrish, 2010):

- Identify at-risk populations
- Close communication gaps among individuals, public health agencies, and clinical care
- Identify cost-effective healthcare delivery models
- Provide access to available public health programs and services
- Improve population health decision making

Health and health problems result from a complex interplay of factors. Social determinants play a key role in the health of each individual. Social determinants of health have gained importance in recent health policy discussions. Existing literature has specified the importance of the social determinants of health in improving the health of populations. Education level, employment, income, family and social support, and community safety are all components of the social and economic determinants of health (County of Los Angeles Public Health, 2013). Unhealthy behaviors

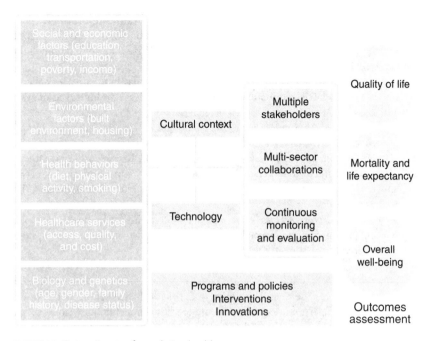

FIGURE 1.2 Determinants of population health

Modified Parrish, R. G. 2010. Measuring population health outcomes. *Preventing Chronic Disease,7*(4): A71. Retrieved from http://www.cdc.gov/pcd/issues/2010
/jul/10_0005.htm

are commonly associated with the lower social and economic position of a population or community. Poor education, lack of affordable housing, and insufficient income affect not just the individuals and families who have fewer resources, but also all the communities in which they live. Researchers estimate that access to quality medical care may prevent less than 20% of avoidable deaths. The remaining 80% of avoidable deaths are attributable to genetics (20%), and social, behavioral, and environmental determinants of health (60%; Taylor et al., 2016). Improvements in healthcare resources and other determinants are likely to have a large impact on prevention and the management of some illnesses (Starfield, 2006).

Gathering social determinants of health data would result in effective risk assessment to ultimately support population health management. It can help healthcare professionals to identify care gaps. Healthcare organizations can also get better insight into individual drivers of patient engagement and can match individuals to specific interventions, preventive services, or resources that are most likely to enhance outcomes. Social determinants of health have not been sufficiently recognized despite the knowledge of their impact on health outcomes and longevity. The interventions that address social, behavioral, and environmental determinants of health are also less developed. There is a need to generate integrated, evidence-based approaches to have a better impact on health outcome and lowering of healthcare costs. This gap has slowed health policymakers in promoting innovative models of care, even though these nonmedical determinants of health are worthy of attention.

Several challenges limit the integration of social determinants of health data. These impact evidence-based decision making, resulting in barriers to improving overall population health. Some of these challenges are (Robert Wood Johnson Foundation, 2016):

- *Limited knowledge of what works best:* Clinicians, healthcare providers, program operators, and researchers are utilizing data on social determinants of health to identify the best ways to collate and use these data so that guidelines can be evidence based.
- *Lack of standardization and tools:* The absence of standard measures for collecting data on social determinants leads to inconsistencies. This limits the analysis and decisions that can be made using such data.
- *Limited knowledge in connecting patient, population, and public health data:* Development of effective, targeted health interventions requires linking of data at multiple levels, from patient-level to population and social determinants of health.
- *Health systems need to understand their communities better:* Community needs and requirements to create programs, policies, and interventions need to be well understood.
- *Sharing data across sectors:* Data sharing and its utility in health decision making presents a fundamental challenge that involves issues of trust, system interoperability, sector, and workflows.
- *Identifying and developing the right technologies:* Integrating social determinants of health data into electronic health records (EHRs) has also been a major challenge. The main alternative to EHRs for the collection, sharing, and use of social determinants of health data are custom technology, cloud-based technology, and geo-visual analytics.

Some of the outcomes facilitated by the analysis of social determinants of health data include the following (Falk, 2016):

- Increased advocacy to address health inequalities
- Better policymaking
- Improved health outcomes
- Cost-effective interventions
- Leadership action plans that positively impact safety, cost, and clinical outcomes
- Improved clinical decision making and evidence-based practice
- Improved practice guidelines

Different stakeholders have different interests, which are not often unified. Although policymakers focus on health policy decision making, advocacy groups typically focus on improving outcomes related to one disease or its determinant. If the goal is overall health improvement, individual groups working in silos are not productive (Kindig & Stoddart, 2003). Population health improvement as a goal creates an overarching need for a population health perspective that encompasses health outcomes across determinants.

▶ II. The Growth of the Internet and Social Media

Information and communication technology (ICT) has continued to proliferate at a rapid pace. The beginning of the 21st century has ushered in the possibility of an unprecedented era of scientific discovery and promise. New ICTs are being explored to effectively and efficiently communicate with, engage, and educate the diverse public. Such technologies can be utilized as web-based apps, mobile phones, and alert systems. Technology continues to improve (Maynard & Harper, 2011). Computers

TABLE 1.1 Overview of the Definitions of Population Health

Definition of Population Health	Source
Exploring reasons about some populations being healthier than others	Young, T. K. (2005). *Population health: Concepts and methods.* New York, NY: Oxford University Press.
Improve health and reduce health inequalities of diverse populations	Health Canada. (1998). *Taking action on population health.* Ottawa, Ontario: Health Canada.
Paradigm for understanding why some populations have better health outcomes than others	Young, T. K. (1998). *Population health: Concepts and methods.* New York, NY: Oxford University Press.
Focuses on factors that influence the health of populations over the life course, variations in their patterns of occurrence resulting in actions, and policies to improve health and well-being of populations	Dunn, J. R., & Hayes, M. V. (1999). Toward a lexicon of population health. *Canadian Journal of Public Health, 90,* S7.
Highlight[s the] role of social and economic forces in combination with biological and environmental factors that shape the health of entire populations	Kreuter, M., & Lezin, N. (2001). *Improving everyone's quality of life: A primer on population health.* Atlanta, GA: Group Health Community Foundation.
Health outcomes of a group of individuals, including the distribution of such outcomes within the group	Kindig, D., & Stoddart, G. (2003). What is population health? *American Journal of Public Health, 93*(3), 380–383.
Improve[s] the health of populations as one element in the Institute for Healthcare Improvement's (IHI) Triple Aim	Berwick, D. M., Nolan, T. W., & Whittington, J. (2008). The triple aim: Care, health, and cost. *Health Affairs, 27*(3), 759–769.
Approach that fosters decision making by policymakers, allowing them to assess the implications of non-health-related policies	Bostic, R. W., Thornton, R. L., Rudd, E. C., & Sternthal, M. J. (2012). Health in all policies: The role of the US Department of Housing and Urban Development and present and future challenges. *Health Affairs, 31*(9), 2130–2137.

- Is less associated with health departments at the government level (Stoto, 2013)
- Includes the healthcare delivery system and is seen as separate from governmental public health (Stoto, 2013)
- Is more than the sum of its individual parts (Stoto, 2013)
- Includes a broader array of the determinants of health than is typical in public health (Stiefel & Nolan, 2012)
- Has outcomes that go beyond state and local public health agencies and healthcare delivery systems (Ayana, 2016)

are now available at much lower, affordable prices. The Internet is a massive network, connecting millions of computers (FIGURES 1.3 and 1.4). The World Wide Web allows individuals to access information via a computer, mobile telephone, tablet, gaming device, or digital TV (Internet Live Stats, 2017).

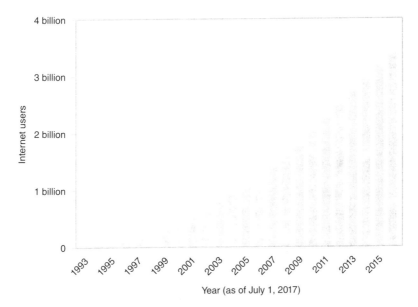

FIGURE 1.3 Internet users in the world

Data from Internet Live Stats. (2017). Internet users by region. Retrieved from http://www.internetlivestats.com/internet-users/

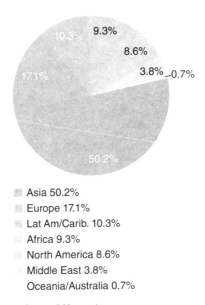

Asia 50.2%
Europe 17.1%
Lat Am/Carib. 10.3%
Africa 9.3%
North America 8.6%
Middle East 3.8%
Oceania/Australia 0.7%

FIGURE 1.4 Internet users in the world by region

Reproduced from Internet World Stats. (2017b). World Internet users and 2017 population stats. Basis: 3,731,973,423 Internet users on March 31, 2017. Retrieved from www.internetworldstats.com/stats.htm. Copyright © 2017, Miniwatts Marketing Group.

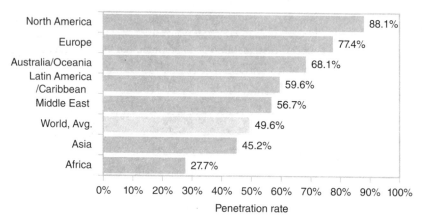

FIGURE 1.5 Internet world penetration rates by regions of the world

Reproduced from Internet World Stats. (2017a). Internet usage statistics: The Internet big picture. Retrieved from http://www.internetworldstats.com/stats.htm

Currently, around 40% of the world's population has an Internet connection (Pew Research Center, 2016). As **FIGURE 1.5** shows, North America has the highest Internet penetration rate (88%), and Africa has the lowest Internet penetration rate (27.7%) (Poushter, 2016; Internet World Stats, 2017a). Nearly half of Internet users are from Asia (50.2%), as compared to 8.6% in North America.

Mobile and Internet technology use has become a daily, routine activity in most parts of the world. Internet use is proliferating, especially for obtaining health information (Atkinson, Saperstein, & Pleis, 2009). In addition to making and receiving calls, cell phones are widely used for multiple purposes including sending messages and capturing pictures and videos. Mobile health technologies constitute one of the most rapidly growing markets globally. Growth is primarily attributed to an increasing penetration of smartphones, tablets, and other mobile platforms, and the mHealth Solutions Market is predicted to be worth 59.15 billion USD by 2020 (Markets and Markets, 2017).

The use of mobile devices has transformed many aspects of health care. More than half of the Internet users in the United States (65%) reported using social networking sites in 2011 (Pew Research Center, 2016) (**FIGURE 1.6**). Facebook is the most popular social networking site globally (Capurro et al., 2014), with an estimated 1 billion active users in total, including 580 million daily users. Twitter, with 500 million users worldwide, detects and predicts events and sentiments by observing users' posts (tweets) in real time (Capurro et al., 2014). Social networking sites offer a range of possibilities for establishing multidirectional communication and interaction, as well as quickly monitoring public sentiment and activity (Capurro et al., 2014).

▶ III. The Intersection of ICTs and Health Care

The advent of ICT has transformed healthcare delivery into patient-centered care. ICTs allow the delivery of healthcare services, particularly to isolated communities. Integration of clinical and nonclinical data sources by using ICTs to enhance population health outcomes across diverse geographic settings is a growing need.

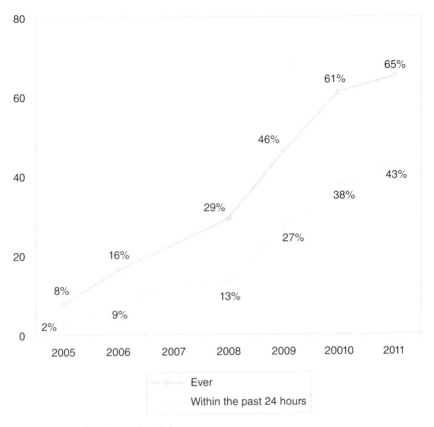

FIGURE 1.6 Social media use by adults

Modified from Madden, M., & Zickuhr, K. (2011). 65% of online adults use social networking sites. Retrieved from http://www.pewinternet.org/2011/08/26/65-of
-online-adults-use-social-networking-sites/

Policymakers on a global scale are encouraging the use of such technologies to improve health and healthcare systems. Mobile health technologies, remote wearable devices, and sensors have demonstrated immense potential in preventing diseases and improving well-being in numerous settings (Capurro et al., 2014). Future technological innovation is going to keep transforming health care. Previously, technology played a minimal role in health, and healthcare professionals were the only way to take care of people (Friede & O'Carroll, 1996). Technology is now playing a significant role in health management information systems (HMISs), public health surveillance, geographic information systems (GISs), and EHRs and facilitates access to both public health programs and services. Technology is used to monitor patterns of illness and to detect emerging or imminent threats to public health (Araujo et al., 2009).

Public health professionals have been among the first users of information technology. Technology can help providers identify and address nonmedical factors that affect population health (Institute of Medicine, 1997). More and more organizations are beginning to record population-level data using cloud-based tools and technologies. Mobile devices including smartphones, tablet computers, and remote monitoring devices have ample potential for use in disease prevention, early risk identification, healthcare delivery, and timely support to populations living in diverse settings (Centers for Disease Control and Prevention, 2006). These emerging technologies present an opportunity to address global health challenges in both developed and developing countries. Healthcare organizations around the globe are forming technological infrastructures that enable several stakeholders to make better informed, faster decisions and individuals to better manage their health outside of the hospital setting (Deloitte, 2016). Innovative technologies cover multiple areas including surveillance for disease, environmental monitoring, pollution mitigation and prevention, behavior modification, screening, and chronic disease management (Eng, 2004). The wide-scale adoption of health information technology has enabled diverse stakeholders, such as providers, payers, and government agencies, to collaborate using new digital tools to improve the health of defined populations.

▶ IV. The Emerging Role of Population Health Informatics

Informatics is the science of information, where information is defined as data with meaning (Bernstam, Smith, & Johnson, 2010). Informatics serves as a bridge across practitioners and professions to support collaboration and electronic communication. Informatics tools provide benefits to both administrative and clinical aspects of healthcare delivery and assist in collaborative practice by enhancing communication across team members. TABLE 1.2 lists some of the key global accomplishments in the field of health informatics.

TABLE 1.2 Key Global Health Informatics Accomplishments		
Year	**Country**	**Key Accomplishments**
1949	Germany	First professional organization for Informatics was founded
1950	United Kingdom	Medical Informatics initiated in the UK
1952	United States	First computer was used in clinical practice at the American Society for Clinical Pathology (Rappoport Arthur M-Bee)
1959	United States	First CT scanner was developed by Robert Ledley, one of the founding fathers of Informatics

1960	France	Training programs for Informatics in France began
1968	Brazil	Computers were first used in Medical care
1987	Hong Kong	Hong Kong Society for Medical Informatics (HKSMI) was established
1988	United States	American Medical Informatics Association (AMIA) established
1989	Switzerland	International Medical Informatics Association formed
1993	Nigeria	First International Working Conference on Health Informatics in Africa
1996	United States	A 2-year fellowship program was established by the Centers for Disease Control and Prevention
1997	Argentina	Biomedical Informatics group was established
2000	New Zealand	Health Informatics program established in New Zealand
2001	Canada	Canada Health Infoway was established
2002	Australia	Australasian college of health informatics established
2004	United States	Office of the National Coordinator for Health Information Technology was created
2005	United States	National Center for Public Health Informatics was created by CDC
2006	Saudi Arabia	Saudi Association for Health Informatics was established
2009	United States	The Health Information Technology for Economic and Clinical Health (HITECH) Act established
2017	India	Digital Health Technology Ecosystem incorporated into National Health Policy

Modified from Ng, S. K., & Wong, L. (2004). Accomplishments and challenges in bioinformatics. *IT Professional, 6*(1),.44–50.

Public Health Informatics

Public health informatics (PHI) is the science of applying information-age technology to serve the specialized needs of public health (Friede, Blum, & McDonald, 1995). PHI is a systematic application of information, computer science, and technology in the practice of public health (Yasnoff et al., 2000). It addresses three core functions of public health: (1) assessment of population health, (2) policy development, and (3) assurance of the availability of high-quality public health services. The scope of PHI expands beyond conceptualization and design and development (Yasnoff et al., 2000).

Members of the public health and informatics community discussed key PHI issues during the American Medical Informatics Association Meeting that was held in Atlanta during May 15–17, 2001 (Yasnoff et al., 2001). The issues were related to funding and governance; architecture and infrastructure; standards and vocabulary; research, evaluation, and best practices; privacy, confidentiality, and security; and training and workforce (Yasnoff et al., 2001). All stakeholders perceived the role of information systems to be beneficial in improving the health of individuals (Yasnoff et al., 2000). Some of the PHI-related challenges included developing integrated national public health information systems, enhancing integration efforts between public health and clinical care systems, and addressing the concerns of information technology on confidentiality and privacy (Yasnoff et al., 2001).

A follow-up PHI conference was held in 2011 to revisit the PHI agenda developed in 2001 (Massoudi et al., 2012). Three key themes were identified: the need to (1) increase communication and information sharing within the PHI community; (2) improve evaluation methods, competency training, and the use of public health; and (3) enhance leadership and coordination to move the field forward. Further recommendations included finding ways to strengthen prevention in the public health and clinical continuum and to build health at the community level (Massoudi et al., 2012).

Population Health Informatics

The U.S. HITECH Act of 2009 was designed to boost health information technology adoption nationwide. President Obama signed the act into law on February 17, 2009, as part of the American Recovery and Reinvestment Act of 2009 (ARRA) economic stimulus bill. Some of the key processes included care coordination, cohort management, clinician engagement, and reporting and knowledge management. Managing public health practice effectively and enhancing societal well-being require multiple resources that provide accurate, high-quality, and timely information. PHI focuses on population-level, preventive-based information. It also serves as an applied science in relevant government settings with a central goal of public health promotion (Yasnoff et al., 2000). PHI is a combination of medicine, public health, computer science, and information processing (Kukafka, 2005). It has also been defined as the application of ICTs in public health practice while integrating health research with information technology (Reeder, Hills, Demiris, Revere, & Pina, 2011). Application of PHI principles provides unprecedented opportunities to build healthier communities (Savel & Foldy, 2012).

A paradigm shift toward the area of population health informatics (PopHI) has begun. This shift is because of the increasing focus on social health determinants and use of technology in health care, combined with stakeholder initiatives including the ACA, HITECH Act, and other relevant reforms (Vest & Gamm, 2010). PopHI is the systematic application of information technologies and electronic information to the improvement of the health and well-being of a defined community or other target population (Kharrazi et al., 2017). For a health risk assessment to be conducted effectively at the population level, aggregate data are needed from a variety of sources including health facilities, social services, law enforcement agencies, departments of labor and industry, population-level surveys, and on-site inspections (O'Carroll, Yasnoff, Ward, Ripp, & Martin, 2003). PopHI can also be described as an integration of social determinants of health data sources (both clinical and nonclinical) by combining principles of ICT to enhance population health outcomes across diverse geographic settings (Joshi, Arora, & Malhotra, 2017; FIGURE 1.7).

The current need for PopHI arises from dramatic improvements in information technology, new pressures on the public health system, and changes in healthcare delivery. PopHI systems involve creation, storage, and processing of data to generate information and knowledge. PopHI facilitates data-driven, well-informed, evidence-based decision making for populations living in diverse settings. In addition to the informatics developments, elements of the PopHI system are a means to generate and process data to achieve meaningful information and knowledge about geographic areas that have concentrations of unfavorable health indicators or are composed of populations of underserved groups (Kharrazi et al., 2017). The development of such systems aims to help stakeholders gather timely and accurate information about entire population groups and permit assessment of disparities of health status among different populations (FIGURE 1.8).

PopHI also refers to the application of emerging technologies to improve the health of populations (Eng, 2004). Some of the challenges that exist in relation to the PopHI tools and technologies include privacy and security of patient data, confidentiality, quality, sustainability, and the existing technology divide (Eng, 2004; FIGURE 1.9).

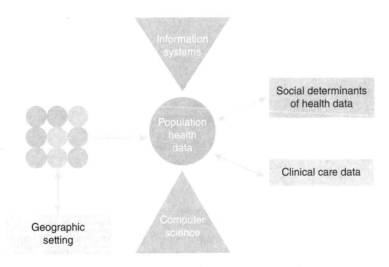

FIGURE 1.7 Intersections of population health, information systems, and computer science among populations in diverse geographic settings

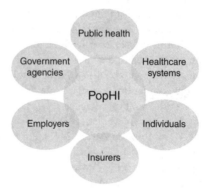

FIGURE 1.8 Diverse stakeholder involvement in PopHI

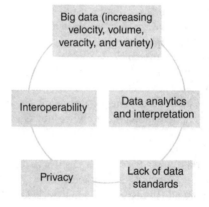

FIGURE 1.9 Challenges in the use of healthcare technologies

Modified from Harbinger Systems. (2016). Healthcare IT: Role of EDI in Affordable Care Act reforms. Retrieved from http://www.slideshare.net/hsplmkting/healthcare-it
-role-of-edi-in-affordable-care-act-reforms

Despite these challenges, health information technology, including mobile health technology, holds significant potential for engaging individuals in disease prevention and health promotion. It provides individuals with the necessary tools to record their data and make data meaningful. More research is needed to assess when, where, and for whom the population health technologies are efficacious. **TABLE 1.3** lists the key comparisons between PopHI and PHI.

▶ V. Challenges and Opportunities Related to PopHI

Experts at a symposium sponsored by the National Library of Medicine identified six key domains of PopHI as significant (Kharrazi et al., 2017). Symposium attendees included national experts and leading researchers in academia, the public sector, provider organizations, and the information technology industry. These six domains were as follows:

TABLE 1.3 Distinguishing Between Population Informatics and Public Health Informatics

	Population Health Informatics (PopHI)	Public Health Informatics (PHI)
Context	Both governmental and nongovernmental	Predominantly governmental context
Common intervention targets	Total population Target population Healthcare organizations Healthcare systems Nongovernmental organizations	Total population Health departments
Main operational goals	Outreach and prevention Care integration Disease management	Assessment Prevention Assurance
Action arm	Population health organizations Care management organizations	Public health agencies Not-for-profit and nongovernmental organizations
Key stakeholders	Provider and payer systems Government and community	Federal, state, and local governments
Key information challenges	Capturing nonmedical information Interoperability across sectors	Expanding public health IT systems Medical and public health interoperability

Modified from Kharrazi, H., Lasser, E. C., Yasnoff, W. A., Loonsk, J., Advani, A., Lehmann, H. P., . . . Weiner, J. P. (2017). A proposed national research and development agenda for population health informatics: Summary recommendations from a national expert workshop. *Journal of the American Medical Informatics Association, 24*(1), 2–12.

- *Interoperability and information infrastructure:* Having an interoperable platform that can facilitate data sharing can potentially help advance the agenda of PopHI.
- *Cross-organization collaboration:* Well-established programs or policies for population health data sharing across diverse stakeholders do not exist.
- *PopHI-based indicators and metrics:* There is a need to have an understanding of how advanced population health metrics can be derived from the health information technology systems.
- *Applying PopHI within integrated provider systems:* Current state-of-the-art tools represent an imbalance between focusing on the population vs. individual providers.

- *Computer science and informatics methods for population health:* There is a great potential to utilize some of the computational methods from the field of computer science to address the challenges of population health data integration and analysis.
- *Integration of social and nonmedical factors into PopHI systems:* Linking social and other nonmedical information with clinical data can enhance population health methods and models.

For each of the domains identified, existing challenges and potential opportunities were assessed, alongside future research directions to address them (TABLE 1.4).

TABLE 1.4 Challenges and Opportunities Across Population Health Domains

Domains	Challenges and Opportunities	Research and Development Issues
Interoperability and information infrastructure	Need for a clear, shared vision for a common, interoperable, and robust information infrastructure	Methods for securely and privately linking patient medical records across stakeholders
	Need for effective patient identification methods to share data across systems	Promote a shared knowledge base for community health trends and population decision support
	Inconsistent adoption of interoperability standards	Design end-user tools that incorporate usability methods and heuristics
	Challenges associated with silo functions and service provisions	Foster the integration of social science data into PopHI's overarching architecture
Cross-organization collaboration	Collaboration challenges among stakeholders	Consensus on what data to collect, integrate, and share as part of PopHI
	Limited PopHI data use and exchange agreements	Discover and share new PopHI analytic solutions and models among stakeholders
	Lack of aligned incentives	Define population health data-sharing methods using established standards
	Instability of many partnerships between private and public organizations	Develop a set of metrics and decision support guidelines
	Difficulty of blending medical, public health, and consumer-targeted interventions.	Create methods to assess the quality of shared data and techniques for linking disparate data sources

PopHI-based indicators and metrics	Understanding how new data sources, such as patient-generated data and unstructured EHR data, can be utilized	Develop actionable predictive models for population health metrics
	Need appropriate informatics methods for improving the reliability, accessibility, and comparability of such measures	Build a health information technology framework to capture and integrate patient-reported outcomes on the population scale
	Develop a prioritized population/community report card	Create a methodology to align existing population health metrics across programs
		Establish a framework to support the roll-out of new population-health–focused metrics by expanding collection of critical data elements
Applying PopHI within integrated provider systems	Lack of appropriate population health electronic quality measures	Integration of practice needs for population health data management and governance
	Absence of proof-of-concept and return-on-investment of enterprise-level tool implementation	Improvement of human factors and workflow issues for all stakeholders
	Up-to-date meaningful use policy, and a lack of governance structures for effective and efficient data sharing	Identification of a unifying framework for PopHI infrastructure and stakeholder incentives for adoption
Computer science and informatics methods for population health	Heterogeneity and complexity of population health data sources	Develop and disseminate a "grand computing challenge" for PopHI
	Privacy issues associated with population-level analytics	Encourage collaboration between computer scientists and trigger the development of advanced, innovative methods
	Limited collaboration between health information technology and population health experts	Develop synthetic population-level datasets that can be shared freely
	Lack of standardized data architectures for population health	Develop guidelines for large-scale data sharing as well as analytic frameworks for non-health researchers
		Advance interdisciplinary research in applied PopHI focus areas, such as change management and workflow reasoning

(continues)

4 Challenges and Opportunities Across Population Health Domains (*continued*)

Domains	Challenges and Opportunities	Research and Development Issues
Integration of social and nonmedical factors into PopHI systems	Poor understanding of the information that needs to remain protected or confidential when using nonclinical data	Solutions need to integrate nonpersonal data to person-specific data Develop population-based decision-support tools for both public health/community officials and clinicians Develop analytic tools that work across disparate population health data types

Modified from Kharrazi, H., Lasser, E. C., Yasnoff, W. A., Loonsk, J., Advani, A., Lehmann, H. P., . . . Weiner, J. P. (2017). A proposed national research and development agenda for population health informatics: Summary recommendations from a national expert workshop. *Journal of the American Medical Informatics Association, 24*(1), 2–12.

▶ VI. Adoption of PopHI Solutions

Apart from the challenges, opportunities, and research and development issues related to PopHI, the following 13 overarching themes of PopHI were identified (Kharrazi et al., 2017):

- *Policy alignment:* There is a need to align the PopHI strategies with desired outcomes that will facilitate adoption and implementation of appropriate PopHI solutions.
- *Data governance:* Data governance and data privacy policies need to be in place to ensure data sharing agreements so that it can further facilitate adoption and implementation of PopHI solutions.
- *Data quality:* A suboptimal rate of completeness, accuracy, timeliness, reliability, or validity of a data source can produce uncertainty when the data are incorporated into PopHI solutions.
- *Data management:* Differences in granularity and heterogeneity across various data sources create many data management challenges.
- *Sustainability and incentives:* Lack of funding and difficulty attracting new funding streams may affect the scalability of a project and limit the flexibility of its core business model.
- *Population metrics:* The lack of accurate and reproducible e-metrics may reduce the effectiveness of PopHI solutions.
- *Interoperability standards:* Limited PopHI standards and interoperability frameworks affect the development of new PopHI solutions.
- *Stakeholder collaboration:* If stakeholders do not collaborate effectively, this will produce suboptimal results.

- *Tools and infrastructure:* Limited PopHI data infrastructure and tools hinder the development of a robust health technology platform for population health.
- *Ethics and security:* Concerns about the privacy, confidentiality, and security of data restrict the expansion of population-wide health information technology solutions.
- *Best practices and dissemination:* Insufficient best practices for PopHI and limited dissemination mechanisms to introduce them among stakeholders have restricted the adoption of new PopHI solutions.
- *Education and training:* Properly training PopHI experts in both payer and provider settings can help empower cross-organizational PopHI programs.
- *Evaluation methods:* The development and evaluation of new PopHI methods are essential to advancing the science of population health.

The emerging field of PopHI addresses a broader-level population dimension as compared to PHI owing to increased adoption of value-based, technology-supported healthcare delivery paradigms (Moreno, Peikes, & Krilla, 2010). The HITECH Act has produced several desirable outcomes including increased use of information technology by healthcare providers (HITECH Act, 2009; Hsiao, Hing, & Ashman, 2014), data interoperability, integration, consolidation, and standards adoption (Centers for Medicare and Medicaid Services, 2012; Clinical Data Interchange Standards Consortium, 2016; Dolin et al., 2001; S&I Framework, n.d.), the creation of mega health data repositories (National Patient-Centered Clinical Research Network, 2015), and advances in the utilization of big data from multiple sources (Barrett, Humblet, Hiatt, & Adler, 2013). All of these factors have significantly improved the extent of the application of informatics to the population health domain.

Three structural barriers exist to the greater adoption of technology in health care. First, the necessary technology is not available; second, the technology exists but is not accessible; and third, technology is not always used, even when accessible. More effective collaboration is a crucial need to address the mechanism of data collection, its dissemination to various stakeholders, and their use of the data in healthcare decision making. An innovative sustainable business model for multisector collaboration is needed.

▶ VII. SMAART: An Innovative PopHI Conceptual Framework

Health status and outcomes do not exist in isolation but are ingrained in a wider array of living conditions (Williams, Costa, Odunlami, & Mohammed, 2008). Including social context in the delivery of healthcare services can have a significant impact in the improvement of individual health. The larger social and economic policies and the economic resources available to the household can also importantly affect health. Improvement in population health involves the integration of complex, multidimensional data that enables diverse stakeholders (such as individuals, healthcare professionals, and policymakers) to identify patterns resulting in meaningful information (Jamison, 2006). There is a need to use the currently available knowledge to improve living conditions and the health of populations.

Defining SMAART

An innovative PopHI framework, Sustainable, Multi-sector, Accessible, Affordable, Reimbursable, Tailored (SMAART) (Joshi et al., 2017) has been proposed that aims to facilitate the integration of determinants of population health (social determinants and clinical data) to guide data-driven, evidence-based, PopHI-related programs, policies, and interventions to enhance population health outcomes across diverse geographic settings (**FIGURE 1.10**).

The SMAART Approach

The SMAART framework combines principles of data, information, and knowledge (DIK) (Chapter 2); human-centered design (HCD) (Chapter 6); cognitive fit theory (Dennis & Carte, 1998); information processing (Miller, 1956); and learning, behavioral, and humanistic theories (Boeree, 1998; Duffy & Jonassen, 1992; Spiro, Feltovich, Jacobson, & Coulson, 1988).

The principles of HCD involve (1) active involvement and understanding of users, (2) understanding task requirements, (3) appropriate allocation of function between user and system, (4) iteration of design solutions, and (5) multidisciplinary design teams. Understanding users is an important aspect of the HCD approach. An individual's ability to work with an HCD application is influenced by multiple demographic factors including age, literacy, spatial skills, and computer familiarity (Slocum et al., 2001). The user model gathers individuals' understanding regarding data, functions, domain, and mapping (Lauesen, 2005). HCD involves users' perspective to create a system that is useful and usable. Tasks classification helps to create useful applications. Common visual tasks performed by users include locating, identifying, distinguishing, categorizing, distributing, comparing, and correlating variables (Wehrend & Lewis, 1990). Interactions enable users to derive meaning and accomplish various analysis goals.

Better results are produced when the task requirement corresponds with the information presented (Joshi et al., 2012). This also improves system and task performance factors.

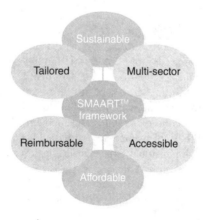

FIGURE 1.10 SMAART framework

Cognitive fit theory reflects how the graphical output affects the decision processes (Dennis & Carte, 1998) and depends upon fit between information presentation and tasks used by the decision maker. Cognitive fit examines the best way in which a user's task output can be presented (Dennis & Carte, 1998).

The principles of information processing theory (Miller, 1956) recommend that information be presented in a meaningful manner in small chunks (like 5–7 pieces of information). It also presents information in a structured format that is simple to understand. According to learning behavioral and humanistic theories, the information presented should be highly interconnected and relevant to the learner, and available in multiple content formats. Feedback should be provided based on responses (Boeree, 1998; Duffy & Jonassen, 1992; Spiro et al., 1988). The evaluation component assesses the process outcomes and the impact of PopHI tools and technologies on the cost of, quality of, and access to healthcare services (FIGURE 1.11).

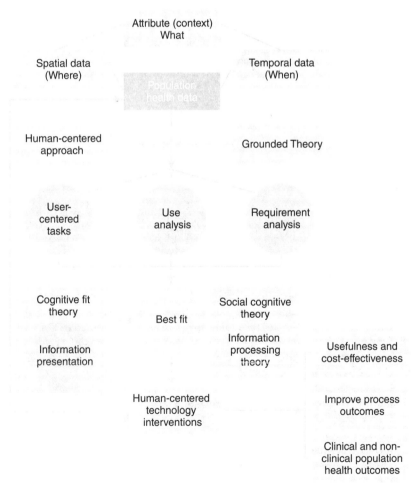

FIGURE 1.11 Theoretical approaches utilized in the SMAART framework

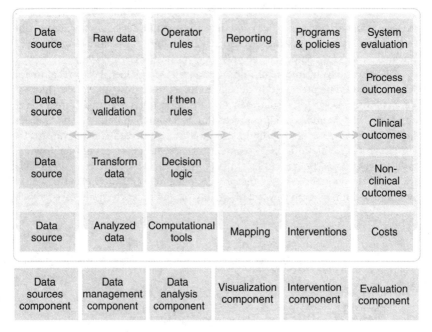

FIGURE 1.12 Elements of the SMAART framework

Components of the SMAART Framework

Some of the elements of the SMAART framework include the following (see **FIGURE 1.12**):

- *Multidimensional data:* Social determinants of health data are typically organized into a geospatial unit that often has three dimensions: (1) attribute (i.e., context), (2) spatial (i.e., geographic), and (3) temporal (i.e., time). The attribute (context) component relates to issues of interest such as social data, environmental data, and health data. The spatial (geographic) component includes data with location attributes (e.g., address, region, or country) and can provide insight into how and where to obtain essential services. The temporal (time) component records the time of the observation and enables users to learn from the past to predict, plan, and build the future. The SMAART framework facilitates the integration of social determinants of health data such as socioeconomic factors, the physical environment, health behaviors, clinical assessment, and knowledge, attitude, and practice (**FIGURE 1.13**). The data are generated into meaningful information to derive an individual/community risk profile, based on existing guidelines and evidence.
- *Data management component:* This component includes several modules such as data recording and storage, data, data validation techniques, and data transformation by making data available in a format that is ready to be analyzed.
- *Data analysis component:* This component includes statistical analysis capabilities to help analyze multisectoral data at both the individual and aggregate levels.

Cognitive fit theory reflects how the graphical output affects the deci. processes (Dennis & Carte, 1998) and depends upon fit between information pre sentation and tasks used by the decision maker. Cognitive fit examines the best way in which a user's task output can be presented (Dennis & Carte, 1998).

The principles of information processing theory (Miller, 1956) recommend that information be presented in a meaningful manner in small chunks (like 5–7 pieces of information). It also presents information in a structured format that is simple to understand. According to learning behavioral and humanistic theories, the information presented should be highly interconnected and relevant to the learner, and available in multiple content formats. Feedback should be provided based on responses (Boeree, 1998; Duffy & Jonassen, 1992; Spiro et al., 1988). The evaluation component assesses the process outcomes and the impact of PopHI tools and technologies on the cost of, quality of, and access to healthcare services (FIGURE 1.11).

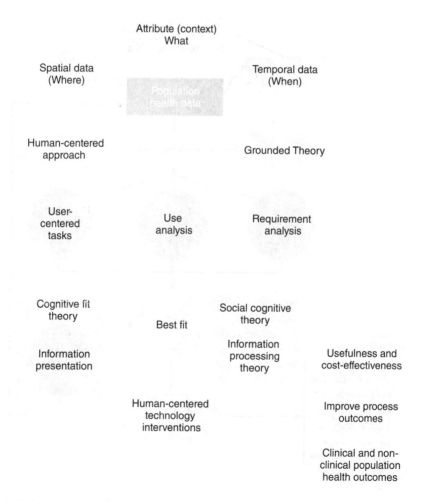

FIGURE 1.11 Theoretical approaches utilized in the SMAART framework

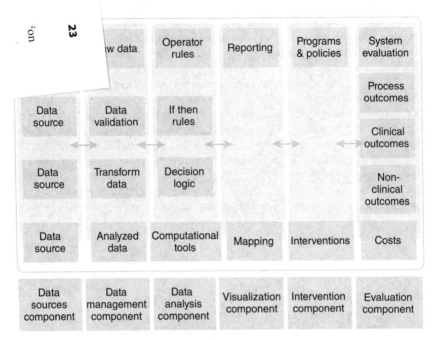

FIGURE 1.12 Elements of the SMAART framework

Components of the SMAART Framework

Some of the elements of the SMAART framework include the following (see FIGURE 1.12):

- *Multidimensional data:* Social determinants of health data are typically organized into a geospatial unit that often has three dimensions: (1) attribute (i.e., context), (2) spatial (i.e., geographic), and (3) temporal (i.e., time). The attribute (context) component relates to issues of interest such as social data, environmental data, and health data. The spatial (geographic) component includes data with location attributes (e.g., address, region, or country) and can provide insight into how and where to obtain essential services. The temporal (time) component records the time of the observation and enables users to learn from the past to predict, plan, and build the future. The SMAART framework facilitates the integration of social determinants of health data such as socioeconomic factors, the physical environment, health behaviors, clinical assessment, and knowledge, attitude, and practice (FIGURE 1.13). The data are generated into meaningful information to derive an individual/community risk profile, based on existing guidelines and evidence.
- *Data management component:* This component includes several modules such as data recording and storage, data, data validation techniques, and data transformation by making data available in a format that is ready to be analyzed.
- *Data analysis component:* This component includes statistical analysis capabilities to help analyze multisectoral data at both the individual and aggregate levels.

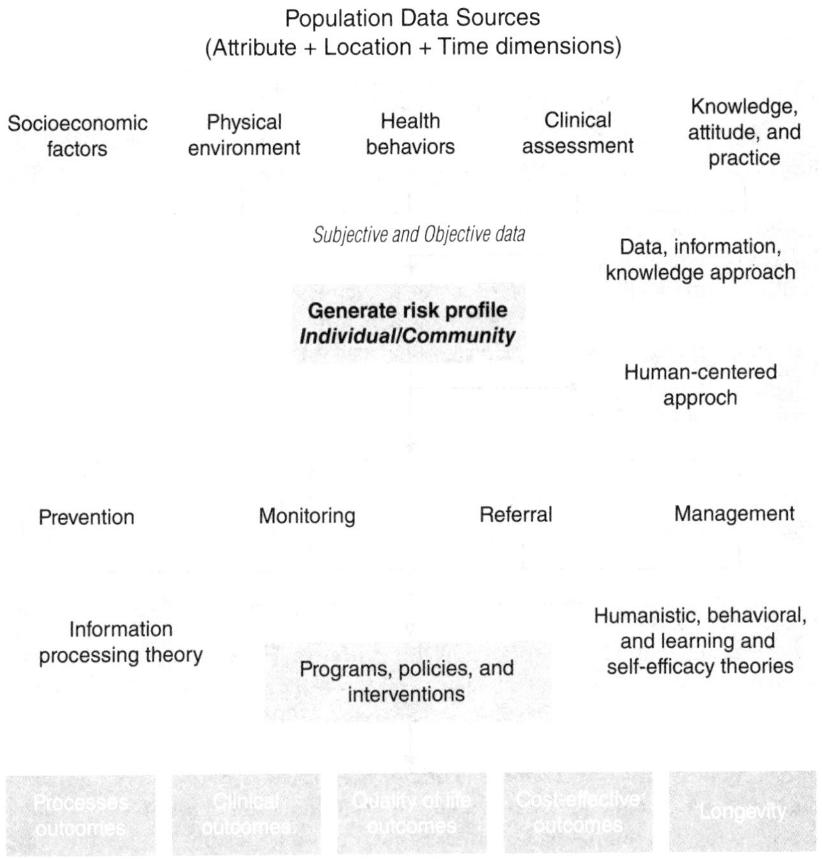

Population Data Sources
(Attribute + Location + Time dimensions)

| Socioeconomic factors | Physical environment | Health behaviors | Clinical assessment | Knowledge, attitude, and practice |

Subjective and Objective data

Data, information, knowledge approach

Generate risk profile
Individual/Community

Human-centered approch

| Prevention | Monitoring | Referral | Management |

Information processing theory

Humanistic, behavioral, and learning and self-efficacy theories

Programs, policies, and interventions

Processes outcomes   Clinical outcomes   Quality of life outcomes   Cost-effective outcomes   Longevity

FIGURE 1.13 Applying the SMAART framework toward social determinants of health data to enhance population health outcomes

- *Visualization component:* The visualization component contributes to displaying meaningful information in various formats including tables, charts, graphs, and maps. This component allows individuals to actively interact with the data to conduct specific analyses and visualize the information based on the needs of the individual or organization.
- *Intervention component:* This component involves several programs, policies, and interventions that can enhance population health outcomes across diverse geographic settings.
- *Evaluation component:* The evaluation component includes system evaluation, process outcomes, and both clinical and nonclinical outcomes.

The SMAART framework can be operationalized as an interactive, a stand-alone, an Internet, or a mobile-enabled platform that (1) facilitates transmission of data and information regarding the health status of the individual/community, (2) interprets data and information using previously established knowledge and/or wisdom and use of evidence-based standards, (3) addresses the specific needs of the individual/community, (4) provides timely feedback to the consumer addressing specific requirements, and (5) uses regular repetition of the feedback loop. Prior research has shown the need to have customized technology solutions to address the gaps that exist in the integration of social determinants of health data and clinical data to enhance population health outcomes.

Several recommendations have been proposed for PopHI interventions to be successful (Kharrazi et al., 2017). Barriers such as cost, poor infrastructure, lack of or limited Internet access, and inadequately trained human resources often prevent or delay the adoption of technology in health care (Buitenhuis, Zelenika, & Pearce, 2010). Overcoming these barriers is crucial if the potential of technology for global health is to be realized. Decisions about implementation of a health technology solution should combine a range of considerations, from cost per unit to how to encourage uptake, to whether a technology can work in a particular setting and the best way to achieve implementation. This presents an urgent need to implement sustainable, low-cost, accessible, and affordable technology-enabled health solutions to meet the needs of local communities, especially those living in low-resource settings.

▶ VIII. Conclusion

Effective use of data determines the extent to which population health stakeholders can sufficiently address societal health concerns. There is an increasing need for tools and technologies that facilitate knowledge construction (Bhowmick, Griffin, MacEachren, Kluhsman, & Lengerich, 2008). Technical constraints, including connectivity, bandwidth provision, and reliability, also need to be taken into account during PopHI implementations (Panth & Acharya, 2015). Expanding the development and dissemination of health data standards and vocabulary tools is critical to improving access. New and upcoming health technologies have shown tremendous value in reducing healthcare costs while improving well-being. Although such technologies are being developed and utilized in several domains of care, intensive research is required to fully explore their potentials, challenges, and opportunities (Eng, 2004). There is an urgent need for PopHI training with an emphasis on competence in population health, data analytics, systems thinking, evaluation, and transdisciplinary approaches to problem solving, communication, leadership, advocacy, and technology. Economic evaluations also need to be taken into consideration when designing, developing, implementing, and evaluating PopHI interventions.

The present century has unraveled a plethora of scientific innovations and discoveries with the potential for better outcomes. Emerging technologies provide enormous opportunities for population health improvement (Eng, 2004). These also present an opportunity for addressing global health challenges in both developed and developing countries. The adoption of population health technologies will require optimal research in the field of PopHI.

References

Affordable Care Act. (2011). *Federal Sentencing Reporter, 23*(3).

Araujo, J., Pepper, C., Richards, J., Choi, M., Xing, J., & Li, W. (2009). The profession of public health informatics: Still emerging? *International Journal of Medical Informatics, 78*(6), 375–385.

Atkinson, N., Saperstein, S., & Pleis, J. (2009). Using the internet for health-related activities: findings from a national probability sample. *Journal of Medical Internet Research, 11*(1), e5.

Ayana, C. (2016). DSRIP statewide learning collaborative, population health. Retrieved from https://hhs.texas.gov/sites/hhs/files/documents/laws-regulations/policies-rules/1115-docs /082916/Triple-Aim-State-Data-Clark.pdf

Barrett, M. A., Humblet, O., Hiatt, R. A., & Adler, N. E. (2013). Big data and disease prevention: From quantified self to quantified communities. *Big Data, 1*(3), 168–175.

Bernstam, E. V., Smith, J. W., & Johnson, T. R. (2010). What is biomedical informatics? *Journal of Biomedical Informatics, 43*(1), 104.

Berwick, D. M., Nolan, T. W., & Whittington, J. (2008). The triple aim: Care, health, and cost. *Health Affairs, 27*(3), 759–769.

Bhowmick, T., Griffin, A. L., MacEachren, A. M., Kluhsman, B. C., & Lengerich, E. J. (2008). Informing geospatial toolset design: Understanding the process of cancer data exploration and analysis. *Health and Place, 14*(3), 576–607.

Boeree, G. (1998). Personality theories: B. F. Skinner. Retrieved from http://webspace.ship.edu /cgboer/skinner.html

Bostic, R. W., Thornton, R. L., Rudd, E. C., & Sternthal, M. J. (2012). Health in all policies: The role of the US Department of Housing and Urban Development and present and future challenges. *Health Affairs, 31*(9), 2130–2137.

Buitenhuis, A. J., Zelenika, I., & Pearce, J. M. (2010). Open design-based strategies to enhance appropriate technology development. *Proceedings of the 14th Annual National Collegiate Inventors and Innovators Alliance Conference: Open*, March 25–27, 2010, pp. 1–12.

Capurro, D., Cole, K., Echavarría, M. I., Joe, J., Neogi, T., & Turner, A. M. (2014). The use of social networking sites for public health practice and research: A systematic review. *Journal of Medical Internet Research, 16*(3), e79.

Centers for Disease Control and Prevention. (2006). Advancing the nation's health: A guide to public health research needs (2006–2015). Retrieved from http://www.ipacohio.org/Websites /ipac/images/LinksResources/AdvancingTheNationsHealth.pdf

Centers for Medicare and Medicaid Services (CMS). (2012). Health information technology: Standards, implementation specifications, and certification criteria for electronic health record technology, 2014 edition. *Federal Register, 77*(171), 53968–54162.

Clinical Data Interchange Standards Consortium (CDISC). (2016). CDISC vision and mission. https://www.cdisc.org/

County of Los Angeles Public Health. (2013). Social determinants of health: How social and economic factors affect health. Retrieved from http://publichealth.lacounty.gov/epi/docs /sociald_final_web.pdf

Deloitte. (2016). 2016 global healthcare outlook: Battling costs while improving healthcare. Retrieved from https://www2.deloitte.com/content/dam/Deloitte/global/Documents/Life -Sciences-Health-Care/gx-lshc-2016-health-care-outlook.pdf

Dennis, A. R., & Carte, T. A. (1998). Using geographical information systems for decision making: Extending cognitive fit theory to map-based presentations. *Information Systems Research, 9*(2), 194–203.

Dolin, R. H., Alschuler, L., Beebe, C., Biron, P. V., Boyer, S. L., Essin, D., . . . Mattison, J. E. (2001). The HL7 clinical document architecture. *Journal of the American Medical Informatics Association, 8*(6), 552–569.

Drummond, M., & Stoddart, G. (1995). Assessment of health producing measures across different sectors. *Health Policy, 33*(3), 219–231.

Duffy, T., & Jonassen, D. H. (1992). *Constructivism and the technology of instruction: A conversation.* Hillsdale, NJ: Lawrence Erlbaum Associates.

Dunn, J. R., & Hayes, M. V. (1999). Toward a lexicon of population health. *Canadian Journal of Public Health, 90*, S7.

Eng, T. R. (2004). Population health technologies: Emerging innovations for the health of the public. *American Journal of Preventive Medicine, 26*(3), 237–242.

Evans, R. G., Barer, M. L., & Marmor, T. R. (1994). *Why are some people healthy and others not? The determinants of health of populations* (pp. 27–64). New York, NY: Aldine de Gruyter.

Falk, L. H. (2016). What is population health and how does it compare to public health? Retrieved from https://www.healthcatalyst.com/what-is-population-health/

Field, M. J., & Gold, M. R. (Eds.). (1998). *Summarizing population health: Directions for the development and application of population metrics.* Washington, DC: National Academies Press.

Friede, A., Blum, H. L., & McDonald, M. (1995). Public health informatics: How information-age technology can strengthen public health. *Annual Review of Public Health, 16*(1), 239–252.

Friede, A., & O'Carroll, P. W. (1996). CDC and ATSDR electronic information resources for health officers. *American Journal of Infection Control, 24*(6), 440–454.

Harbinger Systems. (2016). Healthcare IT: Role of EDI in Affordable Care Act reforms. Retrieved from http://www.slideshare.net/hsplmkting/healthcare-it-role-of-edi-in-affordable-care-act-reforms

Health Canada. (1998). *Taking action on population health.* Ottawa, Ontario: Health Canada.

Health Information Technology for Economic and Clinical Health (HITECH) Act, Title XIII of Division A and Title IV of Division B of the American Recovery and Reinvestment Act of 2009 (ARRA). (2009). Washington, DC: 111th Congress.

Hsiao, C. J., Hing, E., & Ashman, J. (2014). *Trends in electronic health record system use among office-based physicians, United States, 2007–2012.* Washington, DC: U.S. Department of Health and Human Services, Centers for Disease Control and Prevention, National Center for Health Statistics.

Institute of Medicine, Division of Health Care Services. (1997). *The future of public health* (12th ed.). Washington, DC: National Academy Press.

Internet Live Stats. (2017). Internet users by region. Retrieved from http://www.internetlivestats.com/internet-users/

Internet World Stats. (2017a). Internet usage statistics: The Internet big picture. Retrieved from http://www.internetworldstats.com/stats.htm

Internet World Stats. (2017b). World Internet users and 2017 population stats. Basis: 3,731,973,423 Internet users on March 31, 2017. Retrieved from www.internetworldstats.com/stats.htm

Jamison, D. T. (2006). *Disease control priorities in developing countries.* Washington, DC: Oxford University Press.

Joshi, A., Arora, M., & Malhotra, B. (2017). Design, development and implementation of an informatics enabled SMAART intervention framework. Manuscript accepted by *Global Journal of Health Sciences.*

Joshi, A., de Araujo Novaes, M., Machiavelli, J., Iyengar, S., Vogler, R., Johnson, C., . . . Hsu, C. E. (2012). A human centered GeoVisualization framework to facilitate visual exploration of telehealth data: A case study. *Technology Health Care, 20*(6), 457–471.

Kharrazi, H., Lasser, E. C., Yasnoff, W. A., Loonsk, J., Advani, A., Lehmann, H. P., . . . Weiner, J. P. (2017). A proposed national research and development agenda for population health informatics: Summary recommendations from a national expert workshop. *Journal of the American Medical Informatics Association, 24*(1), 2–12.

Kindig, D., & Stoddart, G. (2003). What is population health? *American Journal of Public Health, 93*(3), 380–383.

Kreuter, M., & Lezin, N. (2001). *Improving everyone's quality of life: A primer on population health.* Atlanta, GA: Group Health Community Foundation.

Kukafka, R. (2005). Public health informatics: The nature of the field and its relevance to health promotion practice. *Health Promotion Practice, 6*(1), 23–28.

Lauesen, S. (2005). *User interface design: A software engineering perspective.* Reading, MA: Addison-Wesley.

Madden, M., & Zickuhr, K. (2011). 65% of online adults use social networking sites. Retrieved from http://www.pewinternet.org/2011/08/26/65-of-online-adults-use-social-networking-sites/

Markets and Markets. (2017). Telehealth market by component (hardware (blood glucose monitors), software (integrated), services (remote monitoring, real-time interactions), end user (providers, payers, patients), & mode of delivery (web, cloud)) - Global Forecast to 2021. Retrieved from http://www.marketsandmarkets.com/Market-Reports/telehealth-market-201868927.html

Massoudi, B. L., Goodman, K. W., Gotham, I. J., Holmes, J. H., Lang, L., Miner, K., . . . Fu, P. C. (2012). An informatics agenda for public health: Summarized recommendations from the 2011 AMIA PHI Conference. *Journal of the American Medical Informatics Association, 19*(5), 688–695.

Maynard, A. D., & Harper, T. (2011). Building a sustainable future: Rethinking the role of technology innovation in an increasingly interdependent, complex and resource-constrained world. Retrieved from http://cientifica.com/wp-content/uploads/downloads/2011/01/White-Paper -Building-a-Sustainable-Future.pdf

Miller, G. A. (1956). The magical number seven, plus or minus two: Some limits on our capacity for processing information. *Psychological Review, 63*(2), 81–97.

Moreno, L., Peikes, D. N., & Krilla, A. (2010). *Necessary but not sufficient: The HITECH Act and health information technology's potential to build medical homes*. Rockville, MD: Agency for Healthcare Research and Quality, U.S. Department of Health and Human Services.

National Patient-Centered Clinical Research Network (PCORnet). (2015). About PCORnet. Retrieved from http://www.pcornet.org/about-pcornet/

Ng, S. K., & Wong, L. (2004). Accomplishments and challenges in bioinformatics. *IT Professional, 6*(1), 44–50.

O'Carroll, P. W., Yasnoff, W. A., Ward, M. E., Ripp, L. H., Martin, E. L., Ross, D. A. (Eds.). (2003). *Health informatics and informatics systems*. New York, NY: Springer.

Panth, M., & Acharya, A. S. (2015). The unprecedented role of computers in improvement and transformation of public health: An emerging priority. *Indian Journal of Community Medicine, 40*(1), 8.

Parrish, R. G. 2010. Measuring population health outcomes. *Preventing Chronic Disease,7*(4): A71. Retrieved from http://www.cdc.gov/pcd/issues/2010/jul/10_0005.htm

Pew Research Center Internet, Science and Tech. (2016). Retrieved from http://www.pewinternet .org/2011/08/26/65-of-online-adults-use-social-networking-sites/

Poushter, J. (2016). Smartphone ownership and Internet usage continues to climb in emerging economies. Retrieved from http://www.pewglobal.org/2016/02/22/smartphone-ownership -and-internet-usage-continues-to-climb-in-emerging-economies/

Reeder, B., Hills, R. A., Demiris, G., Revere, D., & Pina, J. (2011). Reusable design: A proposed approach to public health informatics system design. *BMC Public Health, 11*(1), 1.

Robert Wood Johnson Foundation. (2016). Using social determinants of health data to improve health care and health: A learning report. Retrieved from https://healthleadsusa.org /wp-content/uploads/2016/06/RWJF-SDOH-Learning-Report.pdf

S&I Framework. (n.d.). What is the S&I framework? Retrieved from http://www.siframework.org /whatis.html

Savel, T. G., & Foldy, S. (2012). The role of public health informatics in enhancing public health surveillance. *Morbidity and Mortality Weekly Report Surveillance Summary, 61*(Suppl.), 20–24.

Slocum, T. A., Blok, C., Jiang, B., Koussoulakou, A., Montello, D. R., Fuhrmann, S., & Hedley, N. R. (2001). Cognitive and usability issues in geovisualization. *Cartography and Geographic Information Science, 28*(1), 61–75.

Spiro, R. J., Feltovich, P. J., Jacobson, M. J., & Coulson, R. L. (1988). Advanced knowledge acquisition in ill-structured domains. In V. Patel (Ed.), *Proceedings of the 10th Annual Conference of the Cognitive Science Society*. Hillsdale, NJ: Lawrence Erlbaum Associates.

Starfield, B. (2006). State of the art in research on equity in health. *Journal of Health Politics, Policy and Law, 31*(1), 11–32.

Stiefel, M., & Nolan, K. (2012). A guide to measuring the triple aim: Population health, experience of care, and per capita cost. *White paper*.

Stoto, M. A. (2013). Population health in the Affordable Care Act era. Retrieved from http://www .academyhealth.org/files/publications/files/AH2013pophealth.pdf

Taylor, L. A., Xulin Tan, A., Coyle, C. E., Ndumele, C., Rogan, E., Canavan, M., . . . Bradley, E. H. (2016). Leveraging the social determinants of health: What works? *PLoS One, 11*(8), 1–20.

Vest, J. R., & Gamm, L. D. (2010). Health information exchange: persistent challenges and new strategies. *Journal of the American Medical Informatics Association, 17*(3), 288–294.

Wehrend, S., & Lewis, C. (1990). A problem-oriented classification of visualization techniques. *Proceedings from the 1st Conference on Visualization '90, 139–143.* Los Alamitos, CA: IEEE Computer Society Press.

Williams, D. R., Costa, M. V., Odunlami, A. O., & Mohammed, S. A. (2008). Moving upstream: How interventions that address the social determinants of health can improve health and reduce disparities. *Journal of Public Health Management and Practice, 14*(Suppl.), S8.

Yasnoff, W. A., O'Carroll, P. W., Koo, D., Linkins, R. W., & Kilbourne, E. M. (2000). Public health informatics: Improving and transforming public health in the information age. *Journal of Public Health Management and Practice, 6*(6), 67–75.

Yasnoff, W. A., Overhage, M. A., Humphreys, L. B., & LaVenture, M. (2001). A national agenda for public health informatics. Summarized recommendations from the 2001 AMIA Spring Congress. *Journal of the American Medical Informatics Association, 8*(6), 535–545.

Young, T. K. (1998). *Population health: Concepts and methods.* New York, NY: Oxford University Press.

Young, T. K. (2005). *Population health: Concepts and methods.* New York, NY: Oxford University Press.

Zelenika, I., & Pearce, J. M. (2011). Barriers to appropriate technology growth in sustainable development. *Journal of Sustainable Development, 4*(6), 12–22.

CHAPTER 2

Population Health Informatics Workforce, Competencies, and Training Programs

Ashish Joshi

KEY TERM

Healthcare Information and Management Systems Society (HIMSS)

LEARNING OBJECTIVES

- Identify the need for population health informatics professionals in the 21st century.
- Examine barriers to implementing population health informatics solutions in diverse settings.
- List the competencies needed by informatics professionals to address population health challenges.
- Explore current and future job prospects for population health informatics professionals.
- Assess existing training opportunities in the field of population health informatics.

QUESTIONS FOR THOUGHT

- Why is there a growing need for population health informatics professionals?
- What are the barriers in implementing population health informatics solutions in diverse settings?
- Which of the existing informatics competencies are applicable in low- and middle-income countries?
- What are the job roles, skills, and expertise required by a population health informatics professional?
- How can informatics training be incorporated into existing public health programs?

CHAPTER OUTLINE

▶ I. The Need for a Trained Population Health Informatics Workforce in the 21st Century

Public health workers operate in a complex, information-rich environment. They are experiencing an increasing dependence on technology and data. Public health practice faces extraordinary challenges and opportunities driven by the advent of new technologies. The U.S. HITECH Act of 2009 promoted the role of health information technology (HIT) in enhancing the quality and efficiency of health care and improving public health (Buntin, Jain, & Blumenthal, 2010). Leaders of public health organizations must enhance their skills and advance their levels of expertise to promote and protect the health of the public.

In this chapter we use the terms *population health informatics (PopHI)* and *public health informatics (PHI)* interchangeably due to the overlap of PopHI with other informatics fields, such as public health informatics, clinical informatics, and consumer health informatics. This overlap is partly due to the similarity of data sources, stakeholders, and/or operational goals (Kharazzi et al., 2017).

The Centers for Disease Control and Prevention (CDC; Thacker, Qualters, & Lee, 2012), the Council of State and Territorial Epidemiologists (Smith, Hadler, Stanbury, Rolfs, & Hopkins, 2013), and the Association of Schools and Programs in Public Health (Petersen & Weist, 2014) consider workforce in the area of PopHI to be an integral component for public health practice. The World Health Organization (WHO) has also recognized the role of information and communication technology (ICT) in supporting patient care (WHO, 2005). In the last two decades, the number of professionals trained in the field of health informatics (HI) has grown worldwide (WHO, 2006). Health professionals are increasingly reliant on ICT to (1) assess community health, (2) provide preventive services, (3) perform treatment and follow-up procedures, (4) evaluate the effectiveness of preventive services and programs, and (5) identify resources for improving health initiatives within their communities. With the rapid increase in the scale and scope of electronic health information, health organizations are increasingly dependent on the skills of health informatics specialists. These specialists are essential to the ongoing transformation of healthcare agencies and will continue to design and manage public health information systems. They provide support to healthcare professionals to facilitate public health practice and policy development by providing quality information in a timely manner (National Association of County and City Health Officials [NACCHO], 2007). There is a growing need for the workforce to be trained and competent in emerging technologies that can enhance information gathering, analysis, and dissemination.

Computer and communication infrastructure and systems have been slow to develop in local health departments (LHDs), owing to limited financial resources (NACCHO, 2007). This is a critical issue because information gathering is performed at the local level. Most LHD officials felt an urgent need to provide informatics training to the staff already working in public health agencies so they could effectively implement public health information systems (Savel & Foldy, 2012). Trainings should range from general information about PHI to specialized skills on knowledge management for managers, decision makers, and high-level health officials (Lisco, n.d.; NACCHO, 2007).

▶ II. Barriers to the Implementation of PopHI Solutions

Information transfer within and across public and private health programs and structures is on the increase (Yasnoff, O'Carroll, Koo, Linkins, & Kilbourne, 2000). Barriers faced in implementing public health solutions include (1) technical issues (e.g., data standards and systems interoperability), (2) professional issues (e.g., workforce, skills, and practices), (3) legal and regulatory issues (e.g., privacy, access, and confidentiality), and (4) issues related to funding and work processes (Luck, Chang, Brown, & Lumpkin, 2006). Overcoming these barriers will require preparation of a workforce with training in health informatics, data literacy, and systems science methods to enhance population health.

Common difficulties such as poor economics, political uncertainty, and lack of cutting-edge infrastructure have hampered the quality of health care in developing countries. Several challenges that are particularly relevant for developing countries exist in the implementation of technology-enabled solutions. These include

- *Infrastructure and financial needs:* The infrastructure needed to support implementation of technology-enabled solutions is scarce and irregularly distributed. Examples include lack of reliable electricity (Latourette et al., 2011) and expensive Internet access (Shiferaw & Zolfo, 2012). Regional disparities are prevalent in multiple countries, and the situation is not similar in all developing countries. Infrastructure challenges are also very different when comparing private or public initiatives, and are most relevant in rural areas (Simba, 2004). The use of mobile phones and wireless networks can help to ameliorate this issue (Asangansi & Braa, 2010). Prioritizing investments in building the capacity for technology innovations for citizens of low- and middle-income countries is challenging (Cinnamon & Schuurman, 2010).
- *Hardware and software:* Hardware acquisition is another difficult issue. Hardware costs are constantly falling, giving developing countries access to technologies that were previously unattainable. Various initiatives are being implemented by governments to bridge the digital divide. Examples include the Ceibal program in Uruguay,

which a few years ago distributed its millionth computer (Plan Ceibal, 2016), and the Conectar Igualdad program in Argentina, which has distributed more than 3,500,000 netbooks (Conectar Igualdad, n.d.). The rise of open-source software is helping resource-limited countries to implement health information systems. One software platform, OpenMRS, enables the design of customized electronic health records (EHRs) with no programming experience (Mamlin et al., 2006). It has been implemented across several continents including Africa, Asia, and Central and Latin America (Mohammed-Rajput, Smith, Biondich, Mamlin, & Doebbeling, 2011).

■ *Direct costs:* Costs can be very high during health technology implementations. The biggest challenge is during the scaling up of these system implementations, so a well-thought-out, sustainable plan is needed. This can be a much bigger challenge in countries with limited resources where health technology investments are in competition with basic needs like food, housing, education, and health care (Lewis, Synowiec, Lagomarsino, & Schweitzer, 2012). One example of this challenge occurred with the One Laptop per Child (OLPC) initiative. The goal was to transform education among children in resource-poor settings by enhancing their learning abilities. In spite of the innovative features of the XO laptop, including its ability to run on low power, a visual display adapted to bright sunlight, and a sealing component to prevent entry of dirt, critical cost barriers could not be addressed by governments in low-income countries. Each laptop cost $199, plus the cost of deployment (about 10% extra), additional infrastructure, teacher training, maintenance, and support. The projected goal of deploying 5 million laptops by 2008 could not be attained, with only about 1.4 million laptops deployed by the end of 2009 (Kraemer, Dedrick, & Sharma, 2009).

■ *Ethical and legal considerations:* Ethical considerations must be recognized at an early stage (Luna, Almerares, Mayan, Gonzalez Bernaldo de Quiros, & Otero, 2014). Security and legal issues pose critical barriers during implementation. Personnel at the LHDs require an understanding of ethics and legal frameworks. Obtaining voluntary informed consent when conducting research in cross-cultural settings has been consistently reported as a critical challenge. Some other common challenges are related to low education levels, language barriers, religious beliefs, and limitations in autonomous decision making. Recommendations focus on acquiring adequate cultural competency on the part of the researchers, conducting sufficient focus groups to ensure relevant participation of the study participants to address any concerns raised, and presenting consent materials concisely (Brothers & Rothstein, 2015).

■ *Lack of use of common interoperability standards:* The effective use of informatics standards is of fundamental importance (Hammond, Bailey, Boucher, Spohr, & Whitaker, 2010). Use of data interchange standards ensures interoperability and ensures that data are accurate and relevant (Hammond et al., 2010).

■ *Lack of a trained workforce:* There are too few well-trained health informaticians to meet the needs and expertise necessary for HIT implementations (Detmer, 2010). There is widespread agreement that an appropriately trained workforce is a critical dimension if sustained progress is to be achieved.

Global research projects need to incorporate recurrent training and capacity building for field workers and data collectors to account for these challenges (Mbuagbaw, Thabane, Ongolo-Zogo, & Lang, 2011). There is an urgent need for committing to informatics as a core competency for all public health workers (BOX 2.1).

- Develop regional, national, and global agendas that will facilitate implementation of technology-enabled solutions in healthcare settings.
- Provide incentives to use technologies to address population health challenges.
- Reduce the digital divide by encouraging widespread use of open source technologies.
- Develop clear guidelines to address the ethical and legal challenges related to the adoption of population health information systems.
- Promote the common and consistent use of standards.
- Implement educational programs or establish partnerships with organizations with qualified PopHI skilled professionals.

▶ III. Informatics Competencies to Enhance Population Health

Informatics combines a fundamental set of methodologies that are applicable for managing data, information, and knowledge. The central theme of informatics suggests that individuals supported by technology will perform better than those performing a similar task unassisted (Friedman, 2009).

PopHI systems support the needs of various stakeholders including biologists, clinicians, epidemiologists, health services researchers, and policymakers. Informatics is not limited to just the basic sciences. The basic domain of informatics includes information science, computer science, cognitive science, and organizational science, and the application domain includes biological, imaging, clinical, and public health fields (FIGURE 2.1).

The workforce's need for skilled health informatics professionals will rapidly increase as HIT systems support meaningful use objectives. Health professionals at all levels (e.g., clinicians, public health agencies) should be adequately skilled in the applications of information and computer science and technologies to enhance population health. Future research needs to study the advancement of the field of informatics education and informatics positions in the workforce. Defining competencies is a key way of communicating the message of informatics (Kulikowski et al., 2012).

FIGURE 2.1 The intersection of information sciences and application domains to enhance population health using PopHI

Public Health Informatics Competencies

Health professionals must be able to use information effectively as well as use and manage information technology (IT) projects effectively. The PHI competencies describe the needed skills that can help evaluate, measure, and promote employees; describe career pathways; and provide educational guidelines for academic programs. PHI competency has been defined as a "public health worker's observable or measurable performance, skill, or knowledge related to the systematic application of information and computer science and technology to public health" (U.S. Department of Health and Human Services [DHHS], CDC, & University of Washington, 2009). The expertise of PHI professionals is still evolving. The initial PHI competencies were developed during the 2001 Spring Congress of the American Medical Informatics Association (AMIA; Yasnoff, Overhage, Humphreys, & LaVenture, 2001). Two key themes were discussed, and 74 recommendations were made. The two themes were that (1) all stakeholders need to be engaged in coordinated activities related to public health information architecture, standards, confidentiality, best practices, and research; and (2) informatics training is needed throughout the public health workforce (Yasnoff et al., 2001). Six tracks were examined: (1) funding and governance; (2) architecture and infrastructure; (3) standards and vocabulary; (4) research, evaluation, and best practices; (5) privacy, confidentiality, and security; and (6) training and workforce (Yasnoff et al., 2001). The informatics competencies identified complemented the set of core competencies for public health professionals that were developed by the Council on Linkages between Academia and Public Health Practice (Yasnoff et al., 2001). The three classes of PHI competencies were (1) development, deployment, and maintenance of information; (2) use of information; and (3) use of IT. Three expertise levels were suggested for the PHI professional workforce segments: front-line staff, senior-level technical staff, and supervisory and management staff. The expertise levels were further categorized based on skill levels and included being (1) *aware:* a basic level of understanding in which individuals are able to identify the concept or skill but have a relatively limited ability to perform skills; (2) *knowledgeable:* able to apply and describe the skills; and (3) *proficient:* able to synthesize, critique, or teach the skills (TABLE 2.1).

Several domains under each competency were identified (O'Carroll, 2002). (See FIGURE 2.2.)

- *Effective use of information:* The following domains are covered under this competency (O'Carroll, 2002):
  - *Analytics assessment skills:* These skills allow individuals to determine appropriate collection, analysis, interpretation, communication, and dissemination of both qualitative and quantitative data findings in the most ethical and effective manner.
  - *Policy development/program planning:* This gives individuals the ability to utilize collected and summarized information in population health decision analysis and health planning.
  - *Communication skills:* The ability to communicate effectively by using the media and advanced technologies so that information can be presented accurately.
  - *Community dimensions of practice:* The ability to develop, implement, and evaluate community-based public health assessments.

- Develop regional, national, and global agendas that will facilitate implementation of technology-enabled solutions in healthcare settings.
- Provide incentives to use technologies to address population health challenges.
- Reduce the digital divide by encouraging widespread use of open source technologies.
- Develop clear guidelines to address the ethical and legal challenges related to the adoption of population health information systems.
- Promote the common and consistent use of standards.
- Implement educational programs or establish partnerships with organizations with qualified PopHI skilled professionals.

▶ III. Informatics Competencies to Enhance Population Health

Informatics combines a fundamental set of methodologies that are applicable for managing data, information, and knowledge. The central theme of informatics suggests that individuals supported by technology will perform better than those performing a similar task unassisted (Friedman, 2009).

PopHI systems support the needs of various stakeholders including biologists, clinicians, epidemiologists, health services researchers, and policymakers. Informatics is not limited to just the basic sciences. The basic domain of informatics includes information science, computer science, cognitive science, and organizational science, and the application domain includes biological, imaging, clinical, and public health fields (FIGURE 2.1).

The workforce's need for skilled health informatics professionals will rapidly increase as HIT systems support meaningful use objectives. Health professionals at all levels (e.g., clinicians, public health agencies) should be adequately skilled in the applications of information and computer science and technologies to enhance population health. Future research needs to study the advancement of the field of informatics education and informatics positions in the workforce. Defining competencies is a key way of communicating the message of informatics (Kulikowski et al., 2012).

FIGURE 2.1 The intersection of information sciences and application domains to enhance population health using PopHI

Public Health Informatics Competencies

Health professionals must be able to use information effectively as well as use and manage information technology (IT) projects effectively. The PHI competencies describe the needed skills that can help evaluate, measure, and promote employees; describe career pathways; and provide educational guidelines for academic programs. PHI competency has been defined as a "public health worker's observable or measurable performance, skill, or knowledge related to the systematic application of information and computer science and technology to public health" (U.S. Department of Health and Human Services [DHHS], CDC, & University of Washington, 2009). The expertise of PHI professionals is still evolving. The initial PHI competencies were developed during the 2001 Spring Congress of the American Medical Informatics Association (AMIA; Yasnoff, Overhage, Humphreys, & LaVenture, 2001). Two key themes were discussed, and 74 recommendations were made. The two themes were that (1) all stakeholders need to be engaged in coordinated activities related to public health information architecture, standards, confidentiality, best practices, and research; and (2) informatics training is needed throughout the public health workforce (Yasnoff et al., 2001). Six tracks were examined: (1) funding and governance; (2) architecture and infrastructure; (3) standards and vocabulary; (4) research, evaluation, and best practices; (5) privacy, confidentiality, and security; and (6) training and workforce (Yasnoff et al., 2001). The informatics competencies identified complemented the set of core competencies for public health professionals that were developed by the Council on Linkages between Academia and Public Health Practice (Yasnoff et al., 2001). The three classes of PHI competencies were (1) development, deployment, and maintenance of information; (2) use of information; and (3) use of IT. Three expertise levels were suggested for the PHI professional workforce segments: front-line staff, senior-level technical staff, and supervisory and management staff. The expertise levels were further categorized based on skill levels and included being (1) *aware:* a basic level of understanding in which individuals are able to identify the concept or skill but have a relatively limited ability to perform skills; (2) *knowledgeable:* able to apply and describe the skills; and (3) *proficient:* able to synthesize, critique, or teach the skills (TABLE 2.1).

Several domains under each competency were identified (O'Carroll, 2002). (See FIGURE 2.2.)

- *Effective use of information:* The following domains are covered under this competency (O'Carroll, 2002):
  - *Analytics assessment skills:* These skills allow individuals to determine appropriate collection, analysis, interpretation, communication, and dissemination of both qualitative and quantitative data findings in the most ethical and effective manner.
  - *Policy development/program planning:* This gives individuals the ability to utilize collected and summarized information in population health decision analysis and health planning.
  - *Communication skills:* The ability to communicate effectively by using the media and advanced technologies so that information can be presented accurately.
  - *Community dimensions of practice:* The ability to develop, implement, and evaluate community-based public health assessments.

TABLE 2.1 PHI Workforce Segments and Associated Competencies in 2002

Workforce Category	Description	Applicable Competencies	Expertise Level	Tasks
Front-line staff	Individuals carrying out the bulk of day-to-day tasks	Effective use of information technology	Moderate	▪ Basic data collection ▪ Data analysis ▪ Program planning ▪ Outreach activities ▪ Organizational tasks
		Information systems development	Basic	
Senior-level staff	Increase technical knowledge in areas of epidemiology, program planning, and evaluation	Effective use of information technology	Advanced	▪ Budget development ▪ Grant writing ▪ Program coordination and oversight
		Information systems development	Moderate	
Supervisory staff	Perform the major functions in an organization	Effective use of information technology	Moderate	▪ Program development ▪ Program implementation ▪ Program evaluation ▪ Community relations ▪ Manage timelines ▪ Policy recommendations
		Information systems development	Advanced	

Competency 1: Effective Use of Information
- Analytics assessment skills
- Policy development/program planning
- Communication skills
- Community dimensions of practice
- Basic public health sciences
- Financial planning and management
- Leadership and systems thinking

Competency 2: Effective Use of Information Technology
- Digital literacy
- Electronic communications
- Selection and use of IT tools
- Online information utilization
- Data and system protection
- Distance learning
- Strategic use of IT to promote health
- Information and knowledge development

Competency 3: Effective Management of IT Projects
- System development
- Cross-disciplinary communication
- Databases and standards
- Confidentiality and security systems
- Project management
- Human resources management
- Procurement and accountability
- Research

FIGURE 2.2 Core competencies for PHI professionals

> *Basic public health sciences:* The ability to apply basic public health sciences and research methods, and to identify current scientific evidence and related gaps so that determinants of health and illness can be defined.
>
> *Financial planning and management:* The ability to conduct cost-effective analysis.
>
> *Leadership and systems thinking:* The ability to conduct strategic planning, and promote team and organizational building.

- *Effective use of information technology:* This competency describes an individual's ability to use IT to improve professional effectiveness (O'Carroll, 2002). The competency includes the following domains:

  > *Digital literacy:* The ability to utilize ITs for working with documents and other computerized files.
  >
  > *Electronic communications:* The ability to utilize electronic communication.
  >
  > *Selection and use of IT tools:* The ability to select and utilize software tools to facilitate data collection, storage, analysis, and dissemination.
  >
  > *Online information utilization:* The ability to locate and interpret online public health–related information and data.

Data and system protection: The ability to ensure integrity of all electronic files and apply all means to ensure protection of confidential information.

Distance learning: The ability to utilize distance-learning technologies to support lifelong learning.

Strategic use of IT to promote health: The ability to utilize technology to enhance population health.

Information and knowledge development: The ability to integrate data from disparate sources to make informed decisions.

Effective management of IT projects: This competency describes the ability to effectively develop and manage information systems to improve the effectiveness of a public health enterprise. It includes the following domains (O'Carroll, 2002):

System development: Individuals should have the ability to put together and manage a team of professionals in areas ranging from information systems and computer science to epidemiology that can participate in the design, development, and evaluation of cost-effective public health information systems.

Cross-disciplinary communication: Individuals should have the ability to effectively communicate with IT and public health professionals regarding proven technologies that enhance public health practice.

Databases: Individuals should have the ability to apply good principles of database design.

Standards: Individuals should have the ability to utilize data standards for storage and transmission.

Confidentiality and security systems: Individuals should have the ability to develop confidentiality and privacy policies for the enterprise and support their implementation.

Project management: Individuals should have the ability to use informatics principles to manage population health information projects.

Human resources management: Individuals should have the ability to manage IT staff and health technology projects.

Procurement: Individuals should have the ability to procure cost-effective technologies for public health organizations.

Accountability: Individuals should ensure that technology is used to facilitate the openness of public health agency processes.

Research: Individuals should have the ability to monitor and apply informatics research findings relevant to public health practice.

TABLE 2.2 outlines the informatics competencies with proficiency levels by workforce segment across the different domains.

The 2002 competencies did not define competencies for those with a core identity and expertise in informatics. BOX 2.2 shows the inherent gaps in the 2002 PHI competencies.

In 2006/2007 the CDC formed a new working group consisting of public health professionals, informaticians, and educators from representative governmental, nongovernmental, and academic organizations to define the competencies for public health informaticians. The working group agreed to develop definitions of PHI

TABLE 2.2 Cross Comparisons of PHI Domains and Professional Workforce Segments

	Effective Use of Information		
	Informatics Professionals to Enhance Population Health		
Domains	**Front-Line Staff**	**Senior-Level Technical Staff**	**Supervisory and Management**
Analytic/ assessment skills	Aware to proficient	Knowledgeable to proficient	Knowledgeable to proficient
Policy development/ program planning	Aware to knowledgeable	Knowledgeable to proficient	Proficient
Communication skills	Aware to Proficient	Proficient	Proficient
Community dimensions of practice	Knowledgeable	Proficient	Proficient
Basic public health sciences	Aware to knowledgeable	Proficient	Proficient
Financial planning and management	Aware	Knowledgeable to proficient	Proficient
Leadership and systems thinking	Aware to knowledgeable	Knowledgeable to proficient	Proficient
Effective Use of Information Technology			
Digital literacy	Proficient	Proficient	Proficient
Electronic communications	Proficient	Proficient	Proficient
Selection and use of IT tools	Aware	Proficient	Knowledgeable
Online information utilization	Knowledgeable to proficient	Proficient	Knowledgeable to proficient

Data and system protection	Knowledgeable to proficient	Proficient	Knowledgeable to proficient
Distance learning	Knowledgeable to proficient	Knowledgeable to proficient	Knowledgeable to proficient
Strategic use of IT to promote health	Aware	Proficient	Proficient
Information and knowledge development	Aware	Proficient	Knowledgeable
Effective Management of Information Technology Projects			
System development	Aware to knowledgeable	Knowledgeable to proficient	Proficient
Cross-disciplinary communication	Knowledgeable	Proficient	Proficient
Databases	Knowledgeable	Proficient	Knowledgeable to proficient
Standards	Aware	Proficient	Knowledgeable to proficient
Confidentiality and security systems	Aware	Knowledgeable	Proficient
Project management	Aware	Knowledgeable	Proficient
Human resources management	Aware	Knowledgeable	Proficient
Procurement	Aware	Knowledgeable	Proficient
Accountability	Aware	Proficient	Knowledgeable to proficient
Research	Aware	Proficient	Proficient

BOX 2.2   Gaps in 2002 PHI Competencies

- The competency levels were not necessarily precise.
- The competencies were primarily focused on the U.S. public health workforce.
- They did not address the competencies needed for those who worked in specialized roles in health information systems.
- There was no clear understanding of the roles of public health informatics professionals.

---

roles and recognized that at least two tiers of PHIs are employed in public health agencies (see TABLE 2.3). The working group clearly outlined the competency language to help differentiate between the different tiers.

PHIs uniquely differ from IT specialists. All individuals working in the field of PHI require knowledge of public health as well as IT (Savel & Foldy, 2012). BOX 2.3 contains some of the distinguishing features between informaticians and IT professionals.

Fourteen core competencies were identified for both PHIs and senior PHIs (SPHIs). These competencies reflect best practices and describe the expectations

---

TABLE 2.3   The Two Tiers of PHI Roles and Functions

	Tier I Professionals	Tier II Professionals
Types of professionals	Public health informatics professionals	Senior public health informatics professionals
Roles	Narrow	More experienced
Functions	Develop and evaluate innovative health technological applications Ability to analyze how information is utilized Maintain critical health information systems	Oversee complex IT projects, policies, and concerns Manage IT systems using proper strategies Manage agency IT resources Implement innovative emerging informatics principles and IT systems for public health problems
Job titles (examples)	Researchers Scientists Project managers Program advisers	Public health informatics officers Policy advisers Strategic information specialists Standardized vocabulary specialists Health informatics scientists Professor of public health informatics

BOX 2.3 Differences Between PHI Professionals and IT Specialists

- IT specialists implement and operate information systems; PHIs focus more on how technology can enhance population health.
- IT specialists have a limited focus; PHIs function and evaluate impact within the broader spectrum of public health including the political, cultural, economic, and social environments.
- IT specialists primarily provide system support and management; PHIs focus on science and the development of public health information systems.

of what personnel in the PHI field should be doing. The major differences between PHI and SPHI professionals are variations in the level of judgment and experience; TABLE 2.4).

The 2011 AMIA Public Health Informatics Conference brought together members of the public health and health informatics communities to assess the progress and develop recommendations to further guide the field of PHI. Five discussion tracks were convened: (1) technical framework; (2) research and evaluation; (3) ethics; (4) education, professional training, and workforce development; and (5) sustainability (Massoudi et al., 2012). Participants determined the progress achieved and the possible recommendations that were needed in each of these identified themes. Three key themes were identified and 62

TABLE 2.4 Distinctions Between the Job Responsibilities of Senior- and Junior-Level PHIs

Strategic Direction for Public Health Informatics (Competency I)	
Public Health Informatician (PHI)	**Senior Public Health Informatician (SPHI)**
Directs health informatics planning for particular projects	Directs health informatics planning for particular projects
Makes significant recommendations on project decisions	Makes significant recommendations on project decisions
Significantly contributes to strategic decision making	Significantly contributes to strategic decision making
Develops policies related to information management	Participates in development of IT and information management policies for the enterprise

(continues)

TABLE 2.4 Distinctions Between the Job Responsibilities of Senior- and Junior-Level PHIs *(continued)*

Knowledge Management for the Enterprise (Competency II)	
Public Health Informatician (PHI)	**Senior Public Health Informatician (SPHI)**
Assesses knowledge requirements among various groups by collaborating with various public health professionals	Determines core knowledge required by groups within the enterprise
Assists in identifying solutions for information access	Identifies solutions for information access
Develops knowledge repositories	Identifies or creates a knowledge repository

Informatics Standards (Competency III)	
Public Health Informatician (PHI)	**Senior Public Health Informatician (SPHI)**
Disseminates information on the relevance of standards in various projects	Disseminates information on the relevance of standards in various projects
Uses informatics standards in all projects and systems, where relevant standards exist	Monitors and ensures that standards are properly used and applied
Contributes to standards development efforts	Contributes to standards development efforts
Supports orderly migration to a standards-based framework	Oversees orderly migration to a standards-based framework

Knowledge, Information, and Data Needs of Project Are Met (Competency IV)	
Public Health Informatician (PHI)	**Senior Public Health Informatician (SPHI)**
Assesses stakeholder and data needs	Assesses stakeholder and data needs
Designs user-centric information systems by collaborating with the necessary stakeholders	Ensures design of information systems that meet user and stakeholder needs

Development, Procurement, and Implementation of Information Systems (Competency V)	
Public Health Informatician (PHI)	**Senior Public Health Informatician (SPHI)**
Responsible for integrating system requirements into the development and implementation process	Ensures that public health requirements are integrated into information system development, procurement, and implementation
Ensures that projects meet standard public health requirements	Ensures that acquisitions associated with projects meet the public health requirements of the enterprise
Responsible for managing information system projects	Responsible for managing information system projects
Creates a clear project or operating framework	Establishes adequate frameworks for managing public health projects
Minimizes impact on ongoing operations when changing or implementing information systems	Minimizes impact on ongoing operations when changing or implementing information systems

Public Health Agencies with Internal IT Operations (Competency VI)	
Public Health Informatician (PHI)	**Senior Public Health Informatician (SPHI)**
Manages project or program resources	Evaluates agency resources
Manages user support for projects or programs	Ensures effective user support across the enterprise
Manages risks to information systems and applications	Manages risk-related issues in information systems
Follows enterprise operational policies	Participates in developing operational policies

IT Operations Managed by External Organizations (Competency VII)	
Public Health Informatician (PHI)	**Senior Public Health Informatician (SPHI)**
Assesses operational needs of the IT team on health projects	Participates in negotiating IT operational support with the organization that manages the IT resources based on the needs of the public health enterprise

(continues)

TABLE 2.4 Distinctions Between the Job Responsibilities of Senior- and Junior-Level PHIs (*continued*)

Disseminates information on the performance of the IT management team	Ensures that IT operational needs are being met
Ensures that best practices are utilized in management of IT operations	Ensures that best practices are utilized in management of IT operations

Communication with Various Stakeholders (Competency VIII)	
Public Health Informatician (PHI)	**Senior Public Health Informatician (SPHI)**
Communicates effectively with staff across enterprise disciplines	Communicates effectively with staff across enterprise disciplines, stakeholders, and the public
Advocates for the use of best practices in resource management	Advocates for the use of best practices in resource management
Collaborates with neighboring agencies on the use of codes and interoperability issues	Collaborates with neighboring agencies on the use of codes and interoperability issues

Evaluates Information Systems and Applications (Competency IX)	
Public Health Informatician (PHI)	**Senior Public Health Informatician (SPHI)**
Provides assistance in developing evaluation frameworks	Establishes evaluation frameworks and their ability to meet public health objectives
Establishes a framework for evaluating the implementation process for information systems and applications	Establishes a framework for evaluating the implementation process for information systems and applications
Evaluates information systems according to established frameworks	Ensures that frameworks are applied in systems evaluation

Public Health Informatics Research for New Insights and Innovative Solutions to Health Problems (Competency X)	
Public Health Informatician (PHI)	**Senior Public Health Informatician (SPHI)**
Maintains infrastructure for research work in public health	Creates and maintains applied public health informatics research infrastructure within the enterprise and/or through partnerships

Examines the role of IT in improving public health practices through research methods	Examines the role of IT in improving public health practices through research methods
Assists in developing new insights for various PHI programs	Assists in developing new insights for various PHI programs
Makes significant contributions to informatics agendas and provides adequate input	Makes significant contributions to informatics agendas and provides adequate input
Collaborates with researchers in informatics field	Collaborates with researchers in informatics field
Disseminates findings and contributes to science	Disseminates findings and contributes to science
Attends informatics conference and forums for knowledge exchange	Represents the organization at conferences such as that of the American Medical Informatics Association (AMIA) and various other forums
N/A	Responsible for mentoring in public health research

Public Health Information Systems Interoperable with Other Relevant Information Systems (Competency XI)	
Public Health Informatician (PHI)	**Senior Public Health Informatician (SPHI)**
Identifies interoperability concerns	Equips staff to identify interoperability issues within an organization
Determines whether interaction with other relevant information systems (e.g., clinical, environmental, or emergency response) is necessary for information systems being developed	Interacts with other clinical and environmental systems in public health to identify opportunities for improvement
Assesses clinical data for use in public health projects	Ensures relevant clinical data are available automatically and electronically to public health organizations
Supports the implementation of systems on environmental-related data	Ensures relevant environmental data are available automatically and electronically to public health organizations

(continues)

TABLE 2.4 Distinctions Between the Job Responsibilities of Senior- and Junior-Level PHIs *(continued)*

Informatics to Integrate Clinical Health, Environmental Risk, and Population Health (Competency XII)

Public Health Informatician (PHI)	Senior Public Health Informatician (SPHI)
Integrates several domains of informatics including genomics, clinical informatics, nursing informatics, consumer health, etc., with public health.	Integrates several domains of informatics including genomics, clinical informatics, nursing informatics, consumer health, etc., with public health
Supports informatics and its use in disease prevention	Uses informatics to promote disease prevention at the clinical, environmental, and personal health interfaces
Ensures effective clinical service provision using informatics	Ensures effective clinical service provision using informatics
Improves access to public health through informatics systems	Improves access to public health through informatics systems

Ensuring Security, Integrity, and Confidentiality in Public Health Data Management (Competency XIII)

Public Health Informatician (PHI)	Senior Public Health Informatician (SPHI)
Protects personal health information	Ensures protection of personal health information
Ensures compliance with institutional review boards and other ethical boards	Ensures compliance with institutional review boards and other ethical boards
Monitors integrity of public health information systems	Assesses integrity of public health information systems

Education and Training in Public Health Informatics (Competency XIV)

Public Health Informatician (PHI)	Senior Public Health Informatician (SPHI)
Facilitates integration of informatics knowledge within organizations and communities	Facilitates integration of informatics knowledge within organizations and communities

| Advances the profession of public health informatics | Advances the profession of public health informatics |
| Updates personal informatics knowledge with recent literature and conferences | Updates personal informatics knowledge with recent literature and conferences |

recommendations were made (Massoudi et al., 2012). Some of the themes are outlined in BOX 2.4.

A set of core informatics competencies for health professionals of the future has also been framed according to the Accreditation Council for Graduate Medical Education (2016; FIGURE 2.3).

These competencies may vary internationally, especially due to the wide disparities in public health infrastructure including hardware, software, financing, telecommunications, data exchange, and related privacy and security issues (O'Carroll, 2002). Access to computers has become common, resulting in greater demand for more advanced informatics tools. Substantial advances have occurred in IT, and significant investments have been made in health information systems. The increased availability of public health–related datasets emphasizes the need to provide training in new methods for data acquisition and analysis; to integrate large, complex data into decision making; and to focus on solutions rather than technologies. There is an urgent need to integrate informatics training into all aspects of public health.

▶ IV. Public Health Informatics Workforce

Jobs in the healthcare sector are projected to grow more than twice as fast as those in the general economy (Center for Health Workforce Studies [CHWS], 2012). The modern health professional must have competency in informatics as part of a larger goal to provide patient-centered care (Greiner & Knebel, 2003). The funds for the HITECH Act were expanded to enhance the HIT workforce. Of the $20 billion allocated, $116 million was designated for workforce development. Several assessments that characterize the need for PHI-trained professionals have been conducted, mainly in the United States, Europe, and Australia (Garde, Harrison, & Hovenga, 2005; Mantas et al., 2011; Murphy et al., 2004; Staggers, Gassert, & Skiba, 2000). A needs assessment for health informatics was also conducted by the Andean Global Health Informatics Research and Training Center across 11 Latin American countries. The survey was conducted in partnership with the

BOX 2.4 Key Themes During the 2011 AMIA Conference

- Facilitate information sharing with the informatics communities
- Ensure proper use of public health terminologies and evaluation methods in informatics
- Promote effective coordination and leadership

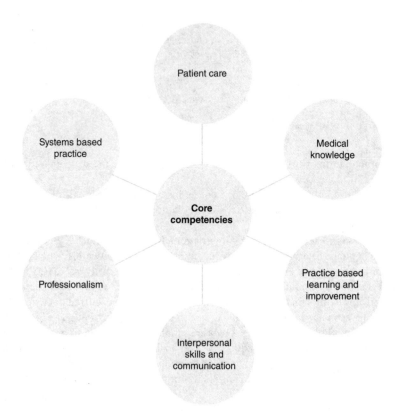

FIGURE 2.3 Core informatics competencies for health professionals, according to the Accreditation Council for Graduate Medical Education

International Medical Informatics Association for Latin America and the Caribbean (IMIA-LAC).

Public health professionals tend to lack needed skills in making efficient use of information for public health. Informatics capacities are considered important to providing surveillance and other important public health functions and services. A large proportion of state and local public health employees may not even be aware of the importance of informatics. Findings indicate the low capacity for, but high importance of, assessing the informatics-related needs of all public health employees. There is also a clear need to improve informatics capacity to analyze data. Designing reports and project management have also been identified as important training needs for informatics staff. Information should also be gathered on how local informaticians utilize informatics in public health. LHDs have various capacities and expertise in informatics, and institutes developing PHI educational programs need to be aware of the training needs at the local level. There is an urgent need to develop a skilled workforce that understands health care, ICT, and the people and organizational challenges involved.

The HITECH Act of 2009 called for rapid and extensive dissemination of HIT (DHHS, 2009). Research showed the need for over 40,000 informatics professionals as the United States rapidly increased its use of IT in health care. However, this total referred only to workers employed by hospitals (U.S. Bureau of Labor Statistics, 2014). The total number of HIT-related job postings per month increased from just

TABLE 2.5 Emerging Informatics Workforce Needs to Enhance Population Health		
Organization	**Year**	**Findings**
College of Healthcare Information Management Executives	2012	Of the 163 members of the College of Healthcare Information Management Executives, 74% reported lack of sufficient staff for implementation of projects.
U.S. Bureau of Labor Statistics	2012	Predicts a 21% increase in demand for medical records and health information technologists from 2010 to 2020.
Healthcare Information and Management Systems Society (HIMSS) Survey	2012	Lack of health IT staffing.
Burning Glassing report (Jayanthi, 2014)	2014	Informatics job postings are usually open for two additional days compared to regular postings.
		Positions for health informatics stay open twice as long as the positions they are replacing.
		Manager-level job postings in informatics are usually available for longer periods (42 days), compared with medical records and coding (41), and developers and medical coders (40).

453 to 12,950 during the period of 2007–2011 (Wheeler, 2014). Online postings of healthcare IT jobs grew 200% from 2009 to 2012—from 4850 to 14,512 per month (Wheeler, 2014). The number of companies with online health IT job postings increased by 94%, growing from 1659 in February 2009 to 3215 in February 2012 (Furukawa, Vibbert, & Swain, 2012). In 2011, the U.S. Bureau of Labor Statistics predicted a 20% annual growth in healthcare IT (Wheeler, 2014). Employment of health information technicians is projected to grow 22% from 2012 to 2022, much faster than the average for all occupations (Furukawa et al., 2012; TABLE 2.5).

▶ V. Informatics Training Programs to Enhance Population Health

An increase in the various types of data sources, data types, and data formats has created a unique opportunity for individuals to obtain informatics training to address the challenges of population health in the 21st century. The current health IT instructional training materials, developed under the Curriculum Development

Centers' cooperative agreement program, need to be updated to address four areas relevant for improved care delivery: (1) population health, (2) care coordination, (3) new care delivery and payments models, and (4) value-based care (DHHS, Office of the National Coordinator for Health Information Technology [ONC], 2015). Efficient use of interoperable systems, care coordination, and quality improvement are essential areas where improvement is needed by professionals in the field (ONC, 2015). Recent activities, primarily in the United States, have highlighted major advances in the education of the PHI workforce (see BOX 2.5). In 2011, the U.S. ONC for HIT provided grants to undergraduate-level institutions to provide training in PHI (CDC, 2012). Different activities have created opportunities and a pipeline of PHI workers to serve the needs of local, state, and federal agencies. Some of these initiatives include the following:

- *Programs in community colleges:* A grant program sought to rapidly create six-month intensive HIT programs in community colleges. Five regional consortia of 70 community colleges offered short-term training for 10,000 individuals per year (DHHS, 2015; TABLE 2.6).
- *Program of assistance for university-based training:* This was a grant program to enhance specialty roles in HIT requiring university-level training. Funding was given for the education of individuals requiring university-level HIT training at nine universities. Emphasis was also on short-term health informatics certificate programs delivered via distance learning (TABLE 2.7).
- *Curricular materials development centers:* A $10-million grant program was provided to higher institutions to support HIT curriculum development. Five universities, in collaboration with community college partners, developed HIT curricula (BOX 2.6).
- *Development of competency certifications:* Grants worth $6 million were awarded to institutions of higher education to support the development and initial administration of a set of HIT competency examinations.

The de Beaumont Foundation is playing a pivotal role in its sponsorship of the Public Health Informatics Institute's Informatics Academy as a unique training resource

---

BOX 2.5 Limitations of the Population Health Informatics Workforce Statistics

- It is difficult to track HIT workforce needs using existing data sources.
- HIT is not a particular set of occupational skills or tasks.
- Employment data are not generally structured in a way that accounts for the many possible ways a worker must be connected to a particular product.
- Standard occupational and industry codes are too coarse to identify HIT employment more precisely or in more diverse occupational settings.
- HIT staffing level estimates are limited in scope to the hospital setting.

Data from Joshi, A., & Perin, D. M. P. (2012). Gaps in the existing public health informatics training programs: a challenge to the development of a skilled global workforce. *Perspectives in Health Information Management/AHIMA, American Health Information Management Association, 9*(Fall); Schmitz, M., & Forst, L. (2016). Industry and occupation in the electronic health record: An investigation of the National Institute for Occupational Safety and Health Industry and Occupation Computerized Coding System. *JMIR Medical Informatics, 4*(1), e5.

TABLE 2.6 Geographic Distribution of Community Colleges Offering Short-Term Training Programs

Region	Lead Institute	Partners
Region A	Bellevue College, WA	Dakota State University, SD; Lake Region State College, ND; North Idaho College, ID; Pueblo Community College, CO; Salt Lake Community College, UT
Region B	Los Rios Community College District, CA	Butte College, CA; Cosumnes River College, CA; East LA College, CA; Fresno City College, CA; Maricopa College, AZ; Mission College, CA; Orange Coast College, CA; Pima College, AZ; San Diego Mesa College, CA; Santa Barbara City College, CA; Santa Monica College, CA; University of Hawaii College–Kapiolani, HI
Region C	Cuyahoga Community College District, OH	Cincinnati State Technical & Community College, OH; Columbus State Community College, OH; Delta College, MI; Des Moines Area Community College, IA; Johnson County Community College, KS; Kirkwood Community College, IA; Lansing Community College, MI; Macomb Community College, MI; Madison Area Technical College, WI; Metropolitan Community College, NE; Milwaukee Area Technical College, WI; Moraine Valley Community College, IL; Normandale Community College, MN; Sinclair Community College, OH; St. Louis Community College, MO; Wayne Community College District, MI
Region D	Pitt Community College, NC	Atlanta Technical College, GA; Broward College, FL; Catawba Valley Community College, NC; Central Piedmont Community College, NC; Chattanooga State Community College, TN; Dallas County Community College District, TX; Delgado Community College, LA; Dyersburg State Community College, TN; Florence/Darlington Technical College, SC; Hinds Community College, MS; Houston Community College, TX; Indian River State College, FL; Itawamba Community College, MS; Jefferson Community & Technical College, KY; Midland College, TX; National Park Community College, AR; Santa Fe College, FL; Tulsa Community College, OK; Walters State Community College, TN
Region E	Tidewater Community College, VA	Bristol Community College, MA; Bronx Community College, NY; Brookdale Community College, NJ; Burlington Community College, NJ; Camden County College, NJ; Capital Community College, CT; Community College of Allegheny County, PA; Community College of Baltimore County, MD; Community College of DC, Washington, DC; Community College of Vermont, VT; Essex County College, NJ; Gloucester County College, NJ; Kennebec Valley Community College, ME; Northern Virginia Community College, VA; Ocean County College, NJ; Passaic County Community College, NJ; Raritan Valley Community College, NJ; Southern Maine Community College, ME; Suffolk County Community College, NY; West Virginia Northern Community College, WV; Westchester Community College, NY

TABLE 2.7 Distribution of Certificate Programs in Health Informatics

	Clinician Leader	Public Health Leader	Health Information Management and Exchange Specialist	Health Information Privacy and Security Specialist	Research and Development Scientist	Programmers and Software Engineers	Health IT Sub-specialists
Duke University	X	X	X		X	X	X
Indiana University	X	X	X	X	X	X	X
University of Minnesota	X	X	X	X	X	X	X
Johns Hopkins University	X	X	X		X	X	X
Oregon Health and Sciences University	X	X	X	X	X	X	X
Texas State University	X	X	X	X	X	X	X
Columbia University	X	X	X	X	X	X	X
University of Colorado Denver College of Nursing	X	X	X	X	X	X	X
George Washington University	X	X	X	X		X	

Oregon Health and Science University
University of Alabama at Birmingham
Johns Hopkins University
Columbia University
Duke University

Despite these important steps, much more needs to be done to strengthen the
informatics competencies of the public health workforce.

in PHI. The academy has trained several hundred public health workers in online
informatics in the areas of design and management of public health information
systems.

Incorporating PopHI training into the curricula of the informatics, public
health, and care management fields will create a skilled workforce. These employees
will be able to address research and development issues such as data interoperability, the creation of large population health data repositories, and advances in big
data methods of storing, managing, and analyzing large population health datasets (Barrett, Humblet, Hiatt, & Adler, 2013; Kharazzi et al., 2017; Standards and
Interoperability Framework, 2016).

Informatics is considered a key component of a 21st-century MPH degree,
according to the Association of Schools and Programs for Public Health (ASPPH)
(CDC, 2012; Petersen & Weist, 2014). The Council on Education for Public Health
(CEPH) has proposed that informatics should be part of the foundational content
for the MPH and DrPH degrees (Calhoun, McElligott, Weist, & Raczynski, 2012).
The CEPH recommendations will help informatics find its way into curricula at
accredited schools of public health. This will assist both new and existing public
health professionals to support public health practice. In addition to informatics skills and expertise, agencies require highly skilled and well-trained health
informatics managers and leaders to enhance population health. Educational programs are emerging around the world to meet the need to train such individuals,
from graduate education to shorter courses (CDC, 2012). The U.S. CDC Informatics Fellowship has been recognized as a Registered Apprenticeship program
(CDC, 2012; BOX 2.7).

Few institutes currently offer training programs in PHI. These educational programs range from short-term training courses to fellowship, certificate, and masters
programs (TABLE 2.8). Many other institutes offer health informatics training programs and include some courses in public health as a part of their curriculum. Only
a few institutes offer a masters in PHI; all such programs are located in schools of
public health (TABLE 2.9).

TABLE 2.8 U.S. Universities Offering Certificate Programs in Public Health Informatics

University	School/Department Where Program Is Housed	City, State	Program	Website
University of Illinois	School of Public Health, Graduate School of Library and Information science	Champaign, Illinois	Certificate in Public Health Informatics	http://publichealth.uic.edu/public-health-informatics/phi-certificate-program
University of Minnesota	School of Public Health	Minneapolis, Minnesota	Certificate in Public Health Informatics	http://sph.umn.edu/site/docs/degrees-programs/informatics/cert_phi.pdf
Michigan State University	College of Human Medicine	East Lansing, Michigan	Certificate in Public Health Informatics	https://reg.msu.edu/AcademicPrograms/ProgramDetail.aspx?Program=2842
Johns Hopkins University	Bloomberg School of Public Health	Baltimore, Maryland	Certificate in Public Health Informatics	http://www.jhsph.edu/departments/health-policy-and-management/certificates/public-health-informatics/
Nova Southeastern University	College of Osteopathic Medicine	Fort Lauderdale, Florida	Certificate in Public Health Informatics	http://osteopathic.nova.edu/msbi/publichealth.html
City University of New York School of Public Health	School of Public Health	New York, New York	Certificate in Population Health Informatics	http://sph.cuny.edu/academics/non-degree-certificate-programs/phi-certificate/
University of Texas Health Science Center at Houston	School of Biomedical Informatics	Houston, Texas	Certificate in Public Health Informatics	https://sph.uth.edu/academics/graduate-certificate-programs/public-health-informatics/
University of North Carolina, Chapel Hill	School of Public Health/School of Information and Library Science	Chapel Hill, North Carolina	Certificate in Public Health Informatics	http://chip.unc.edu/public-health-informatics-certificate/

TABLE 2.9 Public Health Informatics Masters Programs

University	School/Department Where Program Is Housed	City/State	Program	Website
Emory University	Rollins School of Public Health	Atlanta, Georgia	Master of Science in Public Health: Public Health Informatics	http://sph.emory.edu/departments/bios/degree-programs/msph-phi/index.html
University of Illinois	School of Public Health	Champaign, Illinois	Master of Public Health in PHI	http://publichealth.uic.edu/academics/master-public-health-phi-degree
University of North Carolina	Multidisciplinary	Chapel Hill, North Carolina	Master of Professional Science in Biomedical and Health Informatics	http://chip.unc.edu/mps-bmhi/
University of Texas Health Science Center at Houston	School of Biomedical Informatics	Houston, Texas	Master of Science in Biomedical Informatics	https://sbmi.uth.edu/prospective-students/academics/masters.htm
University of Wisconsin	College of Health Sciences	Milwaukee, Wisconsin	Master of Health Care Informatics	http://uwm.edu/healthsciences/academics/masters-health-care-informatics/
University of Pittsburgh	School of Nursing	Pittsburgh, Pennsylvania	Master of Science in Nursing Informatics	http://www.nursing.pitt.edu/degree-programs/master-science-nursing-msn/msn-program-majors/nursing-informatics-online

(continues)

TABLE 2.9 Public Health Informatics Masters Programs *(continued)*

University	School/Department Where Program Is Housed	City, State	Program	Website
Northeastern University	College of Computer and Information Science; Bouvé College of Health Sciences	Boston, Massachusetts	Master of Science in Health Informatics	http://www.northeastern.edu/online/degrees/masters-health-informatics/
University of Missouri	School of Medicine; Department of Health Management and Informatics	Columbia, Missouri	Master of Science in Health Informatics	http://www.online.missouri.edu/degreeprograms/healthmanagementinformatics/informatics/index.aspx
Indiana University	School of Informatics and Computing	Lansing, Indianapolis	Master of Science in Health Informatics	https://soic.iupui.edu/biohealth/graduate/health-informatics-masters/
Drexel University	College of Computing and Informatics	Philadelphia, Pennsylvania	Master of Science in Health Informatics	http://online.drexel.edu/online-degrees/information-sciences-degrees/ms-hci/index.aspx
Case Western Reserve	Case School of Engineering/Graduate School/School of Nursing	Cleveland, Ohio	Master of Science in Health Informatics	https://engineering.case.edu/eecs/node/466
University of Kansas	KU Medical Center	Kansas City, Kansas	Master of Science in Health Informatics	http://www.kumc.edu/health-informatics/master-in-health-informatics.html
Weil Cornell Medical College	Department of Healthcare Policy and Research	New York, New York	Master of Science in Health Informatics	http://hpr.weill.cornell.edu/education/programs/health-informatics/
Northwestern University	School of Professional Studies	Evanston, Illinois	Master of Science in Health Informatics	http://sps.northwestern.edu/program-areas/graduate/health-informatics/

Current health informatics salaries exceed salaries in other fields by about 31%, with an average national salary of $81,000 (Careers in Public Health, 2016). States with the highest average health informatics salaries were Georgia ($93,000), Massachusetts ($95,000), and New York ($98,000). The lowest average salaries were reported in Idaho ($55,000), Nebraska ($60,000), and South Dakota ($61,000).

Some of the barriers to training and development of the public health workforce are well understood. These include cost, time, funding systems, and distances to be traveled to reach training (Northwest Center for Public Health Practice, 2013). Inadequate incentives for participating in training and continuing education, lack of an integrated delivery system for lifelong learning, and no consensus on necessary competencies are some of the other barriers to training (Rowitz, 2012).

▶ VI. Conclusion

There is an increasing need for health informaticians and an increasing number of health informatics programs to deliver graduates with different kinds of expertise (Hersh, 2009). Informatics specialists differ from IT specialists with respect to skills, salary, and their distribution across agencies of varying size (Hersh, 2009). Studies have also shown that there is a need for greater emphasis on leveraging electronic health information for public health functions (Hersh, 2009).

An urgent need exists for enhanced commitment to informatics as a core competency for all public health workers. The translation of research via informatics into healthcare practice will require a multidisciplinary approach to implementation into the healthcare delivery system. Trainees at varying levels require diverse environments for practice to ensure their learning is well grounded in real-world contexts. There is a need to expose trainees to opportunities where they can demonstrate: (1) heterogeneous data, information, and knowledge representation, analysis, and manipulation; (2) the ability to assess the value and costs of HIT platforms and informatics-based interventions; and (3) the ability to re-engineer and manage organizational and processes changes (Williams, Ritchie, & Payne, 2015).

References

Accreditation Council for Graduate Medical Education. (2016). Accreditation program requirer for graduate medical education in clinical informatics. (2016, February 12). Retrieve https://www.acgme.org/acgmeweb/Portals/0/PFAssets/ProgramRequirements/38 ̂ _informatics_2016.pdf

Asangansi, I., & Braa, K. (2010). The emergence of mobile-supported national heal ̂ systems in developing countries. *Studies in Health Technology Informatics, 160 ̂*

Barrett, M. A., Humblet, O., Hiatt, R. A., & Adler, N. E. (2013). Big data and From quantified self to quantified communities. *Big Data, 1*(3), 168–175

Brothers, K. B., & Rothstein, M. A. (2015). Ethical, legal and social impli ̂ personalized medicine into healthcare. *Personalized Medicine, 12*(1)

Buntin, M. B., Jain, S. H., & Blumenthal, D. (2010). Health inform ̂ infrastructure for national health reform. *Health Affairs, 29*(6), '

Calhoun, J. G., McElligott, J. E., Weist, E. M., & Raczynski, J. ̂ doctoral education in public health. *American Journal of P ̂*

Careers in Public Health. (2016). Informatics specialist ᴠ .careersinpublichealth.net/careers/informatics-specialist

Center for Health Workforce Studies (CHWS). (2012). Healthcare employment projections: An analysis of Bureau of Labor Statistics occupational projections 2010–2020. Retrieved from https://www.healthit.gov/sites/default/files/chws_bls_report_2012.pdf

Centers for Disease Control and Prevention. (2012). Establishment of the CDC public health informatics fellowship program as a Department of Labor registered apprenticeship. Retrieved from http://www.cdc.gov/PHIFP/downloads/PHIF-DOL_4-20-12.pdf

Cinnamon, J., & Schuurman, N. (2010). Injury surveillance in low-resource settings using geospatial and social web technologies. *International Journal of Health Geographics, 9*(1), 1.

Conectar Igualdad. (n.d.). Home page. Retrieved from http://www.conectarigualdad.gob.ar/

Detmer, D. E. (2010). Capacity building in e-health and health informatics: A review of the global vision and informatics educational initiatives of the American Medical Informatics Association. *Medical Informatics,* 101–105.

Friedman, C. P. (2009). A "fundamental theorem" of biomedical informatics. *Journal of the American Medical Informatics Association, 16*(2), 169–170.

Furukawa, M. F., Vibbert, D., & Swain, M. (2012, May). HITECH and health IT jobs: Evidence from online job postings. *ONC Data Brief,* no. 2. Washington, DC: Office of the National Coordinator for Health Information Technology.

Garde, S., Harrison, D., & Hovenga, E. (2005). Skill needs for nurses in their role as health informatics professionals: A survey in the context of global health informatics education. *International Journal of Medical Informatics, 74*(11), 899–907.

Greiner, A. C., & Knebel, E. (2003). *Health professions education: A bridge to quality.* Institute of Medicine (US) Committee on the Health Professions Education Summit. Washington, DC: National Academies Press.

Hammond, W. E., Bailey, C., Boucher, P., Spohr, M., & Whitaker, P. (2010). Connecting information to improve health. *Health Affairs (Millwood), 29*(2), 284–288.

Hersh, W. (2009). The health informatics workforce: Unanswered questions, needed answers. *Studies in Health Technology and Informatics, 151,* 492–503.

Jayanthi, A. (2014). Nation faces shortage of health informatics workers: This and 4 more findings on IT workforce. Beckers Health IT & CIO Review. Retrieved from http://www.beckershospitalreview.com/healthcare-information-technology/nation-faces-shortage-of-health-informatics-workers-this-and-4-more-findings-on-it-workforce.html

Joshi, A., & Perin, D. M. P. (2012). Gaps in the existing public health informatics training programs: a challenge to the development of a skilled global workforce. *Perspectives in Health Information Management/AHIMA, American Health Information Management Association, 9*(Fall).

Kharrazi, H., Lasser, E. C., Yasnoff, W. A., Loonsk, J., Advani, A., Lehmann, H. P., . . . Weiner, J. P. (2017). A proposed national research and development agenda for population health informatics: Summary recommendations from a national expert workshop. *Journal of the American Medical Informatics Association, 24*(1), 2–12.

Kraemer, L. K., Dedrick, J., & Sharma, P. (2009). One laptop per child: Vision vs. reality. *Communications of the ACM, 52*(6).

Kulikowski, C. A., Shortliffe, E. H., Currie, L. M., Elkin, P. L., Hunter, L. E., Johnson, T. R., . . . Williamson, J. J. (2012). AMIA board white paper: Definition of biomedical informatics and specification of core competencies for graduate education in the discipline. *Journal of the American Medical Informatics Association, 19*(6), 931–938.

Latourette, M. T., Siebert, J. E., Barto Jr., R. J., Marable, K. L., Muyepa, A., Hammond, C. A., . . . Taylor, T. E. (2011). Magnetic resonance imaging research in sub-Saharan Africa: Challenges and satellite-based networking implementation. *Journal of Digital Imaging, 24*(4), 729–738.

ris, T., Synowiec, C., Lagomarsino, G., & Schweitzer, J. (2012). E-health in low- and middle-income countries: Findings from the Center for Health Market Innovations. *Bulletin of the World Health Organization, 90*(5), 332–340.

J. D. (n.d.). Public health workforce development. Retrieved from www.phf.org/events/documents/COLMeeting_2013Sep_CDC_Update_Slides.pdf

Chang, C., Brown, E. R., & Lumpkin, J. (2006). Using local health information to promote health. *Health Affairs, 25*(4), 979–991.

Luna, D., Almerares, A., Mayan, J. C., Gonzalez Bernaldo de Quiros, F., & Otero, C. (2014). Health informatics in developing countries: Going beyond pilot practices to sustainable implementations: A review of the current challenges. *Healthcare Informatics Research, 20*(1), 3–10.

Mamlin, B. W., Biondich, P. G., Wolfe, B. A., Fraser, H., Jazayeri, D., Allen, C., . . . Tierney, W. M. (2006, January). Cooking up an open source EMR for developing countries: OpenMRS—a recipe for successful collaboration. *AMIA Annual Symposium Proceedings,* 529–533.

Mantas, J., Ammenwerth, E., Demiris, G., Hasman, A., Haux, R., Hersh, W., . . . Wright, G. (2011). Recommendations of the International Medical Informatics Association (IMIA) on education in biomedical and health informatics—first revision. *European Journal for Biomedical Informatics, 7*(2), 3–17.

Massoudi, B. L., Goodman, K. W., Gotham, I. J., Holmes, J. H., Lang, L., Miner, K., . . . Fu, P. C. (2012). An informatics agenda for public health: Summarized recommendations from the 2011 AMIA PHI conference. *Journal of the American Medical Informatics Association, 19*(5), 688–695.

Mbuagbaw, L., Thabane, L., Ongolo-Zogo, P., & Lang, T. (2011). The challenges and opportunities of conducting a clinical trial in a low resource setting: The case of the Cameroon mobile phone SMS (CAMPS) trial, an investigator initiated trial. *Trials, 12*(1), 145.

Mohammed-Rajput, N. A., Smith, D. C., Biondich, P., Mamlin, B., & Doebbeling, B. N. (2011). OpenMRS, a global medical records system collaborative: Factors influencing successful implementation. *AMIA Annual Symposium Proceedings,* 960–968.

Murphy, J., Stramer, K., Clamp, S., Grubb, P., Gosland, J., & Davis, S. (2004). Health informatics education for clinicians and managers—What's holding up progress? *International Journal of Medical Informatics, 73*(2), 205–213.

National Association of County and City Health Officials. (2007). Informatics at local health departments: Findings from the 2005 National Profile of Local Health Department Study. Retrieved from http://archived.naccho.org/topics/infrastructure/profile/upload/LHD _Informatics-final.pdf

Northwest Center for Public Health Practice. (2013). *Oregon public health workforce training needs assessment: Key informant interviews summary report.* Seattle, WA: Northwest Center for Public Health Practice.

O'Carroll, P. W. (2002). O'Carroll PW and the Public Health Informatics Competency Working Group. Informatics for public health professionals. Seattle, WA: Northwest Center for Public Health Practice.

Petersen, D. J., & Weist, E. M. (2014). Framing the future by mastering the new public health. *Journal of Public Health Management and Practice, 20*(4), 371.

Plan Ceibal. (2016). Entrega la computadora 1 millón. Retrieved from http://www.ceibal.edu .uy/#institucional

Rowitz, L. (2012). *Public health workforce development.* Chicago, IL: Mid-America Regional Public Health Leadership Institute.

Savel, T. G., & Foldy, S. (2012). The role of public health informatics in enhancing public health surveillance. *Morbidity and Mortality Weekly Report Surveillance Summary, 61*(Suppl.), 20–24. Retrieved from http://www.cdc.gov/mmwr/preview/mmwrhtml/su6103a5.htm

Schmitz, M., & Forst, L. (2016). Industry and occupation in the electronic health record: An investigation of the National Institute for Occupational Safety and Health Industry and Occupation Computerized Coding System. *JMIR Medical Informatics, 4*(1), e5.

Shiferaw, F., & Zolfo, M. (2012). The role of information communication technology (ICT) towards universal health coverage: The first steps of a telemedicine project in Ethiopia. *Global Health Action, 5,* 1–8.

Simba, D. O. (2004). Application of ICT in strengthening health information systems in developing countries in the wake of globalisation. *African Health Sciences, 4*(3), 194–198.

Smith, P. F., Hadler, J. L., Stanbury, M., Rolfs, R. T., & Hopkins, R. S. (2013). "Blueprint version 2.0": Updating public health surveillance for the 21st century. *Journal of Public Health Management and Practice, 19*(3), 231–239.

Staggers, N., Gassert, C. A., & Skiba, D. J. (2000). Health professionals' views of informatics education. *Journal of the American Medical Informatics Association, 7*(6), 550–558.

Standards and Interoperability (S&I) Framework. (2016). What is the S&I framework? Retrieved from http://www.siframework.org/whatis.html

Thacker, S. B., Qualters, J. R., & Lee, L. M. (2012). Public health surveillance in the United States: Evolution and challenges. *Morbidity and Mortality Weekly Report Surveillance Summary, 61*(Suppl.), 3–9.

U.S. Bureau of Labor Statistics. (2014). Request/recommendation for new health informatics practitioner standard occupational classification (SOC). Retrieved from http://library.ahima .org/xpedio/groups/public/documents/ahima/bok1_050715.pdf

U.S. Department of Health and Human Services. (2009). HITECH Act enforcement interim final rule. Retrieved from http://www.hhs.gov/hipaa/for-professionals/special-topics/HITECH-act -enforcement-interim-final-rule/index.html

U.S. Department of Health and Human Services. (2015). Workforce development programs; participating community colleges. Retrieved from https://www.healthit.gov/providers-professionals /participating-community-colleges

U.S. Department of Health and Human Services, Centers for Disease Control and Prevention, Office of Workforce and Career Development & University of Washington School of Public Health and Community Medicine's Center for Public Health Informatics. (2009). Retrieved from https://www.cdc.gov/informaticscompetencies/pdfs/phi-competencies.pdf

U.S. Department of Health and Human Services, Office of the National Coordinator for Health Information Technology (ONCHIT). (2015). American Recovery and Reinvestment Act of 2009: Information technology professionals in health care: Workforce training to educate health care professionals in health information technology. Retrieved from http://healthit.gov/sites /default/files/workforcefoa1292015.pdf

Wheeler, B. (2014). Biomedical and health informatics: Future prospects for the field and for our students [president's message]. *Pulse, IEEE, 5*(2), 6–69.

Williams, M. S., Ritchie, M. D., & Payne, P. R. (2015). Interdisciplinary training to build an informatics workforce for precision medicine. *Applied and Translational Genomics, 6*, 28–30.

World Health Organization. (2005). Preparing a health care workforce for the 21st century: The challenge of chronic conditions. *Chronic Illness, 1*(2), 99–100.

World Health Organization. (2006). *Building foundations for eHealth: Progress of member states: Report of the Global Observatory for eHealth*. Geneva, Switzerland: WHO Press.

Yasnoff, W. A., O'Carroll, P. W., Koo, D., Linkins, R. W., & Kilbourne, E. M. (2000). Public health informatics: Improving and transforming public health in the information age. *Journal of Public Health Management and Practice, 6*(6), 67–75.

Yasnoff, W. A., Overhage, J. M., Humphreys, B. L., & LaVenture, M. (2001). A national agenda for public health informatics. *Journal of the American Medical Informatics Association, 8*(6), 535–545.

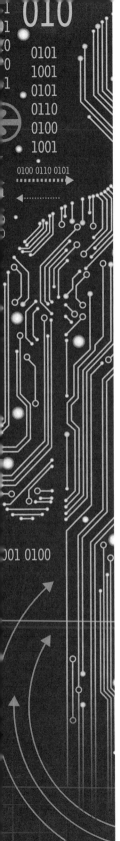

PART 2

Setting the Stage for Population Health Informatics

CHAPTER 3

Role of Population Health Informatics in Understanding Data, Information, and Knowledge

Hadi Kharrazi and Harold P. Lehmann

KEY TERMS

Activities of daily living (ADLs)
Admission, discharge, and transfer
Anatomical Therapeutic Chemical (ATC)
  Classification System (ATC)
Behavioral Risk Factor Surveillance
  System (BRFSS)
Current Procedural Terminology (CPT)
Data, Information, and Knowledge (DIK)
Diagnostic and Statistical Manual of
  Mental Disorders (DSM)
Family Educational Rights and
  Privacy Act (FERPA)
Generalized anxiety disorder (GAD)
Generic Product Identifier (GPI)
Health information exchanges (HIEs)
Health Insurance Portability and
  Accountability Act (HIPAA)

Health risk assessments (HRAs)
Healthcare Common Procedure Coding
  System (HCPCS)
Information
International Classification
  of Diseases (ICD)
International Classification of
  Primary Care (ICPC)
Knowledge
Laboratory information systems
Logical Observation Identifiers Names
  and Codes (LOINC)
Prescription benefit
  management (PBM)
Standardizations
Systematized Nomenclature of
  Medicine (SNOMED)

- Describe data, information, and knowledge in the context of population health.
- Identify common and emerging data types used for population health analytics.
- Examine information systems utilized to capture and organize population health data.
- Explain techniques and tools used to generate knowledge from population-wide information.
- Discuss challenges in managing data, information, and knowledge in population health.

QUESTIONS FOR THOUGHT

- What are the differences among the definitions of data, information, and knowledge in population health informatics compared to other health informatics fields? Explain the differences through real-world examples of population health.
- What are the advantages and disadvantages of using insurance claims versus electronic health records (EHRs) for population health informatics research? Describe the additional advantages and disadvantages of claims and EHRs in the context of a small outpatient clinic, a patient denominator of a large health network, and an entire population of a defined county.
- How can big data address the common challenges of managing data, information, and knowledge in population health informatics? Provide technical examples for each challenge.
- What federal and state health policies have accelerated the adoption and use of population-health informatics solutions? Explain how and why population health informatics can be instrumental in achieving the goals of those policies.

CHAPTER OUTLINE

▶ I. Overview of Data, Information, and Knowledge

Data, information, and knowledge (DIK) are critical elements of the informatics vocabulary. Data are conceived as symbols or signs that represent facts but are not usable in their current raw format (Ackoff, 1989; Rowley, 2007). Information is defined as data that have description and meaning, and thus can answer the questions of "what, when, where, and who" in relation to the data (Ackoff, 1989; Rowley,

2007). Knowledge embraces rules and frameworks to answer why certain relationships within information exist and how the information can be interpreted given these rules and frameworks (Ackoff, 1989; Barrett, Humblet, Hiatt, & Adler, 2013; Rowley, 2007).

The DIK hierarchical model refers to these informatics elements in a structural or functional model in which data are processed into information, information is analyzed and perceived as knowledge, and knowledge is then used to predict future events (Rowley, 2007). The DIK model is often depicted as a pyramid in which data represent the base of the pyramid, information composes the middle layer, and knowledge is the apex of the pyramid (FIGURE 3.1) (Rowley, 2007). Note that some models/pyramids also include wisdom as the fourth informatics element; however, we do not include wisdom here due to the complexities in defining it, especially within the context of population health.

The terms *data, information*, and *knowledge* are often misused in the population health informatics (PopHI) context. For example, a registry of patients with a specific clinical condition may offer a spectrum of capabilities ranging from storing raw facts in a dataset to representing relationships in an information system to providing a complex knowledge repository of rule sets about those patients—and yet may be called, simply, a "database." The poor understanding of these terms and their ambiguous applications often obscure the clear definition of operational and research goals as well as processes and outcomes of PopHI projects, and hence may produce undesirable results. Indeed, *data, information*, and *knowledge* are often used interchangeably in PopHI, thus creating confusion on what different PopHI solutions offer.

This chapter aims to provide an overview of the underlying definitions of DIK and to introduce various types and tasks involved with each of these terms in the context of PopHI. Learning the proper meaning of these terms will enable the informatics specialist to communicate the aims and tasks of PopHI projects clearly, and to improve pinpointing potential challenges or pitfalls of such informatics developments.

Definitions

Data

Data are the measurement, characteristic, or state of an entity/object (Ackoff, 1989). In the context of PopHI, the entity can be a person, provider, payer, health system,

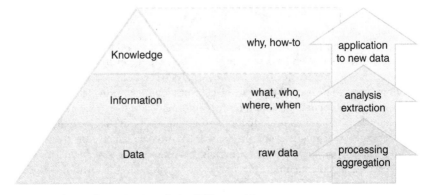

FIGURE 3.1 Data, information, knowledge (DIK) pyramid

community, or any other attributed object. Data in their raw format, without presenting relevant descriptions or relationships, do not carry any meaningful information; for example, the result of a lab test, with no attribution to another entity such as a patient, is considered raw data of perhaps no use in a clinical setting. Similarly, the average risk score of hospitalization is meaningless unless it is attributed to a specific population. Indeed, the meaningfulness of data depends on and differs based on the intended use of the data. As an example, a dataset storing the contact list of a large population, but missing the linkage to individual clinical providers, is useless if the purpose of a PopHI project is to analyze the patient–provider network across the population. Thus, without relations, contexts, or linkage among the data, the isolated data bits do not convey sufficient meaning to inform the end user about the underlying health trends of a population.

Information

Information is data defined and described in a specific context (Ackoff, 1989; Rowley, 2007). In essence, information provides the "who, what, where, and when" about the data. In other words, data will create information if there is some information about what the data means, who has collected it, whom it is attributed to, where it has occurred, or when it was collected. In the context of PopHI, these extra bits of data may contain information about relationships, associations, rankings, and other meaningful explanations of the underlying data. For example, if the existence of a lab test is the intent of a task, then merely knowing if a lab test is associated with a patient can be informative. Another example is a contact database of a large denominator of patients that identifies the relationship between individual patients and providers. This database can convey useful information for a patient–provider network analysis. A wide range of informatics tools captures and manages such attributes or relationships by standardized processes and structures that are commonly used in PopHI solutions (e.g., entity-relationship diagrams in conventional database information systems).

Knowledge

Knowledge is defined in reference to the underlying information (Rowley, 2007; Rowley & Richard, 2008). A knowledge base contains the how-to and why answers to proposed research and operational questions, and can be used to analyze and compare new information to the discovered patterns (Rowley, 2007; Rowley & Richard, 2008). Knowledge contains rules learned from existing information and can be applied to other information as needed for analysis, comparison, or evaluation. For example, in a simple case of a patient's lab test result, the levels of the result can be compared with known standard ranges, and thus various diagnoses can be proposed or ruled out accordingly. In the example of the patient–provider contact database, the result of the network analysis is considered new knowledge, which in turn can be used as a rule to evaluate other patient–provider contact databases. A number of computerized tools help informaticians to extract, generate, and store knowledge that is commonly used for population health projects (e.g., statistical packages, machine-learning programs). Knowledge can also be created, and is generated and captured after information is processed, organized, structured, or analyzed by a specific method. Knowledge can be stored in the form of a process, procedure, or proposition (Zeleny, 2005).

Population Health Informatics Context

In PopHI, DIK are often defined within the broader context of population health missions and goals (see TABLE 3.1). The term *data* usually refers to facts, measures, or characteristics of the entities involved in the health outcome of a population (O'Carroll, Yasnoff, Ward, Ripp, & Martin, 2003). For example, the stand-alone diagnosis list of a patient in a given population is considered population health data. Information is often created when a piece of data is described within the context of PopHI, such as a table of most frequent diagnoses for a defined population. Knowledge is generated when rules are extracted from information or when an existing rule is applied against a new set of information. As an example, knowledge is created when a utilization-risk-score formula is extracted from existing information. In addition, the same extracted knowledge/rule can be applied later against a new set of information to gain insight about the new population presented by the new data.

Within the PopHI context, the progression from data to information to knowledge can be considered as consequential steps in deriving insight about a trend within a defined population and taking action on that basis. Data often include raw administrative, clinical, social, and environmental data collected by a range of entities in various information technology (IT) systems (e.g., clinical data are collected by clinicians in EHRs). Information is produced when patient data across an entire population denominator are processed, aggregated, and joined to present a meaningful picture on the larger population trends. Knowledge is extracted by examining the underlying information with statistical tools, and then applying the extracted knowledge against new populations. FIGURE 3.2 depicts the steps involved in converting data to information, extracting knowledge from information, and applying the new knowledge to new information to generate new data in PopHI. For example, insurance claims records of patients in a population can be considered raw data. These data can be used to generate information with a list of major diagnoses of all patients who sought care at a hospital in a given period. This information can

TABLE 3.1 Data, Information, and Knowledge in the Context of PopHI

Term	PopHI Definition	PHI Example
Data	A fact, measure, or characteristic of a person, provider, payer, or population	A list of diagnoses for a patient
Information	A piece of data contextualized within the purpose of a PopHI solution	A table of most frequent diagnoses for a given population
Knowledge	An information base used to extract or apply a rule representing the knowledge	A utilization-risk-score formula or method derived from the total cost and most frequent diagnoses of a population

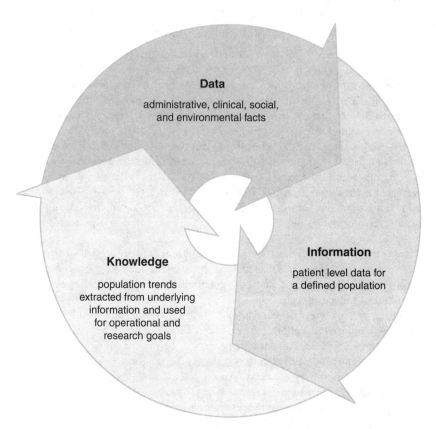

FIGURE 3.2 The cycle of data, information, and knowledge in PopHI

then be turned into knowledge by developing a predicted risk model of unplanned hospitalization for this population. Finally, the produced knowledge can be used on another dataset to generate new data to restart the DIK cycle.

▶ II. Data and Data Types

Patient-Level Data in the Population Health Context

Since the 1980s, PopHI experts have used traditional data sources (e.g., insurance claims) and traditional data types available (e.g., diagnoses) to identify population health trends (Duncan, 2011). However, with the widespread adoption of emerging health IT solutions (Charles, Gabriel, & Furukawa, 2014; Charles, King, Furukawa, & Patel, 2013), new types of data are increasingly captured and used to generate knowledge for population health solutions. Reflecting these trends, this chapter categorizes population-health data types into "common data types" and "emerging data types" (see TABLE 3.2).

Common data types are conventional data formats used in PopHI that are often extracted from traditional data sources. These data sources usually include:

TABLE 3.2	Common and Emerging Types of PopHI Data
Data Type	**Example**
Common Data Types	
Demographics	Age, sex/gender, race
Diagnoses	Diagnosis, severity
Medications	Prescription, dispense
Procedures	Inpatient, outpatient
Surveys	HRA, PHQ9
Utilization	Cost, hospitalization
Grouped variables	ACG, DRG
Emerging Data Types	
Lab orders/values	HbA1c levels
Vital signs	BMI, blood pressure
Social data	Income level
Patient-generated	mHealth, PROs
Community	Community specs
Geospatial	Neighborhood build, environment
Other data	Workflow data

Note: ACG: Adjusted Clinical Group; BMI: Body Mass Index; DRG: Drug Related Group; HbA1c: Glycated Hemoglobin; HRA: Health Risk Assessment; mHealth: Mobile Health; PHQ9: Patient Health Questionnaire; PROs: Patient Reported Outcomes.

(1) medical insurance claims, (2) medication claims, and (3) patient-level surveys such as health risk assessments (HRAs) or activities of daily living (ADLs). Emerging data types include new types of data that are acquired from nontraditional sources of population health. Some of these data sources and their attributed data types include EHRs, which contain multiple data types, and health information exchanges (HIEs), which offer novel types of information, such as admission, discharge, and transfer notifications that could be utilized in real-time population health analytics.

Common Data Types

Common data types used for population health data systems and analytics include demographics, diagnoses, medications, procedures, surveys, and utilization information.

Demographics

The common demographic variables include age and sex, both of which have a direct effect on healthcare utilization. For example, the increasing life expectancy in the U.S. population is leading to an aging population and hence increasing overall healthcare costs (Duncan, 2011). Thus, age and sex are commonly used to predict population health outcomes such as cost and utilization, and are often considered important independent variables in population-health predictive models (Iezzoni, 2012). Demographic-derived variables include age ranges or rule sets to deduct eligibility for insurance plans such as Medicare.

Most patient-level data sources contain demographic variables such as age and sex. For example, insurance claims, EHRs, and HIEs capture demographic data on a regular basis. The quality of demographic data is often acceptable due to various mandates to collect them accurately (Centers for Medicare and Medicaid Services [CMS], 2012, 2014; Jha et al., 2011). However, data quality is usually affected by various factors such as mode of measurement, user mistakes, and data conversion issues.

A number of coding standards for age and sex are published but they are not commonly adhered to, although most age and sex datasets are coded in a recognizable fashion. There are no major interoperability issues with demographic data; however, there are legal limitations on sharing age if it contains the date of birth or includes ages above a certain limit (U.S. Department of Health and Human Services, n.d.). Note that demographic data are used not only for population-health predictive modeling, but also to match patient records across different data sources. Thus, legal limitations on sharing demographic data may hinder the development of multisource population-health data warehouses.

Diagnoses

The term *diagnosis* includes different aspects such as underlying disease, signs, symptoms, injuries, factors influencing health status, family history, and, increasingly, genetic information. Certain diagnoses and various combinations of them—especially chronic conditions—have a direct correlation with healthcare utilization (Duncan, 2011; Iezzoni, 2012). Thus, diagnosis is commonly used as an independent variable to predict population health outcomes such as future cost. Further nuance may include severity of a disease, trajectory of a disease over time, and history of a condition, and all of these could be extracted from a problem list.

Diagnosis data are found in most patient-level data sources; for example, diagnosis codes are included in both insurance claims and EHRs. The quality of diagnosis data is often acceptable due to various mandates to collect them appropriately (CMS, 2012, 2014; Jha et al., 2011); however, data quality differs across different data sources. For example, insurance claims transactions often include a limit on the number of diagnoses that are associated with certain procedures, whereas EHRs do not have such limitations. In addition, EHRs include problem lists that can be used to elicit the active versus nonactive status of a diagnosis; however, the quality of such problem lists often needs further validation.

A few conventional and established coding standards are available to encode diagnoses. These coding standards include, but are not limited to, the International Classification of Diseases (ICD), International Classification of Primary Care (ICPC), Systematized Nomenclature of Medicine (SNOMED), Diagnostic and Statistical Manual of Mental Disorders (DSM), and read codes. ICD is the most commonly used diagnostic coding system for both claims and EHRs.

Some interoperability issues with diagnosis data still prevail, specifically when mapping diagnostic data from one coding system to another one. The mapping challenge also exists when mapping diagnoses across different versions of the same coding system, such as converting diagnostic data from ICD version 9 to ICD version 10. Certain diagnostic codes—such as human immunodeficiency virus (HIV) information and mental illness diagnoses—are protected by various federal and state laws, and population health databases might not include those diagnostic codes.

Medications

The medication data type includes prescribed and filled (dispensed) medications. Prescription information is often extracted from EHRs whereas filled information is usually found in insurance claims. Certain medications, and sometimes various combinations of them, have a direct correlation with healthcare utilization (Duncan, 2011). For the same reason, medication is commonly used as an independent variable to predict population health outcomes such as future healthcare costs. In addition, a number of constructs can be derived from medication data such as medication adherence and reconciliation rates (e.g., polypharmacy counts, medication regimen complexity index, and medication possession ratio).

Most clinical data sources include medication data. Medication codes are included in both insurance claims and EHRs. Medication data can also be extracted from other sources such as prescription benefit management (PBM) systems, commercial electronic medication order systems such as SureScript or specialized HIE datasets such as prescription drug monitoring programs (PDMPs). The quality of medication data is often acceptable due to various mandates to collect medication data (CMS, 2016); however, data quality differs across different data sources. For example, as mentioned previously, insurance claim transactions often capture the filling status of a medication, whereas EHRs collect prescription information only.

Commonly used coding standards for medications include, but are not limited to, National Drug Codes (NDCs), RxNorm, SNOMED chemical axes, Anatomical Therapeutic Chemical (ATC) Classification System (ATC), and a number of commercial drug codes such as MediSpan, Multum, Generic Product Identifier (GPI), and First Databank (FDB). Each coding standard addresses different notions of a medication (e.g., drug class, ingredients, dosage).

Potential interoperability issues may arise with medication data when mapping medication data from one coding system to another. For example, an RxNorm code (drug class) may map to multiple NDC codes (packaged drug) and vice versa. Certain medications—such as those used to treat HIV or mental illnesses—are protected by various federal and state laws, and may be excluded from common population health databases.

Procedures

Procedures include clinical and administrative procedures such as evaluation and management procedures, and procedures representing surgery, radiology, pathology, laboratory, and other clinical domains. Certain procedures have an overall higher cost associated with them, thus creating a direct correlation with healthcare utilization (Iezzoni, 2012). In addition, certain procedures may indicate a potential for higher costs in the future. Procedure data type is commonly used as an independent variable to predict population health outcomes such as future healthcare costs; however, this data type is also used as a dependent variable when the aim is to predict high-cost procedures (Duncan, 2011).

Established coding standards for procedures include, but are not limited to, the ICD's Clinical Modification (ICD-CM) version 9, ICD's Procedure Coding System (ICD-PCS) version 10, Current Procedural Terminology (CPT), and Healthcare Common Procedure Coding System (HCPCS).

Surveys

Certain risk factors and self-reported behaviors affect healthcare utilization (Duncan, 2011); for example, smoking or drinking will likely increase future healthcare costs. Survey data types are commonly used as independent variables to predict population health outcomes such as future healthcare costs. A variety of variables can also be derived from the surveys.

Survey data are collected by self-reported questionnaires. Sometimes survey data are stored within EHRs as part of a population-wide assessment. Moreover, insurers may collect survey data from their members; however, these datasets often are not included in conventional claims datasets. The quality of survey data varies considerably from one questionnaire to another. Inherent data quality issues can be due to the nature of the data being collected. Surveys are also prone to various biases such as sampling, selection, response, and social-desirability biases. In addition, the validity and reliability of questionnaires are often difficult to measure.

There are no standard coding mechanisms for surveys; however, using a standardized questionnaire can help reduce bias and error when utilizing such survey information for population health analytics. Some of the standardized questionnaires include the HRA tools, Patient Health Questionnaires (PHQs), generalized anxiety disorder (GAD) screening tools, and the Life Event Checklist (LEC).

Utilization/Cost

Utilization can be defined as emergency department admission, hospitalization, readmission, or other significant healthcare utilization events. Utilization data are usually used as the dependent or outcome variables in population health analytics (Duncan, 2011); however, prior utilization patterns can also be used to predict future utilization.

Utilization data are often extracted from claims, which include all covered procedures, costs, and other associated utilization events for each patient across all providers. Sometimes utilization data are extracted from other data sources such as EHRs, especially when claims data are not available. Note that EHR-level utilization data are limited to events that have occurred at a particular provider and often do not contain utilization data from other providers. The quality of utilization data is often acceptable due to various mandates to collect them accurately (CMS, 2016); however, as discussed earlier, data quality varies across different data sources.

There are no specific standard coding terminologies for utilization. However, most utilization data are based on claims data, and a number of reimbursement policies and reference-coding systems are available to encode utilization events. Certain utilization events—such as admission to a mental health clinic—are protected by various federal and state laws. Therefore, a population health database might not include those specific utilization and cost data.

Groupers

Groupers are software applications or lookup tables that provide a systematic and logical method for grouping lower-level variables such as ICD codes into larger concepts that can facilitate population-health data management and analytics (Duncan, 2011). These grouped concepts are often designed and generated in a way that can be highly correlated with healthcare utilization or any other outcome of interest. Grouped concepts are often used as independent variables in population-health analytics; for example, a high-level diagnostic concept may categorize all diabetes ICD codes into two grouped concepts of "diabetes with complications" and "diabetes without complications."

There are no specific standard coding terminologies for grouped concepts; however, underlying grouper software usually uses common grouping terms and concepts for internal use. Grouper software applications often use insurance claims data to generate the grouped concepts (see TABLE 3.3). Due to the proprietary aspect of most of these grouping concepts, they have limited interoperability with other systems. Some of the grouped concepts may include sensitive data that should be managed accordingly.

Emerging Data Types

These data types are "emerging" because of the only-recent ubiquity of EHRs and mHealth technologies. How this new availability will affect the predictive models we have used to date is being worked out now.

Lab Data

Lab data include both lab orders and lab results. A number of constructs can be derived from lab data such as the severity of a diagnosis, a missing diagnosis, and even missing medications, although such imputations should be conducted cautiously.

Currently the best sources of lab data are EHRs and other laboratory information systems used by clinical laboratories. The quality of lab data is often acceptable; however, issues with changing coding standards and units of measurement usually affect data quality negatively. There are potential interoperability issues with lab data, specifically when mapping lab data from one coding system to another one. In addition, certain lab results are protected by federal and state laws (e.g., lab test revealing HIV status), and hence might be missing from population-wide databases.

There are a number of well-developed coding standards for lab orders and lab results. These coding standards include, but are not limited to, the Logical Observation Identifiers Names and Codes (LOINC), the SNOMED, and the

TABLE 3.3 Common Groupers, Input Data Types, and Output Data Types

Company/ Institute	Risk Grouper	Data Type
CMS	Diagnostic Risk Groups (DRGs)	Claims (IP)
CMS/DHHS	Hierarchical Condition Categories (HCCs)	Age/sex, ICD9
3M	Clinical Risk Groups (CRGs)	Claims (IP/OP/Rx-NDC)
IHCIS/Ingenix	Impact Pro	Age/sex, ICD9, NDC, Lab
UC San Diego	Chronic disability payment system (Medicaid Rx)	Age/sex, ICD9, NDC
Verisk Sightlines	Diagnostic Cost Groups (DxCGs) RxGroup	Age/sex, ICD9 Age/sex, NDC
Symmetry/ Ingenix	Episode Risk Groups (ERGs) Pharmacy Risk Groups (PRGs)	ICD9, NDC NDC
Summetry/ Ingenix	Episode Treatment Groups (ETGs)	ICD9, NDC
Johns Hopkins	Adjusted Clinical Groups (ACGs)	Age/sex, ICD9, NDC, Lab
CMS	Diagnostic Risk Groups (DRGs)	Claims (IP)

Note: ICD: International Classification of Diseases; NDC: National Drug Codes.

CPT. As of early 2017, the majority of EHRs used localized coding systems for lab orders and results, which made interoperability of lab data for population health challenging.

Vital Signs

Vital sign data include physiological variables such as weight, height, body mass index, blood pressure, temperature, pulse rate, and respiratory rate. Certain long-term trends in vital signs may be predictive of higher healthcare utilization. Vital signs can also be used to impute missing diagnoses or provide a severity measure of a given diagnosis.

LOINC is the de facto coding standard for vital signs; however, most EHRs do not actively adhere to it. Indeed, EHR users often develop internal coding lists for their vital signs that might not be interoperable with other settings.

The best data sources of vital signs are EHRs. The completeness of some vital signs is often acceptable; however, issues with human errors and units of measurement often affect data quality and thus require extensive data cleaning before use for population health analytics. There are interoperability issues with vital signs, specifically when mismatched units are used in different data sources (e.g., inches versus centimeters). Another interoperability issue is the extra data about vital signs that may change the clinical concepts and use of it (e.g., sitting versus standing for blood pressure measurements).

Social Data

Social data include variables such as smoking status, alcohol consumption, addictive behaviors, and socioeconomic status (SES). Many of these predict higher resource utilization in the future; thus, they are used as independent variables to predict healthcare costs. Social data can also be used to derive various constructs such as treatment affordability and medication adherence.

Although a number of coding standards have been proposed to standardize social data, most of the existing social data sources use internally developed coding vocabularies. EHRs often include some social data about individual patients; however, most social data are acquired from nonhealth data sources such as data systems used in social services organizations. Social data often suffer from lower data quality, mainly due to the incompleteness of survey responses and/or a higher possibility of subjective bias. Data interoperability might become challenging if the same underlying survey has not been used to collect a specific social data type. Note that most social data are not subject to the Health Insurance Portability and Accountability Act (HIPAA), but might still be subject to other privacy rules such as the Family Educational Rights and Privacy Act (FERPA) (U.S. Department of Education, n.d.). The challenge of linking between EHR records of individuals and their social-service records thus has both technical and regulatory components.

Patient-Generated Data

Patient-generated data include a growing number of variables such as physical activity levels collected by wearable devices, patient-reported signs and symptoms, and other passive/active variables reported or collected by patients. Certain trends of patient-generated data may improve short-term predictive models of utilization. Patient-generated data can also be used to derive various constructs such as general fitness and ADL levels that could be indicative of frailty. Standards are increasingly becoming more available for mobile health and wearable devices, but operational or research-grade standards are not widely adopted yet.

Patient-generated data are often collected via wearable devices, personal health records, or centralized survey platforms. Patient-generated data have a variety of data quality levels. Data collected by mobile health and wearable devices often have acceptable data quality levels, but the issues of accuracy and comparability are still a challenge when data are collected across a variety of devices. Self-entered data via surveys and other communication means are subject to a variety of biases and errors. Data interoperability might become challenging as more nonstandardized devices enter the market, and for devices that are exempt from being monitored by federal agencies. The distributed consenting process is often complex, and creating large population-wide data warehouses may be infeasible due to certain legal limitations.

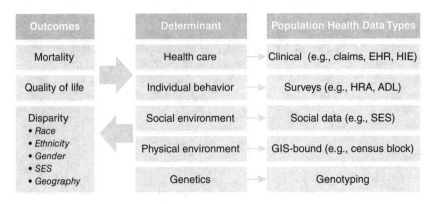

FIGURE 3.3 Health determinants and population health data types

Note: GIS: Geographic Information System

Other Population-Level Data Types

Other data types that can also be used for population health projects include: (1) workflow data types such as care density; (2) environmental data such as geo-bound population health variables and community/neighborhood factors; and (3) marketing data such as shopping behaviors, bankruptcy records, and credit scores. Note that ethical and legal questions of whether certain data types can or should be used for population health projects are still unanswered.

Data Types and Determinants of Health

Determinants of health reflect the range of personal, clinical, social, economic, and environmental factors that influence the health of an individual and/or a population (Kindig & Stoddart, 2003; WHO, n.d.). PopHI data types can be mapped against the various health determinants to depict the variety of potential data sources that can provide such data types (FIGURE 3.3); for example, insurance claims map along healthcare determinants, and geographic data such as U.S. Census data match with the physical environment determinant of health.

▶ III. Information and Information Systems

We discuss information from a population health perspective by examining the diverse sources of data impacting population health. Further, we also outline examples of different data sources and the relevance of information systems to make these sources of data meaningful.

Information in the Population Health Context

In PopHI, information is considered a piece of data that is contextualized within the purpose of a population health solution. For example, a table of most frequent diagnoses for a given population provides information, and not merely raw data, about that population. In operational PopHI, information is usually represented by terms such as *population-wide data sources, databases, data systems, population-health information systems or platforms,* and *informational dashboards* (Friedman & Parrish, 2010). This chapter will use these terms interchangeably.

Factors Affecting Population Health Data Sources

A number of factors have empowered the collection and development of new population-wide data sources: (1) the increasing adoption of health IT solutions among healthcare providers (Hsiao, Hing, & Ashman, 2014), (2) the expanding data variety generated by different population health data systems, (3) the widening continuity of data flow among health IT solutions, and (4) the growing population coverage of health IT solutions.

Variety and Continuity of Population Health Data Sources

The variety and continuity of data sources offering population health data have also grown rapidly. **FIGURE 3.4** shows the variety of data sources that have been populated over the last couple of years within the larger context of PopHI, which spans from private industry to patients, providers, populations, and public health departments. In the near future, a variety of data sources will be used to develop advanced population health solutions that cross the traditional boundaries of clinical care for a patient population.

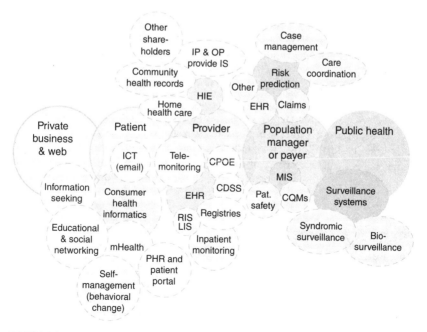

FIGURE 3.4 Variety and continuum of information systems in PopHI

Traditional Data Sources: Insurance Claims

Insurance claims data have traditionally been used for population health over the last couple of decades. Insurance claims are often originated by hospitals, professionals, or pharmacies.

Hospital Claims

Hospital insurance claims include both inpatient and outpatient services that are tied to a hospital facility. The hospital claims are often referred to as the "facility" claims. The inpatient portion of the hospital claims are based on the events and procedures that occurred after admission to the hospital facility. The outpatient facility claims are generated for services such as emergency department visits, ambulatory surgeries, and other services provided in an institutional setting where there is a facility charge. Facility claims are usually billed using the Uniform Billing (UB) form. More specifically, the UB04 (also known as CMS1450; previously UB92) is the main form used for hospital claims (CMS, n.d.a). Most insurers use the same unified form; however, submissions are increasingly being done electronically; for example, the CMS uses the American National Standards Institute (ANSI) ASC X12N 837I standard to receive hospital claims (Davis, 2004). Note that not all fields are required for reimbursement purposes, and the requirements vary between inpatient and outpatient settings.

Hospital insurance claims capture a variety of data elements such as patient information and demographics, provider information, payer information, discharge information, procedure codes, revenue codes, and diagnosis codes. A number of these data elements, such as demographics, procedures, and diagnoses, are commonly used for population health analytics.

Professional Claims

Professional claims (also known as physician claims) include procedures performed by clinicians, respiratory therapists, or physical therapists, regardless of the place of service. Professional claims are billed using the CMS-1500 form (CMS, n.d.b). Because professionals use a different claims form, hospital admissions may produce two claims: the facility services (e.g., room and board, ancillary services, and in-hospital drugs) and the professional services (e.g., physicians, surgeons, and nurse practitioners). Most CMS-1500 forms are electronically submitted. Professional claims include a variety of data elements such as patient information and demographics, provider information, payer information, and procedure and diagnosis codes.

Pharmacy Claims

Most medication claims are submitted electronically and through transactional systems. Medications can be claimed through CMS-1500 or other forms by commercial insurers, although most of the transactions occur electronically. Outpatient drugs are usually assigned an NDC. Medication claims may also contain additional descriptive information about the drug itself. Note that medications that are prescribed by a physician but are never filled will not generate claims. In contrast to medical claims, most medication claims do not include the underlying diagnosis.

Advantages of claims data for population health include the following:

■ Insurance claims usually cover a broad scope of data across a range of health-care providers. The broader coverage of claims gives population health analysts a more complete picture of insured events that have occurred to a patient across various entities in the larger healthcare ecosystem.

■ Insurance claims often have a higher consistency across different claims data sources because of the unified forms and electronic claims submissions. This is critical for merging various claims' data sources and developing a large-enough population-wide data source to predict a given outcome in the underlying population.

■ Population-wide claims datasets already exist. These data sources can be acquired by population health analysts to develop population health solutions.

Disadvantages of claims data include the following:

■ Insurance claims contain a limited number of data types that can be used for population health analytics (i.e., demographics, diagnosis, medication, and utilization).

■ Claims exist only for insured patients; thus, models developed based on claims can be used only for the insured population. (Claims-based predictive models cannot predict healthcare utilization in the uninsured population with high accuracy.)

■ Claims data include only events, procedures, and medications that are covered by the payer depending on the individual member's eligibility. Noncovered procedures and medications—such as over-the-counter medications—are usually missing in claims data.

Emerging Data Sources: Health Records

Health records data are increasingly used for population-health management purposes. The main sources of health records include EHRs and patient registries.

■ *EHR data:* An EHR is an electronic version of a patient's medical history. The federal certification criteria since 2010 for EHRs have helped to shape a minimum required set of data types that EHRs should collect, such as patient demographics, past medical history, problem list, diagnosis, procedures, allergies, and medications (CMS, 2016). Despite the EHR certification criteria, the quality of EHR data collected across different providers is still hindering the common development and use of EHR-based population-wide data sources. In addition, EHR data are usually limited to data collected from patients within a given provider's network and lack the information collected elsewhere. Potential EHR data types that could be useful for population analytics include demographics, diagnoses or problem lists, procedures, medications, family history, social history, vital signs, immunization records, patient-reported outcomes, embedded surveys, and free-text reports.

■ *Registry data:* A patient registry is an organized system that uses observational-study methods to collect uniform data (e.g., clinical data) to evaluate specified outcomes for a population defined by a particular disease, condition, or exposure, and that serves a predetermined scientific, clinical, or policy purpose (Agency for Healthcare Research and Quality [AHRQ], 2013). Registries include a variety of data types depending on the underlying information system. Examples include (1) local EHR-based registries such as a hospital-level registry; (2) clinical trial and condition-based registries; (3) public health registries that often cover a certain geographical boundary; and (4) large-scale reporting registries such as the CDC, Food and Drug Administration (FDA), or National Institutes of Health (NIH) led registries that usually have a national coverage. Registries provide valuable data types for population health analytics such as demographics, diagnoses, medications, family history, social history, immunization records, surveys, and patient-reported outcomes.

Advantages of health records for population health include: (1) health records often include unique data types such as lab values, vital signs, social data, and problem list; (2) health records include procedures and medications that are not covered by insurance, such as over-the-counter medications; and (3) health records include both insured and uninsured patients. Disadvantages in using health records data for population health include: (1) Health records usually include data collected by one provider entity and do not include data collected elsewhere; (2) health records often have a lower consistency across different data providers, especially considering textual data; and (3) population-wide health record datasets are uncommon and very costly to develop.

Nontraditional Data Sources

Nontraditional data sources can be linked to clinical records and used for population health analytics. Some of these nontraditional data sources include the following:

- Public health and vital records data sources such as death and birth records
- Social services data sources such as education, employment, and incarceration records
- Environmental and geographical data sources such as neighborhood information
- Resource-availability data sources such as access to health care
- Consumer and nonmedical data sources such as credit and financial reports
- HIE data sources such as admission, transfer, and discharge
- Other potential data sources, yet to be collected on a population level

Examples of Data Sources with Wide Population Coverage

Multiple population-wide data sources are currently available for developing population health solutions. These data sources include both clinical and nonclinical data sources. Some examples of these data sources include the following:

- Consolidated insurance claims such as the statewide all-payer claims databases (APCD) (Porter, Love, Costello, Peters, & Rudolph, 2015) and insurer databases such as CMS's Medicare
- Centralized or distributed EHR/clinical research data warehouses such as EHR-based data warehouses developed by health maintenance organizations, integrated delivery systems, or accountable care organizations

- Clinical registries such as the National Patient-Centered Clinical Research Network (PCORnet, n.d.)
- Mobile health data that are collected and shared by various smartphone platforms
- Large-scale population-wide surveys and registries such as the CDC's Behavioral Risk Factor Surveillance System (BRFSS) (CDC, n.d.)

▶ IV. Knowledge and Knowledge Management

Knowledge in the Population Health Context

In PopHI, knowledge is considered the result of extracting patterns from an information base or applying an existing rule on an information base. Just as data flow from source (patient) to repository to subsequent use, knowledge has its own flow that we call "knowledge management." This chapter focuses on the overall knowledge management process in population health.

Overall Knowledge Management Process in PopHI

As shown in FIGURE 3.5, the overall knowledge management process for population health involves multiple stages. The first stage involves the merging of various datasets and developing a population-health data warehouse, whether

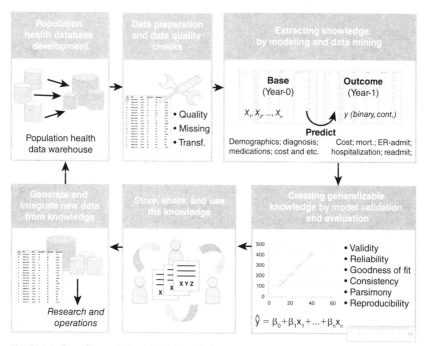

FIGURE 3.5 Overall population health knowledge management process

centralized in a single location or distributed across multiple locations. The second step includes various processes to prepare the data for analysis such as fixing data quality issues, imputing missing data, and transforming the data a second time to meet the assumptions of a given analytic approach. The third step contains the development of the modeling and data mining approaches, and then validating and evaluating the model. In this phase, various statistical and data mining concepts are used to measure how good the model is in differentiating the outcome variable and how reproducible it is when used on other datasets. In the remaining steps, a well-validated model will be stored, shared, and applied against a new population health data source, and the insight generated by such activities will be fed back into the population health database to reflect population trends and risks (e.g., incorporating risk scores and markers in the population health data source). This chapter will provide highlights on data preparation, modeling, and evaluation steps.

Data Preparation

Data preparation is the most time-consuming step in the knowledge management cycle of population health. Data preparation involves multiple tasks such as the following:

- *Data selection:* Selecting appropriate data sources based on prior knowledge of their effect on the outcome
- *Data preprocessing:* Cleaning the data by minimizing potential noise and removing outliers, and applying strategies to handle missing data
- *Data transformation:* Transforming the data to fit the model assumptions
- *Data reduction:* Applying dimensionality reduction functions to reduce the number of variables that will end up in a model

Modeling and Data Mining

A predictive model is an abstraction of the real world and is the result of a modeling or data-mining process. A good model attempts to capture the most important features of the complex health interactions in simple mathematical or statistical terms. A model, however, is never completely representative of a given situation. Indeed, a model should be able to capture the main relationships and predict behaviors in a variety of situations and environments, but is not required to always be correct in predicting the exact outcomes (Duncan, 2011). In population health, a model is often a set of parameters that can be applied within a data environment to generate a prediction of some outcome. For example, if the population health model is defined using a regression method, the model will be presented as an equation where the right side of it represents all of the predictors (i.e., independent variables) and the left side represents the predicted outcome (i.e., dependent variable).

There are usually a series of assumptions about the nature of the data and its types, variance, distribution, and quality when using a statistical method. The common predictive modeling techniques that are used in population health often have restricting assumptions about the underlying data. For example, regression models assume that a linear relationship exists between variables, that error distributions are independent, that multivariate normality exists, that errors are homoscedastic and have a constant variance, and that multicollinearity or correlation between independent variables is minimal. Other statistical methods may have other assumptions. Note that the typical variations in population health data often do not follow all of the assumptions of a given statistical method; thus, it is often required that population health data go through some sort of transformation before being used in the modeling process.

In population health, modeling usually requires a base dataset and an outcome dataset. If developed based on insurance claims data, usually the base dataset includes one year of medical and/or medication claims that would provide most of the independent variables, and the outcome dataset often includes the dependent variable such as cost or other utilization markers. The predictive model is usually developed based on the base dataset, and its predictive accuracy is often measured on the outcome dataset; however, sometimes the accuracy of the model is also measured on the outcome variables available in the same base year. The latter approach is usually referred to as the "concurrent" model, to differentiate it from the former "predictive" models.

Model Validation and Evaluation

Population health models need to be evaluated frequently to ensure high power and accuracy. Models are developed initially with a training data set and then evaluated with a testing data set, before being applied to entirely new data. Overall quality matrix of a population-health model can be defined by various measures, such as the following (Duncan, 2011):

- *Parsimony:* A model needs to be parsimonious and introduce as few variables as necessary to capture the main essence of the phenomenon under study and leave the minor variation to the error. For example, if a model is trying to predict cost for a given population, it is preferred to have the shortest list of independent variables that can explain the highest amount of variation within that cost (Duncan, 2011; Iezzoni, 2012).
- *Goodness of fit:* A model should also have an acceptable level of fitness (Duncan, 2011; Iezzoni, 2012). Indeed, a population health model should explain the variations in the outcome variable, such as cost, hospitalization, or emergency department admission, to a high degree by the explanatory variables.
- *Theoretical consistency:* The relationships expressed by the model should be theoretically plausible (Duncan, 2011; Iezzoni, 2012). For example, some explanations are needed if a population health model turns out to have a negative coefficient for age to predict cost, which does not resemble the real world.
- *Predictive power and reproducibility:* A model should predict accurately when applied to different data and temporal periods. Population health analysts often employ different evaluation techniques to examine the reproducibility of the models, such as cross-validation and bootstrapping (Duncan, 2011).

▶ V. Challenges Managing Data, Information, and Knowledge

Data Management Challenges: Data Quality

Data quality issues stem from the fact that population health data are often extracted from real-world databases, which usually require extensive cleaning and preparation. Data quality can be attributed to the accuracy of the measures, completeness of the data, or timeliness of updates. The quality of data can affect both the models that are developed based on large population health datasets and the application of those models on target population denominators. Data quality can be defined in various perspectives. The most important aspects of data quality for population health research are the following (Chan, Fowles, & Weiner, 2010):

- *Accuracy* of data refers to the extent to which data captured through the health IT system accurately reflect the state of interest. Accuracy is often complex to measure because the true value of a given variable remains inaccessible.
- *Completeness* of data is the level of missing data for a data element in the health IT system. Completeness is the most common measure of data quality in population-health data sources.
- *Timeliness* of data refers to the length of time between the initial capture of a value and the time the value becomes available in the health IT system. Understanding of underlying information flow and the existence of timestamps are required to measure timeliness.

Information Management Challenges

Big Data Challenges

Big data is a collection of datasets so large and complex that it becomes impractical to maintain and process them using traditional database management tools or other common applications (Barrett et al., 2013). Big data is rooted in various advancements in database optimization and computing sciences. These technological advancements have made it possible to efficiently and effectively deal with big data in both research and operational environments, including health care. Big data is often defined as having at least one of the following specifications (Feldman, Martin, & Skotnes, 2012):

- *Volume:* A higher-than-usual quantity or size of data in the population health context
- *Variety:* A wide range of data types or data sources that bring along new data structures, standardizations, or vocabularies that are uncommon to population health
- *Velocity:* A dynamic data source with a high frequency of refreshes, such as real-time data feeds
- *Veracity:* A complex data source with varying accuracy or completeness for a defined population
- *Value:* A data source with ambiguous usefulness in terms of cost, workflow complexity, feasibility, and governance for population health

Note that these specifications should be treated relative to the common practice in a given field. For example, a petabyte (a billion megabytes) of insurance claims is considered "high volume" for population health analysis, hence indicating a big data challenge; in contrast, this volume could be considered routine in other fields such as diagnostic imaging.

Data Interoperability, Linkage, and Exchange Challenges

Data linkage and integration challenges often limit the merger of various data sources and the development of larger population-health data warehouses. The lack of interoperability is one of the main reasons that different population-health data sources cannot be easily integrated. Interoperability is defined as the ability of a system to exchange electronic health information with and use electronic health information from other systems without special effort on the part of the user (Benson, 2010). Interoperability goes through multiple stages, but sending, receiving, finding, and eventually using the data are the end results of interoperability. Interoperability spans multiple dimensions of standards: regulatory, contractual, privacy, exchange formats, content, and technology.

Linking and integrating various data sources for population health also requires the matching of patients in various databases. Often analysts are required to generate master patient indexes (MPIs) to match patients across various data sources such as matching EHRs with insurance claims. Developing and utilizing MPIs is a complex process and may introduce error and bias in population health databases, despite the fact that there are many tools to accomplish this process. Note that most of the data elements needed to create MPIs are considered protected health information (PHI) according to HIPAA regulations and may not be available for the matching process.

Data Access, Privacy, and Use Challenges

HIPAA established national standards to protect individuals' medical records and other personal health information. PHI includes a list of 18 explicit identifiers such as names, geographic data, dates, phone and fax numbers, email addresses, and Social Security numbers, plus implicit unnamed identifiers (such as genome sequence).

Complying with HIPAA and removing PHI may affect population health solutions by: (1) limiting the use of some key population-health data types (e.g., geographic data); (2) making the matching process complex, which introduces errors; (3) shifting population health research into quality improvement efforts; and (4) increasing the development costs of large but anonymized (minimally re-identifiable) population health datasets for research.

Population-Health System Architecture and Design

Population-health data systems can adhere to a variety of system architectures. The two common architectures are the centralized and the federated models. The centralized architecture accumulates and manages all data in a single and centralized repository. The advantages of the centralized model are: (1) simplicity and efficiency, and (2) higher consistency of data and easier patient linkage if the same patient identifiers are used. The disadvantages of the centralized model are: (1) limited scaling to larger and more complex data sets; (2) a single point of control and, therefore, failure; (3) demanding exceptional leadership to get all stakeholders to share their data; (4) requiring everyone to accept the same identifiers for patients; and (5) needing robust communication infrastructures.

The federated architecture permits users to access the data only when needed. An MPI is needed to match the patients across the external data sources. The advantages of the federated model are: (1) data ownership can be managed by defining policies; (2) individual organizations are able to control their own data; (3) it benefits from scalability; (4) it builds on existing infrastructure; and (5) it offers more opportunities for creativity. However, the federated model comes with disadvantages, such as: (1) requiring more coordination, (2) being slower than monolithic databases, and (3) needing to solve the MPI problem.

Knowledge Management Challenges

Denominator and Variable Selection Challenges

There are various challenges with denominator and variable selections while extracting training and testing datasets from population health datasets for analysis. Here is a short list of such challenges:

- Selecting the denominator of the population that should be used for training and testing is always tricky. Multiple factors can be used to modify and refine the definition of a population denominator, such as age, types of diseases, any special conditions such as disability, and insurance coverage.
- Selecting the time frames for the training and testing datasets is also complex.
- Selecting the proper outcome is critical. Outcomes can vary depending on the desired prediction, and hopefully improvement in a given denominator of a population. Typical outcomes are cost, mortality, emergency department admission, hospitalization, and readmission.
- Selecting the best and most parsimonious list of factors to predict an outcome is also a delicate task. There are many factors to choose from, especially from nontraditional data sources. Typical predictors are demographics, diagnoses, medications, and current cost.
- Identifying the purpose of the predictive model is usually a challenge by itself. Often, predictive model development is misaligned with the operational needs and goals of population health programs. The alignment of population health models with organizational goals and integration with existing workflows are critical to the success of any population health solution.

Other Challenges

There are also other challenges with extracting knowledge from population-health data sources (Duncan, 2011):

- *Process of care* refers to the fact that different providers or clinical workflows generate different data values for the same event or fact. Thus, the same fact or event might show up differently in the same population health database.
- *Nature of intervention* suggests that different interventions with different levels of risk may be encoded similarly; thus, the population health database does not contain the true level of risk for those interventions.

■   *Random chance or external factors* indicate that two exactly similar patients in a population health database may develop two different risk profiles due to factors not included in the database or simply because of random chance.

▶ VI. Conclusion

DIK terms reflect crucially different concepts in PopHI. This chapter offers some details and provides a number of examples to define these terms in the context of PopHI. The chapter also reviews traditional and emerging data types and data sources, and describes the overall knowledge management process. Thus empowered, PopHI experts should be better prepared to address the challenges.

References

Ackoff, R. (1989). From data to wisdom. *Journal of Applied Systems Analysis, 16*, 3–9.

Agency for Healthcare Research and Quality (AHRQ). (2013, September). Engaging patients in information sharing and data collection: The role of patient-powered registries and research networks. Retrieved from http://www.ncbi.nlm.nih.gov/books/NBK164513/pdf/Bookshelf _NBK164513.pdf

Barrett, M. A., Humblet, O., Hiatt, R. A., & Adler, N. E. (2013). Big data and disease prevention: From quantified self to quantified communities. *Journal of Big Data, 1*(3), 168–175.

Benson, T. (2010). Principles of health interoperability HL7 and SNOMED. In K. Hanneh & M. Ball (Eds.), *Health informatics series*. London, England: Springer-Verlag.

Centers for Disease Control and Prevention (CDC). (n.d.). Behavioral risk factor surveillance system (BRFSS). Retrieved from http://www.cdc.gov/brfss/

Centers for Medicare and Medicaid Services (CMS). (2012). Medicare health support (formerly CCIP). Retrieved from http://www.cms.gov/Medicare/Medicare-General-Information/CCIP /index.html

Centers for Medicare and Medicaid Services (CMS). (2014). Health information technology: Standards, implementation specifications, and certification criteria for electronic health record technology. *Federal Register, 77*(171), 53968–54162.

Centers for Medicare and Medicaid Services (CMS). (2016). Acute care hospital inpatient prospective payment system. Retrieved from http://www.cms.gov/Outreach-and-Education /Medicare-Learning-Network-MLN/MLNProducts/downloads/AcutePaymtSysfctsht.pdf

Centers for Medicare and Medicaid Services (CMS). (n.d.a). Institutional paper claim form (CMS-1450). Retrieved from https://www.cms.gov/medicare/billing/electronicbillingeditrans/15_1450 .html

Centers for Medicare and Medicaid Services (CMS). (n.d.b). Medicare claims processing manual: Chapter 26—Completing and processing form CMS-1500 data set. Retrieved from https://www.cms.gov/Regulations-and-Guidance/Guidance/Manuals/downloads/clm104c26 .pdf

Chan, K., Fowles, J., & Weiner, J. (2010). Electronic health records and the reliability and validity of quality measures: A review of the literature. *Medical Care Research and Review, 67*(5), 503–527.

Charles, D., Gabriel, M., & Furukawa, M. (2014). Adoption of electronic health record systems among U.S. non-federal acute care hospitals: 2008-2013. Retrieved from http://www.healthit .gov/sites/default/files/oncdatabrief16.pdf

Charles, D., King, J., Furukawa, M. F., & Patel, V. (2013, March). Hospital adoption of electronic health record technology to meet meaningful use objectives: 2008-2012. Retrieved from http://www .healthit.gov/sites/default/files/oncdatabrief10final.pdf

Davis, B. (2004). The evolution of the ANSI ASC X12N 837 format from the UB-92 flat file format. Retrieved from http://www.phdsc.org/standards/pdfs/EvolutionofANSI.pdf

Duncan, I. (2011). *Healthcare risk adjustment and predictive modeling*. Winsted, CT: ACTEX Publications.

Feldman, B., Martin, E. M., & Skotnes, T. (2012). Big data in healthcare: Hype and hope. Retrieved from http://www.west-info.eu/files/big-data-in-healthcare.pdf

Friedman, D. G., & Parrish, G. R. (2010). The population health record: Concepts, definition, design, and implementation. *Journal of the American Medical Information Association, 17,* 359–366.

Hsiao, C.-J., Hing, E., & Ashman, J. (2014, May 20). Trends in electronic health record system use among office-based physicians: United States, 2007-2012. Retrieved from http://www.cdc.gov/nchs/data/nhsr/nhsr075.pdf

Iezzoni, L. (2012). *Risk adjustment for measuring healthcare outcomes.* Chicago, IL: Health Administration Press.

Jha, A., Burke, M., DesRoches, C., Joshi, M., Kralovec, B., Campbell, E., & Buntin, M. (2011). Progress toward meaningful use: Hospitals' adoption of electronic health records. *American Journal of Managed Care, 17*(12 Spec No.), SP117–SP124.

Kindig, D., & Stoddart, G. (2003). What is population health? *American Journal of Public Health, 93*(3), 380–383.

National Patient-Centered Clinical Research Network (PCORnet). (n.d.). About PCORnet. Retrieved from http://www.pcornet.org/about-pcornet/

O'Carroll, P. W., Yasnoff, W. A., Ward, M. E., Ripp, L. H., & Martin, E. L. (2003). *Public health informatics and information systems.* New York, NY: Springer-Verlag.

Porter, J., Love, D., Costello, A., Peters, A., & Rudolph, B. (2015). All-payer claims database development manual: Establishing a foundation for health care transparency and informed decision making. APCD Council and West Health Policy Center. Retrieved from https://www.apcdcouncil.org/manual

Rowley, J. (2007). The wisdom hierarchy: Representations of the DIKW hierarchy. *Journal of Information Science, 33*(2), 163–180.

Rowley, J., & Richard, H. (2008). *Organizing knowledge: An introduction to managing access to information.* Burlington, VT: Ashgate.

U.S. Department of Education. (n.d.). Family Educational Rights and Privacy Act (FERPA). Retrieved from http://www2.ed.gov/policy/gen/guid/fpco/ferpa/index.html

U.S. Department of Health and Human Services, Office of Assistant Secretary for Planning and Evaluation (ASPE). (n.d.). Health Insurance Portability and Accountability Act of 1996. Retrieved from https://aspe.hhs.gov/report/health-insurance-portability-and-accountability-act-1996

World Health Organization (WHO). (n.d.). Health impact assessment (HIA): The determinants of health. Retrieved from http://www.who.int/hia/evidence/doh/en/

Zeleny, M. (2005). *Human systems management: Integrating knowledge, management and systems.* Singapore: World Scientific.

CHAPTER 4

Data Exchange and Interoperability: Foundational Technologies to Enable Population Health

Brian E. Dixon and Saurabh Rahurkar

KEY TERMS

Accountable care organizations (ACOs)
Chesapeake Regional Information System
 for our Patients (CRISP)
Community health workers
Consolidated Clinical Document
 Architecture (C-CDA)
Continuity of care documents (CCDs)
Digital Imaging and Communications
 in Medicine (DICOM)
Emergency departments
Extensible Markup Language (XML)
Fast Healthcare Interoperability
 Resources (FHIR)
Glycated hemoglobin
Health Level Seven (HL7)
Health management information
 system (HMIS)
Hypertext Transfer Protocol (HTTP)
National Council for Prescription Drug
 Programs (NCPDP)

National Trauma Data Standard (NTDS)
Nursing Outcomes Classification (NOC)
Nursing Interventions Classification (NIC)
Open Systems Interconnection (OSI)
Picture archiving and communication
 systems (PACS)
Public Health Information Network's
 Vocabulary Access and Distribution
 System (PHIN VADS)
Public health surveillance
Quality Reporting Document Architecture
 (QRDA)
Reference Information Model (RIM)
Reportable Conditions Mapping Table
 (RCMT)
Representational State Transfer (REST)
Simple Object Access Protocol (SOAP)
Single nucleotide polymorphism (SNP)

LEARNING OBJECTIVES

- Define interoperability and health information exchange (HIE) as these concepts relate to population health.
- Explain why population health management requires HIE because patient information is fragmented and diffuse across the health system.
- Distinguish between syntactic and semantic interoperability, and explain the role of standards in enabling interoperability.
- List and describe common use cases in population health that require HIE.
- List and explain barriers to wider adoption and use of HIE across the health system.
- Discuss future directions and research in HIE shaping the delivery of population health.

QUESTIONS FOR THOUGHT

- How do interoperability and HIE contribute to an organization's ability to perform population health?
- Why does population HIE require both syntactic and semantic standards?
- Which syntactic standards are most pertinent to data exchanged for population health use cases?
- Why do population health informaticians need to understand information architectures?
- How might the governance of health data and information exchanged by providers differ between the United States and low-to-middle income countries?
- Which aspects of interoperability and HIE are most critical to achieving population health management: the technical foundations or the social and political foundations?

CHAPTER OUTLINE

▶ I. Why Population Health Requires Robust Interoperability and Health Information Exchange

P atients seek health care from a variety of settings, including hospitals, primary care clinics, urgent care, pharmacies, and freestanding radiology centers. Therefore, identifying, monitoring, and improving the health of populations fundamentally requires the ability to analyze data from the fragmented settings in which they are captured and stored.

To illustrate the fragmentation of healthcare services, consider three use cases:

▪ *Care coordination:* To effectively coordinate the care of a complex medical patient across primary and specialty care settings, the providers in each setting should ideally know both the outcomes (e.g., diagnoses, procedures, medications prescribed) and recommendations (e.g., notes, opinions) that result from visits the patient makes to other providers. Electronic health records (EHRs) at each setting are excellent for documenting what happens in that setting, but rarely are they exchanged with the other providers in an efficient manner that informs decision making by the other providers. A study by Schoen et al. (2011) demonstrated that, for a majority of patients surveyed, providers are missing lab results or documentation from another care setting. As a work-around, providers often ask the patients if they remember what happened at the other care setting.

▪ *Medication reconciliation:* Patients with complex chronic illness often take multiple medications, and medication regimens can be altered significantly when a patient is admitted to the hospital or sees a specialist for an ailment. Therefore, providers are increasingly asked to reconcile the medications patients are taking—both individually and as a population (e.g., therapy for patients with diabetes, therapeutic plans for patients who have had a stroke). Reconciling this information requires significant effort as physicians, nurses, pharmacists, medical assistants, and patients themselves attempt to track down all current medications and monitor the list of active medications over time. Once again, EHRs likely contain only a partial list of current, active medications for a given patient, let alone a population.

▪ *Disease surveillance:* Public health departments as well as accountable care organizations (ACOs) want to know about emerging trends in disease onset within a population. For example, health departments routinely monitor for outbreaks of influenza. ACOs, on the other hand, are interested in trends related to chronic illnesses like asthma, cardiovascular disease, and diabetes. Understanding the utilization of healthcare resources, and their associated costs, requires more completely capturing the locations, services, and medications consumed by a group of patients from a wide variety of care providers. Individual EHRs, locally stored and managed by individual providers or groups of providers, must be exchanged to more completely analyze disease patterns and trends.

Some health system executives may believe that their particular network of care facilities and/or ACO is large enough to encompass all the care a certain population receives in the community. However, research has shown that patients seek care both in and out of health networks, even large ones. Researchers at the Regenstrief Institute found high levels of patient crossover among emergency departments within and between health system networks (Finnell, Overhage, & Grannis, 2011). Using data from 96 emergency departments representing over 7.4 million visits and 2.8 million patients over a 3-year period, the researchers found that, on average, 40% of visits involved patients with data at more than one emergency department. At 15 emergency departments, more than half of their encounters involved patients with data in other health systems' EHRs. Similarly, within the U.S. Veterans Health Administration (VHA), a nationwide integrated delivery network that provides care to more than 22 million veterans at over 900 ambulatory clinics and 150 large medical centers, health services researchers observed that less than 15% of dual-eligible veterans receive their care exclusively within the VHA (Humensky et al., 2012). Therefore, it is a fallacy to assume that one does not need access to "outside" information in order to effectively manage population health.

Because hospitals and health systems need access to external information "outside the walls of their network," the health system in all nations requires robust interoperability and HIE capabilities. In other words, the information infrastructure of a nation must facilitate the exchange of data for a variety of population health use cases like those previously described. In this chapter, we define the concepts of interoperability and HIE. We further explain how interoperability and HIE work together to support population health. The chapter further describes emerging areas for practice and research with respect to interoperability and HIE because these two areas in informatics are rapidly evolving as the market embraces population health.

▶ II. Interoperability

Interoperability is the ability of two information systems to exchange data, without prior negotiation, and where the receiving system can do something useful with the data (Broyles, Dixon, Crichton, Biondich, & Grannis, 2016). This definition relies on three important assumptions:

- Data can be communicated from the sending system to the receiving system *technically*, usually across a communications network (Healthcare Information and Management Systems Society, 2013).
- The receiving information system can open messages sent by the sending system. This requires the two systems to share a common *syntax* (Vergara-Niedermayr, Wang, Pan, Kurc, & Saltz, 2013).
- The receiving information system can interpret what is inside the message sent from the sending system. This requires the two systems to share a common *semantic understanding* of the contents/information within the message (Dolin & Alschuler, 2011).

These assumptions, depicted in FIGURE 4.1, give rise to three different kinds of interoperability that must exist in order for two disparate systems to seamlessly exchange information and possess a common understanding of the information's meaning (e.g., a report containing summarized performance metrics for clinic operations over the past 90 days).

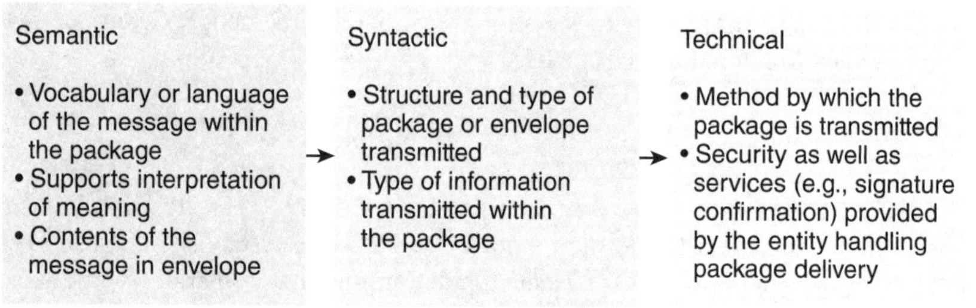

Semantic	Syntactic	Technical
• Vocabulary or language of the message within the package • Supports interpretation of meaning • Contents of the message in envelope	• Structure and type of package or envelope transmitted • Type of information transmitted within the package	• Method by which the package is transmitted • Security as well as services (e.g., signature confirmation) provided by the entity handling package delivery

FIGURE 4.1 Semantic, syntactic, and technical representations

Technical Interoperability

Disparate information systems that wish to exchange information must adhere to a series of standardized communication protocols. Initially, the heterogeneous systems must be linked together to form a communication network. A common method used to connect systems is Transmission Control Protocol/Internet Protocol (TCP/IP) (Gliklich, Dreyer, & Leavy, 2014). Data exchange further requires an application protocol such as the Hypertext Transfer Protocol (HTTP) (Andry & Wan, 2012; Gliklich et al., 2014). Web services such as Simple Object Access Protocol (SOAP) or Representational State Transfer (REST) that define how and where to send the messages are also critical to structured information exchange (Gliklich et al., 2014). Although technical interoperability is necessary, these requirements can be fulfilled relatively easily in comparison to syntactic and semantic interoperability.

Syntactic Interoperability

Successful exchange of data requires messages to be transmitted using a structure and syntax that is ascertainable to both systems (Healthcare Information and Management Systems Society, 2013). Formats such as Extensible Markup Language (XML) are frequently used to satisfy this demand (Gliklich et al., 2014; Vergara-Niedermayr et al., 2013). Enabling successful communication becomes increasingly complex as more heterogeneous systems with their own unique formatting are involved in the information exchange (Gliklich et al., 2014). For this reason, healthcare entities have typically adopted messaging standards such as Health Level Seven (HL7) version 2 or 3 (Barbarito et al., 2012; Gliklich et al., 2014; Lee et al., 2015; Viangteeravat et al., 2011), as described in the next section.

Semantic Interoperability

The ability to successfully receive a message does not ensure that the system receiving the message will be able to interpret and complete a request. If a system attempting to communicate with a second system uses terminology or coding that is incompatible with the internal standards of the second system, then the data must be translated into a standardized format before it can be interpreted. Additionally, any response to the sending system must be translated back into the language used by that system. In many instances, this can be a time-consuming and expensive process (Baorto, Cimino, Parvin, & Kahn, 1998; Dixon, Vreeman, & Grannis, 2014; Lin, Vreeman, McDonald, & Huff, 2011).

The Role of Standards

The technical standards described in this chapter—SOAP, HTTP, HL7, Logical Observation Identifiers Names and Codes (LOINC)—are established, consensus-accepted technical approaches, formats, or definitions that constrain the possible variations in how to structure or represent information down to a normalized form or semantic meaning (Imler, Vreeman, & Kannry, 2016). There are an enormous, almost infinite number of ways in which data and information can be exchanged. As an analogy, think about all the various kinds of paper, envelopes, writing instruments (pens, pencils, markers, crayons), and languages that could be used to send a birthday greeting to a friend. Additional methods and new languages such as emojis are afforded by electronic communications. Therefore, the problem with interoperability is not a lack of methods for communicating between two systems but the ability of two systems to use the same set of conventions for the transfer of data or information. Technical standards are the conventions that enable the systems to both exchange information and share a common understanding of the contents of the message.

Consensus-based technical standards are curated by standards development organizations (SDOs) through voluntary efforts in an industry. As the name implies, a representative group of stakeholders (e.g., physicians, nurses, informaticians, vendors) design and reach consensus on a standard approach to representing, for example, a medication history or problem list for exchange as a patient is discharged from a hospital to a skilled nursing facility. Once consensus is achieved, the SDO publishes the standard, enabling system developers to use the technical approaches, structures, and guidelines to create products in the marketplace that can exchange data or information. More information about SDOs and the process for how standards are developed can be found in books on this subject (Benson, 2012; Imler et al., 2016).

▶ III. Standards for Population Health Informatics

There exists a wide variety of mature, accepted standards in health care that enable interoperability for a wide range of population health functions (Del Fiol, Crouch, & Cummins, 2014; Dixon et al., 2014; Imler et al., 2016). In this section of the chapter, we introduce several of the existing standards as well as emerging standards. These standards represent commonly used ones for population health functions; however, the information is not meant to denote comprehensive coverage of all available technical standards. Because technical standards are in a constant state of evolution or maturity, readers should always seek the latest versions of consensus-based standards. In addition, there now exist published guides on available standards that assess their respective maturity and readiness for adoption and use. These guides, like the annual Interoperability Standards Advisory published by the U.S. Office of the National Coordinator for Health Information Technology (2015), can help readers identify standards for a particular use case in population health.

Syntactic Standards

Technical standards for syntax provide guidance on how the electronic messages exchanged between systems should be structured. These standards pertain to information representation within a message. They enable a system to represent concepts such as a patient or medication, including what types of data should be included to identify a patient versus a medication. How information is structured within a message is critical to the receiving system being able to correctly parse or decode the information within the message.

Health Level Seven

Health Level Seven (HL7) is the most widely recognized and adopted syntactic standard in health informatics. The "level 7" in HL7 refers to the application layer of the Open Systems Interconnection (OSI) model, a conceptual model that characterizes and standardizes interactions within a computer system regardless of its underlying technology (Hosseini & Dixon, 2016). The seventh layer of the OSI model describes application-layer functions that typically include synchronizing communication between computer systems. HL7 is an event trigger model in which the sending application transmits a message after a trigger is fired. The main cause for a trigger is a healthcare event, such as the registration of a patient at a primary care clinic, discharge of a patient from an acute care hospital, or completion of a laboratory test for the presence of a disease. Receiving systems can then act upon the message, inferring the action that occurred based on the message type and responding to that action. For example, an A01 message indicates the registration of a patient. A health information system that receives an A01 message could respond by querying for recent information on the patient available at (1) nearby healthcare settings, (2) the ACO to which the patient is assigned, or (3) a patient portal where he or she may keep personal health records. Alternatively, an A01 message received from an emergency department might trigger a health information system to send an electronic alert to a primary care clinic, providing information to the patient's assigned general practitioner that he or she had an emergent event (e.g., myocardial infarction, stroke).

The first version of the HL7 standard was published in 1987, but there have been many revisions to the standard since its debut. Version 2 (v2) of the HL7 standard has been widely adopted and is used by health information systems in the United States; however, there are a variety of v2 versions, including v2.3, v2.5.1, and v2.6. Successive, incremental improvements to v2 resulted in clearer, more detailed, and better documented versions that sought to expand the standard to additional clinical domains while also supporting better normalization. Because of this, the v2 standard is backward compatible, enabling applications to correctly receive and appropriately handle different versions in the v2 family. Although v2 incrementally improved over time, many in the health IT world felt it only normalized 80% of a given interface between two systems (Corepoint Health, n.d.). This meant that an additional 20% was customized when, for example, an interface was established between a hospital's laboratory information system and that hospital's EHR system. The customization was necessary because many aspects of v2 were inherently designed to be flexible, allowing several "design choices" to be made when implemented.

Because of v2 criticisms and evolving Internet-based communication standards, the HL7 community created version 3 (v3) of the HL7 standard, first released in 2005. Unlike v2, the HL7 v3 standard represents a suite of specifications explicitly designed around the HL7 Reference Information Model (RIM). The RIM provides a comprehensive, consistent data model that contains a combination of storyboards, classes, data types, and use cases, as well as different triggers and events that together create an information framework needed for generating HL7 messages. The v3 standard provides a single source that allows health IT vendors to work with the full set of messages, data types, and terminologies in the RIM needed to build a complete implementation. Furthermore, the RIM and v3 standard were designed with globalization in mind, supporting implementation of HIE around the world.

The following are the benefits of v3 as provided on the HL7 International website (Health Level 7 International, n.d.d):

- Focuses on semantic interoperability by specifying that information be presented in a complete clinical context that ensures that the sending and receiving systems share the meaning (semantics) of the information being exchanged
- Provides consistent representation of data laterally across the various HL7 domains of interest and longitudinally over time as new requirements arise and new fields of clinical endeavor are addressed
- Designed for universal application so that the standards can have the broadest possible global impact and yet be adapted to meet local and regional requirements

The v3 form of HL7 gained popularity in the United States with the "meaningful use" incentive program (Centers for Medicare and Medicaid Services, 2013) for the adoption of EHRs. Criteria and EHR certification standards established by U.S. government agencies for the meaningful use (MU) program require the use of continuity of care documents (CCDs) and, in some cases, Consolidated Clinical Document Architecture (C-CDA) documents (2015 Edition Health Information Technology [Health IT] Certification Criteria et al., 2015; Centers for Medicare and Medicaid Services, 2012; Hosseini, Meade, Schnitzius, & Dixon, 2016). Specific types of CCD or C-CDA documents have been defined and endorsed for MU-based exchange under certain use cases, such as coordination of care after hospital discharge or medication reconciliation. Many of these use cases are relevant to population health, including the following:

- Quality Reporting Document Architecture (QRDA), a document format that provides a standard structure with which to report quality measure data to organizations that will analyze and interpret the data. QRDA documents (Klann & Murphy, 2013), for example, enable hospitals or health systems to transmit quality indicator data to payers or public health agencies.
- Trauma Registry Data Submission (Health Level 7, n.d.a), a document format to support efficient and clinically useful transmission of EHR data to trauma registries by leveraging National Trauma Data Standard (NTDS) data element definitions and the widely understood CDA transmission syntax.

▪ Family History/Pedigree Interoperability (Health Level 7, n.d.c), a document format for transmitting family histories between systems. This includes describing a patient's full pedigree (family and familial relationships) with diseases and conditions, and the option to link genetic data and risk analysis. The model has the ability to transmit complete family history information for clinical decision support and risk assessment. Such a standard would be useful for gathering risk assessment data from a large population for genomics or clinical research as well as public health surveillance or epidemiology.

Digital Imaging and Communications in Medicine

Digital Imaging and Communications in Medicine (DICOM) is the most widely adopted standard in the world for the exchange and management of medical images. Since introducing DICOM in 1993, providers have been able to use fully digital images with high resolution instead of physical X-ray films. Using DICOM, images generated by different types of medical imaging devices (e.g., X-ray, CT, MRI, ultrasound) can be integrated into picture archiving and communication systems (PACs) and exchanged across health system networks (DICOM, n.d.). The DICOM standard not only encodes the image, but also a set of metadata and attributes that describe the image and can be used by other applications in healthcare delivery.

National Council for Prescription Drug Programs

The National Council for Prescription Drug Programs (NCPDP) standardizes electronic exchange of data for prescribing, dispensing, monitoring, managing, and paying for medications and pharmacy services. Currently there are 26 different standards developed by NCPDP; however, only three of them are endorsed for implementation (Telecommunication, SCRIPT, and Manufacturer Rebate). The NCPDP Telecommunication Standard provides a structure to electronically submit third-party drug claims as well as perform eligibility verification and prior authorization. SCRIPT supports transmitting prescription information electronically in support of fulfilling new prescriptions, prescription refill requests, relaying medication history, transactions for long-term care, and manufacturer rebates.

Emerging Technical Standards

Health Level 7 (n.d.b) Fast Healthcare Interoperability Resources (FHIR) is an emerging technical standard. Although HL7 v3 is comprehensive, enabling detailed modeling of health data, many in the industry perceive v3 as overly complex due to the intricacies of the RIM. The HL7 FHIR standard, first introduced in 2011, was designed to overcome the complexity of the RIM and hide all of the v3 complexities from developers' sight. Yet FHIR is designed to be compatible with previous versions of the HL7 standard (v2 and v3) to enable legacy systems to function. Because FHIR is much simpler in its implementation (Kasthurirathne, Mamlin, Grieve, & Biondich, 2015), it is a promising standard for future use cases in which health information is exchanged. The FHIR standard is projected to support population health in two key ways:

- Because population health management tools are perceived to generally have more complete and accurate data than EHR systems, they often serve as better tools for care coordinators or managers who need a complete picture of a patient's health in order to make informed decisions about care plans. Providers, however, generally use their EHR system as their primary clinical application. This discrepancy in workflow can create an information barrier between care managers who update care plans in specialized applications and providers who document care delivery in EHRs. To remedy this, FHIR could facilitate creation of a care plan application programming interface (API), which could be leveraged to push updated care plans from the population health management application to the EHR system for review/use by the provider.
- FHIR may also enable the reverse, allowing EHR systems to push data into population health tools that allow for care coordination and management by specialists as well as community health workers. Applications developed peripherally to the EHR, like a specialized application for management of a population with diabetes, could allow specialists to organize and enter data pertaining to care in ways incongruent with how most EHR systems function today. A FHIR-based API could be engineered to push EHR-based data to the specialized application following each visit by patients with diabetes from primary as well as specialty care settings. A diabetes care coordinator, or specialized endocrinologist, could use the FHIR-enabled specialty application to review data and trends for the population. The care coordinator might further use the application to edit care plans, send urgent alerts to be reviewed by primary care providers, and schedule overdue procedures (e.g., annual eye exam) without the need for emails or superfluous electronic referrals between primary and specialty care providers.

Recent stories in healthcare trade publications suggest that large health systems like Geisinger and the Duke School of Medicine are working on FHIR-based population health tools that may one day be available in the marketplace (Bresnick, 2016; Sullivan, 2016).

Semantic Standards

Once a message has been exchanged, the receiving system must deconstruct the contents in the message and take action. For example, should an admission, discharge, and transfer (ADT) message arrive, then the system will need to interpret which patient has arrived and consequently check the patient in for an appointment. To do this, the system will need to understand concepts beyond simply what is a patient and include recognizing a medical record number, last name, and date of birth. Other kinds of messages will contain more complex data types, such as a glycated hemoglobin test value, a personal single nucleotide polymorphism (SNP), or a concept representing a family history of breast cancer. For the receiving system to understand these concepts and consequently take the appropriate action (e.g., store the data in the right part of the medical record, trigger a decision support alert), it would be helpful to employ standardized terminologies, unlocking semantic interoperability.

A *terminology* is the body of terms used with a particular technical application in a subject of study, theory, or profession. Terminologies vary in their purposes, scopes, and structures. This is especially true in health care, where there is a high degree of specialization. Although there exists a nearly universal terminology for human anatomy that is taught to a variety of health professions, there is a wide array of specialized terminologies used in healthcare settings. Nursing, for example, has three major terminologies: NANDA International (NANDA-I), the Nursing Interventions Classification (NIC), and the Nursing Outcomes Classification (NOC). The nursing terminologies provide sets of terms to describe nursing judgments, treatments, and nursing-sensitive patient outcomes. Terminologies in health care support the documentation of observations, treatments, and outcomes that clinicians put in the patient chart—which is increasingly performed using EHR systems. Although a fair number of "major" or standard terminologies exist, like the NIC and NOC, there are many more terminologies developed for specific purposes. A *local terminology* is one that is created for a specific purpose by a single organization, such as a laboratory, hospital, clinic, or pharmacy. For example, a local terminology may be used by the laboratory supporting a large health system to provide "user-friendly" terms to physicians who order the tests.

Although useful to providers in a particular health system, a local terminology may be difficult for providers in another health system to interpret. For example, Health System A might refer to a glycated hemoglobin (HbA1c) test as "Glycohemoglobin" whereas Health System B may refer to a similar test as "Hemoglobin A1c." Although a clinician can use his or her clinical knowledge and expertise to reason that the two tests likely mean the same thing, computers cannot perform such reasoning in isolation. Therefore, to ensure that meaning or semantics are transferred along with the test results during HIE, health information systems should use a reference terminology. A *reference terminology* is a formal, canonical terminology developed and maintained by a national or international SDO. A reference terminology is often referred to as a *standard*, *terminology standard*, or *standard terminology* (TABLE 4.1).

TABLE 4.1 Commonly Used Terminology Standards in Health Care

Terminology	Full Name	Responsible Organization
CPT	Current Procedural Terminology	American Medical Association (http://www.ama-assn.org)
ICD	International Classification of Diseases	World Health Organization (http://www.who.int)
LOINC	Logical Observation Identifiers Names and Codes	Regenstrief Institute (http://www.loinc.org)
RxNorm	RxNorm	U.S. National Library of Medicine (http://nlm.nih.gov/research/umls/rxnorm/)
SNOMED CT	Systematized Nomenclature of Medicine—Clinical Terms	International Health Terminology Standards Development Organization (http://www.snomed.org/)

Current Use of Terminology Standards

A wide variety of terminology standards are in a mature state of development and are readily available for use in health information systems (Bodenreider, 2008). However, despite availability, actual use in the real world is reported to be limited, and local terms remain highly prevalent. For example, Dixon et al. (2014) examined the use of LOINC and SNOMED CT coding in more than 7 million electronic laboratory messages exchanged in two states between 2010 and 2011. The researchers found that fewer than 17% of all messages reported by laboratories to public health authorities utilized a LOINC term to identify the test performed or a SNOMED CT term to identify the test result. Although this percentage is likely to increase over time, the use of local terminologies will continue (Alyea, Dixon, Bowie, & Kanter, 2016). Further-more, the process of matching local terminology concepts to reference terminology concepts, known as mapping, is complex, costly, and time consuming (Dixon, Hook, & Vreeman, 2015; Imler et al., 2016; Lin et al., 2011; Vreeman, Hook, & Dixon, 2015). The semantic interoperability challenge is one that health systems arguably need the most help with because the process of moving away from local terminologies to refer-ence terminologies is not easy, nor is it strongly supported by vendor systems.

Value Sets for Semantic Interoperability in Population Health

The LOINC terminology has more than 60,000 concepts, and SNOMED CT currently has more than 350,000 concepts. Therefore, adopting the entire termi-nology is likely to be problematic because it would require a significant investment of time and resources. Because of the ever-expanding nature of terminology stan-dards, many organizations rely upon value sets. A value set is a collection of con-cepts drawn from one or more standard vocabularies and grouped together for a specific use case. For example, the U.S. Centers for Disease Control and Prevention (CDC) maintains a standard value set for all of the possible laboratory tests and result values for notifiable diseases—those diseases that must be reported to public health authorities after laboratory-confirmed diagnosis (CDC, 2016)—known as the Reportable Conditions Mapping Table (RCMT) (CDC, 2015). This value set is useful when engineering an informatics system to automatically detect lab-oratory results that should be reported to public health authorities (Fidahussein, Friedlin, & Grannis, 2011) or a system to generate provider case reports that can be integrated into primary care workflow (Dixon, Grannis, & Revere, 2013).

The CDC maintains several value sets beyond the RCMT in a system called the Public Health Information Network's Vocabulary Access and Distribution System (PHIN VADS) (CDC, 2011). Using the PHIN VADS, anyone can download or browse the catalog of available value sets. Here are several examples of useful value sets for population health:

- *Meaningful Use Healthcare Provider Reporting to Central Cancer Registries:* A list of concepts and metadata to be included in documents transmitted from EHR systems to state-based cancer registries.
- *Immunization Messaging—HL7 Version 2.5.1:* A list of data elements and ref-erence terminology concepts that can be used to populate electronic messages sent from EHR systems to state-based immunization registries when patients receive a vaccine.

▣ *National Healthcare Safety Network Healthcare Associated Infection:* A list of data elements and reference terminology concepts for use in CDA documents sent from hospitals to the CDC for the reporting of a healthcare-associated infection.

▶ IV. Health Information Exchange

Interoperability enables HIE, which is defined as the electronic transfer of clinical and/or administrative information across diverse and sometimes competing healthcare settings (Dixon, 2016). The term *HIE* can connote a verb or a noun. As a verb, or action word, HIE refers to movement of data or information electronically among stakeholders in the healthcare sector. The noun use of HIE refers to an organization, usually a legal corporation, that facilitates information exchange (the verb form) within a network of facilities, community, state, or region. Although its connotations vary, HIE nonetheless focuses on leveraging interoperable information systems to exchange data and information so they are available when and where needed by patients, providers, or population health analysts.

Dominant Types of Health Information Exchange Structures

In the current healthcare landscape, the following four types of HIE networks exist:

▣ *Private HIEs:* When a health system interconnects its affiliates, this is referred to as *private HIE*, because the exchange is only within the membership group. For example, the VHA operates 153 medical centers as well as 909 ambulatory care and community-based outpatient clinics across the United States and its territories. In the early 2000s, the VHA interconnected its facilities using a software program referred to as VistaWeb. The software is an Internet-based viewer in which clinicians at the VHA medical center in Indianapolis, Indiana, can access documents such as the discharge summary from the VHA medical center in Palo Alto, California, for a veteran who had a surgery in Palo Alto last year while visiting his grandchildren. This is private HIE, because the VHA medical center cannot look up information on facilities outside the VHA health system, only those facilities managed by the VHA.

▣ *Government-facilitated HIE:* When state governments or other publicly funded organizations act as a primary facilitator of HIE within state boundaries, we refer to this as government-facilitated HIE. This designation distinguishes these activities, which are driven by very public policy priorities (e.g., alignment with Medicaid programs), from the efforts of private HIE, which are usually driven by the priorities of a private health system. Government-facilitated HIE efforts are also unique in that they typically operate at a technical level that supports a "network of networks" in which data and information are "pushed" from provider A to provider B at a single point in time. However, the information pushed is not stored in a central data repository or retained by the state HIE. Such a model allows each state to have multiple, regional HIE initiatives that operate independently of the statewide network.

■ *Community-based HIE:* Community-based HIE involves exchange of data and information among providers and healthcare organizations that may be marketplace competitors or otherwise unaffiliated, meaning they have no financial relationship with each other. For example, an academic medical center, large hospital system, and group of federally qualified health centers might agree to exchange data to better serve low-income populations in an urban area. Although they compete in the marketplace, these organizations recognize they are better served through HIE because they routinely observe patient cross-over, which can lead to repeating tests and procedures for patients who receive uncompensated care. If each organization became more aware of these patients' history, they might be able to save money while sparing patients from unnecessary care.

■ *Vendor-facilitated HIE:* An emerging type is vendor-facilitated HIE, which is a hybrid of government-facilitated and community-based HIEs. As the name implies, this form of HIE is facilitated by an EHR system vendor such as the Cerner Corporation (Kansas City, MO). Like the government-facilitated form, the EHR vendor layers a set of HIE services on top of its EHR infrastructure, enabling its customers to send or receive information to other customers of that vendor's EHR system. And like the community-based form, the vendor services enable exchange of information with hospitals and facilities outside a given integrated delivery network. Unlike a community-based HIE, however, the vendor does not typically facilitate the governance structure of the exchange; it simply provides a technical pathway for HIE. Although it is possible for customers of a different EHR vendor, Epic Systems (Verona, WI), to connect to organizations that use a non-Epic EHR, connecting to non-Epic customers is said to be more challenging, and non-Epic customers report that connecting to Epic-based EHR systems is difficult (Leventhal, 2014).

Key Components of Health Information Exchange

Interoperability and standards are natural prerequisites for any type of HIE. Yet, although necessary, interoperable information systems and technical standards are insufficient. HIE requires that two providers, hospitals, or public health departments fundamentally need and desire to share data or information with each other about a patient or population. Because HIE occurs within the context of a nation, state, or other sociopolitical context, HIE requires that both sociopolitical and technical conditions be met in order for the exchange of data to occur within the bounds of the law, for an authorized use case, and in a technically efficient manner. In this section, we explore the dual foundations that enable HIE within an organization, community, or nation-state.

Social and Political Foundations

Trust, or having confidence in how another party will behave in a given situation, is developed over time through contracts, laws, and regulations, and it is paramount in HIE (Thieme, 2016). Providers, hospitals, clinics, ACOs, and health plans are all trusted by patients or members to safeguard health information. In order for these entities to share health information, a sufficient fabric of trust must be created through contracts and practices, as well as laws and regulations at both state and federal levels. Compliance with HIE-related contracts, as well as applicable laws and regulations, is demonstrated through strong governance (as described later in this section), which breeds further trust. As organizations engaged in HIE work together over time, they develop a higher degree of certainty in how each will act in a given situation, which translates into a higher degree of trust.

With respect to HIE, trust is earned and kept when organizations mutually uphold three key ethical principles: privacy, confidentiality, and security. In this chapter, we briefly review their meaning and application in the context of HIE, as follows:

- *Privacy* is the freedom to choose what information is shared or not shared with other parties. For example, privacy is an individual's right to not disclose personal information to others, such as not disclosing an individual's genetic predisposition to cancer on an employment application. Some legislatures have enacted laws that require individuals to explicitly opt into HIE, authorizing providers to share their information with other care providers or entities that may have a need to know their health information, before information can be shared. Yet in other states or nations, providers can share health information on behalf of individuals in their care unless those individuals have opted out of HIE for certain purposes.

- *Confidentiality* is the obligation to keep secret information with which one is entrusted. For example, confidentially obligations are imposed under the Health Insurance Portability and Accountability Act (HIPAA) by prohibiting providers from disclosing protected health information to the media without a patient's authorization. Confidentiality obligations are often mislabeled as privacy obligations. For example, the HIPAA Privacy Rule would be more appropriately labeled as the Confidentiality Rule, because it imposes obligations upon covered entities not to make certain disclosures of information (i.e., to maintain confidentiality).

- *Security* is the combination of administrative, technical, and physical safeguards that ensure confidentiality and promote privacy. Security is composed of the safeguards that prevent inappropriate uses and disclosures of information. For example, strong passwords, encryption, and door locks all represent security safeguards that exist to keep information out of the wrong hands.

The rules of the road for HIE are defined by a combination of laws and regulations at both the state and federal levels as well as contracts among HIE participants (e.g., two competing health systems that agree to exchange data with each other). Federal and state laws establish a baseline set of guidelines, and then HIE participants may create additional rules through contracts. Contracts among HIE participants cannot override or conflict with federal or state laws and regulations, but they may provide for obligations above and beyond federal or state laws and regulations.

The primary federal laws in the United States applicable to HIE are HIPAA and the Health Information Technology for Economic and Clinical Health Act (HITECH Act). States are free to enact laws that are more stringent, such as requiring providers to obtain patient consent prior to disclosing protected health information for treatment purposes, because imposing such a consent requirement is more stringent than the HIPAA rules. If providers, ACOs, or health systems operate in a state that has more stringent laws, then HIE activities must comply with the more stringent state law requirements, keeping in mind that if a state law is silent on an issue, then the rules of HIPAA must be followed.

Beyond federal and state laws, HIE activities are facilitated by contracts. Legal documents, such as data use agreements (DUAs), multiparty agreements, and terms and conditions govern the relationships between parties engaged in HIE, and they foster trust. Various contracting structures may be used for HIE, as described in TABLE 4.2.

TABLE 4.2 HIE Contracting Structures

Structure	Characteristics
Party-to-party or point-to-point agreements	▪ Direct agreements between individual parties exchanging data. ▪ Example: A health system creates unique or custom data use agreements (DUA) with each of the organizations with which it exchanges data. There would be 12 different DUAs with ambulatory providers, 4 different DUAs with skilled nursing facilities, and 2 unique DUAs with home health agencies, among others.
Two-party HIE participation agreements	▪ Individual agreement between an HIE entity and a participant. ▪ HIE participants do not have a direct contractual legal relationship with each other. ▪ There exists some kind of third-party HIE organization with which providers, hospitals, health plans, and ACOs form agreements. ▪ Example: A community-based HIE establishes 27 customized DUAs with various ACOs, health systems, and independent providers in a single state. The healthcare organizations can all share data with the HIE in order to consume services from the HIE organization, but the providers cannot exchange data directly with each other.
Multiparty agreement	▪ A common set of terms and conditions to which an HIE entity and all participants agree. ▪ The HIE organization and all HIE participants have a direct contractual legal relationship with each other. ▪ There exists some kind of third-party HIE organization. ▪ Example: The CDC negotiates a multiparty agreement among a network of 40 state health departments to collect syndromic surveillance data for its national biosurveillance network. The states can also share data with each other using the HIE platform provided by the CDC.

Technical Foundations

Technical and terminology standards enable health data to be exchanged, yet there are additional technical foundations necessary to perform population health functions. For example, to accurately identify individuals at risk of rehospitalization, a health system or ACO would need to specify that individuals across the many thousands of healthcare observations (e.g., visits, encounters) appropriately attribute characteristics (e.g., onset of diabetes, incident stroke event) the right population of patients of interest. Although technical standards would enable the ACO to query its provider network, and terminology standards would allow it to define a comprehensive concept of "patients with diabetes," the ACO still needs to match individual identities, reconcile all the places where care was delivered, and calculate population-level metrics such as the proportion of patients with diabetes whose 12-month average HbA1c was less than 8.0%.

As outlined in TABLE 4.3, a core set of HIE technologies is necessary for key population health functions beyond movement of data from Provider A to Provider B. Together these functions can support HIE for individual as well as population healthcare delivery and analytics.

TABLE 4.3 Foundational HIE Technologies	
Foundational Technology	**Description**
Client registry or master patient index (MPI)	Software application designed to support uniquely identifying individuals who receive healthcare services from multiple sites and collate these records into a single, longitudinal health record (McFarlane, Dixon, & Grannis, 2016). Client registries can link individuals who have more than one medical record within a health system, and they can link individuals across health systems. Client registries typically use either deterministic or probabilistic algorithms, or a combination thereof, to uniquely link identities.
Facility registry or master facility list	A software application designed to collect, store, and distribute an up-to-date and standardized set of facility (e.g., clinic, hospital) data (McFarlane, Teesdale, & Dixon, 2016). This application can uniquely identify and produce a list of all the places where care was delivered to a patient or population.
Shared health record	A software application that compiles a longitudinal, person-centric record of a patient's clinical encounters that are being shared among the HIE participants (Broyles, Crichton, Jolliffe, Sæbø, & Dixon, 2016). This is like an EHR that spans multiple ACOs or health systems. The software could be an EHR system or a small-scale mobile application.
Health management information system (HMIS)	A software application that stores and distributes cumulative population-level information (Broyles, Crichton, et al., 2016). The HMIS primarily supports management or administration of a health system, and it contains a wide range of aggregate-level data gathered from the shared health record component. An example would be a dashboard of health indicators of interest to a particular stakeholder.

Health Information Exchange Use Cases for Population Health

Numerous applications or use cases of HIE exist for population health—too many to explore in this single chapter. In this section we outline two particularly compelling use cases of HIE in the population health arena given the focus of this text and their growing adoption across the United States.

Care Coordination Alerts

To improve coordination of care across a fragmented health system, many community-based HIE networks have introduced care coordination alerts, also known as event notification services and ADT alerts. These alerts are electronic messages sent to primary care providers, care managers, and/or ACOs following a nonroutine healthcare encounter, such as an inpatient stay or an emergency department visit. The thought is that if a provider, care manager, or ACO is notified of such events, then time and resources can be spent on efforts to identify the root cause (e.g., drug interaction, uncontrolled chronic illness), introduce an intervention (e.g., home visit, enrollment in a diabetes prevention program), and prevent rehospitalization or further consumption of higher cost/acuity resources like the emergency department. The logic extends from the more common use case of public health surveillance (Thacker, Qualters, & Lee, 2012), where systematic collection of information creates awareness of trends leading to better management of population health.

At the Indiana Health Information Exchange, a pilot involving care coordination alerts and subsequent ACO interventions reduced the number of nonurgent emergency department visits by 53% with a corresponding increase in primary care physician office visits by 68%, which, based on the local costs for an emergency department visit versus an office visit, saved one health plan between $2.1 and $4.1 million during the 6-month trial period (Indiana Health Information Exchange, 2013). The event notification service offered by the Chesapeake Regional Information System for our Patients (CRISP) sent 600,000 monthly notifications to more than 400 subscribed healthcare organizations in 2015 (Kharrazi, Horrocks, & Weiner, 2016). Similar services are available from other community-based HIE networks around the United States (Morrissey, 2014).

Population Health Dashboards

Both HIE and ACO networks are interested in monitoring population health. This means tracking various health indicators for populations and subpopulations using dashboards. Dashboards are software applications that summarize multiple indicators for a population or subpopulation, some of which can be configured to drill down into the details such as stratification by gender, age, race, and other individual characteristics that may drive differences between subpopulations. An HMIS component of HIE is particularly useful for supplying the aggregate data needed by dashboards. For example, the OpenHIE initiative uses DHIS 2, an open source application (https://www.dhis2.org/overview), as its HMIS component. The DHIS 2 application has been used in Sierra Leone to track infant mortality, immunization rates, and other population health indicators (Broyles, Crichton, et al., 2016).

▶ V. Challenges to Interoperability and
Health Information Exchange

Despite the theorized benefits, adoption of HIE among healthcare organizations has been limited. In 2015, approximately half of all nonfederal acute care hospitals in the United States had all necessary patient information electronically available from providers or sources outside their health system at the point of care (Patel, Henry, Pylypchuk, & Searcy, 2016). At the physician level, 42% of office-based physicians in 2014 shared electronic patient health information with other healthcare providers (Heisey-Grove, Patel, & Searcy, 2015). In that same year, more than half of all reports from laboratories for communicable diseases arrived at public health departments electronically. Achievement of the public health measures outlined in the MU program for eligible, nonfederal hospitals to encourage electronic submission for immunizations, reportable lab results, and syndromic surveillance observations was reported in 2014 to be 73%, 47%, and 48%, respectively (Heisey-Grove, Chaput, & Daniel, 2015; Wu, 2014).

Several factors contribute to the slow and limited adoption of HIE; the ones presented here are those for which there is consistent evidence in the literature.

Costs: Any health system, hospital, or provider that decides to engage in HIE is faced with the high initial cost associated with the adoption and implementation of HIE (Adler-Milstein, Bates, & Jha, 2009; Akhlaq, McKinstry, Muhammad, & Sheikh, 2016; Cochran et al., 2015; Dixon, Miller, & Overhage, 2013; Eden et al., 2016; Fontaine, Ross, Zink, & Schilling, 2010; Hersh et al., 2015; Markle Foundation, 2006; Vest & Gamm, 2010). In addition to the hardware, software, and labor costs that go into setting up the HIE, the training of staff and personnel to effectively use the new systems contributes to the overall cost (Akhlaq et al., 2016; Dixon et al., 2013). Consequently, there is also a loss of productivity in the period immediately after adopting HIE due to the change in workflow, which may result in lower revenue for providers (opportunity cost) (Adler-Milstein et al., 2009; Akhlaq et al., 2016; Cochran et al., 2015; Dixon et al., 2013; Eden et al., 2016; Fontaine et al., 2010; Hersh et al., 2015). There are also costs associated with the maintenance and management of the HIE, as well as usage fees (Adler-Milstein et al., 2009; Akhlaq et al., 2016; Massoudi, Marcial, Tant, Adler-Milstein, & West, 2016). Usage fees may be in the form of a monthly subscription to use the HIE (Adler-Milstein et al., 2009; Massoudi et al., 2016). Additionally, some EHR vendors may charge physicians and providers between $5000 and $40,000 for each physician who is connected to the HIE while also charging transaction fees for each exchange (Massoudi et al., 2016). In low- and middle-income countries (LMICs), where mobile devices are routinely used to access health information, there are costs related to airtime usage (Akhlaq et al., 2016).

Moreover, although providers bear the financial burden of HIE adoption, only some of the benefits accrue to them. Although there is strong evidence to suggest that HIE is associated with reduced costs due to reduction of medication errors, redundant testing, and unnecessary referrals and generally lower healthcare utilization, these benefits are directed toward the payers (Hersh et al., 2015; Rahurkar, Vest, & Menachemi, 2015). Indeed, it stands to reason that providers may actually lose revenue by adopting HIE. Finally, apart from misaligned incentives, which may not defray the providers' investment in HIE, the sustainability of HIE organizations is an additional concern. Most HIE organizations are sustained by state and federal grants, and thus the uncertainty of their future heightens the financial barrier associated with HIE adoption (Massoudi et al., 2016).

■ *Resources:* Beyond limited financial resources, there are resources in the external environment of a provider organization that may serve as barriers to HIE adoption. The existing computing environment or supporting infrastructure may prevent adoption of HIE technologies without an upgrade (Akhlaq et al., 2016; Cochran et al., 2015). Many provider organizations further lack specialized human resources within their information technology (IT) departments who can focus on interconnecting EHR systems and point-of-care applications across a network or enterprise (Gibson, Dixon, & Abrams, 2015). This is especially true for small providers and local public health departments where IT human resources are limited or outsourced (Dixon, McFarlane, Dearth, Grannis, & Gibson, 2015). In some cases, a healthcare or public health organization may be able to overcome this by partnering with a community-based HIE organization, but this capacity does not exist everywhere (Akhlaq et al., 2016; Patel, Henry, et al., 2016).

■ *Privacy:* Large amounts of protected health information are collected and shared when organizations engage in HIE. Keeping this information from falling into the hands of nefarious parties is a constant concern for stakeholders (Adler-Milstein et al., 2009; Dixon et al., 2013; Eden et al., 2016; Fontaine et al., 2010; Markle Foundation, 2006; Vest & Gamm, 2010). Breaches in confidentiality of these data present a liability in the form of financial penalties and costs associated with damage control and may also result in loss of data. Concerns arise over potential unauthorized access to data, hacking or IT-related incidents, loss, improper disposal, theft, and for other reasons. In 2015, there were 269 breach incidents in which 500 individuals or more were affected in each incident, affecting a total of over 113 million individuals (Office for Civil Rights, 2016). More recently, provider information systems have also been affected by ransomware, which locks providers out of their own HISs (Winton, 2016). Consequently, concerns over privacy are also expressed by patients, who are worried that improper access to their private health information may result in discrimination, social embarrassment, or other negative outcomes (Markle Foundation, 2006). Despite these incidents, patient concerns over privacy of their health data has decreased in recent years (Patel, Hughes, Barker, & Moon, 2016). However, the number of patients who chose not to participate in HIE due to privacy concerns did not change significantly (Eden et al., 2016; Hersh et al., 2015; Patel, Hughes, et al., 2016). Additionally, patients may not understand the benefit to their health care from data sharing or may think that the risk to privacy outweighs the potential benefit from data sharing. Lower patient participation may lead to lack of completeness of information in the EHRs and reduce the value of the health information received from other providers (Eden et al., 2016; Hersh et al., 2015). Indeed, the incompleteness of health data was the most commonly cited reason for not using data received by HIE (Patel, Hughes, et al., 2016). Interestingly, privacy concerns regarding HIE are more commonly cited in the United States than in European countries or LMICs (Akhlaq et al., 2016; Eden et al., 2016; Hersh et al., 2015).

Interoperability: EHR systems developed and evolved as silos that had little incentive or capability to communicate with each other (Adler-Milstein et al., 2009; Dixon, 2007; Fontaine et al., 2010; Vest, 2010). The lack of interoperability was caused by the disparate approaches to EHR systems taken by different vendors. Efforts aimed at facilitating HIE called for the development of standards. Although standards now exist, they are not always embraced by vendors or the health systems in which standards-based EHR systems are implemented (Dixon et al., 2014). Furthermore, despite the availability of standards for transactions between EHR and other health information technologies, there exists a diversity of methods for the exchange of data as well as the presentation of exchanged data to providers. To date, there exists limited evidence-based approaches for how HIE networks should be architected or how the data exchanged among EHR systems should be summarized and presented to end users. Finally, disparities in EHR capabilities may be one of the most common reasons for poor interoperability, with more than half of hospitals citing exchange partners that lack the ability to receive data as a barrier to interoperability (Patel, Henry, et al., 2016).

Competition: Vendors operating in the same market have traditionally resisted data sharing in efforts to maintain competitive advantage (Adler-Milstein et al., 2009; Eden et al., 2016; Fontaine et al., 2010; Hersh et al., 2015; Patel, Hughes, et al., 2016; Vest, 2010; Vest & Gamm, 2010). Thus, vendors may not share patient data with other health systems as part of business policy, or may charge additional fees to exchange information, a practice recently labeled by policymakers as "information blocking." Even when exchange does take place, it may be limited by what the vendor enables to be capable of exchange. Consequently, this may result in inadequate patient information being provided at the point of care, thus reducing the value and utility of data exchange. As discussed previously, given that the benefits of HIE are accrued by the payers, data exchange and the accompanying risk of losing referrals to competitors may discourage HIE (Adler-Milstein et al., 2009; Eden et al., 2016; Fontaine et al., 2010; Vest & Gamm, 2010).

In addition to these barriers, there exist several barriers pertinent to low-resource settings such as those found in LMICs at the sociocultural, political, or environmental level (Akhlaq et al., 2016). Stakeholders in LMICs can place a lower intrinsic value on health data and, as such, do not consider it crucial to providing high quality care. Furthermore, lack of leadership and coordination limits decision making at the national level that may benefit HIE. In addition, political corruption and instability often result in unpredictable changes in policies, which may present additional barriers to HIE. Technical barriers exist in the form of HIE software that is limited to the English language, preventing usage in non-English-speaking nations. Barriers also exist at the individual level with poor English language skills in addition to inadequate data management. Low-resource settings also make it harder to acquire data analysis tools, thus making it difficult to interpret data or present dashboard-level statistics. Despite these barriers, there are several HIE initiatives in 28 LMICs around the world that are trying to improve healthcare delivery and population health outcomes.

▶ VI. Future Directions for Interoperability and Health Information Exchange

The need for interoperability and HIE has never been greater. Therefore, the future looks bright for those who are knowledgeable or specialize in data integration as well as interoperability. Although current skill levels across the health system are not optimized, many informatics as well as public health and clinical sciences programs now offer training in HIE. There will be more programs in the future to help fuel wider integration and exchange of data across the health system. This is especially true in population health, because it is impossible to understand and monitor population health without integration of data across multiple sources. In addition to a wider array of training programs in interoperability and HIE, there will likely be expanded efforts by the federal government in the United States and elsewhere to support nationwide exchange of health data. Whether for population health management or better detection of emerging health threats, nations around the world seek to improve their ability to better understand healthcare delivery and outcomes. In large nations like the United States, greater emphasis on HIE will likely cause greater development and implementation of local and state-based infrastructures in order to create a network-of-networks that will enable national HIE. New players in the healthcare market, including ACOs as well as tech companies and EHR vendors, are likely to emerge with innovative ideas for scaling HIE beyond the limits of current technologies as well as infrastructures that rely on version 1.0 of EHR systems deployed for MU. Emerging standards like FHIR and other API-based solutions will likely help nudge the market toward overcoming the limitations of existing standards-based interfaces.

▶ VII. Conclusion

Interoperability and HIE are critical components of population health informatics. At all levels of the health system, there is a need to integrate data and information systems. Hospitals, EHR systems, and point-of-care applications need to interface to establish longitudinal records of patient care for payment, quality, and legal purposes. There is also a need to connect hospitals and health systems to enable ACO and community-based HIE networks to track patient care and outcomes across organizational boundaries. These networks need to scale to regional and national levels to enable population health management no matter where care is delivered. Informaticians who work on population health applications, including developing, implementing, and evaluating HIE, are in high demand and will likely be in demand for quite some time because the transition toward and realization of population health goals are far from being achieved. Although the road ahead is long, there is much optimism as providers, patients, public health professionals, payers, and policymakers are working together to create better interoperability and HIE.

References

2015 Edition Health Information Technology (Health IT) Certification Criteria, 2015 Edition Base Electronic Health Record (EHR) Definition, and ONC Health IT Certification Program Modifications. Final rule. (2015). *Federal Register, 80*(200), 62601–62759.

Adler-Milstein, J., Bates, D. W., & Jha, A. K. (2009). U.S. regional health information organizations: Progress and challenges. *Health Affairs (Millwood), 28*(2), 483–492. doi:28/2/483[pii]10.1377 /hlthaff.28.2.483

Akhlaq, A., McKinstry, B., Muhammad, K. B., & Sheikh, A. (2016). Barriers and facilitators to health information exchange in low- and middle-income country settings: A systematic review. *Health Policy Plan.* doi:10.1093/heapol/czw056

Alyea, J. M., Dixon, B. E., Bowie, J., & Kanter, A. S. (2016). Standardizing health-care data across an enterprise. In B. E. Dixon (Ed.), *Health information exchange: Navigating and managing a network of health information systems* (pp. 137–148). Waltham, MA: Academic Press.

Andry, F., & Wan, L. (2012). *Health information exchange network interoperability through IHE transactions orchestration.* Paper presented at the International Conference on Health Informatics, Vilamoura, Portugal.

Baorto, D. M., Cimino, J. J., Parvin, C. A., & Kahn, M. G. (1998). Combining laboratory data sets from multiple institutions using the logical observation identifier names and codes (LOINC). *International Journal of Medical Informatics, 51*(1), 29–37.

Barbarito, F., Pinciroli, F., Mason, J., Marceglia, S., Mazzola, L., & Bonacina, S. (2012). Implementing standards for the interoperability among healthcare providers in the public regionalized Healthcare Information System of the Lombardy Region. *Journal of Biomedical Informatics, 45*(4), 736–745. doi:10.1016/j.jbi.2012.01.006

Benson, T. (2012). *Principles of health interoperability HL7 and SNOMED* (2nd ed.). Dordrecht, Netherlands: Springer.

Bodenreider, O. (2008). Biomedical ontologies in action: Role in knowledge management, data integration and decision support. *Yearbook of Medical Informatics,* 67–79.

Bresnick, J. (2016). A FHIR future burns brightly for population health management. Retrieved from http://healthitanalytics.com/features/a-fhir-future-burns-brightly-for-population-health -management

Broyles, D., Crichton, R., Jolliffe, B., Sæbø, J. I., & Dixon, B. E. (2016). Shared longitudinal health records for clinical and population health. In B. E. Dixon (Ed.), *Health information exchange: Navigating and managing a network of health information systems* (pp. 149–162). Waltham, MA: Academic Press.

Broyles, D., Dixon, B. E., Crichton, R., Biondich, P., & Grannis, S. J. (2016). The evolving health information infrastructure. In B. E. Dixon (Ed.), *Health information exchange: Navigating and managing a network of health information systems* (pp. 107–122). Waltham, MA: Academic Press.

Centers for Disease Control and Prevention. (2011). PHIN vocabulary access and distribution system. Retrieved from https://phinvads.cdc.gov/vads/SearchVocab.action

Centers for Disease Control and Prevention. (2015). Reportable condition mapping table (RCMT). Retrieved from http://www.cdc.gov/EHRmeaningfuluse/rcmt.html

Centers for Disease Control and Prevention. (2016, February 3). Current and historical conditions: NNDSS. Retrieved from https://wwwn.cdc.gov/nndss/conditions/

Centers for Medicare and Medicaid Services. (2012). Medicare and Medicaid programs: Electronic Health Record Incentive Program—Stage 2. *Federal Register.* Retrieved from https://www.gpo .gov/fdsys/pkg/FR-2012-09-04/pdf/2012-21050.pdf

Centers for Medicare and Medicaid Services. (2013, August 23). Meaningful use. Retrieved from https://www.cms.gov/Regulations-and-Guidance/Legislation/EHRIncentivePrograms

Cochran, G. L., Lander, L., Morien, M., Lomelin, D. E., Sayles, H., & Klepser, D. G. (2015). Health care provider perceptions of a query-based health information exchange: Barriers and benefits. *Journal of Innovation in Health Informatics, 22*(2), 302–308. doi:10.14236/jhi.v22i2.135

Corepoint Health. (n.d.). The HL7 evolution: Comparing HL7 versions 2 and 3. Retrieved from https://corepointhealth.com/hl7-evolution-comparing-hl7-versions-2-and-3

Del Fiol, G., Crouch, B. I., & Cummins, M. R. (2014). Data standards to support health information exchange between poison control centers and emergency departments. *Journal of the American Medical Informatics Association.* doi:10.1136/amiajnl-2014-003127

Digital Imaging and Communications in Medicine. (n.d.). The DICOM standard. Retrieved from http://medical.nema.org/standard.html

Dixon, B., Miller, T., & Overhage, M. (2013). Barriers to achieving the last mile in health information exchange: A survey of small hospitals and physician practices. *Journal of Healthcare Information Management, 27*(4), 55–58.

Dixon, B. E. (2007). A roadmap for the adoption of e-health. *e-Service Journal, 5*(3), 3–13.

Dixon, B. E. (2016). What is health information exchange? In B. E. Dixon (Ed.), *Health information exchange: Navigating and managing a network of health information systems* (pp. 3–20). Waltham, MA: Academic Press.

Dixon, B. E., Grannis, S. J., & Revere, D. (2013). Measuring the impact of a health information exchange intervention on provider-based notifiable disease reporting using mixed methods: A study protocol. *BMC Medical Informatics and Decision Making, 13*(1), 121. doi:10.1186 /1472-6947-13-121

Dixon, B. E., Hook, J., & Vreeman, D. J. (2015). Learning from the crowd in terminology mapping: The LOINC experience. *Laboratory Medicine, 46*(2), 168–174. doi:10.1309/LMWJ730SVKTUBAOJ

Dixon, B. E., McFarlane, T. D., Dearth, S., Grannis, S. J., & Gibson, P. J. (2015). Characterizing informatics roles and needs of public health workers: Results from the Public Health Workforce Interests and Needs survey. *Journal of Public Health Management Practice, 21*(6), S130–S140. doi:10.1097/phh.0000000000000304

Dixon, B. E., Vreeman, D. J., & Grannis, S. J. (2014). The long road to semantic interoperability in support of public health: Experiences from two states. *Journal of Biomedial Informatics, 49*, 3–8. doi:10.1016/j.jbi.2014.03.011

Dolin, R. H., & Alschuler, L. (2011). Approaching semantic interoperability in Health Level Seven. *Journal of the American Medical Informatics Association, 18*(1), 99–103. doi:10.1136 /jamia.2010.007864

Eden, K. B., Totten, A. M., Kassakian, S. Z., Gorman, P. N., McDonagh, M. S., Devine, B., . . . Hersh, W. R. (2016). Barriers and facilitators to exchanging health information: A systematic review. *International Journal of Medical Informatics, 88*, 44–51. doi:10.1016/j.ijmedinf.2016.01.004

Fidahussein, M., Friedlin, J., & Grannis, S. (2011). Practical challenges in the secondary use of real-world data: The notifiable condition detector. *AMIA Annual Symposium Proceedings, 2011*, 402–408.

Finnell, J. T., Overhage, J. M., & Grannis, S. (2011). All health care is not local: An evaluation of the distribution of emergency department care delivered in Indiana. *AMIA Annual Symposium Proceedings, 2011*, 409–416.

Fontaine, P., Ross, S. E., Zink, T., & Schilling, L. M. (2010). Systematic review of health information exchange in primary care practices. *Journal of the American Board of Family Medicine, 23*(5), 655–670. doi:10.3122/jabfm.2010.05.090192

Gibson, C. J., Dixon, B. E., & Abrams, K. (2015). Convergent evolution of health information management and health informatics: A perspective on the future of information professionals in health care. *Applied Clinical Informatics, 6*(1), 163–184. doi:10.4338/ACI-2014-09-RA-0077

Gliklich, R. E., Dreyer, N. A., & Leavy, M. B. (2014). *Registries for evaluating patient outcomes: A user's guide* (3rd ed., Vol. 2). Rockville, MD: Agency for Healthcare Research and Quality. Retrieved from http://www.effectivehealthcare.ahrq.gov/index.cfm/search-for-guides-reviews-and-reports /?productid=1897&pageaction=displayproduct

Health Level 7. (n.d.a). HL7 CDA® R2 implementation guide: Trauma registry data submission, release 1—US realm. Retrieved from http://www.hl7.org/implement/standards/product_brief .cfm?product_id=355

Health Level 7. (n.d.b). HL7 fast healthcare interoperability resources specification (FHIR®), release 1. Retrieved from http://www.hl7.org/implement/standards/product_brief.cfm?product_id=343

Health Level 7. (n.d.c). HL7 version 3 implementation guide: Family history/pedigree interoperability, release 1. Retrieved from http://www.hl7.org/implement/standards/product_brief .cfm?product_id=301

Health Level 7 International. (n.d.d). HL7 version 3 product suite. Retrieved from http://www.hl7 .org

Healthcare Information and Management Systems Society. (2013). What is interoperability? Retrieved from http://www.himss.org/library/interoperability-standards/what-is-interoperability

Heisey-Grove, D., Chaput, D., & Daniel, J. (2015). Hospital reporting on meaningful use public health measures in 2014. *ONC Data Brief No. 22*, 1–13.

Heisey-Grove, D., Patel, V., & Searcy, T. (2015). Physician electronic exchange of patient health information, 2014. *ONC Data Brief No. 31*. Office of the National Coordinator for Health Information Technology: Washington, DC.

Hersh, W., Totten, A., Eden, K., Devine, B., Gorman, P., Kassakian, S., . . . McDonagh, M. S. (2015). Health information exchange. Retrieved from http://www.ncbi.nlm.nih.gov/books /NBK343580/

Hosseini, M., & Dixon, B. E. (2016). Syntactic interoperability and the role of standards. In B. E. Dixon (Ed.), *Health information exchange: Navigating and managing a network of health information systems* (pp. 123–136). Waltham, MA: Academic Press.

Hosseini, M., Meade, J., Schnitzius, J., & Dixon, B. E. (2016). Consolidating CCDs from multiple data sources: A modular approach. *Journal of the American Medical Informatics Association, 23*(2), 317–323. doi:10.1093/jamia/ocv084

Humensky, J., Carretta, H., de Groot, K., Brown, M. M., Tarlov, E., & Hynes, D. M. (2012). Service utilization of veterans dually eligible for VA and Medicare fee-for-service: 1999-2004. *Medicare and Medicaid Research Review, 2*(3). doi:10.5600/mmrr.002.03.a06

Imler, T. D., Vreeman, D. J., & Kannry, J. (2016). Healthcare data standards and exchange. In J. T. Finnell & B. E. Dixon (Eds.), *Clinical informatics study guide: Text and review* (pp. 233–253). Zurich, Switzerland: Springer International.

Indiana Health Information Exchange. (2013). ADT alerts for reducing ED admissions: A case study. Retrieved from https://az480170.vo.msecnd.net/bd985247-f489-435f-a7b4-49df92ec868e/docs /4f798bc8-4c8f-4dce-b145-cab48f3d8787/ihie-adtalerts-casestudy.pdf

Kasthurirathne, S. N., Mamlin, B., Grieve, G., & Biondich, P. (2015). Towards standardized patient data exchange: Integrating a FHIR based API for the open medical record system. *Studies in Health Technology and Informatics, 216*, 932.

Kharrazi, H., Horrocks, D., & Weiner, J. (2016). Use of HIEs for value-based care delivery: A case study of Maryland's HIE. In B. E. Dixon (Ed.), *Health information exchange: Navigating and managing a network of health information systems* (pp. 313–332). Waltham, MA: Academic Press.

Klann, J. G., & Murphy, S. N. (2013). Computing health quality measures using informatics for integrating biology and the bedside. *Journal of Medical Internet Research, 15*(4), e75. doi:10.2196 /jmir.2493

Lee, M., Heo, E., Lim, H., Lee, J. Y., Weon, S., Chae, H., . . . Yoo, S. (2015). Developing a common health information exchange platform to implement a nationwide health information network in South Korea. *Healthcare Informatics Research, 21*(1), 21–29. doi:10.4258/hir.2015.21.1.21

Leventhal, R. (2014). KLAS report: Epic to non-epic data sharing is real, but challenging. Retrieved from http://www.healthcare-informatics.com/news-item/klas-report-epic-non-epic-data-sharing-real -challenging

Lin, M. C., Vreeman, D. J., McDonald, C. J., & Huff, S. M. (2011). A characterization of local LOINC mapping for laboratory tests in three large institutions. *Methods of Information in Medicine, 50*(2), 105–114. doi:10.3414/ME09-01-0072

Markle Foundation. (2006). The common framework: Overview and principles. Retrieved from http://www.markle.org/sites/default/files/CF-Professionals-Full.pdf

Massoudi, B. L., Marcial, L. H., Tant, E., Adler-Milstein, J., & West, S. L. (2016). Using health information exchanges to calculate clinical quality measures: A study of barriers and facilitators. *Healthcare, 4*(2), 104–108.

McFarlane, T. D., Dixon, B. E., & Grannis, S. J. (2016). Client registries: Identifying and linking patients. In B. E. Dixon (Ed.), *Health information exchange: Navigating and managing a network of health information systems* (pp. 163–182). London, UK: Academic Press.

McFarlane, T. D., Teesdale, S., & Dixon, B. E. (2016). Facility registries: Metadata for where care is delivered. In B. E. Dixon (Ed.), *Health information exchange: Navigating and managing a network of health information systems* (pp. 183–201). London, UK: Academic Press.

Morrissey, J. (2014). Track-and-alert apps enable true care coordination. *Hospitals and Health Networks, 88*(4), 18–19.

Office for Civil Rights. (2016). Breaches affecting 500 or more individuals. Retrieved from http://web.archive.org/web/20160621145042/https://ocrportal.hhs.gov/ocr/breach/breach _report.jsf;jsessionid=E5C858AFDD7FC261EB532C7546595A33.worker1

Office of the National Coordinator for Health Information Technology. (2015). 2015 interoperability standards advisory. Retrieved from http://www.healthit.gov/sites/default/files/2015 interoperabilitystandardsadvisory01232015final_for_public_comment.pdf

Patel, V., Henry, J., Pylypchuk, Y., & Searcy, T. (2016). Interoperability among U.S. nonfederal acute care hospitals in 2015. *ONC Data Brief No. 36*, 1–11.

Patel, V., Hughes, P., Barker, W., & Moon, L. (2016). Trends in individuals' perceptions regarding privacy and security of medical records and exchange of health information: 2012–2014. *ONC Data Brief No. 33*, 1–11.

Rahurkar, S., Vest, J. R., & Menachemi, N. (2015). Despite the spread of health information exchange, there is little evidence of its impact on cost, use, and quality of care. *Health Affairs (Millwood)*, *34*(3), 477–483. doi:10.1377/hlthaff.2014.0729

Schoen, C., Osborn, R., Squires, D., Doty, M., Pierson, R., & Applebaum, S. (2011). New 2011 survey of patients with complex care needs in eleven countries finds that care is often poorly coordinated. *Health Affairs (Millwood)*, *30*(12), 2437–2448. doi:10.1377/hlthaff.2011.0923

Sullivan, T. (2016, March 11). FHIR, the hottest topic at HIMSS16, sets stage for population health. Retrieved from http://www.healthcareitnews.com/news/fhir-hottest-topic-himss16-sets-stage -population-health

Thacker, S. B., Qualters, J. R., & Lee, L. M. (2012). Public health surveillance in the United States: Evolution and challenges. *Morbidity and Mortality Weekly Report: Surveillance Summaries*, *61*, 3–9.

Thieme, E. (2016). Privacy, security, and confidentiality: Toward trust. In B. E. Dixon (Ed.), *Health information exchange: Navigating and managing a network of health information systems* (pp. 91–104). Waltham, MA: Academic Press.

Vergara-Niedermayr, C., Wang, F., Pan, T., Kurc, T., & Saltz, J. (2013). Semantically interoperable XML data. *International Journal of Semantic Computing*, *7*(3), 237–255. doi:10.1142/s1793351 x13500037

Vest, J. R. (2010). More than just a question of technology: Factors related to hospitals' adoption and implementation of health information exchange. *International Journal of Medical Informatics*, *79*(12), 797–806. doi:10.1016/j.ijmedinf.2010.09.003

Vest, J. R., & Gamm, L. D. (2010). Health information exchange: Persistent challenges and new strategies. *Journal of the American Medical Informatics Association*, *17*(3), 288–294. doi:10.1136 /jamia.2010.003673

Viangteeravat, T., Anyanwu, M. N., Nagisetty, V. R., Kuscu, E., Sakauye, M. E., & Wu, D. (2011). Clinical data integration of distributed data sources using Health Level Seven (HL7) v3-RIM mapping. *Journal of Clinical Bioinformatics*, *1*, 32. doi:10.1186/2043-9113-1-32

Vreeman, D. J., Hook, J., & Dixon, B. E. (2015). Learning from the crowd while mapping to LOINC. *Journal of the American Medical Informatics Association*. doi:10.1093/jamia/ocv098

Winton, R. (2016). Hollywood hospital pays $17,000 in bitcoin to hackers; FBI investigating. *Los Angeles Times*. Retrieved from http://web.archive.org/web/20160621144609/http://www.latimes .com/business/technology/la-me-ln-hollywood-hospital-bitcoin-20160217-story.html

Wu, L. (2014). Issue brief: Health IT for public health reporting and information systems. Retrieved from https://www.healthit.gov/sites/default/files/phissuebrief04-24-14.pdf

CHAPTER 5

Informatics in Population Health Surveillance

Lorna Thorpe and Katharine H. McVeigh

QUESTIONS FOR THOUGHT

- How can we identify opportunities to either expand or develop new forms of population health surveillance using informatics-informed approaches?
- How can we evaluate their net benefits versus costs or risks?
- What are some of the potential implications for health departments with respect to workforce and external partnerships in implementing these new approaches?
- How can more data be made publicly available and in ways that are easily understood by the public and policymakers?
- What are the dominant opportunities for improving population health surveillance in developing countries?

CHAPTER OUTLINE

▶ I. Definition of Population Health Surveillance

Population health surveillance is an essential function of public health practice that provides reliable information to the public health community about the health of the population being served. It is formally defined as: "… the ongoing systematic collection, analysis, interpretation and dissemination of health data for the planning, implementation and evaluation of public health practice" (World Health Organization [WHO], 2012).

As implied by its formal definition, three important characteristics of population health surveillance are as follows:

1. Data collection occurs on an *ongoing* basis, so as to be able to monitor trends.
2. Methods of data collection are *systematic* so as not to introduce observed patterns that are a result of changes in how data were collected (data artifact).
3. There is an explicit process for *dissemination* of information to key stakeholders.

Most people are familiar with the concept of tracking infectious diseases to identify the onset of new epidemics. But in the United States and many other countries, population health surveillance has evolved from primarily monitoring infectious diseases and causes of mortality to tracking the occurrence of many different conditions that are now leading causes of morbidity, including chronic conditions, birth outcomes and birth defects, injuries, mental health, risk behaviors, and environmental/

occupational exposures to health risks (Centers for Disease Control and Prevention [CDC], n.d.). Public health institutions and the broader public health community use information generated from population health surveillance for a wide variety of reasons, including to set goals and priorities, identify actions aimed at addressing those priorities, target conditions that are worsening or deemed amenable to change, and monitor the effectiveness of actions over time. The CDC lists the following as a more specific array of potential functions involving population health surveillance (German et al., 2001):

- Guide immediate action for cases of public health importance;
- Measure the burden of a disease (or other health-related event), including changes in related factors, the identification of populations at high risk, and the identification of new or emerging health concerns;
- Monitor trends in the burden of a disease (or other health-related event), including the detection of epidemics (outbreaks) and pandemics;
- Guide the planning, implementation, and evaluation of programs to prevent and control disease, injury, or adverse exposure;
- Evaluate public policy;
- Detect changes in health practices and the effects of these changes;
- Prioritize the allocation of health resources;
- Describe the clinical course of disease; and
- Provide a basis for epidemiologic research.

At the local, state, national, and even broader geographic region levels, public health agencies typically maintain surveillance systems that collect primary data and/or harness data from other sources. That information is disseminated to key stakeholders, which may often include individuals engaged in developing programs to address the conditions under surveillance, policymakers, clinical partners, community-based organizations, and the concerned public. Ultimately, the purpose of capturing, analyzing, and sharing these data is to improve health outcomes.

With advances in data availability and in methods for data capture, analysis, and visualization, the process and scope of population health surveillance is undergoing major changes. CDC authors, in a publication entitled "Public Health Surveillance in the United States: Evolution and Challenges," have highlighted the growing importance of informatics-informed, automated solutions in population health surveillance in the schema shown in FIGURE 5.1, yet they acknowledge that extensive human involvement will remain critical for surveillance to function effectively.

This chapter first reviews long-established surveillance sources, and then introduces emerging modes of population health surveillance, highlighting the different ways informatics is expanding or changing current practice.

▶ II. Public Health Surveillance Data Sources: Past and Present

Hippocrates (460 BC–370 BC) is widely credited as being the first person to systematically collect data on health states and diseases, recognizing acute versus chronic conditions as well as endemic and epidemic patterns (Duncan, Gold, Basch, & Markellis, 1988). However, the first known public health action taken as a result of public health surveillance occurred in Venice in 1348 as a result of a bubonic plague epidemic. Incoming ships

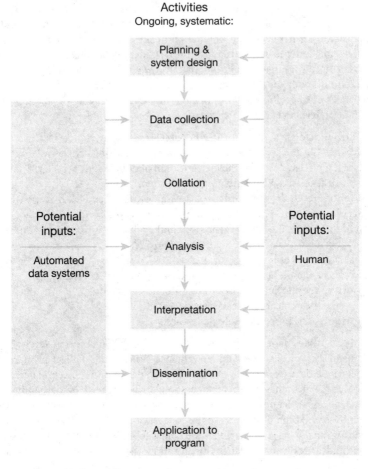

FIGURE 5.1 Optimal balance of human and automated inputs into ongoing, systematic public health surveillance system activities

Reproduced from Thacker, S., Qualters, J. R., Lee, L. M., & Centers for Disease Control and Prevention. (2012). Public health surveillance in the United States: Evolution and challenges. *Morbidity and Mortality Weekly Report, 61*(3), 3–9.

were boarded by local officials to inspect their passengers for evidence of disease prior to disembarking. This soon evolved into a 40-day waiting period before incoming passengers could leave their ships ("quaranta, the Italian word for 40, is the basis for the word quarantine). Quarantine was later used again in Marseilles in 1377 for the same reason.

Vital Statistics

Scientists have been collecting mortality data for more than 400 years in an effort to characterize the health of communities and guide health services. In 1662, John Graunt (1620–1674) was the first to publish a careful analysis of such compiled mortality data from London in his book entitled *Natural and Political Observations upon the Bills of Mortality*. Since the mid-1500s, bills of mortality were statements describing the number of people dying of different causes across parishes of London each week, and Graunt analyzed several years' worth of these statements. Although age at death was not available on these early bills, he estimated that approximately one-third of all deaths occurred from ailments that typically affect children, allowing him to estimate that about 36% of all deaths occurred to young children. Actual civil registration of births and deaths was mandated in England in 1831, and a central vital registration office was opened in 1838, led by William Farr, who became well known for his taxonomy of causes of death.

In the United States, as in Europe, the transition from having birth and death records kept by local churches to secular courts and offices occurred throughout the 17th and 18th centuries. By 1850, states began sending mortality statistics to a common federal office, and in 1910, the United States produced a standard model death certificate to promote uniformity of reporting, followed by a standard birth certificate in 1930. Today, vital registration in the United States remains a voluntary, decentralized system with 57 vital registration reporting jurisdictions, including the 50 states, New York City (NYC), the District of Columbia, and the country's 5 territories (Puerto Rico, U.S. Virgin Islands, Guam, American Samoa, and the Northern Mariana Islands). All jurisdictions report to the National Center for Health Statistics (NCHS), part of the CDC, which is responsible for the collection and analysis of mortality data for the country.

Birth and death registration, in the United States and many other countries, are examples of population-based administrative systems that provide critical legal and identity functions, information on population sizes, as well as important health information to the public health community for surveillance purposes. Death registration provides information on all-cause mortality trends, as well as patterns in causes of death. Cause of death is classified following an internationally recognized standard taxonomy known as the *International Statistical Classification of Diseases and Related Health Problems* (ICD), which is currently in its 10th revision (WHO, 2016). More than 100 countries currently follow this system, which classifies disease by two main criteria: etiology of disease (infectious, neoplasms, diseases originating in the perinatal period, injuries, etc.) and body systems (digestive, respiratory, etc.). The underlying cause of death is determined by: "(a) the disease or injury which initiated the train of morbid events leading directly to death or (b) the circumstances of the accident or violence which produced the fatal injury" (WHO, 2016). This train of morbid events leading directly to death is typically completed by the healthcare provider most familiar with the deceased individual, such as his or her attending or personal physician. Personal and demographic information is completed by a funeral director, who often initiates the death record.

The process of collecting personal and medical information on a decedent is now completed electronically even though there might be some variation in terms of quality and timeliness. The information is collected at the local level by funeral directors and physicians (Brooks & Reed, 2015). Nationally and at the state level, the literal health event descriptions were historically coded by trained nosologists to officially classify the underlying cause of death. Automation of this process began in 1967, and currently the NCHS uses a series of computer programs and algorithms that allow states to automatically enter, classify per ICD codes, select underlying cause, and retrieve cause-of-death information (CDC, 2016a). A variety of informatics solutions to improve electronic death registration and coding are being applied around the country; however, limited funding for vital registration improvements has hampered the speed of progress, with some states achieving more success at garnering health information technology, emergency preparedness, and other resources to do so than others.

On birth certificates, the standardization and coding of health status of mothers and babies has historically been more straightforward, but the content of information collected on birth certificates has grown to include a wide range of health and social factors to identify determinants of perinatal health outcomes. The actual number of items collected on standard recommended birth certificates has grown from 33 items in 1900 to more than 60 items in 2003 (Brumberg, Dozor, & Golombek, 2012). All states have electronic systems to collect birth certificate information, yet systems are disparate, and many are now more than 20 years old. Efforts to standardize birth certificates and electronic systems are actively underway (Brumberg et al., 2012).

Reportable Diseases Registries

The majority of public health surveillance systems developed historically, both nationally and worldwide, were designed to monitor and control infectious diseases, with healthcare professionals always serving as the primary reporting source (Koo & Wetterhall, 1996; Roush, Birkhead, Koo, Cobb, & Fleming, 1999). In the United States, systematic reporting of infectious diseases began in Massachusetts in 1874, with weekly reports submitted from physicians in an attempt to monitor outbreaks of diseases such as yellow fever and cholera (Choi, 2012). State and local public health officials required communicable disease reporting and quarantine of patients with smallpox, cholera, typhoid, and tuberculosis (Birkhead, Klompas, & Shah, 2015). Following nationwide epidemics of influenza and poliomyelitis that struck between 1916 and 1919, all states began participating in reporting some data on communicable diseases nationally by 1925 (Choi, 2012). The Council of State and Territorial Epidemiologists (CSTE), in partnership with the CDC, has guided the formulation of nationally notifiable diseases since the early 1950s, and led development of surveillance case definitions beginning in the 1990s. These efforts have greatly improved standardization of surveillance and comparability of disease rates by state and local health departments (Birkhead et al., 2015; CDC, 2017b). Authority and regulations for notifiable disease reporting exist at the state or local level, with national agencies such as the CDC making annual recommendations on which diseases to report. In the United States, the CDC currently recommends 64 diseases to be notifiable (CDC, 2016a, 2016d); these are published weekly in the CDC publication *Morbidity and Mortality Weekly Report*. Of these, approximately 80% require laboratory confirmation in the definition of a confirmed case (Silk & Berkelman, 2005). Because of state autonomy with respect to determining which diseases are notifiable and in what time period, the actual diseases reported by each state vary. In 1992, the Institute of Medicine released a report voicing concern over the state of the notifiable disease system, stressing the importance of maintaining a strong notifiable disease system (Institute of Medicine [IOM], 2014; Osterholm, Birkhead, & Meriwether, 1996).

In more recent years, laboratories have become an additional important source of case reporting as a result of electronic reporting advances (Roush et al., 1999). Healthcare providers typically have more information on the patient, diagnosis, laboratory test results, and possibly exposures. Laboratory reporting is often more limited in content, with only basic information on the patient, and it may be more difficult to identify duplicate reports of the same case. Beginning in 2010, the CDC began providing resources from the Patient Protection and Affordable Care Act

(ACA) to all 57 state, local, and territorial health departments to support expansion of electronic laboratory reporting (ELR) (CDC, n.d.). Today, the National Notifiable Diseases Surveillance System (NNDSS) involves reporting of state and locally mandated conditions by healthcare providers and clinical laboratories. As of 2014, two-thirds (67%) of all laboratory results received annually for notifiable conditions were received electronically (CDC, n.d.).

Hospital Discharges/Emergency Department Visits

Another longstanding data source for surveillance is hospital (inpatient and ambulatory surgery) and emergency department (ED) data, collected for administrative and billing purposes. Although highly variable in format, scope, and dissemination practices, nearly all states currently collect hospital discharge data. These data are often based on billing data, but health information can be obtained from ICD diagnostic and procedure codes. These data typically exclude laboratory results, clinical measures, or medications prescribed, and demographic data are limited. They are, however, usually representative, recording all hospitalizations, ambulatory surgeries, and ED visits for the entire population, and have been a key source of information on public safety and injury surveillance and contribute data to disease registries. The U.S. Consumer Product Safety Commission's National Electronic Injury Surveillance System (NEISS) is a surveillance network of hospital EDs to detect safety issues. It is weighted to produce national estimates of injuries related to consumer products (Schroeder & Ault, 2001). These data have also been made publicly available for researchers and the public.

These data also have been used, either in conjunction with other data sources or alone, in community-wide health needs assessments. Finally, they are a source of data for clinical quality improvement and health policy initiatives. Another key source of health-related administrative data sources similar to hospital reporting systems are public, private, or all-payer health plan databases.

Health Surveys

National, state, and local surveys have been a mainstay of public health surveillance for more than 50 years, collecting information on health behaviors, diagnoses, environmental exposures, and mental health status relevant to a wide range of health conditions. Routine surveys are a particularly important source of information for monitoring chronic diseases and health-related behaviors. Telephone surveys have been a key source of data collection when random-digit dialing techniques and postsurvey statistical weighting adjustments are employed to attain a representative sample. These methods have allowed states and localities to obtain information on health behaviors, preventive health practices, and healthcare utilization relevant to their geographic jurisdiction, and sometimes with a high level of geographic specificity. Major national surveys in the United States include the National Health and Nutrition Examination Survey (NHANES), the National Health Interview Survey (NHIS), the Behavioral Risk Factor Surveillance System (BRFSS), and the Youth Risk Behavior Survey (YRBS), to name a few. Distinctions among these different national data sources are described in TABLE 5.1. A large array of state and local survey-based surveillance systems also exist.

TABLE 5.1 Distinctions Between National Data Sources

Survey	Geographic Scope	Periodicity	Design	Sample Size	Mode of Data Collection	Other Key Attributes
National Health and Nutrition Examination Survey (NHANES)	United States, national	Continuous, annual	Multistage probability sample (three stages)	5000 people (adults and children)	In-person	Includes extensive health survey, physical exam, and laboratory measures Contains family and individual-level surveys Household-based probability sample (does not require a telephone for participation)
National Health Interview Survey (NHIS)	United States, national	Continuous, annual	Multistage probability sample (four stages)	Approximately 88,000 people from 35,000 households (adults and children)	In-person	Large sample size that allows for multiple stratifications Contains family- and individual-level surveys Household-based probability sample (does not require a telephone for participation)
Behavioral Risk Factor Surveillance System (BRFSS)	United States, national	Continuous, annual	Stratified random-digit dial	Approximately 400,000 adults	Telephone (landline and cell phone)	Anonymous National and state-level components Core questionnaire with optional modules and ability to add state-specific questions
Youth Risk Behavior Survey (YRBS)	United States, national	Continuous, biennial	Multistage probability sample (two stages)	Approximately 15,000 high school students, grades 9–12	In-person	Anonymous National and state-level components Core questionnaire with optional modules and ability to add state-specific questions
National Survey of Family Growth (NSFG)	United States, national	Continuous, biennial	Multistage probability sample (five stages)	Approximately 10,000 adults	In-person	Focuses on gathering information on family life, marriage and divorce, pregnancy, infertility, contraception, and men's and women's health

▶ III. Strengths and Weaknesses of the Existing Surveillance Systems

Vital statistics are essential data sources for public health surveillance and one of the few long-standing surveillance systems with complete data, capturing nearly 100% of birth and death events in the United States. Rigorous coding systems allow for relatively unbiased time and jurisdiction comparisons on cause of death and health conditions. Similarly, the quality of demographic data is reasonably good. The main limitations of vital statistics data are related to accuracy of cause of death data (misclassification) and lower quality data for occupation classification and race.

Notifiable disease reporting has improved tremendously with standardized case definitions, laboratory confirmation, and systems for sharing data. A major strength of reportable conditions surveillance systems is that public health response mechanisms and protocols are more clearly laid out at the state and local level compared to other surveillance systems in order to mount a timely response to concerning conditions or trends (Council for State and Territorial Epidemiologists, 2014). National dissemination occurs routinely through the weekly *Morbidity and Mortality Weekly Report (MMWR)*. However, completeness of reporting is highly variable across conditions, and health department capacity to receive and evaluate urgent reports varies widely across states (Silk & Berkelman, 2005). Conditions with categorical federal funding, such as tuberculosis and HIV/AIDS, have a high level of completeness of reporting and dedicated response teams. However, most communicable diseases do not have such dedicated streams of funding. Improvements in capture, parsing, and analysis of electronic laboratory data can help improve the completeness of reporting.

Hospital and other administrative health data sources also remain highly valuable data sources, mainly due to the fact that the accuracy of diagnoses and completeness of data are generally good, and the data are representative of the population. Because hospitalization discharge data are collected for other administrative purposes, the cost of data collection does not fall on public health and clinical entities using it for surveillance, making them highly cost-efficient (Schoenman, Sutton, Kintala, Love, & Maw, 2005). Linkage with other data sources is also feasible. Hospital discharge databases have important limitations, however, particularly with respect to data quality and missing data, as well as poor timeliness. Some diagnostic coding may be influenced by purposeful attempts to maximize reimbursement, and health institutions may vary in diagnostic coding practices. Race/ethnicity information is also often missing or unreliably reported. Multistate comparisons are also hampered by the lack of national standards in coding payer data.

Health surveys provide valuable information about the prevalence and distribution of chronic diseases as well as about associated upstream risk factors that may contribute to them and their consequences (Mokdad, 2009). Major strengths are the breadth of information they offer and the ability to achieve representativeness through careful sampling. In-person surveys are widely considered to be the most inclusive of the population because they select people independent of whether they have a telephone or respond to mail surveys, and because they often have higher response rates than telephone surveys. Key challenges include the high cost, especially with respect to conducting in-person surveys. Telephone surveys can reach a larger and geographically more dispersed sample at far lower cost per completed interview. Although telephone surveys have begun sampling both persons with landlines and those who rely on cell phones, the representativeness of telephone surveys has been called into question. More generally, steep declines in response rates have affected all surveys, eroding confidence that they include a truly representative sample of the population.

Many population surveys rely exclusively on respondent self-report to questionnaire items, which is perhaps valid for some conditions; however, surveillance of chronic disease also requires reliable examination and laboratory data, which are expensive to collect within the context of a population survey. Examples of population health surveys that rely on respondent self-report include the NHIS, the Youth Risk Behavioral Surveillance System (YRBSS), the BRFSS, and many comprehensive state and local health surveys, such as the California Health Interview Survey (CHIS), the Ohio Family Health Survey (OFHS), and NYC Community Health Survey (NYC CHS). Examples of population health surveys that employ both in-person clinical and laboratory examinations and respondent self-report are the NHANES, Survey of the Health of Wisconsin (SHOW), and NYC HANES.

▶ IV. Emerging Data Sources

Adoption of electronic health records (EHRs) has increased substantially and offers tremendous opportunities for population health researchers to access both structured and unstructured clinical data on large, diverse, and geographically distributed populations. Improved capture of social, behavioral, and environmental data via the Internet and smartphones will enable researchers to reveal insights into treatment and disease prevention and health promotion at an extraordinary population scale. We describe below the several emerging data sources and their relevance.

Electronic Health Records

Although not originally designed for population health surveillance, EHRs are a major new source of information that shows great promise for population health surveillance. They typically include demographic information on patients, their medical histories, vital signs, current diagnoses, medications, allergies, immunizations received, laboratory test results, and radiology images. EHRs are explicitly designed to be able to be shared between providers within a healthcare institution, but also increasingly across different settings through networks, exchanges, or enterprise-wide systems. EHRs have many attractive attributes for population health surveillance. The most important factor that makes the concept of EHR-based surveillance a viable reality has been the rapid uptake of EHRs by primary care providers in the United States since 2001. The proportion of office-based physicians using any EHR system increased from 18% in 2001 to 78% in 2013 (FIGURE 5.2).

EHR networks often have very large samples and could be a highly cost-efficient source of near-real-time information. They contain a wide range of health and disease management indicators and have strong potential to seed and maintain new disease registries. Particularly for chronic diseases, most of which are not notifiable conditions and thus there is little surveillance capacity, EHR networks hold potential for the ability to track short-term disease control outcomes as well as long-term disease trends, internally validated with physical examination, medication, or

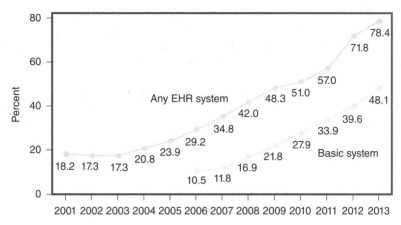

FIGURE 5.2 Percentage of office-based physicians with EHR systems: United States, 2001–2013

Reproduced from Centers for Disease Control and Prevention. (2014, January). Use and characteristics of electronic health record systems among office-based physician practices: United States, 2001–2013. *NCHS Data Brief No. 143*, 1–8.

laboratory data. For infectious notifiable conditions, standard computer algorithms can be developed to identify cases per established case definitions and be automatically reported to public health agencies. More broadly, EHR data can also be used to monitor the effectiveness and equity of care delivery. Indeed, linked bidirectional EHR connections between healthcare institutions and health departments could be developed to deliver time-sensitive information to providers on disease outbreaks and treatment recommendations (Birkhead et al., 2015).

At the same time, EHR technology is still evolving, and multiple hypothesized and confirmed limitations exist (see BOX 5.1). Most broadly, a fundamental limitation of EHR networks is the fact that they reflect only the health status of those who were seen by providers in the network, thus raising concerns for selection bias. From a legal perspective, healthcare institutions have strong privacy concerns about how to properly safeguard the health and identity information of their patient populations. Interoperability problems across EHR platforms and vendor systems also currently limit the capacity of networks to share data with

BOX 5.1 Key Challenges to Be Addressed for EHR-Based Surveillance to Flourish

- Reducing legal and regulatory barriers
- Accessing data from private organizations
- Developing data linkage and harmonization processes
- Ensuring privacy (related to patient and medical organizations)
- Resolving coding issues and delays in access
- Validating behavioral and diagnostic data
- Weighting data for population representativeness
- Linking EHR data with surveillance/administrative data at the local level
- Enriching datasets with data relevant to social determinants (education, income, occupation, ethnicity data, etc.)

Data from World Health Organization, Regional Office for Europe. (2015). Integrated surveillance of noncommunicable diseases (iNCD). Retrieved from http://ec.europa.eu/health/indicators/docs/incd_en.pdf

each other or merge together. Finally, a range of data quality, data standardization, and process automation concerns call into question the scientific validity and technical feasibility of using EHR data for population health surveillance purposes. A body of surveillance validation studies is rapidly emerging that actively addresses these concerns.

Adoption of EHR systems in clinical settings with the aim to improve clinical care has become widespread. Efforts to expand data exchange and aggregation are still in relatively early stages of development. Regarding interoperability, integrated and harmonized formats are needed to exchange information extracts within and across networks (Marco-Ruiz, Moner, Maldonado, Kolstrup, & Bellika, 2015). The adoption of EHR standards such as Health Level 7 (HL7) clinical document architecture (Dolin et al., 2006), openEHR (Beale, 2002), or EN ISO 13606 (International Organization for Standardization, 2008) is needed to exchange health information extracts. By doing so, the exact meaning of clinical data can be delineated, independent of cultural, institutional, or language differences, facilitating data exchange.

Two broad approaches can be used to extract and summarize EHR data: (1) extracting aggregate data from providers or practices in a network (Klann et al., 2014; Klompas et al., 2013; McVeigh et al., 2016), or (2) extracting individual-level data (Marcos-Ruiz et al., 2015). Due to the lack of common data models across clinical systems, both require some level of automated data processing, including identifying and modeling the information requirements, extracting data using Extensible Modeling Language (XML), transforming data into modeled formats, and saving results. However, when only aggregate data are extracted, fewer privacy and security concerns are raised, which can expedite data sharing. Limitations of aggregate practice data include the inability to duplicate records across practices, examine individual-level predictors, or monitor individuals over time.

In a recent IOM report, experts recommended the collection of certain social and behavioral domains in patient health records, given their important impact on health, including factors such as housing, social isolation, and food insecurity (IOM, 2014). As EHR systems and clinical teams adapt to prioritize and collect such data, the possibility of monitoring health status by these determinants and examining health benefits associated with addressing them will become a growing reality. An alternate approach to obtain information on social determinants and other environmental factors includes linking EHR data to community information through geocoding of patient residences and subsequent linkage to external data sources that include geographically organized information such as proximity to parks, healthy food options, air pollution data, and the like. Patient residential address is a standard field in nearly all EHR systems, not requiring system modification. However, linking procedures must often be done by the health institutions themselves in order to protect patient identifying information during the linkage process.

Electronic Laboratory Data

As noted earlier in this chapter, laboratory data are a critical part of surveillance for notifiable diseases to inform prevention, responses to outbreaks, and protection from bioterrorist threats, particularly with respect to

- Pathogen identification/typing
- Antimicrobial resistance detection

Laboratory data are also increasingly recognized to be important for chronic disease surveillance, namely

- Chronic disease diagnoses
- Disease management monitoring

ELR refers to the secure, electronic transmission of laboratory reports to state or local public health authorities, following established reporting standards. Systematic electronic laboratory data capture and ELR to public health agencies began in the late 1990s and expanded steadily over the next decade. Expanded federal resources through the Prevention and Public Health Fund of the ACA beginning in 2010 gave new resources to 57 state, local, and territorial health departments to implement ELR (Lamb et al., 2015). As of mid-2014, two-thirds of approximately 20 million notifiable disease laboratory reports submitted annually were being transmitted electronically from 3269 of 10,600 reporting laboratories (Lamb et al., 2015). Each year, the number of laboratories using ELR and the proportion of reports being sent electronically grows, with variable progress across states (**FIGURE 5.3**). Although four large clinical laboratories contribute nearly 40% of all ELR volume nationally, more than 10,000 public health, hospital, and smaller clinical laboratories comprise the bulk of laboratories that must be certified for standards-based ELR, which implies a lot of work to be overseen by state and public health agencies. A national ELR workgroup, co-chaired by the CDC and CSTE, currently guides this progress (CDC, 2016b).

Potential benefits of ELR for population health surveillance include the potential to improve completeness and timeliness of existing surveillance efforts, as well as introduce new surveillance mechanisms. As with EHR data, however, these opportunities introduce new challenges, both technically and with respect to workforce capacity. A number of early studies examined improvements in timeliness of disease reporting that resulted from a statewide transition from paper to ELR. In one of the first studies to be published assessing the influence of ELR on surveillance, researchers found that statewide mandatory ELR laws

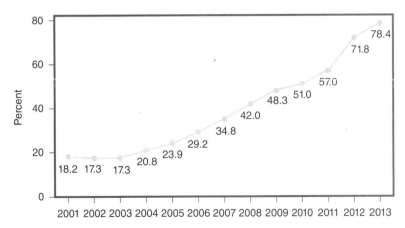

FIGURE 5.3 Percentage of U.S. laboratory reports received electronically by public health jurisdiction: 57 jurisdictions, 2014

Reproduced from Lamb, E., Satre, J., Hurd-Kundeti, G., Liscek, B., Hall, C. J., Pinner, R. W., ... Smith, K. (2015). Update on progress in electronic reporting of laboratory results to public health agencies—United States, 2014. *Morbidity and Mortality Weekly Report, 64*(12), 328–330.

in Hawaii resulted in a 2.3-fold increase in reports for five conditions studied, arriving an average of 3.8 days earlier than conventional reports (Effler et al., 1999). Fields in the electronic reports examined for this study were less likely to be missing than in conventional paper reports. Although completeness and timeliness clearly improved, this early study identified several of the challenges that have affected ELR expansion in all states. During the study's evaluation period, no electronic reports were received on approximately 30% of the days examined, and reporting consistency was variable by laboratory. A range of laboratory information system platforms was used by different laboratories, requiring customized extraction programs. Finally, duplicate reporting was more extensive with electronic reporting than paper records, and automated deduplication efforts were imperfect, requiring substantial staff time. In another evaluation reported several years later by New Jersey researchers, the annual number of Lyme disease reports increased fivefold with the introduction of ELR (from 2460 in 2001 to 11,957 in 2004), yet the number of confirmed cases increased only 18% (CDC, 2008). The evaluation emphasized the workload burden of investigating this larger volume of cases and described how the New Jersey State Health Department introduced a revised Lyme disease definition to allow providers and health departments to classify Lyme disease as "confirmed, probable, and suspected" and modulate priority for investigation accordingly. Other studies have identified similar trade-offs between completeness/timeliness on one hand and the volume and burden of case reports to process and investigate on the other (Dixon, Gibson, & Grannis, 2014; Johnson, Williams, Lee, & Bradley, 2014; Samoff, Fangman, Fleischauer, Waller, & MacDonald, 2013). Other strategies employed to manage the increased workload included revising case definitions and investigation protocols, de-emphasizing certain conditions, and reallocating or hiring additional staff (Dixon et al., 2014) (TABLE 5.2).

TABLE 5.2 Improvements and Drawbacks	
Improvements	**Drawbacks**
■ Improved timeliness from electronic transmission	■ Increased volume of reporting and potential caseload for investigation
■ Increased accuracy by reduction of manual data entry errors	■ Increased false-positive reports
■ More complete reports	■ Increased duplicate reporting
■ More consistent reports across various data sources	
■ Improved effectiveness of public health responses to outbreaks and cases of notifiable conditions	

Reproduced from Centers for Disease Control and Prevention. (2015). ELR/electronic laboratory reporting. Retrieved from http://www.cdc.gov/elr/about.html

A key element in ELR is the use of standardized test codes with standardized measurement units to process ELR messages, most commonly Logical Observation Identifiers Names and Codes (LOINC) for identifying type of laboratory tests, and Systematized Nomenclature of Medicine—Clinical Terms (SNOMED CT) for identifying pathogens, organisms, and diseases. Results are shared with health departments using standardized compliant messaging such as HL7. In 2013, 90% of ELR consisted of HL7-compliant messages (CDC, 2016b). The Centers for Medicare and Medicaid Services (CMS) and the Office of the National Coordinator of Health Information Technology (ONC) published Stage 1 and Stage 2 Meaningful Use (MU) regulations that required hospitals to be able to demonstrate capacity and practice of electronically reporting notifiable disease case reports to health authorities using HL7 standardized formats. The CDC has identified accelerating ELR as one of its four main strategies for improving surveillance nationwide (CDC, 2016b).

Social Media

The rise of the Internet as a source of obtaining and displaying health-related information has been a major new influence on surveillance methods in the past 10–15 years, with varying levels of quality, legitimacy, and sustainability. Approaches include news and social media data mining, web-based triangulation and visualization, and citizen-participatory surveillance. Traditional modes of surveillance rely on filtering case reporting from local to national levels using strict, agreed-upon definitions and processes, a process that is slow but typically highly reliable. In contrast, social media–based surveillance attempts to provide as quickly as possible "event-based reporting," also sometimes referred to as "epidemic intelligence," on public health events that may pose a threat to the public (FIGURE 5.4) (European Centre for Disease Prevention and Control, n.d.; Kostkova, 2013; Velasco, Agheneza,

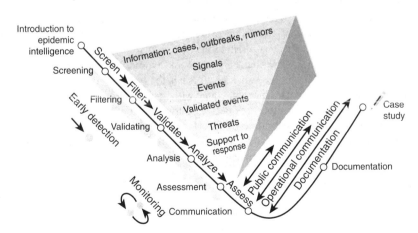

FIGURE 5.4 Schematic of the epidemic intelligence–gathering process, as outlined by the European Centre for Disease Prevention and Control

Reproduced from European Centre for Disease Prevention and Control. (2017). Epidemic intelligence tutorial. Retrieved from http://external.ecdc.europa.eu/EI_Tutorial /course.htm

Denecke, Kirchner, & Eckmanns, 2014). Multiple networks have been developed to harness the Internet to improve the timeliness and sensitivity of monitoring health events. In one of the earliest examples, public health officials at Health Canada and the WHO launched the Global Public Health Intelligence Network (GPHIN) in 1998 to continuously monitor new media from around the world using an automated set of scanning programs with key search terms to identify relevant reports (Noseworthy & Nymark, 1998). Reports were scored according to relevance, and elevated scores were reviewed by a team of trained analysts. The system was developed in response to the fact that news agencies such as CNN were often breaking news about disease outbreaks more quickly than established public health networks. The effectiveness of this and related systems was demonstrated during the severe acute respiratory syndrome (SARS) outbreak, when GPHIN and ProMED-mail detected SARS more than two months before the WHO did (Victor & Madoff, 2004; Wilson & Brownstein, 2009).

Soon after the rise of Internet-scanning systems by expert public health organizations, other digital surveillance approaches emerged, particularly around the early detection and intensity of influenza, including tracking user clicks on certain websites (Eysenbach, 2006; Johnson et al., 2004) and monitoring search queries (Polgreen, Chen, Pennock, Nelson, & Weinstein, 2008). However, this approach began to receive serious attention only after researchers at Google, using an automated approach to select search terms from billions of Google search logs, published a study in *Nature* in 2009 that demonstrated their model to have a high correlation with regional CDC data and detection one to two weeks before existing surveillance reports (Ginsberg et al., 2009). Sizable discrepancies between their estimates and those measured by the CDC quickly became apparent in the next couple of years, leaving public health experts initially doubtful of the validity of such fully automated approaches for reliable surveillance (Olson, Konty, Paladini, Viboud, & Simonsen, 2013).

Subsequent attempts by modelers to improve upon Google's algorithm, however, have led to improvements (Santillana, Zhang, Althouse, & Ayers, 2014; Yang, Santillana, & Kou, 2015; Yuan et al., 2013), showing that Internet-based systems can develop a high congruence with traditional surveillance systems and can indeed sometimes be more timely by accessing information from people even prior to the time when they may seek treatment or from those who do not seek treatment. In populations where Internet usage is high, this has the potential to yield actionable information. The potential for bias associated with increased reporting due to media attention and systematic differences between those inclined to self-report or not remain important potential limitations. Efforts to buffer Internet-based surveillance systems from media-driven spikes have been introduced. For example, Google Dengue Trends employed a model in which spikes above a certain dynamic four-week threshold are replaced by an imputed value (Chan, Sahai, Conrad, & Brownstein, 2011). During the 2009 H1N1 pandemic, in response to heightened attention and public fear, ED visits surged; data from Google Flu Trends displayed similar patterns, leaving its investigators and others to suggest that such data sources might be more valuable in planning required surge capacity as opposed to documenting true disease patterns (Dugas et al., 2012; Milinovich, Williams, Clements, & Hu, 2014). In a review of Internet-based surveillance efforts to track influenza and dengue, researchers concluded that these systems "...do not have the capacity to replace traditional surveillance 'systems; they should not be viewed as an alternative, but rather an extension" (Milinovich et al., 2014). Research is currently underway to assess the utility of Google Trends for surveillance of a wide range of other public health outcomes, including suicide (Arora, Stuckler, & McKee, 2016), cancer screening (Dehkordy et al., 2015), and Ebola (Hossain, Kam, Kong, Wigand, & Bossomaier, 2016).

Other models of Internet-based searches using unstructured data have also emerged, including the use of personal textual data from Twitter, Facebook, Yelp, and other Internet data sources, which are often enhanced by geospatial tags that allow information on the location of reporters. Although Facebook provides users with the ability to restrict their content, Twitter content is available in the public domain and thus is searchable. As with Google Trends, most research regarding the use of Twitter for surveillance has focused on influenza. Twitter surveillance for influenza prediction was first introduced in 2009 (Ritterman, Osborne, & Klein, 2009), and multiple publications have since identified Twitter's ability for timely signal detection (Chew & Eysenbach, 2010; Kim, Seok, Oh, Lee, & Kim, 2013; Signorini, Segre, & Polgreen, 2011). In one article, the authors demonstrated that a predictive model of weekly influenza rates incorporating both Twitter data and historical influenza-like illness data outperformed a model using the historical data only, particularly when compared to "ground truth" (historical influenza-like illness [ILI] data that are no longer being revised with late submission data) (FIGURE 5.5). They also found their model to be more predictive than models incorporating Google Flu Trend data. Their models were built using a

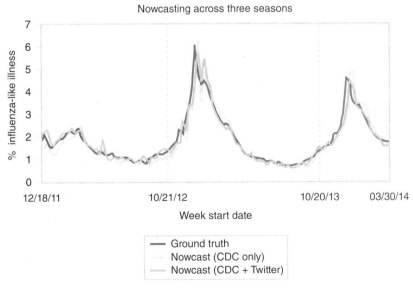

FIGURE 5.5 "Nowcasting" predictions for three influenza seasons using a CDC-only predictive model, compared to a predictive model that includes Twitter

tiered search algorithm based on Twitter message content (Paul, Dredze, & Bronia-towski, 2014). Twitter has been used for surveillance of events not easily tracked through traditional data sources, including tanning bed burns (Seidenberg et al., 2016), eye diseases (Deiner, Lietman, McLeod, Chodosh, & Porco, 2016), and alcohol consumption (Ranney et al., 2016).

Finally, participatory or crowdsourcing systems are rapidly emerging as new data streams that allow citizens to self-report cases or symptoms, allowing the public to take an active part in surveillance. Participatory surveillance emerged in 2003, once again, around the tracking of influenza (Marquet et al., 2006). Since then, several major voluntary symptom reporting systems have emerged, including InfluenzaNet in Europe (InfluenzaNet, 2016), Flu Near You (FNY) in the United States (Smolinski et al., 2015), and FluTracking in Australia (Dalton et al., 2009). These crowdsourcing approaches rely on maintaining dynamic cohorts of participants, who volunteer to respond to short weekly surveys regarding symptoms. For example, FNY allows volunteers in the United States and Canada to report their health information using a brief weekly symptom survey through a website, mobile application, or Facebook. The results are published and compared with data from the CDC sentinel influenza network using maps and charts. The website also hosts a Vaccine Finder tool to let participants identify local sources for influenza vaccine.

To date, few reliability and validity studies have been published regarding these approaches, but initial studies indicate that although participation biases continue to pose threats to performance (Cantarelli et al., 2014), such systems may be able to accurately estimate outbreak characteristics such as disease attack rates (Patterson-Lomba et al., 2014).

Informatics can also be used to better organize and present surveillance data, in both static and interactive forms. For example, the Institute for Health Metrics and Evaluation has many interactive maps, including those related to its global Burden of Disease studies, as well as financing for global health, progress toward international health goals, and social determinants of health (Institute for Health Metrics and Evaluation, 2016). Better data visualization can help engage the public and policymakers, and enables audiences to more easily understand and act on key messages.

▶ V. Role of Meaningful Use in Advancing Population Health Surveillance Efforts

The passing of the ACA in 2010 was largely focused on increasing the quality of, access to, and affordability of health insurance for U.S. residents. Another priority, however, was to transform clinical practices and hospitals financially, technologically, and clinically toward achieving better health outcomes and lower costs. The ACA, in conjunction with the Health Information Technology for Economic and Clinical Health (HITECH) Act of 2009, prompted a major expansion in the use of EHRs, which has been a major resource for population health surveillance efforts (**BOX 5.2**).

BOX 5.2 Five Pillars of Health Outcomes Policy Priorities

The concept of meaningful use rests on the "five pillars" of health outcomes policy priorities, namely

1. Improving quality, safety, and efficiency, and reducing health disparities
2. Engaging patients and families in their health
3. Improving care coordination
4. Improving population and public health
5. Ensuring adequate privacy and security protection for personal health information

Reproduced from Centers for Disease Control and Prevention. (2017a). Meaningful use. Retrieved from https://www.cdc.gov/ehrmeaningfuluse/introduction.html

The HITECH Act provided nearly $30 billion in incentives for clinical practices and hospitals to install and use certified EHRs (Birkhead et al., 2015; Blumenthal, 2010). These federal legislation initiatives also required that providers develop the capability to participate in public health surveillance using EHRs. The largest, single most influential component was the CMS's MU Program, which formally introduced a voluntary, three-stage incentive payment program to build capacity to exchange health data with public health departments (Blumenthal & Tavenner, 2010). MU Stage 1 (data capture and sharing), published in 2010, required that healthcare providers demonstrate capacity to submit electronic data to either a health department immunization registry or its syndromic surveillance system. For hospitals only, another option was to submit laboratory data, essentially expanding its internal ELR capacity. MU Stage 2 (advanced clinical processing) was initiated in 2013 for hospitals and in 2014 for clinical practices. It included a requirement to report electronically to a state cancer registry and another specialized disease registry. It also required that health departments be able to receive and certify those data to demonstrate bidirectional electronic communication. MU Stage 3 (improved outcomes) was published in 2015, along with modified Stage 2 requirements. Although voluntary until 2016, eligible providers or hospitals that have failed to join the EHR incentive program face negative adjustments to their Medicaid/Medicare fees (CMS, 2015).

In addition to electronic transmission of information on notifiable conditions or vaccinations, the CMS EHR incentive program has also expanded chronic disease surveillance opportunities to improve clinical quality of care and disease management. Eligible healthcare providers must also attest they have used their EHR in ways that improve quality and efficiency of care, particularly around at least three of six clinical quality measures (CQMs) endorsed by the National Quality Forum (NQF), several of which aligned with Million Hearts, a federal initiative to prevent 1 million heart attacks and strokes by 2017. Monitoring of progress on these CQMs through CMS now allows public health agencies to monitor disease management goals unaware of healthcare institution (Heisey-Grove, Wall, Helwig, Wright, & CDC, 2015).

▶ VI. Applications of EHR-Based Population Health Surveillance

As mentioned previously, primary care EHRs, in particular, have the potential to extend chronic disease surveillance by assessing the burden of common chronic conditions and related behaviors, as well as monitoring treatment and control patterns for such conditions. Until recently, objectively measured population estimates of chronic disease burden, treatment, and control were obtained only from national population-based examination surveys, such as the NHANES (CDC, 2016c). As EHR networks have expanded to cover defined geographic jurisdictions or population subgroups, a number of initiatives have emerged to track population-based metrics using indicators developed specifically for EHR data (Armed Forces Health Surveillance Center, 2013; Barber, Muller, Whitehurst, & Hay, 2009; Catalán-Ramos et al., 2014; Green et al., 2015; Jones, Nair, & Thakker, 2012; Nichols, 2012; Williamson et al., 2014; Zellweger, Bopp, Holzer, Djalali, & Kaplan, 2014). Few of these systems have been validated for accuracy or reliability (Barber et al., 2009; Williamson et al., 2014).

Here we briefly describe one such validation effort mounted in NYC. Beginning in 2012, public health practitioners in NYC designed a new EHR-based population health surveillance system known as NYC Macroscope using a large distributed EHR network to monitor chronic health conditions, behavioral risk factors, and clinical preventive services among NYC adults (McVeigh et al., 2013). Researchers used cross-sectional survey data from two sources to validate the new system, designed and statistically weighted to represent NYC adults age 20 or older in 2013–2014. NYC Macroscope was developed by the NYC Department of Health and Mental Hygiene (DOHMH). The gold standard reference survey was the 2013–2014 NYC HANES (Thorpe et al., 2015) (BOX 5.3).

To validate the 2013 NYC Macroscope findings, data were first obtained from 392 primary care practices meeting specific inclusion and exclusion criteria. Detailed information regarding methodology and sample characteristics of NYC Macroscope have been described elsewhere (Newton-Dame et al., 2016). For a range of indicators, estimates from 2013 NYC Macroscope were then compared to existing survey estimates, including those generated from 2013–2014 NYC HANES, a representative population-based survey of NYC adults age 20 or older that used household-based sampling and in-person interviews, an examination component, and collection of fasting biological specimens. A priori criteria were established to compare estimates from NYC Macroscope to those obtained from surveys. Criteria included t-test, the two one-sided test of equivalence (TOST) (Barker, Luman, McCauley, & Chu, 2002), prevalence difference (within 5 points), prevalence ratio (0.85–1.15), and a Spearman correlation of ≥ 0.80.

Detailed results of the validation findings have been published elsewhere (McVeigh et al., 2016; Thorpe et al., 2016). Briefly, the authors identified that prevalence measures for smoking, obesity, hypertension, and diabetes were valid and robust, a finding that was corroborated by an exploratory individual-level chart review. Prevalence of high cholesterol, flu vaccination, and depression, along with treatment and control measures for diabetes, hypertension, and

BOX 5.3 New York City's EHR-Based Surveillance System: NYC Macroscope

NYC Macroscope is derived from a large, distributed EHR data network that includes more than 700 ambulatory practices using eClinicalWorks EHR software, serving nearly 2 million individual patients as of 2013. The network is part of a broader DOHMH initiative to help ambulatory practices in NYC adopt and use EHRs to increase delivery of preventative care services, address chronic disease risk factors, and improve disease management.

NYC Macroscope uses a distributed model, where no individual patient data are shared. Using a secured HTTPS connection, SQL queries are pushed from the vendor server, run as a scheduled job at each practice, and returned to an internal data warehouse.

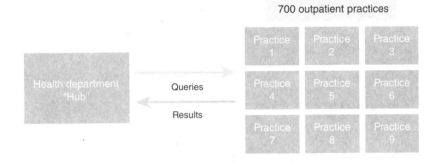

NYC DOHMH. Personal communication

hypercholesterolemia, performed less well, suggesting the need for additional improvements including better consistency and completeness of provider data capture and improving the representativeness of participating provider samples. For flu vaccination, underestimation most likely reflected the fact that vaccination is often received in nontraditional settings, such as pharmacies and workplaces, suggesting that EHR data alone may not provide a reliable measure of vaccination coverage. Although performance across indicators varied, findings confirmed that valid prevalence estimates for chronic diseases can be derived using primary care EHRs, a finding that has been corroborated elsewhere (Barber et al., 2009; Williamson et al., 2014; Zellweger et al., 2014) (TABLE 5.3).

EHRs have also been used to detect disease outbreaks, most commonly through syndromic surveillance of electronic data from hospital EDs. However, community-based EHRs can play an important role in epidemic detection and monitoring. For example, in American Samoa, suspected Zika virus cases were identified through searches of both hospital and clinic EHRs (Healy, 2016). The data were used to estimate population-level incidence of Zika and changes over time, and pregnant women were targeted for testing, treatment, and long-term monitoring. In Massachusetts, EHRs have also been used to supplement other sources of notifiable disease reporting of chlamydia, gonorrhea, active tuberculosis, and acute viral hepatitis (Klompas et al., 2011).

TABLE 5.3 Indicators and Prevalence Estimates

	Indicator						
	Obesity	Smoking	Hypertension Prevalence	Diabetes Prevalence	Hypercholesterolemia Prevalence	Depression	Influenza Vaccination
NYC Macroscope % (95% CI)	27.8 (27.7, 27.9)	15.2 (15.1, 15.3)	32.3 (32.2, 32.4)	13.9 (13.8, 14.0)	49.3 (49.1, 49.5)	8.2 (8.1, 8.2)	20.9 (20.8, 21.0)
NYC HANES	31.3 (28.5, 34.2)	17.7 (15.1, 20.8)	32.5 (29.4, 35.7)	12.6 (10.6, 14.8)	46.9 (42.6, 51.3)	15.2 (13.0, 17.7)	47.6 (44.0, 51.3)
	NYC Macroscope vs. NYC HANES						
Absolute difference < 5 (the value is less than 5)	✔ (3.46)	✔ (2.55)	✔ (0.15)	✔ (1.36)	✔ (2.36)	✘ (10.8)	✘ (26.71)
Prevalence ratio of 0.85–1.15	✔ (0.89)	✔ (0.86)	✔ (1.00)	✔ (1.11)	✔ (1.05)	✘ (0.43)	✘ (0.44)
Test of difference (t-test) $p \geq 0.05$	✘ ($p = 0.02$)	✔ ($p = 0.08$)	✔ ($p = 0.93$)	✔ ($p = 0.19$)	✔ ($p = 0.29$)	✘ ($p < 0.01$)	✘ ($p < 0.001$)
Test of equivalence (TOST) $p < 0.05$	✘ ($p = 0.14$)	✔ ($p = 0.04$)	✔ ($p < 0.01$)	✔ ($p < 0.001$)	✘ ($p = 0.12$)	✘ ($p = 0.99$)	✘ ($p = 0.99$)
Recommendation	Ready for use	Ready for use	Ready for use	Ready for use	Use with caution	Not ready for use	Not ready for use

Modified from McVeigh, K. H., Newton-Dame, R., Chen, P. Y., Thorpe, L. E., Schreibstein, L., Lurie, E., . . . Perlman, S. E. (2016). Can electronic health records be used for population health surveillance? Validating population health metrics against

▶ VII. Conclusion

In the past two decades, the field of population health surveillance has undergone a tremendous explosion, reflecting the opportunities of new data sources, data capture methods, data linkage, and data display. The science of informatics has been integral to these advances. Surveillance teams today benefit greatly from having staff that are knowledgeable in informatics. At the same time, however, recent accumulated experiences underscore the importance of retaining staff with strong epidemiologic training and experience.

Clinical encounter and laboratory data are becoming mainstream data sources, and validation studies have confirmed their utility. At the same time, workforce capacity and technical challenges associated with extracting and parsing data remain high for many state and local health departments, and the full utility of these data are still only beginning to be tapped. The role and utility of social media–based surveillance is still evolving. By distinguishing between the purposes of traditional incident-based reporting and "epidemic intelligence" gathered from event-based reporting, the focused purpose of Internet-based surveillance at improving early detection can be recognized. When triangulated with validated data sources, these can also be useful additions to the surveillance arsenal, not only for outbreaks, but also for monitoring events and conditions for which transitional surveillance data sources do not exist.

Technical advances in data capture, including the use of mobile devices, can facilitate collection of data that were previously not feasible. Similar advances in data extraction can improve data sharing and utilization, thus "liberating" data streams that historically were difficult to access, including linkage to routinely collected administrative data and parsing of data from the Internet. Finally, improved data visualization can improve dissemination of information and key messages to stakeholders and potentially result in greater impact.

References

Armed Forces Health Surveillance Center (AFHSC). (2013). Incidence and prevalence of select cardiovascular risk factors and conditions, active component, US Armed Forces, 2003-2012. *Medical Surveillance Monthly Report, 20*(12), 16.

Arora, V. S., Stuckler, D., & McKee, M. (2016). Tracking search engine queries for suicide in the United Kingdom. *Public Health, 137*, 147–153.

Barber, J., Muller, S., Whitehurst, T., & Hay, E. (2009). Measuring morbidity: Self-report or health care records? *Family Practice, 27*(1), 25–30.

Barker, L. E., Luman, E. T., McCauley, M. M., & Chu, S. Y. (2002). Assessing equivalence: An alternative to the use of difference tests for measuring disparities in vaccination coverage. *American Journal of Epidemiology, 156*(11), 1056–1061.

Beale, T. (2002, November). Archetypes: Constraint-based domain models for future-proof information systems. In *OOPSLA 2002 Workshop on Behavioural Semantics*, Seattle, Washington. (Vol. 105).

Birkhead, G. S., Klompas, M., & Shah, N. R. (2015). Uses of electronic health records for public health surveillance to advance public health. *Annual Review of Public Health, 36*, 345–359.

Blumenthal, D. (2010). Launching HITECH. *New England Journal of Medicine, 362*(5), 382–385.

Blumenthal, D., & Tavenner, M. (2010). The "meaningful use" regulation for electronic health records. *New England Journal of Medicine, 363*(6), 501–504.

Brooks, E. G., & Reed, K. D. (2015). Principles and pitfalls: A guide to death certification. *Clinical Medicine and Research, 13*(2), 74–82.

Brumberg, H. L., Dozor, D., & Golombek, S. G. (2012). History of the birth certificate: From inception to the future of electronic data. *Journal of Perinatology, 32*(6), 407–411.

Cantarelli, P., Debin, M., Turbelin, C., Poletto, C., Blanchon, T., Falchi, A., ... Colizza, V. (2014). The representativeness of a European multi-center network for influenza-like-illness participatory surveillance. *BMC Public Health, 20*(14), 984.

Catalan-Ramos, A., Verdu, J. M., Grau, M., Iglesias-Rodal, M., del Val Garcia, J. L., Consola, A., & Comin, E. (2014). Population prevalence and control of cardiovascular risk factors: What electronic medical records tell us. *Atencion Primaria, 46*(1), 15–24.

Centers for Disease Control and Prevention. (2008). Effect of electronic laboratory reporting on the burden of Lyme disease surveillance—New Jersey, 2001–2006. *Morbidity and Mortality Weekly Report, 57*(2), 42.

Centers for Disease Control and Prevention. (2014, January). Use and characteristics of electronic health record systems among office-based physician practices: United States, 2001–2013. *NCHS Data Brief No. 143*, 1–8.

Centers for Disease Control and Prevention. (2015). ELR/electronic laboratory reporting. Retrieved from http://www.cdc.gov/elr/about.html

Centers for Disease Control and Prevention. (2016a). 2016 nationally notifiable conditions (historical). Retrieved from https://wwwn.cdc.gov/nndss/conditions/notifiable/2016/

Centers for Disease Control and Prevention. (2016b). Electronic Laboratory Reporting (ELR) Task Force overview. Retrieved from http://www.cdc.gov/ehrmeaningfuluse/elrtf.html

Centers for Disease Control and Prevention. (2016c). National Health and Nutrition Examination Survey. Retrieved from http://www.cdc.gov/nchs/nhanes/

Centers for Disease Control and Prevention. (2016d). Nationally notifiable conditions. Retrieved from https://wwwn.cdc.gov/nndss/

Centers for Disease Control and Prevention. (2017a). Meaningful use. Retrieved from https://www.cdc.gov/ehrmeaningfuluse/introduction.html

Centers for Disease Control and Prevention. (2017b). National Notifiable Disease Surveillance System (NNDSS): Case definitions. Retrieved from http://wwwn.cdc.gov/nndss/script/casedefDefault.aspx

Centers for Disease Control and Prevention. (n.d.). *Morbidity and Mortality Weekly Report (MMWR)*. Retrieved from https://www.cdc.gov/mmwr/index.html

Centers for Medicare and Medicaid Services. (2015). CMS fact sheet: EHR incentive programs in 2015 and beyond. Retrieved from https://www.cms.gov/Newsroom/MediaReleaseDatabase/Fact-sheets/2015-Fact-sheets-items/2015-10-06-2.html

Chan, E. H., Sahai, V., Conrad, C., & Brownstein, J. S. (2011). Using web search query data to monitor dengue epidemics: A new model for neglected tropical disease surveillance. *PLoS Neglected Tropical Diseases, 5*(5), e1206.

Chew, C., & Eysenbach, G. (2010). Pandemics in the age of Twitter: Content analysis of tweets during the 2009 H1N1 outbreak. *PLoS One, 5*(11), e14118.

Choi, B. C. K. (2012). The past, present and future of public health surveillance. *Scientifica, 2012*, 1–26.

Council for State and Territorial Epidemiologists. (2014, April). Review of and recommendations for the National Notifiable Disease Surveillance System: A state and local health department perspective. Retrieved from http://www.cste.org/resource/resmgr/PDFs/NNDSS_Report.pdf

Dalton, C., Durrheim, D., Fejsa, J., Francis, L., Carlson, S., d'Espaignet, E. T., & Tuyl, F. (2009). Flutracking: A weekly Australian community online survey of influenza-like illness in 2006, 2007 and 2008. *Communicable Diseases Intelligence Quarterly Report, 33*(3), 316.

Dehkordy, S. F., Hall, K. S., Roach, A. L., Rothman, E. D., Dalton, V. K., & Carlos, R. C. (2015). Trends in breast cancer screening: Impact of U.S. preventive services task force recommendations. *American Journal of Preventive Medicine, 49*(3), 419–422.

Deiner, M. S., Lietman, T. M., McLeod, S. D., Chodosh, J., & Porco, T. C. (2016). Surveillance tools emerging from search engines and social media data for determining eye disease patterns. *JAMA Ophthalmology, 134*(9), 1024–1030.

Dixon, B. E., Gibson, P. J., & Grannis, S. J. (2014). Estimating increased electronic laboratory reporting volumes for meaningful use: Implications for the public health workforce. *Online Journal of Public Health Informatics, 5*(3), 225.

Dolin, R. H., Alschuler, L., Boyer, S., Beebe, C., Behlen, F. M., Biron, P. V., & Shabo, A. (2006). HL7 clinical document architecture, release 2. *Journal of the American Medical Informatics Association, 13*(1), 30–39.

Dugas, A. F., Hsieh, Y. H., Levin, S. R., Pines, J. M., Mareiniss, D. P., Mohareb, A., . . . Rothman, R. E. (2012). Google Flu Trends: Correlation with emergency department influenza rates and crowding metrics. *Clinical Infectious Diseases, 54*(4), 463–469.

Duncan, D., Gold, R. S., Basch, C. E., & Markellis, V. C. (1988). *Epidemiology: Basis for disease prevention and health promotion.* New York, NY: Macmillan.

Effler, P., Ching-Lee, M., Bogard, A., Ieong, M. C., Nekomoto, T., & Jernigan, D. (1999). Statewide system of electronic notifiable disease reporting from clinical laboratories: Comparing automated reporting with conventional methods. *Journal of the American Medical Association, 282*(19), 1845–1850.

European Centre for Disease Prevention and Control. (2017). Epidemic intelligence tutorial. Retrieved from http://external.ecdc.europa.eu/EI_Tutorial/course.htm

European Centre for Disease Prevention and Control. (n.d.). Epidemic intelligence. Retrieved from http://ecdc.europa.eu/en/aboutus/what-we-do/epidemic-intelligence/Pages/epidemic-intelligence.aspx

Eysenbach, G. (2006). Infodemiology: Tracking flu-related searches on the web for syndromic surveillance. In *AMIA Annual Symposium Proceedings.* American Medical Informatics Association, 244–248.

German, R. R., Lee, L. M., Horan, J. M., Milstein, R., Pertowski, C., & Waller, M. (2001). Updated guidelines for evaluating public health surveillance systems. *Morbidity and Mortality Weekly Report Recommendations and Reports, 50*, 1–35.

Ginsberg, J., Mohebbi, M. H., Patel, R. S., Brammer, L., Smolinski, M. S., & Brilliant, L. (2009). Detecting influenza epidemics using search engine query data. *Nature, 457*(7232), 1012–1014.

Green, M. E., Natajaran, N., O'Donnell, D. E., Williamson, T., Kotecha, J., Khan, S., & Cave, A. (2015). Chronic obstructive pulmonary disease in primary care: An epidemiologic cohort study from the Canadian Primary Care Sentinel Surveillance Network. *CMAJ Open, 3*(1), E15.

Healy, J. M. (2016). Notes from the field: Outbreak of Zika virus disease—American Samoa, 2016. *Morbidity and Mortality Weekly Report, 65*(41), 1146–1147.

Heisey-Grove, D., Wall, H. K., Helwig, A., Wright, J. S., & Centers for Disease Control and Prevention (CDC). (2015). Using electronic clinical quality measure reporting for public health surveillance. *Morbidity and Mortality Weekly Report, 64*(16), 439–442.

Hossain, L., Kam, D., Kong, F., Wigand, R. T., & Bossomaier, T. (2016). Social media in Ebola outbreak. *Epidemiology and Infection, 144*(10), 2136–2143.

Influenzanet. (2016). Influenzanet: A network of European citizens fighting against influenza. Retrieved from https://www.influenzanet.eu

Institute for Health Metrics and Evaluation. (2016). Data visualizations. Retrieved from http://vizhub.healthdata.org

Institute of Medicine. (2014). Capturing social and behavioral domains in electronic health records: Summary of selected domains. Retrieved from http://www.nationalacademies.org/hmd/~/media/Files/Report%20Files/2014/EHR-phase-2/EHRfindingsrecs.pdf

International Organization for Standardization. (2008). ISO 13606-1:2008—Health informatics—Electronic health record communication—Part 1: Reference model. Retrieved from http://www.iso.org/iso/catalogue_detail.htm?csnumber=40784

Johnson, H. A., Wagner, M. M., Hogan, W. R., Chapman, W., Olszewski, R. T., Dowling, J., & Barnas, G. (2004). Analysis of web access logs for surveillance of influenza. *Studies in Health Technology and Informatics, 107*(Pt. 2), 1202–1206.

Johnson, M. G., Williams, J., Lee, A., & Bradley, K. K. (2014). Completeness and timeliness of electronic vs. conventional laboratory reporting for communicable disease surveillance—Oklahoma, 2011. *Public Health Reports, 129*(3), 261.

Jones, P. H., Nair, R., & Thakker, K. M. (2012). Prevalence of dyslipidemia and lipid goal attainment in statin-treated subjects from 3 data sources: A retrospective analysis. *Journal of the American Heart Association, 1*(6), e001800. doi:10.1161/JAHA.112.001800

Kim, E. K., Seok, J. H., Oh, J. S., Lee, H. W., & Kim, K. H. (2013). Use of Hangeul Twitter to track and predict human influenza infection. *PloS One, 8*(7), e69305.

Klann, J. G., Buck, M. D., Brown, J., Hadley, M., Elmore, R., Weber, G. M., & Murphy, S. N. (2014). Query health: Standards-based, cross-platform population health surveillance. *Journal of the American Medical Informatics Association, 21*(4), 650–656.

Klompas, M., Eggleston, E., McVetta, J., Lazarus, R., Li, L., & Platt, R. (2013). Automated detection and classification of type 1 versus type 2 diabetes using electronic health record data. *Diabetes Care, 36*(4), 914–921.

Klompas, M., Murphy, M., Lankiewicz, J., McVetta, J., Lazarus, R., Eggleston, E., . . . Platt, R. (2011). Harnessing electronic health records for public health surveillance. *Online Journal of Public Health Informatics, 3*(3).

Koo, D., & Wetterhall, S. F. (1996). History and current status of the National Notifiable Diseases Surveillance System. *Journal of Public Health Management and Practice, 2*(4), 4–10.

Kostkova, P. (2013). A roadmap to integrated digital public health surveillance: The vision and the challenges. In *Proceedings of the 22nd International Conference on World Wide Web* (pp. 687–694). Danvers, MA: Association for Computing Machinery.

Lamb, E., Satre, J., Hurd-Kundeti, G., Liscek, B., Hall, C. J., Pinner, R. W., . . . Smith, K. (2015). Update on progress in electronic reporting of laboratory results to public health agencies— United States, 2014. *Morbidity and Mortality Weekly Report, 64*(12), 328–330.

Marco-Ruiz, L., Moner, D., Maldonado, J. A., Kolstrup, N., & Bellika, J. G. (2015). Archetype-based data warehouse environment to enable the reuse of electronic health record data. *International Journal of Medical Informatics, 84*(9), 702–714.

Marquet, R. L., Bartelds, A. I., van Noort, S. P., Koppeschaar, C. E., Paget, J., Schellevis, F. G., & van der Zee, J. (2006). Internet-based monitoring of influenza-like illness (ILI) in the general population of the Netherlands during the 2003–2004 influenza season. *BMC Public Health, 6*(1), 1.

McVeigh, K. H., Newton-Dame, R., Chen, P. Y., Thorpe, L. E., Schreibstein, L., Lurie, E., . . . Perlman, S. E. (2016). Can electronic health records be used for population health surveillance? Validating population health metrics against established survey data. *eGEMS, 4*(1), 1267.

McVeigh, K. H., Newton-Dame, R., Perlman, S., Chernov, C., Thorpe, L., Singer, J., & Greene, C. (2013). New York City Department of Health and Mental Hygiene. Developing an electronic health record-based population health surveillance system. Retrieved from https://www.researchgate.net/publication/248392412_Developing_an_Electronic_Health _Record-Based_Population_Health_Surveillance_System

Milinovich, G. J., Williams, G. M., Clements, A. C. A., & Hu, W. (2014). Internet based surveillance systems for monitoring emerging infectious diseases. *Lancet Infectious Diseases, 14*, 160–168.

Mokdad, A. H. (2009). The Behavioral Risk Factors Surveillance System: Past, present, and future. *Annual Review of Public Health, 30*, 43–54.

Newton-Dame, R., McVeigh, K. H., Greene, C., Perlman, S. E., Schreibstein, L., & Thorpe, L. E. (2016). Design of the New York City Macroscope: Innovations in population health surveillance using electronic health records. *EGEMS, 4*(1), 1265.

Nichols, G. A. (2012). Construction of a multisite datalink using electronic health records for the identification, surveillance, prevention, and management of diabetes mellitus: The SUPREME-DM project. *Preventing Chronic Disease, 9*, E110.

Noseworthy, T., & Nymark, A. (1998). Connecting for better health: Strategic issues. Interim Report. Advisory Council on Health info-structure. Health Canada. Retrieved from http://publications .gc.ca/collections/Collection/H49-11-1998E.pdf

Olson, D. R., Konty, K. J., Paladini, M., Viboud, C., & Simonsen, L. (2013). Reassessing Google Flu Trends data for detection of seasonal and pandemic influenza: A comparative epidemiological study at three geographic scales. *PLoS Computational Biology, 9*(10), e1003256.

Osterholm, M. T., Birkhead, G. S., & Meriwether, R. A. (1996). Impediments to public health surveillance in the 1990s: The lack of resources and the need for priorities. *Journal of Public Health Management and Practice, 2*(4), 11–15.

Patterson-Lomba, O., Van Noort, S., Cowling, B. J., Wallinga, J., Gomes, M. G. M., Lipsitch, M., & Goldstein, E. (2014). Utilizing syndromic surveillance data for estimating levels of influenza circulation. *American Journal of Epidemiology, 179*(11), 1394–1401.

Paul, M. J., Dredze, M., & Broniatowski, D. (2014). Twitter improves influenza forecasting. *PLOS Currents Outbreaks.* Retrieved from http://currents.plos.org/outbreaks/article/twitter-improves-influenza-forecasting/

Polgreen, P. M., Chen, Y., Pennock, D. M., Nelson, F. D., & Weinstein, R. A. (2008). Using Internet searches for influenza surveillance. *Clinical Infectious Diseases, 47*(11), 1443–1448.

Ranney, M. L., Chang, B., Freeman, J. R., Norris, B., Silverberg, M., & Choo, E. K. (2016). Tweet now, see you in the ED later?: Examining the association between alcohol-related tweets and emergency care visits. *Academic Emergency Medicine, 23*(7), 831–834.

Ritterman, J., Osborne, M., & Klein, E. (2009, November). Using prediction markets and Twitter to predict a swine flu pandemic. In *1st International Workshop on Mining Social Media* (Vol. 9, pp. 9–17). Retrieved from http://homepages.inf.ed.ac.uk/miles/papers/swine09.pdf

Roush, S., Birkhead, G., Koo, D., Cobb, A., & Fleming, D. (1999). Mandatory reporting of diseases and conditions by health care professionals and laboratories. *Journal of the American Medical Association, 282*(2), 164–170.

Samoff, E., Fangman, M. T., Fleischauer, A. T., Waller, A. E., & MacDonald, P. D. (2013). Improvements in timeliness resulting from implementation of electronic laboratory reporting and an electronic disease surveillance system. *Public Health Reports, 128*(5), 393.

Santillana, M., Zhang, D. W., Althouse, B. M., & Ayers, J. W. (2014). What can digital disease detection learn from (an external revision to) Google Flu Trends? *American Journal of Preventive Medicine, 47*(3), 341–347.

Schoenman, J. A., Sutton, J. P., Kintala, S., Love, D., & Maw, R. (2005). The value of hospital discharge databases. Retrieved from https://www.hcup-us.ahrq.gov/reports/final_report.pdf

Schroeder, T., & Ault, K. (2001). *The NEISS sample (design and implementation) from 1979 to 1996.* Washington, DC: U.S. Consumer Product Safety Commission. Retrieved from https://www.cpsc.gov/s3fs-public/2001d010-6b6.pdf

Seidenberg, A. B., Pagoto, S. L., Vickey, T. A., Linos, E., Wehner, M. R., Dalla Costa, R., & Geller, A. C. (2016). Tanning bed burns reported on Twitter: Over 15,000 in 2013. *Translational Behavioral Medicine, 6*(2), 271–276.

Signorini, A., Segre, A. M., & Polgreen, P. M. (2011). The use of Twitter to track levels of disease activity and public concern in the US during the influenza A H1N1 pandemic. *PloS One, 6*(5), e19467.

Silk, B. J., & Berkelman, R. L. (2005). A review of strategies for enhancing the completeness of notifiable disease reporting. *Journal of Public Health Management and Practice, 11*(3), 191–200.

Smolinski, M. S., Crawley, A. W., Baltrusaitis, K., Chunara, R., Olsen, J. M., Wojcik, O., . . . Brownstein, J. S. (2015). Flu near you: Crowdsourced symptom reporting spanning 2 influenza seasons. *American Journal of Public Health, 105,* 2124–2130.

Thacker, S., Qualters, J. R., Lee, L. M., & Centers for Disease Control and Prevention. (2012). Public health surveillance in the United States: Evolution and challenges. *Morbidity and Mortality Weekly Report, 61*(3), 3–9.

Thorpe, L. E., Greene, C., Freeman, A., Snell, E., Rodriguez-Lopez, J. S., Frankel, M., . . . Koppaka, R. (2015). Rationale, design and respondent characteristics of the 2013–2014 New York City Health and Nutrition Examination Survey (NYC HANES 2013–2014). *Preventive Medicine Reports, 2,* 580–585.

Thorpe, L. E., Perlman, S. E., Chan, P., Bartley, K., Schreibstein, L., Rodriguez-Lopez, J., & Newton-Dame, R. (2016). Monitoring prevalence, treatment, and control of metabolic conditions in New York City adults using 2013 primary care electronic health records: A surveillance validation study. *eGEMS, 4*(1), 1266.

Velasco, E., Agheneza, T., Denecke, K., Kirchner, G., & Eckmanns, T. (2014). Social media and Internet-based data in global systems for public health surveillance: A systematic review. *Milbank Quarterly, 92*(1), 7–33.

Victor, L. Y., & Madoff, L. C. (2004). ProMED-mail: An early warning system for emerging diseases. *Clinical Infectious Diseases, 39*(2), 227–232.

Williamson, T., Green, M. E., Birtwhistle, R., Khan, S., Garies, S., Wong, S. T., . . . Drummond, N. (2014). Validating the 8 CPCSSN case definitions for chronic disease surveillance in a primary care database of electronic health records. *Annals of Family Medicine, 12*(4), 367–372.

Wilson, K., & Brownstein, J. S. (2009). Early detection of disease outbreaks using the Internet. *Canadian Medical Association Journal, 180*(8), 829–831.

World Health Organization. (2012). Public health surveillance. Retrieved from http://www.who.int /topics/public_health_surveillance/en/

World Health Organization. (2016). International statistical classifications of diseases and related health problems (10th rev., Vol. 2, 5th ed.). Retrieved from http://www.who.int/classifications/en/

World Health Organization, Regional Office for Europe. (2015). Integrated surveillance of non-communicable diseases (iNCD). Retrieved from http://ec.europa.eu/health/indicators/docs /incd_en.pdf

Yang, S., Santillana, M., & Kou, S. C. (2015). Accurate estimation of influenza epidemics using Google search data via ARGO. *Proceedings of the National Academy of Sciences, 112*(47), 14473–14478.

Yuan, Q., Nsoesie, E. O., Lv, B., Peng, G., Chunara, R., & Brownstein, J. S. (2013). Monitoring influenza epidemics in China with search query from Baidu. *PloS One, 8*(5), e64323.

Zellweger, U., Bopp, M., Holzer, B. M., Djalali, S., & Kaplan, V. (2014). Prevalence of chronic medical conditions in Switzerland: Exploring estimates validity by comparing complementary data sources. *BMC Public Health, 14*(1), 1.

CHAPTER 6

Statistical Issues in Population Health Informatics

Levi Waldron

Application programming
   interface (API)

Human Development Index (HDI)
Null hypothesis (H0)

- Distinguish between descriptive and inferential statistics, and predictive modeling.
- Define population and statistical samples.
- Define types of errors in inference.
- Identify the differences in objectives of inferential statistics and predictive modeling.
- Distinguish between "large n" and "large p" types of big data.
- Define causal inference and distinguish between correlation and causality.
- Define and interpret the *p*-value.
- Identify trade-offs between simple and complex predictive models.

QUESTIONS FOR THOUGHT

- What is big data?
- What are the uses and limitations of the *p*-value?
- What is the bias-variance trade-off? Which is more important in a given application?
- Can a given study prove causality? Can it suggest causality?
- What is overfitting, and how can it be identified?
- What is the difference between prediction or inference, and when are they relevant?
- When should Type I or Type II error be prioritized?
- What is the difference between a sample and a population?
- How do quantitative and qualitative research differ? What was the sampling strategy?
- If analyzing a population, would it be better to analyze a sample instead?

▶ I. Role of Statistics in Population Health Informatics

The Oxford English Dictionary defines statistics as "the practice or science of collecting and analyzing numerical data in large quantities, especially for the purpose of inferring proportions in a whole from those in a representative sample." In all but the simplest of situations, the interpretation of data, and deriving understanding from data, requires statistics. Statistical methods help generate understanding and meaning from potentially large, yet incomplete and noisy, data. They can be used to quantify the amount of uncertainty resulting from incomplete data and noise, and to make interpretable summaries, to test hypotheses, and to make predictions.

We use the term *statistics* to include summarization in graphical or tabular form, inference about the population from a limited sample, and making formal predictions about the future based on past observations. We call these three areas *descriptive*, *inferential*, and *predictive statistics*, respectively. Some of the most well-known uses of statistics, such as the World Health Organization's annual World Health Statistics report (e.g., World Health Organization, 1968) and the annual Cancer Statistics report (Siegel, Miller, & Jemal, 2015) are descriptive in nature, providing tabular summaries of the prevalence of disease and health measures. Inferential statistics are recognizable from statements about hypotheses, for example, about whether intermittent screening and treatment for malaria impact the performance of schoolchildren (Halliday et al., 2014). Predictive statistics, also referred to as predictive modeling and machine learning, are identifiable by statements predicting the outcome of individuals or groups, such as survival after cancer treatment (Waldron et al., 2014), based on contributing factors.

Key Statistical Concepts

Statistical Populations and Statistical Samples

The concept of sampling from populations is important for both qualitative and quantitative research. Whereas inferential statistics make conclusions about entire *populations*, predictive statistics make predictions for *individuals* and *samples*. The terms *population* and *sample* have meanings in statistics that differ from common uses (see BOX 6.1).

Although statistical inference is developed for statistical samples, it is worth noting that many datasets do not meet the definition of a statistical sample, because the data are not collected using a defined procedure where each individual has a known, nonzero probability of being sampled. These problems are described as *sampling bias*, *unrepresentative samples*, or *samples of convenience*. Such datasets can still be useful, but quantitative results of statistical inference are likely to be misleading.

Sampling in Qualitative Research

Although qualitative research is sometimes criticized for lack of scientific rigor, reproducibility, and generalizability, these issues are by no means inherent or unavoidable (Mays & Pope, 1995). However, in any kind of research, drawing generalizable conclusions from a sample requires understanding which population

---

BOX 6.1 Statistical Population vs. Statistical Sample

Statistical population: The entire pool of people, items, or events that is of interest for some question or experiment. A population may be real (such as all people living in the United States in 2017) or hypothetical (such as all schools that are "similar" to one being studied).
Statistical sample: A set of data collected and/or selected from a statistical population by a defined procedure. A "defined procedure" means that the probability of each individual in the statistical population being contained in this sample is known, and that every individual in the population has a nonzero probability of selection for the sample.

the sample is supposed to represent and making it as representative as possible of that population. In quantitative research, this means *probability sampling*, where the probability of every individual in the population being selected for study is nonzero and known. Probability sampling strategies include simple random sampling, stratified random sampling, cluster sampling, and multistage sampling (Diez, 2012).

In qualitative research, including, for example, analysis of data from social media, probability sampling is often impossible. An alternative approach is systematic, nonprobabilistic sampling, where the goal is to "identify specific groups of people who either possess characteristics or live in circumstances relevant to the social phenomenon being studied" (Mays & Pope, 1995). Rather than being labeled participants or subjects, the studied individuals may be more accurately called "informants," who enable exploration of some aspect of behavior being studied. In such sampling, representativeness can be improved by including a wide range of types of informants. Analysis of data collected from social media platforms such as Twitter and Facebook can reach a wider range and larger number of informants than traditional qualitative research methods, although this method has its own drawbacks such as unclear representativeness and difficulty in accessing informants beyond passive observation.

What Is "Big Data"?

Big data has been called a "loosely defined term used to describe data sets so large and complex that they become awkward to work with using standard statistical software" (Snijders, Matzat, & Reips, 2012). Even this loose definition may be hard to apply because modern statistical software such as R (R Development Core Team, 2008) is rapidly adapted to the demands of big data analysis. Big data has been referred to as any data that won't fit in a spreadsheet (Myers, 2013), but even spreadsheets have been adapted to the demands of larger datasets (Shacklett, 2013). It is perhaps more useful to recognize the challenges presented by different types of data (BOX 6.2).

BOX 6.2 Key Terms

Large sample size ("large n"): These datasets provide observations on thousands or millions of individuals. Challenges can include sampling bias, heterogeneity within the sample, and interpretation of statistical results.

High dimensional data ("large p"): These datasets provide many measurements, or variables, on a relatively small number of individuals. Examples include genomics technologies (Sachs, 2015), imaging data (Agrawal, Erickson, & Kahn, 2016), and data generated by "wearable" technologies (Kubota, Chen, & Little, 2016). Such technologies produce large volumes of data (i.e., measurements of many variables) for a single person.

Complex data: This is a generic term for data that cannot be represented in a table and often require specialized programming expertise to manipulate.

▶ II. Correlation, Causality, and Confounding in Causal Inference

Correlation vs. Causality

Correlation describes a relationship between two variables, such as between the height and weight of people. *Causality* means that one of the variables actually causes the other (BOX 6.3). Two variables can be correlated in the absence of any causal relationship; conversely, they may appear uncorrelated even if a causal relationship exists. The only way to prove causation is through experiment, where the hypothesized causal variable is intentionally manipulated, so that its causal effect on other variables can be observed. However, such experimentation is often impossible or unethical in population health studies, and we must rely instead on *observational* data. Challenges and methods of making causal inference from observational data are well reviewed by Pearl, who translates the common phrase "correlation does not imply causation" further as: "one cannot substantiate causal claims from associations alone, even at the population level—behind every causal conclusion there must lie some causal assumption that is not testable in observational studies" (Pearl, 2009).

▶ III. Inferential and Descriptive Statistics

Inference may be the most well-recognized role of statistics, characterized by the *p*-value and by statements like, "Drinking red wine has been found to reduce heart disease." Inherent in such statements is the testing of a hypothesis about a population using a limited sample of individuals, or in other words, inference about a population. Inference is required because it is impractical or impossible to study the entire population; if we could, inference would be unnecessary. A study of the entire population is called a *census*.

BOX 6.3 Correlation vs. Causation from Experimental and Observational Data

Correlation: A mutual relationship or connection between two or more things.
Causation: The action of causing something.
Experimental data: Data collected by manipulating a potentially causal variable of interest. For example, the effectiveness of a new drug for preventing heart disease is determined by randomly assigning the drug or a placebo to clinical trial participants, and then observing those participants for several years after the intervention.
Observational data: Data collected in a way that does not directly interfere with how the data arise, and in particular, does not purposefully manipulate variables of interest. For example, the effectiveness of a diet on preventing heart disease is studied by observing the rates of heart disease among people who follow that diet and people who do not. Or, the effectiveness of the diet is studied by looking at the fraction of heart disease patients who followed the diet, and comparing that to the fraction among healthy individuals.

Inference is used to test hypotheses. Although many kinds of hypotheses may be made in population health, in statistics only a very specific kind of hypothesis is tested: the null hypothesis (H0). The H0 is a hypothesis of no difference between populations, of no effect of an intervention, no relationship between a certain behavior and a health outcome, and the like. The H0 describes a state of the world, something that is either true or not true, but that cannot be observed or measured directly. Inference involves estimating the probability of observing the data at hand if the H0 is true. It is important to remember that the data available to analyze are an incomplete sample of the population, and cannot absolutely prove or disprove anything about the population. It is always possible, by chance, to unknowingly observe an unusual subset of the population.

Types of Errors

Keeping in mind that the H0 is either true or not true, and that statistical inference will lead us either to accept or to reject the H0, then there are four possible outcomes of the inference (TABLE 6.1). We cannot know whether H0 is true or false, so we perform statistical hypothesis tests under the assumption that it is true, and decide to reject it only if the incomplete data we observe are very unlikely under this assumption. This is conceptually similar to a criminal trial, where the defendant is presumed innocent until proven guilty; in statistics, the H0 is presumed true until this is proven improbable.

The H0 is either true or false, but we don't know which is the case. If the observed data seem inconsistent with the H0, we reject H0; the chance of this happening due to random sampling alone is the Type I error probability, or the *p-value*. Conversely, if H0 is false but we fail to reject it due to insufficient evidence, this is a Type II error. But instead of estimating Type II error probability, it is more common to estimate *power*, which is the probability of correctly rejecting the H0 under the assumption that it is false (BOX 6.4).

Note on *p*-Values for Big Data

It is worth emphasizing that the *p*-value captures only the probability of Type I error due to the random nature of sampling. It does not account for errors due to sampling bias (the tendency to observe subsets that are not representative of the population of interest), problematic study design, hidden confounding, or any other reason. For very large samples of thousands or millions of people, very little variation in

TABLE 6.1 Types of Statistical Errors		
	Reject H0	**Fail to Reject H0**
H0 is true.	Type I error, probability is the *p*-value	Correct conclusion
H0 is false.	Correct conclusion, probability is the statistical power	Type II error

Type I error: Rejecting the null hypothesis when the null hypothesis is actually true.
Type II error: Failing to reject the null hypothesis when the null hypothesis is actually false.
Statistical power: The probability of a statistical test rejecting the null hypothesis, estimated under the assumption that the null hypothesis is really false and some other hypothesis is instead true.
p-value: The probability of observing the sample at hand, or one even more inconsistent with the null hypothesis, under the assumption that the null hypothesis is true and the difference observed is due only to random sampling variation. It is also the probability of making a Type I error due to random sampling variation alone.

average properties will occur due to random sampling variation, and *p*-values tend to become vanishingly small and decreasingly meaningful (Lin, Lucas, & Shmueli, 2013). For large samples, Type I error is much more likely due to reasons other than random sampling. Furthermore, the *amount* of difference between samples becomes more meaningful than the *statistical significance* of the difference, because with very large samples, random sampling results in very little variation in average properties. Overreliance on the *p*-value for making conclusions has caused controversy and has even led some academic journals to forbid reporting of *p*-values at all (Wasserstein & Lazar, 2016). In all statistical analysis, and especially analysis of "large n" data, it is important to consider all potential sources of an error when making conclusions, not just the *p*-value, which relates only to variations attributable to random sampling.

▶ IV. Predictive Modeling

Whereas inferential statistics answer questions about the existence and interpretation of relationships between variables, predictive modeling aims to make accurate predictions for an outcome variable, and to estimate what that accuracy is. Sometimes the same interpretable algorithms are used for inference and for prediction (e.g., linear and logistic regression), but the objectives differ. In predictive modeling, making accurate predictions normally takes precedence over understanding how predictor (independent) variables are related to the outcome, response, or dependent variable. Some predictive modeling algorithms, such as random forests (Breiman, 2001) and neural networks (Haykin, 2004), are so complex that they can be interpreted only as a "black box" that takes values of the predictor variables and makes a prediction of the outcome.

Under- and Overfitting

More complex models are not necessarily better than less complex ones. Overfitting is a pervasive problem in predictive modeling, which occurs when a model is fit too closely to the available training data. FIGURE 6.1 provides an example of underfitting, optimal fitting, and overfitting in a simple two-variable case. In this

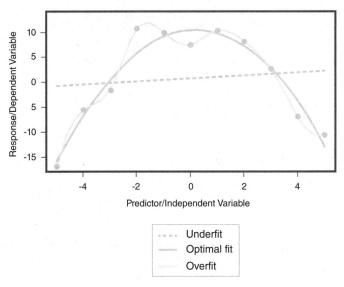

FIGURE 6.1 Underfitting, overfitting, and optimal fitting

example, the response or dependent variable is simulated as a curved (quadratic) function of the predictor or independent variable, plus random noise added. In real situations, it is impossible to know how much of the response variable is due to changes in the predictor variables and how much is due to unknown or random factors. Assuming that all variations in the response variable are due to changes in the predictor variable leads to the extreme overfitting option shown in Figure 6.1, where the model predicts every data point perfectly. Such an overfit model is likely to perform very poorly in predictions on future data. On the other hand, the underfit line in Figure 6.1 fails to account for a systematic relationship between these two variables and likewise will perform poorly in future predictions.

Overfitting is a pervasive problem in predictive modeling, and a primary challenge is finding an appropriate trade-off between fitting too closely and not closely enough to training data. Overfitting refers to models that too closely fit to the training data. Such models vary greatly with sampling variability (high variance, low bias) and produce inaccurate predictions in validation data. resulting in high-variance predictions Conversely, underfitting occurs when an insufficiently flexible model is fit to the data, resulting in biased predictions relative to training or validation data. In real-life data, it is only possible to approximate the optimal fit, using techniques such as cross-validation.

Cross-validation

In data with many predictor variables, it is not nearly so easy to identify under- and overfitting as in the previous example. In fact, most standard predictive modeling algorithms will overfit to training data, and much published research has presented the results of overfitting (Cawley & Talbot, 2010). It is important to keep in mind that the ultimate objective in predictive modeling is to make good predictions in new observations, not just the ones already seen by the algorithm. This is referred to as *validation* performance, or *test set* performance. It is possible to estimate the validation performance of an algorithm in a simulation procedure called *cross-validation*. In cross-validation, available observations are randomly split into a *training* and *validation* set. The training set is used to develop or train the model, and the validation set is used to estimate the accuracy of the model (BOX 6.5).

Take a look at FIGURE 6.2. Panel A shows a high-bias, low-variance solution that is *underfit* to the training data. It provides biased predictions but is not affected much by noise in the training data. Panel B shows a low-bias, high-variance solution

---

BOX 6.5 Key Terminology in the Training and Validation of Predictive Models

Underfitting: The creation of a model that does not sufficiently reflect systematic relationships in the data. Such models are described as *high bias* but *low variance*, because their predictions are systematically biased, but the model does not vary much in response to noise in the data.

Overfitting: The creation of an overly complex prediction model fitted to idiosyncrasies of the training data not likely to be found again in validation data. Such models are also described as having *low bias* but *high variance*, because systematic error is low but the model varies greatly in response to noise in the data.

Cross-validation: A simulation method of randomly partitioning a single dataset into training and validation sets, using these to train and assess a model, and repeating using different random partitions.

Tuning: The process of adjusting the complexity of a model to find an appropriate balance between over- and underfitting.

Training set: Data used to develop or train a predictive model.

Validation set or test set: Data not used for training that are instead used for assessing the accuracy of a predictive model.

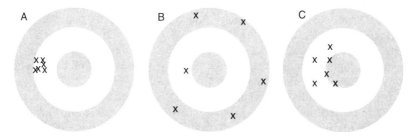

FIGURE 6.2 The overfitting vs. underfitting, or bias vs. variance, trade-off in fitting predictive models

that is *overfit* to the training data. It provides nearly unbiased predictions but is highly sensitive to noise in the training data. Panel C shows a more desirable trade-off between these two extremes, which can be identified by cross-validation. In real-world data it is usually impossible to find a solution that is both very low-variance and low-bias.

▶ V. Example: Gun Violence Worldwide

A dataset created by Tewksbury (2012) provides rates of gun ownership and gun violence for 75 countries around the world, and was collected with the following question in mind: "Do countries whose populations own more guns also have more gun-related deaths?" It also provides a Human Development Index (HDI) (Anand, 1994) summarizing life expectancy, education, and income, as a numeric index and in four tiers (low, medium, high, and very high). This dataset invites descriptive, inferential, and predictive statistics, for example:

- *Descriptive statistics:* What are the rates of gun ownership and gun-related deaths seen in these countries? What are the extremes? What is "normal"?
- *Inferential statistics:* Is the rate of gun violence related to the rate of gun ownership? Is it related to the HDI?
- *Predictive statistics:* How accurately can the rate of gun violence in a country be predicted based on gun ownership and the HDI? Which is more predictive of the rate of gun violence?

Question: Sample or Population?

It is worth questioning whether this dataset, representing 75 countries, is a sample or a population. Seventy-five countries around the world represent enough people that it could certainly be considered to represent a population.

Gun Violence: Statistical Analysis

Descriptive statistics provide a basic orientation to the dataset and help us to understand its basic properties. TABLE 6.2 shows that the mortality rate from gun-related violence is provided for 75 countries, but that ownership rate is missing for 2 countries and HDI is missing for 6 of them. Mean mortality rate of the 75 countries is 5.9 per 100,000, with a very wide range from 0.1 to 50.4 per 100,000. The rate of gun ownership varies from 0.5 to 88.8 guns per person, with an average of 15.1. Certainly, there is large variation in both of these variables, suggesting that the data provide an opportunity to investigate the existence of an association between gun mortality rate and gun ownership.

FIGURE 6.3 provides a visual description of the dataset, showing the variability in gun ownership and gun violence across countries, while also indicating the HDI of each country. It appears that any discussion of relationships between gun ownership and gun violence across countries would be incomplete without discussion of the HDI. Looking at all the countries, no obvious relationship

TABLE 6.2 Descriptive Statistics for the Gun Violence Dataset

	#	Mean	Min	Max
Mortality rate	75	5.9	0.1	50.4
Ownership rate	73	15.1	0.5	88.8
Continuous HDI	69	0.8	0.4	0.9

		Categorical HDI	# countries
Categorical HDI	69	Low	1
		Medium	10
		High	17
		Very high	41

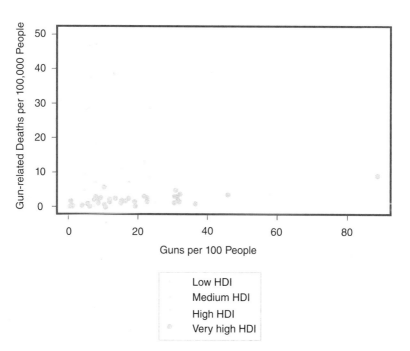

FIGURE 6.3 Scatterplot of the observed relationship between gun deaths and gun ownership, with different plotting symbols showing HDI

between gun ownership and gun violence is apparent, and this holds up in statistical inference: In linear regression, there is no evidence against the H0 of no relationship (p-value $= 0.5$). However, if the linear regression is restricted to only the countries rated as having a "very high" HDI, the relationship becomes highly significant (p-value $< 10^{-6}$), with an estimated additional 14 guns per 100 people adding an additional death per 100,000 people. This example includes all the types of statistics covered so far: descriptive statistics in the form of tables and graphs, which help us to ask the right questions and study meaningful subsets of the data; inference against an H0 of no relationship between gun ownership and gun deaths; and prediction of the expected number of gun deaths per 100,000 people based on the HDI and rates of gun ownership.

This is an alternative example of descriptive statistics that visually inspects the possibility of a relationship among gun ownership, gun violence, and HDI.

▶ VI. Example: Qualitative Analysis of Social Media Data

Social media provides troves of potential data for informatics research, although it is not generally possible to obtain probability samples as required for quantitative research. However, qualitative analysis of social media data provides alternative means of understanding or interpreting public health trends.

Word Clouds

Pursuing the example of gun violence, we created a word cloud for words co-occurring in tweets mentioning the term "AR-15," a popular assault rifle (FIGURE 6.4). This analysis accessed the Twitter application programming interface (API) (https://apps.twitter.com), using the twitteR and wordcloud R packages, after removing punctuation, URLs, common words like "the," and plural word endings such as "es" and "ing." Foul language also was removed. The search reveals words relating to the United States' presidential campaign ("Trump" and "Hillary"), a large number of Spanish words, expected gun-related words ("gun" and "assault"), and a number of difficult-to-interpret terms requiring follow-up. Although this is not a statistical analysis, it could provide insight into gun culture around assault rifles.

Social Networks

Network analysis of social media data can identify key "informants" who are influential and connected to a large number of others. FIGURE 6.5 shows a retweet network for the same tweets used in the word cloud. In this network, nodes are user accounts and edges are retweets, with arrows pointing from the originator of the tweet. Some of these "super-nodes" are connected to each other, indicating the flow of information among highly influential communicators. These accounts would be good targets for in-depth analysis because they provide influential views on assault rifles

FIGURE 6.4 Twitter word cloud

Data from Twitter application programming interface

and likely other aspects of gun culture. Barabási (2016) provides a classic overview of network science, which could be applied to such networks in much greater detail to analyze the flow of information across social networks. In Figure 6.5, red nodes correspond to Twitter accounts, and lines (referred to as "edges") connect accounts where one user retweeted a tweet from another account, with arrows showing the direction of the retweet. Node size is proportional to the number of times tweets from that account were retweeted, showing a pattern of a few influential users whose tweets are widely disseminated, such as the "teenagesleuth" and "william_castro" accounts.

Geographic Analysis

Geographic information is difficult to ascertain from social media data, because it must be provided voluntarily by users. In a larger search of 10,000 "AR-15" tweets, only eight provided the location of the user: five in the United States and three in Europe. The reluctance of social media users to share locational information has been noted previously (Wagner et al., 2010); however, others

myresata Retweet Network

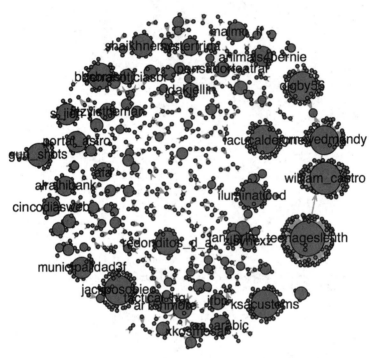

FIGURE 6.5 Retweet network for 2000 tweets mentioning the word "AR-15" during October 2016

Data from Twitter application programming interface

have shown that widely shared phenomena such as earthquakes can be identified and located with high accuracy using social media data (Sakaki, Okazaki, & Matsuo, 2010).

▶ VII. Conclusion

Basic awareness of statistical concepts such as sampling and inference are key to understanding the potential and limitations of population health informatics data for research. Researchers should be aware of and open to methods from both quantitative and qualitative research to make best use of available data.

References

Agrawal, J. P., Erickson, B. J., & Kahn, C. E., Jr. (2016). Imaging informatics: 25 years of progress. *Yearbook of Medical Informatics* (Suppl. 1), S23–S31. Stuttgart, Germany: Schattauer Publishers.

Anand, S. (1994). *Human development index: Methodology and measurement* (No. HDOCPA-1994-02). Human Development Report Office (HDRO), United Nations Development Programme (UNDP). Retrieved from http://EconPapers.repec.org/RePEc:hdr :hdocpa:hdocpa-1994-02

Barabási, A.-L. (2016). *Network science.* Cambridge, UK: Cambridge University Press.

Breiman, L. (2001). Random forests. *Machine Learning, 45*(1), 5–32.

Cawley, G. C., & Talbot, N. L. C. (2010). On over-fitting in model selection and subsequent selection bias in performance evaluation. *Journal of Machine Learning Research, 11,* 2079–2107.

Diez, D. M. (2012). *OpenIntro statistics* (2nd ed.). Lexington, KY: CreateSpace Independent Publishing Platform.

Halliday, K. E., Okello, G., Turner, E. L., Njagi, K., Mcharo, C., Kengo, J., . . . Brooker, S. J. (2014). Impact of intermittent screening and treatment for malaria among school children in Kenya: A cluster randomised trial. *PLoS Medicine, 11*(1), e1001594.

Haykin, S. (2004). Neural networks: A comprehensive foundation. *Neural Networks: The Official Journal of the International Neural Network Society, 2*(2004), 41.

Kubota, K. J., Chen, J. A., & Little, M. A. (2016). Machine learning for large-scale wearable sensor data in Parkinson's disease: Concepts, promises, pitfalls, and futures. *Movement Disorders: Official Journal of the Movement Disorder Society.* Retrieved from https://doi.org/10.1002/mds.26693

Lin, M., Lucas, H. C., & Shmueli, G. (2013). Research commentary—Too big to fail: Large samples and the *p*-value problem. *INFOR. Information Systems and Operational Research, 24*(4), 906–917.

Mays, N., & Pope, C. (1995). Rigour and qualitative research. *BMJ, 311*(6997), 109–112.

Myers, A. (2013, April 17). What is big data? Anything that won't fit in Excel #emetrics. Retrieved from http://www.cmswire.com/cms/information-management/what-is-big-data-anything-that -wont-fit-in-excel-emetrics-020502.php

Pearl, J. (2009). Causal inference in statistics: An overview. *Statistics Surveys, 3,* 96–146.

R Development Core Team. (2008). The R project for statistical computing. Retrieved from http: //www.r-project.org

Sachs, M. C. (2015). Statistical principles for omics-based clinical trials. *Chinese Clinical Oncology, 4*(3), 29.

Sakaki, T., Okazaki, M., & Matsuo, Y. (2010). Earthquake shakes Twitter users: Real-time event detection by social sensors. In *Proceedings of the 19th International Conference on World Wide Web* (pp. 851–860). New York, NY: Association for Computing Machinery.

Shacklett, M. (2013, July 22). Big data spreadsheet products and their potential benefits. *TechRepublic.* Retrieved from http://www.techrepublic.com/blog/big-data-analytics/big-data -spreadsheet-products-and-their-potential-benefits/

Siegel, R. L., Miller, K. D., & Jemal, A. (2015). Cancer statistics, 2015. *CA: A Cancer Journal for Clinicians, 65*(1), 5–29.

Snijders, C., Matzat, U., & Reips, U. D. (2012). "Big data": Big gaps of knowledge in the field of Internet science. *International Journal of Internet Science.* Retrieved from https://kops .uni-konstanz.de/handle/123456789/28647

Tewksbury, J. (2012, December 17). Gun violence and gun ownership—Let's look at the data. Retrieved from http://www.webcitation.org/6jdd7YBwG

Wagner, D., Lopez, M., Doria, A., Pavlyshak, I., Kostakos, V., Oakley, I., & Spiliotopoulos, T. (2010). Hide and seek: Location sharing practices with social media. In *Proceedings of the 12th*

International Conference on Human Computer Interaction with Mobile Devices and Services (pp. 55–58). New York, NY: Association for Computing Machinery.

Waldron, L., Haibe-Kains, B., Culhane, A. C., Riester, M., Ding, J., Wang, X. V., … Parmigiani, G. (2014). Comparative meta-analysis of prognostic gene signatures for late-stage ovarian cancer. *Journal of the National Cancer Institute, 106*(5). Retrieved from https://doi.org/10.1093/jnci /dju049

Wasserstein, R. L., & Lazar, N. A. (2016). The ASA's statement on *p*-values: Context, process, and purpose. *American Statistician, 70*(2), 129–133.

World Health Organization. (1968). World health statistics report. Geneva, Switzerland: WHO Press.

CHAPTER 7

Big Data, Cloud Computing, and Visual Analytics in Population Health

Ashish Joshi

KEY TERMS

Global positioning systems (GPSs)
Information and communication
 technology (ICT)
Information visualization (InfoVis)
National Institute of Standards and
 Technology (NIST)

Social Network Analysis (SNA)
Strengths, weaknesses, opportunities, and
 threats (SWOT) analysis
U.S. Department of Health and Human
 Services (DHHS)

LEARNING OBJECTIVES

- Describe the role of big data in health care.
- List the challenges related to big data in health care.
- Define *cloud computing* and explain how it can be leveraged to improve
  population health.
- Assess the strategies to implement a cloud computing platform.
- Explore various health data visualization techniques.
- Identify the linkages between big data cloud computing and health data
  visualization in making it meaningful.

QUESTIONS FOR THOUGHT

- What are the challenges and opportunities related to big data in population health?
- How can information and communication technology leverage big data for disease prevention and management?
- What are the technological, ethical, and privacy challenges related to cloud computing?
- What are the necessary steps involved in the implementation of a cloud computing platform?
- What role do users play in the design and development of the geovisualization tools?

CHAPTER OUTLINE

▶ I. Introduction to Big Data

Throughout its history, the healthcare industry has generated enormous data (Kudyba, 2010). The current trend is toward rapid digitization of these large amounts of data. Healthcare data are especially challenging to manage owing to their variety in structure. Healthcare data may be structured; unstructured, such as data collected directly by clinicians at the point of service delivery; or semistructured, combining features of both structured and unstructured (Raghupathi & Raghupathi, 2014). Very limited data are readily available in a format that can be processed to derive meaningful information. Several data characteristics such as multiple variables, high signal-to-noise ratio, and a degree of uncertainty limit data exploration, hypothesis generation, exploration, and decision making. However, these large quantities of data hold the potential of supporting a wide range of healthcare functions.

The information technology (IT) revolution in health care has resulted in several advanced methodologies like big data analytics, predictive analytics, and cloud computing. These methodologies have provided stakeholders with the ability to examine data for their specific purpose. Public health programs are limited in aggregating the data they need in order to get an actual picture of population health. Despite the advancement of computational and geographic information system (GIS) technologies, there is an urgent need for novel approaches to represent spatiotemporal (spatial, meaning the location of the event, and temporal, meaning the time of the event) data in a visual form that can guide informed decision making. The growing complexity of public health datasets has created the need for more innovative approaches to facilitate data analysis and decision making through meaningful use of data (Maciejewski et al., 2010).

▶ II. Big Data Classification and Tools

Big data refers to complex and variable data. It has several characteristics: volume/velocity, variety, veracity, and value (Raghupathi & Raghupathi, 2014; see FIGURE 7.1). *Volume* or *velocity* reflects the high rates at which the data are accumulated. *Variety* involves high-volume data in motion and across all specialties. *Veracity* in big data reflects data assurance and that analytics and outcomes are error-free and credible. Big data also derives *value* augmented with new sources of unstructured data (Raghupathi & Raghupathi, 2014). Analysis of big data reveals associations, patterns, and trends and extracts insights for making better-informed decisions.

Big Data Classification

Big data is classified into a variety of categories based on: (1) data sources, (2) content format, (3) data stores, (4) data staging, and (5) data processing (see FIGURE 7.2).

Data Sources

There are several sources of big data, including the following:

- *Social media:* A way of exchanging information or ideas via virtual communities and networks (e.g., blogs, Twitter, Facebook).

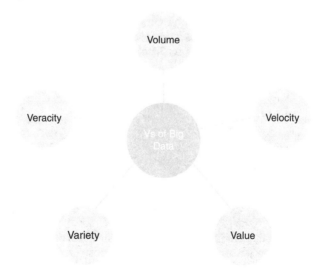

FIGURE 7.1 The five Vs of big data

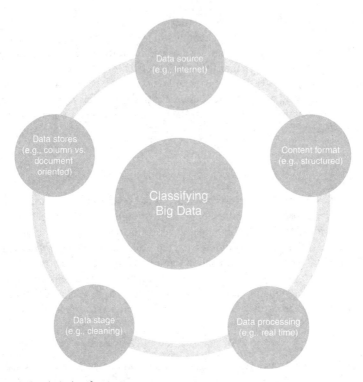

FIGURE 7.2 Big data classification

Modified from Hashem, I. A. T., Yaqoob, I., Anuar, N. B., Mokhtar, S., Gani, A., & Khan, S. U. (2015). The rise of "big data" on cloud computing: Review and open research issues. *Information Systems, 47*, 98–115.

- *Machine-generated data:* Information automatically generated from hardware or software, such as computers or medical devices, without human intervention (e.g., blood pressure device).
- *Sensors:* These devices measure physical quantities and change them into signals.
- *Transaction:* This includes financial and work data and comprises an event that involves a time dimension to describe the data.
- *Internet of things:* Represents a set of objects that are uniquely identifiable as a part of the Internet (e.g., smartphones and tablets). When connected to the Internet, these items produce a huge amount of data and information by enabling smart processes and services (Federal Trade Commission, 2015; Hashem et al., 2015).

Content Format

There are three types of content format:

- *Structured:* This type of data is easy to input, query, store, and analyze (e.g., numbers, words).
- *Semi-structured:* These data do not follow a conventional database system (e.g., structured data that are unorganized in a relational database model such as a table) (Hashem et al., 2015).
- *Unstructured:* These do not follow a specified format (e.g., text messages, videos).

Data Stores

These include a repository that stores and manages collections of data ranging from databases, files (such as audio, image, or video), and emails.

- *Document-oriented:* Designed to store and retrieve collections of documents or information and support complex data forms in several standard formats (e.g., XML format) (Hashem et al., 2015)
- *Column-oriented:* Designed to store content in columns as well as rows. It differs from classical database systems that store entire rows one after another (e.g., big table) (Hashem et al., 2015)
- *Graph database:* Designed to store and represent data that utilize a graph model with nodes, edges, and properties related to one another through relations (Hashem et al., 2015)
- *Key-value:* An alternative relational database system that stores and accesses data designed to scale to a very large size (Hashem et al., 2015)

Data Staging

Data staging is an intermediate storage area used for data processing.

- *Cleaning:* Identifying incomplete and unreasonable data (Hashem et al., 2015)
- *Transform:* Transforming data into an analyzable form
- *Normalization:* Structuring database schema to minimize redundancy (Hashem et al., 2015)

Data Processing

Data processing reflects manipulation of data to generate meaningful information.

- *Batch:* In this scenario, the system allows for the scaling of applications across large clusters of machines comprising thousands of nodes (Hashem et al., 2015).
- *Real time:* This involves developing applications for processing continuous unbounded streams of data (e.g., a simple scalable streaming system [S4]) (Hashem et al., 2015).

Big Data Techniques and Tools

Big data has drawn huge attention from researchers in information sciences and from policy- and decision makers in governments and enterprises (Chen & Zhang, 2014). Considering the various features of big data, innovative techniques are required to adequately manage and analyze it (Gandomi & Haider, 2015; Ward & Barker, 2013). The characteristics of big data require powerful and novel technologies to extract useful information and enable more broad-based healthcare solutions. A fundamental mechanism for managing big data is known as parallel computing. It utilizes large-scale supercomputers and machines in processing complex algorithms simultaneously (Dean & Ghemawat, 2008).

Big Data Techniques

Various techniques are needed to process large amounts of big data within limited run times. Several of these techniques involve disciplines such as statistics, data mining, machine learning, social network analysis, and visualization approaches. A brief description of each of these terms is provided here:

- *Statistics:* Assists in data collection, interpretation, and organization to explore relationships across several variables. However, simple statistical techniques are usually not adapted to manage big data.
- *Data mining:* Assists in extracting meaningful information from data. It includes several approaches such as cluster analysis and rule learning.
- *Machine learning:* Aimed at designing algorithms that can facilitate knowledge discovery based on the behavior of empirical data so that informed decisions can be made.
- *Social network analysis (SNA):* Recently, analysis of online social networks and social media has become popular. SNA consists of nodes (e.g., individual actors or people) and ties (relationships that connect them).
- *Visualization:* Includes techniques that can be used to create tables, images, and diagrams to help in better understanding data.

Big Data Tools

A wide variety of tools has been developed recently to analyze and visualize big data. These tools are categorized into the following three classes:

- *Batch processing tools:* Apache Hadoop is one of the most well-established software platforms that support data-intensive distributed applications (White, 2012). It helps in easily writing applications that process vast quantities of data in parallel. It is a highly scalable and reliable platform. It is a multipurpose, but not a real-time, high-performance engine (Chen & Zhang, 2014).
- *Stream processing tools:* These are a real-time method of processing a large amount of stream data. The tools stream big data and complex data types with real-time data analysis analytics. An example of this type of tool is S4.
- *Interactive analysis tools:* These process the data in an interactive environment, allowing users to undertake their own analysis of information in real time. The data can be reviewed, compared, and analyzed in tabular or graphic format or both at the same time. An example of this type of tool is Apache Drill.

Every big data platform has its own focus and specific functionality, and either is designed for batch processing or is good at real-time analytics. There are seven necessary principles that guide designing big data analytics systems (Chen & Zhang, 2014; Garber, 2012); these are shown in BOX 7.1.

BOX 7.1 Necessary Principles Guiding Design of Big Data Analytics Systems

- Good architectures and frameworks are necessary and are the top priority.
- They must support a variety of analytic methods.
- No size fits all.
- They must bring the analysis to the data.
- Processing must be distributable for in-memory computation.
- Data storage must be distributable for in-memory storage.
- Coordination is needed between processing and data units.

Based on Chen, P. C. L., & Zhang, Y. C. (2014). Data-intensive applications, challenges, techniques and technologies: A survey on big data. *Information Sciences, 275*, 314–347.

▶ III. Big Data in Health Care

Big data in health care consists of enormous volumes of health datasets stored electronically (Frost, 2015). Big data in health care can come from a variety of sources, including internal sources (e.g., electronic health records [EHRs], healthcare decision support systems, etc.) and external sources (government sources, laboratories, pharmacies, insurance companies, etc.) (FIGURE 7.3). They often occur in multiple formats and reside at multiple locations (Frost, 2015).

The adoption and use of health IT is increasing around the world. The volume of healthcare data is expected to increase dramatically in the coming years. Key contributors to this increase include stakeholders in public health data collection including the Centers for Disease Control and Prevention (CDC), the World Health Organization (WHO), and the U.S. National Center for Health Statistics (NCHS), among others, who engage in policymaking using these data-driven results (Raghupathi & Raghupathi, 2014). The $22 billion Health Information Technology for Economic and Clinical Health (HITECH) Act of 2009 allocated $19.2 billion to increase the adoption and use of EHRs (Freedman, 2009). The widespread uptake of EHRs has generated massive datasets. Most EHRs contain quantitative data (e.g., laboratory values), qualitative data (e.g., text-based documents), and transaction-related data (e.g., medication records). Reports suggest that data from the U.S. healthcare system in the year 2011 alone reached 150 exabytes (Raghupathi & Raghupathi, 2014). Exabyte is a multiple of the unit byte for digital information.

Digital healthcare data have also rapidly increased and evolved. Over time, these health-related data will be created and accumulated continuously. Healthcare data are rarely standardized and are often fragmented with incompatible formats (Raghupathi & Raghupathi, 2014). Healthcare applications need more efficient ways to combine and convert varieties of data. New advances in data management and analysis are also enabling organizations to convert this vast resource into information and knowledge (Murdoch & Detsky, 2013). Meaningful use and pay for performance have emerged as two critical factors in today's healthcare environment (Raghupathi & Raghupathi, 2014).

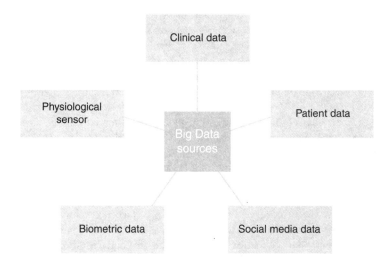

FIGURE 7.3 Multiple big data sources in health care

▶ IV. Leveraging Big Data for Disease Prevention

Digitization of health records is described as a novel revolution in the use of information and communication technology (ICT) in medicine (Labrinidis & Jagadish, 2012). A good population health management approach takes into account the multiple determinants of health, including adequacy of medical care, public health interventions, social and physical environments and related services, genetics, and individual behavior (Kindig & Stoddart, 2003). Traditional public health data are not high volume, high variety, or high velocity (Raghupathi & Raghupathi, 2014). Many aspects of public health could be considered data-poor, due to modest study sample sizes, lack of geographically linked data, and temporal lags due to lengthy data collection and dissemination cycles (Barrett, Humblet, Hiatt, & Adler, 2013). There are four ways big data can enhance healthcare delivery quality and efficiency (Murdoch & Detsky, 2013).

- *Expand the capacity to generate new knowledge:* Big data offers the potential to create an evidence base that would otherwise not be possible.
- *Help with knowledge dissemination:* The big data approach draws from real-time data analysis, rather than solely using rule-based decision trees.
- *Help integrate biomedical and clinical initiatives:* Big data provides the ability to integrate systems biology such as genomics with data stored in EHRs, through its advanced analytic mechanisms.
- *Transform health care by delivering information directly to patients, empowering them to play a more active role:* Big data offers the chance to improve the medical record by linking traditional health data (e.g., family history) to other personal data found on other sites (e.g., income, education, neighborhood, diet habits, exercise regimens, and forms of entertainment) (Brown, 2012).

Big data analytics have a plethora of applications in population health, including (1) translating huge data volumes into meaningful information, (2) enhancing public health surveillance, (3) assessing high-risk population groups for preventive interventions, (4) developing vaccines, (5) clinical diagnosis and care, (6) comparing the cost-effectiveness of treatments, and (6) ensuring the accessibility of health services (Raghupathi & Raghupathi, 2014). Big data plays a key role in both research and intervention activities and can accelerate progress in disease prevention and population health. It has the potential to use daily generated information to improve the quality and efficiency of care. Big data can also help to improve the effectiveness of interventions to help people achieve healthier behaviors in healthier environments (Barrett et al., 2013).

The technological underpinning of health-focused big data is the use of sensors and smartphones. People are increasingly interested in tracking their health care through mobile health sensors and applications. Big data technologies have the potential to allow data collection on a much larger and faster scale than was previously possible. Massive datasets allow not only population-level analysis, but also subpopulation- and personal-level analyses (Barrett et al., 2013). Such analyses enable the discovery of personalized risk factors, giving people more effective information about how to prevent disease. Input can come from EHRs, innovative primary data collection tools (e.g., real-time behavior monitoring), and secondary data sources such as location-linked databases of environmental and neighborhood characteristics (Barrett et al., 2013). Crowdsourcing data are also an important data source for monitoring the spread of infectious diseases (Barrett et al., 2013). HealthMap, for example, collects, filters, and utilizes informal online data sources to analyze, map, and disseminate information about infectious disease outbreaks (Mekaru, Hansen, Freifeld, & Brownstein, 2015). Informal health data on social networking sites such as Facebook and Twitter are currently being studied to assess disease spread in real time (Kass-Hout & Alhinnawi, 2013). Health behaviors can now be monitored remotely using innovative digital smartphone devices including Fitbit for physical activity (Cadmus-Bertram, Marcus, Patterson, Parker, & Morey, 2015), My Meal Mate for diet (Carter, Burley, Nykjaer, & Cade, 2013), Lark for sleep quality, and MyMedSchedule for medication adherence (Coughlin et al., 2015).

A growing understanding of the importance of environmental determinants of health has raised interest in integrating environmental and neighborhood data into health studies. The social and physical environment provide the context that can enable or hinder healthy behaviors (Barrett et al., 2013). Furthermore, the physical environment (e.g., air quality, pollution, crime, noise, public transportation access) has direct impact on health and needs to be better understood at both the population and individual levels (Barrett et al., 2013). A large amount of environmental data is regularly collected in nonhealth sectors and could be an essential component of health-related big data (Raghupathi & Raghupathi, 2014). A few relevant examples of available data on the physical environment include weather patterns, pollution levels, allergens, land use change, forest fires, particulate matter, traffic patterns, pesticide applications, and water quality (Barrett et al., 2013). Geography provides a unifying framework to integrate all of these disparate data sources. Tools such as global positioning systems (GPSs) and GISs allow multiple layers of diverse types of data to be georeferenced and layered. Big data communicates critical educational messages to patients outside the hospital environment in a personalized manner that will increase the likelihood of its impact.

▶ V. Challenges Related to Big Data in Health Care

Problems related to healthcare data are quite similar in many ways to those in other domains (Jagadish et al., 2014; Raghupathi & Raghupathi, 2014). Challenges of data integration, ease of use, and interpretability are all central issues. The lag between data collection and processing is an essential drawback (Raghupathi & Raghupathi, 2014). The important issues of ownership, governance, and standards also have to be considered (Raghupathi & Raghupathi, 2014). Domain-specific challenges include breadth of use, statistical rigor, and data complexity. Other big data challenges related to health care are shown in TABLE 7.1.

Some ethical challenges also require consideration (Vayena, Salathé, Madoff, & Brownstein, 2015).

- *Context sensitivity:* The context of big data in terms of public health differs significantly from other types of big data activity. The public health function is aimed at improving health at the population level (Vayena et al., 2015). There is a clear contrast with other forms of big data in other settings where the exact

TABLE 7.1 Big Data Challenges Related to Health Care

Challenge	Description
Data complexity	Amount of data generated from multiple activities.
Data variety	Multifaceted character of big data with a variety of data dimensions.
Data quality	Missing or invalid data are common due to improper data entry or a lack of system interoperability.
Data heterogeneity	Heterogeneity and linking of data sources across different sources is another growing problem.

Data from Raghupathi, W., & Raghupathi, V. (2014). Big data analytics in healthcare: Promise and potential. *Health Information Science and Systems, 2*(1), 1.

same data (e.g., social networking) may be used for other purposes (e.g., advertising) (Vayena et al., 2015). Another dimension of context is related to global justice. There is a need for some core uniform privacy standards and some variation based on different cultures. The primary ethical challenge is differentiation between commercial versus public health uses of data (Salas-Vega, Haimann, & Mossialos, 2015).

- *Nexus of ethics and methodology:* Methodological robustness is an ethical requirement. This entails consideration of several characteristics such as algorithm validation, managing noisy data, and selecting appropriate data streams (Vayena et al., 2015).
- *Legitimacy requirements:* The validity of the information sources requires proper verification. Monitoring boards should be developed to ensure that risks and costs to individuals and communities are proportional to benefits (Vayena et al., 2015).

The ability of big data to promote the needed value in the health sector calls for rapid changes in current health policies. A balance is critically needed between the societal benefits of big data utilization and ensuring patient data security and confidentiality. Many other important policies related to data use, access, sharing, privacy, and stewardship also need to be revised.

▶ VI. Introduction to Cloud Computing

Defining Cloud Computing

The advent of the digital age has resulted in big data generation, storage, and sharing. There are multiple sources of massive amounts of data ranging from webpages and blogs to audio/video streams. Effective analysis of such complex data

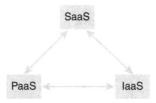

FIGURE 7.4 Cloud computing services

is invaluable in generating relevant information. Cloud computing refers to an on-demand, self-service emerging technology enabling users to access computing resources anytime from anywhere (Chowdhary, Yadav, & Garg, 2011; Mell & Grance, 2011). Essential characteristics of cloud computing include the following:

- On demand self-service
- Broad network access
- Resource pooling
- Rapid elasticity
- Measured services

Cloud computing started to become popular in 2007, and since then it has demonstrated great implications for improving the well-being of society. Cloud computing does not seem to have a common standard or definition. Clouds consist of vast quantities of virtual resources that are easily accessible. These resources, such as hardware, development platforms, and/or services, can be dynamically adjusted to a variable load, allowing for optimum resource utilization (Vaquero, Rodero-Merino, Caceres, & Lindner, 2008). The user can use three key services with cloud computing: (1) software as a service (SaaS), (2) platform as a service (PaaS), and (3) infrastructure as a service (IaaS) (Iyer & Henderson, 2010) (FIGURE 7.4).

- *Software as a service (SaaS):* Hosting for these applications is provided via a cloud service. Consumers are provided access to the software over the Internet (e.g., EHRs, Google Docs) (Iyer & Henderson, 2010).
- *Platform as a service (PaaS):* A browser is used to access the development tools, which reside in the cloud (e.g., Google App Engine and Microsoft Azure). Developers can build and deploy web applications without installing any tools on their computer and without any specialized administrative skills.
- *Infrastructure as a service (IaaS):* Equipment that supports cloud operations, including hardware, servers, networking components, and storage facilities, is outsourced by the user. The provider owns the equipment and is responsible for housing, running, and maintaining it. Payment for services is usually on a per-use basis (e.g., Amazon Elastic Compute Cloud [EC2]) (Iyer & Henderson, 2010).

Models of Cloud Computing

The following four models have been recognized by the U.S. National Institute of Standards and Technology (NIST) for deploying cloud computing systems (FIGURE 7.5):

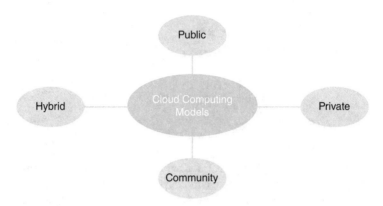

FIGURE 7.5 List of four cloud computing models

- *Public cloud:* Cloud services (including applications and storage features) are made readily accessible to the public on a pay-by-use basis by the provider (e.g., EC2). Users are able to pay for renting virtual computers that allow them to run their own applications and pay only for what they use.
- *Private cloud:* Cloud services and infrastructure are restricted to a single organization securing such service (e.g., Microsoft Azure).
- *Community cloud:* Several stakeholders or organizations pool resources to share cloud services (e.g., the Google GovCloud provides the Los Angeles City Council with a segregated data environment for storing its applications, as well as data that are accessible only to the city's agencies). This attracts policy and compliance concerns.
- *Hybrid cloud:* This comprises two or more clouds (private, public, or community). In this scenario, an organization would provide and manage resources within its own data centers and have others provided externally. An example is the hybrid cloud infrastructure formed by a collaboration between IBM and Juniper Networks (IBM & Juniper Networks, 2009). Cloud computing promises reliable software, hardware, and IaaS delivered over the Internet and remote data centers to perform complex large-scale computing tasks (Armbrust et al., 2010).

▶ VII. Leveraging Cloud Computing in Population Health

The use of cloud computing in health care is rapidly gaining popularity (Griebel et al., 2015). Researchers have proposed cloud computing as a new business paradigm for biomedical information sharing (Rosenthal et al., 2010). Prior research has shown benefit to health services via cloud computing (Kuo, Kushniruk, & Borycki, 2010). Cloud computing infrastructure helps stakeholders to respond to emerging public health threats by facilitating real-time vital data collection via a network of sensors. Further, it eliminates manual data collection and reduces typing errors (Rolim et al., 2010).

In the delivery of mobile health services, the use of cloud computing has helped facilitate processing of multimedia and complex algorithms (Nkosi & Mekuria, 2010). This has resulted in innovative ways of promoting health service delivery to marginalized rural communities. Typical examples of such initiatives include the Dhatri in Chennai, India, which combines wireless technologies with cloud computing services to provide remote access to patient health information by physicians from any location (Rao, Sundararaman, & Parthasarathi, 2010).

Cloud computing software owned by IBM and MedTrak Systems is being utilized by the American Occupational Network to update clinical protocols and digitize patient health records in an effort to improve healthcare delivery (Cloud News Desk, 2009). Acumen Solutions, a cloud-based customer relationship management and project management system, was chosen by the U.S. Department of Health and Human Services (DHHS) for the nationwide hosting of EHR systems in the United States (Kuo, 2011). The software facilitates interactions between the regional extension centers and the healthcare providers related to the selection and implementation of an EHR system (HealthImaging, 2010). In earlier research, an eHealth cloud was built to host healthcare applications and other administrative and clinical services (Korea IT Times, 2010). Many organizations, managers, and experts believe that the cloud computing approach can improve health services and benefit research (Chatman, 2010).

Benefits of Cloud Computing

The main drivers of cloud computing include economics, simplification, and the convenience of how computing-related services are delivered (Erdogmus, 2009). It removes the need for the use of expensive computing hardware, software, and dedicated space. It can also significantly reduce IT costs and complexities while improving workload optimization and service delivery (Lin, Fu, Zhu, & Dasmalchi, 2009). Cloud computing also reduces labor-related costs, because less people will be required to run a cloud-based IT infrastructure (Lin et al., 2009). The quality of service is a critical part of the cloud deployment to ensure that the committed services are readily offered with dynamic deployment of resources (Lin et al., 2009).

Application of Cloud Computing in Telemedicine

One study described 12-lead electrocardiogram telemedicine services based on cloud computing. The study describes processing, visualization, management, and e-learning services deployment within the commercial Microsoft Azure cloud platform. Financial implications and the pricing model were the primary reasons for adopting the Azure platform (Hsieh & Hsu, 2012).

Application of Cloud Computing in Medical Imaging

Medical imaging focuses on the storage, sharing, and computation of images. Archiving is another domain of high relevance for the use of cloud computing (Kagadis et al., 2013).

Application of Cloud Computing in Public Health and Patient Self-Management

The goal of public health is to prevent disease occurrence and promote health outcomes across various populations. HealthATM is a cloud-based personal health infrastructure to provide underserved population groups with instant access to their health information (Botts, Horan, & Thoms, 2011). Another prototype, MyPHR-Machines, utilizes cloud computing for storing health data. Patients can access their health records from remote virtual machines and can share them with selected caregivers (Van Gorp & Comuzzi, 2014). Cloud computing facilitates the use of large volumes of health data for public health reporting (Jalali, Olabode, & Bell, 2013).

Application of Cloud Computing in Hospital Management and Clinical Information Systems

A cloud-based medical service delivery framework (CMSDF) was established to enhance information, resource exchange, and interconnectedness between larger and smaller hospital networks or institutions (Yao et al., 2014). A cloud-based virtual desktop infrastructure was owned and managed by a large hospital that can now share its medical software using SaaS with the smaller healthcare institutions. This resulted in a cost savings (both maintenance and investment) of about 90% by the smaller facilities because they did not have to host such services independently (Yao et al., 2014).

▶ VIII. Cloud Computing Challenges and Opportunities

There are several concerns related to the ability of cloud computing to cope with business process change (Sultan, 2014). Data privacy, governance, integration issues, and security are some of the main concerns for healthcare providers using cloud computing. It takes about five years to realize the economic benefits of cloud computing (Sultan, 2013). Another concern is vendor-lock and failures because many cloud providers offer their services through proprietary application programming interfaces (APIs). Reliability also can be a serious problem for cloud users. Choosing the right cloud provider is a real challenge. Cloud computing requires rigorous evaluation prior to adoption. TABLE 7.2 provides a list of opportunities and challenges related to several aspects of cloud computing (Armbrust et al., 2009; Kuo, 2011).

Predominantly, three types of concerns regarding using cloud computing in health care have been identified. These are shown in TABLE 7.3. The biggest concern is that unauthorized persons might access medical data in a cloud that might hurt patient data confidentiality (ContactBabel, 2015). Reliability and transparency of data handling by third parties and lack of experience or evidence of a new technology are some of the other concerns related to the use of cloud computing in health care.

▶ IX. Strategy to Implement a Cloud Computing Platform

Health organizations need a strategic plan when they are considering moving their services into the cloud. Eight stages are involved in order to commence a cloud computing project: (1) proof of concept/pilot project, (2) strategy and roadmap, (3) modeling and architecture, (4) implementation planning, (5) implementation expansion, (6) integration, (7) collaboration, and (8) maturity. These stages are commonly known as the "cloud computing adoption life cycle" (Marks & Lozano,

TABLE 7.2 Cloud Computing Opportunities and Challenges		
Cloud Computing Aspects	**Opportunities**	**Challenges**
Management	Low cost of new IT infrastructure	Lack of trust by healthcare professionals
	Speeds deployment while maintaining vital flexibility	Cultural resistance
	Computing resources on demand	Loss of governance
	Payments made as needed	Uncertain providers compliance
Technology	Reduction of IT maintenance burdens	Resource exhaustion issues
	Scalability and flexibility of infrastructure	Unpredictable performance
	Advantage for green computing (Baliga, Ayre, Hinton, & Tucker, 2011)	Resource exhaustion
		Performance unpredictability (Durkee, 2010)
		Data lock-in—little capability of data, application, and service interoperability
		Bugs in large-scale distributed cloud systems
Security	Eliminates the new infrastructure cost and IT maintenance burdens (Schweitzer, 2012)	Separation failure
	Provides resources for protection of patient data	Public management interface issues
	Data security is increased through the replication of data in several locations.	Issues due to poor encryptions
	Resilience is strengthened through a variety of defensive resources.	Abuse of privileges

(continues)

TABLE 7.2 Cloud Computing Opportunities and Challenges (*continued*)

Cloud Computing Aspects	Opportunities	Challenges
Legal	Providers are bound by legal constraints to protect their customers' data and privacy.	Issues regarding data jurisdictions and boundaries
	Development of guidelines and technologies to enable the construction of trusted platforms by not-for-profit organizations	Privacy issues (Ward & Sipior, 2010)
	Facilitates government input in regulation of data privacy and protection	Intellectual property rights

TABLE 7.3 Using Cloud Computing in Health Care: Concerns and Recommendations

Concerns	Recommended Solutions
Data security and privacy threats	Secure transmission protocols Have special security certificates Identify users' roles via access control lists Digital signature Data encryption Use of standardized encryption algorithms Secure data transmission using Hypertext Transfer Protocol, Secure (HTTPS)
Reliability and transparency of data handling by third parties	Audit trails
Lack of experience or evidence of a new technology	Rigorous economic assessment is needed to verify the cost-effectiveness of cloud computing.

2010). The various procedures involved in converting traditional IT infrastructure to cloud service include: (1) assessment of demand and readiness for cloud computing, (2) strategic decision-making processes, (3) pilot implementation of cloud computing, (4) internal interconnection, (5) consideration of external resources, and (6) rigorous monitoring and evaluation of the processes (Stanoevska-Slabeva, Wozniak, & Hoyer, 2010; Stanoevska-Slabeva, Wozniak, & Ristol, 2009). The cloud computing strategic planning model consists of several implementation stages when deciding to move toward cloud computing (Lee & Kuo, 2009) (FIGURE 7.6).

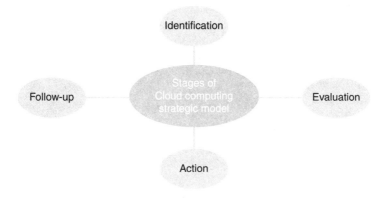

FIGURE 7.6 Strategic model showing the stages of cloud computing

- *Identification stage:* Determine a well-defined scope for the problem being faced. Problems can be analyzed through the use of root-cause techniques (Lee & Kuo, 2009).
- *Evaluation stage:* Evaluate the opportunities and challenges of adopting cloud computing. The European Network and Information Security Agency (ENISA, 2009), the Cloud Security Alliance (2011), and NIST (Jansen & Grance, 2011) have developed comprehensive guides to evaluate the benefits and risks of adopting cloud computing. Strengths, weaknesses, opportunities, and threats (SWOT) analysis should be performed to evaluate the feasibility of the cloud-based approach (Marston, Li, Bandyopadhyay, Zhang, & Ghalsasi, 2011). The user needs to assess methods to handle the identified issues.
- *Action stage:* Once the correct computing model is evaluated, the organization can employ the following five steps to create an implementation plan:
    - *Determine the cloud service and deployment model.* Determine which of the various cloud computing services to choose (SaaS, PaaS, and/or IaaS), as well as their models for deployment (either private, public, community, or hybrid) (Zhang & Liu, 2010).
    - *Compare different cloud providers.* A critical component of cloud computing implementation is identifying a suitable provider (Kuo, 2011).
    - *Obtain assurances from the selected cloud provider.* The cloud provider must provide assurances regarding the quality of service offered, such as technical support, on-demand access, cost per use, elasticity, and transparency in service provision (ENISA, 2009). Privacy and security provisions include data confidentiality, data integrity, system availability, authenticity, and authorization. Providers must ensure that these criteria are adequately met, and data are stored only in agreed-upon locations based on set stipulations.
    - *Consider future data migration.* Data portability must be considered up front as part of the plan (Antonopoulos & Gillam, 2010; Gagliardi & Muscella, 2010).
    - *Start a pilot implementation.* The pilot should be suitable for providing proof of the advantages of cloud computing for the organization (Stanoevska-Slabeva et al., 2009, 2010).
- *Follow-up stage:* This involves deployment of the cloud computing infrastructure and developing a strategic follow-up plan that outlines the service indicators to be measured and how they can be used to gauge improvements (Lee & Kuo, 2009).

There are several management, technology, security, and legal issues that need to be addressed despite the benefits associated with cloud computing applications for health care (Kuo, 2011). Cloud computing adoption is a complex process involving many factors. Rigorous evaluation of the different cloud computing factors is needed before introducing the new cloud computing model to an organization (Kuo, 2011).

▶ X. Introduction to Health Data Visualization

Healthcare datasets are typically multivariate, discrete, and at different granularity levels. They are so large and complex that they are difficult to manage with traditional software and/or hardware (Sharmila & Bhuvana, 2014). It is no longer efficient to perform traditional manual analysis of these datasets across different sources. New tools that can derive contextually relevant and meaningful insights from large data collections need to be developed. Exploratory visual analysis and advanced tool sets are needed to allow the user to interact with their data in a visual environment. One powerful option by which complex data could be made accessible and meaningful is through the use of interactive visualization. Interactive visualization enhances human visual ability in detecting and exploring new patterns (Meyer, Thomas, Diehl, Fisher, & Keim, 2010). Effective visualization technologies have the potential to transform raw data into actionable insights. This enables more effective population management and supports better understanding of health outcomes (Raghupathi & Raghupathi, 2014). Understanding how to best visualize is a central challenge to improving health care.

The graphical visualization of data dates back to the latter part of the 18th century (Playfair, 1801). The use of charts and graphs was considered the most effective way to communicate information about data (Spence, 2006). It shows a linear graph created by Charles Minard, which showed various paths taken by the Napoleonic army during its journey through Moscow and Europe (Tufte & Graves-Morris, 1983). This two-dimensional chart utilizes variables of time, geography, and temperature in visualization (West, Borland, & Hammond, 2015).

A plethora of scales, shapes, and colors have been used in characterizing both small and large datasets. Visual representations in the form of charts, graphs, and scatter plots are often utilized to identify patterns in datasets and inform knowledge discovery. Graphs are routinely used to illustrate data in a way in which comparisons, trends, and associations can be easily understood. However, new visualization techniques beyond graphs and charts are needed to accommodate the growing availability of electronic healthcare data.

▶ XI. Concepts of Geographic Information Science

Geographic information science (or GIScience) is a multidisciplinary field that utilizes innovations in GISs to make data meaningful and facilitate data exploration (Mark, 2003). The field includes many disciplines like cartography, remote sensing, surveying, and image processing (Mark, 2003). GIScience is described as a "science dealing with generic issues surrounding the use of GIS technology" (Goodchild, 1992). Three key dimensions are utilized in characterizing public health: (1) attribute (context), (2) spatial (geographic), and (3) temporal (time) (Joshi et al., 2012). Complexity in geospatial data analysis also arises from the large volumes of data, underlying relationships, and the nature of geographic problems (Gahegan, 2000; Openshaw, 2000).

Public health researchers often examine complex, multidimensional data. This enables them to identify patterns, thereby assembling meaningful information (Janelle & Hodge, 2000). As public health datasets become increasingly complex, there is a growing need for methods and tools to support the construction of knowledge. Public health information users find it challenging to explore datasets to derive insights (Hesse et al., 2010).

Visualization is the use of computer-supported interactive visual representations of data to intensify cognition, acquisition, or use of knowledge (Chen, Floridi, & Borgo, 2014) (FIGURE 7.7). There is a constant search for better visualization tools to allow users to benefit from geospatial analysis results and to support the decision-making process. Interactive visual representations take into account the user's perceptual and cognitive needs (Thomas, 2005).

Interactive visual representations allow stakeholders to control which subset of data needs to be visualized. Different representational forms can impact how cognitive activities are performed (Lee & Kuo, 2009). Interaction as a technique provides the user with the flexibility to tailor the content of the visual display as well as the format of information presented (Sedig & Parsons, 2013). Examples of such actions include filtering, annotating, drilling, selecting, and comparing.

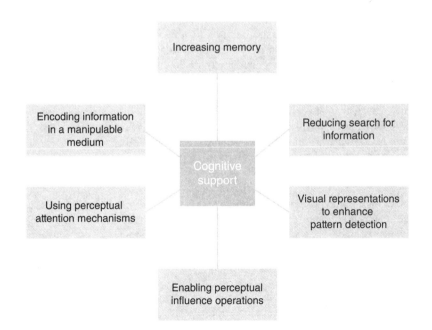

FIGURE 7.7 Features of interactive visualization

▶ XII. Information Visualization with Examples

Information visualization (InfoVis) is an interactive, visual representation of abstract, large-volume, and complex data to amplify cognition (Card, Mackinlay, & Shneiderman, 1999). It aids users in exploring, understanding, and analyzing data through progressive and iterative visual exploration. Users looking at large amounts of complex data can quickly find the information they need. It helps the users to navigate and interact with the data easily. Users can discover errors in the data and recognize patterns and trends. This process has two fundamentally related aspects: structural modeling and graphical representation (Chen, 2006). The structural modeling intends to detect, extract, and simplify underlying relationships. The graphical representation transforms an initial representation of a structure into a graphical one to facilitate visual interaction. InfoVis primarily deals with abstract, nonspatial data (e.g., numerical and nonnumerical data such as text and geographic information). The InfoVis pipeline has five main modules: data transformation and analysis, filtering, mapping, rendering, and user interface (UI) controls (Liu, Cui, Wu, & Liu, 2014). The input consists of data in either a structured or an unstructured format.

- *Data transformation and analysis module:* Extracts structured data from the input data.
- *Filtering module:* Selects data portions to be visualized.
- *Mapping module:* Selects data to geometric primitives (e.g., points, lines) and their attributes (e.g., color, position, size).
- *Rendering module:* Transforms data in geometric form into images.
- *UI controls:* Users interact with data through various UI controls to explore and understand data from multiple perspectives.

Specialized visualization tools are required for different data types with different characteristics and patterns. InfoVis helps users to quickly and accurately process information filtered through domain-specific knowledge to create meaningful abstractions of the data.

Visual representation can often communicate information much more rapidly and effectively than any other method. It expands the capacity of patients, clinicians, and public health policymakers to make better decisions (Schneiderman, Plaisant, & Hesse, 2013; Stadler, Donlon, Siewert, Franken, & Lewis, 2016).

Examples of InfoVis

LifeLines is an InfoVis tool for juvenile records, utilized by the Maryland Department of Juvenile Justice (Plaisant, Milash, Rose, Widoff, & Shneiderman, 1996). LifeLines provides a timeline of a single patient's temporal events. Time is represented on the horizontal axis, and events (problems, allergies, diagnoses, complaints, labs, imaging, medications, immunizations, communications) are listed vertically (West et al., 2015).

LifeLines2 evolved from LifeLines because users wanted to use multiple patient records to see both numerical and categorical data. The ability to drill down into details was recognized as an important feature (Wang, Wongsuphasawat, Plaisant, & Shneiderman, 2010).

TABLE 7.4 Visualization Challenges and Recommendations

InfoVis	Challenge	Solution Recommended
Data (quality, size, diversity)	Amount of EHR data and their display.	Use tools such as zoom, pan, and filter to reduce some of the clutter. Develop better ways to manage the massive amounts of data.
	Data size and complexity in EHRs are challenging.	Color, density, and filtering techniques should be used commonly.
	Data uncertainty in EHR, missing values, and inaccurate data.	Data normalization.
Users (needs, skills)	Users want to see both categorical and numerical data.	Look at detail. Provide training time to learn how to use the system.
Design (easy way to visually explore and analyze results)	Determining the best way to present information.	Give the user the ability to interact so that a great deal of information is available in a single screen.

Longitudinal data from EHRs displayed through innovative visualization techniques have tremendous potential for discovering useful information in the data. InfoVis is now commonly utilized in several applications for data analysis. However, challenges from research to date for EHR visualization can be classified primarily into three areas (West et al., 2015) (see TABLE 7.4).

The potential of InfoVis in facilitating exploration and knowledge discovery in healthcare data is the major factor influencing its adoption and implementation. To fully optimize EHR data, further research is needed to address the presenting challenges in visualization (Aigner, Federico, Gschwandtner, Miksch, & Rind, 2012).

▶ XIII. Geovisualization with Examples

Population health data are typically organized by geospatial unit. Modern computer technologies provide better opportunities for storage, management, visualization, and analysis of dynamic spatiotemporal data (Andrienko, Andrienko, & Gatalsky, 2003). Maps have become a visualization interface for geographic data to facilitate decision making.

GeoVis integrates knowledge and expertise from various related fields such as scientific visualization, InfoVis, and virtual environments. GeoVis uses visual geospatial displays to explore data, generate hypotheses, develop problem solutions, and construct knowledge. It allows users to see the information visually on a map that is otherwise hidden in the complexity of the data. Visual representations enable users to communicate information in a more meaningful and effective manner. It can help stakeholders make evidence-based, informed decisions (Malczewski, 2006). GeoVis focuses on integration of visual, statistical, and computational methods to support knowledge creation with geographically referenced data and information (Dykes, MacEachren, & Kraak, 2005; MacEachren & Ganter, 1990; MacEachren et al., 2004). Features such as lines, dots, and shapes are utilized in representing data elements (e.g., scatter plots, heat maps, bar charts) (Sedig, Parsons, Dittmer, & Ola, 2012). GeoVis analytic tools combine data analytics and interactive visualizations to support users' reasoning (Thomas, 2005). It focuses on space and time and must support visual outputs (Gershon & Page, 2001). For visual exploration, one needs to analyze first, show the important information, zoom/filter, analyze further, and provide details on demand (Abousalh-Neto, 2013).

The geographic visualization pipeline consists of several features, including the following:

- *Data sources:* As mentioned previously, population health data have three dimensions: attribute, spatial, and temporal. Attribute (context) can be illustrated by the social and environmental contexts in population health. The spatial (geographic) component characterizes location attributes of data including address, state, or country, while providing insight into how and where essential services can be located. The temporal (time) component records the time of the observation and enables users to learn from the past to predict, plan, and build the future.
- *Analytics engine:* This stores, transforms, and performs computational analysis on data. It involves three substages:
  - *Data preprocessing:* Data are rapidly retrieved from a variety of sources (e.g., data cleaning, integration, fusion, and synthesis).
  - *Data transformation:* Preprocessed data are converted into a form that is more conducive to data analysis (e.g., data normalization and aggregation).
  - *Data analysis:* Pattern discovery and extraction of valuable information. Managing population health data is often challenging owing to the volume, velocity, veracity, and variety associated with big data (LaPelle, Luckmann, Simpson, & Martin, 2006).
- *Interactive visualization engine:* This takes analyzed data and creates interactive visual representations. It allows the user to access, restructure, analyze, and modify the amount and form of displayed information (e.g., by replacing a line graph with a bar chart). The user has the flexibility to manipulate the subset of information being displayed, directing the process of analysis and sequence of steps involved.

GeoVis analytic tools allow users to represent data in a visual format in the way they want. These tools address most of the persistent data analysis problems of big data. The tools facilitate analytic reasoning from collaboration between the user and the tool (Keim, Mansmann, & Thomas, 2010; Parsons & Sedig, 2014a, 2014b; Sedig & Parsons, 2013). There is a need to align user tasks with the output of the visualization process. External representation conveys information and determines the users' cognitive behavior. The users seek to coordinate their internal representations and the tool's external representations (Zhang, 2001). Interactions should be flexible enough to help users select the subset of data to be displayed, apply the optimal analytic technique needed, and customize the visual displays. The selection of appropriate analysis tools depends on the spatiotemporal data to be analyzed and the goals of analysis. Quality of interaction is an important consideration during the use of GeoVis analytic tools (Sedig, Parsons, & Babanski, 2012). GeoVis analytic tools allow researchers and decision makers to identify patterns and relationships in data as well as other geographic characteristics that were not clearly visible. Visual thinking guides decision making in various public health domains including investigations on disease incidence, public health resource allocation, and policymaking (Bell, Hoskins, Pickle, & Wartenberg, 2006). Results need to be conveyed to different groups of stakeholders including policymakers, hospital directors, and community group leaders who were not involved in the analysis process (O'Carroll, Cahn, Auston, & Selden, 1998).

GeoVis analytic tools can facilitate collaboration and efficiently provide comprehensible assessments to stakeholders. Current GeoVis analytic tools have the potential to enable the use of new sources of data in public health practice.

- *Health assessment:* Stakeholders in public health have historically utilized static representations, as seen in John Snow's mapping technique in characterizing the cholera outbreak of 1850 (Snow, 1855). Public health stakeholders stand to benefit from tools that allow users to manipulate visual representations (Sopan et al., 2012).

- *Policy development:* Stakeholders in public health often utilize visualizations for a variety of tasks including prioritizing needs, identifying supporting evidence, contrasting policy options, and ultimately making evidence-based decisions. Frequently used maps in public health research are dot-density and chloropleth maps. Dot-density maps are the simplest way to display events and are useful for area comparisons. Choropleth maps are "area maps in which polygons are shaded, colored, or patterned according to the value of a given attribute for each polygon" (Schabas, 2002). These maps are also frequently known as thematic or shaded maps. Appropriate color choices, map size, patterns, shapes, and intervals need to be carefully considered because they greatly influence how the information presented is interpreted.

These visualizations present various options and potential outcomes to enable decision makers to select a course of action. Stakeholders are responsible for engaging in a variety of activities including policy enforcement, information dissemination, health resource allocation, workforce education, and evaluation of health services (Bloom, 1999). Visualization tools enable such stakeholders to be able to assess the progress of service delivery indicators, program impact, stakeholder capacity in handling outbreaks, and resource supply during epidemic situations. These tools can be utilized to ensure health resources are managed and dispensed properly.

Sanaviz, an Internet-enabled interactive visualization platform, was implemented to visualize spatiotemporal data (Joshi et al., 2012). Components of the prototype include: (1) a user module that helps to create user profiles based on individual demographics, prior technology expertise, and users' level of understanding about spatiotemporal data; (2) a user management module that helps in providing role-based user access; (3) a data management module that enables users to perform requisite functions such as data import, export, updates, and modifications; (4) a visual display module that enables users to view the data in various formats including charts, graphs, and maps; and (5) a UI module that allows users to engage interactively with the data to gather different insights. The interaction features such as zooming, highlighting, sorting, and multiple linkages provide necessary information to the users to explore their data using different perspectives (FIGURE 7.8).

Geovisual analytic tools for population health show promising results; however, there is an increasing need to assess the usefulness and usability of GeoVis applications as new types of interactions emerge (Muntz et al., 2003). It is essential to focus on the effectiveness, usefulness, and performance of GeoVis applications. Studies have shown that the majority of existing GeoVis applications are designed according to technology and software engineering principles. Recently, there has been a shift toward user-centered design (Fuhrmann et al., 2005; Timpka, Ölvander, & Hallberg, 2008). Domain-specific considerations have been overlooked, and end user input is often incorporated much later when key design and functionality components have already been decided upon.

Some negatives of GeoVis applications are that they are difficult to learn and use, are predominantly generic, and do not address specific users (Robinson, Chen, Lengerich, Meyer, & MacEachren, 2005). Better GeoVis applications can be created through a usability approach and with knowledge of cognitive processes (Slocum et al., 2001).

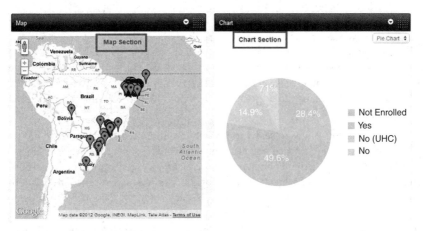

FIGURE 7.8 Sanaviz, a GeoVis platform

▶ XIV. Challenges Related to Interactive Data Visualization

Interactive data visualization in the healthcare domain presents many exciting opportunities along with many challenges. These challenges are related to data complexity, data variety, data quality, and data heterogeneity. Challenges related to data complexity are many of the big data challenges related to data velocity, veracity, volume, variety, and value. Another greater challenge for visualization in the healthcare domain is the variety of data dimensions and the variety of data representations within those dimensions that are available. Data quality issues related to missing or invalid data are common due to improper data entry or a lack of system interoperability. Uncertainty visualization is another critical issue that must be addressed. Heterogeneity of data sources is another growing problem. Efforts are ongoing to federate data across the fragmented systems to enable epidemiological surveillance and population health research activities. In addition, there is a challenge of linking data across different sources. Privacy issues can limit the amount of information available to perform the linking.

Despite these challenges, visualization is well-suited to summarizing large volumes of data. Many common representations, such as bar charts and other proportional symbols, work well regardless of the number of data entities being visualized. Many of the technologies developed, such as Hadoop and Spark, can be adopted in the healthcare field and can help manage ever-growing data stores. Progressive approaches to visual analytics can be employed. Visualization must be developed to enable users to navigate complex variable space. Visualizations must be able to effectively handle and display multiple data types (e.g. numerical, categorical, and hierarchical) and then show relationships between them. Effective visualizations must reveal interesting temporal patterns involving discrete events, interval events, and various measures recorded repeatedly over time. Visualizations must be designed to work effectively with data quality issues and should highlight deficiencies in the underlying data for users to consider as part of their analysis. Visualizations that help users identify interesting trends or insights are often insufficient. Purely statistical approaches have their own limitations, including lack of interpretability and contextualization. Visualizations presenting relationships between data entities and variables should provide effective tools. Visualization further helps users identify and correctly discount relationships that are most likely to be spurious.

▶ XV. Conclusion

New, flexible, and expandable IT infrastructure makes big data analytics in health care possible. However, these innovative promises of big data techniques are likely to be hindered without proper ICT infrastructure, analytic tools, and visualization approaches (Roski, Bo-Linn, & Andrews, 2014). Among the most important issues related to big data is privacy (Barrett et al., 2013). Other challenges are logistical and ethical challenges related to massive protected and personal datasets (Barrett et al., 2013). Long-standing issues surrounding patient consent, data confidentiality, data access, and oversight will need to be addressed (Michael, 2016). There are also technical difficulties, including incompatibility, that exist when combining data from different source datasets.

Cloud computing provides opportunities for improving healthcare services and facilitating research at reduced costs. However, a major issue in cloud computing adoption is in the area of data security and legal issues. Governments foster regulations to protect cloud users' data security and privacy (Minister of Justice, Canada, 2011; U.S. Department of Health and Human Services, n.d.). Negotiations and contract evaluations are necessary tools in resolving the majority of the legal issues and concerns with cloud computing (Schweitzer, 2012). Advancement in big data and cloud computing provides an opportunity to design and develop visual interfaces to represent meaningful data in a format that is easy to understand.

The visual display of data must be tailored for a lay audience with potentially limited numeracy and medical knowledge. Simple, straightforward designs with recognized graphical representations are likely to be the most successful. Visualization tools must be developed to help care managers perform data-driven risk stratification or other forms of population segmentation.

Rapid uptake of information and communication technologies in the health sector have resulted in the massive growth of big data. This has created the need to develop a research agenda in the areas of cloud computing and GeoVis analytics that can drive improvement in the population health outcomes across individuals living in geographic settings. There is also an urgent need to have a trained workforce with a combined expertise in the areas of informatics, data analytics, and population health.

References

Abousalh-Neto, N. (2013). The forest and the trees: See it all with SAS® Visual Analytics.

Aigner, W., Federico, P., Gschwandtner, T., Miksch, S., & Rind, A. (2012). Challenges of time-oriented data in visual analytics for healthcare. In *IEEE VisWeek Workshop on Visual Analytics in Healthcare.*

Andrienko, N., Andrienko, G., & Gatalsky, P. (2003). Exploratory spatio-temporal visualization: An analytical review. *Journal of Visual Languages and Computing, 14*(6), 503–541.

Antonopoulos, N., & Gillam, L. (Eds.). (2010). *Cloud computing: Principles, systems and applications.* London, England: Springer Science & Business Media.

Armbrust, M., Fox, A., Griffith, R., Joseph, A. D., Katz, R. H., Konwinski, A., . . . Zaharia, M. (2009). Above the clouds: A Berkeley view of cloud computing. UC Berkley Technical Report. Retrieved from http://www.eecs.berkeley.edu/Pubs/TechRpts/2009/EECS-2009-28.html

Armbrust, M., Fox, A., Griffith, R., Joseph, A. D., Katz, R., Konwinski, A., . . . Zaharia, M. (2010). A view of cloud computing. *Communications of the ACM, 53*(4), 50–58.

Baliga, J., Ayre, R. W., Hinton, K., & Tucker, R. S. (2011). Green cloud computing: Balancing energy in processing, storage, and transport. *Proceedings of the IEEE, 99*(1), 149–167.

Barrett, M. A., Humblet, O., Hiatt, R. A., & Adler, N. E. (2013). Big data and disease prevention: From quantified self to quantified communities. *Big Data, 1*(3), 168–175.

Bell, B. S., Hoskins, R. E., Pickle, L. W., & Wartenberg, D. (2006). Current practices in spatial analysis of cancer data: Mapping health statistics to inform policymakers and the public. *International Journal of Health Geographics, 5*(1), 1.

Bloom, B. R. (1999). The future of public health. *Nature, 402*, C63–C64.

Botts, N. E., Horan, T. A., & Thoms, B. P. (2011). HealthATM: Personal health cyberinfrastructure for underserved populations. *American Journal of Preventive Medicine, 40*(5), S115–S122.

Brown, J. L. (2012). The unasked question. *Journal of the American Medical Association, 308*(18), 1869–1870.

Cadmus-Bertram, L., Marcus, B. H., Patterson, R. E., Parker, B. A., & Morey, B. L. (2015). Use of the Fitbit to measure adherence to a physical activity intervention among overweight or obese, postmenopausal women: Self-monitoring trajectory during 16 weeks. *JMIR mHealth and uHealth, 3*(4), e96.

Card, S. K., Mackinlay, J. D., & Shneiderman, B. (1999). *Readings in information visualization: Using vision to think.* San Francisco, CA: Morgan Kaufmann Publishers.

Carter, M. C., Burley, V. J., Nykjaer, C., & Cade, J. E. (2013). 'My Meal Mate'(MMM): Validation of the diet measures captured on a smartphone application to facilitate weight loss. *British Journal of Nutrition, 109*(03), 539–546.

Chatman, C. (2010). How cloud computing is changing the face of health care information technology. *Journal of Health Care Compliance, 12*(3), 37–38.

Chen, C. (2006). Extracting salient structures. In C. Chen (Ed.), *Information visualization: Beyond the horizon* (pp. 27–63). London, England: Springer.

Chen, M., Floridi, L., & Borgo, R. (2014). What is visualization really for? In L. Floridi & P. Illari (Eds.), *The philosophy of information quality* (pp. 75–93). Switzerland: Springer.

Chen, P. C. L., & Zhang, Y. C. (2014). Data-intensive applications, challenges, techniques and technologies: A survey on big data. *Information Sciences, 275,* 314–347.

Chowdhary, S. K., Yadav, A., & Garg, N. (2011, April). Cloud computing: Future prospect for e-health. In *Electronics Computer Technology (ICECT), 2011 3rd International Conference on Electronics Computer Technology* (Vol. 3, pp. 297–299). Kanyakumari, India: Institute of Electrical and Electronics Engineers.

Cloud News Desk. (2009). Cloud expo: Healthcare clients adopt electronic health records with cloud-based services. Retrieved from http://cloudcomputing.sys-con.com/node/886530

Cloud Security Alliance. (2011). Security guidance for critical areas of focus in cloud computing v3. 0. Retrieved from https://downloads.cloudsecurityalliance.org/initiatives/guidance/csaguide .v3.0.pdf

ContactBabel. (2015). The US contact center decision-makers' guide 2015. Retrieved from http://www.contactbabel.com/pdfs/jul2015/US%20DMG%202015%20-%20July%2028th%20 2015%20v10%20(optimized).pdf

Coughlin, S. S., Whitehead, M., Sheats, J. Q., Mastromonico, J., Hardy, D., & Smith, S. A. (2015). Smartphone applications for promoting healthy diet and nutrition: A literature review. *Jacobs Journal of Food and Nutrition, 2*(3), 21.

Dean, J., & Ghemawat, S. (2008). MapReduce: Simplified data processing on large clusters. *Communications of the ACM, 51*(1), 107–113.

Durkee, D. (2010). Why cloud computing will never be free. *Queue, 8*(4), 20.

Dykes, J., MacEachren, A. M., & Kraak, M. J. (2005). *Exploring geovisualization.* Amsterdam, Netherlands: Elsevier.

Erdogmus, H. (2009). Cloud computing: Does nirvana hide behind the nebula? *IEEE Software, 26*(2), 4–6.

European Network and Information Security Agency. (2009). Cloud computing: Benefits, risks and recommendations for information security. Retrieved from http://www.enisa.europa.eu/act /rm/files/deliverables/cloud-computing-risk-assessment

Federal Trade Commission. (2015). *Internet of things: Privacy & security in a connected world.* Washington, DC: Author.

Freedman, L. F. (2009). The Health Information Technology for Economic and Clinical Health Act (HITECH Act): Implications for the adoption of health information technology, HIPAA, and privacy and security issues. Retrieved from https://www.nixonpeabody.com//media/Files /Alerts/Health_Law_Alert_02_23_2009.ashx

Frost, S. (2015). Drowning in big data? Reducing information technology complexities and costs for healthcare organizations. Retrieved from https://www.emc.com/collateral/analyst-reports /frost-sullivan-reducing-information-technology-complexities-ar.pdf

Fuhrmann, S., Ahonen-Rainio, P., Edsall, R. M., Fabrikant, S. I., Koua, E. L., Tobón, C., . . . Wilson, S. (2005). Making useful and useable geovisualization: Design and evaluation issues. *Exploring Geovisualization,* 551–566.

Gagliardi, F., & Muscella, S. (2010). Cloud computing—data confidentiality and interoperability challenges. In N. Antonoloulos & L. Gillam (Eds.), *Cloud computing* (pp. 257–270). London, England: Springer.

Gahegan, M. (2000). Visualization as a tool for geocomputation. In D. Martin & P. Atkinson (Eds.), *GeoComputation* (pp. 253–274). London, England: Taylor & Francis.

Gandomi, A., & Haider, M. (2015). Beyond the hype: Big data concepts, methods, and analytics. *International Journal of Information Management, 35*(2), 137–144.

Garber, L. (2012). Using in-memory analytics to quickly crunch big data. *IEEE Computing Society, 45*(10), 16–18.

Gershon, N., & Page, W. (2001). What storytelling can do for information visualization. *Communications of the ACM, 44*(8), 31–37.

Goodchild, M. F. (1992). Geographical information science. *International Journal of Geographical Information Systems, 6*, 31–45. doi:10.1080/02693799208901893

Griebel, L., Prokosch, H. U., Köpcke, F., Toddenroth, D., Christoph, J., Leb, I., . . . Sedlmayr, M. (2015). A scoping review of cloud computing in healthcare. *BMC Medical Informatics and Decision Making, 15*(1), 1.

Hashem, I. A. T., Yaqoob, I., Anuar, N. B., Mokhtar, S., Gani, A., & Khan, S. U. (2015). The rise of "big data" on cloud computing: Review and open research issues. *Information Systems, 47*, 98–115.

HealthImaging. (2010). Acumen nabs ONC cloud computing contract. Retrieved from http://www.healthimaging.com/topics/practice-management/acumen-nabs-onc-cloud-computing-contract

Hesse, B. W., Hansen, D., Finholt, T., Munson, S., Kellogg, W., & Thomas, J. C. (2010). Social participation in health 2.0. *IEEE Computer, 43*(11), 45–52.

Hsieh, J. C., & Hsu, M. W. (2012). A cloud computing based 12-lead ECG telemedicine service. *BMC Medical Informatics and Decision Making, 12*(1), 1.

IBM & Juniper Networks. (2009). IBM and Juniper Networks: Transforming and simplifying your networking infrastructure. Retrieved from https://www-07.ibm.com/smb/in/services/industry_special/hd/images/IBM_Juniper.pdf

Iyer, B., & Henderson, J. C. (2010). Preparing for the future: Understanding the seven capabilities of cloud computing. *MIS Quarterly Executive, 9*(2), 117–131.

Jagadish, H. V., Gehrke, J., Labrinidis, A., Papakonstantinou, Y., Patel, J. M., Ramakrishnan, R., & Shahabi, C. (2014). Big data and its technical challenges. *Communications of the ACM, 57*(7), 86–94.

Jalali, A., Olabode, O. A., & Bell, C. M. (2013). Leveraging cloud computing to address public health disparities: An analysis of the SPHPS. *Online Journal of Public Health Informatics, 4*(3).

Janelle, D. G., & Hodge, D. C. (2000). *Information, place, and cyberspace: Issues in accessibility.* New York, NY: Springer.

Jansen, W., & Grance, T. (2011). Guidelines on security and privacy in public cloud computing. Retrieved from http://nvlpubs.nist.gov/nistpubs/Legacy/SP/nistspecialpublication800-144.pdf

Joshi, A., de Araujo Novaes, M., Machiavelli, J., Iyengar, S., Vogler, R., Johnson, C., & Hsu, C. E. (2012). Designing human centered GeoVisualization application—the SanaViz—for telehealth users: A case study. *Technology and Health Care, 20*(6), 503–518.

Kagadis, G. C., Kloukinas, C., Moore, K., Philbin, J., Papadimitroulas, P., Alexakos, C., . . . Hendee, W. R. (2013). Cloud computing in medical imaging. *Medical Physics, 40*(7), 070901.

Kass-Hout, T. A., & Alhinnawi, H. (2013). Social media in public health. *British Medical Bulletin, 108*(1), 5–24.

Keim, D. A., Mansmann, F., & Thomas, J. (2010). Visual analytics: How much visualization and how much analytics? *ACM SIGKDD Explorations Newsletter, 11*(2), 5–8.

Kindig, D., & Stoddart, G. (2003). What is population health? *American Journal of Public Health, 93*(3), 380–383.

Korea IT Times. (2010). Telstra plans launch of e-health cloud services, tip of the iceberg for opportunity. Retrieved from http://www.koreaittimes.com/story/9826/telstra-plans-launch-e-health-cloud-services-tip-iceberg-opportunity

Kudyba, S. P. (2010). *Healthcare informatics: Improving efficiency and productivity*. Portland, OR: CRC Press.

Kuo, M. H. (2011). Opportunities and challenges of cloud computing to improve health care services. *Journal of Medical Internet Research, 13*(3), e67.

Kuo, M. H., Kushniruk, A., & Borycki, E. (2010). Can cloud computing benefit health services? A SWOT analysis. *Studies in Health Technology and Informatics, 169*, 379–383.

Labrinidis, A., & Jagadish, H. V. (2012). Challenges and opportunities with big data. *Proceedings of the VLDB Endowment, 5*(12), 2032–2033.

LaPelle, N. R., Luckmann, R., Simpson, E. H., & Martin, E. R. (2006). Identifying strategies to improve access to credible and relevant information for public health professionals: A qualitative study. *BMC Public Health, 6*(1), 1.

Lee, T. S., & Kuo, M. H. (2009). Toyota A3 report: A tool for process improvement in healthcare. *Studies in Health Technology and Informatics, 143*, 235–240.

Lin, G., Fu, D., Zhu, J., & Dasmalchi, G. (2009). Cloud computing: IT as a service. *IT Professional Magazine, 11*(2), 10.

Liu, S., Cui, W., Wu, Y., & Liu, M. (2014). A survey on information visualization: Recent advances and challenges. *Visual Computer, 30*(12), 1373–1393.

MacEachren, A. M., Gahegan, M., Pike, W., Brewer, I., Cai, G., Lengerich, E., & Hardistry, F. (2004). Geovisualization for knowledge construction and decision support. *IEEE Computer Graphics and Applications, 24*(1), 13–17.

MacEachren, A. M., & Ganter, J. H. (1990). A pattern identification approach to cartographic visualization. *Cartographica, 27*(2), 64–81.

Maciejewski, R., Rudolph, S., Hafen, R., Abusalah, A., Yakout, M., Ouzzani, M., . . . Ebert, D. S. (2010). A visual analytics approach to understanding spatiotemporal hotspots. *IEEE Transactions on Visualization and Computer Graphics, 16*(2), 205–220.

Malczewski, J. (2006). GIS based multicriteria decision analysis: A survey of the literature. *International Journal of Geographical Information Science*, 703–726.

Mark, D. M. (2003). Geographic information science: Defining the field. *Foundations of Geographic Information Science, 1*, 3–18.

Marks, E. A., & Lozano, B. (2010). *Executive's guide to cloud computing*. Hoboken, NJ: John Wiley and Sons.

Marston, S., Li, Z., Bandyopadhyay, S., Zhang, J., & Ghalsasi, A. (2011). Cloud computing—The business perspective. *Decision Support Systems, 51*(1), 176–189.

Mekaru, S. R., Hansen, A. L., Freifeld, C. C., & Brownstein, J. S. (2015). Appendix D: The HealthMap system (online only). Retrieved from http://wwwnc.cdc.gov/travel/yellowbook/2016/appendices/appendix-d-the-healthmap-system

Mell, P., & Grance, T. (2011). The NIST definition of cloud computing. Retrieved from https://www.nist.gov/sites/default/files/documents/itl/cloud/cloud-def-v15.pdf

Meyer, J., Thomas, J., Diehl, S., Fisher, B., & Keim, D. A. (2010). From visualization to visually enabled reasoning. *Dagstuhl Follow-Ups, 1*, 227–245.

Michael, R. (2016). Does the convergence of big data and health tech mean big brother is coming? Retrieved from https://www.verywell.com/the-convergence-of-big-data-and-health-technology-1739118

Minister of Justice, Canada. (2011). Personal Information Protection and Electronic Documents Act (PIPEDA). Retrieved from http://www.laws-lois.justice.gc.ca/eng/acts/P-8.6/FullText.html

Muntz, R., Barclay, T., Dozier, J., Faloutsos, C., MacEachren, A., Martin, J., & Satyanarayanan, M. (2003). *IT roadmap to a geospatial future, report of the Committee on Intersections Between Geospatial Information and Information Technology*. Washington, DC: National Academy of Sciences.

Murdoch, T. B., & Detsky, A. S. (2013). The inevitable application of big data to health care. *Journal of the American Medical Association, 309*(13), 1351–1352.

Nkosi, M. T., & Mekuria, F. (2010, November). Cloud computing for enhanced mobile health applications. In *Cloud Computing Technology and Science (CloudCom), 2010 IEEE Second*

International Conference on Social Computing (pp. 629–633). Minneapolis, MN: Institute of Electrical and Electronics Engineers.

O'Carroll, P. W., Cahn, M. M. A., Auston, M. I., & Selden, M. C. R. (1998). Information needs in public health and health policy: Results of recent studies. *Journal of Urban Health, 75*(4), 785–793.

Openshaw, S. (2000). GeoComputation. In S. Openshaw & R. J. Abrahart (Eds.), *GeoComputation*. London, England: Taylor & Francis.

Parsons, P., & Sedig, K. (2014a). Common visualizations: Their cognitive utility. In W. Huang (Ed.), *Handbook of human centric visualization* (pp. 671–691). New York, NY: Springer.

Parsons, P., & Sedig, K. (2014b). Distribution of information processing while performing complex cognitive activities with visualization tools. In W. Huang (Ed.), *Handbook of human centric visualization* (pp. 693–715). New York, NY: Springer.

Plaisant, C., Milash, B., Rose, A., Widoff, S., & Shneiderman, B. (1996, April). LifeLines: Visualizing personal histories. In *Proceedings of the SIGCHI conference on Human Factors in Computing Systems* (pp. 221–227). The Hague, Netherlands: Association for Computing Machinery.

Playfair, W. (1801). *The statistical breviary; shewing, on a principle entirely new, the resources of every state and kingdom in Europe; illustrated with stained copper plate charts, representing the physical powers of each distinct nation with ease and perspicuity. To which is added, a similar exhibition of the ruling powers of Hindoostan.* London, England: John Wallis.

Raghupathi, W., & Raghupathi, V. (2014). Big data analytics in healthcare: Promise and potential. *Health Information Science and Systems, 2*(1), 1.

Rao, G. S. V. R. K., Sundararaman, K., & Parthasarathi, J. (2010). Dhatri: A pervasive cloud initiative for primary healthcare services. In *Proceedings of the 2010 14th International Conference on Intelligence in Next Generation Networks (ICIN),* October 11–14, 2010, Berlin, Germany. New York, NY: Institute of Electrical and Electronics Engineers.

Robinson, A. C., Chen, J., Lengerich, G., Meyer, H., & MacEachren, A. M. (2005). Combining usability techniques to design geovisualization tools for epidemiology. *Cartography and Geographic Information Science, 32.*

Rolim, C. O., Koch, F. L., Westphall, C. B., Werner, J., Fracalossi, A., & Salvador, G. S. (2010, February). A cloud computing solution for patient's data collection in health care institutions. In *eHealth, Telemedicine, and Social Medicine, 2010. ETELEMED'10. Second International Conference on eHealth, Telemedicine and Social Medicine* (pp. 95–99). St. Maarten, Netherlands: Institute of Electrical and Electronics Engineers.

Rosenthal, A., Mork, P., Li, M. H., Stanford, J., Koester, D., & Reynolds, P. (2010). Cloud computing: A new business paradigm for biomedical information sharing. *Journal of Biomedical Informatics, 43*(2), 342–353.

Roski, J., Bo-Linn, G. W., & Andrews, T. A. (2014). Creating value in health care through big data: Opportunities and policy implications. *Health Affairs, 33*(7), 1115–1122.

Salas-Vega, S., Haimann, A., & Mossialos, E. (2015). Big data and health care: Challenges and opportunities for coordinated policy development in the EU. *Health Systems and Reform, 1*(4), 285–300.

Schabas, R. (2002). Is public health ethical? [Editorial]. *Canadian Journal of Public Health, 93*(2), 98–99.

Schneiderman, B., Plaisant, C., & Hesse, B. W. (2013). *Improving health and healthcare with interactive visualization methods.* IEEE Computer, Special Issue on Challenges in Information Visualization, *46*(5), 58–66.

Schweitzer, E. J. (2012). Reconciliation of the cloud computing model with US federal electronic health record regulations. *Journal of the American Medical Informatics Association, 19*(2), 161–165.

Sedig, K., & Parsons, P. (2013). Interaction design for complex cognitive activities with visual representations: A pattern-based approach. *AIS Transactions on Human-Computer Interaction, 2*(5), 84–133.

Sedig, K., Parsons, P., & Babanski, A. (2012). Towards a characterization of interactivity in visual analytics. *Journal of Manipulative and Physiological Therapeutics, 3*(1), 12–28.

Sedig, K., Parsons, P., Dittmer, M., & Ola, O. (2012). Beyond information access: Support for complex cognitive activities in public health informatics tools. *Online Journal of Public Health Informatics, 4*(3).

Sharmila, K., & Bhuvana, R. (2014). Role of big data analytic in healthcare using data mining. Retrieved from http://www.ejerm.com/vol1_spl_sep2014/img/Role_of_Big_Data_Analytic_in _Healthcare_Using_Data_Mining.pdf

Slocum, T. A., Blok, C., Jiang, B., Koussoulakou, A., Montello, D. R., Fuhrmann, S, & Hedley, N. R. (2001). Cognitive and usability issues in geovisualization. *Cartography and Geographic Information Science, 28*(1), 61–75.

Snow, J. (1855). *On the mode of communication of cholera.* London, England: John Churchill.

Sopan, A., Noh, A. S. I., Karol, S., Rosenfeld, P., Lee, G., & Shneiderman, B. (2012). Community health map: A geospatial and multivariate data visualization tool for public health datasets. *Government Information Quarterly, 29*(2), 223–234.

Spence, I. (2006). William Playfair and the psychology of graphs. In *2006 JSM Proceedings* (pp. 2426–2436). Alexandria, VA: American Statistical Association.

Stadler, J. G., Donlon, K., Siewert, J. D., Franken, T., & Lewis, N. E. (2016). Improving the efficiency and ease of healthcare analysis through use of data visualization dashboards. *Big Data, 4*(2), 129–135.

Stanoevska-Slabeva, K., Wozniak, T., & Hoyer, V. (2010). Practical guidelines for evolving IT infrastructure towards grids and clouds. In K. Stanoevska-Slabeva, T. Wozniak, & S. Ristol (Eds.), *Grid and cloud computing: A business perspective on technology and applications* (pp. 225–243). Berlin, Germany: Springer.

Stanoevska-Slabeva, K., Wozniak, T., & Ristol, S. (Eds.). (2009). *Grid and cloud computing: A business perspective on technology and applications.* Berlin, Germany: Springer Science & Business Media.

Sultan, N. (2013). Knowledge management in the age of cloud computing and Web 2.0: Experiencing the power of disruptive innovations. *International Journal of Information Management, 33*(1), 160–165.

Sultan, N. (2014). Making use of cloud computing for healthcare provision: Opportunities and challenges. *International Journal of Information Management, 34*(2), 177–184.

Thomas, J. J. (2005). Illuminating the path: The research and development agenda for visual analytics. Los Alamitos, CA: IEEE Computer Society.

Timpka, T., Ölvander, C., & Hallberg, N. (2008). Information system needs in health promotion: A case study of the safe community programme using requirements engineering methods. *Health Informatics Journal, 14*(3), 183–193.

Tufte, E. R., & Graves-Morris, P. R. (1983). *The visual display of quantitative information, 2*(9). Cheshire, CT: Graphics Press.

U.S. Department of Health and Human Services. (n.d.). The Health Insurance Portability and Accountability Act of 1996 (HIPAA) privacy and security rules. Retrieved from https://www .hhs.gov/sites/default/files/privacysummary.pdf

Van Gorp, P., & Comuzzi, M. (2014). Lifelong personal health data and application software via virtual machines in the cloud. *IEEE Journal of Biomedical and Health Informatics, 18*(1), 36–45.

Vaquero, L. M., Rodero-Merino, L., Caceres, J., & Lindner, M. (2008). A break in the clouds: Towards a cloud definition. *ACM SIGCOMM Computer Communication Review, 39*(1), 50–55.

Vayena, E., Salathé, M., Madoff, L. C., & Brownstein, J. S. (2015). Ethical challenges of big data in public health. *PLoS Computational Biology, 11*(2), e1003904.

Wang, T. D., Wongsuphasawat, K., Plaisant, C., & Shneiderman, B. (2010, November). Visual information seeking in multiple electronic health records: Design recommendations and a process model. In *Proceedings of the 1st ACM International Health Informatics Symposium* (pp. 46–55). New York, NY: Association for Computing Machinery.

Ward, B. T., & Sipior, J. C. (2010). The Internet jurisdiction risk of cloud computing. *Information Systems Management, 27*(4), 334–339.

Ward, J. S., & Barker, A. (2013). Undefined by data: A survey of big data definitions. *arXiv preprint arXiv:1309.*

West, V. L., Borland, D., & Hammond, W. E. (2015). Innovative information visualization of electronic health record data: A systematic review. *Journal of the American Medical Informatics Association, 22*(2), 330–339.

White, T. (2012). *Hadoop: The definitive guide.* Sebastopol, CA: O'Reilly Media.

Yao, Q., Han, X., Ma, X. K., Xue, Y. F., Chen, Y. J., & Li, J. S. (2014). Cloud-based hospital information system as a service for grassroots healthcare institutions. *Journal of Medical Systems, 38*(9), 1–7.

Zhang, J. (2001). External representations in complex information processing tasks. *Encyclopedia of Library and Information Science, 68*(31), 164–180.

Zhang, R., & Liu, L. (2010). Security models and requirements for healthcare application clouds. *Proceedings of the 2010 IEEE 3rd International Conference on Cloud Computing (CLOUD),* July 5–10, 2010, Miami, FL. New York, NY: Institute of Electrical and Electronics Engineers.

© VLADGRIN/Shutterstock

PART 3

Specialized Population Health Informatics Applications

© VLADGRIN/Shutterstock

CHAPTER 8

Design, Development, and System Evaluation of Population Health Informatics Applications

Ashish Joshi and Chioma Amadi

LEARNING OBJECTIVES

- Understand the importance of the design stage in population health tools and technologies.
- List the challenges encountered in the design of population health informatics tools.
- Discuss the theoretical approaches commonly employed in the design and development of population health informatics tools.
- Explore various perspectives of the users for the design and development of health technology solutions.
- Assess the factors that need to be considered during the design and development of population health technologies.
- Evaluate population health tools and technologies.

▶ I. Importance of the Design Stage in the Development of Population Health Informatics Tools

The 21st century has been characterized by an exponential increase in the volume of health datasets, growing digital data, and limited cognitive capacity. There is a need for innovative tools and technologies that can convert data into meaningful information for effective population health decision making (Raghupathi & Raghupathi, 2014). The concept of information system design originated in Europe in the 14th and 15th centuries. According to Jacobson, "design can be said to constitute a separation of hand and brain, of manual and intellectual work, of the conceptual part of work from the labor process" (Jacobson, 2000).

The design stage is widely recognized as the pivotal phase in the development of health technology applications (Jacobson, 2000). Creating accessible, functional, and user-friendly interfaces has frequently been the focus of health systems design (U.S. Department of Health and Human Services [DHHS], 2016). User interfaces reflect the visual part of a system and consist of (1) input devices through which end users interact with the system, (2) output devices (e.g., display screen), (3) input devices and navigational components (e.g., keyboard, mouse, touchpad, joystick), (4) input controls (e.g., text fields, buttons, list boxes, toggles), and (5) informational components (e.g., icons, notifications, message boxes) (DHHS, 2016). User interfaces also extend to the aesthetic appearance, software, content displayed, and response time in carrying out specific tasks (DHHS, 2016). They help users to perform specific tasks and obtain required output from a system, making them the central focus of a successfully designed product.

Poorly designed user interfaces introduce a lack of trust and limit user willingness to actually use the system. Users deal with frustrations encountered in navigating excessively complex systems that inhibit user activity and workflow (Shneiderman & Plaisant, 2010). The goal is to produce quality interfaces that are useful, acceptable, and appreciated by the user. Well-designed and usable systems are easy to learn, easy to remember, efficient to utilize, produce fewer errors, and are pleasing to the users (Elkin, 2012).

Efficient user interfaces in medical information systems promote patient care coordination and physician diagnosis, and enhance decision support (Shneiderman & Plaisant, 2010). A limited focus on human factors has been highlighted as the most crucial design challenge facing health information systems (Elkin, 2012). These challenges have been associated with high rates of medical errors and increased mortality (Elkin, 2012). Evidence-driven research on health information technology systems reports that human errors are largely preventable by incorporating user perspectives and employing rigorous usability testing procedures at all stages of design and development (Elkin, 2012).

Designing health technology applications often requires an iterative approach involving continuous input from multiple stakeholders including developers, consumers, healthcare providers, informaticians, and other related multidisciplinary teams to ensure a satisfactory and user-friendly product (Keselman, Logan, Smith, Leroy, & Zeng-Treitler, 2008). Best practices for improving user experience employ a variety of approaches for gathering user perspectives. These include needs assessment, intensive requirements analysis, and evaluations (Shneiderman & Plaisant, 2010). The system designers obtain a thorough understanding of the users, their perceptions, their communities, and their level of engagement in the individual tasks to be performed on the system (Shneiderman & Plaisant, 2010). Creating this ideal user experience is often an arduous task that extends beyond the efforts of the designer (Shneiderman & Plaisant, 2010). The user-friendly designs should satisfy the following criteria: (1) minimize user skills and training, (2) achieve desired task outputs, (3) support standardization within and between systems, and (4) promote reliability of software use. The ISO 9241 standard defines user-friendliness as the ability of a system to meet the goals of effectiveness, efficiency, and satisfaction in a unique defined context (International Organization for Standardization [ISO], 2015). Effectiveness refers to the extent to which desired system tasks are achieved. Efficiency is the ability to maximize the use of resources to achieve optimal outcomes with each task (ISO, 2015). Other attributes of user-friendliness identified in the literature include the following (Shneiderman, 1998):

- *Learnability:* The capacity of a system to support comprehension
- *Speed of performance:* Duration of task completion
- *Error handling:* Ability to recover from errors
- *Retention:* Ability of users to recall prior tasks with ease
- *Satisfaction:* Acceptance in using the system

▶ II. Challenges Associated with the Design and Development of Population Health Informatics Tools

System designers and developers encounter critical challenges in their goal to produce simple, user-friendly, and cost-effective tools that support diverse users (both lay and experienced). Some of these challenges are outlined in the following sections.

Technical Focus

Designers and developers frequently utilize a technology-centered approach during the design process. This process fails to adequately incorporate the psychosocial characteristics, literacy levels, health-seeking behaviors, and familiarity of users as well as their impact on the desired outcomes (Marquard & Zayas-Cabán, 2012). The designers' limited insight into the users' information needs ultimately decreases the satisfaction and utility of the technology, while increasing designers' efforts and investments (Marquard & Zayas-Cabán, 2012).

> Results of one of the prior studies reported that 63% of physician users disagreed that software providers take the opinions of users into account in the design process, 60% believed that software providers were not interested in the feedback provided by end users, and 73% reported that modifications or corrections are rarely implemented frequently. (Martikainen, Korpela, & Tiihonen, 2014)

Health Literacy

Health literacy, health vocabulary knowledge, technological fluency, and health information–seeking skills have been identified as barriers to the use of population health technologies, especially among underserved population groups (Keselman et al., 2008). About 50% of the U.S. adult population lack adequate health literacy, which disproportionately affects the economically disadvantaged, seniors, and minorities (Keselman et al., 2008). In Canada and Australia, 60% of the population have low health literacy, and 47% of Europeans were categorized as having limited health literacy (Weinstein, Gilligan, Morgan, & von Hapsburg, 2015). Inadequate health literacy ultimately influences negative health outcomes.

Studies report that almost 73% of individuals seek online health information for managing their chronic conditions (Keselman et al., 2008). However, those with lower health literacy experience difficulty in following basic self-care procedures or instructions regarding prescriptions. This has been attributed to lack of confidence and fear in taking medications without any form of assistance or proper understanding of simple health terminologies (Institute of Medicine [IOM], 2004). Consequently, guidelines recommend that consumer health information materials be written at the sixth-to-eighth-grade level, to facilitate easier comprehension (Keselman et al., 2008).

Cultural Competency

Limited English language proficiency has been linked to lower income and educational attainment, especially among Latinos (Victorson et al., 2014). Further, those with limited English proficiency lack trust in receiving health information from a variety of other sources (such as TV, the Internet, newspapers, and physicians), making this group highly vulnerable (Victorson et al., 2014). Latinos place greater relevance on cultural and linguistic factors in receiving health messages. Hence, tailoring is critical to ensure that these messages are relevant, accessible, and culturally acceptable to the recipients (Carpentier et al., 2007; Kinney, Gammon, Coxworth, Simonsen, & Arce-Laretta, 2010; Victorson et al., 2014).

Access and the Digital Divide

Access and the digital divide have also been identified as barriers to effective consumer health communication (Keselman et al., 2008). Global Internet usage statistics report that 49.6% of the world population had access to the Internet in 2017. Africa remains the continent with the lowest prevalence of Internet access (27.7 %), compared to more developed continents like the Americas and Europe, where more than 50% of the population have access (Internet World Stats, 2017) (FIGURE 8.1). Better Internet access in developed countries is also marked by demographic disparities (Council of Economic Advisers, 2015).

Differences in consumer knowledge and skills in health terminologies and the use of health systems have continued to widen competency gaps among diverse users. This has resulted in a digital divide between those who are able to benefit from the advances in health technological resources (Keselman et al., 2008). These disparities limit the ability of certain groups to engage in essential e-health tasks (Chan & Kaufman, 2011).

Data Security and Privacy

Remote health monitoring systems pose critical security and privacy issues in terms of data transmission, which are yet to be fully addressed (Baig & Gholam-hosseini, 2013). User acceptance of this innovative technology is widely hampered

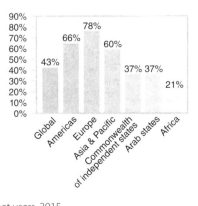

FIGURE 8.1 Global Internet users, 2015

Data from Richter, F. (2015). The digital divide is still a thing. Retrieved from http://www.etcases.com/media/clnews/1433757345994424296.pdf

by data security and privacy challenges extensively discussed in the literature (Li, Lou, & Ren, 2010). Design challenges with health monitoring systems are summarized in TABLE 8.1.

TABLE 8.1 Challenges Encountered in the Design, Development, and Implementation of Health Monitoring Systems		
Population Health Informatics Tools	**Challenges**	**References**
Wearable health monitoring systems	▪ User discomfort ▪ Poor quality of data ▪ Internet connectivity ▪ Generation of false alarms with intelligent sensors	Pandian et al., 2008
	▪ Excessive power consumption ▪ Discomfort in wearability due to complex design components	Dieffenderfer et al., 2016
Remote health monitoring systems	▪ Delay in data transmission ▪ Security and privacy concerns	Shih, Chiang, Lin, & Lin, 2010
Mobile health monitoring systems	▪ High data rates ▪ Decline in productivity ▪ Power consumption ▪ Energy efficiency ▪ Scalability ▪ User-friendliness	Chan, Ray, & Parameswaran, 2008
	▪ Data upload	Anthony et al., 2015
	▪ Restriction in the use of open-ended responses	Drott, Vilhelmsson, Kjellgren, & Berterö, 2016
E-health monitoring systems	▪ Limited Bluetooth coverage ▪ Lengthy training needs ▪ User unfamiliarity	Raad & Yang, 2009
E-health	▪ Tailoring of e-health messages	Carpentier et al., 2007
	▪ Need for Internet connection to assess device and record data	Anton et al., 2012

User Discomfort

Wearable health monitoring systems (WHMSs), which include all forms of wearable electronic health devices or biosensors, have been associated with significant user discomfort (Baig & Gholamhosseini, 2013). Critical challenges persist in the design and utilization of these systems despite being widely recognized for their essential roles in reducing hospitalization, physician consultations, and patient wait times. The need for regular wearing by the users and restriction to a particular range often lead to patient discomfort.

Energy Efficiency and Data Rates

Mobile health monitoring systems (which comprise mobile devices, personal digital assistants, and tablets) have recorded tremendous success in health communications. However, they still face limitations in the analysis and processing of the data collected. The limitation is largely attributed to phone-battery efficiency because battery life is significantly reduced with frequent data transfer (Baig & Gholamhosseini, 2013).

Lack of User Feedback

The importance of user feedback has been extensively documented in the literature (Cresswell, Bates, & Sheikh, 2013). This is a critical issue affecting system design, development, and implementation. Poorly designed systems have been associated with poor usability, acceptance, and satisfaction with use (Cresswell et al., 2013). Hence, the top-down approach in system design is highly discouraged, because user feedback must be an iterative process throughout system development (Kodama, 2011).

▶ # III. Theoretical Approaches Utilized to Design and Develop Population Health Informatics Tools

Design and development of informatics tools and technologies should have a theoretical framework. These theories help to develop and replicate consistent, evidence-based products over time (Shneiderman & Plaisant, 2010). The widespread use of multiple theories reflects the complex processes involved in user-interface design (TABLE 8.2). Design theories are categorized based on various functions including descriptive, predictive, performance-based, perceptual, or cognitive (Shneiderman & Plaisant, 2010). Several theoretical frameworks have been described that are utilized in the design and development of health information systems (TABLE 8.3).

Cognitive Task Analysis

Cognitive task analysis (CTA) is a design principle employed in assessing the users' cognitive processes to complete a given task (User Experience Professionals' Association, 2010). Task analysis provides a better understanding and

TABLE 8.2 Design Theories Based on Functional Classifications

Functions	Description, Definition, or Characteristics	Examples
Descriptive	Used to provide explanation for various features/actions	Developing basic terminologies
Predictive	Utilizes prior information to make projections of user activities	Examining several designs to compare and contrast error rates
Performance-based	User activity to execute specific tasks	Predicting the user's ability to carry out a specific task(s)
Perceptual	User attributes are used as an index for decision making	Ability to locate an item on a display
Cognitive	Use of memory skills in problem solving	Estimating the amount of time a user takes in reading visuals

Modified from Shneiderman, B., & Plaisant, C. (2010). *Designing the user interface: Strategies for effective human-computer interaction*. Reading, MA: Pearson Addison-Wesley.

description of the task by examining essential features such as (1) task duration, (2) variability, (3) frequency, (4) complexity, (5) allocation, (6) required tools, (7) environmental conditions, (8) data needs, (9) user attributes (literacy, training needs), and (10) data dependencies (User Experience Professionals' Association, 2010). CTA involves several steps (Klein, 1993), including: (1) task mapping, (2) identifying major decision points, (3) clustering, (4) linking, (5) prioritization, and (6) strategy evaluation. It also encompasses a variety of strategies and frameworks (User Experience Professionals' Association, 2010), including the following:

- *Critical decision method (CDM):* Structured interview probes to understand how design experts engage in decision making.
- *Task-knowledge structures (TKS):* An in-depth task analysis is conducted to evaluate the steps involved in a given task.
- *Skill-based CTA framework:* This operationalizes cognitive task research by identifying specific skills needed to perform a given task and facilitating linkage between them.
- *Applied CTA:* Interviews are conducted to extract information on the specific demands and skills necessary to carry out a given task.
- *Cognitive function model:* This is geared toward understanding the role of individuals and users in the design of complex systems.

TABLE 8.3 Selected Theoretical Design Frameworks and Their Applications

Design Framework/ Theories	Description	Application in Health Systems Design	References
Cognitive task analysis (CTA)	A cognitive engineering method that decomposes a task to uncover knowledge	CTA was used to study system usability, develop training protocols, and assess the knowledge needed to execute an e-health task.	Schraagen, Chipman, & Shalin, 2000
Community-based participatory research (CBPR)	Engages all stakeholders and prospective users throughout the design, development, and evaluation process	CBPR was used to conduct user needs assessments, enhance study participant recruitment and retention, and evaluate intervention strategies and data collection using an iterative approach.	Henderson et al., 2013
Theory of self-efficacy	Utilizes approaches that enhance users' confidence in their ability to perform specific tasks	Used to design web-based diabetes training initiative for enhancing self-management practices	Catherine et al., 2012
Social cognitive theory	Reflects the interplay of cognitive, personal, behavioral, and environmental factors in determining self-motivation and behavior change	Used to design educational materials for a culturally and linguistically adapted, computer-tailored physical activity intervention for Latinas	Pekmezi et al., 2012
Theory of health information–seeking behavior/health information model	Encompasses key constructs that enhance active information seeking, passive information receiving, and health literacy	Used to design a web-based diabetes training initiative for enhancing self-management practices	Catherine et al., 2012

(continues)

TABLE 8.3 Selected Theoretical Design Frameworks and Their Applications (*continued*)

Design Frameworks/ Theories	Description	Applications in Health Systems Design	References
Knowledge to action framework	Focused on adapting knowledge to the local context, while emphasizing the need for collaboration of key stakeholders including producers and knowledge users' framework, while improving sustainability in knowledge diffusion and usage	Used to design a web-based diabetes training initiative for enhancing self-management practices	Catherine et al., 2012
Sociotechnical model	The social and organizational context of workplaces significantly impacts the technical aspect.	This model informed the design of a clinical decision support system for trauma patients.	Sheehan et al., 2013
Human-centered design	Incorporates users' experience in the entire design process	Applied in the development of patient decision aids	Witteman et al., 2015
Ergonomics	Focuses on human factors as a core element combining physiological, psychological, and engineering principles in the interaction between people and machines	Approach applied in cardiovascular risk assessment, risk communication, and risk management in a community pharmacy	Hubbard, Regan, Strath, & Vosper, 2015
Participatory design principles	Engages all relevant stakeholders in all aspects of the design process to ensure that user needs are met	Applied in validating information needs, personas, and scenarios in the design of an integrated information system for public health nurses	Reeder, Hills, Turner, & Demiris, 2014

Although CTA methods have been widely used in generating data on user performance of a given task, critics argue that data gathering during this process can be time intensive. It also may not fully capture other noncognitive features (e.g., physical capabilities) and may not be representative of user populations, because cognitive abilities differ widely (User Experience Professionals' Association, 2010).

Community-Based Participatory Research

Community-based participatory research (CBPR) has been defined as a

> . . . collaborative approach to research that equitably involves all partners in the research process and recognizes the unique strengths that each brings. CBPR begins with a research topic of importance to the community, has the aim of combining knowledge with action and achieving social change to improve health outcomes and eliminate health disparities. (Kellogg Health Scholars, 2016)

Core differences between CBPR and traditional research approaches include the role played by the community in identifying problems, and engaging with the researchers as full partners rather than as research subjects (Lee & Barnett, 2013).

Social Cognitive Theory

The social cognitive theory was proposed by Albert Bandura and reflects the interplay of cognitive, personal, behavioral, and environmental factors in determining self-motivation and behavior change (Bandura, 1995). It consists of four major constructs: self-observation, self-evaluation, self-reaction, and self-efficacy (Bandura, 1995). Self-observation refers to the regular observation of one's behaviors. Self-evaluation compares an individual's performance to another's or to a set standard using specific, measurable goals. Self-reaction is an assessment of progress or failure in performing a given task and its influence on individual actions. Finally, self-efficacy implies the belief or confidence in carrying out a specific activity (Bandura, 1995). Taken together, the interplay of these factors determines motivation and behavior (Francis, 2016; Lunenburg, 2011).

Theory of Self-Efficacy

The theory of self-efficacy was derived from the social cognitive theory developed by Albert Bandura (1995). The self-efficacy theory reflects the confidence or conviction in one's ability to perform a given task with positive outcomes. According to this theory, the more self-efficacy individuals demonstrate, the more likely they are to complete a given task, and vice versa (Francis, 2016; Lunenburg, 2011; van der Bijl & Shortridge-Baggett, 2002). Three scales utilized in measuring self-efficacy are magnitude (reflects the difficulty level of the task), strength (the confidence of the individual in performing at various difficulty levels), and generality (the extent of generalizing self-efficacy across multiple tasks) (Francis, 2016).

Theory of Health Information–Seeking Behavior/Health Information Model

This theory, developed by Longo et al. (2010) is used to identify and understand patterns in health information–seeking behaviors. This theory investigates the influence of personal factors (sociodemographics, medical history, current health status, cultural factors, cognitive factors, and interpersonal attributes) and contextual factors (health condition, healthcare system, healthcare delivery, family history of disease, and social networks) on the healthcare-seeking patterns of individuals (Lalazaryan & Zare-Farashbandi, 2014).

Knowledge to Action Framework

The Knowledge to Action (K2A) Framework was derived from 31 existing theories (Graham et al., 2006). This framework facilitates the identification of problems, and subsequent structuring into questions, for which answers can be provided from existing literature or through further research (Graham et al., 2006). It employs a cyclical approach consisting of seven key constructs: (1) identify the problem; (2) adapt knowledge to context; (3) understand existing barriers to knowledge use; (4) tailor interventions; (5) monitor utilization of knowledge; (6) evaluate the outcomes; and (7) sustain the use of knowledge. At these various stages of knowledge generation, identified problems are documented and gaps in research are noted; these are then used in developing solutions (Graham et al., 2006).

▶ IV. User Involvement in the Design and Development of Population Health Informatics Tools

A variety of perspectives and approaches to system design and development continue to emerge. These perspectives often incorporate one or more individual overlapping components, reflecting the consensus that there is a need for a multistructured, multidisciplinary, and consolidated approach to systems design and development. A few of these approaches are identified in this section.

Sociotechnical Systems Perspective

Sociotechnical systems design (STSD) is a design approach that integrates human, social, and organizational factors in the process of systems design and development. It emphasizes the complex relationships among organizations, individuals, and systems, which are largely ignored by highly technology-driven processes of system design (Baxter & Sommerville, 2011). The rationale behind this approach is that technical requirements often take center stage in system design; however, such systems often fail due to inadequate consideration of the environmental and organizational context of these systems (Baxter & Sommerville, 2011). Although the benefits of integrating a sociotechnical perspective in systems design are widely recognized, this approach is rarely utilized due to difficulties in operationalizing these methods.

Empirical literature has identified the following four significant scientific communities that have successfully integrated a sociotechnical perspective into the systems design process:

- *Workplace research:* Sociotechnical perspectives have their origin in workplace research. Research in this field has been centered on the interaction between individuals and computers in their work environments, and how this improves or constrains their activities (Mumford, 1983).
- *Information systems research:* The focus is on the relationships between an organization or enterprise and the use of large-scale systems. It supports workflow processes at a macro level rather than specific aspects of computer-supported work activities (Taylor, 1982).
- *Computer-supported cooperative work (CSCW):* Emphasis is placed on the more detailed aspects of a work environment and its influence on the use of varied computer systems.
- *Cognitive systems engineering (CSE):* The main focus has been on healthcare systems (Hollnagel & Woods, 2005; Woods & Hollnagel, 2006). Research groups in this field are primarily interested in interrelations between human factors and organizational issues and how this impacts system success or failure.

In addition to these approaches, other systems design processes that incorporate sociotechnical ideas include: (1) soft systems methodology, (2) cognitive work analysis, (3) ethnographic workplace analysis, (4) contextual design, (5) cognitive systems engineering, and (6) human-centered design (HCD) (Baxter & Sommerville, 2011). One of the major limitations of the sociotechnical systems perspective has been in defining the different constructs and laying out a coherent process that needs to be considered in employing this approach in systems design. Most of the guiding principles have been merely philosophical. Five key characteristics of sociotechnical systems design are noted in TABLE 8.4.

The lack of clear constructs in operationalizing guiding principles in sociotechnical systems designs has led to failure in adopting the use of sociotechnical perspectives in systems design. TABLE 8.5 lists some issues with the sociotechnical approach.

A practical framework provided a means of linking organizational change processes with technical systems engineering, using the following five defined constructs (FIGURE 8.2) (Baxter & Sommerville, 2011):

1. *Extensive needs assessment of sociotechnical requirements:* Addresses how system requirements can fully incorporate sociotechnical perspectives
2. *Modeling and abstraction in software engineering:* Addresses what models are useful when considering systems design and interaction in organizational settings
3. *Integrated HCD:* Addresses how sociotechnical systems can adequately incorporate human factors
4. *Organizational learning:* Addresses how organizational learning can be incorporated into sociotechnical methods
5. *Global systems approach:* Addresses how sociotechnical methods can integrate organizational processes and systems located in different regions

TABLE 8.4 Key Characteristics of Sociotechnical Systems Design
Must include interdependent parts
Must meet specified goals of their environmental context
Must consist of interdependent technical and social subgroups
Must have multiple methods of performing similar tasks
Must include synchronization of technical and social subsystems for optimal utility

TABLE 8.5 Challenges of the Sociotechnical Approach
Inconsistent terminology in the definition of sociotechnical systems
Lack of consensus on success criteria
Does not provide suggestions on how to re-engineer and improve these systems
Difficulty in defining clear roles of the various disciplines and practitioners

The Ergonomists' Perspective

User participation in systems development has received significant attention in recent years (Martikainen et al., 2014). Growing research in the fields of health information technology systems design and development has identified that significant failures in product satisfaction and utilization often stem from a poor understanding of end users' role in system development (Martikainen et al., 2014). Thus, end user involvement in the life cycle of system development is a critical success factor. Ergonomics as a relatively new field examines the combined role of physiological, psychological, and engineering principles in the interaction between people and machines (Ball, Edwards, & Hannah, 2006). Ergonomics focus on human factors as a core element in the design of health information systems, and thus emphasize user needs assessment throughout the system design and development process (Ball et al., 2006).

Typical techniques employed by ergonomists in user assessment include interviews (Karwowski & Salvendi, 1998), questionnaires (University of Wisconsin–Madison, n.d.), ethnography (Privitera, 2009), storyboarding (Lenté, Berthelot, & Buisine, 2014), and prototyping (Plaisance et al., 2016). Following user assessment, the identified user needs are then translated into system requirements and specifications, which often comprise a variety of system performance variables including natural language statements, response time, load balancing, data backup, system availability, and usability (Samaras & Horst, 2005). System requirement generation is an iterative process involving routine assessment and validation of the various system factors against user needs to ensure

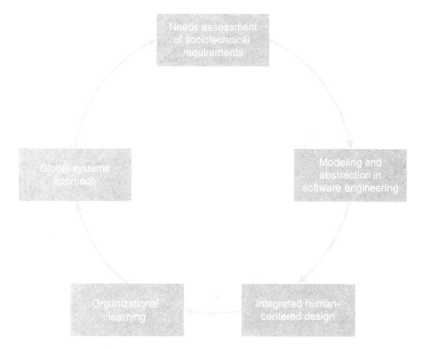

FIGURE 8.2 Framework for organizational change processes and technical systems engineering

internal consistency. This intensive process of operationalizing the various system requirements with the end user emphasizes the critical role of ergonomists in the design process, because defective requirements are the major determinants of failed systems (Samaras & Horst, 2005). The primary flaws in requirements generation include the use of the wrong target audience and the assumption by system engineers that they are familiar with user needs (Samaras & Horst, 2005). Hence, user needs must be clearly defined early in the design process. Requirements formulation has been described as an "interdisciplinary engineering activity" that relies heavily on ergonomists' expertise to fully represent user perspectives in the system design process, especially when engineering trade-offs are made (FIGURE 8.3) (Samaras & Horst, 2005).

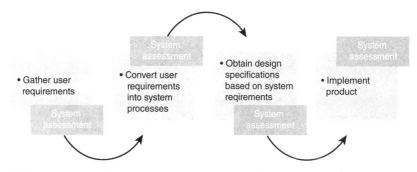

FIGURE 8.3 Workflow of the ergonomist in the system engineering process

Modified from Samaras, G. M., & Horst, R. L. (2005). A systems engineering perspective on the human-centered design of health information systems. *Journal of Biomedical Informatics, 38*(1), 61–74.

The Developers' and Physicians' Perspectives

Health professionals are reported to be highly critical of the approach utilized in the design and development of healthcare information technology systems. The variety of concerns include the following (Martikainen et al., 2014):

- *Limited contribution of the end users' perspective in the system design process*
- *Limited knowledge of healthcare taxonomies and systems by the computer technologists or developers*
- *Absence of end users during the early phases of healthcare systems design*

Users should be actively engaged in healthcare systems design from conceptualization to system deployment (Martikainen et al., 2014). Developers need adequate resources to facilitate intensive collaboration with the end users, especially in analyzing and incorporating user feedback (Martikainen et al., 2014).

▶ V. Factors Influencing the Design and Development of Population Health Informatics Tools

Technical, social, organizational, and sociopolitical factors have been identified as the key broad factors influencing design, development, and adoption of health information systems (Cresswell et al., 2013) (FIGURE 8.4). These factors are described in the following sections.

Technical Factors

Planning for technical factors often begins once the need for a system is defined and goals are examined. Resources are then committed to exploring networks, system options (customizing an existing system vs. creating a new one), system types

FIGURE 8.4 Considerations in designing and developing health technology systems

Data from Cresswell, K. M., Bates, D. W., & Sheikh, A. (2013). Ten key considerations for the successful implementation and adoption of large-scale health information technology. *Journal of the American Medical Informatics Association, 20*(e1), e9–e13.

(homegrown vs. standardized solutions), cost of the system, feasibility of integrating the new system with the existing system, time needed to develop the system, resources available, infrastructure, and setting (Cresswell et al., 2013). The pros and cons of the various listed factors are then carefully considered with respect to system development. For instance, local and international vendors often prefer commercial systems to be homegrown because they are cost-effective, easier to facilitate interoperability due to common standards, and hence easily adaptable (Cresswell et al., 2013). In addition, inappropriate infrastructure such as unsteady wireless connections may influence system utility (Cresswell et al., 2013).

Social Factors

It is essential that the system design and development process fully addresses end user needs. Highly efficient systems with poor user-friendliness have largely limited system utility. Prior literature has outlined numerous challenges in systems that satisfy technical requirements and organizational efficiency, but do not appeal to users' workflow processes (Cresswell et al., 2013; Sheikh et al., 2011). A variety of stakeholders' input is critical during the system design process. User requirements for system design and development are outlined in TABLE 8.6.

Organizational Factors

Organizational factors include strategies, planning, and leadership input for the implementation and adoption of health information systems in various organizational settings. Key considerations to facilitate organizational change include engaging with supplier networks and similar organizations that have implemented the system in question (Cresswell et al., 2013). Evaluation of system acceptance and integration needs to be carried out intermittently because system adoption is often

TABLE 8.6 Factors to Be Considered in the Design and Development of Population Health Informatics Tools and Technologies

Factor Impacting Design	Description	
Expertise/research team	Variety of technical and nontechnical experts	Horvath et al., 2014
Identification of consumers' health information needs	Information about interests and perceptions of seeking health information on the Internet, user-driven content	Horvath et al., 2014
User characteristics/ needs	User demographics, cultural and linguistic factors, familiarity with computer use, interface preferences, and functional needs	Lucero et al., 2014

(continues)

TABLE 8.6 Factors to Be Considered in the Design and Development of Population Health Informatics Tools and Technologies (*continued*)

Factor Impacting Design	Description	References
Health literacy screening	Use of health literacy screening methods in assessing and tailoring consumer literacy levels	Keselman et al., 2008; Zeng & Tse, 2006
Health literacy guidelines	Use of recommended guidelines and readability formulas in developing health messages	Keselman et al., 2008; Zeng & Tse, 2006
Use of consumer health vocabularies	Use of consumer-friendly vocabularies that facilitate health-oriented communication for a particular task or need	Keselman et al., 2008; Zeng & Tse, 2006
Optimizing information retrieval	Facilitating retrieval of precise, accurate, actionable health information based on desired search terms	Keselman et al., 2008; Zeng & Tse, 2006
Evaluating information quality control	Utilization of quality criteria standards (credibility, content, disclosure, design, links, interactivity, caveats) in compiling online health information	Ahmann, 2000
Workflow challenges	Time to address communication issues, internal testing, and debugging Funding for maintaining the website after launch Understanding the target population and user tasks Utilizing a content management system Complexity of intervention and extent of evaluation needed	Horvath et al., 2014

gradual, and changes may not be immediately observed (Cresswell et al., 2013). Key stakeholders in the organization need to be engaged during every stage of implementation to ensure that expectations are clearly defined and consensus is reached on them (Cresswell et al., 2013).

Sociopolitical Factors

Sociopolitical factors consist of larger scale influences on system implementation and adoption including technical policies, interoperability with other healthcare systems, economic influences, and ultimate sustainability.

▶ VI. Design Methods for Developing Population Health Informatics Tools

Design process involves the end user throughout the product development and testing process. It is critical to ensure that the product meets the needs of the user.

Participatory Design

Participatory design (PD), formerly known as cooperative design, places priority on engaging all stakeholders (e.g., users and designers) during the various design stages to ensure an end product that satisfies their needs (Kushniruk & Nøhr, 2016). Originally introduced in the 1970s in Scandinavia, PD was widely used by researchers interested in understanding the mechanisms of human–computer interactions, computer-assisted work, and related topics (Spinuzzi, 2005). PD has mainly been applied to smaller scale systems in local settings (Kushniruk & Nøhr, 2016). Challenges of PD include: (1) complexity to implement, (2) lack of formalization, (3) emphasis on early stages of design with little attention to later stages, (4) impractical in efforts to gather all stakeholder views, (5) time consuming, and (6) rarely repeated by organizations (Spinuzzi, 2005). PD approaches frequently consist of three main stages (FIGURE 8.5).

■ *Exploration stage:* The goal is for designers to understand user interactions consisting of workflow, procedures, routines, and critical pathways. Inquiry tools such as ethnography, interviews, observations, and direct visits to workplaces are utilized by the designers (Spinuzzi, 2005).
■ *Discovery stage:* The discovery stage involves designers working closely with a number of users to set the desired work goals. Inquiry tools utilized during the stage are workplace games, roleplaying, workshops, storyboarding, and interpretations (Spinuzzi, 2005).
■ *Prototyping:* The findings of the exploratory and discovery stages will be utilized by the designers along with the involvement of the end users,

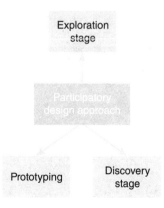

FIGURE 8.5 Stages of participatory design

resulting in a product that meets the desired goals of the users (Spinuzzi, 2005). Techniques employed include mock-ups, paper prototyping, and cooperative prototyping. Eventually, results are disseminated to all users (Serrano et al., 2015).

Human-Centered Design

HCD has been defined as a design thinking process prioritizing the needs, preferences, and values of the users of a system in all steps of the design process. The goal is to make systems usable, interactive, and satisfactory (Vechakul, Shrimali, & Sandhu, 2015). HCD encompasses three critical phases of development (**FIGURE 8.6**).

- *Discovery phase:* The designers gather information about possible user challenges and ways to approach them.
- *Ideation phase:* This is the problem-solving phase that involves significant brainstorming, idea generation, and testing.
- *Implementation phase:* In this phase, the solution or product is further translated into a prototype and deployed (Vechakul et al., 2015).

HCD approaches have been widely used for designing products and services in a variety of healthcare organizations (Vechakul et al., 2015) and a variety of basic products such as stoves and toilets (Acumen HCD Workshop, 2016). Typical human factor considerations include: (1) how the design process of a cooking stove can reduce the quantity of smoke inhaled by a user, (2) how toilets can be designed for families where there is lack of sanitation infrastructure, (3) how hospital waiting rooms can be designed to reduce the spread of airborne diseases, (4) how water delivery services can provide clean water in addition to other nutritional benefits, (5) how community housing can be structured to encourage neighborhood interaction, and (6) how systems can be designed to connect social entrepreneurs globally (Acumen HCD Workshop, 2016).

The HCD approach has also been applied extensively to the design of population health information tools and technologies, including Sanaviz, a geovisualization platform (Joshi et al., 2012), Interactive Surveillance System (ISS; a

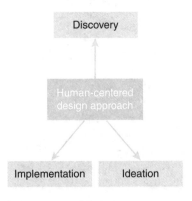

FIGURE 8.6 Approaches in human-centered design

disease surveillance system for monitoring acute bacterial infections) (Joshi, Amadi, Trout, & Obaro, 2014), a bilingual breastfeeding educational system (Joshi, Amadi, Meza, Aguire, & Wilhelm, 2016), a metabolic syndrome educational portal (Joshi, Mehta, Talati, Malhotra, & Grover, 2013), and more (Rinkus et al., 2005).

The HCD approach encompasses multiple levels of analysis: (1) user analysis, (2) functional analysis, (3) task analysis, and (4) representational analysis (TABLE 8.7).

- *User analysis:* Differences in the user characteristics are responsible for differences in the way users interact with the various components of the system. Some of these differences include: (1) demographic characteristics, (2) literacy levels, (3) prior knowledge base, (4) technology experience, (5) educational background, (6) cognitive abilities, and (7) time constraints (Rinkus et al., 2005). User analysis also reflects the unique needs and complexity involved when a variety of users, for instance, physicians, nurses, patients, pharmacists, administrators, technicians, and medical billing agents, utilize a given health information system, and how their different backgrounds influence their acceptance of, satisfaction with, and utilization of the system (Rinkus et al., 2005). The purpose of user analysis is to develop systems that match user needs (Rinkus et al., 2005).
- *Functional analysis:* This is the identification of domain structures, broader system functions, objectives, and goals. The various functions of a system are clearly defined (Rinkus et al., 2005).
- *Task analysis:* This outlines the specific procedures required for a given task. Its primary objective is to ensure that specific tasks that have been adequately matched to the user needs are incorporated into the system (Rinkus et al.,

TABLE 8.7 Levels of Analysis and Assessment Approaches in HCD

Analysis Level	Assessment Approaches
User analysis	Direct approaches: questionnaires, interviews, focus groups, field visits, and ethnography Indirect approaches: journals, manuals, procedures, and textbooks
Functional analysis	Domain structure analysis and broader system functions (analysis of cognitive activities in the work domain)
Task analysis	Detailed task components and the relationships between them, procedures required for a given task, and ranking of procedures and user approaches
Representational analysis	Visual display structures outlining workflow and taskflow processes Assessing display formats for user fit Representations affect task efficiency and completion.

Data from Rinkus, S., Walji, M., Johnson-Throop, K. A., Malin, J. T., Turley, J. P., Smith, J. W., & Zhang, J. (2005). Human-centered design of a distributed knowledge management system. *Journal of Biomedical Informatics, 38*(1), 4–17.

2005). Task analysis also serves to prioritize the various procedures based on their importance, which ultimately enhances user workflow (Rinkus et al., 2005). FIGURE 8.7 shows a simplified task analysis scenario.

■ *Representational analysis:* This deals directly with the user interface. It is focused on displaying how users interact with the system while performing various tasks to generate the desired outcomes. The display formats for various tasks are assessed to determine an appropriate fit for the users to engage in the task performance (Rinkus et al., 2005). The way a task is presented is most likely to influence the information perceived by a user and the cognitive capacity required. The goal is to simplify this process as much as possible (Rinkus et al.,

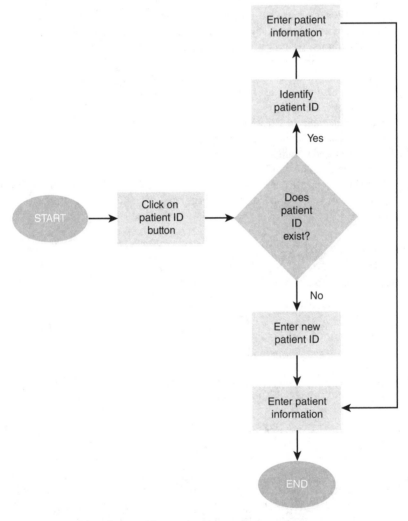

FIGURE 8.7 User task analysis workflow example

Data from Dabbagh, N. (n.d.). The Instructional Design Knowledge Base. Retrieved from http://cehdclass.gmu.edu/ndabbagh/Resources/IDKB/index.htm

2005). These analytic approaches employ a variety of tools and technologies in their assessment, including: (1) interviews, (2) questionnaires, (3) ethno-methodological studies, (4) brainstorming, (5) problem domain storyboarding, (6) prototyping, (7) literature reviews, (8) ergonomics laboratory, and (9) personas that create reliable and real representations of audience segments for reference (Rinkus et al., 2005).

Scenario-Based Design

Scenario-based design is a system design process that involves using narratives in describing human experiences and human–computer interaction processes in performing specific tasks (Rosson & Carroll, 2009). Scenario-based designs incorporate a user-centered method by focusing more on the process by which individuals utilize systems in accomplishing their various activities, and less on the system design specifications and requirements (Rosson & Carroll, 2009). Scenarios employ sketches and stories to create workflow processes and tasks in a contextual manner. The benefit of this design strategy is that it provides designers with a thorough analysis of the design context and needs while preventing a solution-focused approach, which may lead to poorly designed products (Rosson & Carroll, 2009). FIGURE 8.8 has frequently been used in characterizing scenario-based design (Rosson & Carroll, 2009).

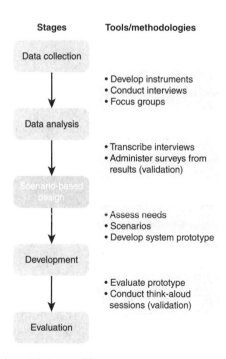

FIGURE 8.8 Scenario-based design workflow

Data from Reeder, B., & Turner, A. M. (2011). Scenario-based design: A method for connecting information system design with public health operations and emergency management. *Journal of Biomedical Informatics, 44*(6), 978–988.

Designing a system starts off as a vague concept with some defined objectives and goals that need to be met. This is then followed by an iterative exploratory approach to analyze the concept to identify opportunities, barriers, and the feasibility of addressing them using certain technologies. The output of this process is then communicated using scenarios to describe stakeholder views and claims to assess possible consequences of the various scenarios (Reeder & Turner, 2011; Rosson & Carroll, 2009).

▶ VII. Evaluation of Population Health Informatics Tools and Technologies

Evaluation is defined as "a systematic process carried out at different time periods of an intervention to gather information which is often utilized in improving the structure, implementation, function, adoption and use of that intervention" (Eng, Gustafson, Henderson, Jimison, & Patrick, 1999). Evaluation is an iterative process that should be conducted throughout the process of system design and development, with the goal of making necessary modifications prior to system deployment (Eng et al., 1999). Evaluation is necessary for several reasons.

- The rapid increase in the consumer demand for health information
- The availability of a variety of interactive health technology applications
- To address concerns regarding the quality, effectiveness, and impact of health technology platforms
- To foster innovation in the design and development of consumer health applications
- To prevent harm to potential consumers
- To maximize resources and ensure informed decisions by appropriate stakeholders
- To encourage the contributions of end users in the development and implementation process

Evaluation methods should be applied and practical, taking into consideration real world scenarios (FIGURE 8.9). Evaluation methods need to be proactive in order to maximize use of resources and minimize wastage. Evaluation steps should be SMART (Specific, Measurable, Achievable, Relevant, and Time-bound) and must involve the collective efforts of all relevant stakeholders. TABLE 8.8 outlines the various approaches utilized in the evaluation process.

Stages of Evaluation

The evaluation process is an iterative one frequently characterized by the following three stages (Eng et al., 1999):

- *Formative evaluation:* Formative evaluation is carried out during the early stages of system design. The goal is to gather useful data that will inform the design process (Kamberelis & Dimitriadis, 2013). Typical tools utilized in formative evaluation include needs assessments, focus groups, and interviews. During this stage, reviews of prior similar tools and technologies are often conducted to identify gaps and opportunities (Kamberelis & Dimitriadis, 2013).

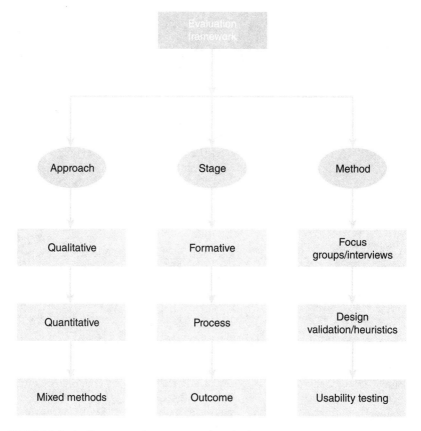

FIGURE 8.9   Evaluation approaches, stages, and methods

▣   *Process evaluation:* This second stage of evaluation is usually ongoing through-out the system design and development process. It is conducted to monitor and ensure that set procedures and standards are adhered to. Operational charac-teristics including accuracy, functionality, and other essential parameters are measured.

▣   *Outcomes assessment:* This third stage of the evaluation process is usually carried out following system deployment (Kamberelis & Dimitriadis, 2013). It involves the use of empirical study design approaches to assess the impact of the intervention. Quantitative measurements, randomized trials, and quasi-experimental approaches are employed to assess the impact of the system (Kamberelis & Dimitriadis, 2013).

Evaluation Methods

There are several methods of health technology evaluation including the following.

TABLE 8.8 Evaluation Approaches, Features, and Tools

Approach	Purpose	Features	Tools Utilized
Qualitative	To seek understanding of phenomena that are not fully developed	Subjective Semistructured approach to data collection Use of descriptive data Contextual Research questions are broader and exploratory Informal procedure	Focus groups Interviews Observations Open-ended surveys
Quantitative	To test hypotheses	Objective Structured data collection Use of numerical data Quantifiable outcomes Research questions are predefined and fixed Formal procedure	Use of experimental design methods, employing comparison groups
Mixed methods	Complementing results from both qualitative and quantitative methods	Combines features of both qualitative and quantitative approaches	Combines tools of both qualitative and quantitative approaches

Focus Groups

A focus group is not necessarily a group discussion where participants take turns answering the same questions, but rather involves participants engaged in talking to one another (Ziebland, Coulter, Calabrese, & Locock, 2013). Features of focus groups include the following:

- Use of a qualitative method of data collection
- Ideally between 6 and 10 people participating
- Moderated informal sessions with study participants/end users
- Commonly used to gather user perceptions, experiences, knowledge, attitudes, practices, or behavior regarding an intervention
- Semistructured and exploratory approach
- Potentially demographically diverse participants
- Usually last for about 45–90 minutes
- Frequently audio-recorded

Heuristic Evaluation

Heuristic evaluation is a system engineering process (Nielsen & Molich, 1990). This systematic process is employed in detecting inconsistencies or errors within the prototype so that modification can be done prior to the system deployment (Nielsen & Molich, 1990). Heuristic evaluation is usually conducted by system designers using a collection of 10 criteria known as Nielsen's heuristics (Nielsen & Molich, 1990). Multiple evaluators or raters are needed for this process, and it does not involve the end users of the program. Raters use a coding severity index range from 0 (no usability issues) to 4 (usability catastrophe) to evaluate the system (Nielsen & Molich, 1990). An outline of Nielsen's heuristic principles is shown in FIGURE 8.10.

Usability Testing

Usability testing is a system evaluation process that assesses system performance with a sample of end users (Brooke, 1986; Eng et al., 1999; Jaspers, 2009). The focus is to ensure end user satisfaction with the health technology system. Usability testing incorporates the preferences and choices of the users to ensure a tailored, easy-to-use, and user-friendly application (Jaspers, 2009). The benefits of usability include: (1) increased acceptance of the system by end users, (2) reduced user errors, (3) rapid adoption, and (4) maximum utilization of resources.

Usability testing employs several tools including the system usability scale (SUS), developed by John Brooke in 1986. The scale is described as a rapid tool for assessing usability (Brooke, 1986). It consists of a 10-item questionnaire on a 5-point Likert scale. Response options range from "Strongly disagree" (1) to "Strongly agree" (5). Total scores above 68 are considered above average (Brooke, 1986) (TABLE 8.9).

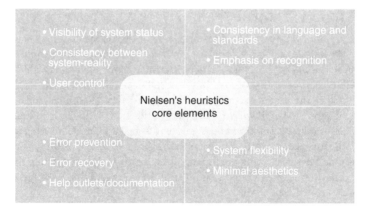

FIGURE 8.10 Nielsen's heuristic principles

Data from Nielsen, J., & Molich, R. (1990). *Heuristic evaluation of user interfaces. Proceeding CHI '90 proceedings of the SIGCHI conference on human factors in computing systems* (pp. 249–256). New York, NY: ACM.

TABLE 8.9 Usability Tools and Links

Usability Tool	Link	References
System Usability Scale (SUS)	http://hell.meiert.org/core/pdf/sus.pdf	Brooke, 1986
Perceived usefulness and ease of use	http://garyperlman.com/quest/quest.cgi?form=PUEU	Davis, 1989
Nielsen's attributes of usability	http://garyperlman.com/quest/quest.cgi?form=NAU	Nielsen, 1993
Nielsen's heuristic evaluation	http://garyperlman.com/quest/quest.cgi?form=NHE	Nielsen, 1993
After-scenario questionnaire	http://garyperlman.com/quest/quest.cgi?form=ASQ	Lewis, 1995
Practical heuristics for usability evaluation	http://garyperlman.com/quest/quest.cgi?form=PHUE	Perlman, 1997
Purdue usability testing questionnaire	http://garyperlman.com/quest/quest.cgi?form=PUTQ	Lin, Choong, & Salvendy, 1997
Usefulness, Satisfaction, and Ease of Use questionnaire (USE)	http://garyperlman.com/quest/quest.cgi?form=USE	Lund, 2001

Think Aloud Protocol

The think aloud protocol is a critical method for evaluating usability flaws (Eng et al., 1999; Jaspers, 2009). Individuals employed in this evaluation should represent expected users of the system. A representative sample of about eight subjects is needed to draw valid conclusions (Jaspers, 2009). Users are assigned a set of predefined tasks in the system to complete. They are instructed to think aloud (i.e., verbalize their thoughts) while performing each of the given tasks. The tasks assigned to the users should be practical and equivalent to real scenarios. Information provided by the users is subjective. The users should be given an opportunity to practice thinking aloud before starting the process, because they might not be familiar with it. Data collection is often done by audio and/or video recording. Coding schemes are then developed (Eng et al., 1999).

Cognitive Walkthrough

Cognitive walkthrough is focused on evaluating a system for learnability through exploration. It analyzes cognitive processes that users would undergo to carry out given tasks on the system. In this process, the evaluator acts like a user without any guidance (Jaspers, 2009). The evaluator/user sets a goal/task to be carried out. He or she examines the available options on the interface and chooses a specific option to complete the task. Upon completion of the given task, the evaluator examines the system response using the following criteria (Jaspers, 2009):

- Did the user try to achieve the correct effect?
- Was the user able to make the correct choice for the given task?
- Was the correct action associated with the desired effect?

Usability is critical to the safety and effectiveness of population health informatics tools, and regulators and policymakers have been increasingly focused on this area.

▶ VIII. Conclusion

Creating an ideal user experience is often a function of the critical processes of system design, development, and evaluation. More important to consider is the iterative process involved during transition between these phases, and the role of various stakeholders such as developers, providers, informaticians, and evaluators. Hence, evaluation of system prototypes using multiple stakeholders is pertinent throughout the course of system development to ensure an acceptable, functional, and user-friendly system.

References

Acumen HCD Workshop. (2016). An introduction to human-centered design. Retrieved from http://plusacumen.org/wp-content/uploads/2013/07/Week1_readings.pdf

Ahmann, E. (2000). Supporting families' savvy use of the Internet for health research. *Pediatric Nursing, 26*(4), 419.

Anthony, C. A., Polgreen, L. A., Chounramany, J., Foster, E. D., Goerdt, C. J., Miller, M. L., . . . Polgreen, P. M. (2015). Outpatient blood pressure monitoring using bi-directional text messaging. *Journal of the American Society of Hypertension, 9*(5), 375–381.

Anton, S. D., LeBlanc, E., Allen, H. R., Karabetian, C., Sacks, F., Bray, G., & Williamson, D. A. (2012). Use of a computerized tracking system to monitor and provide feedback on dietary goals for calorie-restricted diets: The POUNDS LOST study. *Journal of Diabetes Science and Technology, 6*(5), 1216–1225.

Baig, M. M., & Gholamhosseini, H. (2013). Smart health monitoring systems: An overview of design and modeling. *Journal of Medical Systems, 37*(2), 1–14.

Ball, M. J., Edwards, M. J., & Hannah, K. J. (2006). *Introduction to nursing informatics.* New York, NY: Springer.

Bandura, A. (1995). Exercise of personal and collective efficacy in changing societies. In A. Bandura (Ed.), *Self-efficacy in changing societies* (pp. 1–45). New York, NY: Cambridge University Press. Retrieved from https://books.google.com/books?id=ZL7qN4jullUC&dq =editions%3AitTbpOYuAYgC&source=gbs_book_other_versions

Baxter, G., & Sommerville, I. (2011). Socio-technical systems: From design methods to systems engineering. *Interacting with Computers, 23*(1), 4–17.

Brooke, J. (1986). SUS—A quick and dirty usability scale. Retrieved from http://hell.meiert.org /core/pdf/sus.pdf

Carpentier, F. R. D., Mauricio, A. M., Gonzales, N. A., Millsap, R. E., Meza, C. M., Dumka, L. E., & Genalo, M. T. (2007). Engaging Mexican origin families in a school-based preventive intervention. *Journal of Primary Prevention, 28*(6), 521–546.

Catherine, H. Y., Parsons, J., Mamdani, M., Lebovic, G., Shah, B. R., Bhattacharyya, O., & Straus, S. E. (2012). Designing and evaluating a web-based self-management site for patients with type 2 diabetes—systematic website development and study protocol. *BMC Medical Informatics and Decision Making, 12*(1), 1.

Chan, C. V., & Kaufman, D. R. (2011). A framework for characterizing eHealth literacy demands and barriers. *Journal of Medical Internet Research, 13*(4), e94.

Chan, V., Ray, P., & Parameswaran, N. (2008). Mobile e-Health monitoring: An agent-based approach. *IET Communications, 2*(2), 223–230.

Council of Economic Advisers. (2015). Mapping the digital divide. Retrieved from https://obamawhitehouse.archives.gov/sites/default/files/wh_digital_divide_issue_brief.pdf

Cresswell, K. M., Bates, D. W., & Sheikh, A. (2013). Ten key considerations for the successful implementation and adoption of large-scale health information technology. *Journal of the American Medical Informatics Association, 20*(e1), e9–e13.

Dabbagh, N. (n.d.). The Instructional Design Knowledge Base. Retrieved from http://cehdclass.gmu.edu/ndabbagh/Resources/IDKB/index.htm

Davis, F. D. (1989). Perceived usefulness, perceived ease of use, and user acceptance of information technology. *MIS Quarterly, 13*(3), 319–340.

Dieffenderfer, J., Goodell, H., Mills, S., McKnight, M., Yao, S., Lin, F., . . . Zhu, Y. (2016). Low power wearable systems for continuous monitoring of environment and health for chronic respiratory disease. *IEEE Journal of Biomedical and Health Informatics, 20*(5), 1251–1264.

Drott, J., Vilhelmsson, M., Kjellgren, K., & Berterö, C. (2016). Experiences with a self-reported mobile phone-based system among patients with colorectal cancer: A qualitative study. *JMIR mHealth and uHealth, 4*(2), e66.

Elkin, P. L. (2012). Human factors engineering in HI: So what? Who cares? And what's in it for you? *Healthcare Informatics Research, 18*(4), 237–241.

Eng, T. R., Gustafson, D. H., Henderson, J., Jimison, H., & Patrick, K. (1999). Introduction to evaluation of interactive health communication applications. Science Panel on Interactive Communication and Health. *American Journal of Preventative Medicine, 16*(1), 10–15.

Francis, B. F. (2016). Self-efficacy and social-cognitive theories. Retrieved from https://wikispaces.psu.edu/display/PSYCH484/7.+Self-Efficacy+and+Social+Cognitive+Theories

Graham, I. D., Logan, J., Harrison, M. B., Straus, S. E., Tetroe, J., Caswell, W., & Robinson, N. (2006). Lost in knowledge translation: Time for a map? *Journal of Continuing Education in the Health Professions, 26*(1), 13–24.

Henderson, V. A., Barr, K. L., An, L. C., Guajardo, C., Newhouse, W., Mase, R., & Heisler, M. (2013). Community-based participatory research and user-centered design in a diabetes medication information and decision tool. *Progress in Community Health Partnerships: Research, Education, and Action, 7*(2), 171.

Hollnagel, E., & Woods, D. D. (2005). *Joint cognitive systems: Foundations of cognitive systems engineering.* Boca Raton, FL: CRC Press.

Horvath, K. J., Ecklund, A. M., Hunt, S. L., Nelson, T. F., & Toomey, T. L. (2014). Developing Internet-based health interventions: A guide for public health researchers and practitioners. *Journal of Medical Internet Research, 17*(1), e28.

Hubbard, R., Regan, K., Strath, A., & Vosper, H. (2015). Ergonomic assessment of a community pharmacy-based cardiovascular risk assessment: A new strand to an existing teaching and learning activity. *Communicare, 1*(2).

Institute of Medicine. (2004). *Health literacy: A prescription to end confusion.* Washington, DC: National Academies Press. Retrieved from http://www.nationalacademies.org/hmd/~/media/Files/Report%20Files/2004/Health-Literacy-A-Prescription-to-End-Confusion/healthliteracyfinal.pdf

International Organization for Standardization. (2015). Ergonomics of human-system interaction. Retrieved from https://www.iso.org/standard/60317.html

Internet World Stats. (2017). Internet users in the world by regions. Retrieved from http://www .internetworldstats.com/stats.htm

Jacobson, R. (2000). *Information design.* Cambridge, MA: MIT Press.

Jaspers, M. W. (2009). A comparison of usability methods for testing interactive health technologies: Methodological aspects and empirical evidence. *International Journal of Medical Informatics, 78*(5), 340–353.

Joshi, A., Amadi, C., Meza, J., Aguire, T., & Wilhelm, S. (2016). Evaluation of a computer-based bilingual breastfeeding educational program on breastfeeding knowledge, self-efficacy and intent to breastfeed among rural Hispanic women. *International Journal of Medical Informatics, 91,* 10–19.

Joshi, A., Amadi, C., Trout, K., & Obaro, S. (2014). Evaluation of an interactive surveillance system for monitoring acute bacterial infections in Nigeria. *Perspectives in Health Information Management, 11.*

Joshi, A., de Araujo Novaes, M., Machiavelli, J., Iyengar, S., Vogler, R., Johnson, C., . . . Hsu, C. E. (2012). Designing human centered GeoVisualization application—the SanaViz—for telehealth users: A case study. *Technology and Health Care, 20*(6), 503–518.

Joshi, A., Mehta, S., Talati, K., Malhotra, B., & Grover, A. (2013). Evaluation of metabolic syndrome related health information on Internet in Indian context. *Technology and Health Care, 21*(1), 19–30.

Kamberelis, G., & Dimitriadis, G. (2013). *Focus groups: From structured interviews to collective conversations.* Abingdon, Oxon: Routledge.

Karwowski, W., & Salvendy, G. (Eds.). (1998). *Ergonomics in manufacturing: Raising productivity through workplace improvement.* Dearborn, MI: Society of Manufacturing Engineers.

Kellogg Health Scholars. (2016). Community track. Retrieved from https://cultureofhealthequity .org/our-work/khsp/khsp-community-track/

Keselman, A., Logan, R., Smith, C. A., Leroy, G., & Zeng-Treitler, Q. (2008). Developing informatics tools and strategies for consumer-centered health communication. *Journal of the American Medical Informatics Association, 15*(4), 473–483.

Kinney, A. Y., Gammon, A., Coxworth, J., Simonsen, S. E., & Arce-Laretta, M. (2010). Exploring attitudes, beliefs, and communication preferences of Latino community members regarding BRCA1/2 mutation testing and preventive strategies. *Genetics in Medicine, 12*(2), 105–115.

Klein, G. A. (1993). *Naturalistic decision making: Implications for design.* Wright Patterson AFB, OH: Crew Systems Ergonomics Information Analysis Center.

Kodama, M. (2011). *Interactive business communities: Accelerating corporate innovation through boundary networks.* New York, NY: Gower Publishing.

Kushniruk, A., & Nøhr, C. (2016). Participatory design, user involvement and health IT evaluation. *Evidence-Based Health Informatics, 222,* 139.

Lalazaryan, A., & Zare-Farashbandi, F. (2014). A review of models and theories of health information seeking behavior. *International Journal of Health System and Disaster Management, 2*(4), 193.

Lee, R., & Barnett, L. (2013). Community-based participatory research & health equity. Retrieved from https://www.une.edu/sites/default/files/6%20Maine%20CBPR%20training%20slides%20 -%20FINAL.pdf

Lenté, C., Berthelot, S., & Buisine, S. (2014, October). Storyboarding to improve collaboration between ergonomics, design and engineering. In *Proceedings of the 2014 Ergonomie et Informatique Avancée Conference-Design, Ergonomie et IHM: Quelle articulation pour la co-conception de l'interaction* (pp. 80–87). New York, NY: Association of Computing Machinery.

Lewis, J. R. (1995). IBM computer usability satisfaction questionnaires: Psychometric evaluation and instructions for use. *International Journal of Human-Computer Interaction, 7*(1), 57–78.

Li, M., Lou, W., & Ren, K. (2010). Data security and privacy in wireless body area networks. *IEEE Wireless Communications, 17*(1), 51–58.

Lin, H. X., Choong, Y.-Y., & Salvendy, G. (1997). A proposed index of usability: A method for comparing the relative usability of different software systems. *Behaviour and Information Technology, 16*(4/5), 267–278.

Longo, D. R., Schubert, S. L., Wright, B. A., LeMaster, J., Williams, C. D., & Clore, J. N. (2010). Health information seeking, receipt, and use in diabetes self-management. *Annals of Family Medicine, 8*, 334–340.

Lucero, R., Sheehan, B., Yen, P., Velez, O., Nobile-Hernandez, D., & Tiase, V. (2014). Identifying consumer's needs of health information technology through an innovative participatory design approach among English- and Spanish-speaking urban older adults. *Applied Clinical Informatics, 5*(4), 943–957.

Lund, A. M. (2001). Measuring usability with the USE questionnaire. *STC Usability SIG Newsletter, 8*, 2.

Lunenburg, F. (2011). Self-efficacy in the workplace: Implications for motivation and performance. *International Journal of Management, Business, and Administration, 14*(1), 1–22.

Marquard, J. L., & Zayas-Cabán, T. (2012). Commercial off-the-shelf consumer health informatics interventions: Recommendations for their design, evaluation and redesign. *Journal of the American Medical Informatics Association, 19*(1), 137–142.

Martikainen, S., Korpela, M., & Tiihonen, T. (2014). User participation in healthcare IT development: A developers' viewpoint in Finland. *International Journal of Medical Informatics, 83*(3), 189–200.

Mumford, E. (1983). *Designing human systems for new technology: The ETHICS method*. Manchester, England: Manchester Business School.

Nielsen, J. (1993). *Usability engineering* (pp. 26, 115). San Diego, CA: Academic Press.

Nielsen, J., & Molich, R. (1990). *Heuristic evaluation of user interfaces. Proceeding CHI '90 proceedings of the SIGCHI conference on human factors in computing systems* (pp. 249–256). New York, NY: ACM.

Pandian, P. S., Mohanavelu, K., Safeer, K. P., Kotresh, T. M., Shakunthala, D. T., Gopal, P., & Padaki, V. C. (2008). Smart vest: Wearable multi-parameter remote physiological monitoring system. *Medical Engineering and Physics, 30*(4), 466–477.

Pekmezi, D., Dunsiger, S., Gans, K., Bock, B., Gaskins, R., Marquez, B., . . . Marcus, B. (2012). Rationale, design, and baseline findings from Seamos Saludables: A randomized controlled trial testing the efficacy of a culturally and linguistically adapted, computer-tailored physical activity intervention for Latinas. *Contemporary Clinical Trials, 33*(6), 1261–1271.

Perlman, G. (1997). Practical usability evaluation. *Based in part on Nielsen's 1993 Heuristics and Norman's 1990 principles*. Retrieved from http://garyperlman.com/quest/quest.cgi?form=PHUE

Plaisance, A., Witteman, H. O., Heyland, D. K., Ebell, M. H., Dupuis, A., Lavoie-Bérard, C. A., & Archambault, P. M. (2016). Development of a decision aid for cardiopulmonary resuscitation involving intensive care unit patients' and health professionals' participation using user-centered design and a wiki platform for rapid prototyping: A research protocol. *JMIR Research Protocols, 5*(1), e24.

Privitera, M. B. (2009, September). Applied ergonomics: Determining user needs in medical device design. In *Conference Proceedings for the IEEE Engineering in Medicine and Biology Society, 2009*, 5606–5608.

Raad, M. W., and Yang, L. T. (2009). A ubiquitous smart home for elderly. *Information Systems Frontiers, 11*(5), 529–536.

Raghupathi, W., & Raghupathi, V. (2014). Big data analytics in healthcare: Promise and potential. *Health Information Science and Systems, 2*(1), 1.

Reeder, B., Hills, R. A., Turner, A. M., & Demiris, G. (2014). Participatory design of an integrated information system design to support public health nurses and nurse managers. *Public Health Nursing, 31*(2), 183–192.

Reeder, B., & Turner, A. M. (2011). Scenario-based design: A method for connecting information system design with public health operations and emergency management. *Journal of Biomedical Informatics, 44*(6), 978–988.

Richter, F. (2015). The digital divide is still a thing. Retrieved from http://www.etcases.com/media/clnews/1433757345994424296.pdf

Rinkus, S., Walji, M., Johnson-Throop, K. A., Malin, J. T., Turley, J. P., Smith, J. W., & Zhang, J. (2005). Human-centered design of a distributed knowledge management system. *Journal of Biomedical Informatics, 38*(1), 4–17.

Rosson, M. B., & Carroll, J. M. (2009). Scenario based design. In *The human-computer interaction handbook* (145–162). Boca Raton, FL: CRC Press.

Samaras, G. M., & Horst, R. L. (2005). A systems engineering perspective on the human-centered design of health information systems. *Journal of Biomedical Informatics, 38*(1), 61–74.

Schraagen, J. M., Chipman, S. F., & Shalin, V. L. (Eds.). (2000). *Cognitive task analysis.* New York, NY: Psychology Press.

Serrano, J. A., Larsen, F., Isaacs, T., Matthews, H., Duffen, J., Riggare, S., . . . Graessner, H. (2015). Participatory design in Parkinson's research with focus on the symptomatic domains to be measured. *Journal of Parkinson's Disease, 5*(1), 187–196.

Sheehan, B., Nigrovic, L. E., Dayan, P. S., Kuppermann, N., Ballard, D. W., Alessandrini, E., . . . Mark, D. G. (2013). Informing the design of clinical decision support services for evaluation of children with minor blunt head trauma in the emergency department: A sociotechnical analysis. *Journal of Biomedical Informatics, 46*(5), 905–913.

Sheikh, A., Cornford, T., Barber, N., Avery, A., Takian, A., Lichtner, V., . . . Morrison, Z. (2011). Implementation and adoption of nationwide electronic health records in secondary care in England: Final qualitative results from prospective national evaluation in "early adopter" hospitals. *BMJ, 343,* d6054.

Shih, D. H., Chiang, H. S., Lin, B., & Lin, S. B. (2010). An embedded mobile ECG reasoning system for elderly patients. *IEEE Transactions on Information Technology in Biomedicine, 14*(3), 854–865.

Shneiderman, B. (1998). The standard interaction design process. Retrieved from https://thestandardinteractiondesignprocess.wordpress.com/process/specify-user-requirements/optimising-usability-requirements/

Shneiderman, B., & Plaisant, C. (2010). *Designing the user interface: Strategies for effective human-computer interaction.* Reading, MA: Pearson Addison-Wesley.

Spinuzzi, C. (2005). The methodology of participatory design. *Technical Communication, 52*(2), 163–174.

Taylor, J.C., 1982. Designing an organization and an information-system for central stores—a study in participative socio-technical analysis and design. *Systems Objectives Solutions 2*(2), 67–76.

University of Wisconsin–Madison. (n.d.). W-Madison occupational health program analysis and implementation guide for office ergonomics. Ergonomic symptom survey. Retrieved from https://www.uhs.wisc.edu/eoh/ergonomics/

U.S. Department of Health and Human Services. (2016). User interface design basics. Retrieved from https://www.usability.gov/what-and-why/user-interface-design.html

User Experience Professionals' Association. (2010). Cognitive task analysis. Retrieved from http://www.usabilitybok.org/cognitive-task-analysis

van der Bijl, J. J., & Shortridge-Baggett, L. M. (2002). The theory and measurement of the self-efficacy construct. In E. A. Lentz & L. M. Shortridge-Baggett (Eds.), *Self-efficacy in nursing: Research and measurement perspectives* (pp. 9–28). New York , NY: Springer. Retrieved from http://books.google.com/books?id=J6ujWyh_4_gC

Vechakul, J., Shrimali, B. P., & Sandhu, J. S. (2015). Human-centered design as an approach for place-based innovation in public health: A case study from Oakland, California. *Maternal and Child Health Journal, 19*(12), 2552–2559.

Victorson, D., Banas, J., Smith, J., Languido, L., Shen, E., Gutierrez, S., . . . Flores, L. (2014). eSalud: Designing and implementing culturally competent ehealth research with Latino patient populations. *American Journal of Public Health, 104*(12), 2259–2265.

Weinstein, B. E., Gilligan, J., Morgan, S., & von Hapsburg, D. (2015). Health literacy and hearing healthcare. Retrieved from http://www.slideshare.net/JenniferGilligan/25healthliteracy

Witteman, H. O., Dansokho, S. C., Colquhoun, H., Coulter, A., Dugas, M., Fagerlin, A., . . . Ivers, N. (2015). User-centered design and the development of patient decision aids: Protocol for a systematic review. *Systematic Reviews, 4*(1), 1.

Woods, D. D., & Hollnagel, E. (2006). *Joint cognitive systems: Patterns in cognitive systems engineering.* Boca Raton, FL: CRC Press.

Zeng, Q. T., & Tse, T. (2006). Exploring and developing consumer health vocabularies. *Journal of the American Medical Informatics Association, 13*(1), 24–29.

Ziebland, S., Coulter, A., Calabrese, J. D., & Locock, L. (2013). *Understanding and using health experiences.* New York, NY: Oxford University Press.

CHAPTER 9

Electronic Health Records and Telehealth Applications

Ashish Joshi

KEY TERMS

Agency for Healthcare Research and Quality (AHRQ)
American Society for Testing and Materials (ASTM)
Certified Health IT Product List (CHPL)
Clinical decision support systems
Integrated Services Digital Network (ISDN)

Model for Assessment of Telemedicine Applications (MAST)
National Ambulatory Medical Care Survey (NAMCS)
Notice of Proposed Rule Making (NPRM)
Safety-enhanced design (SED)

LEARNING OBJECTIVES

- Describe the significance of electronic health records (EHRs) and telehealth applications to enhance healthcare delivery.
- Identify the components of EHR essential for their certification.
- Examine the factors influencing the adoption and utilization of EHR and telehealth applications.
- Explore the clinical, organizational, and societal benefits of EHRs and telehealth applications.
- Assess the importance of the evaluation of EHRs and telehealth applications.
- List the factors that drive the future of telehealth.

QUESTIONS FOR THOUGHT

- Is the adoption of EHRs and telehealth applications cost-effective?
- Can a HITECH Act–like policy contribute to the institutionalization of EHRs in global settings?
- What are the challenges and opportunities related to the adoption of EHR and telehealth applications?
- Compare and contrast the factors that can impact EHR and telehealth implementation in developed versus low- to middle-income countries.
- What requirements need to be taken into consideration before the implementation of EHR and telehealth applications?
- Why it is important to have an evaluation of EHR and telehealth applications?
- What are the recommended solutions to address some of the issues that impact the future of telehealth applications?

CHAPTER OUTLINE

▶ I. Introduction to Electronic Health Records

The Centers for Medicare and Medicaid Services (CMS) define electronic health records (EHRs) as

An electronic version of a patients' medical history, that is maintained by the provider over time, and may include all of the key administrative clinical data relevant to that person's care under a particular provider, including demographics, progress notes, problems, medications, vital signs, past medical history, immunizations, laboratory data and radiology reports. (2012, n.d.)

The term *electronic health record* has been used interchangeably with various other terms, including *automated health records, electronic medical records,* and *computer-based patient records*. EHRs do not refer to a mere replacement of the conventional paper-based records (World Health Organization [WHO], 2006). The design of the EHR mainly facilitates information access and helps in streamlining the workflow of healthcare providers, while supporting other healthcare-related activities and decision making (CMS, 2012) (BOX 9.1).

The WHO, in an effort to ascertain the need for EHRs, identified a set of rationales for their adoption based on critical unmet needs of nonelectronic health record systems (WHO, 2006). Several factors, such as the absence of integrated medical records, unique identifiers, patient master indices, discharge lists, and demographic and morbidity statistics, result in the lack of a seamless flow in healthcare access and provision (WHO, 2006). EHRs can address these issues, provided that healthcare practitioners are properly trained to adhere to best practices in documentation efforts (WHO, 2006).

An increasing trend in health information technology (HIT) development and adoption has been recorded around the world, with EHRs most commonly taking center stage in European and North American countries (Stone, 2014). The highest EHR adoption rates are recorded in Denmark, New Zealand, and Sweden, where almost 100% of primary care physicians utilize EHRs with full functionality (Gray, Bowden, Johansen, & Koch, 2011). France has surpassed the United States in its process of implementing a nationwide EHR (Stone, 2014). Since the implementation, France has recorded better efficiency in terms of system interoperability, privacy laws, health information exchange, and an overall improved framework to support advanced functionalities (Stone, 2014). These achievements have been attributed to the top-down structure of governance making it easier to adhere to privacy laws and facilitate health information exchange with minimal barriers (Stone, 2014). Similar to France, the United Kingdom has made significant efforts to implement a national EHR, and 96% of medical practices have some form of EHR (Gray et al., 2011).

Canada's national framework guides the development of an interoperable EHR across its jurisdictions. EHR adoption rates by physicians and other healthcare professionals in Canada increased from 20% in 2006 to about 62% in 2013 (Chang & Gupta, 2015); however, Canadian physicians use only limited functionalities of the EHR system (Chang & Gupta, 2015). India is one of the developing countries that has made great strides in EHR development (Stone, 2014). The National Knowledge Commission of India is currently working on establishing national standards that facilitate interoperability; however, challenges in privacy and security functionalities

---

BOX 9.1 Definition of an Electronic Health Record

"The Electronic Health Record contains all personal health information belonging to an individual."

". . . is entered and accessed electronically by healthcare providers over the person's lifetime."

". . . extends beyond acute inpatient situations including all ambulatory care settings at which the patient receives care."

Reprinted from World Health Organization. (2006). Electronic health records: Manual for developing countries (p. 12). Retrieved from http://www.wpro.who.int/publications/docs/EHRmanual.pdf

remain (Stone, 2014). Of the approximately 1500 hospitals in India, very few have adopted some form of EHR (Rustagi & Singh, 2012).

A steady increase has been observed in the utilization of EHRs among U.S. physicians, from 18.2% in 2001 to 48.3% in 2009 following the launch of the Health Information Technology for Economic and Clinical Health (HITECH) Act (FIGURE 9.1) (Hsiao & Hing, 2012). National average rates for adoption of EHRs with basic systems in 2013 was at 48%, with a range from 66% in the state of New Jersey to about 94% in the state of Minnesota (Hsiao & Hing, 2012).

▶ II. HITECH Act and Meaningful Use

There has been a rapid transition from paper-based records in health care to the use of computer-based systems for patient data storage and clinical decision making. Implementation and utilization of EHRs was stimulated by the HITECH Act of 2009. It provided incentives to encourage the use of EHRs among physicians and healthcare providers (Hsiao & Hing, 2012). The HITECH Act was a segment of the 2009 American Recovery and Reinvestment Act (ARRA), which was intended to establish a foundation for the implementation and adoption of EHR systems (Blumenthal, 2010). In 2009, the U.S. government took critical steps toward the establishment of a national, interoperable EHR system. These included the following (Blumenthal, 2010):

▪ A Notice of Proposed Rule Making (NPRM) represented the various criteria that were required for healthcare professionals and health facilities to qualify for numerous monetary incentives following the meaningful use of EHRs.

▪ A final regulation describing the various certifications and standards that must be met by those EHRs in order for the implementers (physicians and hospital facilities) to receive the intended incentives.

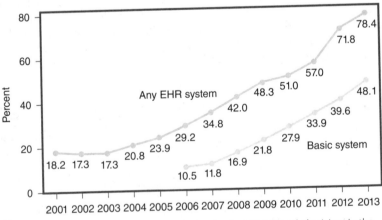

FIGURE 9.1 Trends in electronic health record adoption by office-based physicians in the United States, 2001–2013

Modified from Hsiao, C. J., & Hing, E. (2012). Use and characteristics of electronic health record systems among office-based physician practices, United States, 2001–2012 (pp. 1–8). Washington, DC: U.S. Department of Health and Human Services, Centers for Disease Control and Prevention, National Center for Health Statistics.

The two-step process emphasized not only the installation of EHR systems, but the maximization of their utility using appropriate standards in order to realize the intended benefits of EHRs. See FIGURE 9.2 for some examples for programs developed per the HITECH Act.

Meaningful use of EHRs is an invaluable component needed to foster improved health delivery and outcomes (Blumenthal, 2010) (FIGURE 9.3).

The goals of meaningful use under the HITECH Act can best be described as follows: (1) define meaningful use, (2) encourage and support the attainment of meaningful use through incentives and grant programs, (3) encourage public trust in electronic information systems by ensuring their privacy and security, and (4) foster continued HIT innovations (Blumenthal, 2010).

Meaningful use has been described in different ways by varying stakeholders (BOX 9.2). Meaningful use demonstrates that providers can utilize an EHR technology that is certified, quantifiable, and has measurable outputs (U.S. Department of Health and Human Services [DHHS], 2016).

FIGURE 9.2 Programs and regulations developed according to the HITECH Act

Data from Blumenthal, D. (2010). Launching HITECH. *New England Journal of Medicine, 362*(5), 382–385.

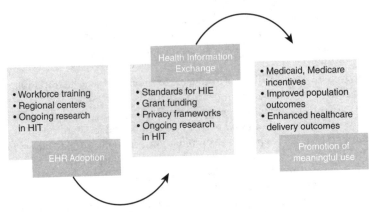

FIGURE 9.3 The HITECH Act's framework for meaningful use of EHRs

Modified from Blumenthal, D. (2010). Launching HITECH. *New England Journal of Medicine, 362*(5), 382–385.

The DHHS's definition of meaningful use is geared toward advancing five major healthcare goals: (1) improvement in healthcare quality, safety, and efficiency while alleviating health disparities; (2) fostering active engagement of patients and their families in their health care; (3) improving population health; (4) increasing efficiency in patient care coordination; and (5) ensuring privacy and security in EHR use (Blumenthal, 2010).

The healthcare professionals and Medicaid providers who satisfy meaningful use requirements may receive about $44,000 to $63,750 in incentives between 2011 and 2021 to help in addressing financial and technical challenges (Blumenthal, 2010). More importantly, the HITECH Act allocated a total of $650 million to create a network of about 70 regional HIT extension centers to assist primary care providers in achieving meaningful use (Blumenthal, 2010). In addition, about $560 million was allocated to state governments to foster exchange capabilities at multiple levels in their jurisdictions (Blumenthal, 2010). According to the CMS, physicians must satisfy three requirements to be considered for incentive payments (Stages 1, 2, and 3 meaningful use requirements) (CMS, 2012, n.d.).

■ *Stage 1 objectives:* Covered the period of 2011–2012. They included initial requirements for EHRs to be used in data entry and the ability for patients to access their medical records.

BOX 9.2 Criteria for Meaningful Use of Electronic Health Records

The use of a certified EHR in a meaningful manner
The electronic exchange of health information to improve quality of health care
The use of certified EHR technology to submit clinical quality

Data from Hsiao, C. J., & Hing, E. (2012). Use and characteristics of electronic health record systems among office-based physician practices, United States, 2001–2012 (pp. 1–8). Washington, DC: U.S. Department of Health and Human Services, Centers for Disease Control and Prevention, National Center for Health Statistics.

- *Stage 2 objectives:* Required certain conditions to be fulfilled for the meaningful use of EHRs to facilitate quality improvement during 2014.
- *Stage 3 objectives:* The year 2016 and beyond aimed with the goal of realizing improved outcomes.

CMS's meaningful use objectives represent a set of core objectives that must be met; providers can design their own path toward meaningful use (Blumenthal & Tavenner, 2010) (FIGURE 9.4).

The 2013 National Ambulatory Medical Care Survey (NAMCS) reported that about 81% of physicians lacked EHR systems with all the structural and functional capabilities to satisfy the stage 2 meaningful use requirements of the HITECH Act (see Figure 9.1) (Hsiao & Hing, 2012). Adoption of EHRs that satisfy meaningful use requirements has continued to proceed gradually; as of 2013, adoption rates for seven of the stage 2 meaningful use requirements ranged from 39% (data reporting to immunization registries) to 83% (recording of patient demographic information) (Hsiao & Hing, 2012).

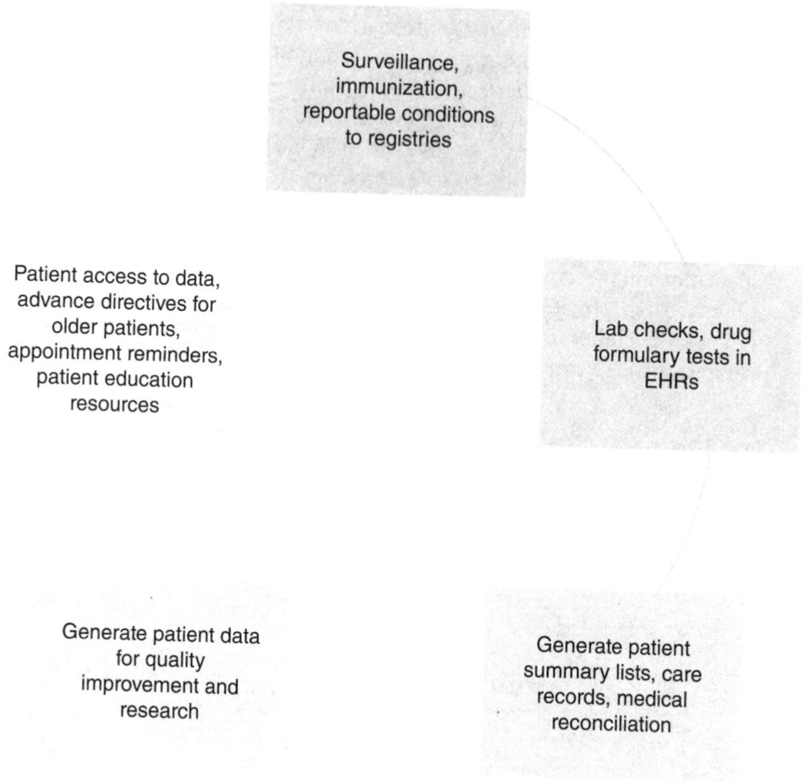

Surveillance, immunization, reportable conditions to registries

Patient access to data, advance directives for older patients, appointment reminders, patient education resources

Lab checks, drug formulary tests in EHRs

Generate patient data for quality improvement and research

Generate patient summary lists, care records, medical reconciliation

FIGURE 9.4 Objectives of meaningful use

Data from Blumenthal, D., & Tavenner, M. (2010). The "meaningful use" regulation for electronic health records. *New England Journal of Medicine, 363*(6), 501–504.

▶ III. Electronic Health Record Certification

A certified EHR demonstrates the technological capability, functionality, and security requirements and has received certification by the Office of the National Coordinator (ONC) for Health Information Technology.

Electronic Health Record Components

EHRs consist of multiple components (Yina, 2010), outlined here (**FIGURE 9.5**).

- *Administrative components:* Administrative components of an EHR include registration, admissions, discharge, and transfer data sections (RADT) (Yina, 2010). These sections frequently contain data on demographics, patient complaints, and patient disposition (Yina, 2010). The key component of this section is the patient identifier or master patient index, which uniquely identifies each patient using either numeric or alphanumeric sequences (Yina, 2010).
- *Laboratory components:* Laboratory systems are generally interfaced with EHRs as standalone systems and commonly consist of lab results, schedules, lab orders, billing, and other administrative services (Yina, 2010). Laboratory systems are rarely linked directly to EHRs, but rather can be accessed through a link within the EHR interface (Yina, 2010).
- *Radiology components:* Radiology systems are frequently used with picture archiving communication systems (PACS) to facilitate the tracking of patient data and images. This aspect includes tracking, reporting, and scheduling functions (Yina, 2010).
- *Pharmacy components:* Pharmacy system components incorporate all aspects of medication prescriptions and requirements.
- *Computerized physician order entries (CPOEs):* Computerized order entries provide the ability to place orders electronically for radiology, pharmacy, or laboratory services (Yina, 2010). CPOEs range in complexity from simple

FIGURE 9.5 EHR system components

Modified from Blumenthal, D., & Tavenner, M. (2010). The "meaningful use" regulation for electronic health records. *New England Journal of Medicine, 363*(6), 501–504.

systems with pharmacy ordering abilities to more complex systems with a variety of functions including alerting, customizing orders, ancillary services, and reporting (Yina, 2010). Although CPOEs have demonstrated success in reducing medical errors, some physicians have resisted adoption (Yina, 2010).

- *Clinical documentation:* Clinical documentation in EHRs enhances physician note taking, physician assessments of patients, and medical reports (Yina, 2010).

Requirements for Electronic Health Record Implementation and Its Certification

The EHR implementation framework integrates three critical dimensions that affect organizational change processes (Boonstra, Versluis, & Vos, 2014).

- *Context:* This is divisible into internal and external components. Internal components reflect the structure, capabilities, politics, and resources available to an organization, whereas external components consist of the social, political, economic, and competitive nature of different environments (Boonstra et al., 2014). Findings indicate that health facilities that are larger in size, located in urban settings, and teaching hospitals will generally possess greater capabilities in implementing an EHR system. Other critical context components that influence successful implementation of an EHR include the presence of a reliable vendor, health staff with prior knowledge of HIT, and a working organizational culture (Boonstra et al., 2014).
- *Content:* This aims to unify technology requirements with work practices by ensuring a proper fit between them. Content-related factors that influence EHR implementation include hardware and software reliability, protective guards for privacy and security of patient data, and the adaptiveness of these processes to the work environment (Boonstra et al., 2014).
- *EHR implementation process:* This ensures smooth integration of the EHR into work processes (Boonstra et al., 2014). Successful implementation of an EHR also involves collaborative efforts among different stakeholders such as hospital staff, developers, and physicians.

The certification for the EHRs and qualification for incentives can be achieved only if they fulfill the meaningful use objectives (DHHS, 2015). These standards for certification of EHRs were established by the ONC (DHHS, 2015). The 2015 HIT goals for EHR certification criteria included the following:

- Improvement in interoperability
- Enhancing data exchange and access
- Improvement in privacy and security capabilities
- Reduction in health disparities
- Enhancing patient safety
- Enhancing reliability and transparency of certified HIT
- Providing support for stage 3 EHR incentive provisions
- Providing support for the care continuum using the ONC HIT certification

The Certified Health IT Product List (CHPL) provides a comprehensive and authoritative listing of all certified HIT that has been successfully tested and certified by the ONC HIT Certification program (CHPL, 2016). The CHPL website allows comparison of EHR products and provides in-depth details on each product. Information is also provided on the various certification editions required to satisfy meaningful use requirements. They include the following (Neal, 2011):

- *Physician-hosted systems:* The physician takes responsibility for data storage and server hosting. The physician is tasked with system maintenance, security checks, and data backup. However, the EHR vendor still possesses administrative access to the physician-hosted data.
- *Remotely hosted systems:* A separate entity that owns and provides the services. The physician is charged with data storage, maintenance, security, and backup. Remotely hosted systems are classified into the following three types:
  - *Subsidized system:* The physician partners with an entity, such as a hospital, to obtain subsidized costs for the EHR. The subsidizing entity provides servers to host the data, and so they obtain ownership of the data, with no control by the physician. Legal concerns and data ownership issues are often major concerns with this method.
  - *Dedicated host system:* Data are also stored using a vendor's software and servers, rather than the physician's servers. However, the physician has minimal control in terms of knowing the physical location of the data, and has no control over data storage.
  - *Cloud system:* Also known as Internet-based computing, data are stored by vendors using cloud systems. Vendors providing these services are called software as a service (SAAS), and the data are usually stored in the cloud. Physicians can access the software only through the vendor website and do not know the physical location of the data. Cloud systems are frequently associated with liability issues because the vendor has complete control over the data. There are also minimal terms of negotiation for the physicians.

▶ IV. Benefits of Electronic Health Records

The implementation and adoption of EHRs have produced definite improvements in clinical outcomes, organizational outcomes, and societal outcomes (HealthIT.gov, 2014).

Clinical Outcomes

Clinical outcomes consist of improvement in patient- and system-level measures that increase efficiency of care. These include:

- *Improved healthcare quality and safety:* In terms of quality of care, the focus of EHRs has been on patient safety, effectiveness, and efficiency (Menachemi & Collum, 2011). EHR adoption has been linked to an increased adherence to guidelines for effective care provision, especially for preventive services (Menachemi & Collum, 2011). Computerized reminders as part of EHRs have also been associated with significant improvement in health outcomes (Menachemi & Collum, 2011).

- *Reduction in medical errors:* Medical error rates often serve as a proxy for patient safety. Use of CPOE, a component of EHRs, has been linked to a decline in medication errors (Campbell, Sittig, Ash, Guappone, & Dykstra, 2006; Menachemi & Collum, 2011).

- *Improved patient care:* EHRs facilitate rapid access to patient health records, both locally and remotely. They facilitate decision making, act as reminder and alert systems, and enable real-time connection with laboratories, pharmacies, and registries, as well as other EHRs (HealthIT.gov, 2014).

- *Improved patient convenience and participation:* Patients are no longer required to fill out the same forms during each doctor's visit, and e-prescriptions are electronically sent to the pharmacy at the convenience of the patient. EHRs also incorporate patient portals, which provide patients direct access to their health information and enable them to communicate directly and get feedback from physicians (HealthIT.gov, 2014). In addition, physicians are able to obtain reliable point-of-care information and receive reminders regarding essential health interventions (HealthIT.gov, 2014).

- *Improved clinical endpoints:* The use of EHRs has been associated with reduced mortality rates, fewer health complications, and lower costs (Amarasingham, Plantinga, Diener-West, Gaskin, & Powe, 2009; DesRoches et al., 2010; Menachemi, Chukmaitov, Saunders, & Brooks, 2008). These results have been inconsistent, however; several studies have reported little or no significant change in outcomes with EHR utilization (DesRoches et al., 2010; Jones, Adams, Schneider, Ringel, & McGlynn, 2010; McCullough, Casey, Moscovice, & Prasad, 2010).

Organizational Outcomes

EHR utilization in both inpatient and outpatient settings has been associated with a variety of organizational outcomes, including physician job satisfaction, legal compliance, increase in revenue, and cost savings (Menachemi & Collum, 2011). The influx of revenue with EHR adoption is a product of a combination of factors, including reduced billing errors, reduced errors in financial data capture, timeliness in balancing accounts, and improved cash flow (Menachemi & Collum, 2011). Cost savings are a product of reduced costs linked to paper data capture, transcription and chart audits, and other related documentation needs (Wang et al., 2003). By enhancing data security and patient confidentiality, EHRs facilitate improved legal compliance and have been linked to a 4% reduction in physician malpractice (Menachemi & Collum, 2011).

Societal Outcomes

A critical public health outcome of EHR adoption and implementation is the facilitation of research to enhance population health outcomes (Menachemi & Collum, 2011). The electronic availability of data and EHR interoperability makes integration easier (Menachemi & Collum, 2011). These data enable public health experts to conduct better surveillance of disease and health conditions (Menachemi & Collum, 2011).

▶ V. Factors Impacting Adoption of Electronic Health Records

Performance expectancy has been highlighted as a major influence on EHR adoption and usage by healthcare professionals, both locally and globally (Kim, Lee, Hwang, & Yoo, 2016; Kruse, Kothman, Anerobi, & Abanaka, 2016). It is described as the perceived ability of electronic systems to improve workflow, efficiency, and performance output. Another very influential factor is "facilitating conditions" comprising an array of physical, behavioral, and environmental attributes that directly or indirectly influence intention to utilize EHRs (Kim et al., 2016). Other factors include the following:

- *Implementation costs:* Some implementation costs associated with adoption of EHRs include installation costs for hardware and software, conversion of paper to electronic charts, maintenance costs, and revenue costs with initial loss of productivity (Menachemi & Collum, 2011). Recent studies reported EHR installation costs (including software and training) of almost $50,000 per physician (Menachemi & Collum, 2011). Maintenance costs (largely consisting of hardware and software maintenance, support systems, and IT staff) also rise as high as $8000 per provider annually (Menachemi & Collum, 2011). These costs have been reported as the highest barriers to EHR adoption among physicians (Menachemi & Collum, 2011).

- *Workflow disruption:* Physicians and other healthcare professionals frequently encounter disruption in their work activities during the installation and training process in EHR implementation, which has been linked to a loss of productivity (Menachemi & Collum, 2011). Some clinics report a decline in productivity of up to 35% during a three-month implementation period, resulting in revenue loss of about $11,200 per clinician (Wang et al., 2003). Contributing factors to decline in productivity include long training hours (up to 134 hours) and reduced patient visits (Miller, West, Brown, Sim, & Ganchoff, 2005).

- *Patient privacy and security issues:* The availability of EHRs poses threats to the privacy and security of patient data (Parver, 2009). However, Health Insurance Portability and Accountability Act (HIPAA) legislation enforces the use of audit measures to identify individuals who access patient health records as well as the activities performed (Parver, 2009).

- *Increased technology dependence:* The computerization of health records increases reliance on technology (Menachemi & Collum, 2011). It is critical to ensure that basic physician activities can be carried out when technical issues with the EHRs occur (Menachemi & Collum, 2011). In addition, loss of physician autonomy often accompanies the use of clinical decision support systems, because physicians may not be able to counter certain decisions made by the system (Campbell et al., 2006). The WHO outlines several drawbacks encountered in the adoption and implementation of EHRs (WHO, 2006) (BOX 9.3).

Several factors that positively influenced EHR adoption in the United States include larger hospital size, benefits of improved efficiency, quality, data access, perceived value, and improved information transfer (Kruse et al., 2016) (TABLE 9.1).

The cost of EHR implementation and its related training and maintenance were the most commonly identified barriers to EHR adoption (Kruse et al.,

BOX 9.3 Drawbacks in the Adoption of Electronic Health Records

- Lack of standards and terminology in clinical data entry
- Poor familiarity with computers and resistance to computer technology
- Resistance to workflow change among healthcare professionals
- Cost of computer systems and limited financial resources
- Provider concerns regarding availability of information on request
- Privacy and confidentiality of electronically generated stored data
- Quality of electronically stored health records and data entry accuracy
- Limited staff with adequate training in disease classification systems
- Limited human resources—lack of staff with adequate skills
- Environmental issues—electrical wiring and supply of electricity, amount and quality of space needed for computers, etc.
- Involvement of clinicians and hospital administrators

Reprinted from World Health Organization (2006). Electronic Health Records; Manual for developing countries., chapter. Issues and Challenges, Pages No. 27, Copyright (2006).

TABLE 9.1 Facilitators to EHR Adoption and Implementation in the United States

EHR Adoption Determinants		Components
Inputs (These factors initially determine adoption)	**Demographics/ Organizational level factors**	Location of facility in urban setting Alignment with organizational strategy Size of facility Incentives Availability of training support Availability of technical support Perceived usefulness to facility
	Provider work efficiency/ effectiveness	Enhanced provider communication Care continuity Improved time efficiency Rapid information transfer
Outputs (These observed outcomes facilitate adoption)	**Patient-level outcomes**	Improved population health Better data security Increased system utility Improved quality Accessibility of health data to patients Patient empowerment
	Provider/ facility level outcomes	Facility cost savings Staff retention Reduced medical errors Management support Competitiveness Effectiveness

Data from Kruse, C. S., Kothman, K., Anerobi, K., & Abanaka, L. (2016). Adoption factors of the electronic health record: A systematic review. *JMIR Medical Informatics, 4*(2), e19.

2016). Other identified barriers included poor timeliness in implementation, perceived lack of usefulness, hurdles with data transfer/integration, patient resistance, limited staff training, and organizational characteristics (such as the size and location of the facility) (Kruse et al., 2016). Facilities located in rural communities tend to have reduced capacity to take on capital-intensive tasks (Kruse et al., 2016).

EHR design and other technical concerns were also commonly identified barriers to its adoption and utilization by physicians and other healthcare professionals (McGinn et al., 2011). Although all groups of health professionals expressed concerns over patient data security, patients felt that EHRs could lead to compromise of their health information, either within the health facility or through communication between other health facilities (McGinn et al., 2011). Patients perceived EHRs to negatively influence patient–provider communication due to decline in physical contact of patients with their physicians and increased technology reliance (McGinn et al., 2011) (TABLE 9.2).

Healthcare professionals indicated cost as a barrier to EHR adoption, mostly related to lack of funding, startup costs, maintenance, and concerns with return on investments (McGinn et al., 2011). Physicians indicated concerns including lack of time to learn to use the EHR properly and concerns of disrupting workflow. Healthcare professionals, managers, and patients were more likely to report positive influence on productivity from EHRs whereas nurses had mixed responses (McGinn et al., 2011). Nurses felt that on the one hand, EHRs reduce time spent during patient–nurse interactions, while on the other hand, they perceived increasing productivity with better documentation and access to patient records (McGinn et al., 2011).

TABLE 9.2 User Perspective on EHR Adoption

Physicians	▪ Design/technical issues
	▪ Cost issues
	▪ Increased workload/no time
Health professions	▪ Design/technical issues
	▪ Motivation to use EHR
	▪ Increased workload/no time
Managers	▪ Cost issues
	▪ Privacy/security concerns
	▪ Design, workload, productivity, interoperability
Patients	▪ Privacy and security concerns
	▪ Motivation to use EHR
	▪ Patient-provider interaction concerns

Data from McGinn, C. A., Grenier, S., Duplantie, J., Shaw, N., Sicotte, C., Mathieu, L., & Gagnon, M. P. (2011). Comparison of user groups' perspectives of barriers and facilitators to implementing electronic health records: A systematic review. *BMC Medicine, 9*(1), 1.

▶ VI. Evaluation of Electronic Health Record Systems

Usability and information design are critical components in the development, implementation, and adoption of EHR (Middleton et al., 2013). The mode in which information is organized and presented in the EHRs determines its ability to support the healthcare processes while minimizing the occurrence of human errors (Middleton et al., 2013). The EHR user interface with which the healthcare providers interact must be user-friendly, intuitive, and responsive to user needs (Middleton et al., 2013). Four primary functions describe the impact of EHRs on user needs: (1) memory aid (minimize the need for complete reliance on human memory), (2) computational aid (minimize the need for complex computations using human memory), (3) decision support aid (facilitate decision making through triangulation of information from multiple sources), and (4) collaboration aid (make collaboration between multiple entities of the hospital facilities easier).

The Agency for Healthcare Research and Quality (AHRQ) identified the need for a uniform framework in assessing the usability of EHRs. Safety-enhanced design (SED) certifications were established as a requirement by the ONC for HIT for EHR vendors to certify their products (Ratwani, Hettinger, Kosydar, Fairbanks, & Hodgkins, 2017). The rationale for the SED arises from findings that most vendors lack legitimate usability testing procedures and standards (Ratwani et al., 2017). The ONC for HIT also outlines several questions that should be addressed in conducting a postimplementation evaluation of EHRs to foster workflow efficiency, while ensuring continuous quality improvement (HealthIT.gov, 2013; BOX 9.4). According to this report, post-EHR implementation evaluation should be conducted about three to four weeks following installation (HealthIT.gov, 2013).

▶ VII. Telehealth: A Global Perspective

Telehealth is defined as the use of healthcare information exchanged from one site to another via information and communication technologies (ICTs) to improve the patient's health status (Paul & McDaniel, 2016). Different terminologies have been utilized to characterize telehealth, including: *telemedicine, telemonitoring,* and *teleconsultations* (Fatehi & Wootton, 2012). Telemedicine involves remote provision of medical services; this is in contrast to telehealth, which includes a wider array of services including education and administration (Fatehi & Wootton, 2012). Presently, all terms are collectively referred to as remote ICT tools that facilitate healthcare access between geographically distant areas (Paul & McDaniel, 2016).

ICT has been the driver of telehealth development and implementation to deliver healthcare services (WHO, 2009). The rapid decline in the cost of ICTs and the increased transformation of digital methods, alongside rapid Internet penetration, has fostered substantive interest in the use of telehealth (WHO, 2009). However, striking disparities are prevalent in the adoption and utilization of telehealth in developed versus developing settings (WHO, 2009). In western world regions such as the United Kingdom, North America, Australia, and Scandinavia, telehealth applications are primarily focused on patient monitoring and management of chronic diseases, creating a gradual paradigm shift in healthcare delivery from hospital settings

BOX 9.4 Requirements to Be Addressed During Postimplementation Evaluation of EHRs

Culture and Adoption

- What did we learn about ourselves that we did not know before?
- Have all of our providers/departments migrated to an EHR or are some providers still waiting?
- Do workflow processes need to be re-evaluated? Are providers returning to pre-EHR workflows?
- Do any staff need additional training?
- Are we capturing the required data elements needed for internal clinical priorities, as well as for reportable quality measures and meaningful use objectives?
- Have unplanned consequences arisen due to the implementation of the EHR?

Network and Infrastructure

- If there are network bottlenecks and downtimes, have we logged and reported them?
- Is technology (hardware, software) in the right places?
- Are technology tools reliable?
- Have we ensured personal health information is used and disclosed in a secure environment?

EHR Vendor

- What did we learn about our EHR vendor that we didn't know before?
- What issues must be resolved before the practice is handed over to the vendor's Technical Support and Maintenance division?

Reproduced from HealthIT.gov. (2013). How do I conduct a post-implementation evaluation? Retrieved from https://www .healthit.gov/providers-professionals/faqs/how-do-i-conduct-post-implementation-evaluation

to patient homes (WHO, 2009). However, in developing settings where infrastructure is limited and ICTs are gradually gaining momentum, telehealth services primarily serve as tools for connecting patients to specialist services, tertiary centers, and hospitals through referrals (WHO, 2009). In addition, significant barriers such as cost, infrastructure, culture, and policy still preclude the scalability and sustainability of telehealth interventions in low- and middle-income settings (WHO, 2009).

There has been a gradual increase in the adoption and utilization of telehealth in the 21st century. Europe, North and South America, and Southeast Asia have recorded high adoption rates, with Africa and the Mediterranean closely lagging behind (Wilson & Maeder, 2015). Telehealth adoption has been projected to increase by 10-fold between 2012 and 2018. It is largely attributed to the growth in mobile and e-health applications for self-management of chronic conditions (Wilson & Maeder, 2015). Telehealth is broadly influenced by three factors: clinical specialty, connectivity technology, and care model (Wilson & Maeder, 2015). New clinical specialties emerging in telemedicine include intensive care, wound care, dermatology, and emergency medicine; areas such as orthopedics, neurology, pediatrics, and rehabilitation are becoming less common in telemedicine. The most advanced area in the field of telehealth is teleradiology. According to a WHO global assessment on telehealth services, over 60% of countries offered initiatives in teleradiology; however, only 30% had established services (WHO, 2009). Other up-and-coming fields include telepathology, teledermatology, and telepsychiatry, reporting 40%, 38%, and 24% of telehealth initiatives, respectively. Several medical specialties that are gaining increasing recognition in the telehealth market include gynecology, neurology, orthopedics, oncology, radiology, and pathology (Transparency Market Research, 2014).

Progress in telehealth and other associated video conferencing strategies is linked to three main factors: system manufacturers, network providers, and system integrators (Transparency Market Research, 2014). These have cumulatively contributed to the proliferation of video conferencing and telehealth applications (Transparency Market Research, 2014). Previous use of audio conferencing tools and technologies has been rapidly replaced by broadband systems, webcams, and video sensors (Transparency Market Research, 2014). The cumulative progress of these industry segments has led to an overall growth in video-enabled telehealth applications. Various 4G technologies are frequently used in developed settings and are gradually gaining popularity in developing markets, especially in the Asia-Pacific region (Transparency Market Research, 2014). This is closely followed by 3G technologies and Integrated Services Digital Network (ISDN).

▶ VIII. Mechanisms of Telehealth Delivery

Three distinct mechanisms are predominant in telehealth delivery: store and forward, self-monitoring, and interactive services. Each of them is outlined in the following sections.

Store-and-Forward Approach

With the store-and-forward approach, the focus is on patient monitoring through data gathering and storage. The telehealth system facilitates the collection of various patient indicators, biosignals, and physiologic parameters, and these are processed in the form of medical reports, images, and history. This information is then sent to the primary care physician, who will utilize it in decision making and diagnosis, or send it to a specialist (Casadevall, 2015). This approach is widely adopted in the radiology, dermatology, and pathology fields (Smith, 2015). The benefits include the time-saving nature and the flexibility for physicians to serve more people (Smith, 2015). A major disadvantage of this mechanism is an increased reliance on records and reduced emphasis on patient–physician interaction (Casadevall, 2015).

Self-Monitoring

In the self-monitoring approach, the patients take the lead in utilizing the telehealth device(s) and conducting various self-measurements from their homes. The data gathered are then transmitted directly to the system and to the healthcare providers. This model is frequently employed in the management of chronic conditions such as cancer, heart conditions, and diabetes, which constitute over two-thirds of healthcare costs in the United States (Casadevall, 2015). Inherent risks lie in patient data accuracy, because measurement is carried out by the patients, but outcomes are generally similar to traditional reports carried out by physicians (Smith, 2015).

Interactive Monitoring

Interactive monitoring is also known as real-time monitoring. Interactive monitoring promotes patient–physician interaction during teleconsultations. These consultations mimic virtual conferencing between patients and one or more physicians, thus providing a dynamic interface for patient health assessment and diagnosis (Casadevall, 2015). This approach is gaining rapid popularity in the United States. Nearly 22 states have mandated reimbursement for such teleconsultations at similar rates to traditional health delivery models (Casadevall, 2015). Teleneuropsychology is a field that largely employs this approach. Other applicable areas include telenursing, telepharmacy, and telerehabilitation (Smith, 2015).

▶ IX. Benefits of Telehealth

Prior research has highlighted numerous benefits of telehealth. Some of the key benefits are highlighted in the following sections (FIGURE 9.6).

Enhanced Continuity of Care

Telehealth enhances continuity of care by providing an avenue for healthcare providers to directly relate to and communicate with patients, and monitor patient activity beyond the hospital environment (Knight et al., 2016). Telehealth consultations allow for triangulated communication among the patient and various healthcare providers including physicians and nurses, thus facilitating improved patient care (Knight et al., 2016).

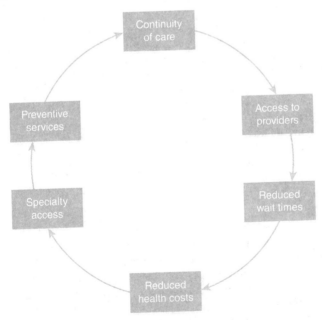

FIGURE 9.6 Benefits of telehealth

Improved Access to Healthcare Providers

Telehealth bridges the gap of geographic proximity in providing access to healthcare services to wider populations. Telehealth also enables a wider variety of specialists to provide coordinated care to patients remotely with a lot of flexibility. It addresses the critical issue of long wait times that is frequently encountered by patients when scheduling doctors' appointments (Knight et al., 2016).

Enhanced Patient Monitoring

Chronic health conditions currently represent the majority of health conditions in westernized countries, and chronic healthcare management frequently incorporates home monitoring technologies (Reed, 2005). Telehealth technologies have been shown to significantly improve the management of heart conditions, while ensuring compliance and reducing the cost of care (Benatar, Bondmass, Ghitelman, & Avitall, 2003).

Preventive Services

Substantive evidence has been gathered regarding the potential of telehealth as a tool in promoting preventive health care including health education and disease screening. Telehealth technology can be utilized in capturing high resolution digital images of the retina, as a procedural screening for diabetic retinopathy. This is especially relevant for isolated population groups at high risk for this condition. Using telehealth technology, rapid screening can be conducted in real time, thus reducing patient wait times and transportation costs (Reed, 2005; Stumpf, 2003).

Specialty Access

Teleconsultation services facilitate access to multiple health professionals simultaneously, effectively reducing patient costs (Reed, 2005). Telehealth systems have been employed in hospital logistics and patient care management, providing clinicians with real-time information on bed space availability and physician schedules (Reed, 2005). Telehealth systems reduce wait times and have the potential to address patient needs in a timely manner (David & Tavenner, 2015). According to Gold (2014), an average of approximately 19 days is required to schedule a doctor's appointment in the traditional health delivery system, compared to less than one hour for scheduling telehealth appointments (David & Tavenner, 2015). Telehealth also promotes simultaneous access to multiple physicians (David & Tavenner, 2015).

Reduced Health Costs

Existing evidence has shown that patients incur fewer costs from telehealth appointments compared to traditional doctors' visits (David & Tavenner, 2015). On average, doctors' visits cost about $45 to $120, compared to $40 or less for teleconsultations. These cost benefits are believed to provide improved value to patients (David & Tavenner, 2015; Dizik, 2012).

▶ X. Barriers to Implementation of Telehealth Applications

Some of the barriers to the implementation of telehealth applications are discussed in the following sections.

Perceptions about Technology

Lack of in-person contact, confidentiality issues, and lack of familiarity with telehealth benefits largely influence telehealth adoption among varying population groups (Reginatto, 2012). The adoption of new technology is particularly low among older populations (Reginatto, 2012). Remote consultations have the potential to impair the decision-making ability of healthcare professionals, especially when more objective measurements requiring physical contact are needed. Patients also express confidentiality concerns with health data accessibility and sharing (Reginatto, 2012).

Technology-Related Barriers

Limited familiarity with technology, system usability, broadband access, incompatibility, and interoperability challenges are the most frequently highlighted technical concerns with telehealth (Reginatto, 2012). Usability concerns are still undergoing exploration as telehealth systems continue to emerge in different settings. These design challenges are especially critical because the majority of the population catered to are the elderly. Hence, maximum consideration should be given to their user characteristics, abilities, needs, and preferences. Designers do not adequately incorporate health professionals' views into system design and development, creating unnecessary strain in the training process and a decline in productivity (Reginatto, 2012). Consumers also express concerns about the ability of health professionals to utilize the data generated during telehealth (Reginatto, 2012).

Internet access is a critical limiting factor affecting the functioning of telehealth systems. Recommendations have been made to make broadband free for patients to address this issue.

The compatibility and interoperability of telehealth systems remain issues because they affect physician–physician communication in terms of data sharing (Reginatto, 2012). The relevance of the data becomes questionable if patients receiving consultations in their homes are unable to share their data with providers due to such limitations.

Organizational Barriers

Limited integration into the healthcare system, trust issues among stakeholders, and organizational readiness for change are key organizational barriers influencing telehealth adoption (Reginatto, 2012). Physicians express resistance to changing their usual practices and adopting telehealth models (Reginatto, 2012). This is further complicated by the lack of champions in healthcare systems who are willing to promote telehealth interventions.

Financial Barriers

The high cost of infrastructure and issues with affordability for patients influence telehealth design, implementation, and adoption. The lack of governmental support through subsidies, incentives, and clearly defined reimbursement models frequently deters physician and healthcare professionals from engaging in telehealth practice, even though its benefits are widely recognized (Reginatto, 2012). Cost of access is a key factor, especially when insurance models are not clearly laid out (Reginatto, 2012). Telehealth penetration in the healthcare market is facing numerous challenges because it interferes with the regular workflow of clinicians in hospitals, without an added incentive to make up for this. Another large problem is that the current healthcare systems are more likely to incentivize poor health rather than preventive health or continuity in the monitoring process (Reginatto, 2012).

Regulatory Issues

Numerous challenges accompany the use of telehealth among providers and patients residing within the same country (Jordanova & Lievens, 2011). A typical example is a 2009 incident where a psychiatrist based in Colorado was imprisoned for writing an antidepressant prescription for a teenager based in California, without having a license from California (Jordanova & Lievens, 2011). This constituted a potential hindrance to the practice of telemedicine, because physicians would need to be licensed in virtually every state they consult in (Jordanova & Lievens, 2011).

Legislation

Laws governing the use of telehealth are lacking in most countries (Jordanova & Lievens, 2011). Where these laws are present, controversies often accompany them. For instance, the Malaysian Telemedicine Act of 1997 regulates telemedicine practice in Malaysia, with the view of protecting its citizens and penalizing negligent physicians. However, it mandates that all practicing physicians who provide teleconsultation in the country be registered with the Director General, thereby limiting telemedicine practice with foreign physicians (Jordanova & Lievens, 2011). In addition, foreign physicians are subject to the malpractice laws and penalties in the patient's country of residence.

Varying standards exist governing different aspects of telehealth. However, the absence of uniform guidelines for telehealth poses a significant barrier to its adoption and practice (Jordanova & Lievens, 2011). Core standards for telemedicine operations, evidence-based practice for telemental health, practice guidelines for teledermatology, and telehealth practice recommendations for diabetic retinopathy are some of the examples of telehealth standards developed by various organizations, including the American Society for Testing and Materials (ASTM), Standards Australia e-health, and the International Organization for Standardization (Jordanova & Lievens, 2011). Other barriers to telehealth adoption include language challenges, ethics, differences in clinical practice, informed consent, privacy, taxes, and insurance issues (Jordanova & Lievens, 2011) (TABLE 9.3).

TABLE 9.3 Barriers to Telehealth Adoption and Implementation Among Key Stakeholders

Barriers	Consumers	Health Professionals	Service Providers	Technology Providers	Health System Context Experts
Poorly defined incentives for health professionals		X	X	X	X
Usability of telehealth system	X	X	X	X	X
Lack of reimbursement methods		X	X	X	X
Organizational readiness for change		X	X	X	X
Infrastructural costs		X	X	X	X
Technology skills	X	X	X	X	X
Organizational readiness for change		X	X	X	X
Trust among stakeholders	X	X	X	X	X
Confidentiality	X	X	X	X	X
Disincentives due to payment models			X	X	X
Regulatory issues for data		X	X	X	X

Barrier					
Liability issues			X		
Higher professional responsibility	X	X	X	X	
Reduced broadband access	X	X	X		
Lack of champions in the health system	X	X	X		
Consumer cost of care					X
Interoperability issues	X	X	X		
Reduced physical contact during care	X	X	X	X	X
Insufficient evaluation methods	X	X	X	X	X
System compatibility issues		X	X		
Technology stability and reliability		X			

Modified from Reginatto, B. M. B. (2012). Understanding barriers to wider telehealth adoption in the home environment of older people: An exploratory study in the Irish context. *International Journal on Advances in Life Sciences*, 4(3/4), 63–76.

▶ XI. Factors Influencing Adoption and Sustainability of Telehealth Applications

Several factors contribute to the successful adoption and sustainability of telehealth applications. Some of these factors are discussed in the following sections.

Time Constraints

Healthcare providers tend to not consider teleconsultations as a significant aspect of their work, especially when they are overwhelmed with workload (Paul & McDaniel, 2016). These findings were identified in areas where healthcare providers and caregivers are engaged in numerous responsibilities, and time allocation for teleconsultations is minimal (Paul & McDaniel, 2016).

Patient Participation

Healthcare providers are often limited by patients' financial constraints in traveling to specific locations or hubs where the telehealth services are housed (Paul & McDaniel, 2016). This results in sparse use of these hubs by patients and frustrations on the part of providers waiting for patients on the other end. Some of these challenges are overcome by situating telehealth workstations within health facilities for providers and at easily accessible community locations for patients. One telehealth study discussed an oncology teleconsultation project that failed due to the lengthy amount of time it took for the healthcare providers to get to a workstation (Paul & McDaniel, 2016). Early scheduling of teleconsultations was mostly preferred by healthcare providers because it did not interrupt their regular routines (Paul & McDaniel, 2016).

Fit with Patient Characteristics

The fit between telehealth systems and patient needs, environment, literacy, and capacity influences patient comfort and the feasibility of continuing with such processes (Vassilev et al., 2015). Evidence shows that simplified technologies routinely used by patients are likely to be sustainable when applied in telehealth systems (Vassilev et al., 2015).

Project Design Strategy

The teleconsultations need to be designed in a manner that provides learning and empowers patients more, as opposed to healthcare provision–based consultations (Paul & McDaniel, 2016). This facilitates collaborative efforts between patients and providers to implement healthy and corrective practices (Paul & McDaniel, 2016). The educational component of teleconsultations is therefore critical. Evidence suggests that healthcare provider collaborations during teleconsultations should involve multidisciplinary teams of health professionals including psychiatrists, disease specialists, and physicians (Paul & McDaniel, 2016).

There are several other obstacles to achieving widespread adoption of tele-health: acceptance of technology by patients and clinicians, economically sus-tainable reimbursement systems, interoperability among electronic patient record systems, and technological capacity to accommodate bandwidth-heavy telehealth programs in smaller hospitals, clinics, and patients' homes (Dinesen et al., 2016).

▶ XII. Telehealth Evaluation

Telehealth evaluation can potentially generate evidence-based information in promoting sound policies and strategies (WHO, 2009). Europe, North America, and Southeast Asia reported the highest frequency of evaluating telehealth proj-ects, with disparities evident in the African, Eastern Mediterranean, and Western Pacific regions (WHO, 2009). Results suggest a shortage of trials and evaluation results on telehealth globally. Only 20% of countries reported publishing a recent tele-project evaluation. This challenge has been attributed to several factors, including: (1) limited research expertise in evaluation processes, (2) financial constraints, (3) sample size limitations, and (4) duration taken to observe visible and measurable outcomes in telehealth projects (WHO, 2009). These challenges are significantly higher in developing regions because the majority of telehealth initiatives are informal, limiting their ability to become readily established with published evidence (WHO, 2009). These regions frequently require external assistance in conducting and publishing results on telehealth projects. Proper evaluation is essential to convince the various stakeholders of the added value of telehealth and to come to sustainable implementation in daily clinical practice. Evaluation of telehealth services begins with an evaluation of technical efficacy such as accuracy and reliability of the application. During subsequent deploy-ment a comprehensive evaluation is necessary, using multiple endpoints such as accessibility, quality, and cost of care (Jansen-Kosterink, Vollenbroek-Hutten, & Hermens, 2016). The next step in telehealth evaluation is to examine whether the overall evaluation of a technology in a particular system applies in other settings (DeChant, Tohme, Mun, Hayes, & Schulman, 1996) (TABLE 9.4).
The stages of telehealth evaluation include:

- *Stage 1:* This can be conducted using an experimental design with a small number of subjects or even case studies. This type of evaluation design allows researchers to gain detailed information that can be used for further improve-ment of telehealth services.
- *Stage 2:* Evaluation is focused on gaining an initial idea about the potential added value for clinical practice. Suitable designs are cohort studies with a small sample size ($n < 50$) or single-case design (or $N = 1$ designs) (Jansen-Kosterink et al., 2016).
- *Stage 3:* The evaluation focuses on showing the effectiveness of the telehealth service and/or adoption of the service by its end users. Randomized controlled trials (RCTs) fit well with the evaluation of telehealth services. The evaluation also takes into account the way the telehealth service is being implemented in daily clinical practice.

TABLE 9.4 Stages and Objectives of Evaluation

Evaluation Stage	Description	Evaluation Objective
Stage 1	Technical efficacy	Feasibility and usability of the system
Stage 2	Specific system objectives	Potential added value on technology used and clinical service
Stage 3	System analysis	Effectiveness and adoption
Stage 4	External validity	Adoption and business models

Data from Jansen-Kosterink, S., Vollenbroek-Hutten, M., & Hermens, H. (2016). A renewed framework for the evaluation of telemedicine. In 8th International Conference on eHealth, Telemedicine, and Social Medicine, Venice, Italy, eTELEMED (Vol. 2016). Retrieved from https://www.thinkmind.org/index.php?view=article&articleid=etelemed_2016_4_30_40183

- *Stage 4*: Evaluation here should focus on the business models, or else the decision makers run the risk of introducing telehealth services that are not cost-effective. The studies performed in this stage are large-scale cohort studies ($n \geq 50$) (Zanaboni & Wootton, 2012).

The Model for Assessment of Telemedicine Applications (MAST) is a multidisciplinary telehealth assessment tool (Kidholm et al., 2012) that involves three stages.

- *Stage 1*: Preliminary assessment in which the maturity of the technology and the organization using it is assessed.
- *Stage 2*: Outcome assessment of the telehealth application is conducted within seven domains: (1) health problem and characteristics of the application; (2) safety; (3) clinical effectiveness; (4) patient perspectives; (5) economic aspects; (6) organizational aspects; and (7) sociocultural, ethical, and legal aspects.
- *Stage 3*: Transferability assessment in which the transferability of the evidence to the local setting is considered.

The MAST model is currently the most widely used framework for evaluating telemedicine in the European Union (EU) and is used in a number of EU projects (Rosenbek et al., 2015).

▶ XIII. Future of Telehealth Applications

Key issues driving the future of telehealth include the following (Dinesen et al., 2016) and those listed in BOX 9.5.

- *Personalization of health care:* Technology must engage patients in their care, enhance collaboration with the healthcare system, and be personally meaningful.
- *Matching patients with appropriate technologies:* Novel telehealth platforms require a match based on the patient's age, education, interests, physical

BOX 9.5 Issues Driving the Future of Telehealth Applications

Personalization of health care
Matching patients with the right technologies
Optimal use of healthcare data
New education paradigm for patients and providers
New communities of knowledge and practice
New care and business models tailored to sustainability and scalability of telehealth initiatives
Transfer of scientific knowledge from research to implementation and practice
Innovative research methodologies within telehealth

Data from Dinesen, B., Nonnecke, B., Lindeman, D., Toft, E., Kidholm, K., Jethwani, K., . . . Gutierrez, M. (2016). Personalized telehealth in the future: A global research agenda. *Journal of Medical Internet Research, 18*(3), e53.

capabilities, familiarity, access to technology, and support to help with self-care and functional independence. Perceptual, motor, and cognitive abilities need to be considered when matching technology to patients. Matching patients with a proper device and gathering large amounts of meaningful data will lead to improved insight into a person's disease state and better assessment of the success of care management strategies (Dinesen et al., 2016).

Optimal use of healthcare data, including developing a secure interface between patient-generated data and the EHR: There is a lack of clarity regarding the conditions under which personal data become protected data and how to handle the lack of accessibility to one's own personal health information. Further, the policies related to EHR technology are more focused on provider-centric HIT, with minimal incentive for patients to engage with and use the system. Hence, there is a focus on having standards that require the EHR to incorporate patient-generated data from remote monitoring devices (Dinesen et al., 2016).

New education paradigms for patients and providers: Mobile phones and other emerging handheld applied telehealth-based tools and devices store a great amount of information and can become the source tool for information sharing and education. Adoption of high-technology medical communication enables greater collaboration and learning between healthcare providers.

New communities of knowledge and practice: With the rapid uptake of telehealth applications, it is of paramount importance to ensure that the experts within the communities have the right understanding of the needs of specific patient populations. This will ensure that the educational message content can match the proper telehealth system (Dinesen et al., 2016).

New care and business models tailored to sustainability and scalability of telehealth initiatives: There has been a growing need for innovative business models for telehealth applications to ensure their sustainability, scalability, and success. New telehealth models should address care coordination across multiple sectors and multiple care practices and develop guidelines that can assist patients on how to use technology (Chen, Cheng, & Mehta, 2013).

Transfer of scientific knowledge from research to implementation and practice: Telehealth can deliver care that is accessible, convenient, and patient-centered (Lustig, 2012). Widespread implementation will require attention to systems engineering approaches to healthcare design so that it can address incentives, technical and human requirements, work processes, and payment issues (President's Council of Advisors on Science and Technology, 2014).

■ *Innovative research methodologies within telehealth:* RCTs are the most effective method of evaluating the efficacy of telehealth application; however, they are time consuming and cumbersome. Stakeholders are keen to gather information about patient perceptions, clinical impact, cost-effectiveness, and organizational aspects of telehealth (Kidholm et al., 2015).

▶ XIV. Conclusion

EHR adoption and implementation have rapidly increased in the past decade. Although the majority of EHR use has been in clinical settings, EHRs are gradually gaining momentum in population health research. Studies on EHR use in population health show an improved collection of social and behavioral indicators, linkage with vital statistics and records, as well as EHR integration with emerging technologies such as wearable sensor devices as a means to improve both clinical and population health outcomes (Casey, Schwartz, Stewart, & Adler, 2016). Data stored in EHRs have immense potential to enhance healthcare quality, safety, and efficiency, especially when they are combined with mortality data or other relevant records (van Velthoven, Mastellos, Majeed, O'Donoghue, & Car, 2016). Hence, it is imperative for countries implementing EHRs to identify ways of improving accessibility to these data for such purposes (van Velthoven et al., 2016). Better strategies are needed to ensure data confidentiality and address other privacy and security concerns common to EHRs. More research also is needed to explore patient perceptions on the use of their medical records for secondary purposes beyond direct clinical care (van Velthoven et al., 2016). In addition, improving EHR data availability at the national level for policymakers is critical for evidence-based decision making in healthcare planning and provision (van Velthoven et al., 2016). Hence, data accessibility, completeness, cost-effectiveness, efficiency, and their associated risks are essential topics that will drive future EHR adoption, implementation, and sustainability (van Velthoven et al., 2016).

Telehealth is an innovate solution to facilitating remote healthcare management. Evidence has shown increasing patient acceptance toward telehealth, with the potential for it to grow rapidly and overtake prior traditional delivery models (David & Tavenner, 2015). The competitive advantages of telehealth systems include its cost-effectiveness, accessibility, enhanced patient referrals, and reduced wait times (David & Tavenner, 2015). These benefits have shown potential in addressing health service delivery in areas experiencing a shortage of health professionals, poverty, and limited proximity to health services (David & Tavenner, 2015). Telehealth implementations continue to face pushbacks from healthcare providers due to lack of sustainable reimbursement models, with patients expressing concerns of privacy, security, and trust in health decision making (David & Tavenner, 2015). The lack of integration of telehealth into existing health systems is also a core issue that must be addressed to facilitate its adoption (David & Tavenner, 2015). WHO has offered evidence-based recommendations to be considered in tackling these challenges in diverse settings (WHO, 2009) (FIGURE 9.7).

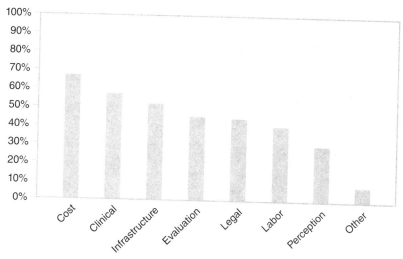

FIGURE 9.7 Global information needs for the future of telehealth services

Reproduced from World Health Organization. (2009). Telemedicine opportunities and development in member states. Retrieved from http://www.who.int/goe/publications/goe_telemedicine_2010.pdf

A WHO assessment on telehealth projects showed that cost, clinical infrastructure, and evaluation were the top information needs for telehealth adoption, implementation, and sustainability (WHO, 2009). Information on the cost-effectiveness of telehealth projects was requested by about 70% of respondents, closely followed by clinical relevance and utility (60%) and infrastructural requirements (50%). Low-income countries were more likely to request information on cost and infrastructure, whereas high-income countries were more interested in legal, ethical, and policy issues as well as cost-effectiveness (WHO, 2009). Middle-income countries were major drivers of information needs on clinical relevance. Specific inquiries from low-income countries were potentially driven by a lack of sufficient human resources for health and limited access to quality health care (WHO, 2009). Among high- and middle-income countries, access to quality health care is not as critical owing to more advanced health systems; hence, more scrutiny is placed on issues like clinical relevance and policy issues to rationalize telehealth adoption (WHO, 2009). It will be vital to develop a robust evidence base of successful, innovative telehealth solutions that lead to scalable and sustainable telehealth programs.

References

Amarasingham, R., Plantinga, L., Diener-West, M., Gaskin, D. J., & Powe, N. R. (2009). Clinical information technologies and inpatient outcomes: A multiple hospital study. *Archives of Internal Medicine, 169*(2), 108–114.

Benatar, D., Bondmass, M., Ghitelman, J., & Avitall, B. (2003). Outcomes of chronic heart failure. *Archives of Internal Medicine, 163*(3), 347–352.

Blumenthal, D. (2010). Launching HITECH. *New England Journal of Medicine, 362*(5), 382–385.

Blumenthal, D., & Tavenner, M. (2010). The "meaningful use" regulation for electronic health records. *New England Journal of Medicine, 363*(6), 501–504.

Boonstra, A., Versluis, A., & Vos, J. F. (2014). Implementing electronic health records in hospitals: A systematic literature review. *BMC Health Services Research, 14*, 370.

Campbell, E. M., Sittig, D. F., Ash, J. S., Guappone, K. P., & Dykstra, R. H. (2006). Types of unintended consequences related to computerized provider order entry. *Journal of the American Medical Informatics Association, 13*(5), 547–556.

Casadevall, S. (2015). Retrieved from https://www.wecounsel.com/3-ways-telehealth-technology -is-changing-the-health-care-landscape/

Casey, J. A., Schwartz, B. S., Stewart, W. F., & Adler, N. E. (2016). Using electronic health records for population health research: A review of methods and applications. *Annual Review of Public Health, 37*, 61–81.

Centers for Medicare and Medicaid Services. (2012). Electronic health records. Retrieved from https://www.cms.gov/Medicare/E-health/EHealthRecords/index.html

Centers for Medicare and Medicaid Services. (n.d.). Electronic health records (EHR) incentive programs. Retrieved from https://www.cms.gov/Regulations-and-Guidance/Legislation /EHRIncentivePrograms/index.html?redirect=/ehrincentiveprograms/

Certified Health IT Product List. (2016). CHPL overview. Retrieved from https://chpl.healthit .gov/#/resources/overview

Chang, F., & Gupta, N. (2015). Progress in electronic medical record adoption in Canada. *Canadian Family Physician, 61*(12), 1076–1084.

Chen, S., Cheng, A., & Mehta, K. (2013). A review of telemedicine business models. *Telemedicine and e-Health, 19*(4), 287–297.

David, C., & Tavenner, M. (2015). Information systems blog of Christine David & Marilyn. Retrieved from https://davidmarilyn.wordpress.com/2015/01/30/telemedicine-increases-access-to-underserved -markets/

DeChant, H. K., Tohme, W. G., Mun, S. K., Hayes, W. S., & Schulman, K. A. (1996). Health systems evaluation of telemedicine: A staged approach. *Telemedicine Journal, 2*(4), 303–312.

DesRoches, C. M., Campbell, E. G., Vogeli, C., Zheng, J., Rao, S. R., Shields, A. E., . . . Jha, A. K. (2010). Electronic health records' limited successes suggest more targeted uses. *Health Affairs, 29*(4), 639–646.

Dinesen, B., Nonnecke, B., Lindeman, D., Toft, E., Kidholm, K., Jethwani, K., . . . Gutierrez, M. (2016). Personalized telehealth in the future: A global research agenda. *Journal of Medical Internet Research, 18*(3), e53.

Dizik, A. (2012). A doctor's visit without the cold stethoscope. *Wall Street Journal.* Retrieved from http://www.wsj.com/articles/SB10000872396390444025204577545170233085602

Fatehi, F., & Wootton, R. (2012). Telemedicine, telehealth or e-health? A bibliometric analysis of the trends in the use of these terms. *Journal of Telemedicine and Telecare, 18*(8), 460–464.

Gold, J. A. (2014). In cities, the average doctor wait time is 18.5 days. Retrieved from https://www .washingtonpost.com/news/wonk/wp/2014/01/29/in-cities-the-average-doctor-wait-time-is -18-5-days/?utm_term=.30c2dee6750a

Gray, B. H., Bowden, T., Johansen, I., & Koch, S. (2011). Electronic health records: An international perspective on "meaningful use." *Issue Brief (Commonwealth Fund), 28*, 1–18.

HealthIT.gov. (2013). How do I conduct a post-implementation evaluation? Retrieved from https:// www.healthit.gov/providers-professionals/faqs/how-do-i-conduct-post-implementation -evaluation

HealthIT.gov. (2014). Benefits of EHRs. Retrieved from https://www.healthit.gov/providers -professionals/health-care-quality-convenience

Hsiao, C. J., & Hing, E. (2012). *Use and characteristics of electronic health record systems among office- based physician practices, United States, 2001-2012* (pp. 1–8). Washington, DC: U.S. Department of Health and Human Services, Centers for Disease Control and Prevention, National Center for Health Statistics.

Jansen-Kosterink, S., Vollenbroek-Hutten, M., & Hermens, H. (2016). A renewed framework for the evaluation of telemedicine. In *8th International Conference on eHealth, Telemedicine, and Social Medicine, Venice, Italy,* eTELEMED (Vol. 2016). Retrieved from https://www.thinkmind.org /index.php?view=article&articleid=etelemed_2016_4_30_40183

Jones, S. S., Adams, J. L., Schneider, E. C., Ringel, J. S., & McGlynn, E. A. (2010). Electronic health record adoption and quality improvement in US hospitals. *American Journal of Managed Care*, 16(12 Suppl. HIT), SP64–SP71.

Jordanova, M., & Lievens, F. (2011, November). Global telemedicine and eHealth (a synopsis). In *E-Health and Bioengineering Conference (EHB), 2011* (pp. 1–6). Proceedings of the 3rd International Conference on E-Health and Bioengineering, Belgium.

Kidholm, K., Ekeland, A. G., Jensen, L. K., Rasmussen, J., Pedersen, C. D., Bowes, A., . . . Bech, M. (2012). A model for assessment of telemedicine applications: MAST. *International Journal of Technology Assessment in Health Care*, 28(1), 44–51.

Kidholm, K., Ølholm, A. M., Birk-Olsen, M., Cicchetti, A., Fure, B., Halmesmäki, E., . . . Sampietro-Colom, L. (2015). Hospital managers' need for information in decision-making—An interview study in nine European countries. *Health Policy*, 119(11), 1424–1432.

Kim, S., Lee, K. H., Hwang, H., & Yoo, S. (2016). Analysis of the factors influencing healthcare professionals' adoption of mobile electronic medical record (EMR) using the unified theory of acceptance and use of technology (UTAUT) in a tertiary hospital. *BMC Medical Informatics and Decision Making*, 16(1), 1.

Knight, P., Bonney, A., Teuss, G., Guppy, M., Lafferre, D., Mullan, J., & Barnett, S. (2016). Positive clinical outcomes are synergistic with positive educational outcomes when using telehealth consulting in general practice: A mixed-methods study. *Journal of Medical Internet Research*, 18(2), e31.

Kruse, C. S., Kothman, K., Anerobi, K., & Abanaka, L. (2016). Adoption factors of the electronic health record: A systematic review. *JMIR Medical Informatics*, 4(2), e19.

Lustig, T. A. (2012). *The role of telehealth in an evolving health care environment: Workshop summary.* Washington, DC: National Academies Press.

McCullough, J. S., Casey, M., Moscovice, I., & Prasad, S. (2010). The effect of health information technology on quality in US hospitals. *Health Affairs*, 29(4), 647–654.

McGinn, C. A., Grenier, S., Duplantie, J., Shaw, N., Sicotte, C., Mathieu, L., & Gagnon, M. P. (2011). Comparison of user groups' perspectives of barriers and facilitators to implementing electronic health records: A systematic review. *BMC Medicine*, 9(1), 1.

Menachemi, N., Chukmaitov, A., Saunders, C., & Brooks, R. G. (2008). Hospital quality of care: Does information technology matter? The relationship between information technology adoption and quality of care. *Health Care Management Review*, 33(1), 51–59.

Menachemi, N., & Collum, T. H. (2011). Benefits and drawbacks of electronic health record systems. *Risk Management and Healthcare Policy*, 4, 47–55.

Middleton, B., Bloomrosen, M., Dente, A. M., Hashmat, A. B., Koppel, J. R., Overhage J. M., . . . Zhang, J. (2013). Enhancing patient safety and quality of care by improving the usability of electronic health record systems: Recommendations from AMIA. *Journal of the American Medical Informatics Association*, 20(e1), e2–e8.

Miller, R. H., West, C., Brown, T. M., Sim, I., & Ganchoff, C. (2005). The value of electronic health records in solo or small group practices. *Health Affairs.* 24(5), 1127–1137.

Neal, D. (2011). Choosing an electronic health records system. *Innovations in Clinical Neuroscience*, 5(6), 43–45.

Parver, C. (2009). How the American Recovery and Reinvestment Act of 2009 changed HIPAA's privacy requirements. *CCH Health Care Compliance Letter*, 4–7.

Paul, D. L., & McDaniel, R. R. (2016). Facilitating telemedicine project sustainability in medically underserved areas: A healthcare provider participant perspective. *BMC Health Services Research*, 16(1), 1.

President's Council of Advisors on Science and Technology. (2014). Better health care and lower costs: Accelerating improvement through systems engineering. Retrieved from https://obamawhitehouse.archives.gov/sites/default/files/microsites/ostp/systems_engineering _and_healthcare.pdf

Ratwani, R. M., Hettinger, A. Z., Kosydar, A., Fairbanks, R. J., & Hodgkins, M. L. (2017). A framework for evaluating electronic health record vendor user-centered design and usability testing processes. *Journal of the American Medical Informatics*, 24(e1), e35–e39.

Reed, K. (2005). Telemedicine: Benefits to advanced practice nursing and the communities they serve. *Journal of the American Academy of Nurse Practitioners, 17*(5), 176–180.

Reginatto, B. M. B. (2012). Understanding barriers to wider telehealth adoption in the home environment of older people: An exploratory study in the Irish context. *International Journal on Advances in Life Sciences, 4*(3/4), 63–76.

Rosenbek, M. L., Hansen, L. W., Pedersen, C. D., Titlestad, I. L., Christensen, J. K., Kidholm, K., ... Møllegård, L. (2015). Early telemedicine training and counselling after hospitalization in patients with severe chronic obstructive pulmonary disease: A feasibility study. *BMC Medical Informatics and Decision Making, 15*, 3.

Rustagi, N., & Singh, R. (2012). Electronic medical record: Time to migrate? *Perspectives in Clinical Research, 3*(4), 143.

Smith, Y. (2015). Types of telemedicine. Retrieved from http://www.news-medical.net/health/Types-of-Telemedicine.aspx

Stone, C. P. (2014). A glimpse at EHR implementation around the world: The lessons the US can learn. Health Institute for E-Policy. Retrieved from http://www.e-healthpolicy.org/docs/A_Glimpse_at_EHR_Implementation_Around_the_World1_ChrisStone.pdf

Stumpf, S. (2003). Telemedicine awaits. Reimbursement will mean big change and real money. *Healthcare Informatics, 10*(5), 54–57.

Transparency Market Research. (2014). Video telemedicine market (communication technologies: 3G, 4G, ADSL, B-ISDN, and satellite communication; applications: cardiology, dermatology, neurology, orthopedics, oncology, pathology, radiology, gynecology, & dentistry) - global industry analysis, size, share, growth, trends and forecast 2014 - 2020. Retrieved from http://www.transparencymarketresearch.com/v-telemedicine-market.html

U.S. Department of Health and Human Services. (2015). 2015 edition health information technology (health IT) certification criteria, 2015 edition base electronic health record (EHR) definition, and ONC health IT certification program modifications. Retrieved from https://www.federalregister.gov/documents/2015/10/16/2015-25597/2015-edition-health-information-technology-health-it-certification-criteria-2015-edition-base#h-32

U.S. Department of Health and Human Services. (2016). What is meaningful use? Retrieved from https://www.healthit.gov/providers-professionals/meaningful-use-definition-objectives

van Velthoven, M. H., Mastellos, N., Majeed, A., O'Donoghue, J., & Car, J. (2016). Feasibility of extracting data from electronic medical records for research: An international comparative study. *BMC Medical Informatics and Decision Making, 16*(1), 1.

Vassilev, I., Rowsell, A., Pope, C., Kennedy, A., O'Cathain, A., Salisbury, C., & Rogers, A. (2015). Assessing the implementability of telehealth interventions for self-management support: A realist review. *Implementation Science, 10*(1), 1.

Wang, S. J., Middleton, B., Prosser, L. A., Bardon, C. G., Spurr, C. D., Carchidi, P. J., ... Kuperman, G. J. (2003). A cost-benefit analysis of electronic medical records in primary care. *American Journal of Medicine, 114*(5), 397–403.

Wilson, L. S., & Maeder, A. J. (2015). Recent directions in telemedicine: Review of trends in research and practice. *Healthcare Informatics Research, 21*(4), 213–222.

World Health Organization. (2006). Electronic health records: Manual for developing countries. Retrieved from http://www.wpro.who.int/publications/docs/EHRmanual.pdf

World Health Organization. (2009). Telemedicine opportunities and development in member states. Retrieved from http://www.who.int/goe/publications/goe_telemedicine_2010.pdf

Yina, W. (2010). Application of EHR in health care. In *Proceedings of the 2010 Second International Conference on Multimedia and Information Technology* (Vol. 1, pp. 60–63). Washington, DC: IEEE Computer Society.

Zanaboni, P., & Wootton, R. (2012). Adoption of telemedicine: From pilot stage to routine delivery. *BMC Medical Informatics and Decision Making, 12*(1), 1.

CHAPTER 10

Personal Health Records

Ashish Joshi

Health Information National Trends Survey (HINTS)

- Describe the role of the Internet as a source of health information.
- Understand the role of personal health records (PHRs) in disease self-management.
- Identify the characteristics and types of PHRs.
- Examine the factors influencing the adoption of PHRs among individuals living in diverse settings.
- Explore the clinical impact and cost-effectiveness of PHRs.

- What is a PHR?
- What factors can motivate an individual to adopt a PHR?
- What are the technical architecture requirements for PHRs?
- Are PHRs cost-effective in supporting chronic disease self-management and improving health outcomes?
- What strategies can be employed to overcome the technical, societal, organizational, and privacy-related barriers that influence use of PHRs?

▶ I. Health Information–Seeking Behavior on the Internet

The Internet has become an important source from which individuals obtain health information (see BOX 10.1). Trends show that today, patients have greater access to and control over their medical information. The increasing pace of health information–seeking behavior of the consumers creates an emerging need for more research into consumer engagement (Maaike, Dijkhorst-Oei, & Rutten, 2014). The accessibility of information on the Internet has been shown to facilitate patients learning more about their health conditions, symptoms, and various treatment procedures (Archer, Fevrier-Thomas, Lokker, McKibbon, & Straus, 2011). The literature reports that the web serves as the initial source of health information for most people, even before their physicians (Hesse, Moser, & Rutten, 2010). Nearly 72% of Internet users in the United States looked online for health information within the past year. About 70% of Canadians also obtain their health information on the web (Statistics Canada, 2011).

BOX 10.1 Health Information on the Internet

- 87% of U.S. adults use the Internet.
- 72% of Internet users looked online for health information within the past year.
- The most common topics searched for were specific diseases or conditions, treatments or procedures, and doctors or other health professionals.

Data from Pew Research Center (2013). Health Fact Sheet. Highlights of the Pew internet's project research related to health and healthcare. Retrieved from http://www.pewinternet.org/2013/01/15/health-online-2013/

Great momentum has surfaced in the private healthcare sector, with employers, the government, and consumers desiring a commonly accessible health record. Reports show that 78% of respondents were interested in having online access to medical records and test results provided by doctors. Nearly 76% were interested in online access to an integrated medical record, 72% in online scheduling of appointments, and 69% in a website providing information about health conditions or treatments (Deloitte Consulting, 2008). Providing patients with access to health records alone is insufficient unless it is integrated into the patients' existing health and social infrastructure (Archer et al., 2011). The patient's role has emerged as a central one that will facilitate health information exchange among consumers and providers (Serocca, 2008; Wells, Rozenblum, Park, Dunn, & Bates, 2014).

▶ II. Introduction to Personal Health Records

PHRs are one of the newest health information exchange technologies to promote patient engagement, patient–clinician communication, and continuity of care. "A Personal Health Record (PHR) is a tool used in sharing health information, increasing health understanding, and helping transform patients into better-educated consumers of health care" (Kahn, Aulakh, & Bosworth, 2009). Almost 50% of U.S. adults reported keeping some form of PHR (Serocca, 2008). These approaches have been associated with improvements in clinical outcomes, health service efficiency, and positive business metrics (Charmel & Frampton, 2008; Hibbard & Greene, 2013). The United States, France, Denmark, Canada, Taiwan, and the United Kingdom have already identified the need to establish a PHR to assist in the coordination of care. The information contained in the PHR is populated by both patients and healthcare providers (Tang, Ash, Bates, Overhage, & Sands, 2006). PHRs help patients to manually key in their health data, communicate with their caregivers, share their health information, and easily obtain access to information from their health records, as well as other health sources (Tang et al., 2006). "An electronic PHR is a universally accessible, layperson comprehensible, lifelong tool for managing relevant health information, promoting health maintenance and assisting with chronic disease management via an interactive, common data set of electronic health information tools" (IBM, 2008).

Patients hold full rights of access and can determine with whom the access needs to be shared. PHRs do not serve as a replacement for the legal record of healthcare providers (Wiljer et al., 2008). Adequate security must be provided to ensure the protection of patients' health information.

"PHRs have also been defined as an 'electronic application through which individuals can access, manage and share their health information, and that of others for whom they are authorized, in a private, secure and confidential environment'" (Tang et al., 2006). An ultimate potential of the PHR is to serve as a single, comprehensive record that will reflect the entire history of a patient's medical care throughout his or her lifetime (Serocca, 2008). It enables healthcare providers to gain easier access to patient information. It also opens channels of communication with other healthcare providers and entities (Serocca, 2008). PHRs have the potential to enhance the efficiency and quality of health care. Restricting patient healthcare records to physicians or caregivers is a norm that is changing, especially due to the fragmentation of the healthcare system, with multiple points of care. There is a need for an integrated record that consolidates health professionals' electronic health record (EHR) alongside the patients' health record for seamless healthcare provision (Serocca, 2008).

The data within PHRs can be subjective or objective (TABLE 10.1). Data represented in the PHR must be in a format that is usable and enables the patient to fully understand the information (Tang et al., 2006).

The PHR attributes can vary from system to system based on the following: (1) information scope, (2) information source, (3) system features/functions, (4) technical approach to design, (5) record custodian, and (6) security administrator (Jones, Shipman, Plaut, & Selden, 2010; National Committee on Vital and Health Statistics et al., 2006). These attributes include (1) content, (2) architecture, (3) privacy and security, (4) functionality, and (5) costs and financing (TABLE 10.2).

The earliest estimate for when minimally functional PHRs entered the marketplace was around the year 2001 (Etherton-Beer, Venturato, & Horner, 2013). The year 2007 was identified as when the first PHRs were accessed through providers (Halamka, Mandl, & Tang, 2008). Kaiser Permanente, a U.S. managed care provider, made its clinically linked PHR available to all members in 2007 (Zhou, Medo, Cimini, Zhang, & Zhang, 2011). Further advancements in PHR development came through innovations by Google and Microsoft, which developed web-based PHRs that provided consumers direct access to their health records using the Internet, without the need for organizational protocols (Zhou et al., 2011). These enhanced PHRs—Google Health and Microsoft HealthVault—served to promote data sharing from multiple sites (Zhou et al., 2011).

PHR functionality has been measured by the Health Information National Trends Survey (HINTS), which is a nationally representative survey regularly carried out by the U.S. National Cancer Institute. It uses the following assessments (Nelson et al., 2004):

- "In the last 12 months, have you used the Internet to keep track of personal health information such as care received, test results, or upcoming medical appointments?"
- "In the last 12 months, have you used email or the Internet to communicate with a doctor or a doctor's office?"

These surveys assess two critical requirements for effective use of a PHR: the ability to store medical data electronically and the ability to facilitate web-based communication with healthcare providers. Based on survey weighting, approximately 8 million people were using the two basic PHR functionalities tracked in 2008 (i.e., storing data on the Internet and communicating electronically with a clinical provider) (Ford, Hesse, & Huerta, 2016). In 2013, 31 million people were using these PHR functionalities, similar to social media penetration rates (Feeley & Shine, 2011). Consumers' PHR use continues to increase in both the number of people engaged and the degree of technological functionality they can manage (Baudendistel et al., 2015).

TABLE 10.1 Description of Data Sources and Categories in Personal Health Records

| | Data Sources | | | | |
Commercial Laboratories	Immunization Registries	Monitoring Surgery/ Medical Devices	Claims	EHR	Patient
Lab test results	Immunization records	Self-monitoring data	Disease history	Medical problem	Medical problem
			Record of health providers	Medical procedure	Medical procedures
			Prescriptions	Record of health providers	Disease history
			Lab test results	Patient allergies	Record of health providers
				Immunization records	Patient allergies
				Prescriptions	Self-monitoring data
				Lab test results	Family, social, lifestyle data
					Immunization records
					Prescriptions
					Lab test results

Data from Tang, P. C., Ash, J. S., Bates, D. W., Overhage, J. M., & Sands, D. Z. (2006). Personal health records: Definitions, benefits, and strategies for overcoming barriers to adoption. *Journal of the American Medical Informatics Association, 13*(2), 121–126.

TABLE 10.2 Attributes and Features of Personal Health Records

PHR System Attribute	Features
Content	Easy-to-understand language Complete Accurate/credible Organized Complete
Architecture	Ability to enter or view their own healthcare data Share medical records System interoperability Centralization of all individual records Portability Authentication
Privacy and security	Confidentiality of the data Authentication and authorization of the users
Functionality	Information collection Information sharing and exchange Information self-management
Costs and financing	Who will pay and how much will be paid?

Data from Archer, N., Fevrier-Thomas, U., Lokker, C., McKibbon, K. A., & Straus, S. E. (2011). Personal health records: A scoping review. *Journal of the American Medical Informatics Association, 18*(4), 515–522.

▶ III. Types of Personal Health Records

PHRs vary based on their number of users and levels of functionality, and are frequently classified as either standalone PHRs, tethered or connected PHRs, or hybrid PHRs (TABLE 10.3). These three types are described in the following sections.

Standalone Personal Health Records

This type of PHR is a standalone application that does not connect with any other system. Its functionality allows patients to view their own health information. PHRs depending solely on the patient input are unlikely to be a trusted channel for transmission of medical record data among healthcare institutions. PHRs must serve as more than a repository for an individual's health information. Some examples of standalone PHRs include Access My Records, Active Doctors Online, Elder Issues, EMRy Stick, GlobalPatientRecord, Medsfile, and RelayHealth (Fuji et al., 2012).

TABLE 10.3 Comparison of Personal Health Records

PHR	Standalone	Integrated	Tethered	Hybrid
Owned solely by patient	X			X
Consists of data from multiple providers	X	X		X
Changes made by medical providers		X	X	X
Portable	X	X		X
Integrated review process				Planned

Data from Israelson, J., & Cankaya, E. C. (2012, January). A hybrid web based personal health record system shielded with comprehensive security. In *System Science (HICSS), 2012, 45th Hawaii International Conference on System Sciences* (pp. 2958–2968). Institute of Electrical and Electronics Engineers.

Personal Health Records Interconnected with Electronic Health Records

These interconnected systems often possess enhanced functionality, including patients' ability to schedule doctor appointments and initiate prescription refills, and also allow direct patient–physician communication. Hence, the PHRs interconnected with EHRs generally provide much improved benefits when compared to standalone PHRs. In addition, the integrated PHR/EHR is more meaningful and useful to patients. The majority of consumers using a PHR today use one that is integrated in a single healthcare organization. Examples of integrated PHRs include Health Record Bank, DIRAYA (Spain), and The Health Portal, Sundhed (Denmark) (Detmer, Bloomrosen, Raymond, & Tang, 2008).

Hybrid Personal Health Records

Hybrid PHRs incorporate additional features into the integrated PHRs, including patient ownership of the PHR with the ability of only health professionals to change it, and the presence of a review process that involves both patient and physician participation (Israelson & Cankaya, 2012). These features provide added security controls over sensitive data (Israelson & Cankaya, 2012). Hybrid PHRs may be used to acquire and transmit data by connecting to other health data sources. The individual data sources must be visible to the user. Data contained in PHRs should be as comprehensive as possible to enable maximal utility by both patients and healthcare providers. An example of a hybrid PHR is SynChart.

New innovations in PHR technologies such as Google Health and Microsoft HealthVault are likely to facilitate PHR adoption. They are equipped to enhance data sharing at multiple sites, thereby allowing consumers to access their health information online without organizational protocols. Some of these recent tools are described in the following sections.

HealthVault

The HealthVault was developed by Microsoft in 2007 and was expanded to the United Kingdom in 2010. It serves as a platform that provides information to both patients and healthcare professionals. Some key features of the HealthVault include multiple authentication options, built-in privacy and security components, enhanced user control and authorization, vendor neutrality, system interoperability, cloud storage, device connectivity (using weight scales, blood pressure monitors, blood glucose monitors, etc.), data auditing, continuous platform enhancement, and international access (Microsoft, 2017). HealthVault facilitates the sharing of information between patients and caregivers. It also allows the use of third-party applications such as fitness applications or diet stores in self-management of health conditions (Microsoft, 2017). According to Microsoft (2017), "HealthVault enables a connected ecosystem that currently includes more than 300 applications and more than 80 connected health and fitness devices in the U.S."

Dossia Health Management System

Dossia is one of the largest PHRs deployed globally. It operates as open-source software, unlike the Microsoft HealthVault (Dossia, 2014). Dossia was formed by a group of 10 companies: "AT&T, Applied Materials, BP America, Cardinal Health, Intel, Pitney Bowes, Sanofi-aventis, Walmart, Abraxis BioScience, and Vanguard Health Systems" (Dossia, 2014). Dossia differs from other PHRs by providing users access to their health information regardless of the user plan, physician, or employer (Dossia, 2014). The Dossia platform provides a customizable system that enables users to create and personalize their EHRs. The users initially populate the PHR with their data; then, the initial data are further built on through physician chart reports and health insurance companies (Dossia, 2014). According to Critelli (2012), "the Dossia platform has no financial incentive to lock the consumers into a particular provider system, health plan, pharmacy, test lab, or applications provider." It is flexible to accommodate new applications over time, while providing multiple options to consumers based on their preferences and the requirements of their health plan sponsor (Critelli, 2012).

MyChart

MyChart, developed by Epic, is one of the most widely used PHRs by health systems such as Kaiser Permanente. MyChart provides controlled access to electronic medical records used by healthcare providers. It allows central access to patient health information (Epic, 2016).

Other PHRs include The Patient Portal, from Cerner Corp; Centricity Patient Online; MedSeek's PHR; RelayHealth's PHR; eClinicalWorks; Allscripts Patient Portal; and HealthSpace (HealthIT.gov, 2013).

Retail Clinics

Retail clinics typically serve as ambulatory care sites. They provide basic screening, diagnostic, and treatment services. These clinics have expanded their service offerings to include behavioral health screenings, and are accessed for basic primary and preventive care services. Retail clinics offer several convenient features such as walk-in availability, reduced wait times, and extended weekday and weekend hours of operation. Prices are typically fixed and transparent, generally posted on-site and online (Thygeson, van Vorst, Maciosek, & Solberg, 2008). Physicians provide oversight of the nurse practitioners and physician assistants who provide most of the care in these clinics. Retail clinics are distinct from urgent care clinics and freestanding emergency departments (EDs), which treat more acute cases. Retail clinics are also required to have board-certified physicians on staff. Some examples of stores with retail clinics include Walmart, CVS, and Target. Results from one study estimated that up to 27% of emergency department visits can be handled appropriately at retail clinics and urgent care centers. This would provide a cost savings of $4.4 billion per year (Weinick, Burns, & Mehrotra, 2010).

▶ ## IV. Benefits of Personal Health Records

The absence of a comprehensive information architecture limits the ability to design and develop cohesive strategies to tackle issues affecting population health (Tang et al., 2006). Use of modern information technology tools like PHRs will provide a seamless care continuum among patients with chronic diseases. PHRs possess immense potential to significantly enhance healthcare efficiency and quality remotely. PHR portals have been identified as an essential technology that can adequately support self-management of health conditions (Collins, Vawdrey, Kukafka, & Kuperman, 2011). PHRs also enhance consumer participation in healthcare decision making (Collins et al., 2011). Prior literature has indicated a high degree of interest in PHRs for sharing health information such as health finances, diagnoses, allergies, immunizations, insurance information, and medications in an easy way to help patients manage their own health (Kahn et al., 2009).

In addition to capturing patient health records, PHR systems provide information on patients' healthcare patterns (Tang et al., 2006). PHRs have the potential to change and improve patient–provider relationships, enhance patient–physician shared decision making, and enable the healthcare system to evolve toward a more personalized medical model (Nazi, 2013). They can also include decision support capabilities that can assist patients in managing chronic conditions. Empirical evidence on PHR benefits, however, have been inconsistent (Ko, Turner, Jones, & Hill, 2010). There has been early positive evidence as well as dramatic challenges in adoption of PHRs (Greenhalgh, Hinder, Stramer, Bratan, & Russell, 2010). Some of the long-term benefits of PHRs include improved quality, access, and cost of care (Tang et al., 2006). The benefits largely differ depending on the stakeholders' (patients, providers, or payers) perspectives, described here (Price et al., 2015).

- *Patient–provider communication:* PHRs have facilitated direct, easier access and better communication with healthcare professionals (Bouri & Ravi, 2014).

- *Education and lifestyle changes:* PHR can store data on healthy lifestyles including diet, exercise, smoking, weight loss, and work habits (Archer et al., 2011).

Patients can also access education and automated advice programs, and add their own information to hospital systems (Archer et al., 2011). Resources such as online patient communities, electronic forums, and messaging features provide patients with the ability to share their information with other patients experiencing similar health issues and get support. An example of such a resource is the Caring Voices site at the Princess Margaret Hospital in Toronto, Canada (Archer et al., 2011).

■ *Health self-management:* By providing a platform for individuals to access their records without assistance, as well as edit and retrieve their various health parameters, PHRs support self-management and monitoring of various chronic health conditions. In addition, advances in PHRs promote decision support by providing guidance in patient self-monitoring (Archer et al., 2011).

PHRs have many potential benefits across several stakeholders including patients, healthcare professionals, payers, caregivers, and governments (**FIGURE 10.1**).

■ *Patient benefits:* PHRs benefit patients by providing them greater access to a wider array of credible health information. Patients with chronic diseases (Ko et al., 2010) or mental health–related problems (Ennis, Rose, Callard, Denis, & Wykes, 2011) are able to track their diseases and receive timely personalized interventions when needed. PHRs have the ability to assist consumers in managing their health conditions and treatment protocols (Kahn et al., 2009). PHRs also provide an ongoing connection between patients and physicians.

■ *Caregiver benefits:* For caregivers, PHRs make it easier to care for patients. The technology-based interventions can empower patients and their caregivers and help them maintain a healthy lifestyle in the community (Archer et al., 2011).

■ *Healthcare professional benefits:* Patients enter data into their health records and can decide to submit the data to their clinician's EHR. Asynchronous PHR-mediated electronic communication can free clinicians from the limitations of telephone and face-to-face communication.

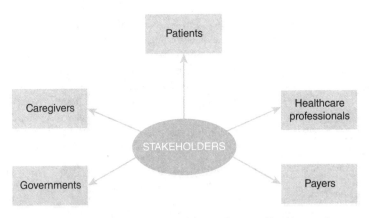

FIGURE 10.1 Stakeholders and beneficiaries in the use of personal health records

■ *Payer and purchaser benefits:* PHRs have been associated with enormous cost savings. They have been shown to lower chronic disease management costs, medication costs, and wellness program costs (Maaike et al., 2014). A cost savings of $21 billion is expected if 80% of the U.S. population were to use PHRs (Center for Information Technology Leadership, 2008). However, these outcomes have been not well researched. The greatest area of benefit accrues to chronic disease management, where costs are typically high (Walker et al., 2005). Relevant agencies should sponsor research to assess the clinical and health behavior benefits of PHRs. An initiative like a tax deduction for PHR-related expenses may promote PHR adoption. Payers need to evaluate and assess various incentive options to facilitate PHR implementation by providers. There is a critical need for comprehensive education of providers and patients on the use of PHRs and their benefits, in order to facilitate its adoption (Serocca, 2008). Policy issues within organizations frequently arise with new innovations such as PHRs, and these policies have been shown to influence integration of patient care (Reti, Feldman, Ross, & Safran, 2010). The literature has recognized 10 categories related to PHR policy issues, which are shown in FIGURE 10.2 (Reti et al., 2010).

For the majority of PHR-related policy issues, the responses to the patient-centered policies were "yes," except for the third-party web advertising, which was "no." The availability of normal lab results to the patients should be as soon as they are available to the clinician. Further, the clinician should respond to patient emails in less than 24 hours (Reti et al., 2010).

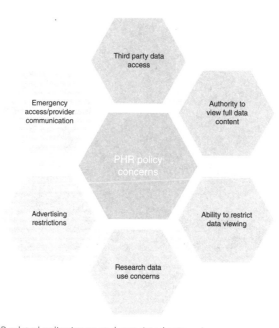

FIGURE 10.2 PHR-related policy issues and associated categories

Data from Reti, S. R., Feldman, H. J., Ross, S. E., & Safran, C. (2010). Improving personal health records for patient-centered care. *Journal of the American Medical Informatics Association, 17*(2), 192–195.

▶ V. Factors Impacting Adoption of Personal Health Records

A study was conducted of the uptake and utilization of PHRs by the U.S. population to examine individual use of web applications in performing two basic PHR functionalities: (1) storing health information, and (2) communicating with providers (Ford et al., 2016). The HINTS also provides comprehensive data for projecting usage of PHRs in coming years (FIGURE 10.3).

Consumer usage of electronic media for storing health information and for provider communication has rapidly increased from 8 million people in 2008 to 31 million people in 2013 (Ford et al., 2016). Some of the key motivators of PHR adoption are outlined in BOX 10.2.

Diffusion of full patient access to their EHR-tethered portal or personally controlled PHR has been slow historically. A large proportion of the U.S. population has yet to adopt PHRs, with critical challenges persisting among the early adopters (Ford et al., 2016). These challenges include poor adoption rates (Logue & Effken, 2012), poor integration into care processes (Koch & Vimarlund, 2012), and policy limitations (Hordern, Georgiou, Whetton, & Prgomet, 2011). Several barriers also exist at multiple levels that influence adoption of PHRs.

- *System-level barriers:* Failure of PHR adoption can be linked to limited consumer involvement during planning, design, and implementation (Archer et al., 2011). Variation in consumers' abilities to use PHRs, fear of technology, and poor computer and Internet skills are also some of the factors that impact PHR adoption. Additional challenges relate to time and resources that are needed to maintain

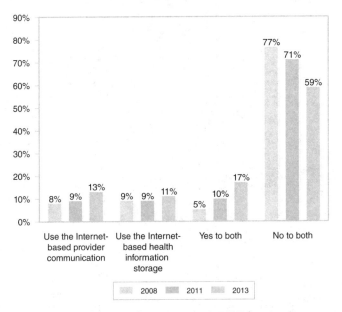

FIGURE 10.3 Response rates for items of interest measuring PHR functionality

Data from Ford, E. W., Hesse, B. W., & Huerta, T. R. (2016). Personal health record use in the United States: Forecasting future adoption levels. *Journal of Medical Internet Research, 18*(3), e73.

BOX 10.2 Key Motivators of PHR Adoption

- Ability to learn new behaviors
- Elders receiving more care in multiple locations
- Perceptions that PHR makes access to care easier
- Those who preferred to work together with their healthcare provider as a team
- Those with Internet access and confidence in using the Internet
- Likelihood of receiving incentives
- Usefulness of technology rather than ease of use
- Compatible with current healthcare needs

Data from Vydra, T. P., Cuaresma, E., Kretovics, M., & Bose-Brill, S. (2015). Diffusion and use of tethered personal health records in primary care. *Perspectives in Health Information Management, 12*, 1c.

and use PHRs (Kim & Nahm, 2012). The technical nature of web-based medical information could create a health literacy burden (D'Amore et al., 2014).

Technology literacy: Inadequate access, low health literacy, and limited physical and cognitive abilities are the factors influencing individual's understanding related to technology literacy.

PHR reimbursement: More patients will start to use PHR as they become aware of its benefits. Establishing a clear-cut payment model for PHR use is critical to facilitating its adoption among consumers (Tang et al., 2006). Healthcare payers and purchasers are the primary beneficiaries and should probably be the predominant stakeholders to bear the costs of PHR.

Patient barriers: There are several challenges that influence adoption of PHRs at the patient level, including: (1) relative unfamiliarity and inexperience with using electronic PHRs; (2) low computer and health literacy; (3) limited provider participation; (4) visual, cognitive, and physical limitations; and (5) lack of trust in the provider. Others include patient concerns about privacy and security breaches to their health information. Factors influencing patients' adoption of PHR include prior Internet use, magnitude of benefits, and ability of physicians to inform patient use (Vydra et al., 2015).

Provider barriers: Low levels of physician awareness and lack of familiarity with PHRs represented significant barriers to PHR adoption and use (Vydra et al., 2015). Other factors adversely affecting the adoption of PHRs among healthcare providers include: (1) new workflow demands resulting from PHR use (Vydra et al., 2015), (2) general resistance to change, (3) lack of technological literacy, and (4) concerns relating to confidentiality and privacy (Vydra et al., 2015). Physicians also expressed concern over the ability of patients to understand the working of the PHR (Vydra et al., 2015).

The barriers to PHR adoption and related recommendations to address those challenges have been outlined in TABLE 10.4.

Physician knowledge and familiarity with PHR use is one of the strongest predictors of patient adoption (Vydra et al., 2015). Physicians have the ability to encourage patient use while addressing existing concerns (Vydra et al., 2015). Future use of PHRs largely depends on the level of satisfaction derived from PHR education (Vydra et al., 2015). Although the increased efficiency realized from using PHRs may offset the workload of communicating with patients, financial reimbursement

TABLE 10.4 Barriers to PHR Adoption and Recommendations to Overcome Them

Barrier	Suggested Recommendations
Incentives and initiatives in the healthcare system	Obtaining a balance between autonomy of patients and healthcare providers
	Instituting training for new technologies and incentives to enhance physician interest
	Working on healthcare providers' resistance to change efforts
	Clearly defining the workflows, scope, and responsibilities of physicians and other healthcare providers regarding technology use
	Boosting incentives and compensation packages for physicians
	Addressing provider concerns regarding liability risks
Patient/consumer confidence	Enhancing privacy and security inputs to protect consumer health information
System interoperability and standards	Establishing standards for data exchange
	Creating unique standards for individual provider specifications
	Defining standards for user privacy and security
	Providing certification of health technology tools and products
Absence of infrastructure for health technologies and tools	Need for resources to improve system integration
	Reducing existence and use of systems that are incompatible
	Supporting integration by mediating organizational structures and networks
	Improving online service provision at institutions for healthcare providers
Digital divide	Accounting for disparities in race, socioeconomic position, and education
	Improving health literacy rates
	Considering disability and other visual or cognitive needs of users
	Funding
Evidence base	Improved effectiveness and cost efficiency
Lack of certainty in market demand	Limited success rates among smaller vendors
	Improved certainty to foster investment in better quality or advanced PHRs
	Barriers posed by economic and market forces in PHR uptake

Environmental barriers	Health information on each patient resides in multiple locations. Integrated PHRs must reach across organizational boundaries to interface with multiple EHR systems. Lack of ubiquitous EHR usage presents the greatest environmental barrier to integrated PHR adoption. Exploring what functions of the PHR that patients use the most and what changes in health-related behaviors arise from using PHRs would contribute to future development.
Legal barriers	For example, courts might apply negligence standards in cases where practitioners rely on inaccurate patient-entered PHR information to make suboptimal decisions about care.
Individual-level barriers	Healthcare consumers must understand and accept their roles and responsibilities related to their own health care. Need to have understanding of patients' work flow processes.

Modified from Archer, N., Fevrier-Thomas, U., Lokker, C., McKibbon, K. A., & Straus, S. E. (2011). Personal health records: A scoping review. *Journal of the American Medical Informatics Association, 18*(4), 515–522.

models for PHR use by physicians are still a pertinent challenge. They need to be addressed in order to facilitate PHRs' adoption and meaningful use by physicians. Limited PHR-related billing codes are more likely to impact physicians operating under a fee-for-service model (Vydra et al., 2015).

Technical security measures require connections to be encrypted and that they do not cache. In addition, local laws need to be followed. Accurate authentication is critical to maintaining the medical integrity of the PHR and protecting its privacy. Patients should be enabled with privileges to reconcile their medications using PHR, a requirement of the Joint Commission Outpatient Medication Reconciliation (Halamka et al., 2008).

Personal Health Records Adoption Model

The Personal Health Records Adoption Model (PHRAM) was developed based on social cognitive theory (Hood, 2013). The goal was to provide an explanation of why individuals may choose to utilize PHRs (Hood, 2013). Five major factors were found: (1) behavioral, (2) personal, (3) environmental, (4) technological, and (5) chronic disease (Logue & Effken, 2013) (FIGURE 10.4).

Personal factors constitute demographic, biological, and cognitive features that influence individual intention to carry out a specific action. Environmental factors consist of psychosocial and physical conditions that may influence human behavior. Technological factors consist of technical attributes and resources that contribute to feasibility of system use. Chronic disease factors surround the nature and characteristics of the health condition to be managed (Hood, 2013). These factors play a key role in the adoption of PHRs to self-manage their chronic health conditions.

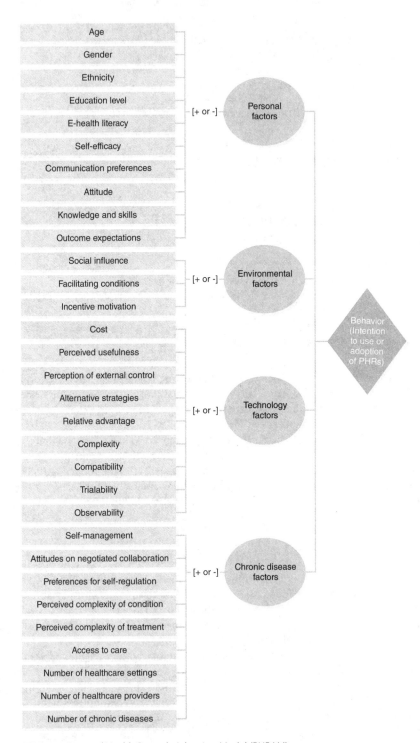

FIGURE 10.4 Personal Health Records Adoption Model (PHRAM)

Data from Logue, M. D., & Effken, J. A. (2013). An exploratory study of the personal health records adoption model in the older adult with chronic illness. *Journal of Innovation in Health Informatics, 20*(3), 151–169.

The Bass model is a diffusion of commercial applications model that predicts the number of customers that embrace a given product, as well as the time period in which they do so (Bass, 1969). It identifies technology diffusion patterns as a function of external and internal influences.

▪ *External influences:* Represent the impact of innovation and advertising and the environmental context in which the innovation is embedded (Gladwell, 2000).

▪ *Internal influences:* Reflect the impact of relationships on diffusion. Internal influences are often referred to as the limitation coefficient, the word-of-mouth effect, or social contagions in the diffusion literature (Gladwell, 2000).

These influences serve as measures that reflect how a new technology will diffuse in the future. One study utilized the Bass model to estimate the future uptake of PHR functionalities among the U.S. population (Ford et al., 2016). Results of the HINTS showed rapid increase in the use of electronic media for both health data storage and health provider communication (Ford et al., 2016). PHR uptake or adoption among consumers informs better decision making by policymakers, providers, and technology vendors.

▶ VI. Consumer Perspectives on the Use of Personal Health Records

Access and security of patient health data are the primary concerns related to PHRs (Kim & Nahm, 2012; Lester, Boateng, Studeny, & Coustasse, 2016). Limited usage has also been associated with difficulty in navigating the system and poor comprehension of health information (Kim & Nahm, 2012). PHR designs also pose significant challenges for its adoption among elderly patients (Lester et al., 2016). However, these populations indicate value in their control over activities such as viewing their health records, interacting with providers, and sharing health information with other providers (Lester et al., 2016).

Although PHRs have been successfully used among patients and providers in the self-management of chronic care conditions, especially among the elderly, their impact on preventive healthcare practices among younger adults has been understudied. Younger adults have been found to be less likely to adopt and use PHRs (Nguyen, Bartlett, Rodriguez, & Tellier, 2016). Some participants reported a reluctance to input sensitive information into their PHRs for fear of privacy breaches; others felt that insurance, marketing, and advertising companies, or their own employer, could easily access their private information and use it for unintended purposes (Nguyen et al., 2016). However, they also recognized potential advantages of PHR use including its ability to facilitate increased efficiency in patient–caregiver collaboration and an improved ability to monitor their health parameters for preventive purposes. Recommendations provided by young participants to enhance the adoption of PHRs included improve user-friendliness, enhance user interfaces, allow customization based on preferences, provide visual data displays in the form of charts or graphs, include feedback and reminder features, remove associated user costs, and ensure the interoperability of PHRs to facilitate easier input and transfer of medical records in new systems (Nguyen et al., 2016).

Literacy issues, language barriers, privacy, and security are the major concerns expressed regarding use of PHRs (Groenen, Faber, Kremer, Vandenbussche, & van Duijnhoven, 2016). MyPregn@ncy, a novel personal healthcare record, was implemented in Nijmegen, a Dutch primary healthcare setting that records about 4500 deliveries each year, on average, with over 250 health professionals involved in maternal care (Groenen et al., 2016). The aim was to facilitate the coordination of maternal and newborn care before, during, and after pregnancy (Groenen et al., 2016). Evaluation of the MyPregn@ncy PHR was conducted by employing randomized controlled trials and focus groups with pregnant women and healthcare professionals in 13 primary care maternity centers for a period of 21 months. Critical themes identified from focus groups included safety, access, communication, cultural change, legal issues, and patient empowerment (Groenen et al., 2016).

Major factors inhibiting the adoption of PHRs among healthcare professionals include limited familiarity with the features of PHRs and time constraints in learning about these systems (Nazi, 2013). The ideology that PHRs are patient-focused tools also restricts caregivers from experiencing patients' use of the systems (Nazi, 2013). Healthcare provider perspectives toward PHRs also varied with their respective roles and designations. Whereas physician concerns were centered on their inability to access patient self-reported data, nurses emphasized the lack of patient motivation in system use, and pharmacists reported being overwhelmed by workload, especially with medication reconciliation (Nazi, 2013).

▶ VII. Evaluation of Patient Health Records

PHRs need to be integrated into patients' current health portfolios in order to be meaningful and useful (Archer et al., 2011). PHRs have recorded success in improving patient outcomes, quality of life, hospital readmission rates, and mortality (Archer et al., 2011). The results of the few reported PHR randomized controlled trials are disappointing in that few significant effects were seen in clinical endpoints. Users are likely to utilize PHRs when they are able to realize a significant improvement in their health outcomes (Archer et al., 2011). Following are some of the evaluation measures of PHRs.

Adoption, Acceptance, and Usability

Determinants of PHR adoption include workflow demands, familiarity with technology, resistance to change, integrity and security of health information across interconnected systems, confidentiality, and privacy concerns (Archer et al., 2011). The Delone and McLean model includes multiple measures for evaluating information systems' success, such as quality of use, satisfaction of users, and individual and organizational impacts (Delone & McLean, 2003). A sustainable PHR implementation will depend on positive results from all these characteristics as well as favorable individual and organizational impacts. Sustainability is a measure of adoption success and was rarely mentioned in the literature. Usability is another critical factor impacting system evaluation; it largely incorporates consumer perspectives, acceptance, and satisfaction. User interface and support are key to the adoption and use of PHRs. Users with limited technology literacy may encounter barriers including low contrast, poor navigation features, and small font size, which could impede their uptake of the tool. Despite the emphasis on the role of PHRs as mediators in patient self-management, minimal attention has been directed to usability and other key predictors of successful uptake.

Clinical and Cost-Effectiveness of Personal Health Records

Empirical studies have evaluated the clinical effectiveness of PHRs and have shown improvements in essential health indicators including reduced blood pressure, HbA1c, and cholesterol levels among intervention groups, though the significance of these results has been inconsistent across studies (Riippa, Linna, & Rönkkö, 2015). PHR use has been associated with better patient satisfaction and improvement in self-management of chronic health conditions (O'Reilly, Holbrook, Blackhouse, Troyan, & Goeree, 2012; Riippa et al., 2015). Results of prior research have reported an association between high patient activation and low cost of care. Findings have also shown the willingness of individuals to pay for PHR use with evidence of improved outcomes (Greene, Hibbard, Sacks, Overton, & Parrotta, 2015; Hibbard & Greene, 2013; Hibbard, Greene, & Overton, 2013; Hibbard, Mahoney, Stock, & Tusler, 2007; Riippa et al., 2015). More longitudinal research is required to provide a suitable evidence base for assessing cost-effectiveness in patients' use of PHRs.

▶ VIII. Conclusion

PHRs over the next several years should be able to allow patients to link to and aggregate a variety of health data sources from hospitals to pharmacies. Existing PHR systems need to be modified to support a service-oriented architecture. This will permit multiple applications to retrieve institutional data with patient control and consent. A comprehensive coordinated care model for the PHR is required to allow patients to readily integrate data from multiple providers when using their PHRs. Patients may also want to access health information by communicating with other patients experiencing similar health conditions, through mediums such as online chat rooms, discussion forums, and subscription features for health information. This would require modification of a PHR to provide a private, secure matchmaking mechanism to enable patients to connect to communities.

Patients may also be motivated by the societal benefit of sharing their deidentified PHR data with researchers, public health entities, or regulatory bodies. Hence, systems need to be designed to incentivize data sharing among patients for secondary purposes such as population health research, quality assessments, and trials. These added features of controlled data sharing require a higher level of PHR functionality. Technical security measures should include requiring secure connections. Enhanced authentication features are invaluable in maintaining the integrity of individual health records and ensuring maximum privacy protection. The increasing prevalence of PHRs in coming years will create many policy and technical challenges for the healthcare institutions, payers, and employers. Providing patient control of healthcare information exchange is extremely relevant to providing an effective solution for privacy and consent issues that are currently limiting organizations' data exchange (Halamka et al., 2008).

It is clear that there is an emerging need for a future research agenda regarding PHRs in the areas of infrastructure and technology readiness, economics, interoperability, technology development and its applications, user and consumer acceptance, legal and privacy concerns, awareness, alignment of policy, and technology access. More research is needed to develop a more detailed understanding of what motivates people to not only adopt, but also continue using PHRs. The long-term sustainability of PHRs needs further exploration and has rarely been mentioned in the literature. Randomized controlled trials are needed to test assumptions about the comparative effectiveness of PHRs on outcomes for various patient populations.

References

Archer, N., Fevrier-Thomas, U., Lokker, C., McKibbon, K. A., & Straus, S. E. (2011). Personal health records: A scoping review. *Journal of the American Medical Informatics Association, 18*(4), 515–522.

Bass, F. (1969). A new product growth for model consumer durables. *Management Science, 15*(5), 215–212.

Baudendistel, I., Winkler, E., Kamradt, M., Längst, G., Eckrich, F., Heinze, O., . . . Ose, D. (2015). Personal electronic health records: Understanding user requirements and needs in chronic cancer care. *Journal of Medical Internet Research, 17*(5), e121.

Bouri, N., & Ravi, S. (2014). Going mobile: How mobile personal health records can improve healthcare during emergencies. *Journal of Medical Internet Research, 2*(1), e8.

Center for Information Technology Leadership. (2008). The value of personal health records. Retrieved from http://www.partners.org/cird/pdfs/CITL_PHR_Report.pdf

Charmel, P., & Frampton, S. (2008). Building the business case for patient centered care. *Healthcare Financial Management, 62*, 80–85.

Collins, S. A., Vawdrey, D. K., Kukafka, R., & Kuperman, G. J. (2011). Policies for patient access to clinical data via PHRs: Current state and recommendations. *Journal of the American Medical Informatics Association, 18*(Suppl. 1), i2–i7.

Critelli, M. (2012). Dossia Health Management System reduces healthcare costs and improves health quality. Retrieved from http://dossia.org/white-papers/Dossia%20Health%20Management%20System%20Reduces%20Healthcare%20Costs%20and%20Improves%20Healthcare%20Quality.pdf

D'Amore, J. D., Mandel, J. C., Kreda, D. A., Swain, A., Koromia, G. A., Sundareswaran, S., . . . Ramoni, R. B. (2014). Are meaningful use Stage 2 certified EHRs ready for interoperability? Findings from the SMART C-CDA collaborative. *Journal of the American Medical Informatics Association, 6*, 1060–1068.

Deloitte Consulting, Deloitte Center for Health Solutions. (2008). 2008 survey of health care consumers: Executive summary. Retrieved from http://www.medretreat.com/templates/UserFiles/Documents/DeloitteConsumerHealthcareSurvey2008.pdf

Delone, W. H., & McLean, E. R. (2003). The DeLone and McLean model of information systems success: A ten-year update. *Journal of Management Information Systems, 19*(4), 9–30.

Detmer, D., Bloomrosen, M., Raymond, B., & Tang, P. (2008). Integrated personal health records: Transformative tools for consumer-centric care. *BMC Medical Informatics and Decision Making, 8*(1), 1.

Dossia. (2014). About. Retrieved from http://dossia.com/about.html

Ennis, L., Rose, D., Callard, F., Denis, M., & Wykes, T. (2011). Rapid progress or lengthy process? Electronic personal health records in mental health. *BMC Psychiatry, 11*, 117.

Epic. (2016). Epic MyChart Central: Frequently asked questions. Retrieved from https://www.mychartcentral.com/FAQ.aspx

Etherton-Beer, C., Venturato, L., & Horner, B. (2013). Organisational culture in residential aged care facilities: A cross-sectional observational study. *PLoS One, 8*(3), e58002.

Feeley, T. W., & Shine, K. I. (2011). Access to the medical record for patients and involved providers: Transparency through electronic tools. *Annals of Internal Medicine, 155*(12), 853–854.

Ford, E. W., Hesse, B. W., & Huerta, T. R. (2016). Personal health record use in the United States: Forecasting future adoption levels. *Journal of Medical Internet Research, 18*(3), e73.

Fuji, K. T., Abbott, A. A., Galt, K. A., Drincic, A., Kraft, M., & Kasha, T. (2012). Standalone personal health records in the United States: Meeting patient desires. *Health and Technology, 2*(3), 197–205.

Gladwell, M. (2000). *The tipping point: How little things can make a big difference.* Boston, MA: Little, Brown.

Greene, J., Hibbard, J. H., Sacks, R., Overton, V., & Parrotta, C. D. (2015). When patient activation levels change, health outcomes and costs change, too. *Health Affairs (Millwood), 34*(3), 431–437. doi:10.1377/hlthaff.2014.0452

Greenhalgh, T., Hinder, S., Stramer, K., Bratan, T., & Russell, J. (2010). Adoption, non-adoption, and abandonment of a personal electronic health record: Case study of HealthSpace. *BMJ, 341,* c5814.

Groenen, C. J., Faber, M. J., Kremer, J. A., Vandenbussche, F. P., & van Duijnhoven, N. T. (2016). Improving maternity care using a personal health record: Study protocol for a stepped-wedge, randomised, controlled trial. *Trials, 17*(1), 1.

Halamka, J., Mandl, K., & Tang, P. (2008). Early experiences with personal health records. *Journal of the American Medical Informatics Association, 15*(1), 1–7.

HealthIT.gov. (2013). What is a personal health record? Retrieved from https://www.healthit.gov/providers-professionals/faqs/what-personal-health-record

Hesse, B. W., Moser, R. P., & Rutten, L. J. (2010). Surveys of physicians and electronic health information. *New England Journal of Medicine, 362*(9), 859–860.

Hibbard, J. H., & Greene, J. (2013). What the evidence shows about patient activation: Better health outcomes and care experiences; fewer data on costs. *Health Affairs (Millwood), 32*(2), 207–214. doi:10.1377/hlthaff.2012.1061

Hibbard, J. H., Greene, J., & Overton, V. (2013). Patients with lower activation associated with higher costs: Delivery systems should know their patients' 'scores'. *Health Affairs (Millwood), 32*(2), 216–222. doi:10.1377/hlthaff.2012.1064

Hibbard, J. H., Mahoney, E. R., Stock, R., & Tusler, M. (2007). Do increases in patient activation result in improved self-management behaviors? *Health Services Research, 42*(4), 1443–1463. doi:10.1111/j.1475-6773.2006.00669.x

Hood, L. (2013). *Leddy & Pepper's conceptual bases of professional nursing.* Philadelphia, PA: Lippincott Williams & Wilkins.

Hordern, A., Georgiou, A., Whetton, S., & Prgomet, M. (2011). Consumer e-health: An overview of research evidence and implications for future policy. *Health Information Management Journal, 40,* 6–14.

IBM. (2008). Addressing the state of the electronic health record (EHR). Retrieved from ftp://ftp.software.ibm.com/software/ae/arab_health/state_of_the_ehr_arab_health08_y_moosa_v2.pdf

Israelson, J., & Cankaya, E. C. (2012, January). A hybrid web based personal health record system shielded with comprehensive security. In *System Science (HICSS), 2012, 45th Hawaii International Conference on System Sciences* (pp. 2958–2968). Institute of Electrical and Electronics Engineers.

Jones, D. A., Shipman, J. P., Plaut, D. A., & Selden, C. R. (2010). Characteristics of personal health records: Findings of the Medical Library Association/National Library of Medicine Joint Electronic Personal Health Record Task Force. *Journal of the Medical Library Association, 98*(3), 243–249. http://doi.org/10.3163/1536-5050.98.3.013

Kahn, J. S., Aulakh, V., & Bosworth, A. (2009). What it takes: Characteristics of the ideal personal health record. *Health Affairs, 28*(2), 369–376.

Kim, K., & Nahm, E. (2012). Benefits of and barriers to the use of personal health records (PHR) for health management among adults. *Online Journal of Nursing Informatics, 16*(3), 1–9.

Ko, H., Turner, T., Jones, C., & Hill, C. (2010). Patient-held medical records for patients with chronic disease: A systematic review. *BMJ Quality and Safety, 19,* e41.

Koch, S., & Vimarlund, V. (2012). Critical advances in bridging personal health informatics and clinical informatics. *Yearbook of Medical Informatics, 7*(1), 48–55.

Lester, M., Boateng, S., Studeny, J., & Coustasse, A. (2016). Personal health records: Beneficial or burdensome for patients and healthcare providers? *Perspectives in Health Information Management, 13,* 1h.

Logue, M. D., & Effken, J. A. (2012). Modeling factors that influence personal health records adoption. *Computers, Informatics, Nursing, 30*(7), 354–362.

Logue, M. D., & Effken, J. A. (2013). An exploratory study of the personal health records adoption model in the older adult with chronic illness. *Journal of Innovation in Health Informatics, 20*(3), 151–169.

Maaike, C. M. R., Dijkhorst-Oei, L. T., & Rutten, G. E. H. M. (2014). Reasons and barriers for using a patient portal: Survey among patients with diabetes mellitus. *Journal of Medical Internet Research, 16*(11), e263.

Microsoft. (2017). HealthVault: A platform for connected health information and innovation. Retrieved from https://msdn.microsoft.com/en-us/healthvault/healthvault-introduction.aspx

National Committee on Vital and Health Statistics, U.S. Department of Health and Human Services, National Cancer Institute, National Institutes of Health, National Center for Health Statistics, & Centers for Disease Control and Prevention. (2006). Personal health records and personal health record systems: A report and recommendations from the National Committee on Vital and Health Statistics. Retrieved from http://www.ncvhs.hhs.gov/wp-content/uploads/2014/05/0602nhiirpt.pdf

Nazi, K. M. (2013). The personal health record paradox: Health care professionals' perspectives and the information ecology of personal health record systems in organizational and clinical settings. *Journal of Medical Internet Research, 15*(4), e70.

Nelson, D. E., Kreps, G. L., Hesse, B. W., Croyle, R. T., Willis, G., Arora, N. K., . . . Alden, S. (2004). The Health Information National Trends Survey (HINTS): Development, design, and dissemination. *Journal of Health Communication, 9*(5), 443–460.

Nguyen, Q., Bartlett, G., Rodriguez, C., & Tellier, P. P. (2016). Young adults on the perceived benefits and expected use of personal health records: A qualitative descriptive study. *Journal of Innovation in Health Informatics, 23*(1), 466–475.

O'Reilly, D., Holbrook, A., Blackhouse, G., Troyan, S., & Goeree, R. (2012). Cost-effectiveness of a shared computerized decision support system for diabetes linked to electronic medical records. *Journal of the American Medical Informatics Association, 19*(3), 341–345.

Pew Research Center. (2013). Health fact sheet. Highlights of the Pew Internet's project research related to health and healthcare. Retrieved from http://www.pewinternet.org/2013/01/15/health-online-2013/

Price, M., Bellwood, P., Kitson, N., Davies, I., Weber, J., & Lau, F. (2015). Conditions potentially sensitive to a personal health record (PHR) intervention, a systematic review. *BMC Medical Informatics and Decision Making, 15*(1), 1.

Reti, S. R., Feldman, H. J., Ross, S. E., & Safran, C. (2010). Improving personal health records for patient-centered care. *Journal of the American Medical Informatics Association, 17*(2), 192–195.

Riippa, I., Linna, M., & Rönkkö, I. (2015). A patient portal with electronic messaging: Controlled before-and-after study. *Journal of Medical Internet Research, 17*(11), e250.

Serocca, A. B. (2008). Personal health record use by patients as perceived by ambulatory care physicians in Nebraska and South Dakota: A cross-sectional study. *Perspectives in Health Information Management, 5*(15), 1.

Statistics Canada. (2011). 2009 Canadian Internet use survey. Retrieved from http://www.statcan.gc.ca/

Tang, P. C., Ash, J. S., Bates, D. W., Overhage, J. M., & Sands, D. Z. (2006). Personal health records: Definitions, benefits, and strategies for overcoming barriers to adoption. *Journal of the American Medical Informatics Association, 13*(2), 121–126.

Thygeson, M., van Vorst, K. A., Maciosek, M. V., & Solberg, L. (2008). Use and costs of care in retail clinics versus traditional care sites. *Health Affairs, 27*(5), 1283–1292.

Vydra, T. P., Cuaresma, E., Kretovics, M., & Bose-Brill, S. (2015). Diffusion and use of tethered personal health records in primary care. *Perspectives in Health Information Management, 12*, 1c.

Walker, J., Pan, E., Johnston, D., Adler-Milstein, J., Bates, D. W., & Middleton, B. (2005). The value of health care information exchange and interoperability. *Health Affairs (Millwood),* Suppl. Web Exclusives, W5-10–W5-18.

Weinick, R. M., Burns, R. M., & Mehrotra, A. (2010). Many emergency department visits could be managed at urgent care centers and retail clinics. *Health Affairs, 29*(9), 1630–1636.

Wells, S., Rozenblum, R., Park, A., Dunn, M., & Bates, D. W. (2014). Personal health records for patients with chronic disease: A major opportunity. *Applied Clinical Informatics, 5*(2), 416–429.

Wiljer, D., Urowitz, S., Apatu, E., DeLenardo, C., Eysenbach, G., Harth, T., . . . Leonard, K. (2008). Patient accessible electronic health records: Exploring recommendations for successful implementation strategies. *Journal of Medical Internet Research, 10*(4), e34.

Zhou, T., Medo, M., Cimini, G., Zhang, Z., & Zhang, Y. (2011). Emergence of scale-free leadership structure in social recommender systems. *PLoS One, 6*(7), e20648.

CHAPTER 11

Mobile Health Interventions: Opportunities, Challenges, and Applications

Ashish Joshi

KEY TERMS

Federal Communications Commission (FCC)

Federal Food, Drug, and Cosmetic Act (FD&C Act)

mHealth Evidence Reporting and Assessment (mERA)

mHealth Technical Evidence Review Group (mTERG)

Mobile App Rating Scale (MARS)

Operating systems (OSs)

Personal digital assistants (PDAs)

Short Message Service (SMS)

LEARNING OBJECTIVES

- Examine the growing usage of mHealth technologies.
- Discuss the opportunities and challenges related to mHealth technologies.
- Understand the classification of mHealth apps.
- Recognize the importance of regulatory standards for mHealth apps.
- Examine mHealth applications in diverse settings.
- List the tools reporting the quality of evidence about mHealth apps.

- What are the pros and cons of various mobile devices?
- What opportunities are available to enhance population health outcomes with the growing usage of mobile technologies?
- What essential factors need to be considered when choosing mHealth apps?
- What are the opportunities and challenges related to mHealth interventions in low resource settings?
- What outcomes are impacted through mHealth interventions?

CHAPTER OUTLINE

▶ I. The Growing Number of Mobile Device Users

The introduction of mobile computing devices has greatly impacted many fields. These devices include personal digital assistants (PDAs), patient monitoring devices, smartphones, and tablet computers. Both smartphones and tablets combine computing and communication features in a single device. These can be held in a hand or stored in a pocket, allowing easy access and use at point of care (Ventola, 2014). These devices incorporate digital features including audio, text messaging, global positioning systems (GPSs), web browsing, camera systems, and voice recording (Ventola, 2014). Mobile devices have powerful processers and operating systems (OSs), large memories, and high-resolution screens (Boulos, Wheeler, Tavares, & Jones, 2011). Recent estimates state that there are more than 5 billion mobile phone subscriptions, and more than 85% of the world's population is covered by a commercial wireless signal (Baig, GholamHosseini, & Connolly, 2015). The availability of mobile technology has also advanced infrastructure development in low- and middle-income countries (LMICs).

Mobile subscriptions are growing around 3% year-on-year globally while Mobile broadband subscriptions are growing by around 20% year-on-year (Ericsson, 2017). Mobile phones like Apple's iPhone and the various Android devices have taken over the mobile market (Istepanian, Jovanov, & Zhang, 2004). Mobile devices have evolved since 1973, when the first mobile phone, the DynaTac, was introduced (Jordan, Ray, Johnson, & Evans, 2011). The PDA was first introduced in 1992, and the Blackberry came on the market in 2002 (Jordan et al., 2011). Several other handheld mobile devices were introduced after the Blackberry. In January 2007, Apple launched the first-generation iPhone, and in October 2008, Google's Android OS was introduced (Mosa, Yoo, & Sheets, 2012). A novel product known as the iPad, a tablet computer system, was introduced by Apple in 2010 (Mosa et al., 2012). Mobile device ownership has increased rapidly because of the easy touchscreen user interface and advanced features that the iPhones and other smartphones offer. Tablets that run the Google Android OS also are in widespread use (FIGURE 11.1).

Wireless communication subscribers in the United States have increased from about 270 million in 2008 to over 300 million in 2013 (Federal Communications Commission, 2015). Smartphone ownership in the United States has increased from 35% of adults in 2011 to 64% in 2014 (Azenkot et al., 2011). Smartphones are the most recent technology with advanced connectivity and computing capability (Bashshur, Shannon, Krupinski, & Grigsby, 2011; Boulos et al., 2011). They combine the functions of a mobile phone and a PDA, in addition to enabling Internet access and imaging and video functionality. According to the U.S. Federal Communications Commission (FCC), "Smartphones are mobile devices with cell-phone capability having an HTML browser that allows easy access to the full, open Internet" (Hall, Fottrell, Wilkinson, & Byass, 2014).

FIGURE 11.1 Evolution of iPhones and smartphones

A report by the Telecommunications Industry Association (TIA) in 2010 defined a "smartphone as a mobile device that offers the most advanced computing ability and connectivity available today" (Wallace, Clark, & White, 2012). Smartphones have large screens, greater processing power than the basic phones, memory, and multiple connections such as WiFi and Bluetooth (Wallace et al., 2012). Smartphones also have features including email access; calendars; Internet access; multimedia applications such as photos, music, and videos; and GPS functions (Kay, Santos, & Takane, 2011). Smartphone platforms are usually based on a specially designed OS platform or mobile computing and phone services. These OS platforms are capable of running third-party applications including medical and healthcare applications. Several smartphone OS platforms include: Windows Phone, Blackberry, iOS, and Android. All of these platforms provide standard features such as organizers, contact lists, email, web browsers, and photo galleries (Boulos et al., 2011). Some of the other features include the following:

- *Multitasking:* Allows multiple applications to run concurrently.
- *Notification system:* Displays system status and notification while the user works on an application window.
- *Toolbar:* Facilitates control buttons for applications.
- *Customizable:* Allows users to add or remove application shortcuts on the home screen.
- *App folder:* Stores applications in a special system-defined folder.
- *Recent apps:* Displays all recently used applications.
- *Universal search:* Search box combines searching of the web and the device internally.
- *Adobe Flash:* Allows all the Flash-based resources (e.g., games, videos) from the web.
- *Encryption:* Enhances data security.
- *WiFi security:* Allows for wireless connection to the Internet and secure data transmission.

Accessibility features are also supported by some mobile devices to provide enhanced services for the disabled, as well as multiple languages. An overview of the OS features of smartphone platforms is provided in FIGURE 11.2.

Some of the common functions of several smartphone OS platforms have also been described (Bashshur et al., 2011). These include touchscreens, multitouch user interfaces, virtual keyboards, external keyboards, cameras, and video recording (FIGURE 11.3). Smartphone rankings showed Facebook as the most popular app, followed by Facebook Messenger, YouTube, and Google Maps (Perez, 2016). The results are similar to the previous results that also showed similar trends in the ranking of the smartphone apps (Free et al., 2013).

▶ II. The Growing Usage of mHealth Applications

The term *mobile health* (*mHealth*) was coined over a decade ago (National Institutes of Health, 2016). The utilization of mobile devices in the healthcare domain has grown worldwide. According to the Director of the Earth Institute, Jeffrey Sachs, "Mobile phones and wireless Internet end isolation, and will therefore prove to be the most transformative technology of economic development of our time" (Kahn,

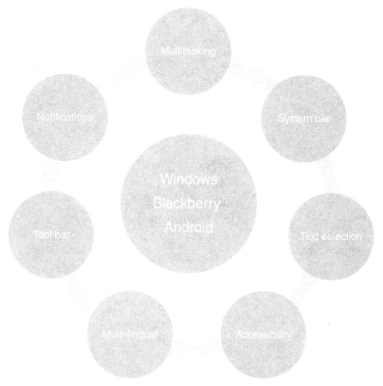

FIGURE 11.2 Common OS features across smartphone operating system platforms

Data from Mosa, A. S. M., Yoo, I., & Sheets, L. (2012). A systematic review of healthcare applications for smartphones. *BMC Medical Informatics and Decision Making, 12*(1), 1.

Yang, & Kahn, 2010). An initial search of Google Trends for the term "mHealth" revealed increased growth over time (Ventola, 2014) (FIGURE 11.4).

Fitness apps were the most popular way consumers utilized Mobile Health prior to 2014. However, this changed in 2014 when there was a spike in searches for "health app". Searches for "Pregnancy app" have been higher than other medical conditions such as diabetes, cholesterol, and blood pressure (Tseng, 2016).

Making phone calls has now become just one of many interesting features of mobile technologies. Other commonly used features include simple Short Message Service (SMS) texts and voice messaging. Mobile Internet browsers, Voice over Internet Protocol services (e.g., Skype), instant messaging services, photographic capabilities, and a wide variety of device-based software applications (commonly known as apps) have also been introduced (Fjeldsoe, Marshall, & Miller, 2009; Ventola, 2014). Apps are defined as "Software programs that have been developed to run on a computer or mobile device to accomplish a specific purpose" (Payne, Wharrad, & Watts, 2012).

Faster processors, improved memory, smaller batteries, and highly efficient systems that perform complex functions have paved the way for rapid development of mHealth apps for both professional and personal use (Ventola, 2014). mHealth broadly encompasses health-related uses of mobile technologies within the delivery of healthcare services and the public health systems. These services range from

FIGURE 11.3 Smartphone operating-system platforms, features support with hardware

Data from Mosa, A. S. M., Yoo, I., & Sheets, L. (2012). A systematic review of healthcare applications for smartphones. *BMC Medical Informatics and Decision Making, 12*(1), 1.

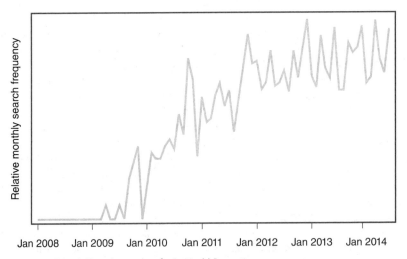

FIGURE 11.4 Google Trends searches for "mHealth" over time

Data from Google Trends, July 25, 2014.

facilitating communication between individuals and health systems to health monitoring and surveillance to providing point-of-care access to information.

The World Health Organization (WHO) defines mHealth as the "[s]pread of mobile technologies as well as advancements in their innovative application to address health priorities" (Azenkot et al., 2011). mHealth is also defined as the "[d]elivery of healthcare services via mobile communication devices" (Med Data Group, 2015). mHealth also has been referred to as "Delivery, facilitation and communication of health-related information via mobile technologies—including cell phones, tablet devices, PDAs and wireless infrastructure" (Shieh, Tsai, Anavim, Wang, & Lin, 2008). The National Institutes of Health defines mHealth as the "[u]se of mobile and wireless devices to improve health outcomes, healthcare services, and health research" (McGowan, Cusack, & Bloomrosen, 2012). mHealth is also defined as the "[u]se of portable electronic devices for mobile voice or data communication over a cellular or other wireless network of base stations to provide health information" (Kahn et al., 2010).

The Apple iTunes Appstore was launched in July 2008 as a platform or service area where iPad, iPhone, and iPod users can search for and download apps from a variety of online vendors (Murfin, 2013). In 2011, Apple created the Apps for Healthcare Professionals section within the medical category of the Appstore (iMedical Apps, 2016). In 2013, the medical section was further divided into subcategories including reference, medical education, electronic medical record and patient monitoring, nursing, imaging, patient education, and personal care (Mobi-HealthNews, 2016). Google similarly launched Google Play, which provides a wide variety of apps for mobile devices that use the Android OS (Payne et al., 2012). In 2014, more than 62% of smartphone users searched for health information using their cell phones, reflecting a 10% increase from 2012 (Smith & Page, 2015). In 2014, 34% of all U.S. adults downloaded at least one app meant to support healthy living (Med Data Group, 2015). There has been a rapid proliferation of mHealth solutions throughout developing and developed countries (TABLE 11.1). The potential exists for technology-based health interventions to impact populations like never before.

The incredible volume of apps makes it difficult for consumers to keep track of which apps are available for use by patients. There is limited guidance on how to judge the validity and worth of commercially available apps. The implication is that serious consequences can result from recommending an app with inaccurate content or that could be harmful to a patient.

TABLE 11.1 Percentage of mHealth Apps Utilized in Developing and Developed Countries

Type of mHealth App	Developing Countries	Developed Countries
Manage overall health	57%	42%
Payers pay for telephone-based consultations	43%	29%
Payers pay for SMS text-based consultations	37%	23%

▶ III. Opportunities and Challenges in mHealth

Mobile technologies play a key role in shaping mobile health. mHealth presents an opportunity to improve access to and use of health services both in the United States and globally. mHealth extends the reach of health information and services to remote populations. It also helps to improve health system efficiency and health outcomes (Shieh et al., 2008). SMS texting is among the most commonly used mobile technologies (Shieh et al., 2008). Key benefits of mHealth globally include the following:

- Increased access to health care
- Increased access to health-related information
- Improved efficiency and reduced service delivery costs
- Improved ability to diagnose, treat, and track diseases
- Timely and actionable public health information
- Enhanced access to modalities for health worker training and medical education

Developments in wireless technologies have provided a variety of opportunities to address public health challenges (Shieh et al., 2008). Mobile health care empowers stakeholders with mobility, uninterrupted access, and real-time decision making at the point of care. The role of mHealth in promoting population health outcomes and mitigating health disparities remains a widely untapped field with numerous opportunities. Continuing efforts are needed to utilize several opportunities and overcome the various challenges related to the mobile technologies (Shieh et al., 2008).

Opportunity 1: Paradigm Shift from Wired Access to the Internet to Universal Access

The Internet has become a global storage system of data, information, and knowledge (Yu, Wu, Yu, & Xiao, 2006). The availability of portable wireless computing devices enables users to maintain wireless Internet connectivity at all times (Shieh et al., 2008). The majority of healthcare institutions have migrated toward electronic recordkeeping and away from paper-based medical recordkeeping. Healthcare consumers are willing to actively seek the best provider regardless of the distance, resulting in a patient's clinical data residing in multiple healthcare facilities (Shieh et al., 2008).

Related challenges include the following:

- Interoperability
- Balance between good signal strength and no adverse interference
- Small display screen
- Security vulnerability of portable devices

Opportunity 2: Paradigm Shift from Clinically Focused Systems to Community-Focused Systems

The availability of wearable, wireless monitoring devices makes it possible for individuals to have the measurement devices at all times. Further, these devices also keep the patient connected with the caregivers on the remote end. A related challenge is data volume reduction—meaning the process of minimizing the amount of data to make it meaningful and stored in a data storage environment.

Opportunity 3: Paradigm Shift from Physician-Centered Decision Making to Collaborative Physician–Patient Decision Making

The concept of collaborative decision making between the patient and the physician to determine suitable treatment creates new opportunities to maximize patient satisfaction (Shieh et al., 2008).

Related challenges include the following:

- Loss of traditional authority
- Elevation of the consumer's level of medical literacy

Opportunity 4: Paradigm Shift from Generic Health Care to Personalized Health Care

Wireless communication provides a uniquely convenient way for the physician and patient to maintain a continuous ongoing evaluation of treatment and related health outcomes. A phone call or text message can be initiated to inform the individual whenever a new change occurs.

Opportunity 5: Patient Engagement

The Health Information Technology for Economic and Clinical Health (HITECH) Act has provided a platform that could serve as the policy model for mHealth technologies (McGowan et al., 2012). It serves as an enabler of mHealth deployment because it creates an incentive structure to increase the utilization of technology in health care. Texting and smartphone apps are important tools to meet the objectives of meaningful use to improve population health.

Related challenges include the following:

- A number of mobile phone services do not provide texting capabilities, so inclusion of SMS within federally funded programs for enabling health-based texting should be considered.
- Use of texting still requires a certain level of literacy, especially for the elderly and those living in rural settings (Shieh et al., 2008).

Some of the other numerous challenges that have been attributed as reasons for the slow uptake of mHealth technologies include poor infrastructure, cultural and ethical barriers, legal and policy issues, limited technical capacity, lack of awareness, and uncertainty on mHealth cost-effectiveness (Mburu, Franz, & Springer, 2013). Various other challenges related to mHealth uptake have been classified into seven other categories (see FIGURE 11.5).

A number of other critical issues considered important in mHealth monitoring include the following:

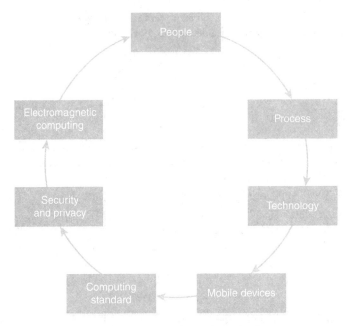

FIGURE 11.5 Challenges related to the uptake of mHealth technologies

- *Reliability, efficiency, and acceptability:* mHealth apps must provide reliable and efficient vital data for evaluating patients' needs. End user acceptability is becoming an important aspect in the design of such systems. Several factors that need to be taken into consideration when analyzing user needs are the attitudes, perceptions, and concerns of the mHealth users (Lee et al., 2014).
- *Smartphone platform variability:* Multiple OSs and variability between the programming language and application environment are important considerations for mHealth apps.
- *Cost-effectiveness:* The costly mobile phone contracts, and expensive termination fees create barriers to accessing specific services such as health data processing.
- *Involvement of healthcare professionals:* Policy discussions around mHealth apps would be a key to achieving the maximum potential of mHealth apps.
- *Energy use and battery life:* Low energy consumption devices are needed for battery-operated systems such as smartphones. Long-term use can pose a serious threat to mobile device battery life and compromise the transmission of essential data.
- *User interface:* The smartphone's graphical user interface is one of its most important features. Any app's user interface design should be simplistic and easy to use. Using high-quality data in mHealth apps is important for reliable communications (Shieh et al., 2008).
- *Security and privacy:* mHealth apps deal with personal information and therefore require security to maintain a safe and secure system. Wireless transmission of data in mHealth results in various security threats; this is a major area of research. The security issues can be classified into two categories (**TABLE 11.2**).

A trust-based security framework using encryption and decryption is designed to secure mobile wireless-networked sensors (Arora, Yttri, & Nilsen, 2014). A robust

TABLE 11.2 mHealth-Related Security Challenges	
System Security	**Information Security**
Administrative	Data encryption
Physical level	Data integration
Technical level	Authentication

and secure system is built on many functions including (1) data protection on the device, secure authentication, and data encryption; and (2) design consideration for the long term and monitoring of vital signs (Arora et al., 2014). One of the possible ways of addressing fundamental mHealth deployment challenges is a multidimensional approach that integrates principles of sociocognitive theories into the design science (von Alan, March, Park, & Ram, 2004). There is a need for a well-grounded model to accelerate acceptance and utilization of mHealth innovations.

▶ IV. Classification of mHealth Apps

There are several approaches to classifying mHealth apps (see FIGURE 11.6). These will be discussed in the following sections.

Device-Level Apps

Mobile devices are classified into basic mobile phones, smart devices, and PDAs and other devices (Ali, Chew, & Yap, 2016).

- *Basic and feature phones:* Includes mobile phones with Internet and media functionalities. They usually have a limited, proprietary OS, and may not necessarily support third-party software. Push email is often nonexistent. Calendar syncing and document editing is a problem. However, they do have GPS, full HTML browsers, 3G speeds, and some popular social networking abilities like Twitter and Facebook (Ali et al., 2016).

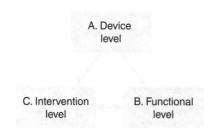

FIGURE 11.6 Levels of classification of mHealth apps

- *Smart devices:* These consist of smartphones, tablet PCs, iPod Touch, or any similar devices that have the ability to run third-party apps. Email is a necessary feature along with a push email feature. Calendar syncing and document editing are essential as well.
- *PDAs and other devices:* Pagers, wireless communication devices, and wearable devices are classified under the category of other devices.

Prior to 2007, more articles reported on the use of PDAs (Sabol, Emonds, Soltys, & Disch, 1993). From 2007 to 2012, mHealth research was concentrated on the healthcare uses of mobile phones (Ali et al., 2016). From 2013 on, the direction of mHealth research was geared more toward the use of smart devices such as smartphones, tablet PCs, iPads, or other variations of these devices (Ali et al., 2016).

Functional-Level Apps

Mobile device functionalities have been classified into six types (see FIGURE 11.7). Any software installed on mobile devices is classified as an app. Automated sensing systems include electronic devices that connect to mobile devices that process the data (Ali et al., 2016).

Intervention-Level Apps

The purpose of mHealth interventions was categorized into five major classes (see FIGURE 11.8). The health conditions addressed by mHealth interventions have been broadly categorized into nonspecific conditions, noncommunicable conditions, infectious diseases, and other conditions.

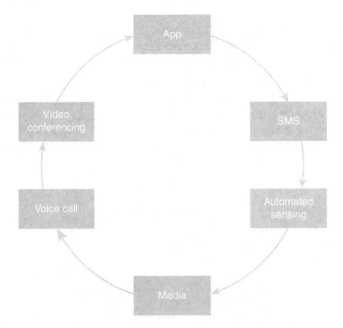

FIGURE 11.7 Classification of mobile device functionalities

Security and Privacy Concerns

mHealth apps are classified into three dimensions in terms of their privacy and security concerns: mHealth, security, and privacy (see FIGURE 11.9).

mHealth Dimension

This dimension includes the following categories (Ozdalga, Ozdalga, & Ahuja, 2012; see FIGURE 11.10):

▪ *Patient care and monitoring:* These apps observe patients via mobile devices (e.g., the Android app iWander for patients with Alzheimer's disease uses a GPS to track their location [Sposaro, Danielson, & Tyson, 2010]).

FIGURE 11.8 Classification of mHealth apps at the intervention level

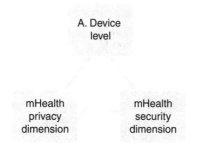

FIGURE 11.9 Classification of mHealth apps in terms of security and privacy concerns

FIGURE 11.10 Taxonomy of mHealth apps

Data from Plachkinova, M., Andrés, S., & Chatterjee, S. (2015, January). A taxonomy of mHealth apps—security and privacy concerns. In *System Sciences (HICSS), 2015 48th Hawaii International Conference* (pp. 3187–3196). IEEE. doi:10.1109/HICSS.2015.385

- *Health apps for the layperson*: There is not sufficient evidence of trends for patient apps. An example of this type of app is weight loss apps such as Lose It!. Using the built-in GPS and accelerometer, smartphones can be turned into navigators and pedometers (Lose It, 2016).
- *Communication, education, and research:* These are critical smartphone apps. They allow users to receive information in a timely manner and be more efficient. Examples include integration with electronic records and data on disease outbreaks by location (Santoro, Castelnuovo, Zoppis, Mauri, & Sicurello, 2015).
- *Physician or student reference apps:* There is limited evidence on such apps. There is significant potential to enhance medical decision making and mitigate medical errors using certain apps. An example of this type of app is 'Mersey Burns App', which is a smartphone/tablet application that aids in the assessment of total burn surface area and calculation of fluid resuscitation protocols in burns (Barnes et al., 2015).

mHealth Security Dimension

This dimension includes the following categories (Stavrou & Pitsillides, 2005; see Figure 11.10):

- *Authentication:* Proof of identity is an essential component of any app that handles confidential information.
- *Authorization:* This is the act of determining whether a particular user has the right to carry out a certain activity.
- *Accountability:* A user who has misused the app account can be tracked down and made accountable.
- *Integrity:* Information may be altered when it is exchanged in an insecure network.
- *Availability:* People authorized to get information should be able to get what they need.
- *Ease of use:* The security component must be easy to use, or else users will switch security off or bypass it.
- *Confidentiality:* The app must ensure that information is available only to those who are authorized to access it.
- *Management:* Proper management of apps is key to ensure the normal flow of operation and information involved.
- *Physical security:* This is essential in maintaining the security of the mobile device as well as the back end data center used by the app developer.

mHealth Privacy Dimension

This dimension includes the following categories (Kotz, 2011; see Figure 11.10):

- *Identity threats:* These are related to patients losing or sharing their identity credentials.
- *Access threats:* Patients must have control over the collection, use, and disclosure of protected health information. Patient data may be shared and health records might be modified.
- *Disclosure threats*: These are related to several factors including secure data transmission to comply with the Health Insurance Portability and Accountability Act (HIPAA) and the HITECH Act.

▶ V. Selection of mHealth Apps

Mobile health apps are rapidly proliferating. With thousands of health apps in the marketplace, guidance is needed to identify apps that provide accurate information, are user-friendly, and are effective (Powell, Landman, & Bates, 2014). There is limited quality control or regulations in existence to ensure that health apps are user friendly, accurate in content, evidence-based, or efficacious. Some limited strategies that can be employed to identify relevant mHealth apps are outlined here (Powell et al., 2014) (FIGURE 11.11):

- *Scientific literature search:* One strategy is to search for papers reviewing apps in a content domain. This approach reveals the capabilities and limitations of

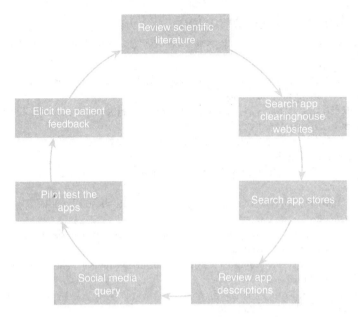

FIGURE 11.11 Strategies employed to identify relevant mHealth apps

existing mHealth apps. Challenges associated with this search include limited published literature on health apps, it is time consuming, evaluations predominantly focus on one OS, and the literature is often outdated because of the constantly evolving market.

- *Apps clearinghouse:* Another strategy is to search app clearinghouse websites that can help with identifying the apps' strengths and weaknesses. This is highly efficient and includes access to systematic evaluations. The evaluation methods chosen by each clearinghouse largely determine the quality of apps. Reviewing apps can be resource intensive and time consuming. Different clearinghouses may yield more useful recommendations when searching for different types of apps (TABLE 11.3).

- *App stores:* These are challenging to navigate. It is important to conduct app searches with the most relevant and targeted key words. Using ineffective search terms may display apps that are not a good fit owing to how the apps are indexed by developers. No method exists to search all app stores together. There is a lack of systematic evaluation of the apps. Apps designed for smaller audiences or those that are new to the market are harder to find. Lower app ranks do not necessarily reflect poor quality of the apps.

- *User ratings reviews:* Looking over user ratings and reviews can offer evidence of app usability, functionality, and efficacy. However, this approach is time consuming, is not evidence based, and might not ensure the validity or accuracy of the app. Social networks may reveal new app trends and likability by certain user groups. This approach, however, may oversample the patients with positive experiences with a particular app. It fails to elicit the experiences that result in the patient no longer using the app for health promotion.

TABLE 11.3 Examples of mHealth Websites

Site	URL
National Health Service (NHS) Health Apps Library	http://apps.nhs.uk
Happtique	http://www.happtique.com
iMedicalApps	http://www.imedicalapps.com
Eat Right App Reviews	http://www.eatright.org/appreviews

▪ *Apps piloted:* This method has the healthcare provider examine the functionality, content accuracy, and usability of apps (Bastien, 2010). Many of the apps can be evaluated with only a few minutes of navigation. It rarely takes more than one day of using an app before major pros and cons are observed (Haskins et al., 2014). However, piloting an app may seem laborious.

Patients may provide valuable insight after they have used the app a provider recommends. A follow-up is needed to determine if the patient has successfully changed his or her behavior after using the app. Providers may need to elicit feedback from multiple patients to increase their confidence in an app's potential benefit. These strategies should be viewed as a list rather than a stepwise approach; any one or a combination of them can be employed to best suit the needs of users.

More guidance is needed on identifying apps that provide accurate information and are user-friendly, and more research is needed to establish evidence for health apps' efficacy. Building better app clearinghouses that review health apps for usability, privacy, security, and functionalities, as well as information on the relationship between the app platform and existing evidence, may represent the most important direction.

The Mobile App Rating Scale (MARS) is a reliable, multidimensional tool for classifying and assessing the quality of mHealth apps (Stoyanov et al., 2015). The 23-item MARS tool includes four objective quality scales and one subjective quality scale (TABLE 11.4). The tool has a five-point rating: (1) Inadequate, (2) Poor, (3) Acceptable, (4) Good, and (5) Excellent. The score is determined by calculating the mean scores of the objective subscales and an overall mean app quality total score. Mean scores are reported instead of total scores because an item can be rated as not applicable. The subjective quality items can be scored separately as individual items or as a mean subjective quality score.

Innovators are continually developing apps with growing complexity. Although some of these innovative apps are focused on enhancing individual self-management of health and wellness, others are geared toward facilitating patient care delivery by healthcare providers.

TABLE 11.4 Mobile App Rating Scale to Evaluate mHealth Apps

Objective Scales	Criteria
Engagement	Entertainment, interest, customization, interactivity, and target group
Functionality	Performance, navigation, gestural design, and ease of use
Aesthetics	Layout, graphics, and visual appeal
Information	Accuracy of app description, goals, quality of information, quantity of information, visual information, credibility, and evidence base
Subjective quality	Would you recommend this app? How frequently would you use it? Would you pay for this app? What is your overall star rating of the app?

▶ VI. Regulation of mHealth Apps

A mobile app is a software application that can be executed on a mobile platform with or without wireless connectivity. It can also be a web-based software app tailored to a mobile platform but that is executed on a server. Mobile medical apps are defined as "apps that meet the definition of device in section 201(h) of the Federal Food, Drug, and Cosmetic Act (FD&C Act)" (Barton, 2012). Their intent is to be used as an accessory to a regulated medical device or to turn a mobile platform into a regulated medical device. TABLE 11.5 provides some examples of these types of apps.

FIGURE 11.12 represents mobile apps for which the U.S. Food and Drug Administration (FDA) intends enforcement discretion (Barton, 2012).

Some of the mHealth apps that the FDA does not consider to be devices and with no regulatory requirements include the following (Barton, 2012; Buijink, Visser, & Marshall, 2013):

- Apps providing access to electronic copies of medical textbooks or other reference materials. Examples include medical dictionaries and libraries of clinical descriptions for diseases and conditions.
- Apps used as educational tools and not for use in the diagnosis of disease. Examples include medical flash cards with medical images, pictures, graphs, and interactive videos.
- Apps supporting patient-centered health care. Examples include an educational portal for healthcare providers and patients to find the closest healthcare facilities.

TABLE 11.5 Mobile Medical Apps Meeting the Definition of a Device

Type of App	Examples
An extension of one or more medical devices. Connect to devices for the purpose of inactive patient monitoring or analysis of medical device data.	Medical image display from picture archiving and communication systems (PACS)
Mobile platform can be transformed into a regulated medical device (e.g., by using attachments, display screens, or sensors).	Attachment of a blood glucose strip reader
Perform patient-specific analysis and provide patient-specific diagnosis or treatment recommendations.	Apps that use patient-specific parameters and calculate dosage or create a dosage plan

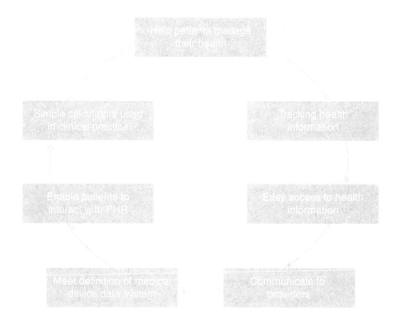

FIGURE 11.12 Mobile apps for which the FDA intends enforcement discretion

- Apps with the purpose of automating general office operations in a healthcare setting.
- Apps not intended for use in the prevention, diagnosis, or cure of diseases. Examples include billing codes like ICD-9.

The FDA's oversight approach to mHealth apps is focused on their functionality and not determined by the platform (Buijink et al., 2013). Although the FDA does not regulate mobile device sales, it does provide oversight of mobile apps performing medical device functions (Buijink et al., 2013). The FDA guidelines inform the various stakeholders about how the FDA intends to apply its regulatory authorities to select mobile software apps.

▶ VII. mHealth Apps

Cell phones, tablet computers, and other wireless devices all play a role in shaping mHealth. It is often presented as a low-cost option for increasing communication between patients and providers. The growing utilization of smartphones and enhanced bandwidth and computing power have provided greater opportunities for individuals to use mobile devices for improving health. SMS allows messages containing a maximum of 160 characters from a mobile phone or a computer to one or many mobile phones simultaneously (Déglise, Suggs, & Odermatt, 2012). SMS is available on all cellular phones, including cheap low-end handsets, making them a preferred choice for those who cannot afford expensive handsets or those living in the rural settings. Prior research has focused largely on the use of SMS for health purposes in developed countries (Franklin, Waller, Pagliari, & Greene, 2006; Krishna, Boren, & Balas, 2009). The affordability of mobile handsets and SMS is very attractive in resource-poor areas with little electricity and slow Internet connections.

Mobile devices have emerged globally as a platform to engage and educate patients. mHealth apps are available in every area of health care, such as physical activity (Bexelius et al., 2010); obesity (O'Malley, Dowdall, Burls, Perry, & Curran, 2014), diet (Wang, Egelandsdal, Amdam, Almli, & Oostindjer, 2016), and weight loss (Pellegrini et al., 2012); diabetes self-management (Liang et al., 2011); and asthma self-management (Ryan, Cobern, Wheeler, Price, & Tarassenko, 2005).

Smartphones serve as key computing and communication mobile devices of choice and also come with a rich set of advanced and embedded sensors. These sensors include an accelerometer, digital compass, gyroscope, GPS, microphone, and camera. The majority of vital sign monitoring systems use built-in Bluetooth technology to receive information from various devices. They use mobile Internet or WiFi to transfer information. Smartphones using General Packet Radio Service (GPRS), 3G, and 4G for data transfer are a technically attractive solution to establishing reliable communication links between patients and clinicians (Déglise et al., 2012). Smartphones' widescreen graphical display of data can facilitate transmission and receiving of data in real time. In addition, the microphone of smartphones can act as a stethoscope to get heart sounds. However, data processing on a mobile device poses a serious disadvantage in terms of accuracy, delay, and power/battery life. Another critical challenge is the security and privacy of user data, especially in terms of patient identification and confidentiality of medical information.

mHealth Apps in Developing Countries

There is growing enthusiasm to leverage the rapid uptake of mobile phones and mobile broadband services in low- and middle-income countries (LMICs). The evidence regarding the health impacts of mHealth interventions was categorized into 12 common applications of mHealth (Labrique, Vasudevan, Kochi, Fabricant, & Mehl, 2013). TABLE 11.6 shows the various health impact indicators. These include: (1) behavior change (measured by improvement in knowledge, self-efficacy,

TABLE 11.6 Findings Regarding Utilization of mHealth Apps in Developing Countries

Utilization of mHealth App	Findings
Client education and behavior change (Hunchangsith, Barendregt, Vos, & Bertram, 2012)	Treatment adherence was studied extensively. Mixed and limited evidence of mHealth effectiveness on noncommunicable diseases in LMICs.
Sensors and point-of-care diagnostics (Frühauf et al., 2013)	Improved medical diagnostics (e.g., mobile-based light microscopy, images using cameras)
Data collection and reporting (Blaschke et al., 2009)	Lower rates of data loss, sped-up data collection, and fewer errors
Electronic health records (World Bank, 2012)	Health records are generally problematic in LMICs. Access of electronic health records on mobile devices is a challenge.
Electronic decision support: information protocols, algorithms, and checklists (Iyengar & Florez-Arango, 2013)	Improved health systems functionality
Patient–provider and provider–provider communication (Ngabo et al., 2012)	Facilitated communication, greater time efficiency, and better access to medical information
Provider work planning and scheduling (Da Costa, Salomão, Martha, Pisa, & Sigulem, 2010)	Improved speed of data collection and follow-up rates
Provider training and education (Lee, Chib, & Kim, 2011)	Benefits of access to medical apps with condensed medical information
Supply chain management (UNICEF, 2016)	Improved medication transparency and accountability. Ability to track counterfeit and poor-quality drugs

attitudes, or other related behaviors), (2) mortality, (3) morbidity, (4) disability adjusted life years, (5) improved detection rates of diseases, and (6) change in other clinical parameters (Labrique et al., 2013). Small-scale implementations and scalability challenges frequently limit the potential of mHealth projects.

The following are some of the limitations of mHealth apps in developing countries:

- Need to examine the importance of frequency and timing of messages.
- More rigorous studies (e.g., randomized controlled trials) are needed.
- Large sample size studies and more rigorous user testing are needed.
- Limited infrastructure.
- Inadequate workforce training in health informatics.
- Lack of evidence-based treatment protocols.

SMS has two methods of communication: one-way and two-way (Déglise et al., 2012). TABLE 11.7 provides some examples of their use.

TABLE 11.7 SMS Modes of Communication

	Communication Method	
SMS	**One-Way**	**Two-Way**
Definition	SMS sent outbound to large numbers of subscribers No opportunity to respond to messages	Opportunities for individuals to both receive and send messages
Purpose	Standardized communication	Tailored messages
Examples	Cell Phone for Life (Déglise et al., 2012) Text Me! Flash Me! (Shillingi & Mayo, 2009)	Sex-Ed Text (Communication Initiative Network, 2016) Cell Life project (De Tolly, Skinner, Nembaware, & Benjamin, 2012)
Challenges	Network fluctuations, spam issues, limited access for women and rural populations, limited access for poor people, device maintenance and cost of sending SMS, high mobile phone turnover, potential misuse or private use of SMS, lack of incentives, language and culturally relevant barriers, and confidentiality concerns	
Considerations	Careful planning regarding capacity of systems and staff. Use of games and interactive communication strategies. Integrating SMS with other channels. High-quality SMS-based intervention studies and their impact on outcomes are needed.	

Unfortunately, there is very limited evidence on the effects of SMS within health systems. Data collection and reporting continue to be a major mHealth issue in LMICs.

mHealth Apps for Healthcare Professionals

Smartphone adoption has rapidly increased in recent years among healthcare professionals as well as the general public (Mosa et al., 2012). Point-of-care access to technology is a common need among healthcare professionals (Mosa et al., 2012). Features of hospital information systems include electronic health records, picture archiving and communication systems, laboratory information systems, and clinical decision support systems (CDSSs) (FIGURE 11.13). Evidence-based resources include PubMed and Up-to-Date, and clinical applications include medical calculators, drug databases, and disease diagnosis applications. Clinical communication includes voice calling, video conferencing, text messaging, and email messaging.

Increased smartphone adoption among healthcare professionals demonstrates the potential for enhanced clinical communication as well as information systems access. There are many smartphone-based applications for healthcare professionals. These mHealth apps have been grouped into six categories: (1) disease diagnosis apps, (2) drug reference apps, (3) medical calculator apps, (4) literature search apps, (5) clinical communications apps, and (6) health information system client apps (Ventola, 2014) (TABLE 11.8).

mHealth Apps for Community Health Workers

The majority of countries globally are limited by health worker shortages. This crisis has been largely attributed to a variety of factors including migration of qualified

FIGURE 11.13 Adoption of mHealth apps among healthcare professionals

TABLE 11.8 mHealth Apps for Healthcare Professionals

mHealth App	Description	Platforms	Examples
Disease diagnosis apps	Assist in diagnosis and treatment of infectious diseases by clinicians	iOS, Android, Windows Mobile, Blackberry	Johns Hopkins antibiotic guide (Burdette, Herchline, & Oehler, 2008)
Drug reference apps	Drug database app	Palm OS, Windows Mobile, iOS, Blackberry, Android	Epocrates (Oehler, Smith, & Toney, 2010)
Medical calculator apps	Provide medical formula calculator	Android and iOS	QxMD (http://www.qxmd.com/) and MedCalc (Busis, 2010)
Literature search apps	Medical search tools	Android and iOS	Medical Search (http://www.lookformedical.com/) Pubmed on Tap (Pope, Silva, & Almeyda, 2010)
Clinical communication apps	Incorporate message and alert systems	iOS, Blackberry, Android	Voalte One (Gamble, 2009)
Health information system client apps	A digital imaging and communications in medicine (DICOM) viewing program	Android and iOS	Epocrates (Gaudette, 2015) Osirix Mobile (Choudhri & Radvany, 2011)

health workers to better countries, poor investment in local and national health systems, and predominance of epidemics (Braun, Catalani, Wimbush, & Israelski, 2013). Community health workers (CHWs) help to build bridges between health systems and communities in low resource settings (Braun et al., 2013). CHWs serve many functions including (1) conducting home visits, (2) disease assessment and treatment, (3) data collection, (4) education and counseling, (5) referrals for care, and (6) accessing difficult-to-reach populations. The use of mobile technologies by CHWs has been shown to improve healthcare services. Four key strategies have been identified to improve the delivery of health services by CHWs through the use of mHealth tools (Braun et al., 2013) (FIGURE 11.14).

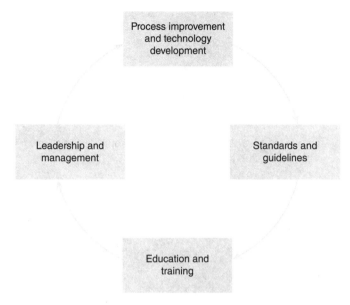

mHealth apps for community health workers (CHWs)

Fewer data errors and limited data loss were realized when CHWs used mHealth tools (Bernabe-Ortiz et al., 2008; Tomlinson et al., 2009). They also enable real-time quality review and analysis for decision making (Jones et al., 2012). mHealth tools ensure CHWs' compliance with standards and guidelines for health services via decision support, and alert and reminder tools (Jones et al., 2012). CHWs use mHealth tools to reach difficult-to-reach populations with accurate and timely interactive health information (Lemay, Sullivan, Jumbe, & Perry, 2012). mHealth tools facilitate the creation of professional networks of CHWs for providing real-time advice, information, and support (Lee et al., 2011). mHealth tools have also been used to facilitate better practices in leadership and management (DeRenzi et al., 2012). mHealth tools have also improved outcomes related to CHW performance. Improvement in efficiency has been measured in terms of cost savings and time and increased work capacity (Mahmud, Rodriguez, & Nesbit, 2010). Policies are needed to support the integration of CHWs into national strategies for health system strengthening. There remains a great need for more rigorous measurement of improvements in performance and outcomes.

Evidence-Reporting and Quality Evaluation mHealth Apps

Several tools evaluate quality and standardize the reporting of scientific evidence of mHealth tools (Agarwal et al., 2016) (TABLE 11.9).

CONSORT-EHEALTH is one tool aimed at web-based intervention trials, is study-design specific, and focuses on methodological rigor (Schulz et al., 2010). It does not provide recommendations for reporting of technical details, feasibility, and sustainability of the intervention strategies. However, in comparison, several mHealth interventions do not have an active web-based component. These typically use more descriptive and observational study designs in addition to randomized trials.

TABLE 11.9 Evidence Reporting and Quality Evaluation of mHealth Apps

Tool	Description
CONSORT (Schulz, Altman, & Moher, 2010)	Consolidated standards for reporting of randomized controlled trials
CHEERS (Husereau et al., 2013)	Consolidated health economic evaluation reporting standards
PRISMA (Liberati et al., 2009)	Preferred reporting of systematic reviews and meta-analyses
AMSTAR (Shea et al., 2007)	Assessing methodological quality of systematic reviews
MOOSA (Stroup et al., 2000)	Meta-analyses and systematic reviews of observational studies
TREND (Des Jarlais, Lyles, & Crepaz, 2004)	Reporting of evaluations with nonrandomized designs
STROBE (von Elm et al., 2007)	Strengthening the reporting of observational studies in epidemiology
CONSORT-EHEALTH (Eysenbach, 2011)	Reporting of trials involving web-based interventions (eHealth) and mHealth

The mHealth Technical Evidence Review Group (mTERG) convened by WHO included global experts in the field of mHealth research and program implementation. The goal of the mHealth Evidence Reporting and Assessment (mERA) checklist was to define mHealth interventions (content), where they are implemented (context), and the mode of their implementation (technical features), in order to facilitate replication (Agarwal et al., 2016) (TABLE 11.10). The checklist attempts to standardize reporting of mHealth evidence, and guide reviewers and policymakers in synthesizing high-quality evidence (Agarwal et al., 2016).

▶ VIII. Conclusion

Despite the existence of thousands of mHealth apps and their potential to enhance health behaviors, evaluation remains a major challenge. Most of the studies in the literature were small sample pilot or feasibility studies, instead of more rigorous randomized controlled trials with adequately powered samples. Most of the apps had lower behavior change potential. Researchers recommended that developers partner with experts in behavior change to increase app utility. Further integrating rewards into the interventions with smartphone apps may drive better behavioral outcomes. If promising mHealth initiatives in LMICs are to be adequately scaled up,

TABLE 11.10 mHealth Evidence and Reporting Assessment Tool

Criteria	Description
Infrastructure	Presents availability of infrastructure to support technology operations (i.e., includes physical infrastructure)
Technology platform	Provides justification for the technology architecture and includes a description of software and hardware
Health information systems (HISs) interoperability	Refers to the integration of mHealth interventions into current HISs
Intervention delivery	Frequency of mobile communication, mode of delivery of intervention, timing, and duration over which delivery occurred
Intervention content	Intervention content source, and modifications carried out
Usability	Describes formative research and/or content and/or usability testing, with target group(s) clearly identified
User feedback	Includes user opinions about content or user interface, and their perceptions about usability, access, and connectivity
Access to participants	Mentions individual-level, structural, economic, and social barriers or facilitators to the adoption of intervention among study participants
Cost assessment	Presents basic assessment of costs
Adoption inputs	Description of promotional activities and/or training to implement the mHealth solution among the user population of interest
Limitations for delivery at scale	Describes limitations clearly
Contextual adaptability	Describes the adaptation, or not, of the solution to a different language, different population, or different context
Replicability	Describes source code, screenshots, and algorithm flowcharts

(continues)

TABLE 11.10 mHealth Evidence and Reporting Assessment Tool *(continued)*

Criteria	Description
Data security	Describes the data security procedures/confidentiality protocols
Compliance with national guidelines or regulatory statuses	Guidance/information provided related to intervention content
Intervention fidelity	Did the intervention follow the planned delivery steps? Describe strategies utilized in assessing fidelity.

more rigorous evaluations are needed, and interventions have to demonstrate effectiveness in terms of both outcomes and cost before they can be implemented on a routine basis. New and advanced smartphone features such as wireless connectivity, high-quality images, and videos make them suitable for more advanced healthcare applications. End user consideration is often ignored. It is very important to consider the broad community, the target group/disease, and healthcare professionals from the early stages of design so that user-centric approaches can be implemented throughout development. Issues of acceptability as well as trust of healthcare professionals and patients should also be considered. Security and privacy are crucial phenomena to the success and adaptation of mHealth systems. Potential improvements in smartphone OSs and cloud computing systems in the next few years will offer a wider range of opportunities in mHealth research and its applications.

References

Agarwal, S., LeFevre, A. E., Lee, J., L'Engle, K., Mehl, G., Sinha, C., & Labrique, A. (2016). Guidelines for reporting of health interventions using mobile phones: Mobile health (mHealth) evidence reporting and assessment (mERA) checklist. *BMJ, 352,* i1174.

Ali, E. E., Chew, L., & Yap, K. Y. L. (2016). Evolution and current status of mHealth research: A systematic review. *BMJ Innovations, 2*(1), 33–40.

Arora, S., Yttri, J., & Nilsen, W. (2014). Privacy and security in mobile health (mHealth) research. *Alcohol Research: Current Reviews, 36*(1), 143.

Azenkot, S., Prasain, S., Borning, A., Fortuna, E., Ladner, R. E., & Wobbrock, J. O. (2011, May). *Enhancing independence and safety for blind and deaf-blind public transit riders.* Paper presented at the Proceedings of the SIGCHI Conference on Human Factors in Computing Systems.

Baig, M. M., GholamHosseini, H., & Connolly, M. J. (2015). Mobile healthcare applications: System design review, critical issues and challenges. *Australasian Physical & Engineering Sciences in Medicine, 38*(1), 23–38.

Barnes, J., Duffy, A., Hamnett, N., McPhail, J., Seaton, C., Shokrollahi, K., . . . Pritchard Jones, R. (2015). *Emergency Medicine Journal, 32*(8), 637–641.

Barton, A. J. (2012). The regulation of mobile health applications. *BMC Medicine, 10*(1), 1.

Bashshur, R., Shannon, G., Krupinski, E., & Grigsby, J. (2011). The taxonomy of telemedicine. *Telemedicine and e-Health, 17*(6), 484–494.

Bastien, J. C. (2010). Usability testing: A review of some methodological and technical aspects of the method. *International Journal of Medical Informatics, 79*(4), e18–e23.

Bernabe-Ortiz, A., Curioso, W. H., Gonzales, M. A., Evangelista, W., Castagnetto, J. M., Carcamo, C. P., . . . Holmes, K. K. (2008). Handheld computers for self-administered sensitive data collection: A comparative study in Peru. *BMC Medical Informatics and Decision Making, 8*(1), 1.

Bexelius, C., Löf, M., Sandin, S., Lagerros, Y. T., Forsum, E., & Litton, J. E. (2010). Measures of physical activity using cell phones: Validation using criterion methods. *Journal of Medical Internet Research, 12*(1), e2.

Blaschke, S., Bokenkamp, K., Cosmaciuc, R., Denby, M., Hailu, B., & Short, R. (2009). *Using mobile phones to improve child nutrition surveillance in Malawi*. Brooklyn, NY: UNICEF Malawi, UNICEF Innovations, Mobile Development Solutions.

Boulos, M. N. K., Wheeler, S., Tavares, C., & Jones, R. (2011). How smartphones are changing the face of mobile and participatory healthcare: An overview, with example from eCAALYX. *Biomedical Engineering Online, 10*(1), 1.

Braun, R., Catalani, C., Wimbush, J., & Israelski, D. (2013). Community health workers and mobile technology: A systematic review of the literature. *PloS One, 8*(6), e65772.

Buijink, A. W., Visser, B. J., & Marshall, L. (2013). Medical apps for smartphones: Lack of evidence undermines quality and safety. *Evidence-Based Medicine, 18*(3), 90–92.

Burdette, S. D., Herchline, T. E., & Oehler, R. (2008). Practicing medicine in a technological age: Using smartphones in clinical practice. *Clinical Infectious Diseases, 47*(1), 117–122.

Busis, N. (2010). Mobile phones to improve the practice of neurology. *Neurologic Clinics, 28*(2), 395–410.

Choudhri, A. F., & Radvany, M. G. (2011). Initial experience with a handheld device digital imaging and communications in medicine viewer: OsiriX mobile on the iPhone. *Journal of Digital Imaging, 24*(2), 184–189.

Communication Initiative Network. (2016). Special report: ICT is effective in supporting behavior change communication, strengthening peer outreach and facility-based services, and increasing service uptake among MSM and FSW. Retrieved from http://www.comminit .com/c-change-picks/content/special-report-ict-effective-supporting-behavior-change -communication-strengthening-peer

Da Costa, T. M., Salomão, P. L., Martha, A. S., Pisa, I. T., & Sigulem, D. (2010). The impact of Short Message Service text messages sent as appointment reminders to patients' cell phones at outpatient clinics in Sao Paulo, Brazil. *International Journal of Medical Informatics, 79*(1), 65–70.

Déglise, C., Suggs, L. S., & Odermatt, P. (2012). Short Message Service (SMS) applications for disease prevention in developing countries. *Journal of Medical Internet Research, 14*(1), e3.

DeRenzi, B., Findlater, L., Payne, J., Birnbaum, B., Mangilima, J., Parikh, T., . . . Lesh, N. (2012, March). Improving community health worker performance through automated SMS. In *Proceedings of the Fifth International Conference on Information and Communication Technologies and Development* (pp. 25–34). New York, NY: Association of Computing Machinery.

Des Jarlais, D. C., Lyles, C., & Crepaz, N. (2004). Improving the reporting quality of nonrandomized evaluations of behavioral and public health interventions: The TREND statement. *American Journal of Public Health, 94*(3), 361–366.

De Tolly, K., Skinner, D., Nembaware, V., & Benjamin, P. (2012). Investigation into the use of Short Message Services to expand uptake of human immunodeficiency virus testing, and whether content and dosage have impact. *Telemedicine and e-Health, 18*(1), 18–23.

Ericsson. (2017). Ericsson mobility report. Retrieved from https://www.ericsson.com/res/docs/2016 /ericsson-mobility-report-2016.pdf

Eysenbach, G. (2011). CONSORT-EHEALTH: Improving and standardizing evaluation reports of web-based and mobile health interventions. *Journal of Medical Internet Research, 13*(4), e126.

Federal Communications Commission. (2015). Annual report and analysis of competitive market conditions with respect to mobile wireless, including commercial mobile services. *WT Docket 11-186*.

Fjeldsoe, B. S., Marshall, A. L., & Miller, Y. D. (2009). Behavior change interventions delivered by mobile telephone Short-Message Service. *American Journal of Preventive Medicine, 36*(2), 165–173.

Franklin, V. L., Waller, A., Pagliari, C., & Greene, S. A. (2006). A randomized controlled trial of Sweet Talk, a text-messaging system to support young people with diabetes. *Diabetic Medicine, 23*(12), 1332–1338.

Free, C., Phillips, G., Watson, L., Galli, L., Felix, L., Edwards, P., . . . Haines, A. (2013). The effectiveness of mobile-health technologies to improve health care service delivery processes: A systematic review and meta-analysis. *PLoS Medicine, 10*(1), e1001363.

Frühauf, J., Hofman-Wellenhof, R., Kovarik, C., Mulyowa, G., Alitwala, C., Soyer, H. P., & Kaddu, S. (2013). Mobile teledermatology in sub-Saharan Africa: A useful tool in supporting health workers in low-resource centres. *Acta Dermato-venereologica, 93*(1), 122–123.

Gamble, K. H. (2009). Beyond phones. With the proper infrastructure, smartphones can help improve clinician satisfaction and increase EMR use. *Healthcare Informatics, 26*(8), 23–24.

Gaudette, R. F. (2015). Are you connected to the best apps? *The Consultant Pharmacist, 30*(11), 634–642.

Hall, C. S., Fottrell, E., Wilkinson, S., & Byass, P. (2014). Assessing the impact of mHealth interventions in low- and middle-income countries—what has been shown to work? *Global Health Action, 7*, 25606.

Haskins, B., Le, R., Terrian, L., Grissom, G., Ziedonis, D., & Boudreaux, E. D. (2014). Evaluation of websites and web-based applications targeting alcohol and drug use. In *Annals of Behavioral Medicine* (Vol. 47, p. S139). New York, NY: Springer.

Hunchangsith, P., Barendregt, J. J., Vos, T., & Bertram, M. (2012). Cost-effectiveness of various tuberculosis control strategies in Thailand. *Value in Health, 15*(1), S50–S55.

Husereau, D., Drummond, M., Petrou, S., Carswell, C., Moher, D., Greenberg, D., . . . Loder, E. (2013). Consolidated health economic evaluation reporting standards (CHEERS) statement. *Cost Effectiveness and Resource Allocation, 11*(1), 1.

iMedicalApps; Husain, I., Wodajo, F., Mistra, S., Schultz, C., Lewis, T., & Aungst, T. (2016). The iMedical Apps Reviews and Commentary by medical professionals. Retrieved from http://www .imedicalapps.com/about/

Istepanian, R. S., Jovanov, E., & Zhang, Y. (2004). Guest editorial introduction to the special section on m-health: Beyond seamless mobility and global wireless health-care connectivity. *IEEE Transactions on Information Technology in Biomedicine, 8*(4), 405–414.

Iyengar, M. S., & Florez-Arango, J. F. (2013). Decreasing workload among community health workers using interactive, structured, rich-media guidelines on smartphones. *Technology and Health Care, 21*(2), 113–123.

Jones, C. O., Wasunna, B., Sudoi, R., Githinji, S., Snow, R. W., & Zurovac, D. (2012). "Even if you know everything you can forget": Health worker perceptions of mobile phone text-messaging to improve malaria case-management in Kenya. *PLoS One, 7*(6), e38636.

Jordan, E. T., Ray, E. M., Johnson, P., & Evans, W. D. (2011). Text4Baby. *Nursing for Women's Health, 15*(3), 206–212.

Kahn, J. G., Yang, J. S., & Kahn, J. S. (2010). 'Mobile' health needs and opportunities in developing countries. *Health Affairs, 29*(2), 252–258.

Kay, M., Santos, J., & Takane, M. (2011). mHealth: New horizons for health through mobile technologies. *World Health Organization, 64*(7), 66–71.

Kotz, D. (2011, January). A threat taxonomy for mHealth privacy. In *International Conference on Communication Systems and Networks COMSNETS. In Proceedings of the Workshop on Networked Healthcare Technology (NetHealth)* (pp. 1–6). IEEE Press.

Krishna, S., Boren, S. A., & Balas, E. A. (2009). Healthcare via cell phones: A systematic review. *Telemedicine and e-Health, 15*(3), 231–240.

Labrique, A. B., Vasudevan, L., Kochi, E., Fabricant, R., & Mehl, G. (2013). mHealth innovations as health system strengthening tools: 12 common applications and a visual framework. *Global Health: Science and Practice, 1*(2), 160–171.

Lee, J. A., Nguyen, A. L., Berg, J., Amin, A., Bachman, M., Guo, Y., & Evangelista, L. (2014). Attitudes and preferences on the use of mobile health technology and health games for self-management: Interviews with older adults on anticoagulation therapy. *JMIR mHealth and uHealth, 2*(3), e32.

Lee, S., Chib, A., & Kim, J. N. (2011). Midwives' cell phone use and health knowledge in rural communities. *Journal of Health Communication, 16*(9), 1006–1023.

Lemay, N. V., Sullivan, T., Jumbe, B., & Perry, C. P. (2012). Reaching remote health workers in Malawi: Baseline assessment of a pilot mHealth intervention. *Journal of Health Communication, 17*(Suppl. 1), 105–117.

Liang, X., Wang, Q., Yang, X., Cao, J., Chen, J., Mo, X., . . . Gu, D. (2011). Effect of mobile phone intervention for diabetes on glycaemic control: A meta-analysis. *Diabetic Medicine, 28*(4), 455–463.

Liberati, A., Altman, D. G., Tetzlaff, J., Mulrow, C., Gøtzsche, P. C., Ioannidis, J. P., . . . Moher, D. (2009). The PRISMA statement for reporting systematic reviews and meta-analyses of studies that evaluate health care interventions: Explanation and elaboration. *Annals of Internal Medicine, 151*(4), W-65.

Lose It! (2016). Home page. Retrieved from https://www.loseit.com

Mahmud, N., Rodriguez, J., & Nesbit, J. (2010). A text message-based intervention to bridge the healthcare communication gap in the rural developing world. *Technology and Health Care, 18*(2), 137–144.

Mburu, S., Franz, E., & Springer, T. (2013, July). A conceptual framework for designing mHealth solutions for developing countries. In *Proceedings of the 3rd ACM MobiHoc Workshop on Pervasive Wireless Healthcare* (pp. 31–36). New York, NY: Association of Computing Machinery.

McGowan, J. J., Cusack, C. M., & Bloomrosen, M. (2012). The future of health IT innovation and informatics: A report from AMIA's 2010 policy meeting. *Journal of the American Medical Informatics Association, 19*(3), 460–467.

Med Data Group. (2015). Infographic: Physician adoption and predictions of mobile in 2015. Retrieved from https://www.meddatagroup.com/2015-physician-use-of-mobile/

MobiHealthNews. (2016). Apple helps MDs cut thru medical apps clutter. Retrieved from http://www.mobihealthnews.com/13254/apple-helps-mds-cut-thru-medical-apps-clutter

Mosa, A. S. M., Yoo, I., & Sheets, L. (2012). A systematic review of healthcare applications for smartphones. *BMC Medical Informatics and Decision Making, 12*(1), 1.

Murfin, M. (2013). Know your apps: An evidence-based approach to evaluation of mobile clinical applications. *Journal of Physician Assistant Education, 24*(3), 38–40.

National Institutes of Health. (2016). Consensus Development Program. Retrieved from https://consensus.nih.gov

Ngabo, F., Nguimfack, J., Nwaigwe, F., Mugeni, C., Muhoza, D., Wilson, D. R., . . . Binagwaho, A. (2012). Designing and implementing an innovative SMS-based alert system (RapidSMS-MCH) to monitor pregnancy and reduce maternal and child deaths in Rwanda. *Pan African Medical Journal, 13*(31).

Oehler, R. L., Smith, K., & Toney, J. F. (2010). Infectious diseases resources for the iPhone. *Clinical Infectious Diseases, 50*(9), 1268–1274.

O'Malley, G., Dowdall, G., Burls, A., Perry, I. J., & Curran, N. (2014). Exploring the usability of a mobile app for adolescent obesity management. *JMIR mHealth and uHealth, 2*(2), e29.

Ozdalga, E., Ozdalga, A., & Ahuja, N. (2012). The smartphone in medicine: A review of current and potential use among physicians and students. *Journal of Medical Internet Research, 14*(5), e128.

Payne, K. F. B., Wharrad, H., & Watts, K. (2012). Smartphone and medical related app use among medical students and junior doctors in the United Kingdom (UK): A regional survey. *BMC Medical Informatics and Decision Making, 12*(1), 1.

Pellegrini, C. A., Duncan, J. M., Moller, A. C., Buscemi, J., Sularz, A., DeMott, A., . . . Spring, B. (2012). A smartphone-supported weight loss program: Design of the ENGAGED randomized controlled trial. *BMC Public Health, 12*(1), 1.

Perez, S. (2016). Facebook and google dominate the list of 2016's top apps. Retrieved from https://techcrunch.com/2016/12/28/facebook-google-dominate-the-list-of-2016s-top-apps/

Plachkinova, M., Andrés, S., & Chatterjee, S. (2015, January). A taxonomy of mHealth apps–security and privacy concerns. In *System Sciences (HICSS), 2015 48th Hawaii International Conference* (pp. 3187–3196). IEEE. doi:10.1109/HICSS.2015.385

Pope, L., Silva, P., & Almeyda, R. (2010). CPD EDITORIAL: i-Phone applications for the modern day otolaryngologist. *Clinical Otolaryngology, 35*(4), 350–354.

Powell, A. C., Landman, A. B., & Bates, D. W. (2014). In search of a few good apps. *Journal of the American Medical Association, 311*(18), 1851–1852.

QxMD. (2017). *Calculate by QxMD.* Retrieved from http://www.qxmd.com/apps/calculate-by-qxmd

Ryan, D., Cobern, W., Wheeler, J., Price, D., & Tarassenko, L. (2005). Mobile phone technology in the management of asthma. *Journal of Telemedicine and Telecare, 11*(Suppl. 1), 43–46.

Sabol, J., Emonds, B., Soltys, M., & Disch, J. (1993). An innovative approach to telemetry monitoring. *Medsurg Nursing, 2*(2), 99–103.

Santoro, E., Castelnuovo, G., Zoppis, I., Mauri, G., & Sicurello, F. (2015). Social media and mobile applications in chronic disease prevention and management. *Frontiers in Psychology, 6*, 567.

Schulz, K. F., Altman, D. G., & Moher, D. (2010). CONSORT 2010 statement: Updated guidelines for reporting parallel group randomised trials. *BMC Medicine, 8*(1), 1.

Shea, B. J., Grimshaw, J. M., Wells, G. A., Boers, M., Andersson, N., Hamel, C., . . . Bouter, L. M. (2007). Development of AMSTAR: A measurement tool to assess the methodological quality of systematic reviews. *BMC Medical Research Methodology, 7*(1), 1.

Shieh, Y. Y., Tsai, F. Y., Anavim, A., Wang, M. D., & Lin, C. M. C. (2008). Mobile healthcare: Opportunities and challenges. *International Journal of Electronic Healthcare, 4*(2), 208–219.

Shillingi, M., & Mayo, C. (2009). Text Me! Flash Me! Helpline. Retrieved from http://www.comminit .com/content/text-me-flash-me-helpline

Smith, A., & Page, D. (2015). *U.S. smartphone use in 2015.* Washington, DC: Pew Internet & American Life Project.

Sposaro, F., Danielson, J., & Tyson, G. (2010, August). iWander: An Android application for dementia patients. *Conference Proceedings IEEE Engineering in Medicine and Biology Society,* 3875–3878.

Stavrou, E., & Pitsillides, A. (2005). Security challenges in a mobile healthcare environment. *International Workshop in Wireless Security Technologies,* 121.

Stoyanov, S. R., Hides, L., Kavanagh, D. J., Zelenko, O., Tjondronegoro, D., & Mani, M. (2015). Mobile app rating scale: A new tool for assessing the quality of health mobile apps. *JMIR mHealth and uHealth, 3*(1), e27.

Stroup, D. F., Berlin, J. A., Morton, S. C., Olkin, I., Williamson, G. D., Rennie, D., . . . Thacker, S. B. (2000). Meta-analysis of observational studies in epidemiology: A proposal for reporting. *Journal of the American Medical Association, 283*(15), 2008–2012.

Tomlinson, M., Solomon, W., Singh, Y., Doherty, T., Chopra, M., Ijumba, P., . . . Jackson, D. (2009). The use of mobile phones as a data collection tool: A report from a household survey in South Africa. *BMC Medical Informatics and Decision Making, 9*(1), 51.

Tseng, D. (2016). Data from Google trends in mobile health shows interesting growth in certain medical specialties. Retrieved from http://www.imedicalapps.com/2016/11/google -trends-mobile-health/#

UNICEF. (2016). Innovations. Retrieved from https://www.unicef.org/uganda/9903.html

Ventola, C. L. (2014). Mobile devices and apps for health care professionals: Uses and benefits. *Pharmacy and Therapeutics, 39*(5), 356.

von Alan, R. H., March, S. T., Park, J., & Ram, S. (2004). Design science in information systems research. *MIS Quarterly, 28*(1), 75–105.

von Elm, E., Altman, D. G., Egger, M., Pocock, S. J., Gøtzsche, P. C., Vandenbroucke, J. P., & Strobe Initiative. (2007). The Strengthening the Reporting of Observational Studies in Epidemiology (STROBE) statement: Guidelines for reporting observational studies. *Preventive Medicine, 45*(4), 247–251.

Wallace, S., Clark, M., & White, J. (2012). 'It's on my iPhone': Attitudes to the use of mobile computing devices in medical education, a mixed-methods study. *BMJ Open, 2*(4), e001099.

Wang, Q., Egelandsdal, B., Amdam, G. V., Almli, V. L., & Oostindjer, M. (2016). Diet and physical activity apps: Perceived effectiveness by app users. *JMIR mHealth and uHealth, 4*(2), e33.

World Bank. Information, Communication Technologies, & infoDev. (2012). *Information and communications for development 2012: Maximizing mobile.* World Bank Publications.

Yu, P., Wu, M. X., Yu, H., & Xiao, G. Q. (2006, June). The challenges for the adoption of M-health. In *2006 IEEE International Conference on Service Operations and Logistics, and Informatics* (pp. 181–186). Institute of Electrical and Electronics Engineers.

PART 4

Other Population Health Informatics Topical Areas

© VLADGRIN/Shutterstock

315

© VLADGRIN/Shutterstock

CHAPTER 12

The Economic Value of Informatics Applications in Population Health

Edward Mensah

KEY TERMS

Contingent Valuation Methods (CVMs)
National Institute for Occupational Safety
    and Health (NIOSH)

Willingness to pay (WTP)

LEARNING OBJECTIVES

- Define clinical, public, and population health informatics.
- Discuss lock-in and high switching costs that result in low adoption rates for health information technologies.
- Discuss the economic value of improved decision making.
- Identify the factors that contribute to the success or failure of information systems.
- Discuss the need for economic evaluation of investments in health information technologies.
- Discuss the use of traditional economic models to evaluate population health information technologies.
- Discuss the relevance of using the Contingent Valuation Method (CVM) to evaluate population health improvement applications.
- Discuss the application of population health informatics to workplace health promotion.

QUESTIONS FOR THOUGHT

- How can informatics applications be employed to facilitate the delivery of better population health outcomes under the pay-for-performance system as compared to the fee-for-service system?
- Discuss the investment approach for measuring the returns on investment in information technologies by healthcare providers to improve health status?
- What are the phases of information systems development and the information value cycle?
- What are some of the barriers that have to be overcome in order for health information technologies to deliver value to providers and other stakeholders?
- How can lock-in and switching costs slow the optimal adoption of health information technologies?
- Why is the CVM a superior approach for valuing the economic benefits that result from utilization of population health improvement technologies?

CHAPTER OUTLINE

▶ I. Introduction

Although health care is an information-intensive industry, there is very little connectivity among physicians, their patients, and relevant stakeholders outside their respective networks. This tendency to work in silos has been reinforced by a lack of standards and appropriate incentives, resulting in an inefficient healthcare market with service duplications, lack of care coordination among members of a patient care team, lack of interoperability between information from disparate healthcare entities, inconsistent quality, more errors, and a high cost of service delivery. The Health Information Technology for Economic and Clinical Health (HITECH) Act of the American Recovery and Reinvestment Act (ARRA) of 2009 has provided incentives for providers to implement certified electronic medical records (EMRs). Subsidies from the federal government coupled with other aspects of the healthcare reform, such as pay-for-performance and patient-centered medical homes, have also encouraged the use of health information technologies and informatics applications by clinics and health departments to improve access to and quality of care, and to reduce costs.

Investments in information and communication technologies (ICTs) have contributed to a massive transformation of the healthcare system to a system in which authorized providers and other stakeholders can share patient data electronically. Authorized providers who are in the same network can request the medical records of their patients who visit other facilities in the same network. Continuity of care documents can electronically follow patients who are discharged to other facilities for specialty care, thereby avoiding duplication of diagnoses. Researchers (Choudhry et al., 2013; Daniell, Fulton-Kehoe, Smith-Weller, & Franklin, 1998; Enyia, 2016; Friedman, 2009) have shown that hospitals that invested in EMRs and health information exchanges have seen benefits in terms of reductions in emergency department waiting times, drug–drug interactions, and readmissions after 30 days of discharge.

▶ ## II. Medical and Population Health Informatics

The fundamental theorem of informatics, according to Friedman (2009), states that informatics is about the use of technology to help people carry out cognitive tasks more effectively rather than about constructing technological infrastructure to replace experts. It is about the use of information systems to help domain experts to improve the delivery of clinical services, public and population health, and research. According to Detmer, Lumpkin, and Williamson (2009), informatics transforms health care by "analyzing, designing, implementing, and evaluating information and communication systems that enhance individual and population health outcomes, improve patient care, and strengthen the clinician–patient relationship."

In recent years there has been an increasing demand for health information technologies or informatics applications by individuals, communities, or corporations in order to address certain health problems. Hospitals and clinics have invested in electronic health records and care coordination technologies in order to improve efficiency and quality of care, increase access, and reduce costs. Entrepreneurs and corporations have invested in ICTs and mobile applications in order to engage patients in the treatment of their health by modifying behavior. Individuals need access to credible health information in order to monitor their health. A recent Pew Research Center publication stated that 95% of adults in the United States owned a cell phone and 77% owned a smartphone (Pew Research Center, 2017). Approximately 50% of smartphone owners access health information from their devices.

The meaningful use provisions of the Affordable Care Act and the movement from fee-for-service to pay-for-performance all point to a future where the main focus of the healthcare industry will be on improvements in patient outcomes. Realizing that the current fee-for-service architecture is unsustainable, population health management is the focus of a future healthcare delivery system. In the current information age, effective population health management requires the integration of primary care and secondary care, as well as information gained from patient mobile apps and web portals.

Major components of care under this system are electronic health records, health information exchanges, web-based health information systems, and mobile applications. These technologies can be used to create a healthcare equivalent of an "air traffic control system" that will provide the right information to the right providers and patients in order to maintain continuity of care during transition and optimize patient engagement postdischarge.

How do we measure the economic value of the improvement in health status? There is evidence that the adoption of chronic disease monitoring systems and patient-centered care technologies has improved the health of communities and specific populations (Chiauzzi, Rodarte, & DasMahapatra, 2015). However, without demonstration of returns on investment it will be difficult to sustain the adoption and utilization of these technologies and informatics applications when the federal incentives run out; that is, the technologies must deliver value to the stakeholders. The problem is, what is the economic value of investments in health information technology (HIT) and informatics applications for population health improvement? Responding to that question is the essence of this chapter.

▶ III. Barriers to Successful Implementation of Information Systems

To create value, providers and other stakeholders must be willing to adopt and implement health information technologies and systems necessary to provide care. The main components of the health information systems, especially the EMRs and health information exchanges, will not be adopted optimally if certain conditions are not satisfied. The vendors of EMRs must be willing to develop technologies that will allow providers to share patient data with other providers, including those out of network. Providers must be willing to share patient data without the fear of losing business or market share. Privacy and security must be guaranteed in order for patients to trust the system. Patients must believe that their health data will not be released to unauthorized agents. A study of providers, clinics, and hospitals in Illinois by Mensah (2010) identified the following major barriers to optimum adoption of certified electronic health records in the state:

- Concerns about capital needed to acquire and implement the system
- Uncertainty about return on investment of the system
- Ongoing operational costs associated with licensing fees and technical/maintenance support
- Finding a system that meets providers' needs
- Lack of productivity during transition
- Legal liability if patients have more access to their health records
- Changes in the role of and regulations from federal and state governments
- Privacy and security

Incentives must be aligned such that investors will be rewarded for taking risks. In addition, those who benefit from the implementation and use of electronic health records and health information exchanges must be willing to pay for access to the data and information.

The cost of implementation and uncertainty about return on investment were the biggest concerns. Depending on the size of the operations, it can be quite expensive to implement EMRs. A study of 26 primary care practices in North Texas (McBride, 2012) showed that the implementation cost to a typical multiphysician practice was $162,000. The maintenance cost in the first year was $85,000. In addition, McBride (2012) reported that the end users (physicians and clinical and nonclinical staff members) required 134 hours per individual, on average, to become familiar with the technology. At present, the implementation of certified electronic health records is being subsidized by the federal government.

The barriers identified by the Illinois providers are universal in the healthcare industry. Factors such as high costs of implementation and maintenance, uncertainty about return on investment, lack of productivity during transition, and lack of knowledge about finding a system that meets the needs of providers all contribute to high switching costs. EMRs deliver functionalities such as patient scheduling, accessing medical histories, warning alerts for drug interactions, guideline-based interventions, knowledge-based decision support systems, public health surveillance, and the like. These functionalities are valued by providers. When a clinic or medical center installs an EMR from Cerner or Epic (the two largest EMR vendors in the United States), the clinic gets used to the functionalities built into the EMR and is therefore locked into the given EMR system. If an alternative EMR vendor creates a more effective functionality, such as a decision support system capable of bidirectional data exchange with external systems, providers find it very difficult to switch to the competing EMR. The demand for compatibility and high switching costs have increased the monopoly of the large EMR vendors, reducing competition in the EMR market. Switching costs and lock-in effects are characteristic of the "new economy," which is dominated by ICT industries (Sammut-Bonnici, 2010). The modern healthcare industry is a network economy. Providers are very cautious when adopting a new ICT. This caution slows down the rate of adoption for all providers, thereby limiting the social value of health information technologies.

▶ IV. Evaluation of Health Information Systems

The development of population health information systems involves the following phases: planning, data capture, data management and analysis, data utilization to improve population health, and system evaluation. All these phases involve the use of resources and processes. For example, the data capture phase involves the identification of data sources, development and use of methods to capture data, and adherence to data standards and quality. The management phase involves storage/retrieval, transformation, exchange, security, and data integration. Data are analyzed to create information and knowledge to improve population health. Evaluation may be carried out for all the phases in terms of input evaluation, process evaluation, outcomes evaluation, and impact evaluation. This description is based on the concept of the information value cycle (Taylor, 1982; Thacker, Qualters, Lee, & Centers for Disease Control and Prevention, 2012).

Value is created at each phase of the information systems development for employees and administrators who have different occupational responsibilities, from clerks to clinical and nonclinical staff, supervisors, managers, and executives. When we say that information systems create value, the logical question is, value to whom? Conceptually, the total value created by an information system must be the aggregate of all values created to all the stakeholders. This is beyond the scope of this chapter. The focus of the remaining chapter will be on outcomes and impact evaluation. The idea behind this choice is to concentrate on health status, the ultimate objective of population health management, rather than the input and process evaluations, which are also very relevant.

We need information about the value of health in order to make decisions about how much to spend on health care, disease prevention, and health control. The main economic evaluation models require that the costs and benefits of health improvement projects be estimated. Project planning, development, and implementation costs, as well as the costs of screening for illnesses, treatment, and follow-up, must be estimated. The benefits to individuals and society must be estimated over the life span of the project. The costs must be compared to the benefits in order to make decisions about the efficacy of investment(s) in the health improvement project or projects compared to all other alternative ways of spending the limited resources. The major groups of economic evaluation methods that rely on this reasoning are cost-benefit analysis, cost-effectiveness analysis, and cost-utility analysis.

Cost-benefit analysis requires that all costs and benefits be converted to monetary values. Before a decision is made about the measurement of the costs and benefits, one must decide on the following:

- *The perspective of the project:* This could be an individual patient, a household, a targeted group of people (e.g., workers, diabetic patients in a given community), a clinic or medical center, or society in general. The perspective determines which costs and benefits are included in the economic evaluation.
- *The time horizon over which to consider the project's costs and benefits:* The time horizon captures the fact that although major costs may be incurred in the early years of the project, the benefits in health improvements may occur in the distant future. In some instances, the benefits may extend to generations yet to be born. Consider the use of a mobile health app to educate obese individuals or communities about behavior modifications that encourage exercising, smoking cessation, proper diets, and the like. The benefits of obesity control in terms of diabetes management and reductions in cardiovascular diseases could have intergenerational impacts.
- *A discount rate or rate of time preference:* This will be used to convert future costs and earnings into present values. The choice of discount rate depends on the risk preference of the stakeholders. People discount future costs and benefits differently. Young people, for example, discount future events very heavily and place more weight on short-term costs and benefits. However, people who are more forward looking would invest in health promotion even if the outcomes are expected to occur in the distant future.

A sensitivity analysis must be carried out in order to identify the input and output factors most likely to change over the life span of the project.

Another approach to estimating the value of a health improvement project is the cost-effectiveness approach. Unlike the cost-benefit approach, the cost-effectiveness approach compares the costs to the health outcome achieved. This means the benefit is not monetized but expressed in health outcome units; for example, the cost per person could be identified as a diabetic using a screening process.

An alternative version of cost-effectiveness analysis is cost-utility analysis, in which the benefits are valued in terms of quality adjusted life years. For more details about cost-benefit, cost-effectiveness, or cost-utility analyses, see Tolley and Kenkel (1994), Banta and De Wit (2008), and Jakubiak-Lasocka and colleagues (2014). These economic evaluation methods have no foundation in the economic theory of consumer choices. They are, however, captured in the cost-of-illness approach.

The avoidance of disease damages has been a traditional approach to estimating the benefits of improved health for the purposes of cost-benefit analyses. This approach is also called the damage avoidance, earnings expenditure, or cost-of-illness approach. It considers people as production machines, and expenditures on health services to improve health are carried out in order to improve future productivity (Tolley & Kenkel, 1994). This is an investment approach to valuing health. Expenditures on health improvement technologies will be valued as investments in future productivity. The returns on this type of investment can be measured as the sum of the monetary value of increase in labor productivity plus the savings from the prevention of illnesses due to health promotion activities. The costs can be classified as direct and indirect costs, where the direct costs are the health expenditures and resources used to deliver health care, and the indirect costs are the sum of the lost productivity and the earnings lost due to illness. The value of health improvements is the sum of the reductions in direct and indirect costs. The idea behind this approach is that because illness imposes medical expenditures as well as foregone earnings, a technology or strategy that reduces illness must necessarily result in benefits to individuals, corporations, or society, depending on the perspectives of the investment. In the cost-of-illness approach, retirees, homemakers, senior citizens, and all those not in the workforce are ascribed zero value of health. The value of improved health for these people is assumed to be, at best, a fraction of those who have full-time employment. Individual consumers play a passive role in the cost-of-illness approach to health valuation. There are no health benefits to behavior modifications except in situations that make one more productive. The choices they make in selecting alternative strategies to improve their health status are irrelevant. The cost-of-illness approach, therefore, has no foundation in economic or public health theory.

The investment theory approach assumes that the value to society of human life is equivalent to the output of that life. It therefore favors "productive" people over retired people, and children. Mishan (1971) argued that this method will be acceptable only if the major objective of society is the maximization of gross national product. It is doubtful whether this is the goal of health promotion programs.

▶ V. The Demand for Health Information

We demand health ICTs because of our demand for the services that they produce, in the same way that we demand cotton because of the apparel that cotton produces. Although this might sound simple, it is the foundation of what economists term *derived demand*. Manufacturers or farmers do not demand machines for their own sake but for producing the goods and services that consumers demand. In the education industry, the demand for instructors is derived from the demand for information or knowledge to address a given problem. Similarly, the demand for certain types of wood is derived from the special types of furniture that can be produced from the wood. When the demand for these end products is reduced due to shifts in tastes, the availability of superior alternatives, technology, or price changes, the demand for the intermediate products will be reduced.

The characteristic downward sloping demand curve is derived from the individual utility maximization function subject to budget constraints. With goods where the positive income effect is strong enough to outweigh the negative substitution effect, the demand curve is always downward sloping. The demand curve also represents the maximum amount consumers are willing to pay for a given quantity of good or service. This implies that the area under the demand curve at a given price represents the extra value gained by consumers (consumers' surplus) over and above the price they are willing to pay. A common methodology for estimating the value of information is to examine the demand price, which is the maximum amount the decision maker is willing to pay in order to make an informed decision. The willingness-to-pay concept forms the foundation of economic valuation models for goods and services that are nontradable. Health outcome or status, the final product from the application of population health management technologies, is nontradable.

▶ VI. Valuing Improvements in Health Status

If a population health informatics application is developed to increase the probability of improving health, what value should society place on this technology? Alternatively, how much should society or a corporation spend to improve workplace safety or mental health? These are very interesting questions because all societies have to make choices among alternative uses of scarce resources. For efficient allocation of resources, these questions have to be answered because society does not have an unlimited supply of funds. The focus is on the reduction of the statistical risk to health or life. Mishan (1971) argues that if we are to compare alternative resource allocations on the basis of the "potential Pareto improvements" (allocations that do not make anyone worse off), then it will be more efficient to recommend public investment projects that increase the safety of human life only if the aggregate amount that individuals would be willing to pay to realize such improvements in health exceeds the cost of the project. According to Becker (1974), this model accounts for altruism in the family and community; that is, people will be willing to pay for technologies that will improve the health of others even if they themselves will not directly benefit.

The estimation of the value of reductions in the probability of spreading a disease or improving health is part of the general issue of valuing the risk to human life, which has attracted the attention of economists in recent years. We present a simple theoretical model of the amount of money an individual would be willing to pay to avert a small probability of contracting a nonfatal disease. This value represents the compensating variation in wealth for small changes in health status. If problems associated with the perception of risk are solved, the value an individual would be willing to pay to improve health is not unique—it is a nonlinear (and inverse) function of the existing health status.

In the last half century, health economists and cost-benefit analysts have been attempting to solve the problem of how much to spend to improve human health. The issue of valuing life for the purpose of cost-benefit analysis has been addressed from many angles. Some economists have computed an implicit value of life from the political process (Acton, 1976). The problem with this approach is that it is impossible to eliminate the influence of political pressures in valuing human life. Life insurance may be seen as a proxy for the value of life. The major criticism of the life insurance method is that although it reflects concern for family and dependents, life insurance does not accurately represent the policyholder's (end user's) valuation of his or her own life (Bailey, 1968; Mishan, 1971).

▶ VII. The Contingent Valuation Method

Empirical research must strive to search for a hypothetical WTP that is derived from utility maximization theory. This amount must leave the individual as well-off without the disease as with the disease.

The most theoretically sound approach to the valuation of improvements in health status is the willingness to pay (WTP) concept. This concept, which was first introduced by Tolley and Fabian (1988) emphasizes the consumption side of health services; that is, individuals derive satisfaction from good health. Note that the life valuation methods that are based on investment theory emphasize the role of good health in the production of goods and services. These methods implicitly conclude that once the individual cannot contribute to national production, his or her life is not worth saving. This conclusion makes the investment theory approach unacceptable for the valuation of technologies that improve health.

The WTP concept asks the question: What is it worth to the individual to reduce the probability of his or her death? Mishan (1971) formulates the WTP concept in the framework of the Hicksian compensating variation in wealth. The value of life can therefore be derived from how much an individual is willing to pay in order to have a program that reduces risk from which he or she benefits, or the compensation the individual would be willing to accept to live with the risk.

Let us assume that an individual starts the current period facing two states of the world for each level of wealth. The individual may either live through the current period without contracting any risk to his or her life, in which case he or she gets to enjoy the full value of his or her wealth (W) or he or she may contract a disease and need treatment. When this happens, the individual incurs treatment costs and suffers loss of productivity due to temporal disability. He or she also suffers some loss in utility due to pain. It is hence assumed that the individual prefers the state of the world "good health" over "bad health." Let us further assume that in this single-period model, the individual faces a probability (p) of contracting a disease. If the individual behaves as an expected utility maximizer, then during the current period, he or she will select the state of the world "good health" or "bad health" with probabilities p or $(1 - p)$, respectively, such that he or she maximizes the mathematical expectation of the utility function:

$$E(U) = pU_A(W) + (1-p)U_B(W) \qquad (1)$$

where $U_A(W)$ is the indirect utility associated with wealth given that the person is in good health, and $U_B(W)$ is the indirect utility associated with wealth given that the person is in bad health. Let us assume the functions $U_A(W)$ and $U_B(W)$ are unique up to the same linear transformation and are both continuous and twice differentiable.

Let W^i be the individual's initial wealth, and assume he or she faces probability p^i ($0 < p^i < 1$) of contracting the disease during the current period. The individual's expected utility function can be represented by:

$$E(U) = (1 - p^i)U_B(W^i) + p^iU_A(W) \tag{2}$$

Assume that an informatics application is being developed that, when adopted, will reduce the individual's probability of contracting a disease from pi to p^* where $p^* < p^i$. Because the individual prefers the condition of good health to bad health, he or she must be willing to pay an amount V in order to realize the probability reduction from p^i to p^*.

The magnitude of V must be such that it leaves him or her indifferent between the state of the world where he or she has a probability pi of incurring the disease and p^* where $p^* <$ pi. Assuming that utility is a function of wealth in both states of the world, V can be computed from the following equation:

$$p^*U_A(W^i - v) + (1 - p^*)U_B(W^i) = p^iU_A(W^i) + (1 - p^i)U_B(W^i) \tag{3}$$

On the other hand, if the informatics application required to improve health is not adopted, then the individual is faced with an increase in the probability of incurring the disease. In this case, he or she must be compensated at least by an amount that will increase his or her wealth to a level that satisfies the last equation. The value of V is recognized as the Hicksian compensating variation in wealth for an increase in the probability of safety.

Given realistic assumptions about $U_A(W^i - V)$ and $U_B(W^i)$ and subjective evaluations of p^i and p^*, it will be possible to estimate V. It will, however, be expected that V will not be unique. An individual faced initially with a very large probability of getting involved in an accident will be willing to pay more money to avert such a probability than a relatively safer individual. This implies that the Hicksian compensating variation in wealth (W) is a function of both pi and p^*; that is, the WTP is a function of initial risk to life and the expected reduction in risk due to adoption of the technology, controlling for all socioeconomic factors.

▶ VIII. The Trade-Off Between Income and Health Status

The main outcome from the adoption and utilization of health information systems and technologies is the improvement in wellness (health status). Health status is a nonmarket good, so existing cost-benefit models are inadequate for valuing the economic benefits that result from utilization of health improvement technologies. Although CVM is also used to value goods available in regular markets, the method is mostly used for valuing nontradable goods such as improvements in environmental amenities or health status. CVM is the only valuation technique for measuring nonuse value. CVM was used to estimate both the use and nonuse values of improvements in health status and environmental amenities (Tolley & Fabian, 1988). Mensah (1999) used CVM to identify the nonuse values of providing access to education using ICTs. The adoption of health applications that facilitate the delivery of primary care services to home-based or disabled patients, especially elder care, yields nonuse value to caregivers, family members, and friends. Also, health applications that improve the hearing of workers in a noisy workplace have significant nonuse values (Bertsche & Stevens, 2006). Those who do not purchase the technology, such as family members and friends, also benefit from being able to communicate with the hearing impaired who use such technologies. The use of conventional capital budgeting techniques such as cost-benefit or cost-effectiveness methods will yield underestimations of the total value of such technologies.

In order to estimate the amount individuals are willing to pay for access to technologies that improve health, Equation 3 can be reformulated as follows:

$$U\left(y-V,p,S_1;X\right)=U\left(y,p,S_0;X\right) \tag{4}$$

where U represents the indirect utility function, y represents income, and p is a vector that represents the prices of all goods and services the individual faces. The alternative levels of health or safety are represented by S_1 and S_0, where $S_1 > S_0$, showing that S_1 is a state of improved health or safety. The individual characteristics such as risk preference, insurance status, age, education, gender, and the other social factors (e.g., housing, race) that influence the trade-off between income and health status are represented by X. WTP and WTA (willingness to accept) depend on the factors enumerated previously and must be included in the CVM. In practice, the WTP questionnaires use dichotomous or multinomial response functions where respondents are asked to state whether they will pay a given amount of money for access to the health-improving technology. This is usually the situation in actual markets where consumers have to make a decision between buying and not buying a commodity at a given price. The exception here is that there is no actual market for "*improved* health." Although the technology that improves health may exist, people do not have panel data or experience with all the factors that may influence adoption, such as usability, implementation and maintenance costs, satisfaction with the product, existence of alternative products, and the quality and reliability of the product. In using CVM to estimate the WTP for the technology, researchers usually use the dichotomous choice model.

Respondents are asked to state whether they are willing to purchase the technology at a given price. If $Y = 1$ represents the decision to purchase the technology at a given price whereas $Y = 0$ is the decision to decline, then we have the following (Greene, 1993):

$$Prob\left(Y=1\right)=F\left(B^1X\right) \tag{5}$$

$$Prob\left(Y=0\right)=1-F\left(B^{1X}\right) \tag{6}$$

The factors that influence the decision to adopt are represented by X, whereas the parameter B represents the impact of changes in X on the probability of adoption. When we assume a logistic probability distribution,

$$Prob\left(Y=1\right)=\frac{\ell^{B^1X}}{\left(1+\ell^{B^1X}\right)} \tag{7}$$

Equation 7 can be estimated using R, SAS, SPSS, or STATA statistical packages.

The impact of individual factors on WTP can be estimated, and the mean WTP can also be estimated holding all factors constant at their mean values. For more details about the design of WTP experiments, see Loomis, Brown, Lucero, and Peterson (1997) and Calia and Strazzera (2000).

▶ IX. Some Applications of CVM and WTP Models

Environmental economists have used Contingent Valuation Methods (CVMs) to estimate the value of environmental amenities that are not traded in the marketplace. Holmes and colleagues (2004) used CVM to estimate the benefits and costs of the restoration of the ecosystem along the Little Tennessee River in Western North Carolina. The benefits considered were water clarity, allowable water uses, and ecosystem naturalness. The estimated economic benefit of full restoration was $2,835,373. The benefits enjoyed by individuals and populations from restoring the ecosystem are nontradable in the marketplace. Due to the absence of market transactions, these public goods are underproduced. This project demonstrated that the Tennessee Valley Authority needs to spend almost $3 billion of tax money in order to implement projects and technologies that restore the ecosystem for the enjoyment of present and future generations.

CVM also was employed to estimate the economic value of improvements in tap water quality in Pusan, South Korea (Kwak, Yoo, & Kim, 2013). The result showed that households were willing to pay an additional $2.20 per month over the monthly water bill in order to have access to clean drinking water.

A common characteristic of all of these environmental improvement projects is that they generate benefits (clean water, clean air, sustainable ecosystem) that are not traded in the marketplace. Yet individuals and populations are willing to pay for these benefits because, in most cases, their lifestyles, businesses, or the lifestyles of their loved ones and future generations depend on the existence of these resources.

In recent years, the use of CVM has become increasingly popular among health economists. Klose (1999) reviewed the use of CVMs to estimate the monetary value of the effects of health technologies. O'Conor and Blomquist (1997) and Brandt, Lavin, and Hanemann (2012) employed CVM to study the value of asthma treatment. The study demonstrated that, controlling for sociodemographic variables as well as the perception by families of the risk of asthma symptoms, the mean household WTP for a 50% reduction in symptom days was $56.48 per month (Brandt et al., 2012). If an informatics application is developed to control the incidence or severity of asthma in a specific community, individuals will be willing to pay an average of $56.48 per month for a 50% reduction in symptom days.

Note that the demand for the health technology is derived from the value placed on reductions in symptoms or severity of the chronic illness. Modern health information technologies, such as web-based applications, mobile or wearable applications, care coordination technologies, EMRs, health information exchanges, telemedicine applications, and the like, generate different types of benefits to different stakeholders. The effectiveness of communication between providers saves time and allows providers and other stakeholders to devote scarce resources to the delivery of healthcare services. The use of care coordination applications and decision support systems enables providers to minimize medication prescription errors, reduce duplication of diagnoses, reduce emergency department waiting times, reduce readmissions, and improve quality and costs. Management can use well-designed executive information systems for effective managerial control and improve productivity. Web-based and mobile applications provide clinicians with the capability to deliver care to patients where they reside or work and, most importantly, improve patient satisfaction and health status. Patients also are able to be engaged in the treatment process. The use of care coordination technologies, web-based and mobile applications, interoperable electronic health records, and health information exchanges for health services delivery has been shown to generate values for hospitals, providers, and consumers.

Roettl, Bidmon, and Terlutter (2016) studied German patients' WTP more for online treatment. The results showed that monthly household net income and educational level were major determinants of the WTP extra for online treatment.

The third most common cause of death in the United States is chronic obstructive pulmonary disease (COPD). In 2010, the annual cost of COPD was projected to be $50 billion (Guarascio, Ray, Finch, & Self, 2013). COPD is a preventable and a treatable disease with fast increasing morbidity and mortality around the world (Chen, Ying, Chang, & Hsieh, 2016). Chen et al. (2016) used CVM to study Taiwanese patients' WTP for a cure for COPD based on the severity of the disease, health-related quality of life, and smoking behavior. The results showed that the average annual WTP was $1422. Patients who were 55 years old or younger were willing to pay significantly more per year ($5709). WTP also increased with income. The results also showed that current smokers were willing to pay $2380 more for a cure than either former smokers or those who never smoked.

Mammography screening and early detection of breast cancer reduce mortality rates from breast cancer. The Australian government established the National Program for Early Detection of Breast Cancer in 1994 in order to reduce the breast cancer mortality rate. Clarke (2000) employed the CVM to estimate the use and nonuse benefits of mobile mammography screening among women in rural Australian towns. Use benefits accrue to those who undergo the screening, whereas nonuse benefits represent the amount that individuals are willing to pay in order for others (relatives and friends, for example) to have access to the screening services. These towns were too small to afford permanent mammography screening facilities, although the services were free. However, without the availability of mobile mammography services, women had to travel long distances in order to be screened. Those who could not afford the travel cost were not screened. The availability of the mobile screening facility in the small towns provided access to many poor women. A good example of a nonuse value is when we observe a woman with a double mastectomy who is willing to fund a mobile mammography project in order to make the services available to her relatives or friends. The results showed that the average WTP for a visit by a mobile mammography screening unit was AU$149.

Recognizing the improvements in patient engagement and cost reductions from the adoption of health ICTs as well as informatics applications, many healthcare facilities have invested in telemedicine facilities. These facilities allow major healthcare systems, such as academic medical centers, to deliver healthcare services to patients in remote areas of the country. A small clinic in a rural area that cannot afford certain medical services can receive consultations from specialists in major academic centers.

There has been an increase in the development of health promotion websites and mobile applications that serve special populations and illnesses. These applications, modern-day versions of the mobile mammography services in rural Australia, enable patients and targeted populations to receive relevant health information in order to manage their health. The following section presents a case study of mobile health (mHealth) applications that facilitate the delivery of care to employees in a noisy workplace. Models that combine traditional cost analysis with CVM will be recommended for estimating the value of the population health informatics applications.

▶ X. A Case Study of Population Health Informatics Applications

Hearing and vision are major contributory factors to the quality of life of an individual. According to Kochkin and Rogin (2000), hearing loss has a "detrimental impact on every aspect of life including: physical health, emotional and mental health, perceptions of mental acuity, social skills, family relationships, self-esteem not to mention work and school performance."

Kochkin (2005) also showed that, depending on the degree of impairment, the loss of hearing can reduce household income by approximately $12,000 per year, which translates to approximately $100 billion per year in the United States. According to Blackwell, Lucas, and Clarke (2014), hearing loss is the third most common chronic physical condition in the United States, and is more prevalent than diabetes or cancer. About 500,000 to 750,000 Americans have severe hearing impairment (Mohr et al., 2000). A meta-analysis of secondary data by Mohr et al. (2000) also demonstrated that the expected lifetime cost per individual to society of severe and profound hearing loss is $297,000. Research by Tak, Davis, and Calvert (2009) showed that 22 million U.S. workers are exposed to hazardous levels of noise. Exposure to high noise at the workplace is the most common work-related illness determinant in the United States. In addition to productivity losses, a study by the Hearing Industries Association (Mohr et al., 2000) showed that compared to their non-hearing-impaired colleagues, employees with severe hearing loss are expected to earn 30% to 50% less. These employees could lose as much as $440,000 in earnings over their careers. There are also social costs in terms of relationships with friends and family.

A multinational healthcare products corporation developed a Noise Medical Surveillance Procedure in all countries where it did business in 2002. Noise conservation programs were implemented at all sites with the purpose of tracking changes in employees' standard threshold shifts (STS), where an STS represents changes in an employee's hearing threshold relative to an initial audiogram of 10 decibels or more in each year. An inclusion criterion was that employees must be exposed to noise levels equaling or exceeding 8 hours of 85 decibels. The presence of an STS informs supervisors to recommend employees for intervention to minimize current and future adverse effects.

For the purpose of this case study, imagine implementing additional mHealth applications (smartphone apps, and tablet computers) that collect workplace noise exposure data in addition to ototoxic chemicals, which include organic solvents (styrene, trichloroethylene, mixtures), heavy metals (mercury, lead, trimethyltin), and asphyxiants (carbon monoxide, hydrogen cyanide). Exposure to these chemicals could cause hearing impairment. The system collects worker hearing data, exposure data, and related information for analysis. These data are also integrated into employees' EMRs. Employees' data are also stored on cloud servers after appropriate security and privacy procedures are followed. The surveillance system sends alerts to supervisors when noise threshold levels are within reach or these ototoxic chemicals are identified. The identified employees will be referred to hearing loss nurse practitioners for an early healthcare intervention.

▶ XI. The Economic Evaluation Model

We must estimate the cost of an effective workplace hearing loss abatement program. This would include (1) noise exposure monitoring that tracks noise levels in the workplace, (2) installation of mufflers, and (3) measurement and evaluation of individual employees' hearing. The costs of the wearable devices, smartphones and tablet computers, and cloud server subscription must be estimated. The costs of hearing conservation training materials must also be estimated.

In the absence of long-term data or panel data on costs that can be used for credible cost-benefit analysis, one can rely on costs from the government estimates. The National Institute for Occupational Safety and Health (NIOSH) (2014) reported that the cost per work-related hearing loss case in British Columbia was $16,838. Bertsche and Stevens (2006) found that the cost of complying with the Global Occupational Health Services Noise Medical Surveillance Procedure was $19,509 to screen 390 workers. Using data from Washington State, Daniell et al. (1998) showed that the median settlement for a work-related hearing loss case was $4726. This implies that the Noise Medical Surveillance Procedure will be cost-effective if at least four work-related hearing loss cases per year are prevented.

A CVM should be used to estimate the use and nonuse value to employees who are exposed to work-related noise that could lead to hearing loss. The idea is to estimate workers' WTP for the avoidance of hearing loss. There is no market for the outcome of the implementation of a noise abatement surveillance system at workplaces: improvement in hearing. However, people value good hearing because, as explained earlier, hearing loss can have a detrimental impact on every aspect of life, including physical, emotional, and mental health; perceptions of mental acuity; social skills; family relationships; self-esteem; and work and school performance. It is common knowledge that many people, especially the middle aged, try to cover the early stages of hearing loss by pretending they did not hear the conversation. If identified earlier by the noise surveillance application, these people will be willing to pay for the use of a noise surveillance information system (application).

In order to estimate the economic value of the noise surveillance technology, we have to sample workers in manufacturing and construction companies likely to be exposed to loud noises. Relevant data on sociodemographic variables, income, and employment status (e.g., assembly worker, supervisor, manager) must be collected. These will represent the independent variables. The dependent variable in the contingent variation model will be the WTP a given amount for the implementation of the workplace noise surveillance information system. The specific amount will depend on the sample size and the total cost of the surveillance information system. The results of the CVM will provide decision makers with data about how much workers (and their family) value good hearing. This estimate can be compared to the cost of developing and implementing the hearing loss surveillance system.

▶ XII. Conclusion

Health care is an information-intensive industry and will benefit significantly if patient data and information are shared among authorized stakeholders to facilitate continuity of care along the care continuum, from admission to discharge and follow-up. However, this is not the case in most healthcare settings. The fragmented healthcare industry in the United States has resulted in structural inefficiencies leading to duplication of services, poor quality of care and lack of access to many citizens, and excessive expenditures. The traditional fee-for-service payment system has not helped matters because the more providers treat a patient, the more money they make, resulting in perverse incentives to providers to optimize revenue from treatment of individuals. Disease prevention and health promotion do not factor into this unsustainable business model.

Since 2009, the U.S. government has provided over $40 billion to encourage the implementation of certified electronic health records and health information exchanges to enable providers to share patient data in order to improve efficiency, quality of care, and access, and reduce costs.

Payment reforms that emphasize pay-for-performance have been designed to provide incentives to providers to improve the health status of patients and to move away from simply treating patients to health promotion. We need to concentrate on improving the health of communities and populations rather than individuals; that is, the focus must be on population health management. The implementation and use of EMRs, health information exchanges, mobile health applications, smartphones, tablet computers, and cloud-based servers will enable providers to deliver services to their patients wherever they may be. Patients are already using their smartphones to access health information for behavior modifications and participation in the treatment process. Corporations and school districts are using ICTs to encourage their employees to comply with their treatment protocols. Providers are focusing on postdischarge treatments in order to improve the health of the individual and populations. In effect, the traditional healthcare delivery architecture is being disrupted with ICTs in order to improve efficiency and access at reduced costs.

Population health informatics and the relevant ICTs are the competencies and tools needed to facilitate this transformation process. The transformation will be incomplete without the optimum adoption and utilization of the ICTs. A major problem being faced by investors, corporations, and providers is how to measure the value of health ICTs in health care. The emphasis should be on value of the improved health status. Economists have traditionally relied on using cost-benefit analyses to value the returns on investment in ICTs. These methods have no foundation in economic theory. They also miss the fact that health is not only a private good, but also a mixed good with a significant public good component. An improved health status generates value to corporations in terms of productivity improvements and reduced absenteeism. It also generates nonuse value to friends, family members, and the community at large. This chapter recommends the use of the CVM to estimate the value that consumers place on improved health. This method has strong foundations in economic theory and captures the fact that people react to incentives and are also altruistic. The end of this chapter provided a case study for the use of CVM to value the use of hearing loss technologies in noise workplaces.

The optimum design of the healthcare architecture to promote population health should incorporate mobile and wearable applications, clinic- or hospital-based electronic health records, regional health information exchanges, and cloud-based computers. Vital health data from patients can be collected and stored on secure cloud servers. Alerts can be sent to patients to comply with their treatments and also engage in health promotion protocols, most importantly after discharge from clinics. This architecture can be used to address both chronic and acute care problems. Home-based elderly and disabled patients and populations can benefit from this model. The CVM can be developed to measure the monetary value of health improvements resulting from the implementation of these health information technologies.

References

Acton, J. P. (1976). Measuring the monetary value of lifesaving programs. *Law and Contemporary Problems, 40*(4), 46–72.

Bailey, M. J. (1968). Comment on TC Schelling's paper. In S. B. Chase Jr. (Ed.), *Problems in public expenditure analysis*. Washington, DC: Brookings Institute.

Banta, H. D., & De Wit, G. A. (2008). Public health services and cost-effectiveness analysis. *Annual Review of Public Health, 29*, 383–397.

Becker, G. (1974). A theory of social interactions. *Journal of Political Economy, 82*(6), 1063–1093.

Bertsche, P. K., & Stevens, T. (2006). Complying with a corporate global noise health surveillance procedure—Do the benefits outweigh the costs? *Workplace Health and Safety, 54*(8), 369.

Blackwell, D. L., Lucas, J. W., & Clarke, T. C. (2014). Summary health statistics for US adults: National Health Interview Survey, 2012. *Vital and Health Statistics, 260*, 1–161.

Brandt, S., Lavín, F. V., & Hanemann, M. (2012). Contingent valuation scenarios for chronic illnesses: The case of childhood asthma. *Value in Health, 15*(8), 1077–1083.

Calia, P., & Strazzera, E. (2000). Bias and efficiency of single versus double bound models for contingent valuation studies: A Monte Carlo analysis. *Applied Economics, 32*(10), 1329–1336.

Chen, Y. T., Ying, Y. H., Chang, K., & Hsieh, Y. H. (2016). Study of patients' willingness to pay for a cure of chronic obstructive pulmonary disease in Taiwan. *International Journal of Environmental Research and Public Health, 13*(3), 273.

Chiauzzi, E., Rodarte, C., & DasMahapatra, P. (2015). Patient-centered activity monitoring in the self-management of chronic health conditions. *BMC Medicine, 13*, 77.

Choudhry, S. A., Li, J., Davis, D., Erdmann, C., Sikka, R., & Sutariya, B. (2013). A public-private partnership develops and externally validates a 30-day hospital readmission risk prediction model. *Online Journal of Public Health Informatics, 5*(2), 219.

Clarke, P. M. (2000). Valuing the benefits of mobile mammographic screening units using the contingent valuation method. *Applied Economics, 32*(13), 1647–1655.

Daniell, W. E., Fulton-Kehoe, D., Smith-Weller, T., & Franklin, G. M. (1998). Occupational hearing loss in Washington state, 1984–1991: I. Statewide and industry-specific incidence. *American Journal of Industrial Medicine, 33*(6), 519–528.

Detmer, D. E., Lumpkin, J. R., & Williamson, J. J. (2009). Defining the medical subspecialty of clinical informatics. *Journal of the American Medical Informatics Association, 16*(2), 167–168.

Enyia, O. U. (2016). Effects of health information technology implementation on clinical outcomes and quality of care. Ann Arbor, MI: Proquest LLC.

Friedman, C. P. (2009). A "fundamental theorem" of biomedical informatics. *Journal of the American Medical Informatics Association, 16*(2), 169–170.

Greene, W. H. (1993). *Econometric analysis, 2000* (5th ed.). New York, NY.

Guarascio, A. J., Ray, S. M., Finch, C. K., & Self, T. H. (2013). The clinical and economic burden of chronic obstructive pulmonary disease in the USA. *ClinicoEconomics and Outcomes Research, 5*, 235–245.

Holmes, T. P., Bergstrom, J. C., Huszar, E., Kask, S. B., & Orr, F. (2004). Contingent valuation, net marginal benefits, and the scale of riparian ecosystem restoration. *Ecological Economics, 49*(1), 19–30.

Jakubiak-Lasocka, J., Lasocki, J., Chłopek, Z., & Siekmeier, R. (2014). The economic burden of air pollution impact on health of Warsaw population. *Economic and Environmental Studies, 3*(14), 265–282.

Klose, T. (1999). The contingent valuation method in health care. *Health Policy, 47*(2), 97–123.

Kochkin, S. (2005). The impact of untreated hearing loss on household income. *Better Hearing Institute*, 1–10.

Kochkin, S., & Rogin, C. M. (2000). Quantifying the obvious: The impact of hearing instruments on quality of life. *Hearing Review, 7*(1), 6–34.

Kwak, S. Y., Yoo, S. H., & Kim, C. S. (2013). Measuring the willingness to pay for tap water quality improvements: Results of a contingent valuation survey in Pusan. *Water, 5*(4), 1638–1652.

Loomis, J., Brown, T., Lucero, B., & Peterson, G. (1997). Evaluating the validity of the dichotomous choice question format in contingent valuation. *Environmental and Resource Economics, 10*(2), 109–123.

McBride, M. (2012). Understanding the true costs of an EHR implementation: Plan for unanticipated expenses so they don't slow your progress or delay a 'return to normalcy'. *Medical Economics, 89*(14), 52–54.

Mensah, E. (1999). *Valuing the returns on investment of University of Illinois online education: A case study of the library education experimental program (LEEP)*. Champaign, IL: University of Illinois, Urbana-Champaign.

Mensah, E. (2010). *State of Illinois electronic health records survey. Report by the Health Information Exchange Working Group*. Chicago, IL.

Mishan, E. J. (1971). Evaluation of life and limb: A theoretical approach. *Journal of Political Economy, 79*(4), 687–705.

Mohr, P. E., Feldman, J. J., Dunbar, J. L., McConkey-Robbins, A., Niparko, J. K., Rittenhouse, R. K., & Skinner, M. W. (2000). The societal costs of severe to profound hearing loss in the United States. *International Journal of Technology Assessment in Health Care, 16*(4), 1120–1135.

National Institute for Occupational Safety and Health. (2014). NIOSH Hearing Loss Prevention Program, Our Research is Sound. DHHS Publication Number 2012-174.

O'Conor, R. M., & Blomquist, G. C. (1997). Measurement of consumer-patient preferences using a hybrid contingent valuation method. *Journal of Health Economics, 16*(6), 667–683.

Pew Research Center. (2017). Device ownership. Retrieved from http://www.pewresearch.org /data-trend/media-and-technology/device-ownership/

Roettl, J., Bidmon, S., & Terlutter, R. (2016). What predicts patients' willingness to undergo online treatment and pay for online treatment? Results from a web-based survey to investigate the changing patient-physician relationship. *Journal of Medical Internet Research, 18*(2), e32.

Sammut-Bonnici, T. (2010). Network strategy in the digital economy. Retrieved from https://mpra .ub.uni-muenchen.de/50620/

Tak, S., Davis, R. R., & Calvert, G. M. (2009). Exposure to hazardous workplace noise and use of hearing protection devices among US workers—NHANES, 1999–2004. *American Journal of Industrial Medicine, 52*(5), 358–371.

Taylor, R. S. (1982). Value-added processes in the information life cycle. *Journal of the American Society for Information Science, 33*(5), 341–346.

Thacker, S. B., Qualters, J. R., Lee, L. M., & Centers for Disease Control and Prevention. (2012). Public health surveillance in the United States: Evolution and challenges. *Morbidity and Mortality Weekly Report: Surveillance Summary, 61*(Suppl.), 3–9.

Tolley, G., & Fabian, R. G. (Eds.). (1988). *The economic value of visibility*. Mount Pleasant, MI: Blackstone Books.

Tolley, G. S., & Kenkel, D. S. (1994). *Valuing health for policy: An economic approach*. Chicago, IL: University of Chicago Press.

CHAPTER 13

Privacy, Confidentiality, Security, and Ethics

Luk Arbuckle, Michelle Chibba, Khaled El Emam, and Ann Cavoukian

CHAPTER OUTLINE

▶ I. Introduction

Information and communication technologies (ICTs) have enhanced progress across various aspects of the health system including the use of electronic health records; electronic medical records; wireless networks; assistive technologies that enable individuals to remain in their homes, permitting the growth of a mobile health workforce; and personal health and wellness apps, to name but a few. This movement toward the digitization of healthcare data, events, and occurrences will produce a wealth of data that has never before been available. The value of ICTs and health data is not limited to advanced health systems, but also includes those populations without ready access to health care, such as in poorer areas of the world. Regardless of the location, however, health data are highly sensitive in nature, requiring privacy, confidentiality, and security to be addressed as essential considerations of any technological implementation involving such health data.

This chapter will introduce fundamental concepts of privacy as related to health data, and also identify the various privacy and security challenges in population health informatics. It will also introduce a widely recognized paradigm—Privacy by Design (PbD)—which incorporates solutions to enhance privacy protection. The second part of this chapter describes risk-based data deidentification, a PbD approach to using health data for research and evidence-based practice. The chapter provides definitions of common terms and a proper understanding of the methods used to protect against identity disclosure through data deidentification, and introduces a repeatable risk-based framework for estimating reidentification risk in health data sets, and a categorization of risk based on the context in which it is shared.

▶ II. Privacy and Personal Health Information

Although the definition of informational privacy may differ among jurisdictions, the essence of privacy relates to freedom—the ability of individuals to maintain control and freedom of choice relating to the collection, use, and disclosure of one's personal data flows. Personal health information (PHI) consists of sensitive details such as health history; hence, it requires adequate privacy protections for individuals. A privacy breach in the form of unauthorized access to PHI can have significant consequences for the individual involved and the overall healthcare system. Unauthorized access to an individual's PHI will likely dissuade the individual from seeking health care or encourage individuals to provide false information (Ontario Hospital Association & Information and Privacy Commissioner of Ontario, 2012). Unauthorized access to PHI may also result in stigmatization and psychological consequences. PHI must also be accurate, complete, and accessible to providers of health care to enable them to deliver necessary services. In addition, patient health information is utilized for numerous secondary purposes that benefit overall population health. This includes such varied uses as population health monitoring, quality improvement, and health research. The question of how to maximize both personal privacy and the benefits that may be derived from secondary use becomes more challenging as the uptake of ICTs has become more prevalent in the health sector. Advances in technology that permit usage of PHI also pose novel challenges for privacy, confidentiality, security, and ethics.

On the one hand, the transition away from paper-based systems can enable immediate access to large volumes of PHI and transactional data, often over great distances, which can vastly improve primary care and facilitate secondary uses that will enhance population health management. On the other hand, these technology advancements pose critical concerns regarding issues of security and privacy because of the accessibility of electronically stored information by both authorized and unauthorized users who may be far removed from the site of the original collection. Data stored in large repositories can be readily linked to other repositories and used for multiple purposes. The increasing use of wireless mobile technologies requires particular attention to securing data in motion. From an ethical standpoint, privacy is seen as a right of individuals that may have to be compromised or sacrificed for socially competing goals; for example, in the health sector, some believe that patient privacy may be sacrificed in the interests of health research and quality improvement.

How do we promote transparency about the uses and disclosures for secondary purposes? How do we maintain public trust and confidence in the ability of electronic systems to protect privacy, particularly given the growth of health-based ICTs and the potential expansion in secondary uses of health data? If there is a lack of public trust in the capacity of health systems to protect sensitive information, it may limit the ability to utilize health data for both primary and secondary purposes of improving health care.

The authors are committed to bringing about a paradigm shift by demonstrating how information technology, introduced to serve one function, may be properly implemented to ensure privacy without deviating from the technology functionality. To achieve this, privacy needs to be integrated into the design phase as well as the implementation of such technologies. This process, called *Privacy by Design*, shifts the traditional zero-sum (win/lose) paradigm to a positive-sum (win/win) paradigm, in which both goals are maximized to the greatest extent possible.

▶ III. Privacy by Design

In the same way that security by design has moved from relating to purely technical matters to a much broader consideration of the organization's operations, the concept of PbD has emphasized the need to adopt a proactive rather than a reactive compliance approach to the protection of personal information (Cavoukian, 2011). Our views on privacy concerns change with time; privacy was previously regarded as an individual responsibility. Jurisdictions around the world started to adopt laws based on practices that were founded on fair information practices (FIPs), which are universally recognized principles for managing personal data. FIPs tended to reflect the fundamental concepts of responsible data management, the first and most essential of which was purpose specification and use limitation (Cavoukian, 2011). This meant that the reasons for the collection, use, and disclosure of personally identifiable information (PII) should be disclosed to subjects during or before the time of data collection. Hence, PHI should be utilized only under the stipulations for which it was collected (Cavoukian, 2011). The next concept was that of user participation and transparency, which indicates the role that individuals need to play in the use and disclosure of their PHI. Finally, the FIPs indicated the relevance of security (Cavoukian, 2011). This implied that confidentiality, integrity, and availability should be safeguarded based on the sensitivity of the information—personal health and financial information being the most obvious categories of highly sensitive information.

FIPs represented an important development in the evolution of data privacy because they provided an essential starting point for responsible information management practices. However, many organizations began to view enabling privacy via FIPs and associated laws as regulatory burdens that inhibited innovation (Cavoukian, 2011). This zero-sum mindset viewed the task of protecting personal information as a "balancing act" of competing organizational and privacy requirements. This balancing approach tended to overemphasize the significance of notice and choice as the primary method for addressing personal information data management (Cavoukian, 2011). As technologies develop, the possibility for individuals to meaningfully exert control over their personal information becomes far more difficult. Taking a regulatory compliance approach is no longer feasible or a sufficient condition for protecting privacy (Cavoukian, 2011). Accordingly, the thinking around how best to approach privacy began to shift from reactive compliance to proactive system design (Cavoukian, 2011). With advances in technologies, it became increasingly apparent that systems needed to be complemented by a set of norms that reflected broader privacy dimensions.

The current challenges to privacy are a result of the dynamic relationship among the forces of innovation, competition, and the global adoption of ICTs. Given the complex and rapid nature of these developments, it became apparent that privacy needed to become the default mode of design and operation. This was the central motivation for PbD, which aimed at preventing privacy violations from arising in the first place (Cavoukian, 2011).

PbD is a globally recognized framework based on the seven foundational principles. The framework emphasizes respect for user privacy and the need to embed privacy as a default requirement. It also integrates functionality in a doubly enabling "win-win," or positive-sum strategy. This approach transforms consumer privacy from a pure policy or compliance issue into a business imperative. Getting privacy right has become a critical success factor to any organization handling personal information, so a neutral approach is now more relevant than ever. PbD is focused on processes rather than a singular focus on technical outcomes. This indicates how difficult it is in practice to favorably impact both consumer and user behavior after the fact. Instead, privacy is best dealt with proactively.

To achieve this, privacy must be considered early on—during architecture planning, system design, and the development of operational procedures (Cavoukian, 2011). These principles, where possible, should be rooted into actual code, with defaults aligning both privacy and business imperatives. PbD requires the integration of privacy into technology design, but also into how a system is operationalized (e.g., work processes, operational practices, management structures, and networked infrastructure) (Cavoukian, 2011).

Implementing PbD means focusing on, and living up to, the following seven foundational principles, which form the essence of PbD (Cavoukian, 2011):

1. *Proactivity and prevention:* The PbD approach involves proactive approaches that anticipate events. Risks are not allowed to materialize, and infractions are not allowed to occur; rather, they are prevented from occurring. Hence, PbD comes before the fact, not after.

2. *Privacy as a default requirement:* The maximum degree of privacy is assured through PbD default requirements, which ensures automatic protection of personal data in a system. The individual is not required to perform any action for privacy protection.

3. *Privacy integrated into design:* Privacy is integrated into the initial stage of systems design and architecture, rather than afterwards. This ensures that privacy concerns are addressed as part of the core functionalities without devaluing them.

4. *Full functionality—"positive-sum, not zero-sum":* PbD accommodates legitimate concerns in a positive or "win-win" manner, rather than a zero-sum approach of either/or, thereby preventing trade-offs. It mandates that both privacy and security are desirable.

5. *Full lifecycle protection—"end to end security":* Privacy, which is integrated prior to data collection, extends beyond the data life cycle, from beginning to end. In so doing, it ensures adequate protection of data even after their use and destruction. Hence, PbD follows a cradle-to-grave approach.

6. *Visibility and transparency—keep it open:* PbD assures stakeholders that it operates based on stipulated standards that can be verified. The components and operations are visible and transparent to both healthcare providers and users.

7. *Respect for user privacy—keep it user-centric:* Above all, PbD requires that user interests be prioritized by making a variety of user-friendly features available. The individual is the ultimate focus. User privacy is not a stand-alone principle but is linked with other PbD principles, thereby allowing users to play an active role in their data management. This helps ensure better data quality.

Currently, PbD is an internationally recognized standard for privacy compliance development. Its focus is to encourage organizations to show higher privacy commitments above meeting technical requirements.

▶ IV. Data Minimization Through Deidentification

As electronic systems become more widely implemented in the health sector, the clinical and population benefits of electronic health data continue to emerge. PHI is widely collected throughout the care provision process; ensuring that consent is properly obtained for its use in various secondary purposes much later on is a challenge (Cavoukian, 2011). Hence, the use of safeguards, such as the anonymization of PHI and transparency about secondary uses, are critical. Data minimization, an essential element of PbD principle 2, privacy as a default requirement, requires that personally identifying information not be collected, used, or disclosed if alternative information could serve a similar purpose, and also that unnecessary identifying information should not be collected (Cavoukian, 2011).

In the context of designing and implementing systems to support population health informatics, PbD protects individual privacy while meeting multiple goals of privacy, security, and confidentiality, as well as societal benefits. By so doing, PbD protects both primary and secondary uses of health information (Cavoukian, 2011).

Identifying information is frequently defined as "information that identifies an individual or for which it is reasonably foreseeable in the circumstances that it could be utilized, either alone or with other information, to identify an individual" (Government of Ontario, 2004).

Health information that is deidentified in a manner such that it is highly unlikely that an individual may be reidentified would fall outside the scope of such privacy laws. However, when ad-hoc methods of deidentification are used, it may be possible to reidentify individuals. To the extent that it is reasonably foreseeable that it would be possible to reidentify individuals, the information would be considered to fall within the scope of the definition of PHI and be subject to all of the limitations and restrictions imposed by privacy laws governing PHI (Dalenius, 1986).

To reduce the risk to a level where reidentification is not reasonably foreseeable, identifiers may be altered or removed prior to using or disclosing health information for secondary purposes. It is important to note, however, that the more variables that are altered or stripped from a database, the less useful the database may be for secondary purposes. Thus, individual privacy may be achieved through a high level of deidentification, but perhaps at the expense of data quality. Alternatively, data quality may be preserved, but at the expense of patient privacy. This is the classic zero-sum paradigm, which we make every effort to avoid. In its place, we prefer to use a positive-sum paradigm, which maximizes the positive attributes of *both* interests (Dalenius, 1986).

Proper deidentification provides an excellent example of what can be achieved using a doubly enabling, positive-sum approach that maximizes both goals—in this case, individual privacy and data quality. Provided that proper deidentification techniques are used in conjunction with reidentification risk management procedures, the collection, use, and disclosure of deidentified information has a number of advantages over the use of PII (Dalenius, 1986).

- Proper deidentification greatly reduces the risk of a privacy breach in the event that the information is lost, stolen, or accessed by unauthorized persons, because it is far less likely that individuals can be identified from information that has been strongly deidentified.

▪ Deidentification allows organizations to comply with data minimization principles—principles that are the cornerstone of privacy legislation and FIPs, all across the globe.

▪ Greater use may be made of deidentified information because properly deidentified information falls outside the scope of privacy legislation and is not subject to the same restrictions and limitations that are imposed on the collection, use, and disclosure of PII (Dalenius, 1986).

The next sections of this chapter delve deeper into the art and science of the data and methods for handling the highly sensitive nature of PHI to achieve both privacy and the value of such data to population health management.

▶ V. Types of Disclosure Risk

Attribute Disclosure

In the context of protecting privacy, concerns are often raised over learning characteristics about a specific person or a population subgroup. This is known as *attribute disclosure* when it is possible to associate the data to a target individual, or *inferential disclosure* when it is only possible to infer the new characteristics to a target individual (Duncan & Lambert, 1989). Because both concepts are limited to sensitive variables, they are often simply referred to as attribute disclosure in a more general sense.

The concern is that a group could be stigmatized or discriminated against based on information learned from a released dataset, resulting in people not wanting to share data in the future. For example, it could be inferred from a released dataset that parents of a certain private school are not vaccinating their children against mumps, measles, and rubella. An outbreak in any one of these preventable diseases could result in local media or community members pointing blame at the parents of children in private schools, whether it is justified or not (Hogue, 1991).

Although a legitimate and important concern, attribute disclosure is a separate issue from anonymization. Preventing attribute disclosure can be managed through some form of governance framework, such as an ethics review process (Hogue, 1991), rather than imposing data transformations that may prove insufficient to protect against identity disclosure or decreasing a dataset's utility for research or other secondary analyses when applied after protecting against identity disclosure. This distinction will be made clearer in the next section.

Identity Disclosure

In statistical disclosure control, the purpose of deidentification is to "prevent third parties working with these data to recognize individuals in the data" (Willenborg & de Waal, 2001). The Health Insurance Portability and Accountability Act (HIPAA) Privacy Rule in the United States, for example, concerns itself only with this type of disclosure, as is the case for the different federal and provincial privacy and health privacy laws in Canada and the European Union (EU). There are no known cases of attribute disclosure leading to identity disclosure. By its very definition, identifiable attributes must be considered in preventing identity disclosure. Provided identity disclosure is controlled, attribute disclosure is therefore limited to sensitive variables that are not already considered identifiable.

The distinction between attribute and identity disclosure is important because methods to protect against attribute disclosure alone can seem to provide better quality data but leave the data at risk of identity disclosure. This is why protecting against identity disclosure is generally considered to be a more restrictive condition (Skinner, 1992). However, protecting against both identity disclosure and attribute disclosure could render the data useless because there is nothing to learn from the data (depending on how strictly attribute disclosure is controlled). The purpose of these secondary analyses is most often to learn about the characteristics of subgroups in the data.

Motivations for Deidentification

There is some concern that if explicit consent for sharing these data for secondary analyses is sought at the outset, the responses themselves could be biased (Furnham, 1986). For example, patients could engage in privacy-protective responding behaviors by lying about their health condition or omitting important details, switching physicians to avoid providing the data, or not responding to certain questions altogether (Malin, El Emam, & O'Keefe, 2013). Privacy-protective responses have been shown to be more prevalent when the subject matter is more sensitive in nature. Seeking consent after the collection of data is equally problematic, due to biases between consenters and nonconsenters (e.g., on age, race, and level of education), and the difficulty in contacting a large number of people who may have moved, died, or simply do not wish to discuss private healthcare matters (El Emam, Jonker, Moher, & Arbuckle, 2013).

Anonymization, on the other hand, allows the sharing of information and does not require explicit consent. Several guidelines and standards for anonymizing data are in existence (Committee on Strategies for Responsible Sharing of Clinical Trial Data, 2015; Expert Panel on Timely Access to Health and Social Data for Health Research and Health System Innovation, 2015; HITRUST Alliance, 2015; Information Commissioner's Office, 2012; Office for Civil Rights, 2012; PhUSE De-Identification Working Group, 2015). Under the appropriate security and privacy controls, access to health data can be of clear benefit to the public by facilitating greater public health surveillance and research. It also plays an important role in making the healthcare system more efficient and responsive to the needs of the public, through the planning, delivery, evaluation, and monitoring of health programs or services, and by improving the quality of care (Cavoukian & El Emam, 2011). Anonymization is an effective strategy for obtaining full and complete datasets, and for also ensuring adequate data protection by data custodians.

The growth and prevalence of electronic health data have produced a growing number of breaches, from inappropriate access or handling of data to the growing number of hackers whose sole purpose is to attack datasets and demonstrate where security flaws exist. White hat attackers are often employed by organizations and function to find and patch holes (Taylor, Fritsch, & Liederbach, 2014); black hat attackers aim to attack data, reidentify it, and release it publicly (Pandurangan, 2014). There are even academics who attack datasets to show how poorly anonymized or how poorly secured they are (Sweeney, 2013), and who have their own code of ethics (Erlich, 2013).

When properly anonymized, the likelihood of a successful attack on a dataset is small (Cavoukian & El Emam, 2011; El Emam, Jonker, Arbuckle, & Malin, 2011). Furthermore, if there is a data breach, the cost is minimal because no identifying information is included in the dataset. This means that there is no legal requirement to notify affected patients or other entities (such as regulators or the media).

Healthcare data breaches are already relatively common (occurring in 19–27% of organizations [Solutions, 2012]), so the cost of anonymizing data is small in relation to the savings from the reduced likelihood of experiencing a notifiable data breach.

▶ VI. Justifying a Risk-Based Framework

In Canada and the EU, the regulations follow a "reasonableness" standard for defining identifiability (Personal Information and Electronic Documents Act, 2000). Under the expert determination method of the HIPAA Privacy Rule, the wording is even more clear: the risk must be "very small" that the information in the data could be used, with or without other information that is reasonably available, to reidentify a data subject (U.S. Congress, 1996a, 1996b, 1996c).

The regulations therefore suggest a framework for anonymization that is risk based (El Emam, 2013) (i.e., that considers the context of the data release) to have strong assurances that the risk is "reasonable" or "very small." Subjective interpretations or opinions about the risk are unlikely to be acceptable to regulators. In the United States, audits by the Office of Civil Rights have included findings of weak anonymization practices, suggesting that such practices are targeted by audits and that it is important that these practices meet the appropriate standards (Sanches, 2012).

A trade-off needs to be made between the level of privacy protection and the utility in the data, as shown in FIGURE 13.1, conceptually the same as a concept known as a risk-utility confidentiality map (Duncan, Keller-McNulty, & Stokes, 2001). Anonymization will always result in some loss of information, and hence a reduction in data utility. We want to make sure this loss is minimal so that the data can still be useful for data analysis afterwards. The goal when anonymizing data is to find the right balance between privacy and utility.

One could argue that the data are never truly anonymous, because there will always remain some probabilistic risk that the data and other sources of information could be used to reidentify people (Expert Panel, 2015). Imagine a dataset with every resident in the Littleton suburb of Denver, Colorado, with ZIP code 80123 and no other identifying information. There are about 44,097 residents in Littleton. If you know one person in Littleton, there will be a $1/44,097 = 0.000027$ chance that you can correctly match that person to his or her record in this dataset. This would certainly be considered a reasonable level of risk.

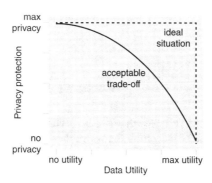

FIGURE 13.1 Trade-off between privacy protection and data utility

In a risk-based framework, the term "anonymous" is taken more broadly than an absolute interpretation regarding identifiability. It is not whether data subjects are anonymous or not, but *to what degree* they are anonymous (Marsh et al., 1991). The interpretation of anonymity must also account for the context of data sharing, such as who will be working with the data, who will have access to the data, how this will be ensured (via security and privacy protocols), and what contracts or data sharing agreements must be signed (Jabine, 1993).

The regulations clearly highlight the need to consider other reasonable sources of information that could be used to reidentify the data. However, if contracts prohibit the linking to external sources of data without explicit information, then this risk is lessened and should be factored into the analysis (Office for Civil Rights, 2012).

▶ VII. Classifying Identifiers

We need to determine whether or not a given field is identifying to determine potential risks. It is important that an analyst familiar with the data be involved in the determination of whether a field is identifying, and preferably more than one unless he or she has expertise in this area, because the analyst will understand what is contained in the fields being considered in a data release. Three properties of identifiers can be used to make this determination: they must be replicable, distinguishable, and knowable (Office for Civil Rights, 2012).

- *Replicable:* A field in a dataset is replicable if its values are stable over time, so that an identity thief can reliably use the background information to reidentify an individual. For example, blood sugar level will vary considerably and therefore would not be a good identifier.
- *Distinguishable:* A field is distinguishable if it has sufficient variation to distinguish among individuals in the dataset. For example, the diagnosis of breast cancer in a breast cancer database is not distinguishable, although secondary diagnoses would be.
- *Knowable:* Identifiers must characterize information that an identity thief can know and then use to reidentify the records in the dataset (i.e., identifiers must be knowable). The adversary might know this information because he or she is an acquaintance of individuals in the dataset (e.g., relatives or neighbors), because that information exists in a public registry (e.g., a voter registration list), or because the adversary can get access to the information through social engineering (e.g., pretending to be a healthcare provider).

Decision Tree

Once we have a set of identifiers, we need to classify them as either *direct identifiers* or *quasi-identifiers*.

- *Direct identifiers* are variables that can be used to uniquely identify an individual, either alone or by combining with other readily available information. Many people will have a name that is unique for a specific population group (such as the geographic location provided in the dataset or implied by the data collection method), and generally a person's name is considered "too close to home" to be included in a dataset. Some other common examples are the data subject's email address, mailing address, Social Security number, credit card number, and medical record number. These numbers, in particular, are identifying because public and/or private databases exist that an identity thief can plausibly get access to that can lead directly, and uniquely, to a person's identity.

■ *Quasi-identifiers* are variables for which their relationship (marginal distribution) is used to identify an individual, based on background knowledge available to an identity thief (Dalenius, 1986). The way in which an adversary will obtain this background knowledge will determine which attacks on a dataset are plausible. For instance, background knowledge may be accessible if the adversary knows an individual, an individual has a visible characteristic that is also described in the dataset, or the background knowledge exists in a public or semi-public registry. Quasi-identifiers include age, sex, birthdate, location markers (postal codes, census coordinates, landmark proximity), language, ethnicity, aboriginal identity, education, marital status, criminal history, income, visible minority status, activity difficulties/reductions, profession, event dates (admission, discharge, procedure, death, specimen collection, visit/encounter), codes (such as diagnosis codes, procedure codes, and adverse event codes), country of birth, birth weight, and birth plurality.

We treat direct and quasi-identifiers very differently, and we therefore need a systematic process by which we classify identifiers in a dataset, which we summarize in the decision tree shown in FIGURE 13.2. Essentially, if a variable uniquely identifies an individual (e.g., a Social Security number), it will be treated as a direct identifier; if it is not unique and it will be used for analytic purposes, it should be treated as a quasi-identifier.

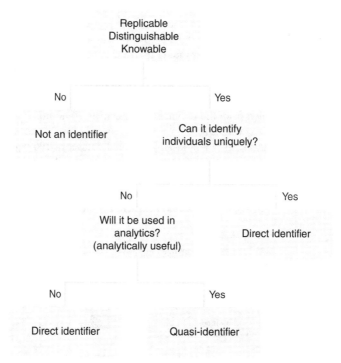

FIGURE 13.2 Decision tree to distinguish between direct and quasi-identifiers

Reproduced from El Emam, K., & Arbuckle, L. (2013). *Anonymizing health data: Case studies and methods to get you started.* Sebastopol, CA: O'Reilly Media Inc.

There will be cases when it is not clear whether an identifier is a direct or quasi-identifer. Use the best available evidence and have more than one person provide input. But if it will be used for analytic purposes, treat it as a quasi-identifier. Otherwise you lose that information entirely, because masking does not produce fields that are useful for analytics, whereas a major objective of deidentifying indirect identifiers is to preserve analytic integrity.

▶ VIII. Classifying Anonymization

We distinguish between two classes of methods for anonymization using the terms *masking* and *deidentification*, based on the concern for the analytic quality of the resulting data. Masking techniques remove the identity of the data subjects from the data without concern for the analytic utility of the resulting data; deidentification techniques remove the identity of the data subjects from the data while maintaining analytic utility of the resulting data, as shown in FIGURE 13.3 (El Emam & Arbuckle, 2013).

Masking Techniques

Masking is typically applied to direct identifiers. Three general approaches are used to mask data: field suppression, randomization, and pseudonymization, which we will explain in turn.

- *Field suppression* (i.e., dropping a column in a database) is used to remove data elements that are not needed in the anonymized data. Names, for example, are removed from research datasets because they are not used to conduct research.
- *Randomization* is used to create fake entries that make the data look like the original source data. This is commonly used for datasets that will be used in software testing, where all data elements need to be preserved to ensure software can be deployed on the source data once all quality checks are complete. Unlike research datasets, names would be needed in this case. The names could be randomly sampled from the phone book or census. Randomizing from the source data, however, would introduce risk that would need to be accounted for in the risk analysis. In our randomly sampled dataset of 100 people from Littleton, without names we would assess risk at the population level of the 44,097 residents of Littleton. With their names in place, even if randomized, we could no longer consider this a random sample from the perspective of reidentification risk. Suddenly, the name Bob Pendleton is indicative of who is in the

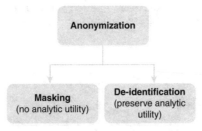

FIGURE 13.3 Classifying methods by analytic utility

dataset, and the risk would therefore be assessed at the level of the cohort. This would increase risk considerably.

▪ *Pseudonymization* replaces direct identifiers with some other unique value (International Organization for Standardization, 2008). The two general methods to create pseudonyms are hashing and encryption. For hashing, a random element, called a salt, needs to be added to be considered acceptable in the field of health informatics. However, encryption is the more secure method to use. In order to track patients across records and tables, to maintain referential integrity, the pseudonym needs to be created in the same manner across records and tables. That way, MRN 12345 becomes 67890 for every instance of MRN 12345, regardless of record or table.

Deidentification Techniques

Deidentification is applied to indirect or quasi-identifiers. Masking can also be applied to quasi-identifiers, which implies removing them from any form of analytics. Five general approaches are used to deidentify data: generalization, local suppression, subsampling, security and privacy practices, and contracts. The first three deidentification techniques are the ones generally thought of when discussing deidentification, that is, transformations to the data itself.

▪ *Generalization* replaces a field with a broader characterization of the information in the original field. The population of Littleton, for example, could be represented with each person's date of birth, but this is known to dramatically increase reidentification risk (Golle, 2006). Replacing date of birth with age is a common generalization used in practice, as are age ranges. The degree of generalization can also vary from one group to another within the same dataset (e.g., redheads get an age generalization of 5-year increments, whereas blonds get an age generalization of 1-year increments because they are more common [De Waal & Willenborg, 1999]).

▪ *Suppression* in this context removes quasi-identifier values that make a record highly identifiable with missing values. In the case of our record of a 20-year old female with red hair, we could have the entry for age or hair color, or both, removed from the record, without affecting the other records in the dataset. An alternative would be to remove the entire record, rather than having to decide on which quasi-identifier value to suppress.

▪ *Subsampling* can also be used as a means of deidentification, because an adversary will not know if a target individual is in the random subsample or not (Elliot & Dale, 1999). When trying to reidentify someone from a sample of 100 people in Littleton, the adversary will not know if the person being targeted is in the subsample or in the rest of the population. There certainly could be someone that looks the same on quasi-identifiers outside of the sample.

In a risk-based framework, the controls and contracts put in place are also factored into the analysis because they can significantly reduce the risk that someone will have access to the data or even attempt a reidentification.

▪ Unless there are strong security and privacy practices in place, a rogue employee may not be bound by contracts. This will have a direct impact on the chance that an adversary will attempt a reidentification. The specific practices that are followed can be imposed by the data custodian, such as requiring that data recipients keep deidentified data in a secure environment that adheres to a specific implementation level of the HITRUST Common Security Framework (HITRUST Alliance, 2015) or to the HIPAA Security Rule (Health Insurance Portability and Accountability Act, 1996). These practices can also be assessed to determine their impact on risk (El Emam, 2013). Public data releases, however, have no security and privacy practices in place, which increases the risk dramatically.

- Enforceable contracts will discourage companies, and their employees, from trying to reidentify data subjects. Such a contract will also outline the security controls that are expected to be in place. Some specific clauses are needed in a data sharing agreement (El Emam & Arbuckle, 2013):

  - Prohibit reidentification, contacting people in the data, and linking to other datasets without permission from the data custodian.
  - Include an audit requirement so that the data custodian or a third party can ensure compliance with the agreement in place.
  - Prohibit sharing the data without permission from the data custodian, or a requirement to transfer the same set of restrictions outlined in the agreement.

▶ IX. Measuring Reidentification Risk

The public is uncomfortable disclosing their personal information. Individuals often cite privacy and confidentiality concerns as reasons for not having their health information used for research purposes.

Data Risk

We assume that direct identifiers are appropriately masked; otherwise, the risk of reidentification has probability 1. The most common technique considered for deidentifying data uses the concept of k-anonymity to transform the quasi-identifiers in the data using generalization and suppression (El Emam et al., 2009). In a k-anonymous dataset, there are at least k people with the same quasi-identifier values. The risk of reidentification for a k-anonymous group is $1/k$, because an adversary cannot distinguish between those k individuals using their quasi-identifiers. For example, if there are three 20-year-old men in Littleton with red hair, they are 3-anonymous on these quasi-identifiers, and the probability of reidentifying any one of them is 1/3 or 0.33, because we cannot tell them apart.

Many datasets will, in fact, be samples from a larger population, and therefore the data must be considered within that sampling context (Marsh et al., 1991). Imagine we now have a dataset with 100 people randomly selected from Littleton, and only one person in this sample has red hair. Without considering the context from which this sample was drawn, we might be tempted to conclude that this red-haired person is uniquely identifiable ($k = 1?$). After all, there is only one such person in the dataset of 100 people. We know, however, that this dataset of 100 people is a random sample from a population of 44,097 people. There is a lower probability of having only one red-haired person in Littleton. The context of this sample data is therefore the population of Littleton.

On the other hand, if we had selected a cohort with all 20-year-old females in Littleton, and found there was only one with red hair, then we would come to a different conclusion. In this case the subpopulation is not a random sample, but was instead chosen based on an identifiable attribute—age. That means that we have one 20-year-old with red hair in Littleton, and that person is uniquely identifiable ($k = 1$). The context of these data is the data themselves and any additional information that can be reasonably attached to them for the purposes of reidentification.

This distinction between the identifiability in the sample and the identifiability in the population is very important. If the population is not taken into consideration, risk measures will be overestimated. When the identifiable attributes in the population are known (e.g., how many people there are with red hair in Littleton), the risk can be measured at the population level. In most cases, however, this must be estimated from the data. Estimators exist to measure the risk at the population level based on the sample data themselves (Dankar, El Emam, Neisa, & Roffey, 2012).

Contextual Risk

The risk of reidentification is not just the risk in the data. We can be realistic and consider plausible attacks on the data. When we measure the risk in the data alone, we are assuming there will be an adversary that will attempt to reidentify the data. Consider the probability of reidentification from quasi-identifiers given that an attacker makes an attempt as Pr (reid | attempt) (Marsh et al., 1991). We can therefore formulate the problem as the probability of reidentification and an attack using

$$\text{Pr (reid, attempt)} = \text{Pr (reid | attempt)} \times \text{Pr (attempt)}$$

In a risk-based approach to deidentification, the risk from the quasi-identifiers in the data is combined with the risk from contextual factors (i.e., the security and privacy practices, and contracts). The latter incorporates a subjective assessment of risk based on expert opinions (Morgan, Henrion, & Small, 1992; Vose, 2008). There are many strong precedents from reputable data-releasing institutions that can be used as benchmarks of what is acceptable risk (e.g., Centers for Disease Control and Prevention, 2014; Statistics Canada, 2007; Subcommittee on Disclosure Limitation Methodology, 2005). These precedents can be divided by the contextual factors in which data were released to create a repeatable framework for risk assessments (El Emam, 2013). We will return to this topic in the next section.

Overestimating the risk will lead to more deidentification, and therefore less granular data—which is why context is such an important aspect to consider. Public datasets carry the most risk, because everyone has access and there are no controls on how they are used; nonpublic datasets, however, can have contracts and security controls to protect the data.

Public Versus Nonpublic

For a public data release, a demonstration attack by a researcher or journalist aimed at the most identifiable individuals in the dataset is assumed; therefore, an attempt is certain. This implies that the only protection against reidentification is the algorithms used to deidentify the dataset. For this reason, maximum risk is advised, in line with census and other public data releases, meaning that the risk for the dataset is based on the individual(s) that are the most identifiable. For example, if there are $k = 2$ people with the same quasi-identifier values, and they represent the smallest set of k, then the max risk is 1/2 or Pr (reid | public attempt) = 0.5.

For a nonpublic data release, the three attacks we model—representing different ways to "attempt" a reidentification—are consistent with the modeling of threats in information security: deliberate, accidental (or inadvertent), and catastrophic (a breach). Compared to a public data release, the recipient(s) will be known, and there will be security and privacy controls in place, as well as data use agreements to enforce these practices. These controls will reduce the chance of an attempt to reidentify individuals, and can be evaluated to determine the relative strength of these safeguards. Once this is done, these estimates can be incorporated into the overall risk of reidentification (i.e., data and contextual risk).

Average risk is advised in the case of a nonpublic data release, because a demonstration attack, which requires publicizing the results to be successful, would carry serious legal implications. Because the attack could be on any individual in the dataset, the risk is averaged across all individuals. For example, if there are $k = 2$ people with the same quasi-identifier values, and $k = 5$ people with the same quasi-identifier values, for a total of 7 people in the dataset, then the average risk is 2/7 or Pr (reid | non-public attempt) = 0.285.

▶ X. Risk Threshold

Measuring risk demonstrates the impact deidentification will have on the overall risk in a data release, but a benchmark of acceptable risk is needed to determine how much deidentification to apply. There are many strong precedents going back multiple decades as to what constitutes significant risk of reidentification for both public and nonpublic data sources (see El Emam, 2013 for a summary of these precedents). These precedents are based on minimum cell sizes, equivalent to k-anonymity for tabular data; they have not changed recently and remain in wide use. In general, they vary from an acceptable probability of 0.33 ($k = 3$) to 0.05 ($k = 20$) for data risk, as shown in FIGURE 13.4.

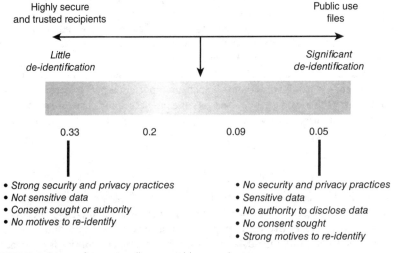

FIGURE 13.4 Range of operationally acceptable precedents

To decide which threshold to use, we look at the potential invasion of privacy using the sensitivity of the data (Carr, 2010), potential harms in the case of an inappropriate disclosure, as well as the mechanism for obtaining consent. For instance, highly sensitive data require a lower threshold whereas a higher threshold is accorded to data for which patients have consented to their release and public use. We developed a detailed checklist in El Emam (2013) to determine an appropriate risk threshold to use.

There are instances where anonymization schemes do not include risk measurement or setting thresholds to ensure an acceptable probability of reidentification. For example, these schemes provide a fixed list of identifiers that should be removed from the dataset (Hughes, Wells, McSorley, & Freeman, 2014; U.S. Congress, 1996c). These approaches cannot provide assurance that the probability of reidentification is small for any single dataset because the actual identifiers may differ from the list. Moreover, their application may result in significant transformation of datasets. Hence, such approaches cannot be applied to complex datasets. Knowing when to stop deidentifying the data is important to balance privacy protection and data utility.

Repeatable Process

Having reviewed all the necessary steps needed to anonymize health data using a risk-based framework, we can now define a process that is consistent and repeatable (El Emam & Arbuckle, 2013).

1. *Classify variables:* Variables need to be classified into direct identifiers (they are uniquely identifying but they are of no analytic utility) and quasi-identifiers (their relationship is used to identify an individual and they are of analytic utility). Recall that identifiers need to be replicable, distinguishable, and knowable.
2. *Set risk threshold:* A defensible risk threshold is needed based on strong precedent and the potential invasion of privacy (sensitivity of the information, potential harm in the event of an inappropriate disclosure, and appropriateness of the consent mechanism).
3. *Examine plausible attacks:* Using contextual risk factors, attacks on the data need to be evaluated. In a public data release, you need to concern yourself with a demonstration attack; in a nonpublic data release, you need to concern yourself with deliberate attempts, accidental attempts, or a catastrophic breach.
4. *Mask and deidentify:* Direct identifiers are masked using the best standards; quasi-identifiers are deidentified using data transformations, and security and privacy controls are set with enforceable contracts to reduce the risk below your defensible risk threshold.
5. *Document:* The entire process and reasoning for all decisions made need to be documented, with a reference to a process or methodology text. The resulting report is your legal defense in case of an audit or investigation. Include a summary of the dataset and data flow, the risk assessment process, the risk threshold used, assumptions, data transformations, and evidence that the risk is below the threshold.

Although presented as a five-step process, there are iterations that can be applied within a step and also between steps. Step 4, masking and deidentification, in particular, is often repeated until a desired balance is achieved between the deidentification of variables. One variable can be transformed more or less from its original form depending on how other variables are transformed. For example, geography could be less generalized if demographics are more generalized.

The resulting solution from Step 4 that is needed to achieve an acceptable level of risk may not have the desired utility for the given application. In this case, you have the option to iterate on Steps 2 to 4, as shown in FIGURE 13.5.

Take, for example, a researcher looking to perform geospatial analysis on the data. If the geographic information in the data is highly generalized, the deidentified data may not be suitable to his or her research. We can repeat the process at Step 2, set risk threshold, and consider removing sensitive information (e.g., HIV/AIDS, abortions) to increase the level of acceptable risk. This will not always be an option, depending on the use case, but it is worth considering.

Next we could evaluate Step 3, examine plausible attacks, to determine how risk levels may be modified by strengthening security and privacy controls and contractual obligations (i.e., lowering the probability of attempt), thereby allowing for fewer data transformations to achieve the same overall level of risk. Finally in Step 4, masking and deidentification, we would apply the needed data transformations to achieve a level of risk that is below our threshold.

Reidentification Attacks

A dataset with direct identifiers that have been masked, and the quasi-identifiers left intact, is considered pseudonymous. Almost all known successful reidentification attacks have been performed on pseudonymous data (El Emam et al., 2011). In the EU, the Article 29 Working Party made clear that pseudonymous data are

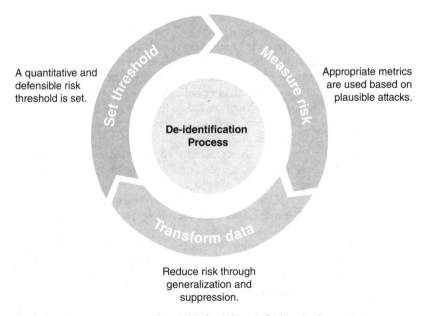

FIGURE 13.5 Iterative process to achieve the desired level of risk and utility

considered personal information (El Emam & Alvarez, 2015). HIPAA requirements mandate that data be pseudonymized, and it is still considered protected health information (U.S. Congress, 1996c).

There are two particularly egregious examples of demonstration attacks on pseudonymous data that are constantly raised as examples of failed "anonymization" or "deidentification." (We use quotes to emphasize that these datasets were not anonymized or deidentified in a defensible way.)

- *AOL search queries:* In 2006, a team at AOL released the 20 million web search queries for 657,000 individuals, hoping it would be of use to researchers. They replaced user names with a randomly generated numeric code to protect the identity of the searchers. These search terms included personal names that were identifiers (e.g., vanity searches, friends, and neighbors), location names related to residence, as well as other important identifiers that could link users to demonstration attacks (Barbaro & Zeller Jr., 2006). The searches also contained sensitive personal information (e.g., possible depression, infidelity). These search data demonstrate the risk from identifiers in free-form text. Properly anonymizing the data would have started, at the very least, with terms-of-use agreements that prohibit reidentification and linking to external databases. However, given the possibility of having direct identifiers in the searches themselves, it would have been necessary to use a natural language processing engine to find and eliminate them (El Emam & Arbuckle, 2013).

- *Netflix prize:* Also in 2006, Netflix launched a data analytics competition to predict subscribers' movie ratings based on their past movie ratings. They publicly released the movie ratings with dates of nearly 500,000 subscribers, replacing subscriber names with pseudonyms. Researchers claimed that subscribers in the dataset were unique based on a handful of ratings outside the top 500 movies and approximate dates (+/−1 week) (Narayanan & Shmatikov, 2008). Whether an adversary could know this level of detail and confirm their target was in the sample dataset is debatable. The researchers, however, attempted to match 50 of the public profiles on the Internet Movie Database to the Netflix dataset and claimed to have two especially strong candidates for reidentification (although never validated). Again, there was the lack of a terms-of-use agreement to prohibit reidentification and linking to external databases. Because the uniqueness of a subscriber's profile is not typically useful for data analytics, rare attributes can often be removed from a data release. In this case, the probabilistic estimation of movie ratings did not require rare films, so they could have been either eliminated or substituted with an indicator of having watched certain classes of rare films (e.g., foreign films, documentaries). Dates could also have been perturbed by generalizing or shifting (up to the release date of films).

Often the risk of disclosure from a public data release can be significantly decreased with the use of a terms-of-use agreement, making it a quasi-public data release. A terms-of-use agreement will reduce the probability of attempt considerably, especially that of a demonstration attack, although to be clear it is the least that can be done. Stronger contracts are possible, with the inclusion of security and privacy controls. In a risk-based framework, these contextual controls are always considered, which often leads to the inclusion of at least some of them. At this point data transformations can also be considered, with reasonable assumptions and considering plausible attacks.

There have been other demonstration attacks, beyond just pseudonymous data, all with debatable success rates. We will consider only two more, because each provides a different lesson.

- *Credit card metadata:* A sample of financial transactions—including date, place, and amount paid—was used to demonstrate the potential risks of space–time data, even when generalized to various levels of accuracy. The researchers claimed that only four transactions were needed to make people unique in the data. Generalizing the data decreased how unique they were, but could be overcome by collecting more transactions (Montjoye, Radaelli, Singh, & Pentland, 2015). There are several problems with this study, beyond neglecting the potential inclusion of contextual controls. First and foremost, the researchers failed to differentiate between uniqueness in the sample of metadata versus uniqueness in the population (i.e., they assumed that a unique profile in their sample of credit card metadata implied a unique profile in the population). Furthermore, they assumed there is an external source of data that can be used to match against and thereby provide direct identifiers to the metadata, and generalization will be overcome with more external data.

- *State inpatient database:* In 2013, the Washington State Inpatient Database (SID) from 2011 was subject to a demonstration attack using publicly available news reports. A researcher found 81 news reports from 2011 with the word "hospitalized" in it and uniquely identified 35 patients in the SID of 648,384 hospitalizations (Sweeney, 2013). On the one hand, one could argue that 35/81 is not a very small risk (the conditional probability of reidentification, given a public news report exists of the patient's hospitalization); on the other hand, one could argue that 35/648,384 is a very small number. This study is informative in that it demonstrated many of the quasi-identifiers relevant to health data that need to be considered in properly estimating risk, which have been raised before (El Emam & Arbuckle, 2013; El Emam et al., 2012). It also demonstrated that seemingly unjustified generalizations to quasi-identifiers will not properly account for risk, especially from a demonstration attack when there are few restrictions on who can access the data and what the data recipients can do with it. (Unfortunately this is a lesson that bears repeating, as we have seen time and again.)

The previous research has provided important lessons regarding reidentification risks and emphasizes the need to consider all risk factors and the context of a data release. Unfortunately, the results are often inflated and misunderstood to emphasize a storyline that attracts more interest than a balanced risk-based perspective would. The purpose of anonymization is not to eliminate all risks, but to manage them in a reasonable way.

▶ XI. Categorizing Risk

The concepts of personal information and identifiability have been discussed considerably in this field, because they largely influence legislative requirements. There is a general view that identifiability falls on a spectrum, from no risk of reidentification to fully identifiable, with many precedents in between (El Emam, 2008). This spectrum has been defined previously in terms of a probability, as we have described in this chapter (Skinner & Elliot, 2002).

There is also the ongoing distinction between deidentified and pseudonymous data, whereby the latter is considered personal information by regulatory authorities. Recall that pseudonymization replaces direct identifiers with some other unique value, and therefore pseudonymous data are considered to be data in which direct identifiers have been masked (according to our distinction between masking and deidentification).

Seven States of Data

We can define a framework for categorizing risk and the methods needed to address them on the spectrum of identifiability, which we call the *states of data*. To characterize the states of data, we consider five characteristics about the data or the data sharing transaction itself.

- *Verifying the identity of the data recipient:* This is used to assess whether the custodian of the data can recognize the identity of an individual or an organization receiving such data. This can be achieved through signing a contract or by more automated identity authentication schemes. The main purpose of identity verification is to be able to hold the data recipient accountable for any breach of contract or terms-of-use.
- *Masking of direct identifiers, as previously described:* Another term that is used for this kind of data is "pseudonymous" or "pseudonymized" data.
- *Deidentification of quasi-identifiers, as previously described:* It can also range from low perturbation (e.g., a date of birth converted to month and year of birth) to high perturbation (e.g., a date of birth converted to a 5-year interval).
- *Contractual controls:* Requiring the data recipient to sign an enforceable contract that prohibits reidentification attempts is considered a strong control.
- *Security and privacy controls:* These can vary in their strength, but greatly minimize the risks of attempts at reidentification and reduce the likelihood of a data breach occurring.

These characteristics are not independent. For example, it is not possible to have contractual controls unless the data recipient can be identified, and there is no mechanism to enforce security and privacy controls unless there are also contractual controls. Using these characteristics, we can describe the seven states of data, as shown in TABLE 13.1.

Personally Identifiable

Starting from the bottom of the table up, the first three states of data are considered PII. Because they define identifiable states of data, they are all nonpublic releases of data. They require consent for reusing the data for anything other than the primary purpose for which the data were collected.

- *Personal data* have not been modified in any way, or have been minimally modified with a high probability of reidentification. They still include all direct and indirect identifiers more or less intact.
- *"Vanilla" pseudonymous data* are the plain old pseudonymous data without any of the additional contractual, security, or privacy controls that we have discussed in place. As personal data, the identity of the recipient is already assumed to be known.

TABLE 13.1 The Seven States of Data and How They Categorize Risk on the Spectrum of Identifiability

		Verify Identity of Recipient	Masking	Deidentification	Contractual Controls	Security and Privacy Controls
Not Publicly Identifiable Information	Public release of anonymized data	No	Yes	High	No	None
	Quasi-public release of anonymized data	Yes	Yes	Medium-high	Yes	None
	Nonpublic release of anonymized data	Yes	Yes	Low-medium	Yes	Medium-high
No Consent	Flexible† pseudonymized data	Yes	Yes	None	Yes	High
Publicly Identifiable Information	Protected pseudonymized data	Yes	Yes	None	Yes	High
	"Vanilla" pseudonymized data	Yes	Yes	None	No	None
	Personal data	Yes	No	None	None	None

†Additional constraints imposed to ensure very low risk of reidentification (see text for details).

Pseudonymous data that are protected incorporate additional security controls that minimize reidentification risk significantly, but do not necessarily bring them below the threshold to be considered non-PII.

Not Personally Identifiable

Data releases that have a very low risk of reidentification are considered anonymized or not PII, and do not require consent for reusing the data for other purposes. There is one state in which pseudonymous data can be considered anonymized, consistent with guidance provided by regulators, and it demonstrates the flexibility of a risk-based framework for anonymization.

Flexible pseudonymous data have contractual, security, and privacy controls in place, and also conditions that ensure a very low risk of reidentification. There would be no processing of data by humans, the analysis results would not disclose personal information (O'Keefe & Chipperfield, 2013), and the data would not be considered sensitive.

An example of flexible pseudonymous data is secure computation—which requires all analyses be conducted under encryption, without decrypting the data to run the analyses—with appropriate contractual obligations and measures to ensure there are no leakages of personal information from the results themselves. With secure computation, the highest levels of security controls are implied, and there would be no processing of PHI by humans. Under these conditions, the risk of reidentification is very low (Arbuckle & El Emam, 2016).

On the assumption that proper deidentification methods have been applied, and the contractual, security, and privacy controls are reasonable, the data in the last three states can credibly be said to be not personally identifiable.

Nonpublic data are limited to qualified individuals, such as research investigators at a recognized academic institution, or a recognized business with a legitimate purpose to use the data. Because strong contractual controls will be in place, specific security and privacy controls may be imposed by the data custodian to determine how much deidentification is needed.

Quasi-public data are anonymized data that are available to anyone, except the identity of the data recipients is verified and they must sign a terms-of-use agreement. The terms of use would include the contractual controls we described earlier, with a requirement for reasonable efforts to protect the data.

Public data are anonymized data that are made available to the public. Restrictions do not apply in data access, and prior request is not made to verify the identity of the person(s) requesting such data. It is subject to considerable deidentification because of the lack of controls in place to protect the data.

▶ **XII. Conclusion**

Using the proper tools and techniques for deidentification and reidentification embodies the PbD approach in managing sensitive PHI, while enforcing stringent security measures for data at various levels of usage. In addition, it ensures the availability of quality health information for secondary purposes to advance population health outcomes. Proper deidentification is a critical tool for providing a PbD approach to population health informatics where innovative technologies are constantly being leveraged in capturing, communicating, aggregating, storing, and analyzing huge health-related datasets.

References

Arbuckle, L., & El Emam, K. (2016). Practical applications of secure multiparty computation for public health and post-marketing drug surveillance. In *JSM Proceedings*. Seattle, WA: American Statistical Association.

Barbaro, M., & Zeller Jr., T. (2006). A face is exposed for AOL searcher no. 4417749. *New York Times*. Retrieved from http://www.nytimes.com/2006/08/09/technology/09aol.html

Carr, J. M. (2010). *Recommendations regarding sensitive health information*. Washington, DC: National Committee on Vital and Health Statistics.

Cavoukian, A. (2011, January). *Privacy by design: The 7 foundational principles*. Toronto, Canada: Information and Privacy Commissioner of Ontario.

Cavoukian, A., & El Emam, K. (2011). Dispelling the myths surrounding de-identification: Anonymization remains a strong tool for protecting privacy. *Canadian Law Review, 8*(9), 89–100.

Centers for Disease Control and Prevention and Health Resources and Services Administration (2014). *Integrated guidance for developing epidemiologic profiles: HIV prevention and Ryan White HIV/AIDS Programs Planning*. Atlanta, GA: Centers for Disease Control and Prevention. Retrieved from http://www.cdc.gov/hiv/guidelines/

Committee on Strategies for Responsible Sharing of Clinical Trial Data, Board on Health Sciences Policy, Institute of Medicine. (2015). *Sharing clinical trial data: Maximizing benefits, minimizing risk*. Washington, DC: National Academies Press. Retrieved from http://www.ncbi.nlm.nih.gov/books/NBK269030/

Dalenius, T. (1986). Finding a needle in a haystack or identifying anonymous census records. *Journal of Official Statistics, 2*(3), 329–336.

Dankar, F., El Emam, K., Neisa, A., & Roffey, T. (2012). Estimating the re-identification risk of clinical data sets. *BMC Medical Informatics and Decision Making, 12*, 66.

De Waal, T., & Willenborg, L. (1999). Information loss through global recoding and local suppression. *Netherlands Official Statistics, 14*, 17–20.

Duncan, G., & Lambert, D. (1989). The risk of disclosure for microdata. *Journal of Business and Economic Statistics, 7*(2), 207–217. Retrieved from https://doi.org/10.1080/07350015.1989.10509729

Duncan, G. T., Keller-McNulty, S. A., & Stokes, S. L. (2001). *Disclosure risk vs. data utility: The R-U confidentiality map* (No. LA-UR-01-6428). National Institute of Statistical Sciences. Research Triangle Institute, NC.

El Emam, K. (2008). Heuristics for de-identifying health data. *IEEE Security and Privacy, 6*(4), 58–61.

El Emam, K. (2013). *Guide to the de-identification of personal health information*. Boca Raton, FL: CRC Press (Auerbach).

El Emam, K., & Alvarez, C. (2015). A critical appraisal of the Article 29 Working Party Opinion 05/2014 on Data Anonymization Techniques. *International Data Privacy Law, 5*(1), 73–87.

El Emam, K., & Arbuckle, L. (2013). *Anonymizing health data: Case studies and methods to get you started*. Sebastopol, CA: O'Reilly Media Inc.

El Emam, K., Arbuckle, L., Koru, G., Eze, B., Gaudette, L., Neri, E., . . . Gluck, J. (2012). De-identification methods for open health data: The case of the Heritage Health Prize claims dataset. *Journal of Medical Internet Research, 14*(1), e33. Retrieved from https://doi.org/10.2196/jmir.2001

El Emam, K., Dankar, F., Issa, R., Jonker, E., Amyot, D., Cogo, E., . . . Bottomley, J. (2009). A globally optimal k-anonymity method for the de-identification of health data. *Journal of the American Medical Informatics Association, 16*(5), 670–682.

El Emam, K., Jonker, E., Arbuckle, L., & Malin, B. (2011). A systematic review of re-identification attacks on health data. *PLoS ONE, 6*(12). Retrieved from http://www.plosone.org/article/info%3Adoi%2F10.1371%2Fjournal.pone.0028071

El Emam, K., Jonker, E., Moher, E., & Arbuckle, L. (2013). A review of evidence on consent bias in research. *American Journal of Bioethics, 13*(4), 42–44.

Elliot, M., & Dale, A. (1999). Scenarios of attack: The data intruders' perspective on statistical disclosure risk. *Netherlands Official Statistics, 14*(Spring), 6–10.

Erlich, Y. (2013, May 13). Breaking good: A short ethical manifesto for the privacy researcher. Retrieved from http://blogs.law.harvard.edu/billofhealth/2013/05/23/breaking-good-a-short -ethical-manifesto-for-the-privacy-researcher/

Expert Panel on Timely Access to Health and Social Data for Health Research and Health System Innovation. (2015). *Accessing health and health-related data in Canada.* Ottawa, Canada: Council of Canadian Academies.

Furnham, A. (1986). Response bias, social desirability and dissimulation. *Personality and Individual Differences, 7*(3), 385–400.

Golle, P. (2006). Revisiting the uniqueness of simple demographics in the US population. In *Proceedings of the 5th ACM Workshop on Privacy in Electronic Society* (pp. 77–80). New York, NY: Association of Computing Machinery. Retrieved from https://doi.org/10.1145/1179601.1179615

Government of Ontario. Personal Health Information Protection Act, Pub. L. No. S.O. 2004, CHAPTER 3, Schedule A (2004).

Health Insurance Portability and Accountability Act, Pub. L. No. 104-191, 110 Stat. 1936. (1996).

HITRUST Alliance. (2015). *HITRUST updates common security framework to include privacy controls.* Retrieved from https://hitrustalliance.net/hitrust-includes-csf-privacy-controls/

Hogue, C. (1991). Ethical issues in sharing epidemiologic data. *Journal of Clinical Epidemiology, 44*(Suppl. I), 103S–107S.

Hughes, S., Wells, K., McSorley, P., & Freeman, A. (2014). Preparing individual patient data from clinical trials for sharing: The GlaxoSmithKline approach. *Pharmaceutical Statistics, 13*(3), 179–183. Retrieved from https://doi.org/10.1002/pst.1615

Information Commissioner's Office. (2012). *Anonymisation: Managing data protection risk code of practice.* Wilmslow, England: Information Commissioner's Office.

International Organization for Standardization. (2008). *Health informatics. Pseudonymization.* Geneva, Switzerland: Author. Retrieved from https://www.iso.org/standard/42807.html

Jabine, T. B. (1993). Procedures for restricted data access. *Journal of Official Statistics, 9*(2), 537–589.

Malin, B. A., El Emam, K., & O'Keefe, C. M. (2013). Biomedical data privacy: Problems, perspectives, and recent advances. *Journal of the American Medical Informatics Association, 20*(1), 1–5.

Marsh, C., Skinner, C., Arber, S., Penhale, B., Openshaw, S., Hobcraft, J., . . . Walford, N. (1991). The case for samples of anonymized records from the 1991 census. *Journal of the Royal Statistical Society, Series A (Statistics in Society), 154*(2), 305–340.

Montjoye, Y.-A. de, Radaelli, L., Singh, V. K., & Pentland, A. (2015). Unique in the shopping mall: On the reidentifiability of credit card metadata. *Science, 347*(6221), 536–539. Retrieved from https://doi.org/10.1126/science.1256297

Morgan, M. G., Henrion, M., & Small, M. (1992). *Uncertainty: A guide to dealing with uncertainty in quantitative risk and policy analysis* (reprint ed.). Cambridge, MA: Cambridge University Press.

Narayanan, A., & Shmatikov, V. (2008). Robust de-anonymization of large sparse datasets. In *Proceedings of the 2008 IEEE Symposium on Security and Privacy* (pp. 111–125). Washington, DC: IEEE Computer Society.

Office for Civil Rights. (2012). *Guidance regarding methods for de-identification of protected health information in accordance with the Health Insurance Portability and Accountability Act (HIPAA) privacy rule.* Washington, DC: Department of Health and Human Services.

O'Keefe, C., & Chipperfield, J. (2013). A summary of attack methods and confidentiality protection measures for fully automated remote analysis systems. *International Statistical Review, 81*(3), 426–455.

Ontario Hospital Association & Information and Privacy Commissioner of Ontario. (2012, November). Preventing/reducing unauthorized access to personal health information. Toronto, Canada: Ontario Hospital Association.

Pandurangan, V. (2014, June 21). On taxis and rainbows: Lessons from NYC's improperly anonymized taxi logs. Retrieved from https://medium.com/@vijayp/of-taxis-and-rainbows-f6bc289679a1

Personal Information and Electronic Documents Act (PIPEDA). (2000). Directive 95/46/EC on the protection of individuals with regard to the processing of personal data and on the free movement of such data. *Official Journal of European Communities.* No L 281/31.

PhUSE De-Identification Working Group. (2015). Providing *de-identification standards to CDISC DATA Models 3.2*. Vienna, Italy: Author. Retrieved from https://www.pharmasug.org/proceedings/2015/DS/PharmaSUG-2015-DS10.pdf

Sanches, L. (2012, June). *2012 HIPAA privacy and security audits*. Presented at the Safeguarding Health Information: Building Assurance through HIPAA Security Conference, Washington, DC. Retrieved from http://csrc.nist.gov/news_events/hiipaa_june2012/day2/day2-2_lsanches_ocr-audit.pdf

Skinner, C. J. (1992). On identification disclosure and prediction disclosure for microdata. *Statistica Neerlandica, 46*(1), 21–32. Retrieved from https://doi.org/10.1111/j.1467-9574.1992.tb01324.x

Skinner, C. J., & Elliot, M. J. (2002). A measure of disclosure risk for microdata. *Journal of the Royal Statistical Society: Series B (Statistical Methodology), 64*(4), 855–867. Retrieved from https://doi.org/10.1111/1467-9868.00365

Solutions, K. A. (2012). *HIMSS analytics report: Security of patient data*. New York, NY: Kroll Advisory Solutions.

Statistics Canada. (2007). Therapeutic abortion survey. Retrieved from http://www23.statcan.gc.ca/imdb/p2SV.pl?Function=getSurvey&SDDS=3209

Subcommittee on Disclosure Limitation Methodology. (2005). Statistical policy working paper 22—Report on statistical disclosure limitation methodology. Federal Committee on Statistical Methodology. Retrieved from https://www.hhs.gov/sites/default/files/spwp22.pdf

Sweeney, L. (2013). Matching known patients to health records in Washington State data. Harvard University. Data Privacy Lab. White Paper 1089-1.

Taylor, R. W., Fritsch, E. J., & Liederbach, J. (2014). *Digital crime and digital terrorism* (3rd ed.). Upper Saddle River, NJ: Prentice Hall.

U.S. Congress. (1996a). The Health Insurance Portability and Accountability Act of 1996; 45 Code of Federal Regulations 164.154(b)1 Expert Determination. Retrieved from https://www.law.cornell.edu/cfr/text/45/164.514

U.S. Congress. (1996b). The Health Insurance Portability and Accountability Act of 1996; 45 Code of Federal Regulations 164.154(b)2 Safe Harbor. Retrieved from https://www.law.cornell.edu/cfr/text/45/164.514

U.S. Congress. (1996c). The Health Insurance Portability and Accountability Act of 1996; 45 Code of Federal Regulations 164.154(b)5(e) Limited Data Set. Retrieved from https://www.law.cornell.edu/cfr/text/45/164.514

Vose, D. (2008). *Risk analysis: A quantitative guide* (3rd ed.). Hoboken, NJ: Wiley.

Willenborg, L., & de Waal, T. (2001). *Elements of statistical disclosure control*. New York, NY: Springer-Verlag.

CHAPTER 14

Innovations and Sustainability in Population Health Technologies

Ashish Joshi

- What are the driving factors for health technology innovations?
- Which factors influence the adoption and implementation of health technology innovations?
- What steps are required in implementing health technology innovations?
- How can health technology innovations be sustained in diverse settings?
- How do you translate innovative ideas of enhancing population health outcomes into practice?

▶ I. Innovations in Population Health

Defining Innovation

Advancement of technology has facilitated socioeconomic growth and enhanced overall human welfare and well-being. Technology is making a substantial contribution to global health. Information and communication technology (ICT) should be suitably used and applied to accomplish national and global health goals. The focus is primarily to create affordable and quality healthcare services for everyone. Most industrialized countries actively support the development of health innovations ranging from medical devices to biotechnologies (Lehoux, Miller, & Daudelin, 2016). Several policy instruments have been targeted at building research capacity, facilitating industry–university collaborations, and encouraging academic entrepreneurship (Guimón, 2013). The ability of academic spin-offs to successfully pass the threshold of sustainability is uneven (Lehoux, Daudelin, Williams-Jones, Denis, & Longo, 2014). Academic researchers tend to rely predominantly upon venture capitalists that tend to foster short-term financial growth (Lehoux et al., 2014).

West (1990) defined innovation as "the intentional introduction and application within a role, group, or organization of ideas, processes, products, or procedures, new to the relevant unit of adoption, designed to significantly benefit the individual, group, or the wider society."

An innovation is a new product or service that an organization, developer, or inventor has created for the market. Innovation is a technology or a practice being used for the first time by members of an organization, whether or not other organizations have used it previously (Klein & Sorra, 1996). Implementation of innovation within an organization is the process of gaining targeted employees' appropriate and committed use of an innovation. It presupposes innovation adoption. According to the United Nations Educational, Scientific and Cultural Organization (UNESCO), "Innovation is the implementation of a new or significantly improved product (good or service), or process, a new marketing method, or a new organizational method in business practices, workplace organization or external relations" (Omachonu & Einspruch, 2010).

Quality of healthcare services and costs are the two important factors that determine healthcare standards, whereas innovation acts like a driving force to balance out the two factors (Omachonu & Einspruch, 2010). Innovation is a basic segment of business growth and competition survival. UNESCO describes the following four types of innovations (Omachonu & Einspruch, 2010):

- *Product innovation:* New kinds of goods and services are introduced to generate incremental revenues for the external market.
- *Process innovation:* Improvises on internal capabilities and safeguarding to improve quality and enhance production processes.
- *Marketing innovation:* Improvises the design and packaging of products, their promotion strategies, or pricing.
- *Organizational innovation:* Implementation of a new organizational method in the business practices, workplace organization, or external relations.

Three types of innovations can make health care better and cheaper (FIGURE 14.1).

- *Consumer focused:* Innovations in healthcare delivery should be convenient, more effective, and less expensive than what currently exists. Patients are like consumers who want a good product in addition to quality care at a good price that is easy to use.
- *Technology:* ICT connects many islands of information in the healthcare system, and it vastly improves the quality and lowers costs.
- *Business model:* Innovative business models integrate healthcare activities that can increase efficiency, improve care, and save time for consumers (Herzlinger, 2006; Klein & Sorra, 1996).

Two types of stage models are commonly used to describe the innovation process.

- *Source-based stage models:* These are based on the perspective of the innovation developed or source.
- *User-based stage models:* These are based on the perspective of the user.

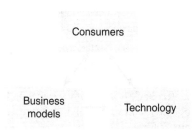

FIGURE 14.1 Role players in innovations

The health sector has witnessed tremendous progress due to the rise in health technology innovations. Healthcare innovation takes novel ideas, inventions, or processes and applies them to achieve health improvement and greater health equity (Greenhalgh, Robert, Macfarlane, Bate, & Kyriakidou, 2004). Advanced, innovative products help to tackle health-related problems more efficiently with limited human errors.

Why Innovation in Health Care Is a Challenge

Modern health care is highly specialized, and innovations are pushing the frontiers of what is knowable and doable. There is limited information about the effectiveness, cost, and impact of technologies on the healthcare system (Klein, Conn, & Sorra, 2001). A significant waste of resources and preventable problems occur because innovation processes are not sufficiently informed by these factors (Klein et al., 2001). The two policy domains of health care and innovation rarely interact. One of the challenges involves struggle with local adoption of innovations by the patients, clinicians, and decision makers. Another challenge is to increase the efficiency of the innovation process and avoid investing resources in technologies for which there is inadequate clinical evidence. The adoption of innovation is also largely constrained by the health policy branch, which seeks evidence-based decision making and sets priorities given available resources (Klein & Sorra, 1996). The health policy branch fosters innovation regulation and evaluation prior to the entry of these products into market settings. It usually focuses on one technology at a time. The innovation branch tends to intervene early. It supports a range of public and private innovators operating in places that are seen as commercially promising but without an explicit and detailed assessment of healthcare priorities (Greenhalgh et al., 2004).

Innovation designers rarely tap into the knowledge generated by health service researchers. They do not provide information on comparative effectiveness and value of these innovations in relation to one another. There is an acute lack of knowledge about ways to promote the design of more valuable innovations (Greenhalgh et al., 2004). From a healthcare perspective, a desirable innovation is a technology that matches the following description (Omachonu & Einspruch, 2010):

- Is effective and costs less than the current alternative
- Can be used safely and effectively by less skilled and less costly personnel
- Can be used safely and effectively in any kind of setting and in all geographic areas
- Solves a health problem permanently or produces diagnostic certainty
- Does not trigger side effects or reduce patients' mobility or autonomy
- Does not raise ethical dilemmas or give rise to equivocal social transformers

The idea of having a new, collaborative, policy-oriented research agenda can bridge design processes and healthcare needs and priorities (Omachonu & Einspruch, 2010). Clear and strong incentives are needed for innovators to design more desirable innovations. Appropriate feedback from health services and policy research about the level of fit between potential innovations and their likely real-world use needs to be established (Omachonu & Einspruch, 2010).

Drivers of Innovation in Health Care

Health care has several stakeholders with different competing interests. It is important to work with the interests of the different players or else the uptake of the innovation will be hindered. Innovation in health care presents two kinds of financial challenges: funding the innovation's development and determining who will pay how much for the product or service it yields (Klein & Sorra, 1996). In addition, many traditional sources of capital aren't familiar with the healthcare industry, so it's difficult to find investors. Government regulation of health care can also sometimes either aid or hinder innovation. Understanding how and when to adopt or invest in technology is also critical (Omachonu & Einspruch, 2010). Infrastructure to support the innovation might not be in place if the technology deployment is too early, and waiting too long might be a risk because the time to gain competitive advantage may pass (Omachonu & Einspruch, 2010). The empowered and engaged consumers of health care can greatly enhance the adoption of an innovation. There are several features that make certain innovations more compelling than others. These include the following:

- *Respective relevance:* The appropriateness of the purpose when compared to other existing or feasible interventions given the population health needs and the healthcare delivery problems to be addressed.
- *Usability:* Direct and active cooperation between users and designers enhances the quality, functionality, usability, effectiveness, and adoption of innovations (Vicente, 2010).
- *Sustainability:* A rigorous analysis and understanding are needed to learn of the various ways in which a manufacturer's commercial viability can be established. Comparative studies of business models and their implications for design may help strengthen sustainable innovation.
- *Implementation effectiveness (IE):* This is another important driving factor of healthcare innovations (Klein & Sorra, 1996; Klein et al., 2001). IE is a function of an organization's climate for the implementation of a given innovation and the targeted organizational members' perceptions of the fit of the innovation to their values (Klein & Sorra, 1996). Targeted organizational members are individuals who are expected either to use the innovation directly or to support the innovation's use. Innovation implementation may result in one of three outcomes: (1) implementation is effective, and use of implementation enhances an organization's performance; (2) implementation is effective, but use of the innovation does not enhance the organization's performance; or (3) implementation fails (Klein & Sorra, 1996). The majority of the time, researchers have identified implementation failure, not innovation failure, as the cause of the organization's inability to achieve the intended benefits of innovations (Michaelis, Stegmaier, & Sonntag, 2009). There are six factors that can either help or hinder the efforts of the three levels of innovation (consumer, technology, and business models) (FIGURE 14.2).

Health interventions are defined as complex innovations. Evidence suggests that the nature of innovations, their complexity as perceived by the adopters, contextual circumstances, and health system factors play crucial roles in influencing adoption and ultimately diffusion (Atun, de Jongh, Secci, Ohiri, & Adeyi, 2010). Constraints on

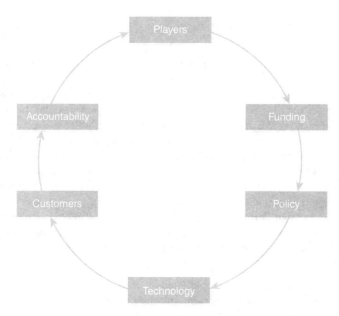

FIGURE 14.2 Factors influencing innovation

scaling up interventions operate at five different levels: (1) community and house-hold, (2) health services delivery, (3) health sector policy and strategic management, (4) public policies cutting across sectors, and (5) environmental and contextual characteristics. According to Simmons and Shiffman (2007), innovation is propa-gated through multiple channels, including a team of promoters, users, a channel or strategy for its transfer, and an enabling environment that fosters the transfer of innovation. FIGURE 14.3 outlines the factors contributing to scaling health interven-tions (Yamey, 2011).

The attributes of scaling health interventions exemplify that technology should be simple, easy to use, and governed by scientifically robust policies. A variety of implementers should be employed in the process. Qualities of implementers should include strong leadership and governance, and the ability to engage with other stakeholders. In terms of delivery strategy, diffusion and social network theories should be applied and interventions need to be tailored to suit the local context, while decentralizing implementation.

Factors that influence diffusion of innovation include (Rogers, 2010): (1) type of adopter (innovator, early adopter, early majority, late majority, or lag-gard) and (2) stages of adoption (awareness stage, interest stage, evaluation stage, trial stage, and finally adoption). The theory of diffusion has been widely applied and has contributed immensely to the success of various interventions and pro-grams (Rogers, 2010). Cultural and normative beliefs and values largely influ-ence adoption and diffusion of innovations within the adoption system (Atun et al., 2010). Factors that affect the ability of an innovation to be integrated into existing health system functions include: (1) the nature of the problem, (2) the actual intervention, (3) the system in which adoption takes place, (4) health sys-tem characteristics, and (5) the context (Grossman, Goolsby, Olsen, & McGinnis, 2011) (TABLE 14.1).

FIGURE 14.3 Attributes of scaling health interventions

Data from Yamey, G. (2011). Scaling up global health interventions: A proposed framework for success. *PLoS Medicine, 8*(6), e1001049.

TABLE 14.1 Attributes of Adoption and Diffusion of Innovation

The problem	Problem characteristics influence the rate at which a designed intervention is integrated into the general health system.
The intervention	Consists of innovations, new practices, institutional arrangements, or ideas for adoption.
	Incorporates various innovation attributes, including relative advantage, compatibility, trialability, observability, and complexity. These serve to impact the degree of acceptance and integration of the innovation.
The adoption system	Includes key actors and institutions in the health system with differing perceptions of the benefits and risks of an intervention.
Health system characteristics	Interventions need to be integrated into the broader context of the health system and its governance.
	Functions will involve alignment with existing regulatory mechanisms and establishment of a common performance management system.
Broader context	Influence of environmental and nonenvironmental factors including demographics, economic conditions, political status, and ecological, sociocultural, and legal factors.
	Adoption and assimilation of a health intervention into a health system.
	A variety of contextual factors influence sustainability.
	Critical events and technological change also provide opportunities for integration of interventions into health systems (Atun et al., 2010).

Innovation Frameworks

Innovation frameworks describe methods to generate transformative innovation to bring about changes in the healthcare delivery or payment models. The innovation integrates four business catalysts: (1) technology, (2) business model, (3) market adoption strategy, and (4) policy (Omachonu & Einspruch, 2010). All four catalysts must work collaboratively for transformative innovation to work effectively. The two principal dimensions of healthcare innovation are environmental and operational (Omachonu & Einspruch, 2010).

- *Environmental dimension:* Involves organizational leadership, organizational culture, regulatory acceptance and physician acceptance, complexity of innovation, and partnerships and collaboration
- *Operational dimension:* Includes patient satisfaction, profitability, effectiveness, efficiency, patient safety, aging population, productivity, cost containment, labor shortage, clinical outcomes, and quality

Together these two dimensions affect the introduction of innovation in healthcare organizations (Omachonu & Einspruch, 2010). TABLE 14.2 describes the various innovation frameworks related to the innovation's adoption and implementation (Omachonu & Einspruch, 2010).

▶ II. Health Technology Innovations

Health information technology (IT) solutions developed by vendors are required to meet the meaningful use criteria resulting from the HITECH Act (HealthIT.gov, 2013). These healthcare technology systems often satisfy unmet needs in various aspects of patient care provision (McKesson, 2016). Innovation systems respond best to the needs of those who can afford their outputs. Numerous initiatives have been created or proposed to reengineer those systems to address the needs of poor people. Innovators should show the cost-effectiveness and long-term safety requirements for the health technology innovations.

- *Reengineering innovation systems:* Product development partnerships are explicitly modeled after partnerships in the private sector. Industrial policies including tax breaks and liability protection are regularly evaluated by a lot of countries as a means of stimulating innovation (e.g., Global Fund to Fight AIDS, Tuberculosis, and Malaria). There is a need for implementation research to include research on policies and practices affecting distribution, adoption, and availability.
- *Innovative developing countries:* A handful of innovative developing countries have emerged as world leaders in the manufacture of essential drugs and vaccines. These countries regularly engage in modifying and adjusting their national strategies on innovation (Gardner, Acharya, & Yach, 2007). They continue to aspire toward developing and adopting social innovations that foster technology development (Gardner et al., 2007).
- *Public–private investments:* Funding of health research by public sources continues to proliferate in developing countries. The local public investment has much better chances to be sustainable. However, private research and development investments by both local and global organizations have grown rapidly in developing countries.

TABLE 14.2 Healthcare Innovation Frameworks and Adoption Constructs

	Related to Adoption
Factors related to adoption effort	Early involvement of influential potential users Use of outside consultant to advise on adoption strategy Personal contact between developer of innovation and potential users Building methods for rewarding adoption Social network (intersystems) Leadership and champion of innovation Network with innovation developers Training readiness and efforts Complexity, relative advantage, and observability Evidence and compatibility Innovation fit with users' norms and values
Factors related to the adopting organization effort	Primary implementer Psychosocial resistance to change Contextual influence Trialability, relevance, and ease of use Attitudes, motivation, readiness toward quality improvement, and reward Readiness for change and capacity to adopt
Factors related to innovation characteristics	Current practice similarity Cost Observability Trialability Relevance Relative advantage Ease of understanding and use

(continues)

TABLE 14.2 Healthcare Innovation Frameworks and Adoption Constructs *(continued)*

Healthcare Innovation Frameworks	Summary	Adoption Constructs
Social network models in diffusion of innovation	Opinion leadership and external influences Threshold for adoption Critical mass for early adopters, early majority, late majority, and laggards	Social network (intersystems) Social network (interorganizations) Social network (individual's personal network)
Full contingency model of innovation adoption	Factors that affect innovation adoption on three levels: ■ Individual ■ Organization ■ Environment	Government policy and regulations Social network (intersystems) Leadership and champion of innovation Operational size and structure Complexity Relative advantage Observability Trialability Relevance and ease of use Attitudes, motivation, readiness toward quality improvement, and reward
Theory of reasoned action and theory of planned behavior	Personal-level attributes Behavior change related to decision making Innovation adoption	Operational size and structure Attitudes, motivation, readiness toward quality improvement, and reward

Precaution adoption process model (PAPM)	How an individual comes to a decision to take action. Translate decision into action in stages. 1. Unaware of issue 2. Unengaged by issue 3. Undecided about acting/decided 4. Acting 5. Maintenance	Innovation fit with users' norms and values Attitudes, motivation, readiness toward quality improvement, and reward
Adoption Within the Context of Implementation		
Reach, effectiveness, adoption, implementation, and maintenance (RE-AIM)	A design for dissemination along five dimensions: ▪ Reach target population ▪ Effectiveness of innovations ▪ Adoption of innovations ▪ Implementation of consistent and accurate delivery ▪ Maintenance of innovations	Government policy and regulation complexity, relative advantage, observability Attitudes, motivation, readiness toward quality improvement, and reward Feedback on execution and fidelity Readiness for change and capacity to adopt
Evidence-based model for diffusion of innovations in health service organizations	Individual adoption System readiness Dissemination and implementation Adopters characterized as active seekers of knowledge. It has seven aspects: general psychological antecedents, context-specific, meaning, adoption decision, concerns in preadoption stage, concerns during early use, and concerns in established users.	Absorptive capacity Leadership and champion of innovation Network with innovation developers Norms, values, and cultures Operational size and structure Social network (interorganizations) Complexity, relative advantage, and observability Evidence and compatibility Innovation fit with users' norms and values Trialability, relevance, and use Attitudes, motivation, readiness toward quality improvement, and reward Individual characteristics Social network (individual's personal network)

(continues)

TABLE 14.2 Healthcare Innovation Frameworks and Adoption Constructs *(continued)*

Healthcare Innovation Frameworks	Summary	Adoption Constructs
Framework of dissemination in healthcare intervention research	Integrate diffusion process with evaluation process.	Reinforcing regulation with financial incentives to improve quality service delivery Social network (intersystems) Network with innovation developers and consultants Norms, values, and culture Operational size and structure Social climate Cost-efficacy and feasibility Innovation fit with users' norms and values Individual characteristics Social network (individual's personal network)
Practical, robust implementation and sustainability model (PRISM)	Considers how innovation/intervention design, the external environment, the implementation and sustainability infrastructure, and the recipients influence adoption, implementation, and maintenance Synthesizes four existing models of implementation and diffusion research: ■ Diffusion of innovations ■ Chronic care model ■ Model for improvement ■ RE-AIM	Government policy and regulation Leadership and champion Network with innovation developers Cost-efficacy and feasibility Evidence and compatibility Facilitators and barriers Innovation fit with users' norms and values Feedback on execution and fidelity Readiness for change and capacity to adopt

The increasing capacity of developing countries coupled with a growing recognition of the need for innovations reflect a new paradigm that fosters global health interventions. An "innovation systems lens" highlights the need to create and implement both social and technological solutions (Gardner et al., 2007). The implementation of health information technology interventions is at the forefront of most policy agendas. However, such undertakings require systemic organizational changes and complex strategic planning. Sustained government support for research, availability of venture capital, regulations, and policies and practices affecting public–private partnerships (PPPs) are important factors of innovation to meet healthcare needs (Morel et al., 2005). Although healthcare systems in high-income settings utilize technology extensively, individuals in most low- and middle-income countries (LMICs) lack access to basic healthcare needs. Greater use of effective health technologies in LMICs should benefit productivity (Gardner et al., 2007). The key is to ensure that only effective technologies receive investment. Decisions to introduce health technologies into resource-poor settings should be evidence based. Currently, most of the infrastructure for health research in developing countries resides in the public sector. Governments of LMICs encounter critical challenges and competing priorities when it comes to investing in innovations due to the array of unmet basic needs that citizens struggle with (Gardner et al., 2007). Careful consideration should be given to successful implementation and scale-up. Innovation through partnering of local public and private research organizations deserves particular attention (Crowley et al., 2004). These partnerships can translate the research findings into practice to enhance population health (Crowley et al., 2004).

Implementation of Health Technology Innovations

Improving the quality and safety of health care using health information technology innovations is a priority area. Implementation is a complex process of integrating innovations within a setting (Damschroder et al., 2009). It is the means by which an innovation is translated into practice and assimilated into an organization. Implementation steps are invaluable because a plethora of interventions deemed to be effective do not necessarily yield the desired health outcomes (Damschroder et al., 2009). Evidence has shown that about 75% of efforts by organizations to foster change fail (Damschroder et al., 2009). Barriers to implementation may arise at multiple levels of healthcare delivery including: (1) patient level, (2) provider level, (3) organizational level, (4) policy level, and (5) market level (Damschroder et al., 2009).

Implementation frameworks can be characterized based on their orientation, type, stage of implementation, domains addressed, and the level at which the elements are included (Omachonu & Einspruch, 2010). These frameworks have been categorized into four types (Damschroder et al., 2009; Omachonu & Einspruch, 2010).

- *Descriptive:* Describes properties, characteristics, and qualities of implementation
- *Prescriptive:* Provides direction on the implementation process via a series of steps or procedures

- *Explanatory:* Specifies the linkage and/or relationships between framework concepts
- *Predictive:* Proposes directional relationships between the concepts of implementation

The Consolidated Framework for Implementation Research (CFIR) reflects a professional consensus within a particular scientific community. This framework constitutes five domains: (1) intervention characteristics, (2) inner setting, (3) outer setting, (4) individuals, and (5) implementation process (Damschroder et al., 2009). Each of these domains is described here:

- *Intervention characteristics and related constructs:* These are often complex and multifaceted with many interacting components. Interventions can be conceptualized as having core and adaptive peripheral components. Constructs related to intervention characteristics include the source of intervention, strength and quality of evidence, relative advantage, adaptability (degree to which an intervention can be adapted), trialability (ability to test the intervention and its usability on a small scale), complexity (perceived difficulty reflected by duration, scope, disruptiveness, and number of steps to implement), design quality and packaging, and costs of the intervention (Damschroder et al., 2009).
- *Outer setting characteristics and related constructs:* This involves two types: the external system (economic, political, and professional setting) and the local environment (circumstances surrounding the organization including patient, community, and network). The constructs related to the outer setting include patient needs and resources, cosmopolitanism (support and promote staff roles), peer pressure, and external policies and incentives (Damschroder et al., 2009). The changes in the outer setting can influence implementation.
- *Inner setting characteristics and related constructs:* The constructs related to inner setting include structural characteristics (organization size influences implementation of an innovation), high-quality networks and communications, and cultural norms (Damschroder et al., 2009).
- *Individual characteristics and related constructs:* Individuals play a significant role because they reflect various cultural, professional, organizational, and individual perspectives (Greenhalgh et al., 2004). Organizational change starts with individual behavior change. Theories of change have highlighted predominant measures for individual change: knowledge, beliefs toward changing behavior, and level of self-efficacy (Grol, Bosch, Hulscher, Eccles, & Wensing, 2007). Individuals' perception toward the organization and their relationship and degree of commitment to the organization affect staff readiness toward implementation activities.
- *Implementation process:* Successful implementation usually requires an active change process at multiple levels within the organization (Grol et al., 2007).

The choice of an implementation framework is quite challenging. It is possible that not all frameworks targeting a particular innovation cover all implementation concepts (FIGURE 14.4). It is imperative for an individual or an organization to decide

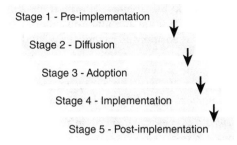

Stage 1 - Pre-implementation

Stage 2 - Diffusion

Stage 3 - Adoption

Stage 4 - Implementation

Stage 5 - Post-implementation

FIGURE 14.4 Implementation stages of the framework

Modified from Damschroder, L. J., Aron, D. C., Keith, R. E., Kirsh, S. R., Alexander, J. A., & Lowery, J. C. (2009). Fostering implementation of health services research findings into practice: A consolidated framework for advancing implementation science. *Implementation Science*, 4(1), 1.

whether an implementation framework for the innovation to be implemented is most applicable. The consequence of using a framework lacking degree or depth of an implementation concept may be poor results.

▶ III. Implementation of Health Technology Innovations

The World Health Organization (WHO) describes a health system as consisting of all health-related activities with the key purpose of promoting, restoring, or maintaining health (WHO, 2005). Three fundamental barriers exist to the greater adoption of technology in health care. First, the necessary technology is not available. Second, the technology may be in existence but may be inaccessible. This barrier is often caused by price, problems with distribution, energy supply, or inadequate human resources (Howitt et al., 2012). Third, technology is not always used, even when accessible. Overcoming these barriers is crucial if the potential of technology for global health is to be realized. The feasibility of deploying an intervention in a resource-poor setting is largely influenced by multiple factors including financial/cost, economic impact, distribution challenges, human resource capacity, and energy supply (WHO, n.d.). Other factors that can influence implementation include persuading people to use the technology, scale-up of use, effective assessment and regulation, and issues of equity.

Decisions about implementation of a technology in an LMIC should be based on a variety of factors that range from cost of intervention to methods of facilitating adoption (WHO, n.d.). This process is known as a health technology assessment (HTA). An HTA is described as the "systematic evaluation of properties, effects, and/or impacts of health-care technology" (WHO, n.d.). It describes whether a technology can work in a particular setting and the best way to achieve implementation. It should be used effectively in resource-poor settings (WHO, n.d.). Donor funding cannot be relied on to cover the cost of beneficial health technologies in resource-poor settings. Methods of prompting buy-in from the private sector should be explored (Howitt et al., 2012). Two examples already in use are cross-subsidization and micro-insurance (Howitt et al., 2012). In cross-subsidization, users can afford to pay more so that those unable to afford it pay less. Micro-insurance aims to aggregate a large number of poor consumers through their health insurance scheme.

The following important characteristics need to be taken into consideration for the successful implementation of health technology innovations:

- *Technical characteristics:* A new system needs to be at least as quick as the system that was previously in operation (Boonstra & Broekhuis, 2010; Yarbrough & Smith, 2007). Other features of technology that are repeatedly found to facilitate adoption include early demonstrable benefits, perceived ease of use, costs, and the extent to which a system is interoperable with existing technology in the organization and fits in with existing organizational processes. Technology has the potential to be adapted to support changing needs and individual/organizational contexts of use.

- *Social aspects:* These include information technology literacy and general competencies of users, personal and peer attitudes toward an innovation (including colleagues and patients) (Yarbrough & Smith, 2007), financial considerations (Boonstra & Broekhuis, 2010; Gagnon et al., 2010), and the extent to which the technology supports interprofessional roles and working (Gurses & Xiao, 2006). Ongoing involvement of key stakeholders at the conception and design stages, and an opportunity for field testing of early prototypes and open communication channels, can help to ensure that systems are likely to be valued and used by professionals and patients (Keshavjee et al., 2006; Yusof, Stergioulas, & Zugic, 2007).

- *Organization factors:* Larger, more complex health systems have proven particularly receptive to the introduction of technological innovation. Senior leadership supports results surrounding implementation activities (Gagnon et al., 2010; Keshavjee et al., 2006). They can also facilitate the redesign of workflows, provide adequate training and support to users, and highlight problematic issues (Gagnon et al., 2010). Management also needs to plan for potentially extreme contingencies, such as technology failing (Keshavjee et al., 2006).

The human, organization, and technology–fit framework reflects that human, technology, and organizational factors are equally important, as is the fit between them (Yusof et al., 2007). Organizational strategies that support innovative uses of health information technology include supportive organizational culture, recognizing that technology and the organization evolve together with a common goal and purpose. Specific organizational strategies include educational sessions about innovative uses, champions to facilitate innovative uses in different specialties, effective communication and feedback about innovative uses throughout planning and implementation, and involving suppliers and working together to discover and disseminate innovative uses (Cresswell & Sheikh, 2013). Proctor et al. (2011) have developed a framework of implementation outcomes that can be applied to evaluate implementation endeavors. The framework proposes eight conceptually distinct outcomes for potential evaluation (**FIGURE 14.5**).

FIGURE 14.5 Framework for evaluation of health information technology

Modified from Proctor, E., Silmere, H., Raghavan, R., Hovmand, P., Aarons, G., Bunger, A., . . . Hensley, M. (2011). Outcomes for implementation research: Conceptual distinctions, measurement challenges, and research agenda. *Administration and Policy in Mental Health and Mental Health Services Research, 38*(2), 65–76.

▶ **IV. Examples of Health Technology Innovations in Global Settings**

Several technology innovations to enhance population health have been deployed in global settings. TABLE 14.3 outlines some of these health technology innovations, which have been characterized based on the health problem addressed, description of the solution, technology requirements, and the country of focus (WHO, 2015). The majority of these innovations have been directed at preventing and managing chronic health conditions including hypertension, diabetes, and hearing loss. Others were geared toward addressing gaps in existing healthcare delivery processes including accessibility of medications in pharmacies, stock outs and supply chain disruption, lack of access to quality health care in remote settings, and workforce shortage/training programs. The technology solutions were mostly mobile health services; other types included self-monitoring devices, kiosks, and telemedicine. Internet access was a common technology requirement for the function of these innovations, with a few of them being able to function without Internet. Interestingly, these innovations were likely to originate from developed countries including Canada and the United States, as well as LMICs such as Kenya, Benin, Malawi, Tanzania, and Uganda.

TABLE 14.3 Examples of Health Technology Innovations in Global Settings

Technology	Health Problem	Solution Description	Technology Requirements	Countries
Blood pressure eReader/ ICD-10 (WHO, 2013a)	High blood pressure	Self-measured blood pressure (SMBP) e-reader positioned in social points; accessed by community members	Access to the Internet, access to a mobile phone, use of a computer and a stable power supply that will be solar powered	Canada, Kenya
ePharmacy Netsystem/ HL-7 (WHO, 2013b)	Accessibility of medicine in pharmacies	Connect patients to pharmacies within their location, and provide listings for available medications	Internet access and mobile device that uses unstructured supplementary service data (USSD), SMS, or specific SIM	Benin
Hearing screen eRecord/ HL-7 (WHO, 2015)	Hearing loss	Optimized screening, diagnosis, and care audiogram screening	A touchscreen device and headphones; iOS platform	South Africa
Maternal and child health mobile services (WHO, 2015)	Maternal, neonatal, and infant mortality	Mobile interactive voice response	Basic mobile phone	India
Mobile supply chain management material (WHO, 2015)	Stock outs and other supply chain disruptions	Support health workers to manage commodities in low-resource settings	Mobile phones with SMS capabilities	United States; used in Ghana, India, Malawi, Tanzania, and Uganda

SMAART Portable Health Information Kiosk (Joshi, Puricelli Perin, & Arora, 2013)	Chronic NCD prevention	Identification of individuals at risk of chronic NCDs; tailored recommendation based on individual's category in either prevention, monitoring, or management	Windows computer, touchscreen, multilingual platform; physiological sensors including blood pressure, weight scale, glucometer; Internet and without Internet and printer	United States/India
SMS-DMCARE (WHO, 2015)	Diabetes	Coaching program	Mobile phone with SMS messaging	United States, Canada, Kenya
T1D System (WHO, 2015)	Type 1 diabetes	Mobile technology to better self-manage type 1 diabetes mellitus (T1D)	Access to a cellular/mobile network via mobile phone, personal computer, tablet, or smart TV; Android platform	Worldwide
Smartphones for Tuberculosis (WHO, 2015)	Low capacity to provide high-quality TB-DOTS and TB-HIV	Smartphone collection and analysis of data on tuberculosis	Smartphones, Wi-Fi, SIM cards, cellular network, online database	United States
Telemedicine for HIV/AIDS care (WHO, 2015)	Workforce shortage, training limitations in continuing professional development	Telemedicine is used to provide an online discussion forum for referrals. Patients' medical information is uploaded to the discussion forum for the physicians.	Telemedicine, computers, Internet access	Belgium

(continues)

TABLE 14.3 Examples of Health Technology Innovations in Global Settings (continued)

Technology	Health Problem	Solution Description	Technology Requirements	Countries
Mobile technology to connect patients to remote doctors (WHO, 2015)	Lack of access to quality health care in remote settings	Use of a mobile application platform for health screening, diagnosis, and treatment. The diagnostic application provides remote doctors with immediate actions for care.	Mobile connectivity, source of power	United States
Mobile technology for maternal, newborn, and child health (U.S. Agency for International Development, 2014)	High rates of maternal and neonatal morbidity caused by limited access to healthcare services due to geographic barriers and cultural and security concerns	Use of mobile technology by community health workers in antenatal, postnatal, and pregnancy monitoring to facilitate health facility referrals and counseling	Basic cell phones	Afghanistan
Electronic registry application (MedRegis) (Startup Complete, 2016)	Improve on traditional electronic health records and replace paper-based systems	Comprehensive medical apps for doctors' offices, clinics, and ambulatory settings, transcending electronic health records by creating user-specific apps for nursing, front desk, doctor, and pharmacy	Internet, app technology requirements	Caribbean (Barbados, Lesser Antilles)
Belize Health Information System (Ministry of Health, Belize, 2013)	Need for a centralized system with aggregate data for health performance monitoring and patient outcomes improvement	Integrated multicapacity health information system	Desktop computer, Internet	Belize

Collaborative on Health and Technology (CHAT) (Mental Health Innovation Network, 2015)	Need to address high cost of health care and fragmentation of mental healthcare services	Digital health care consisting of a collaboration among healthcare providers providing mental health services across six countries.		United Kingdom
Mobile telemedicine solution also known as Kgonafalo (Ndlovu, Littman-Quinn, Park, Dikai, & Kovarik, 2015)	Lack of sufficient specialized medical doctors in Botswana, limiting patient access to quality care (doctor to patient ratio of 3:10,000)	Rapid growth in the telecommunication industry supported the development of a mobile telemedicine solution for remote diagnosis.	Smartphones with built-in camera, SIM cards	Botswana
Nutrition RapidSMS Project KiraMAMA (Nutrition RapidSMS, 2014)	High maternal and child mortality due to delay in healthcare-seeking behaviors	Use of cell-phone technology for enhanced nutrition programming and data tracking on essential maternal and child health indicators	Cell phone	Burundi
Digital Disease Detection and Participatory Surveillance System (Chen, 2016)	Need to improve infectious disease detection and surveillance efforts	Web-based tool used for surveying online media to gather information on disease outbreaks and impending epidemics	Cell phone	Cambodia
CardioPad (Hendricks, 2015)	Low doctor-to-patient ratio, creating the need for enhanced access to cardiovascular health services among patients in remote locations	Mobile technology facilitates the transmission of electrocardiograms over the mobile network from remote settings	Wireless electrodes, sensors, touchscreen tablets	Cameroon

Modified from World Health Organization. (2015). WHO compendium of innovative health technologies for low resource settings, 2011–2014: Assistive devices, eHealth solutions, medical devices, other technologies; technologies for outbreaks.

Example Case Study: PopHI SMAART Framework

Sustainable, Multi-sector, Accessible, Affordable, Reimbursable, Tailored (SMAART) is an innovative population health informatics (PopHI) framework that aims to facilitate the integration of social determinants of health data and clinical data to facilitate evidence-based programs, policies, and interventions to enhance population health outcomes across diverse geographic settings. Adding data about social determinants of health, which account for more than 60% of health outcomes, can help healthcare providers to identify more care gaps than they would in a traditional risk model. Healthcare organizations can also gain better insight into individual drivers of patient engagement, which can help providers match patients to interventions, services, or resources that are most likely to improve outcomes. The framework aims to facilitate the policymakers and other government agencies having a better understanding of the population needs in specific geographic settings. Some of the barriers related to adoption of health technologies include the lack of technologies that are easily available, affordable, and accessible to the individuals who need them the most. Barriers to adoption of technology innovations in health care are often caused by cost, poor infrastructure such as lack of or limited Internet, or inadequately trained human resources (Buitenhuis, Zelenika, & Pearce, 2010).

The SMAART framework has been operationalized as an interactive, a standalone, or an Internet-enabled portable health information kiosk (PHIK) facilitating transmission of data and information regarding the health status of an individual/community. Interpretation of data into information was accomplished using previously established knowledge and available evidence-based guidelines. Tailored feedback and reinforcement are given to the consumers, and there is regular repetition of the feedback loop (Joshi et al., 2013).

The PHIK is both a standalone and an Internet-enabled, interactive, multilingual, touchscreen computer program that allows individuals to record self-report data about their sociodemographics, health behaviors, and clinical assessment. It also assesses individuals' knowledge, attitudes, and practices toward self-managing their chronic diseases including obesity, hypertension, type 2 diabetes, and hypercholesterolemia (FIGURE 14.6). Currently PHIK is available in multiple languages including English, Portuguese, Hindi, and a local Indian dialect (Oriya) (Joshi et al., 2013). The goal is to empower consumers to play a critical role in self-management of their health conditions, thereby improving health outcomes. The PHIK gathers both subjective and objective data. Subjective data include the following:

- *Sociodemographics:* Variable information recorded includes age (years), gender (male/female), and education attained.
- *Physical environment:* Data are gathered about the neighborhood location of the individual such as urban/slum/tribal settings.
- *Health behaviors:* Information gathered includes history of smoking and alcohol, drug consumption, and body weight.
- *Clinical status:* This includes variable information such as (1) ever been told by a doctor about high blood sugar, (2) ever been told by a doctor about high blood pressure, and (3) ever been told by a doctor about high blood cholesterol. Information about individual treatment and type of treatment is also

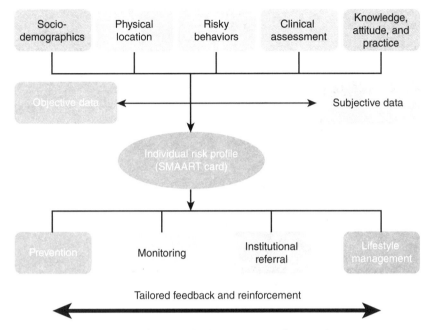

FIGURE 14.6 Portable health information kiosk using SMAART framework

gathered. A decision logic based on available evidence is applied to identify individuals who might already have a chronic disease, those who might be at risk of developing a chronic disease, or those who might have a disease but not know about it.

- *Knowledge, attitudes, and practices:* Information is also gathered about the individual's level of understanding about the disease and its management.

The objective data are gathered using multiple physiological sensors including weight measurements, blood pressure measurements, and blood sugar assessments.

- *SMAART health card:* Based on existing guidelines and available evidence in the literature, decision rules are applied toward the response data of an individual to generate a SMAART health card. The health card visualizes the state of individual risk factors across several variables in a format that is easy to understand. The system creates a personal health record of an individual and can allow the individual to save this health record or transmit it to his or her healthcare provider if the Internet is available. They can also print their SMAART health card (FIGURE 14.7).
- *SMAART intervention:* Based on the individual risk profile, tailored educational messages are delivered. Individuals can also choose the educational modules of their choice and gather more health information.
- *Monitor individual progress:* Individuals are able to track their risk factors over a period of time.

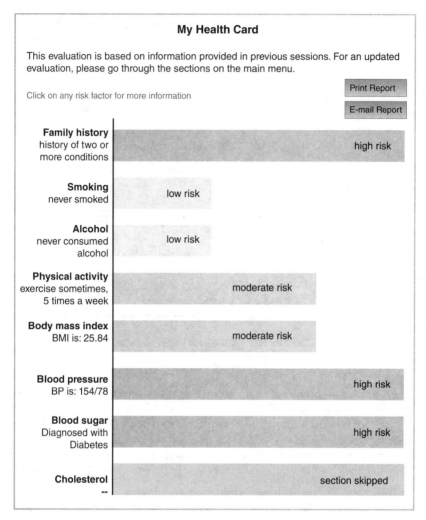

FIGURE 14.7 SMAART health card

- *SMAART reporting portal*: Policymakers and administrators can do population-level analysis to detect the trends of the risk factors of chronic disease across diverse settings. This assists the policymakers in making data-driven, evidence-based, informed decision making so that programs, policies, and interventions can have optimal resources allocated (FIGURE 14.8).

PHIK has been successful as a community-based intervention tool to assess the burden of chronic disease risk and promote self-management among populations living in diverse settings. The platform has widespread reach in areas that normally are not covered due to lack of infrastructure or health personnel (Joshi et al., 2013). The SMAART framework can be utilized to create targeted interventions for individuals, especially among those living in underserved settings. The scalability and sustainability of the PHIK using the SMAART framework is still being investigated.

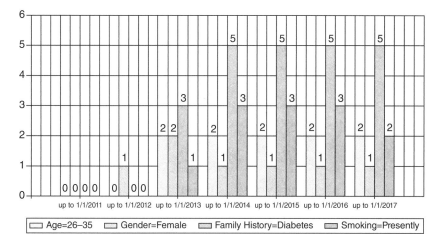

FIGURE 14.8 SMAART reporting tool for policymakers and administrators to track the burden of risk factors of chronic disease

▶ V. Sustainability

Sustainability is a vital aspect of a program's life cycle. Sustainability is defined as a process of ensuring that the innovation is sustainable and that it can be integrated into ongoing operations to benefit diverse stakeholders. Sustainability has several characteristics (Johnson, Hays, Center, & Daley, 2004).

- It is an ongoing, cyclic change process.
- It is receptive to change.
- Adequate infrastructure and capacity building are determinants of sustainability.
- It should be scientifically proven to be beneficial to diverse stakeholders prior to its adoption and after implementation.

Sustainability and *institutionalization* are the terms predominantly used to characterize continuation of innovations (Johnson et al., 2004) (FIGURE 14.9). Interventions need to move beyond their initial state of implementation once evidence reflects their effectiveness. However, sustainability decisions are impaired by a lack of strategies and tools that have been shown to work (Johnson et al., 2004).

Sustainability Planning Model

The sustainability planning model follows a standard planning sequence. Attributes such as infrastructure, capacity building, and sustainable innovation are causally associated with sustainability (Johnson et al., 2004). Each of the goals of the attribute have five objectives. Several things need to be taken into consideration when exploring infrastructure and capacity building and identifying the attributes of sustainable innovation (FIGURE 14.10).

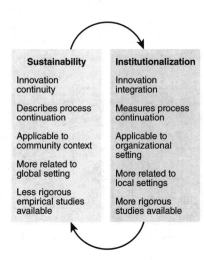

FIGURE 14.9 Comparing sustainability and institutionalization

Data from Johnson, K., Hays, C., Center, H., & Daley, C. (2004). Building capacity and sustainable prevention innovations: A sustainability planning model. *Evaluation and Program Planning, 27*(2), 135–149.

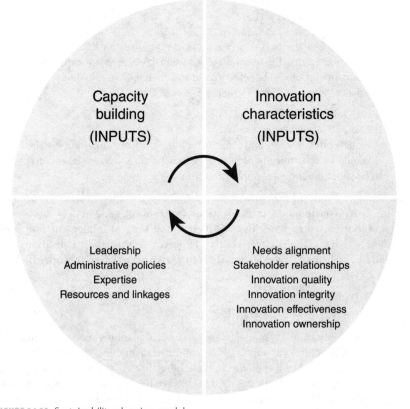

FIGURE 14.10 Sustainability planning model

Modified from Johnson, K., Hays, C., Center, H., & Daley, C. (2004). Building capacity and sustainable prevention innovations: A sustainability planning model. *Evaluation and Program Planning, 27*(2), 135–149.

Several skills are needed to assess and understand the effectiveness of the innovations. These include knowledge of needs assessment, logic model construction, fidelity assessment, and staging intervention components (Johnson et al., 2004). Some of the other skills include knowledge of data collection, process, outcome evaluation and interpretation, communication and data presentation skills, leadership skill, and fundraising expertise. Several steps are associated with the sustainability planning model, including the following (Centers for Disease Control and Prevention, n.d.; Johnson et al., 2004):

- Assessment of prevention infrastructure and innovation readiness
- Development of a sustainability plan including objectives, actions, and protocols
- Executive sustainability actions
- Evaluating sustainability readiness
- Modifying the sustainability plan

These assessments help to determine the sustainability factors that need attention in the planning and implementation steps and to provide baseline data for evaluating the impact of the sustainability actions (FIGURE 14.11).

FIGURE 14.11 Factors to consider in sustainability planning

Modified from Johnson, K., Hays, C., Center, H., & Daley, C. (2004). Building capacity and sustainable prevention innovations: A sustainability planning model. *Evaluation and Program Planning, 27*(2), 135–149.

Sustainability is the ability to maintain program services after the end of financial, managerial, and technical assistance from external donors. Few studies have emphasized the sustainability of electronic health information systems in low resource settings. Some of the determinants of sustainability include: (1) program-specific factors, (2) organizational factors, and (3) contextual factors.

Program-specific factors include the following:

- *Type/goals:* Focuses on the extent to which project goals are clearly specified.
- *Perceived effectiveness:* Describes the level of confidence in the program in achieving the desired outcome.
- *Financing:* There is always a need for substantial external financing.
- *Training:* Institutional capacity is built through trainings, which are seen to increase exposure and buy-in to the adoption and implementation of an electronic health information system.

Organizational factors include the following:

- *Local-level modifiability:* Electronic health information systems should meet local needs.
- *Donor–client and donor–community interactions:* Participatory and consensus-building activities are needed.
- *Project champions:* Governments should take an active role in engaging stakeholders from different sectors.
- *Integration:* A smooth integration within the broader health information system is desired.
- *Institutional capacity:* Software development and technical support have been identified as substantial challenges to system sustainability.

Contextual factors include the following:

- *Concurrent projects:* Activities need to be strengthened by supporting complimentary projects.
- *Community characteristics:* There are various needs of diverse stakeholders.
- *Political, economic, and cultural characteristics:* The majority of care is delivered through the public sector. High reliance on donor funding and a shortage of healthcare workforce have been mentioned as challenges of electronic health information system implementation.

Advances in health technology have the potential to significantly influence the way health care is delivered. These technological advances are helping to facilitate increased access to health information through new communication technologies. This is increasing people's health literacy and is contributing toward a shift to personal responsibility for health. Health innovations around the world are aiming to make the most use of these opportunities so that they can deliver sustainable solutions for current and future healthcare systems.

▶ VI. Conclusion

More research is needed to know which innovative initiatives are most cost-effective. Enormous gaps in our knowledge of health product innovation systems exist. There is a need for collaboration among higher educational institutions, research organizations, and industry to foster the development of cost-effective products and services for the resource-poor. To promote future innovations, there is also a need to explore existing evidence templates and how they can be applied in the various realms of health care. Critical questions that need to be addressed include: (1) What constitutes the elements of existing innovations that have been proven to work? (2) What are the challenges facing those that do not work? (3) What are the roles of these templates in knowledge generation and utilization? (4) What are the various consequences in practice? (5) How do they interface and apply in various settings and contexts? (Kyratsis, Ahmad, & Holmes, 2012). Further research could also assess ways in which innovations are implemented and assimilated into the day-to-day activities of their users.

References

Atun, R., de Jongh, T., Secci, F., Ohiri, K., & Adeyi, O. (2010). Integration of targeted health interventions into health systems: A conceptual framework for analysis. *Health Policy and Planning*, *25*(2), 104–111.

Boonstra, A., & Broekhuis, M. (2010). Barriers to the acceptance of electronic medical records by physicians from systematic review to taxonomy and interventions. *BMC Health Services Research*, *10*(1), 1.

Buitenhuis, A., Zelenika, I., & Pearce, J. M. (2010). Open design-based strategies to enhance appropriate technology development. In 14th Annual National Collegiate Inventors and Innovators Alliance Conference, 1–12.

Centers for Disease Control and Prevention. (n.d.). A sustainability planning guide for healthy communities. Retrieved from https://www.cdc.gov/nccdphp/dch/programs/healthycommunities program/pdf/sustainability_guide.pdf

Chen, D. (2016). Mobile technology innovation to improve public health in Cambodia. Retrieved from http://geeksincambodia.com/mobile-technology-innovation-to-improve-public -health-in-cambodia/

Cresswell, K., & Sheikh, A. (2013). Organizational issues in the implementation and adoption of health information technology innovations: An interpretative review. *International Journal of Medical Informatics*, *82*(5), e73–e86.

Crowley Jr, W. F., Sherwood, L., Salber, P., Scheinberg, D., Slavkin, H., Tilson, H., . . . Genel, M. (2004). Clinical research in the United States at a crossroads: Proposal for a novel public-private partnership to establish a national clinical research enterprise. *Journal of the American Medical Association*, *291*(9), 1120–1126.

Damschroder, L. J., Aron, D. C., Keith, R. E., Kirsh, S. R., Alexander, J. A., & Lowery, J. C. (2009). Fostering implementation of health services research findings into practice: A consolidated framework for advancing implementation science. *Implementation Science*, *4*(1), 1.

Gagnon, M. P., Pluye, P., Desmartis, M., Car, J., Pagliari, C., Labrecque, M., . . . Légaré, F. (2010). A systematic review of interventions promoting clinical information retrieval technology (CIRT) adoption by healthcare professionals. *International Journal of Medical Informatics*, *79*(10), 669–680.

Gardner, C. A., Acharya, T., & Yach, D. (2007). Technological and social innovation: A unifying new paradigm for global health. *Health Affairs*, *26*(4), 1052–1061.

Greenhalgh, T., Robert, G., Macfarlane, F., Bate, P., & Kyriakidou, O. (2004). Diffusion of innovations in service organizations: Systematic review and recommendations. *Milbank Quarterly*, *82*(4), 581–629.

Grol, R. P., Bosch, M. C., Hulscher, M. E., Eccles, M. P., & Wensing, M. (2007). Planning and studying improvement in patient care: The use of theoretical perspectives. *Milbank Quarterly*, *85*(1), 93–138.

Grossmann, C., Goolsby, W. A., Olsen, L., & McGinnis, J. M. (Eds.). (2011). *Engineering a learning healthcare system: A look at the future: Workshop summary*. Washington, DC: National Academies Press.

Guimón, J. (2013). Promoting university-industry collaboration in developing countries. *Policy Brief. The Innovation Policy Platform*, *1*(3), 1–12.

Gurses, A. P., & Xiao, Y. (2006). A systematic review of the literature on multidisciplinary rounds to design information technology. *Journal of the American Medical Informatics Association, 13*(3), 267–276.

HealthIT.gov. (2013). EHR incentives and certification. Retrieved from https://www.healthit.gov/providers-professionals/how-attain-meaningful-use

Hendricks, I. (2015). Africa: A hub for innovations in medical diagnostic solutions? Retrieved from http://www.howwemadeitinafrica.com/africa-a-hub-for-innovation-in-medical-diagnostic-solutions/

Herzlinger, R. E. (2006). Why innovation in health care is so hard. *Harvard Business Review.* Retrieved from https://hbr.org/2006/05/why-innovation-in-health-care-is-so-hard

Howitt, P., Darzi, A., Yang, G. Z., Ashrafian, H., Atun, R., Barlow, J., . . . Cooke, G. S. (2012). Technologies for global health. *The Lancet, 380*(9840), 507–535.

Johnson, K., Hays, C., Center, H., & Daley, C. (2004). Building capacity and sustainable prevention innovations: A sustainability planning model. *Evaluation and Program Planning, 27*(2), 135–149.

Joshi, A., Puricelli Perin, D. M., & Arora, M. (2013). Using portable health information kiosk to assess chronic disease burden in remote settings. *Rural Remote Health, 13*(2), 2279.

Keshavjee, K., Bosomworth, J., Copen, J., Lai, J., Kucukyazici, B., Lilani, R., & Holbrook, A. M. (2006). Best practices in EMR implementation: A systematic review. AMIA Annual Symposium Proceedings, 982.

Klein, K. J., Conn, A. B., & Sorra, J. S. (2001). Implementing computerized technology: An organizational analysis. *Journal of Applied Psychology, 86*(5), 811.

Klein, K. J., & Sorra, J. S. (1996). The challenge of innovation implementation. *Academy of Management Review, 21*(4), 1055–1080.

Kyratsis, Y., Ahmad, R., & Holmes, A. (2012). Making sense of evidence in management decisions: The role of research-based knowledge on innovation adoption and implementation in healthcare. Study protocol. *Implementation Science, 7*(1), 1.

Lehoux, P., Daudelin, G., Williams-Jones, B., Denis, J. L., & Longo, C. (2014). How do business model and health technology design influence each other? Insights from a longitudinal case study of three academic spin-offs. *Research Policy, 43*(6), 1025–1038.

Lehoux, P., Miller, F. A., & Daudelin, G. (2016). How does venture capital operate in medical innovation? *BMJ Innovations, 2*(3), 111–117.

Mansour, M., Mansour, J. B., & El Swesy, A. H. (2010). Scaling up proven public health interventions through a locally owned and sustained leadership development programme in rural Upper Egypt. *Human Resources for Health, 8*(1), 1.

McKesson. (2016). Fostering transformative innovation in healthcare. Retrieved from http://www.mckesson.com/documents/blog/innovation-framework-white-paper/

Mental Health Innovation Network. (2015). Collaborative on Health and Technology (CHaT). Retrieved from http://www.mhinnovation.net/innovations/collaborative-health-and-technology-chat#.WBylqsm7w-U

Michaelis, B., Stegmaier, R., & Sonntag, K. (2009). Affective commitment to change and innovation implementation behavior: The role of charismatic leadership and employees' trust in top management. *Journal of Change Management, 9*(4), 399–417.

Ministry of Health, Belize. (2013). BHIS: Belize health information system. Retrieved from http://health.gov.bz/www/attachments/article/169/BHISBooklet02.pdf

Morel, C. M., Acharya, T., Broun, D., Dangi, A., Elias, C., Ganguly, N. K., . . . Hotez, P. J. (2005). Health innovation networks to help developing countries address neglected diseases. *Science, 309*(5733), 401–404.

Ndlovu, K., Littman-Quinn, R., Park, E., Dikai, Z., & Kovarik, C. L. (2015). Scaling up a mobile telemedicine solution in Botswana: Keys to sustainability. *Front Public Health, 2*, 275.

Nutrition RapidSMS. (2014). Improving maternal and child health care with Project KiraMAMA—Burundi. Retrieved from https://nutritionrapidsms.wordpress.com/2014/09/25/improving-maternal-and-child-health-care-with-project-kiramama-burundi/

Omachonu, V. K., & Einspruch, N. G. (2010). Innovation in healthcare delivery systems: A conceptual framework. *The Innovation Journal, 15*(1), 1–20.

Proctor, E., Silmere, H., Raghavan, R., Hovmand, P., Aarons, G., Bunger, A., . . . Hensley, M. (2011). Outcomes for implementation research: Conceptual distinctions, measurement challenges, and research agenda. *Administration and Policy in Mental Health and Mental Health Services Research, 38*(2), 65–76.

Rogers, E. M. (2010). *Diffusion of innovations.* London, England: Simon & Schuster.

Simmons, R., & Shiffman, J. (2007). Scaling up health service innovations: A framework for action. *Scaling up Health Service Delivery,* 1–30 (P-23). *World Health Organization.* Retrieved from http://www .who.int/immunization/hpv/deliver/scalingup_health_service_delivery_who_2007.pdf#page=23

Startup Complete. (2016). MedRegis. Retrieved from http://startupcompete.co/startup-idea/it /medregis/41797

U.S. Agency for International Development (USAID). (2014). Mobile technology strengthens behavior change communication and referrals by community health workers for maternal, newborn, and child health in rural Afghanistan. Retrieved from https://www.usaid.gov/sites /default/files/documents/1864/WorldVisionORBrief.pdf

Vicente, K. (2010). *The human factor: Revolutionizing the way we live with technology.* Toronto, Canada: Random House of Canada.

West, M. A. (1990). The social psychology of innovation in groups. In M. A. West and J. L Farr (Eds.), *Innovation and creativity at work: Psychological and organizational strategies* (pp. 309–334). Chichester, UK: Wiley.

World Health Organization. (2005). World report on knowledge for better health: Strengthening health systems. *Bulletin of the World Health Organization, 83*(1), 77.

World Health Organization. (2013a). Blood pressure eReader. Retrieved from http://www.who.int /ehealth/resources/compendium_ehealth2013_1.pdf

World Health Organization. (2013b). ePharmacyNet system. Retrieved from http://www.who.int /ehealth/resources/compendium_ehealth2013_2.pdf

World Health Organization. (2015). WHO compendium of innovative health technologies for low resource settings, 2011–2014: Assistive devices, eHealth solutions, medical devices, other technologies, technologies for outbreaks.

World Health Organization. (n.d.). Health technology assessment. Retrieved from http://www.who .int/medical_devices/assessment/en/

Yamey, G. (2011). Scaling up global health interventions: A proposed framework for success. *PLoS Medicine, 8*(6), e1001049.

Yarbrough, A. K., & Smith, T. B. (2007). Technology acceptance among physicians: A new take on TAM. *Medical Care Research and Review, 64*(6), 650–672.

Yusof, M. M., Stergioulas, L., & Zugic, J. (2007). Health information systems adoption: Findings from a systematic review. *Studies in Health Technology and Informatics, 129*(1), 262.

Appendix A

Population Health Informatics Resources

Resource	Website
Agency for Healthcare Research and Quality	https://www.ahrq.gov
American Health Information Management Association	http://www.ahima.org
American Medical Informatics Association	https://www.amia.org
American National Standards Institute	https://www.ansi.org
American Nursing Informatics Association	https://www.ania.org
Centers for Disease Control and Prevention, Division of Health Informatics and Surveillance	https://www.cdc.gov/ophss/csels/dhis/
Centers for Disease Control and Prevention Electronic Laboratory Reporting	http://www.cdc.gov/elr/about.html
Centers for Medicare and Medicaid Services	https://www.cms.gov
Certification Commission for Health Information Technology	https://www.cchit.org
Clinical Data Interchange Standards Consortium	http://www.cdisc.org
Data.gov, Health	https://www.data.gov/health
eHealth Initiative	https://www.ehidc.org
European Federation for Medical Informatics	https://www.efmi.org

Global Standards Organization	http://hrmi.org/gso.htm
GS1 US	https://www.gs1us.org
Health Level Seven International	http://www.hl7.org
Health Resources and Services Administration	https://www.hrsa.gov
Healthcare Cost and Utilization Project	https://www.hcup-us.ahrq.gov
Healthcare Information and Management Systems Society	http://www.himss.org
Healthcare Information Technology Standards Panel	http://www.hitsp.org
International Medical Informatics Association	http://imia-medinfo.org/wp/
International Organization for Standardization	http://www.iso.org
Medical Expenditure Panel Survey	https://meps.ahrq.gov /mepsweb/
National Center for Health Statistics	https://www.cdc.gov/nchs/
National Committee for Vital and Health Statistics	https://www.ncvhs.hhs.gov/
National Informatics Centre, Government of India	http://www.nic.in
National Institute of Standards and Technology	https://www.nist.gov
National Library of Medicine, National Information Center on Health Services Research and Health Care Technology	https://www.nlm.nih.gov /hsrinfo/informatics.html
Office of the National Coordinator for Health Information Technology	https://www.healthit.gov /newsroom/about-onc
Pew Research Center	http://www.pewresearch.org
Substance Abuse and Mental Health Services Administration	https://www.samhsa.gov
Workgroup for Electronic Data Interchange	http://www.wedi.org

Appendix B

Acronyms

Chapter 1	**Emerging Need for Population Health Informatics**	
	Affordable Care Act	ACA
	American Medical Informatics Association	AMIA
	American Recovery and Reinvestment Act	ARRA
	Data, information, and knowledge	DIK
	Electronic health record	EHR
	Geographic information system	GIS
	Health information technology	HIT
	Health Information Technology for Economic and Clinical Health	HITECH
	Health management information system	HMIS
	Human-centered design	HCD
	Information and communication technology	ICT
	Population health	PopH
	Population health informatics	PopHI
	Public health informatics	PHI
	Public health surveillance	PHS
	Sustainable, Multi-sector, Accessible, Affordable, Reimbursable, Tailored	SMAART
Chapter 2	**Population Health Informatics Workforce, Competencies, and Training Programs**	
	Accreditation Council for Graduate Medical Education	ACGME
	American Medical Informatics Association	AMIA
	Association of Schools and Programs for Public Health	ASPPH
	Center for Health Workforce Studies	CHWS
	Centers for Disease Control and Prevention	CDC
	Council on Education for Public Health	CEPH
	Health information technology	HIT
	Information and communication technology	ICT
	International Medical Informatics Association	IMIA
	International Medical Informatics Association for Latin America and the Caribbean	IMIA-LAC
	Local health department	LHD

Application programming interface	API
Centers for Disease Control and Prevention	CDC
Chesapeake Regional Information System for our Patients	CRISP
Consolidated Clinical Document Architecture	C-CDA
Continuity of care document	CCD
Digital Imaging and Communications in Medicine	DICOM
Electronic health record	EHR
Extensible Markup Language	XML
Fast Healthcare Interoperability Resources	FHIR
Glycated hemoglobin	HbA1c
Health information exchange	HIE
Health Information Technology for Economic and Clinical Health	HITECH
Health Insurance Portability and Accountability Act	HIPAA
Health Level Seven	HL7
Hypertext Transfer Protocol	HTTP
Logical Observation Identifiers Names and Codes	LOINC
Low- and middle-income countries	LMICs
National Council for Prescription Drug Programs	NCPDP
National Trauma Data Standard	NTDS
Nursing Interventions Classification	NIC
Office of the National Coordinator for Health Information Technology	ONC
Open Systems Interconnection	OSI
Public Health Information Network's Vocabulary Access and Distribution System	PHIN VADS
Quality Reporting Document Architecture	QRDA
Reference Information Model	RIM
Reportable Conditions Mapping Table	RCMT
Representational state transfer	REST
Simple Object Access Protocol	SOAP
Single nucleotide polymorphism	SNP
Systematized Nomenclature of Medicine	SNOMED

Chapter 5   **Informatics in Population Health Surveillance**

Behavioral Risk Factor Surveillance System	BRFSS
Centers for Disease Control and Prevention	CDC
Centers for Medicare and Medicaid Services	CMS
Clinical Quality Measures	CQMs
Council of State and Territorial Epidemiologists	CSTE
Department of Health and Mental Hygiene	DOHMH
Electronic health record	EHR
Electronic laboratory reporting	ELR
Global Public Health Intelligence Network	GPHIN
Health Information Technology for Economic and Clinical Health	HITECH
Health Level 7	HL7
Institute of Medicine	IOM

Laboratory information system   LIS
Low- and middle-income countries   LMICs
mHealth Evidence Reporting and Assessment   mERA
mHealth Technical Evidence Review Group   mTERG
Mobile App Rating Scale   MARS
Mobile health   mHealth
National Institutes of Health   NIH
Operating system   OS
Personal digital assistant   PDA
Picture archiving and communication system   PACS
Short Message Service   SMS
World Health Organization   WHO

Chapter 12   **The Economic Value of Informatics Applications in Population Health**

American Recovery and Reinvestment Act   ARRA
Chronic obstructive pulmonary disease   COPD
Contingent Valuation Method   CVM
Electronic medical record   EMR
Information and communication technology   ICT
National Institute for Occupational Safety and Health   NIOSH
Willingness to pay   WTP

Chapter 13   **Privacy, Confidentiality, Security, and Ethics**

Fair information practices   FIPs
Healthcare Information and Management Systems Society   HIMSS
Health Insurance Portability and Accountability Act   HIPAA
Information and communication technology   ICT
Personal health information   PHI
Privacy by Design   PbD

Chapter 14   **Innovations and Sustainability in Population Health Technologies**

Consolidated Framework for Implementation Research   CFIR
Health technology assessment   HTA
Information and communication technology   ICT
Low- and middle-income countries   LMIC
Population health informatics   PopHI
Portable health information kiosk   PHIK
Public–private partnership   PPP
Sustainable, Multi-sector, Accessible, Affordable, Reimbursable, Tailored   SMAART
United Nations Educational, Scientific and Cultural Organization   UNESCO
World Health Organization   WHO

Glossary

A

Accountable care organizations (ACOs) Healthcare organizations consisting of a group of doctors and healthcare facilities who come together to provide a more coordinated care to Medicare patients, where payments are directly linked to quality metrics and cost of care.

Activities of daily living A set of indicators reflecting six daily, routine activities—eating, bathing, dressing, toileting, walking, and continence—that individuals are expected to perform without assistance. It is used to classify individuals based on their long-term care needs.

Admission, discharge, and transfer A system utilized by health facilities for tracking patients through the clinical course of hospital arrival, admission, and/or transfer, discharge, or death.

Affordable Care Act A U.S. federal law enacted by President Obama on March 23, 2010, that provides comprehensive healthcare reforms.

Agency for Healthcare Research and Quality (AHRQ) The health services research arm of the U.S. Department of Health and Human Services (DHHS) that specializes in key healthcare research areas including quality improvement and patient safety, outcomes and effectiveness of care, clinical practice and technology assessment, and healthcare organization and delivery systems.

American Medical Informatics Association (AMIA) A U.S.-based professional organization consisting of a large body of experts in the field of informatics with the goal of developing informatics tools, standards, and guidelines to support patient care, research, and education.

American Recovery and Reinvestment Act of 2009 (ARRA) An economic stimulus package signed into law by President Obama on February 17, 2009, consisting of provisions for federal tax relief, unemployment and welfare benefits, and infrastructure spending on various sectors.

American Society for Testing and Materials (ASTM) An international standards organization that develops and publishes voluntary consensus technical standards for a variety of materials, products, systems, and services.

Anatomical Therapeutic Chemical (ATC) Classification System A system for classifying the active ingredients contained in medications based on their chemical and pharmacological effect on the body.

Application programming interface (API) A set of tools used for building software applications that defines the interaction between software components.

B

Behavioral Risk Factor Surveillance System (BRFSS) A national telephone-based survey conducted by the Centers for Disease Control and Prevention to collect data on behavioral risk factors for various health outcomes in the United States.

C

Certified Health IT Product List (CHPL) A website of the Office of the National Coordinator for Health Information Technology showing the complete list of certified health information technology products.

Chesapeake Regional Information System for our Patients (CRISP) A nonprofit organization serving as Maryland's state-designated health information exchange (HIE), currently serving Maryland and the District of Columbia.

Clinical decision support system A health information technology system that supports physicians and other health professionals in patient diagnosis, management, and decision making.

Clinical quality measures (CQMs) Consists of tools for measuring and tracking the quality of health services across health facilities.

Cognitive fit theory A theory developed by Iris Vessey that emphasizes that the way a task is presented largely influences the performance of the users in problem solving.

Cognitive systems engineering (CSE) An all-inclusive systems design that incorporates cognitive, social, and organizational psychology in designing systems through an understanding of human cognitive processes.

Cognitive task analysis (CTA) A set of techniques used for assessing the various mental processes, skills, and thinking patterns needed to solve a given set of tasks.

Community-based participatory research (CBPR) A partnership approach to conducting research where the research team effectively integrates community members and organizational representatives throughout the research process to facilitate decision making.

Community health workers Frontline public health workers who interact directly with community members, linking them to needed care and health services.

Computer-supported cooperative work (CSCW) A community of behavioral researchers and system builders at the intersection of collaborative behaviors and technology.

Consolidated Clinical Document Architecture (C-CDA) Set of standards developed by Health Level 7 that defines the structure of specific medical records including progress notes and discharge summaries to facilitate data exchange among providers.

Consolidated Framework for Implementation Research (CFIR) A theoretical framework that provides standard constructs that can be applied across the spectrum of implementation research.

Contingent Valuation Method (CVM) A method of conducting cost–benefit analysis and environmental impact assessment.

Continuity of care documents (CCDs) Facilitate exchange of patient medical information between providers during transfers, thereby enabling seamless flow in patient care.

Council of State and Territorial Epidemiologists (CSTE) A nonprofit organization working to advance capacity for practicing epidemiologists by providing them with information, education, and developmental support in a wide range of areas.

Critical decision method (CDM) A method of conducting cognitive task analysis in which semi-structured interviews are applied to generate information on how experts engage in their decision-making process.

Current Procedural Terminology (CPT) A set of medical codes used in reporting data related to medical, surgical, and diagnostic procedures to providers, payers, and regulatory bodies.

D

Data A set of facts, figures, and statistics collected together for reference or analysis.

Department of Health and Mental Hygiene (DOHMH) One of several local health departments across states in the United States responsible for developing and implementing programs to prevent disease, promote health, and protect the public from health problems and hazards.

Diagnostic and Statistical Manual of Mental Disorders (DSM) A comprehensive list of standards developed by the American Psychological Association for classifying mental disorders.

Digital Imaging and Communications in Medicine (DICOM) A standard for referencing data or using information in medical imaging.

E

Electronic health record (EHR) A systematic collection of patient and population-health records stored in a digital format.

Electronic laboratory reporting An automated system of sending laboratory reports to public health agencies, which fast-tracks the reporting of notifiable conditions.

Emergency department A hospital department responsible for the provision of medical and surgical care to patients who need immediate care.

Extensible Markup Language (XML) A meta-language used to create other languages. It facilitates text, data, and graphic exchange between applications and operating systems.

F

Fair information practices (FIPs) A set of standards governing the collection and use of personal data and addressing privacy issues.

Family Educational Rights and Privacy Act (FERPA) A federal law aimed at protecting the privacy of student records.

Fast Healthcare Interoperability Resources (FHIR) A standard for exchanging healthcare information electronically. It represents granular clinical concepts.

Federal Communications Commission (FCC) An agency of the U.S. government responsible for regulating interstate and international communications by radio, television, wire, satellite, and cable across U.S. states and territories.

Federal Food, Drug, and Cosmetic Act (FD&C Act) Legislation empowering the Food and Drug Administration of the United States to oversee the safety of foods, drugs, and cosmetics.

G

Generalized anxiety disorder A mental condition characterized by excessive anxiety and a tendency to continually worry.

Generic Product Identifier (GPI) A classification system consisting of 14 characters identifying a drug from its therapeutic use down to its final interchangeable product, irrespective of the manufacturer.

Geographic information system (GIS) A location-oriented computer system designed to capture data at various points on the earth's surface using mapping features.

Geographic visualization A set of techniques used in analyzing geospatial data (data possessing geographic positioning information such as road networks or satellite images).

Global positioning system (GPS) A satellite system that provides location and time data to a GPS receiver anywhere on the earth's surface.

Global Public Health Intelligence Network (GPHIN) An early-warning system developed by Health Canada in collaboration with the World Health Organization to provide real-time information on disease outbreaks and other related occurrences that impact global public health.

Glycated hemoglobin A form of hemoglobin primarily used to measure the 3-month average plasma glucose concentration.

H

Health information exchange Transfer of healthcare-related data among providers, facilities, and governmental organizations according to nationally accepted standards.

Health information National Trends Survey (HINTS) A cross-sectional survey sponsored by the National Cancer Institute that collects data about the use of cancer-related information by the U.S. public.

Health information technology Utilizing computer systems in facilitating the transfer and exchange of health information across key players including patients, providers, and payers.

Health Information Technology for Economic and Clinical Health (HITECH) Act A legislation enacted in 2009 to promote the adoption and meaningful use of health information technology in the United States.

Health Insurance Portability and Accountability Act (HIPAA) A federal law signed in 1996 that protects health insurance coverage for workers and families, and mandates the maintenance of strict standards in electronic health record transactions among providers and payers.

Health Level 7 (HL7) Set of international data standards guiding the exchange of clinical and administrative data between healthcare systems.

Health management information system (HMIS) A system of data collection that supports management, planning, and decision-making activities across all arms of a health organization.

Health risk assessment A screening tool designed to provide a tailored assessment of one's health status, estimate the level of health risk, and provide feedback recommendations for behavior modification.

Health technology assessment (HTA) A systematic evaluation of the design, development, and impacts of health technology.

Healthcare Common Procedure Coding System (HCPCS) A set of healthcare procedure codes based on the American Medical Association's Current Procedural Terminology (CPT).

Healthcare Information and Management Systems Society (HIMSS) A not-for-profit organization that provides a platform for collaboration among stakeholders in healthcare IT, using advocacy and education with the goal of improving healthcare delivery.

Human Development Index (HDI) A composite statistic that includes life expectancy, education, and per capita income indicators. It is used to rank countries into four tiers of human development.

Hypertext Transfer Protocol (HTTP) A set of rules that govern how graphics, images, sounds, text, and multimedia are transferred on the Internet, as well as the actions needed by web browsers and servers in this process.

I

Information and communication technology (ICT) A broad array of electronic tools and devices used in processing and disseminating information, including, but not limited to, radios, televisions, cellular phones, computers, satellites, and videoconferencing.

Information visualization (InfoVis) Communicating abstract data by using interactive visual interfaces to enhance understanding/cognition.

Institute of Medicine A nonprofit organization working independently of the government to provide evidence-based policy recommendations for public health.

Integrated Services Digital Network (ISDN) A set of communication standards for simultaneous digital transmission of voice, video, data, and other network services over telephone networks.

International Classification of Diseases Consists of global health information standards used in reporting morbidity and mortality data and other health trends.

International Classification of Primary Care A method of classification for primary care encounters reflecting three elements: reason for encounter, diagnosis, and process of care.

K

Knowledge to Action (K2A) Framework A conceptual framework designed to facilitate effective knowledge translation while delivering evidence-based interventions.

L

Laboratory information system A software system used in recording, storing, and managing laboratory records for clinical laboratories.

Logical Observation Identifiers Names and Codes (LOINC) Set of comprehensive standards used in identifying and classifying medical laboratory observations.

M

mHealth Evidence Reporting and Assessment (mERA) A checklist developed by the mHealth Technical Evidence Review Group to improve the reporting of mHealth interventions.

mHealth Technical Evidence Review Group (mTERG) A working group convened by the World Health Organization consisting of global experts at the intersection of mHealth and reproductive, maternal, newborn, and child health, across research and program implementation foci, who work to establish methodologies to identify evidence-based mHealth strategies.

Mobile App Rating Scale (MARS) A five-point rating scale used by researchers, developers, and health professionals in evaluating mobile-based applications based on quality, impact, and functionality.

Model for Assessment of Telemedicine Applications (MAST) A framework that guides the design of telemedicine applications.

Morbidity and Mortality Weekly Report A weekly epidemiological digest published by the Centers for Disease Control and Prevention that provides updated public health information and recommendations on essential topics.

N

National Ambulatory Medical Care Survey (NAMCS) A national survey designed to assess and evaluate information on the use of ambulatory medical care services in the United States.

National Center for Health Statistics (NCHS) A principal agency of the U.S. Federal Statistical System responsible for providing statistical information to inform health policy decisions.

National Council for Prescription Drug Programs (NCPDP) A not-for-profit standards development organization composed of major sectors of the pharmacy service industries.

National Electronic Injury Surveillance System (NEISS) A national probability sample of hospitals and emergency departments to collect data on consumer product–related injuries occurring in the United States.

National Health and Nutrition Examination Survey (NHANES) A national survey designed to assess the health and nutritional status of adults and children in the United States.

National Health Interview Survey (NHIS) A national survey designed to track health status, healthcare access, and progress toward achieving U.S. health objectives.

National Institute for Occupational Safety and Health (NIOSH) An agency of the United States responsible for research and recommendations for the prevention of work-related injury and illness.

National Institute of Standards and Technology (NIST) A nonregulatory arm of the U.S. Department of Commerce that specializes in innovations toward improving measurement science and use of standards in science and technology.

National Institutes of Health (NIH) The primary agency of the U.S. government responsible for biomedical and health research.

National Notifiable Diseases Surveillance System (NNDSS) A nationwide collaboration that enables all levels of public health—local, state, territorial, federal, and international—to share notifiable disease-related health information used in monitoring and preventing the occurrence of notifiable diseases.

National Quality Forum (NQF) A nonprofit organization that promotes patient protections and healthcare quality through measurement and public reporting.

National Trauma Data Standard (NTDS) Defines the data elements that make up the National Trauma Data Bank (NTDB).

Notice of Proposed Rule Making (NPRM) A public notice issued by law when modifications need to be made to U.S. government legislation.

Null hypothesis A statistic indicating that there is no significant difference between specified populations; any observed difference is due to sampling or experimental error.

Nursing Interventions Classification (NIC) A classification system describing the activities and processes involved in creating a nursing plan.

Nursing Outcomes Classification (NOC) A classification system describing patient outcomes to evaluate nursing care.

O

Open Systems Interconnection (OSI) A reference model for how applications can communicate over a network.

Operating system Major software present in a computer that manages the memory and processes, as well as all other software and hardware.

P

Personal digital assistant (PDA) A handheld device that functions as a personal information manager and supports an array of computing features including telephone/fax, Internet, and networking features.

Picture archiving and communication system (PACS) A healthcare technology used for capturing, storing, retrieving, distributing, and presenting medical images.

Population health (PopH) Holistic outcomes of a group of individuals who share common characteristics.

Prescription benefit management (PBM) Serves as a third-party administrator of prescription drug programs; responsible for contracting and negotiating discounts with pharmacies and paying prescription drug claims.

Public health informatics (PHI) Application of information science and technology to public health research, education, and practice.

Public Health Information Network's Vocabulary Access and Distribution System (PHIN VADS) A vocabulary system with a wide variety of data for use in both public health and clinical practice.

Public health surveillance A continuous process of systematic data collection, analysis, and interpretation as a means of providing evidence-based information for population health decision making.

Public–private partnerships (PPPs) Working relationships formed by cooperative arrangement between one or more public and private sectors, typically of a long-term nature, to achieve common project goals.

Q

Quality Reporting Document Architecture (QRDA) A subset of Health Level 7 standards for representing information on healthcare quality measurements.

R

Reference Information Model (RIM) Component of the Health Level 7 set of standards that provides a representation of healthcare workflows.

Reportable Conditions Mapping Table (RCMT) Set of standards that provides mappings between reportable conditions and their associated LOINC laboratory tests and SNOMED results.

Representational State Transfer (REST) Service for facilitating interoperability between computer systems on the Internet.

S

Safety-enhanced design (SED) A multidisciplinary process that integrates user feedback during the design and development of systems.

Short Message Service (SMS) A mobile-based service for exchanging messages of up to 160 characters among smartphones, cellular phones, and personal digital assistants.

Simple Object Access Protocol (SOAP) Instructions that guide communication between applications from different operating systems, technologies, or programming languages.

Single nucleotide polymorphism (SNP) Variation in a nucleotide at a specific point in the genome leading to a degree of genetic differences within a population.

Social determinants of health The overall set of conditions in which people are born, grow, live, work, and age (including education, employment, socioeconomic status, and physical environment) that significantly affects their health.

Social network analysis (SNA) The process of mapping relationships between groups of people, organizations, computers, or other connected information.

Specific, Measurable, Achievable, Relevant, and Time-bound (SMART) A mnemonic that provides a set of objectives to be met in order to implement effective tasks or projects.

Standardization The process of implementing and developing technical standards based on the consensus of different parties including firms, users, interest groups, standards organizations, and governments.

Strengths, weaknesses, opportunities, and threats (SWOT) analysis A planning and evaluation strategy that assesses four major elements of a project or business venture: strengths, weaknesses, opportunities, and threats.

Systematized Nomenclature of Medicine (SNOMED) A set of standards that represents clinical terminology used by physicians in the process of exchanging or transferring health information.

T

Task-knowledge structures (TKS) Models of users' domain tasks that are created in the process of system design as a way of matching the user's field of knowledge in their domain to the knowledge required to interact efficiently with a system that supports their work.

Two one-sided test of equivalence (TOST) The TOST test uses Student's test to check the equivalence between the means of two samples.

U

United Nations Educational, Scientific and Cultural Organization (UNESCO) The agency of the United Nations that promotes international collaboration through education, science, and culture in global settings.

U.S. Department of Health and Human Services (DHHS) A cabinet-level department of the U.S. federal government geared toward protecting and enhancing health and human services.

W

Wearable health monitoring systems (WHMSs) Innovative technology-enabled devices used in monitoring body parameters such as heart rate or blood pressure.

Willingness to pay (WTP) An elucidation of the economic theory of value that represents the maximum amount an individual is willing to pay for a product or service.

Y

Youth Risk Behavioral Surveillance System (YRBSS) A national survey of adolescent health risk and health protective behaviors, such as smoking, drinking, drug use, diet, and physical activity, conducted biennially by the Centers for Disease Control and Prevention.

Index

Note: Page numbers followed by *f* indicate figures; those followed by *b* indicate boxes; those followed by *t* indicate tables.

T

Task-knowledge structures (TKS), 202
Technical interoperability, 94–95
Technical security, 275
Technological factors, 275
Technology and health care, 10–12, 15
Technology-based interventions, 270
Technology diffusion patterns, 277
Technology literacy, 273
Telecommunications Industry Association
(TIA), 286
Telehealth
  adoption and sustainability of, 252–253
    fit with patient characteristics, 252
    patient participation, 252
    project design strategy, 252–253
    time constraints, 252
  barriers to implementation of, 248–249,
    250–251t
    financial barriers, 249
    legislation, 249
    organizational barriers, 248
    regulatory issues, 249
    technology perceptions, 248
    technology-related barriers, 248
  benefits, 246–247, 246f
    access to healthcare providers, 247
    enhanced continuity of care, 246
    enhanced patient monitoring, 247
    preventive services, 247
    reduced health costs, 247
    specialty access, 247
  definition, 243
  delivery, mechanisms of, 245–246
    interactive monitoring, 246
    self-monitoring approach, 245
    store-and-forward approach, 245
  driver of, 243
  evaluation, 253–254, 254t
  factors influencing, 244
  future of, 254–256, 255b, 257f
  projects, 257
  video conferencing strategies, 245
Telemedicine, cloud computing in, 173
Temporal (time) component, 24
Tennessee Valley Authority, 328
Terminologies, in healthcare settings,
  100–101
Terminology standards
  current use of, 102
  in health care, 101
Test set performance, 153

Theoretical consistency, 85
Theory of health information, 206
Think aloud protocol, 222
TIA. *See* Telecommunications Industry
  Association (TIA)
Timeliness, of data, 86
TKS. *See* Task-knowledge structures (TKS)
TOST. *See* Two one-sided test of equivalence
  (TOST)
Trade-off between income and health status,
  326–327
Training set, 153
Transmission Control Protocol/Internet
  Protocol (TCP/IP), 95
Trauma Registry Data Submission, 98
Trust-based security framework, 292
Tuning, 153
Twitter, 10, 133, 156
  word cloud, 157f
Two one-sided test of equivalence (TOST), 136
Type I error probability, 150–151
Type II error probability, 150

U

UB form. *See* Uniform Billing (UB) form
UB04/UB92 (Uniform Billing) form, 80
Unauthorized access, 337
Uncertainty visualization, 185
Underfitting, 151, 152f, 153f
UNESCO. *See* United Nations Educational,
  Scientific and Cultural Organization
  (UNESCO)
Uniform Billing (UB) form, 80
United Nations Educational, Scientific and
  Cultural Organization (UNESCO), 363
Universities, training programs in PHIs,
  56–58t
Unstructured content format, 164
U.S. Bureau of Labor Statistics, 51t
U.S. Centers for Disease Control and
  Prevention (CDC), 13t, 32, 102, 167
U.S. Department of Health and Human
  Services (DHHS), 173
U.S. HITECH Act of 2009. *See* Health
  Information Technology for Economic
  and Clinical Health (HITECH) Act
U.S. National Cancer Institute, 264
U.S. National Center for Health Statistics
  (NCHS), 121, 167
U.S. Veterans Health Administration (VHA),
  94

TERRENCE DES PRES

PRAISES
&
DISPRAISES

Poetry and Politics,
the 20th Century

PENGUIN BOOKS

PENGUIN BOOKS
Published by the Penguin Group
Viking Penguin, a division of Penguin Books USA Inc.,
40 West 23rd Street, New York, New York 10010, U.S.A.
Penguin Books Ltd, 27 Wrights Lane,
London W8 5TZ, England
Penguin Books Australia Ltd, Ringwood,
Victoria, Australia
Penguin Books Canada Ltd, 2801 John Street,
Markham, Ontario, Canada L3R 1B4
Penguin Books (N.Z.) Ltd, 182–190 Wairau Road,
Auckland 10, New Zealand

Penguin Books Ltd, Registered Offices:
Harmondsworth, Middlesex, England

First published in the United States of America by
Viking Penguin, a division of Penguin Books USA Inc. 1988
Published in Penguin Books 1989

1   3   5   7   9   10   8   6   4   2

LIBRARY OF CONGRESS CATALOGING IN PUBLICATION DATA
Des Pres, Terrence.
Praises & dispraises: poetry and politics, the 20th century/
Terrence Des Pres.
p.   cm.
Bibliography: p.
ISBN 0 14 01.2760 7
1. Poetry—20th century—History and criticism.   2. Poetry—
Political aspects.   3. Politics and literature.   I. Title.
II. Title   Praises and dispraises.
PN1081.D47   1989
809.1'9358—dc20   89-33633

Printed in the United States of America
Set in Galliard
Designed by Victoria Hartman

For Liz

What looks the strongest has outlived its term.
The future lies with what's affirmed from under.

—Seamus Heaney, "The Haw Lantern"

Acknowledgments

These acknowledgments are based on notes and comments made by Terrence Des Pres prior to his death.

The following individuals provided aid and encouragement during the writing of *Praises & Dispraises:* Carolyn Forché, Paul Mariani, Reg Gibbons, Peter Balakian, and especially Morton Bloomfield. For assistance with individual chapters the author acknowledges: Howard Iger (Brecht); Patricia Hampl and the writers at the Loft in Minneapolis (McGrath); the feminist reading group at Colgate University (Rich). Special thanks to George Hudson for help in moments of computer crisis and to Helen Kebabian for proofreading. For the care he gave this manuscript the author is grateful to Dan Frank at Viking.

Contents

Contents

Prolog

This book has been written for men and women who care about poetry and read it first of all for personal reasons. Such readers, I would like to think, know well enough the violent spirit of our century, and exactly for *this* reason expect at least one kind of language to hold its own against the grim disquiet. If they value it further as a means to poise and self-possession, they do not ask too much of a serious art. Poetry helps us seize our being-in-the-world, the better to enjoy, the better to endure. In this book, accordingly, poetry is prized and spoken of, in Kenneth Burke's fine phrase, as "equipment for living."[1]

About the violence of our century, its lethal strife and endless misery, there seems little doubt that politics has played a central, and too often a ruinous, part. Less clear is the impact of political havoc on poetry, an affliction put this way by Czeslaw Milosz:[2]

> The first movement is singing,
> A free voice, filling mountains and valleys.
> The first movement is joy,
> But it is taken away.

The poetic impulse—hope's proof and finest messenger—arises to fulfill itself in praises and in blessings. Now it finds more exercise in cursing, and Milosz goes on, in another poem, with dispraise of his own:[3]

> We learned so much, this you know well:
> how, gradually, what could not be taken away
> is taken. People, countrysides.

And the heart does not die when one thinks it should,
we smile, there is tea and bread on the table.

That Milosz speaks from a time and place as strange to us as Baltic
woodlands or the streets of occupied Warsaw, that he writes as a witness
to some of the century's worst occasions, makes him not the less but
rather the *more* familiar to us—an unusual circumstance, to say the least.
Yet Milosz is not alone in this oddity. The great Russians, Akhmatova,
Mandelshtam, Tsvetayeva, and Pasternak, lived and wrote amid terrible
upheavals; now they are regarded by us as the patron saints of poetry
in dark times. Others—Neruda and Vallejo, for example—have been
with us some time already, and more recently Milosz's peer in Poland,
Zbigniew Herbert, has been taken up with high esteem, along with
many another poet from traditions not our own—Vasko Popa and Miroslav Holub in Slavic, for example, or Seferis and Ritsos in Greek; nor
do we forget the example of Nazim Hikmet, who from his Turkish cell
wrote prison poems that are among the finest of that twentieth-century
genre. These poets come from places burdened by political torment but
blessed with zealous care for poetry; and now they have gained an
important hearing among us despite the uncertain dignity of translation.
If we should wonder why their voices are valued so highly, it's that they
are acquainted with the night, the nightmare spectacle of politics especially. The sense of familiarity got from their poems resides in an
undervoice, an emerging consciousness in common that we, too, are
beginning to share.

Not that most of us in North America (unless black or female or
native American) find ourselves caught in history's path; not, at least,
in directly damaging ways. The point is rather that now a wretchedness
of global extent has come into view; the spectacle of man-created suffering is *known*, observed with such constancy that a new shape of
knowing invades the mind. From South Africa, here is André Brink's
sense of it:[4]

> One may ask: is there anything new in this condition? Has
> there not always been suffering and injustice and oppression?
> Of course. But until recently the condition of the world was
> not wholly intolerable—because the full measure of the truth
> was not known. . . . Mass communications have propagated
> these events around the world; and "no man can claim that he

has not personally SEEN the intolerable condition of the world."

The miracles of modern communications—the instant replay of events on TV, the surfeit of images provided by photojournalists, the detailed accounts of inhumanity given by survivors of all kinds, and then too the documentation from organizations like Amnesty International and Americas Watch, every page of it open to those who would know what can be known—all these sources combine with the cold-war order of things to make a uniquely twentieth-century sense of reality, a consciousness that began in the wake of World War Two with the film footage, miles of it, that gave us our first window on "the world." That shock of recognition, that climate of atrocity, is now our daily fare.

"The real," said Henry James, is that which "we cannot not know."[5] With his imagination of disaster, James was on the right track but could hardly guess the enormity of things to come. Thanks to the technological expansion of consciousness, we cannot not know the extent of political torment; and in truth it may be said that what others suffer, we behold. If the mechanical reproduction of art diminishes art's aura, as Walter Benjamin argued, he might have said further that the media's reproduction of politics demystifies the exercise of power and makes it into a spectacle that is immediate, encompassing, supercharged with shame and disgust and also, of course, with dread inspired by the tyranny of the Bomb. It's at this point and in this way that the world is too much with us.

The press of the real is problematic for all of us but especially for poets because their art requires attention to humanity's sad still music that now, amid the awful nonstop roar of things, is hard to make out. There is the need for a diction that won't be outflanked by events, and the further need to support, through the stamina of language, the trials of spirit in adversity—a struggle that is often appalling, painful merely to observe. Among poets alert to these conditions, Charles Simic is exactly on target in his "Notes on Poetry and History," written in 1984:[6]

If not for the invention of photography and motion pictures, one could perhaps still think of history in the manner of nineteenth-century painting and Soviet Revolutionary posters. There you meet the idealized masses and their heroic leaders leading them with chests bared and sleeves rolled up. They are marching with radiant faces and flags unfurled through the carnage of the battlefield. The dying young man in the arms of his steadfast comrades has the half-veiled gaze of the visionary. We know that he has glimpsed the future of humanity, and that it looks good. Unfortunately for all concerned, people started taking pictures. I remember, for example, a black-and-white photograph of a small child running toward the camera on a street of collapsing buildings in a city being fire-bombed. The smoke and the flames are about to overtake her. She's wearing a party dress, perhaps a birthday party dress. One is also told that it is not known where and when the picture had been taken.

With a shift in the means of representation, a radical change occurs in the way the world is known. Epic fantasy gives way to stark realism. And now politics is everywhere and hopeless. The photo of the luckless girl is an image of ubiquitous suffering; and in the gaze of the dying hero we behold the end of faith in the future. The myth of Progress has run its course and failed; now no political agenda, East or West, can appeal to the old triumphalism. No glory at some future date, or plan of greatest happiness to come, can dismiss the actualities of power taking its toll. The agony of third-world peoples is with us; terrorism is with us, death squads and torture; and an arms trade boldly supplying the whole of the world with weapons, that too is with us. None of it is going to go away tomorrow, and when this recognition arrives, as indeed it has, politics begins to be seen less as a means than as an end in itself—a condition, in fact, that the human spirit and therefore poetry must take into account.

Politics, then, as the play of impersonal force disrupting personal life; and politics, therefore, as a primary ground of misfortune. Taken to its tragic extreme, this kind of experience is the matter of *Antigone*, a drama of selfhood beset by the state, perhaps also of poetry hemmed in by political power. I therefore take Sophocles as my starting point; and here, too, I align politics with "world" and poetry with the powers of "earth." Moreover, if political experience is felt as a pressure, an intrusion of "the real" for those who absorb its impact, Wallace Stevens' notion of "a violence from within that protects us from a violence without" needs remarking. Then we can go directly to Yeats, whose revival of bardic practice illustrates "the scene of poetry" as I observe it in these pages—namely, as the poet in tribal relation to his or her audience through the force of the poem's occasion.

I shall not argue that all poets embrace a bardic protocol, but only that those studied here—Yeats, Thomas McGrath, and Adrienne Rich especially, but Brecht and Breyten Breytenbach as well—take up, and put to unique use, an ancient institution most accessible in its Irish example, an example long famous, or rather infamous, in the eyes of its English antagonists:[7]

> There is amongst the Irishe a certen kind of people Called Bardes which are to them in stead of Poets whose profession is to sett fourthe the praises and dispraises of menne in their Poems and Rhymes . . .

That was Edmund Spenser's view in 1596, as the British took bloody measures to colonize Ireland and met, thanks to bardic incitements, with a resistance that simply would not die. What this tradition meant in Spenser's time, and what it might entail for poets today, is directly the matter of this book, habits of voice that reach from antiquity into the present and embrace a political scale from Yeats's reactionary bitterness to the radical feminism of Rich. I am after rites of poetic address that emerge when poets and their tribes become embattled. Of course, the poet must have a tribe, an audience; on this condition, by no means common in our time, depends the poet's will to speak *for* and *against*.

In the late years of a discouraging century, the problems poets face are multiple, deeply troubling, and not to be solved by a single idea of the poet's office. The notion of bardic practice, however, helps make sense of relations between poetry and politics more generally. Also to be gained is an outside vantage on the situation of poetry in America, much of it still Emersonian in spirit, still enamored of self, nature, and escape to worlds elsewhere. Insofar as poets stay shut in those imperatives, the results are less than sufficient to hard times. Poetry that evades our being-in-the-world affords no happy fortitude, no language to live by, gifts that have always been the poet's job. At very least, then, the poets studied in this book provide a variety of hopeful examples, not only of an art taking place in the world, but also of the ways in which politics becomes a challenge to, and an occasion for, renewal in American poetics.

Finally, a few words about the role of critics. There has been, recently, a remarkable surge in critical theory, and along with it solid studies—Jameson's *The Political Unconscious*, for example—of politics in the case of fiction. For poetry, on the other hand, there is as yet, in America, no poetics equal to the import of politics in language or in life. All the more reason, therefore, to be glad for Kenneth Burke, whose work is as instructive now as it was when, during my student days, I first encountered his *Attitudes Toward History*, his *Philosophy of Literary Form*, and the *Grammars*. For I thought then, and still do, that in Burke's notion of language as symbolic language is room for politics and as well as for poetry's role in the world. I find useful his way of melding Marx and Freud no less than his alignment of tragedy with social order generally. In particular, I have relied on Burke's notions that "poetic forms are symbolic structures designed to equip us for confronting given historical or personal situations";[8] that formal functions include the poem's occasion; and that the "dramatistic" approach, which takes ritual drama as the model for poetic form in action, best suits the problems of poetry in relation to political experience.

In my own prose I have kept to a style that is aware of, but that declines to employ, the vocabularies of various criticisms now in ascendance. Ordinary language, open to the formalities of bardic tradition, has been my mainstay. I have, however, kept in view the feminist approach to poetry. Feminism's way of connecting the personal and the political is useful. So is its alertness to power and its claim that patriarchal order has perjured institutions generally, not least the study of literature. Insofar as bardic practice has begun to be active again in poetry, its foremost exercise—the poet summoning his or her tribe—is likely to be with embattled groups, women first of all. That Antigone is our sister must now, I think, be conceded.

· ONE ·

POLITICAL
INTRUSION

·I·

Creon's Decree

Terror is the feeling which arrests the mind in the
presence of whatsoever is grave and constant in human
sufferings and unites it with the secret cause.
—Stephen Dedalus[1]

In the beginning, what can be further from politics than Antigone's
grief? Her pain is hers alone. She tries to share it with her sister,
but Ismene is afraid. Creon, after all, has issued a decree. Guards have
been posted and the dead man can't be touched. Even so, a brother
must be buried and Antigone is determined to do it; nothing else matters, not the decree, not the fact that Polynices died attacking the city.
This is a family affair, an obligation to the dead, but certainly it's not a
public issue. Challenging Creon is not part of Antigone's plan. There
is no plan, but only a passion compounded of reverence and love. Therefore she goes out to bury her brother. Birds must not pick his eyes.
Some gesture of blessing there must be. That a king has ruled otherwise
is nothing to her.

It becomes something, however, and reasons of state preempt the
heart's purpose. From the moment Creon puts forth his decree, Antigone's behavior becomes a public issue, with consequences not intrinsic
to her life but that follow nonetheless. For her the springs of action are
interior, while for him they are public and expedient. Creon imposes
his will upon others, but believes that he acts for the good of the *polis*.
Thebes has weathered an attack and order needs restoring. Heroes must
be praised, betrayers cursed. Above all, leadership must demonstrate
control. Creon has only just become king—"the new man for the new
day"—and his authority needs sealing with a sign of his power. Thus
Creon orders a funeral with honor for Eteocles, who died defending

the city, and proclaims that Polynices, who led the attack, shall be left unburied:

> carrion for the birds and dogs to tear,
> an obscenity for the citizens to behold![2]

That is the decree. It is an arbitrary act; but as a law backed up by force it carries the weight of necessity. To the city it's an insult, and to the gods as well. But the stakes are treason and defense, issues anyone in power might exploit, and Creon is no exception. Therefore the dead man rots in public view.

In confrontation, the protagonists in *Antigone* are slowly pushed to extremes by a situation overwhelming them both. Under pressure Creon becomes more and more the tyrant. Antigone grows heroic but also fanatical. Thus does character reveal itself in adversity. But something larger than a contest of wills is at work. At the outset power is exercised, then challenged; and as the drama gains momentum the increasingly irrational logic of power begins to determine much, perhaps all, that happens thereafter. In political tragedy, terror's "secret cause" is the power—the mystery—of politics itself. Notions of hubris or a tragic flaw become irrelevant in drama of this kind. No error in judgment or fault of character accounts for disaster erupting from such depths. Things turn out as they do because a power greater than human will or understanding moves the action to its end.

In the *Poetics*, Aristotle is concerned with the special connection between action and character in tragic situations. More than once he insists that tragedy represents not men but the actions of men. Tragic action is whole—with beginning, middle, and end—and must therefore include, or be prior to, the character of its participants. Aristotle calls this executive aspect of action the "plot," and goes on to say that plot is the "soul" of tragedy—not the foibles of men and women thus caught up, but action in its unstoppable unfolding. Tragedy, therefore, is the literary form that dramatizes human conflicts for which, in the end, fate governs.

Most of the time we (the lucky ones) stay inside the boundaries of a realm where character counts, where options abound, a world where self-determination is effective. Now and then, however, hard circumstances arise and force us to difficult choices. We may then go the way of Ismene or Antigone, and if the latter, freedom gives way to necessity and the world of desire vanishes. Some of our best plays in the tragic mode—*Hamlet* or *King Lear*, for example—include the struggle for and with power. All of them have a political dimension. But not all strike us as, in the first degree, dramas of politics. Political tragedy in the formal sense is rare and involves a contradiction that can be put, to begin with, as a question: If, on the one hand, fatality is the soul of tragedy, and if, on the other hand, politics is the art of the possible, by what coincidence can such contrary realms be brought to occupy each other?

Oedipus meets his fate at a crossroads, a moment of junction in which choice is overtaken by necessity. Political situations, on the other hand, are political to the degree that possibilities stay open. Among power's options, however, is the choice to close things down and turn into a path from which there is no going back. It's here that violence arises; and it's here, in the freedom to resort to force, that the fatality of politics resides.

In *Antigone* the action is best described as the closing down of possibility, very fast in Antigone's case, much more gradually for Creon. Disaster occurs when options are exhausted. The oddity is that while we watch "the art of the possible" destroying itself, the spectacle before us has an aura of anxiety unusual in tragic art. What remains disturbing about *Antigone* is that at any point before the hero's death, we feel the course of action *could* be changed. The plot might take a different turn and violence be averted. Or so we feel. But that is the feeling of any political crisis—the waiting to see, the unnerving hope that maybe the worst won't happen. Even so, the strangeness of tragic action in *Antigone* is that it does not look iron-clad, not even in hindsight. In *Oedipus*, the hero's fate is sealed by the gods before his birth. Nothing so relentless appears to govern *Antigone*. How, then, does fatality enter?

At the beginning of the play we glimpse a pivotal moment of freedom. When the action begins, the attack on Thebes is over, nor is the fact of Polynices' death an issue in itself. True, that is the one circumstance beyond change, but the action is put on its fatal course by, first, the public decree, and then by Antigone's reaction. This initial moment recalls Act One of *King Lear*, the other towering instance of political tragedy. In both cases, a fluid situation becomes fixed after an arbitrary decree is proclaimed and met with unexpected resistance. Creon's reasons of state are less flimsy than Lear's, but both men act officially, both wield the power invested in them, and both are undone by the reluctance—Cordelia's, Antigone's—of the heart to betray itself.

In political tragedy the misuse or squandering of freedom as a political resource is the immediate, although not the ultimate, cause of misfortune. The protagonists refuse or do not see their options. In *Antigone*, tragic necessity reveals itself little by little as choices arise only to be cancelled. Denial of freedom is, in fact, the play's central gesture. Creon did not have to forbid the burial of Polynices. Had he fixed upon some other show of power, Antigone would have been free to fulfill her private need. But once the decree intervenes, she cannot act without destroying herself. Or can she?

There is, in fact, a gap of possibility to be tried—but that Antigone refuses to consider. Hearing the decree, she might go first to Creon and make an appeal, privately or in public, for her brother's burial. She might invoke royal blood or special favor, as well as tradition and the city's honor. She might also ask Haemon, to whom she is betrothed, for help; and if broader support were useful, she might appeal to the chorus of elders. Finally, she might approach Tiresias and enlist an authority backed by the gods themselves. Antigone is not without resources. But to use them would be to descend to political methods—enroll in the game and play politics—and this Antigone will not do. Although she is open to attack, she refuses the defense that is hers. To become "political" and try the art of the possible is not, for Antigone, a possibility.

Her alternatives do indeed look petty compared to the stand she takes and the solemnity of her death. Greatness of soul does not stoop to tactics, and Antigone holds to her heroic course. This nobility of spirit, however, should not obscure the fact that it fails. When Antigone dies, her brother still rots in the sun. All that is certain, when weighing her plight, is that her intensely private perspective denies the public world. Even the decree is seen in personal terms. Speaking to Ismene, Antigone refers to "the martial law our good Creon / lays down for you and me— yes, me, I tell you." She has no point of reference outside of self and family, nor would she seek one. She goes, then, directly to her task.

After her arrest, the initiative passes to Creon, and Creon, of course, is king. His freedom is commensurate with his power, which is nearly absolute and, in time of peace, capable of indulgence. If Antigone will not bend, Creon can turn the occasion to political advantage. He might simply forgive her, either magnanimously or in such a way as to shame her. He can say her case is special, or declare her action the outcome of madness brought on by grief. For these same reasons, he might display his mercy by assigning a lesser punishment—house arrest, for example. Or with loud faith in their judgment, he can turn things over to the elders. Creon has choices. Ways exist to impress the citizens of Thebes with their new king's sagacity. His job is to be tough, but also wise, and negotiation is the natural resource of his office. Yet he too acts as if no alternative were possible. Having issued his decree, Creon becomes as singleminded as Antigone—as blind, and as bent on the absolute course.

For both protagonists the stakes are larger than self-interest. In the moment of confrontation Creon feels responsible to the polis, while Antigone honors the deeper grounds—ancestral, poetic, religious—of selfhood. Her manner is consistently inward, passionate, lyrical. Hers is in fact the poet's way of taking the world. And like most poets of lyrical bent, Antigone becomes more, rather than less, solipsistic as the pressure of politics builds. Her loyalty is to inner vision; in the emergency she falls back upon an inwardness of self that puts her in touch with the whisper of the gods. These interior powers are the ground of her strength, and to three in particular she and the elders of the chorus appeal. First is Eros, fountainhead of desire and builder of life. The most insistent is Hades, guardian of the ancestral dead. Beyond these, vague but the greater for his mystery, is Dionysus, festive giver of dance and poetry, godhead of daemonic commingling and tragedy itself, the presiding power of orphic earth.

It's with these primal energies that Antigone aligns herself; thus empowered she can neither bargain with the king, nor calculate support, nor, by calling on Tiresias, set one authority against another. To enter the public arena would be to forfeit the strength that selfhood derives from at-oneness with its own deepest sources. Integrity is all, or so it must seem to Antigone. Herself she will not compromise. She will not play the game and never sees that politics is anything more than a phantom spectacle, as if Creon were nothing but the "fool" she takes him for. Were her vision dramatic rather than lyrical, she might appreciate, or at least recognize, worldly power's danger. But then she would be a hero of knowledge rather than, as she is, a hero of passionate will. The dead, for whom she speaks, have their powers at one with the earth, but like Eros or the tragic god himself, they are blind to the world. This blindness is Antigone's strength and the cause of her downfall.

But Creon too is blind, and to understand *his* tragedy we need not dwell on his despotic temper, but look to the office he holds as ruler of Thebes. He is not guided by self-interest but by the compulsions of his high position. Within the boundaries of the city-state his power is absolute; but possessing such power is, more than a little, to be possessed in turn. On the one hand, great power confers assurance of omnipotence; on the other hand, it provokes paranoia to an endless degree. These delusions are the price of Creon's position; and when it comes to small mistakes at vast cost, he is neither better nor worse than our own kings and chieftains.

Creon feels almighty, and thinks he does *not need* to negotiate. At the same time, he is beset by chronic suspicion and feels he does *not dare* negotiate. He is faced with a challenge far beneath his majesty and will not, as he says, be swayed by the whim of a girl. However, he also imagines that invisible enemies are working to unseat him, bribing his soldiers, suborning his son. And so, to a king, it must seem. Creon thinks he has enough strength to handle Antigone no matter what happens. But he also thinks negotiation would threaten his authority. And he is misled still further by the sense of commitment that power breeds, the thrust of urgency and mission with which great power invests its agents. Might *feels* right, and for these reasons: because it seems invincible, and because it seems besieged; because its every action carries the weight of necessity, and because the deep excitement of power is godlike and blinding.

Creon does at last relent. This change of heart comes too late, of course, and if we ask why Creon does not reverse himself sooner, the answer is again a function of power. He acts belatedly, as Hegel would say, because the Owl of Minerva flies only at dusk; because power understands itself only in its aftermath. What this means is that the cost of wisdom is excessive, often tragic, always sacrificial. Tiresias is wise, but he comes to speak with Creon only after the king's decree has infested the land. When the altars are polluted and the sacred birds defiled, then the prophet arrives. Tiresias appears in time of need, but the need comes after its cause.

And even then, Creon must first reject the advice he receives. The truth Tiresias offers—that Creon's own decree plagues the land—comes at him as a challenge, and the reaction of power to challenge is entrenchment. Once the king and the seer no longer stand face to face, Creon can drop his guard and consider that Tiresias has always given true counsel. This also accounts, in part, for Creon's inflexible stand toward Antigone. She is a threat that, in the moment of face-to-face encounter, requires quelling. She is not seen as a niece or a grieving sister but as a "criminal." She is not the bride of his son but a force to be met with force. Once Antigone has been condemned and led away, the challenge is over and Creon can take time to reconsider. But by then his time has run out.

Creon wields a power that in turn wields him, and in the encounter with Antigone he is as much the victim as she is. Both of them have been trapped by the decree from the moment it was declared. To make an issue of Polynices' burial, as I suggested earlier, is in itself arbitrary. But once the law exists the king acts in accord with his policy and the decree becomes sovereign. Antigone breaks the law but the law came first. The decree determines everything, Antigone's rebellion and Creon's tyranny no less than the end to which the conflict leads.

The fact that Creon did not have to choose *this* decree must make us wonder why this one was his choice. Here we approach the mainspring of tragedy in political form. Here, in what looks to be an arbitrary sign, we meet the "secret cause." For if we agree that Creon's decree is a political act, meant to show forth a new king's might, we must suppose a symmetry (in this most symmetrical of dramas) between the nature of the decree and the nature of power at its tragic extreme. On this equivalence everything hinges. The decree is one option among many; but in the tragedy of politics, as we shall see, Creon's choice is inevitable.

Vico was among the first to observe that societies "all have some religion, all contract solemn marriages, all bury their dead."[3] These "human customs," as he calls them—religion, kinship systems, and funeral rites— are institutions necessary to social order and they are also, as it happens, at the center of *Antigone*. Creon manages to offend all three, but most pointedly he violates the imperative of ritual burial, our communal rites (and rights) as creatures of earth that Vico (citing Classical sources) calls "compacts of the human race" and "fellowships of humanity."[4]

To bury the dead and dignify death's occasion seems profoundly needful and even, as Vico implies, a constitutive act for human community. Ceremony makes death meaningful; it formalizes our griefs and our fears, and certifies human continuity by binding the past to the present, and the living to the dead. Certainly we feel better for the disburdening that ritual allows. Grief and fear are not, however, the whole of it. Anthropologists use the site of the grave to distinguish human from anthropoid forms of life. There will *be* a grave, and also signs of identity—weapons, jewelry, household utensils, perhaps a death mask—to signal that these bones once lived like you or I, and were returned to earth in a communal ceremony involving the living as much as the dead. Symbolic procedures of this kind are anchored in death, but they are meant for the living, for religious reasons no doubt, but principally because through ritual disposition of the body we certify its human worth despite death's terribly visible negation.

Hegel agreed with Vico that burial rites establish humanness. In the *Phenomenology of Mind* Hegel retraces Antigone's story and calls burial the "ultimate ethical act" in fulfillment of "divine law."[5] The nothingness of death is cancelled through symbolic confirmation of personal significance. Even more important, ritual burial becomes the act that separates human beings from mere nature and, beyond that, mediates individual existence with universal being. Against death, burial is the one thing we can do. By treating the body as a person, we assert that the person was never merely a body, never nature's abstract object. The ceremony performed for a loved one, as Hegel goes on, "weds the relative to the bosom of the earth, the elemental individuality that passes not away."[6] In this special case, the earth is part of the ritual and is not to be confused with mere nature. For Hegel as for Antigone, earth is the concrete substance of eternity. It is the fundament of birth and becoming, the dwelling of creation's nether powers and the place, finally, to which the individual returns "as a member of a community"—a community that is not political but rather human and ancestral.[7]

Opposing blank nature, burial rites affirm at-oneness with the indwelling powers of earth. The distinction is crucial because at the level of the physical body, nature is an amoral field of force and necessity; and insofar as politics rests on force, as it does in Creon's exercise, nature's nothingness is power's real foundation. Insofar as we are creatures of nature and subject to political order, any of us can be reduced, like Polynices, from "thou" to "it." Creon favors, Antigone opposes, this emptying out of human significance. The body of Polynices is the field of their struggle, a vivid reminder that we are the object of politics to the extent that we are things of nature. The function of burial is to keep these two spheres separate, the political (grounded in nature) on the one hand, and the human (sustained by earth) on the other.

And therefore the central place of last rites in *Antigone*. Alive, Polynices was a traitor; but in death he resumes his essential humanity, at one with the earth, free of any social role or political identity. As Hegel puts it, the act of burial "does not concern the citizen . . . [but] takes him as a universal being."[8] For this reason, when Sophocles speaks of "the dead" he sometimes refers to the individual, whereas at other times he refers to all human beings who through death have returned to earth's ancestral realm. But this much is certain: having entered the community of the dead, Polynices is no longer to be judged by worldly power.

In *Antigone*, therefore, the body of Polynices is the drama's central emblem. As we behold Antigone and Creon face to face we cannot forget the man-become-thing in the dust dividing them. It is the mirror of Antigone's wound and the image of Creon's misrule. While one of them strives to sanctify the dead man's humanity, the other insists on reducing it to carrion. At the start a dead man is left unburied; at the end a living person is buried alive. This monstrous symmetry suggests a perversity at the heart of power's exercise, a horrid disorder imposed upon the cosmos of earth and humankind together. In the extremity that results in tragedy it is politics that brings on disaster. The "secret cause" is power itself and its sign is mutilation of the human image.

In *Oedipus* the hero's fate is terrible but at least it is his. If the gods seem hostile, no other agency comes between the oracular dark and what happens. With Antigone the case is otherwise. Her death is not the working out of private destiny (even though she acts for interior reasons) nor does she die in fulfillment of divine design (even though she and the gods are in perfect accord). She is robbed of both by politics, and the immediate and final causes of her fall are therefore one—the public pronouncement of a man who proceeds in good faith, but for whom piety, kinship, human worth, and finally (for so it will turn out) the polis itself are expendable loss in the service of power. Under pressure Creon is deaf to counsel and blind to human need, the perfect slave of politics. Antigone stands up to him; she resists her situation and takes her life to escape the decree, but the decree destroys her nonetheless. Her fate is therefore divided; it is hers but not her own.

There are many ways to read *Antigone*, but no recent reading ignores its political spirit. And increasingly, dramatic revisions of the play have put politics at the center. I think in particular of the stage versions by Jean Anouilh (France, 1944) and Bertolt Brecht (Germany, 1948), and also Athol Fugard's *The Island* (South Africa, 1973). In *Antigones*, his recent study of the play's cultural destiny, George Steiner points to a sudden increase of interest in Antigone's story at the beginning of the nineteenth century, an exaltation of her fate that passed through the whole of that century into our own. The ground of this obsession, in Steiner's estimate, was the impact of the French Revolution. For it was then that historical consciousness began to crystalize; then that men and women began to feel "the new immersion of the private individual in historical extremity," as if after the Terror, after the march from Corunna to Moscow and back, no one could be entirely free from "the burn of history in his or her bones." In *Antigone* we behold "the meshing of intimate and public, of private and historical existence," a drama of consequence because, as Steiner concludes, "after 1789 the individual knows no armistice with political history."[9]

After the Revolution, as was often said at the time, life—and, even more, the *sense* of life—was different. History began to *move*, and the basic metaphor of politics shifted from "the body politic" to "the ship of state." The speed of events increased, and large-scale change became pervasive. Eternity, as William Blake put it, fell in love with the productions of time. It was a love-hate courtship, with more of agitation than of bliss, and poets like Blake and Yeats have given us names— "fearful symmetry," "terrible beauty"—to account for the spectacle, sometimes awesome, sometimes hateful, of the political sublime. In *Mimesis*, Eric Auerbach traces the rise of what he calls "tragic modern realism," and in his chapter on Stendhal he observes of *The Red and the Black* that "contemporary political and social conditions are woven into the action in a manner more detailed and more real than had been exhibited in any earlier novel."[10] In the wake of the Revolution came a general consciousness of participation in history, a process Auerbach sums up as follows:[11]

> for the progress then achieved in transportation and communication, together with the spread of elementary education resulting from the trends of the Revolution itself, made it possible to mobilize the people far more rapidly and in a far more unified direction; everyone was reached by the same ideas and events far more quickly, more consciously, and more uniformly. For Europe there began that process of temporal concentration, both of historical events themselves and of everyone's knowledge of them. . . . Such a development ab-

rogates or renders powerless the entire social structure of orders and categories previously held valid. . . . He who would account to himself for his real life and his place in human society is obliged to do so upon a far wider practical foundation and in a far larger context than before, and to be continually conscious that the social base upon which he lives is not constant for a moment but is perpetually changing through convulsions of the most various kinds.

Since then political turmoil has become an expected part of the environment. To understand even local affairs, we now require a space-time map that covers the whole of the globe. More recently, Milan Kundera has observed the political compression of life as the "world" hems us in:[12]

That life is a trap—well, that we've always known. We are born without having asked to be, locked in a body we never chose, and destined to die. On the other hand, the wideness of the world used to provide a constant possibility of escape. A soldier could desert from the army and start another life in a neighboring country. Suddenly, in our century, the world is closing around us. The decisive event in that transformation of the world into a trap was surely the 1914 war, called (and for the first time in history) a world war. Wrongly, "world." It involved only Europe, and not *all* of Europe at that. But the adjective "world" expresses all the more eloquently the sense of horror before the fact that henceforward, nothing that occurs on the planet will be a merely local matter, that all catastrophes concern the entire world, and that consequently, we are more and more determined by external conditions, by situations no one can escape, and which, more and more, make us resemble one another.

The "Great War" of 1914–18 was not called a "world war" until after World War Two, but Kundera's sense of political reality is accurate, and with good cause. He saw the Russians invade Prague in 1968, saw the Czech spirit founder, and ended up in Paris knowing the slap of history firsthand. The percentage of important writers uprooted by politics has been, in this century, very high. *Mimesis*, for example, was written in

Istanbul during the second of our "world" wars. Auerbach was a scholar trained in the German philological tradition, but also a Jew in flight from the Third Reich. Had there been no earlier world war, no economic collapse, no social unrest to intensify the prior defeat, Hitler might not have happened. Great thinkers like Heidegger and Jaspers and Arendt would not have been faced with such difficult choices. Hitler was their Creon, and his decree—the Nuremberg Laws, for example—entered the world of art and the universities to alter in a single sweep the European mind. Auerbach might otherwise have pursued his career with the usual prospects, advancing quietly in a quiet profession to the eminence that would have easily been his. When he began, the realms of literature and politics seemed comfortably separate. But they did not stay that way, and in a series of dislocations that drove Auerbach to the Bosphorus— that pushed Walter Benjamin to suicide at the Spanish border and Paul Celan to the bridge in Paris—politics intrude to mock the happy notion that we can be in the world but not of it.

Who among us has not known men and women broken or destroyed for refusing to follow their government's will? Ordinary people, burdened with the ordinary problems of birth and love and death, suddenly find private responsibility blocked by public decree. In the era of Cold War, with terrorism on the one hand and nuclear threat on the other, Antigone's fate can be anyone's or everyone's at once. Innocence counts for nothing, if only because terrorism and police-states both require random victims. That is the terrorist's terror, the state's proof of power— and the real threat in nuclear deterrence. One is amazed, and perhaps also instructed, by the way Americans protest their "innocence" when planes are hijacked and hostages taken.

In fact and in spirit, Antigone's drama is the heart of our time. How, then, shall it go unremarked that the hero is a woman? And what's to be said for the fact that she draws her strength from the gods of the earth, in opposition to Creon's worldly authority? This much we know directly from the play: that a patriarchal order is challenged by a woman; that when political power intervenes, it asserts the primacy of world over earth; and finally, that conflict of this kind is kept in motion by the logic of power and can lead to terrible ends. George Steiner has pointed out the "martial" element in Creon's diction, recalling the ruthless world of the *Iliad*, and Creon's remarks, we see from the text, attack Antigone's status as a woman. The struggle of the individual against the state is thus compounded by a premodern, or in fact a perpetual degradation of women to noncitizens, deprived of dignity and public space. That Antigone should challenge this arrangement is not, for Creon, an option. These ancient inequities are now being tested. The coopting of personal being by public force has given rise to the notion that the personal is political. And feminism, even in its milder forms, confounds established order in the same way Antigone stands up to Creon.

But what, finally, of the conflict between world and earth? Greek literature of the Classical period contains a general tension between the *polis*, dedicated to war and public order, and the *oikos*, the zone of immediate life, dedicated to hearth, home, the generative powers of earth. With his high regard for Greek thinking, Heidegger took the poetic notion of an earth-world antagonism and gave it conceptual form in "The Origin of the Work of Art." Here is the heart of his argument:[13]

> The world is the self-disclosing openness of the broad paths of the simple and the essential decisions in the destiny of an historical people. The earth is the spontaneous forthcoming of that which is continually self-secluding and to that extent sheltering and concealing. World and earth are essentially different from one another and yet never separated. The world grounds itself on the earth, and the earth juts through world. . . . The world, in resting upon the earth, strives to surmount it. As self-opening it cannot endure anything closed. The earth, however, as sheltering and concealing, tends always to draw the world into itself and keep it there.

With earth as fundament, humankind builds up and sets forth a world, and in the process attempts to subdue and then negate the primal forces on which it depends. Earth, meanwhile, pushes to displace and shut down world's opened spaces. Each, in this contest, needs the other; earth only comes into view when world provides a perspective, and world, as Heidegger puts it, "cannot soar out of the earth's sight if, as the governing breadth and path of all essential destiny, it is to ground itself on a resolute foundation."[14] But in fact the human world does presume to "soar," a capacity granted us by our genius of artifice and the colossal powers of technology, a kind of illusory flight that men, less often women, have always praised ecstatically. And here the logic of apocalypse asserts itself; here, in our dreams, we would do away with our condition as earth-bound creatures altogether.[15]

In a technological world, the wisdom that allowed premodern peoples to live at one with the blessings of their environment is no longer effective. At some point, as world transgresses its boundaries, we must expect that earth will "jut" back and reclaim its injured dignity. This is, of course, the logic at work in *Antigone*. If, today, world seems to conquer earth's limits, the victory is only apparent. Each time our spacecraft lift off, the terrible pull of earth ascends also, as the tragedy of *Challenger* made clear. At the same time, only by world's utmost exertion—from a precarious station in space—does earth reveal herself whole. In broadest terms, what this imagery suggests is that poetry defends and draws authority from the powers of earth, while politics is authorized by any world it happens to uphold.

In *Antigone* the conflict between earth and world cannot be overlooked so long as Polynices lies in the sun unburied. His decaying body serves the public good, or so Creon decrees; but as Antigone asserts through action and Tiresias backs up with prophecy, failure to bury the dead upsets an order of things that is sacred. Against Creon's authority Antigone's sole resource is her dependence on the powers of earth. It's these powers Creon aims to override, insisting that the polis comes first. And he does override them, only to be undone by forces he thought he had vanquished. The political world exploits the earth and presumes to cancel earthly claims; but in the end no order or regime can sustain itself without respect for, and support from, the finite energies of earth.

At present we are served by a military world-order that holds the planet hostage. We are sustained by an economy that destroys creation's plenitude. These are not sane ways to care for life on earth. They have about them the blindness of a Creon doing what's expedient. How strange it is, how out of joint our time, that hope for the world now depends on the odds of the earth. Poetic justice, we might suppose, were it less disturbing. For as things now stand, the planet is alive and vulnerable and, like Antigone, a sister to us all.

·II·

The Press of the Real

Far in the woods they sang their unreal songs,
Secure. It was difficult to sing in face
Of the object. The singers had to avert themselves
Or else avert the object.

—Wallace Stevens[1]

Thinking of poetry and politics together does not, ordinarily, bring to mind the likes of Wallace Stevens, who is among the grandest of our modernist masters but not a poet of the kind to whom politics mattered, neither in his life nor in his work. But in fact, he was alert to the damage politics can do, not only to life in the world, but to imagination and the spirit's interior life. To say, as he did, that poets must "resist or evade" political reality is to acknowledge quite starkly the loss of earlier freedoms. If Stevens was the last of the great evaders—a strategist whose mainstay tactic was "the intricate evasions of as"—if Stevens managed his feints supremely well, he was also intelligent about the forces he aimed to outfox.

His most pointed statement about politics and poetry is "The Noble Rider and the Sound of Words,"[2] a lecture delivered at Princeton and first published in 1942, at a time when grim messages from Europe were vexing the American dream of detachment. Looking for the difference between the Victorian era and our own, Stevens points to the First World War as a turning point and sums up the spirit of the time this way: "Reality then became violent and so remains." He goes on to say that in a century rife with war and unrest we have been increasingly crowded and diminished by events. It's in this overtly political context that Stevens formulates "the pressure of reality":

> . . . in speaking of the pressure of reality, I am thinking of life
> in a state of violence, not physically violent, as yet, for us in
> America, but physically violent for millions of our friends and
> for still more millions of our enemies and spiritually violent,
> it may be said, for everyone alive.

Stevens takes for granted that the increase in havoc, with its spiritual
repercussions, is political in character. "Reality," he goes on, "has ceased
to be indifferent." Malignity has found its motive and the victims, on
any given day, are those the crossfire catches. Given this state of affairs,
Stevens offers his prescription for poets to come:

> A possible poet must be a poet capable of resisting or evading
> the pressure of reality of this last degree [spiritually violent for
> everyone alive], with the knowledge that the degree of today
> may become a deadlier degree tomorrow.

The notion of "the pressure of reality" is an entrance to the heart of
the problem. For as soon as we ask what happens when poetry and
politics collide, we are speaking of forces external to language, but which
impinge so severely upon imagination's freedom that the poetry, in order
to suffice, must resort to resistance or evasion. To speak of "reality," as
Stevens speaks of it, is to designate a condition in some sense universal—
political intrusion, that is, as the general case arising from countless
special cases. One way to test Stevens' formulation is to ask the following
question: What happens when communal misfortune disrupts the life
of the poet who might otherwise feel free to pursue less noble, more
indulgent matters in his or her art?

By way of answer I shall go to one of C. P. Cavafy's historical parables,
one of the several Hellenistic anecdotes that he invented, or adumbrated
upon, in his poetry. The circumstances of Cavafy's life—that he wrote
in Greek, that he was born and lived most of his life in Alexandria, a
city fabulous with the past—are not coincidental to his ironic grasp of
events, his view of personal stories as marginalia to history's dense and
endless text. That Cavafy was homosexual is also, I think, important to
his work; boundary positions alert us to the limits of the self, to the
loneliness of vision, and also to the flux and hazard that history throws
up along its fault lines. Cavafy made his living as a minor bureaucrat,
and in any political way his life was invisible, a circumstance he seems

to have relished. At the same time, however, and especially when we consider Cavafy's detached, almost exquisite awareness of historical bad luck, it can't be ignored that the span of his life (1863–1933) was one with the arrival of the political moment that, in Stevens' words, "became violent and remains so."

A poet with Cavafy's Old World sensibility would not assume that poetry automatically transcends time, or history's imprint, or the predictable down-slide of empire. He wrote, anyway, a number of famous poems that challenge such assumptions. The best of these are unpretentious portraits from the distant (usually Hellenic) past, in part historical and in part imagined, snapshots that throw their momentary light upon the condition in which men and women find themselves when overtaken by events. One such poem, entitled "Dareios" and written in 1920, is an apt parable for poetry in dark times. The poem's persona, Phernazis, is imagined, but his situation rests in historical fact. Among the ancient Persian kings, Darius was the grandest, and his dynasty, along with his late successor referred to in the poem, eventually fell to the Romans. Here, then, is Cavafy's "Dareios":[3]

> Phernazis the poet is at work
> on the crucial part of his epic:
> how Dareios, son of Hystaspis,
> took over the Persian kingdom.
> (It's from him, Dareios, that our glorious king,
> Mithridatis, Dionysos and Evpator, descends.)
> But this calls for serious thought; Phernazis has to analyse
> the feelings Dareios must have had:
> arrogance, maybe, and intoxication? No—more likely
> a certain insight into the vanities of greatness.
>
> But his servant, rushing in,
> cuts him short to announce very important news:
> the war with the Romans has begun;
> most of our army has crossed the borders.
>
> The poet is dumbfounded. What a disaster!
> How can our glorious king,
> Mithridatis, Dionysos and Evpator,

bother about Greek poems now?
In the middle of a war—just think, Greek poems!

We are, at this point, midway through the poem. The bad news arrives and in an instant all is changed. The situation, so "crucial" a moment ago, now tilts toward real disaster. In what becomes a rush of insight, Phernazis starts to see the folly of his project. The alarm puts an end to inflated ambitions and at the same time raises serious questions. With war under way, what will become of this or any work of art? The poetic enterprise—how valid, how worthy of respect can it be when life and the security of nations are directly at stake? Who bothers, in an emergency, about poems?

Pressured by the turn of events, Phernazis begins to ask hard questions—exactly the kind we who care for poetry have been asking, with increasing bewilderment, since roughly the end of World War Two. How, in bad times, shall the poet be honored? Is poetry equal to the news? And *Greek* stuff to boot—poetry modelled on past glories? In the middle of nuclear buildup, terrorism gone berserk, just think, *poems*?

As the rest of Cavafy's poem make clear, Phernazis has been forced to confront his poem's "crucial" moment in more ways than one. We can see, for example, that in searching after the dynastic motive—the feeling that Darius "must have had"—our poet is divining his own motives. The reference to "our glorious king" in the first stanza is more than parenthetical; it breaks up the call to serious thought and alerts us to the fact that, if the question of empire is pivotal, our poet's scheme for preferment is equally demanding. Before the bad news arrives, fame and the fruits of recognition urge him on at least as much as loyalty to "the poetic idea." As the rest of the poem will make clear, Phernazis begins by seeking critical acclaim and its benefits—equivalents to the grant, the prize, the university slot. Aiming to please, our poet would write a poem irrelevant to life but still of service to a fine career.

Cavafy's Persian poet, by producing a flattering work in an outdated style, aims to win attention from the powers that be, in this case the small king whose preposterous triple name, especially when repeated, suggests his ballooning idea of himself, in particular the arrogance and intoxication he reveals by his decision to take on the Romans. And in this minor despot's example we see something of Phernazis as well. He is arrogant toward his task and exalted by his prospects. He forfeits poetic integrity and turns the "poetic idea" against itself. By opting for the false theme, he attributes nobility of purpose to brute conquest, and would obscure the stupidity of power extending, and then overextending, its reach. Darius, we recall, met his match at Marathon in 490 B.C. Mithridatis VI Evpator went down in similar style. History tells us that he ended against Pompey in 66 B.C., a suicide, betrayed by his own son.

These contextual details give the poem its irony; and as a method this is one of Cavafy's triumphs, the way he uses history to compel prophetic inspection. Any leader's strength, we might agree, is the firmer for its grasp of tragic irony—"a certain insight," as Phernazis puts it, "into the vanities of greatness." But this is an unlikely wisdom, given what we know about leaders then or now. We can suppose, moreover, that until he hears the unfortunate news, our poet has little understanding of greatness, and none at all of vanity, although vanity is what he serves. And thus the "disaster"—the fact that with history on the move and events deflating illusions, the poet's pretensions collapse: "In the middle of a war—just think, Greek poems!"

His pretensions collapse, but what of the poet himself? He turns out to have more character than we—or he himself—might have guessed. Once his careerist schemes are defeated, he begins to see that his personal misfortune is in fact a minute part of full-scale catastrophe. The war, with its dumbfounding impact, jars him into an integrity that, earlier, he thought he could dismiss. A darker, more accurate awareness begins to develop, and the real poem—a kind of poetry equal to its occasion—begins to be possible. The rest of Cavafy's poem traces the stages of this turn:

> Phernazis gets all worked up. What a bad break!
> Just when he was sure to distinguish himself
> with his *Dareios*, sure to make
> his envious critics shut up once and for all.
> What a setback, terrible setback to his plans.
>
> And if it's only a setback, that wouldn't be too bad.
> But can we really consider ourselves safe in Amisos?
> The town isn't very well fortified,
> and the Romans are the most awful enemies.
> Are we, Cappadocians, really a match for them?
> Is it conceivable?

Are we to compete with the legions?
Great gods, protectors of Asia, help us.

But through all his nervousness, all the turmoil,
the poetic idea comes and goes insistently:
arrogance and intoxication—that's the most likely, of course:
arrogance and intoxication are what Dareios must have felt.

As the "setback" becomes more than personal bad luck, and as the
meaning of the historical moment begins to open upon him, Phernazis
looks beyond himself, sees the disaster thus set in motion, and turns
back to his tribe. He loses sight of himself in the fate of his people ("we,
Cappadocians"), is astonished that the king, for all his self-deluding
grandeur, could have gone so far as to provoke the Roman war machine
("Is it conceivable?"), and turns with humility to the gods that his people
might be spared their king's folly. Released from his self-serving plans,
Phernazis the poet can assume his true office. He can allow "the poetic
idea" its hegemony and write the real thing, a poem alive with its time
and the true concerns of its audience. Most interesting is the way "the
poetic idea" persists, awaits the coming of its incarnation. When it asserts
itself it lifts the poet beyond his fear, beyond his pettiness and mere
ambition. Earlier the poetic idea was in his service, but now he serves
it—which is what makes poetry possible. Having faced history and abandoned heroic pretense to "the vanities of greatness," Phernazis escapes
his own delusions and does in fact gain insight into the vanity—its pride
and awful cost—of political "greatness."

Counting his options, Phernazis might have given up altogether, once
the "setback" occurred; or he might have gone vainly on with his initial
plans; or, he might turn as in fact he does turn. He adjusts his art to
the pressure of reality. Now, and perhaps for the first time, he can take
up "the poetic idea," can thrive on its power, can be directed onward
by the interior force of a vision that presses back "insistently," through
personal confusion, through historical trauma, against external forces.
He is no longer troubled by the question of caring for poems in the
middle of a war. The answer is as it always is, a matter of poetic integrity,
an openness to the press of the real. We see, then, that the man's bad
luck becomes the artist's gift of grace. Facing up to politics, he becomes
the poet that earlier he only pretended to be; and in so doing he gains
what had seemed, just seconds ago, to have been lost—the opportunity

to write important poetry. We might even suppose that his audience, waiting for the Romans to arrive, will appreciate and find a fortitude worth having, in poetry "condemned [as Seferis said to Cavafy] to truth."[4]

Cavafy and Stevens both conceive of the poet as an *outside* observer distressed by the march of events but not—not yet—an *inside* participant overwhelmed and mute in the face of events themselves. The poet, here, occupies the same situation most readers of this book are likely to be in—the position of someone apart from political havoc but well within reach of its shock waves. The press of the real, in this situation, is less from politics itself (brute forces that mangle and destroy) than from the impact of politics (more subtle forces that unnerve and undermine) on those of us at a crucial remove. Poetry—anything more than raw cursing—is always language at a crucial remove. For Stevens, however, the question of distance becomes the heart of the matter. With enough space between self and world, the press of the real is diffuse and can be evaded. When this space cramps and shuts down, the real is unavoidable and must be resisted.

Stevens points out, to begin with, that there are "degrees of imagination," differences in poetic language at different times in history, and that "a variation between the sound of words in one age and the sound of words in another age is an instance of the pressure of reality." We know, of course, that the sound of words depends in part upon their sense but also upon the degree of their referential commitment. Words in their sounding register the degree of relation, or its lack, between poetry and the world. This peculiar circumstance leads Stevens to question the notions of his day: "If it is the pressure of reality that controls poetry, then the immediacy of various theories of poetry is not what it was." He cites critical ideas that seem to him discredited, among them the poet's older claim to a "highly complex and unified content of consciousness," which, as he says, cannot compete with the kind of consciousness that "every newspaper reader experiences today." And to Croce's notion of the poet as "the whole man," or of poetry as "the triumph of contemplation," Stevens replies: "Croce cannot have been thinking of a world in which all normal life is at least in suspense, or, if you like, under blockage." Imagination is crowded and cowed by the press of the world, until finally the collapse of distance has "cast us out on reality":

It is not only that there are more of us and that we are actually close together. We are close together in every way. We lie in bed and listen to a broadcast from Cairo, and so on. There is no distance. We are intimate with people we have never seen and, unhappily, they are intimate with us.

These things "constitute," says Stevens, "the drift of incidents, to which we accustom ourselves as to the weather," and the weather, we know, can make itself felt in our bones. Stevens is trying, as he says, "to think of a whole generation and of a world at war, and trying at the same time to see what is happening to the imagination." This leads him to the first of his big definitions:

By the pressure of reality, I mean the pressure of an external event or events on the consciousness to the exclusion of any power of contemplation.

Among the causes of this intrusiveness there is, to begin with, "an extraordinary pressure of news." This is a phenomenon that Stevens insists upon—"news incomparably more pretentious than any description of it, news, at first, of the collapse of our system, or, call it, of life; then of news of a new world, but of a new world so uncertain that one did not know anything whatever of its nature, and does not know now." He is correct, even prophetic, to dwell on the impact of "news." Through the media the world comes at us every day nonstop, and in ways that undermine the distance imagination needs to make sense of what we behold. Gradually what we see informs the limit of what we know until, as Stevens puts it, "the war is only a part of a war-like whole." And it's here, in this degree of intrusion, that the pressure of news and events cannot be ignored or further put off by ordinary means:

Rightly or wrongly, we feel that the fate of a society is involved in the orderly disorders of the present time. We are confronting, therefore, a set of events, not only beyond our power to tranquillize them in the mind, beyond our power to reduce them and metamorphose them, but events that stir the emotions to violence, that engage us in what is direct and immediate and real, and events that involve the concepts and sanctions that are the order of our lives and may involve our very lives;

and these events are occurring persistently with increasing omen, in what may be called our presence. These are the things that I had in mind when I spoke of the pressure of reality, a pressure great enough and prolonged enough to bring about the end of one era in the history of imagination and, if so, then great enough to bring about the beginning of another.

When this point is reached the press of the real is severe enough to instigate a change in imagination's stance toward the world. Stevens notes that imagination "is always attaching itself to a new reality, and adhering to it," but he adds: "It is not that there is a new imagination but that there is a new reality." In Stevens' time and in ours, the cause of reality's change is time's acceleration and the collapse of space, the increasing reach and beat of political clamor—events "that stir the emotions to violence," events beyond the capacity of mind to tranquillize, reduce, or transform them; events, finally, that threaten "the concepts and sanctions that are the order of our lives and may involve our very lives." At this point Stevens is ready to generalize the impact of history upon art:

> To sum it up, the pressure of reality is, I think, the determining factor in the artistic character of an era and, as well, the determining factor in the artistic character of an individual. The resistance to this pressure or its evasion in the case of individuals of extraordinary imagination cancels the pressure so far as those individuals are concerned.

The world is always with us; the question is whether it can be evaded or whether, when it intrudes too far, it must be resisted. If the latter, then how shall the "possible poet" carry on? It's at this point that Stevens makes his remarks (quoted earlier) about "life in a state of violence," and says that "a possible poet must be a poet capable of resisting or evading the pressure of reality of this last degree." This position raises a question about "the social, that is to say sociological or political, obligation of the poet," a question that Stevens answers bluntly: "he has none." Stevens concedes that "if a social movement moved one deeply enough, its moving poems would follow," but at the same time and emphatically: "no politician can command the imagination." Coercion of this directly political kind is itself "a phase of the pressure of reality" that any poet today "is bound to resist or evade." The poet is not absolved of community. On the contrary, Stevens has a definite sense of the poet's role in times of political torment:

> What is his function? Certainly it is not to lead people out of the confusion in which they find themselves. Nor is it, I think, to comfort them while they follow their readers [leaders?] to and fro. I think that his function is to make his imagination theirs and that he fulfills himself only as he sees his imagination become the light in the minds of others. His role, in short, is to help people live their lives.

Poetry can help people live their lives, not by instruction but by creating potent figures that anyone's imagination might kindle to and take hold of—language that takes a place in the mind, allowing us to anchor ourselves and reclaim our self-possession—even amid the grim confusions of politics in dark time. Then especially, works like *Antigone* and *King Lear* serve us as *As You Like It* or even *The Tempest* cannot. Prokofiev's *Romeo and Juliet* rallies the spirit as Tschaikovsky's no longer can. And many a poem not otherwise strong will help restore presence of mind if uttered in a voice to match—or oppose—its occasion. The point, in this last instance, is that the poem is spoken aloud and not merely read. Thinking of the ways language resists the shove of the world, Stevens concentrates on "the sounds of words," and in terms of a force he calls "nobility." This strength of language is the key to Stevens' argument; by way of approaching it he goes on with these questions. "And what," he asks, "about the sound of words? What about nobility, of which the fortunes were to be a kind of test of the value of the poet?"

If we ask how poetry equips us for living, the further answer has something to do with the sounds of words and the character of imagination (here called "nobility") inherent in words and the music of their endless mixing. "Poetry," says Stevens, "is a revelation in words by means of the words." Or again: "A poet's words are things that do not exist without the words." Things, then; but things whose dwelling is sound and the soundings of lyric combination, words as they exist in their audible saying. About this Stevens is adamant; he says "that above everything else, poetry is words; and that words, above everything else, are, in poetry, sounds." He is stressing the importance of art's concreteness, the oracular action of words taking place. He is also endorsing

Heidegger's notion that language, in poetry, is the earth that imaginative worlds are set into.

The odd carnality of words is that they arise *ex nihilo,* become incarnate in their saying, then instantly depart while at the same time they leave an imprint that resounds. Poetry activates memory through its soundings—through rhyme, alliteration, etc., but also tone, inflection, and finally the entire ensemble of "voice," which is the earthly shape of sound in motion. Language of this memorable kind is capable of persisting through a void or, on the other hand, through the dense chaos of language in the world. Poetry—any set of lines we prize—sorts itself out from the infinitude of babble and allows us moments of coherence, of lucidity and self-possession as close to unity of being as most of us shall come:

> The deepening need for words to express our thoughts and feelings which, we are sure, are all the truth that we shall ever experience, having no illusions, makes us listen to words when we hear them, loving them and feeling them, makes us search the sound of them, for a finality, a perfection, an unalterable vibration, which it is only within the power of the acutest poet to give them.

That formal language empowers is a point on which poets and politicians agree. Stevens reserves this executive power for poetry by saying that "the peculiarity of the imagination is nobility," and further that "nobility" of this kind resides in "the sound of words." Language and imagination together constitute a system of grace and a *force,* and by way of analogy Stevens gives an example worth quoting in full, ellipses included:

> Late last year Epstein exhibited some of his flower paintings at the Leicester Galleries in London. A commentator in *Apollo* said: "How with this rage can beauty hold a plea. . . . The quotation from Shakespeare's 65th sonnet prefaces the catalogue. . . . It would be apropos to any other flower paintings than Mr. Epstein's. His make no pretense to fragility. They shout, explode all over the picture space and generally oppose the rage of the world with such a rage of form and colour as no flower in nature or pigment has done since Van Gogh."

"How with this rage shall beauty hold a plea, / Whose action is no stronger than a flower"? That is the whole of Shakespeare's conceit. Stevens cites the catalogue description to suggest how the challenge might be answered. These flowers explode, they rage and oppose, and urge him to conclude; "What ferocious beauty the line from Shakespeare puts on when used under such circumstances! While it has its modulation of despair, it holds its plea and its plea is noble." He has in mind a kind of strength or power generated by imagination in vigorous contest with reality. That his poetic action is elusive, hard to pin down, he does not deny. What he insists upon is that "nobility is a force," an agency that opposes the rage of the world with a rage of its own. Imagination and reality meet as equals, and the former draws its character and strength from the latter. In this way art sustains itself *in* the world, surviving rushes of negative force that to innocent eyes might seem overwhelming. And the way poetry sets itself in relation to the world is summed up in these lines:[5]

> The poem is the cry of its occasion,
> Part of the res itself and not about it.

Without being afraid or self-serving, art of this kind faces its own negation; it meets the pressure of reality and uses the world's force to call forth a counterpoise of its own. That is its nobility. In this view the poet can claim to be a realist, while the realist will always be a poet *manqué*. It's on this ground that Stevens stands when he says, as he often did, "that the structure of poetry and the structure of reality are one." The poem is "part of the res" and draws its force from its occasion.

In the concluding paragraph of "The Noble Rider and the Sound of Words," Stevens tells us that his "description of it as a force" is the best he can do toward explaining what "nobility" means. He then adds: "It is not an artifice that the mind has added to human nature. The mind has added nothing to human nature." At first this remark seems out of place, there having been no mention of "human nature" until this late moment. But Stevens is moving, at this point, from "nobility" as an attribute of poetry to "nobility" as an element of our humanity. He is arguing that *nobility as a force* is a kind of action or behavior needful to our being-in-the-world. It is the human way of keeping dignity alive in violent or demeaning situations, with the added sense that poetry and the arts play a key role in spiritual well-being. With these ideas in mind, here are the last sentences of Stevens' essay:

> It is a violence from within that protects us from a violence without. It is the imagination pressing back against the pressure of reality. It seems, in the last analysis, to have something to do with our self-preservation; and that, no doubt, is why the expression of it, the sound of its words, helps us live our lives.

The formula is famous and often cited, although not always as Stevens intended. Coming at the end of the essay, it sums up the whole of his argument and reveals what hadn't been visible before, namely that the poet as a "noble rider" is a *martial* figure. The way Stevens constructs the poet's situation—imagination contending with reality, powers within against powers without—suggests an art that is embattled, and Stevens speaks not only of violence and pressure, but of help and survival. These are substantial ideas, the more interesting for coming from a poet in whose work the martial element has seldom been recognized. We might all agree on the urbane Stevens, the ornate and carnivalesque Stevens. But Stevens as a noble rider? Stevens embattled?

But of course he was, and not only with old themes like loss and mutability. His deployment of metaphor in sequence—one image or phrase overtaking another to keep poetic consciousness diverging and imagination impossible to pin down—holds him at a distance, yet on occasion also allows him to move in close. Stevens takes his subject by degrees, but he gives "reality" its due, from the early *firecat,* bristling in the way no matter which way the bucks go swerving, to the late gray *rock* that is "the habitation of the whole." His art thrives on "the spirit that goes roundabout," but at the same time Stevens is ever mindful that "a blank underlies the trials of device, / The dominant blank, the unapproachable," against which summer's crickets sing in vain. His deepest strategy, the *basso continuo* of all his airy flights, is to outflank the world's avid uproar by stationing himself upon the bleak and empty backdrop of existence. At the heart of darkness is grim nothing, and the violence of confronting this is, for Stevens, strength. He never loses sight of life's essential poverty, "the nothing that is not there and the nothing that is." Reading him with care, there is a "misery in the sound of the wind." The real nobility, for this poet, is that despite the strain of pushing back he stays so poised. Preferring to bless rather than to blame, he leavens reserve with humor and braids his cursing into larger fabrics of praise.

With language that confronts and resists we mobilize "a violence from within that protects us from a violence without." For poetry to help us live our lives, the force of its diction must be equal to the world in which the poem itself takes place. And these strengths, it seems to me, are of especial value for the late years of this century. The world founders in political torment; it is ours yet not ours, the same world Stevens faced when he says: "I am thinking of life in a state of violence, not physically violent, as yet, for us in America, but physically violent for millions of our friends and for still more millions of our enemies and spiritually violent, it may be said, for everyone alive." That is our predicament but not, in Stevens' view, without resources to help us endure.

·TWO·

BARDIC PRACTICE, THE IRISH EXAMPLE

·III·

Yeats and the Rat-Rhymers

Theare is amongst the Irishe a certen kind of
people Called Bardes. . . .
—Edmund Spenser, 1596[1]

I write it out in a verse. . . .
—William Butler Yeats, 1916[2]

Shortly after his death in 1939, Yeats was praised by T. S. Eliot as "one of those few whose history is the history of their own time, who are a part of the consciousness of an age which cannot be understood without them."[3] As Eliot suggests, Yeats was always alert to politics. More often than not, he confronted history head-on, eagerly, sometimes with venom. But often, too, he sought a "ghostly solitude" apart from the clamor around him. It is not, therefore, his poetry in total that concerns me, but the part of his work that is like backbone to body, the part that Yeats spoke up for when (in 1936) he summed himself up as "a man of my time, through my poetical faculty living its history."[4]

To take Yeats as a man of his time, living his age through his art, is to take for granted that politics is central to his work. This does not mean poetic practice at the cost of political conformity or reductiveness but, exactly as Yeats says, responding to events *through* poetry. The Irish Free State came into being under Yeats's watchful eye, and much of his art responds to affairs of his time, kinds of events that still today set the character of experience for many countries and peoples—in Yeats's case a nationalist movement in politics and the arts; a culmination to centuries of colonial strife in war with empire, terrorism right and left followed by civil war; and at last the setting up of an independent (but not untroubled) republic.

After *Responsibilities* (1914), the greater number of Yeats's poems address an event or public circumstance, a person or persons involved in political affairs, or otherwise come braced with topical references. He was especially attentive to events that looked like signs of the times, and then to men and women who by lonely acts of will stood out from the fray. One of his heroes was Charles Stewart Parnell, whose downfall Yeats described as the last of "Four Bells, four deep tragic notes" sounding disastrous turning points in Irish history, beginning with the Flight and ending with the hysteria surrounding Parnell's death in 1891.[5] Praised as a savior, reviled as a sinner, Parnell was called "the Chief" and then "the dead King." He had united Ireland in an all-out push for independence, but then he found himself dragged down by private issues (adultery and divorce), with the clergy and much of his Catholic constituency against him. As Joyce later said: "To their eternal credit the Irish never threw Parnell to the wolves. They tore him to pieces themselves.[6] The rage that Joyce observed is Yeats's concern in "Parnell's Funeral," a poem not written until 1934, but a good example of "living" one's time through one's art.

The poem begins by sounding the theme of sacrifice, which is introduced by the fall of a star, and then extended into an arcane mythological reference:

> What shudders run through all that animal blood?
> What is this sacrifice? Can someone there
> Recall the Cretan barb that pierced a star?

Yeats goes on, in the next stanza, with language even more obscure, and the first fourteen lines of "Parnell's Funeral" are the least successful part of the poem. The star pierced by an arrow is equated with the extracted heart in ancient ritual, and the theme of sacrifice is expanded to suggest a way of life so ceremonious and whole that what occurs in the body politic is rendered perfectly in public art. This kind of elaboration—not unusual for Yeats—serves to dignify the theme and keep the poet distant.

But Yeats does not stay at a distance, nor does visionary calm prevail. Having seen—over and over—his own programs for the nation rejected, he embraces a mood of defeat and asks if sacrifice, and the communal regeneration that comes of it, can succeed in his own time and country. As late as 1932 Yeats said of Parnell: "from that sacrificial victim I derive

almost all that is living in the imagination of Ireland today."[7] Yeats links
Irish art to Irish politics, a connection that becomes explicit in the poem
as it goes on, along with dramatic or even startling changes in tone and
diction. In his meditation on Parnell's defeat, Yeats is forced out of myth
into history; he falls from detachment into vehement reaction—as if he
were embracing the progress of an actual fall, in language, syntax, and
voice, enacted in the poem's onward plunge:

> . . . . popular rage,
> *Hysterica passio* dragged this quarry down.
> None shared our guilt; nor did we play a part
> Upon a painted stage when we devoured his heart.
>
> Come, fix upon me that accusing eye.
> I thirst for accusation. All that was sung,
> All that was said in Ireland is a lie
> Bred out of the contagion of the throng,
> Saving the rhyme rats hear before they die.
> Leave nothing but the nothings that belong
> To this bare soul, let all men judge that can
> Whether it be an animal or a man.

The progress of the first four stanzas (Part One) suggests that politics
did sometimes provoke Yeats so severely that myth no longer sustained
him. His meditation on Parnell's death becomes so troubled that Yeats
turns into a different *kind* of poet—not a wise and timeless voice beyond
the grave, but the bard in agitated outcry, praising his lost lord while
cursing the tribe's perfidy. Stanzas three and four describe the hero's
downfall, met by a voice that accuses and blames, that lays down the
law ("let all men judge") and then will go on, in Part Two, to praise
the hero's good name.

Yeats has taken up the role of the Irish bard, the kind of poet known
from Ireland's well-documented tradition of bardic schools and tribal
poetry—the kind of poet whose professional calling was to praise, curse,
bless, and cast blame. Yeats was a great curser, but also quick to bless
and be blessed. Much of his work is based on blame and praise, and
these fields of announcement become more insistent as politics becomes
more directly the subject of particular poems. Yeats was nothing if not

confrontational, and often the role of the Irish bard became his preferred office when he responded to political occasions.

Given the importance Yeats placed on voice,[8] and his love of ceremony, we can appreciate that bardic practice is formulaic, rhetorical, and self-aware, a position rather than a posture. In "Parnell's Funeral" we come upon bardic formulae like "one sentence I unsay" and "but I name no more."

In Part Two Yeats offers a chronicle of Irish politics, using the bardic custom of naming to move from 1891 to 1934:

> The rest I pass, one sentence I unsay.
> Had de Valera eaten Parnell's heart
> No loose-lipped demagogue had won the day,
> No civil rancor torn the land apart.

> Had Cosgrave eaten Parnell's heart, the land's
> Imagination had been satisfied,
> Or lacking that, government in such hands,
> O'Higgins its sole statesman had not died.

> Had even O'Duffy—but I name no more—
> Their school a crowd, his master solitude;
> Through Jonathan Swift's dark grove he passed, and there

> Plucked bitter wisdom that enriched his blood.

Part of the "rest" passed over is the Easter uprising of 1916, an omission important to the poem's dark mood. The sentence that the poet would "unsay" (from stanza two) ends with "when we devoured his heart." Some did not partake of Parnell's heart but should have.

"Parnell's Funeral" is an elegy, a lament, a praise-poem. It is also a curse upon "the crowd" and its captains, including "even O'Duffy." The word *even*, with its suggestion of scorn followed by the gesture of dismissal, counts heavily for any poem about Irish politics in 1934. Cosgrave and then de Valera ran the republic in its early years, with O'Higgins as strong man until he was murdered. Then O'Duffy appeared as leader of the Blue Shirts, the Irish fascist movement that, briefly, drew praise from Yeats and lifted his political spirits one last time. "Politics are growing heroic," he wrote in July 1933—"Our chosen colour is blue."[9] To this ludicrous low point Yeats came in his yearning for an order that could make the world cohere, an outcome his own art contradicted. The Blue Shirts were not defeated but simply fell apart. And with O'Duffy's collapse Yeats recognized overwhelmingly, just as his life was ending, that politics was not heroic and, except for the Easter uprising of 1916, that it had never been so in his lifetime. In 1936 he admitted that "Communist, Fascist, nationalist, clerical, anti-clerical, are all responsible according to the number of their victims."[10]

Yeats's own brand of politics—an aristocratic order embracing a tragic sense of life—had been improbable from the start. In 1934 he would have done better to depend for fortitude on the wisdom of an earlier time, a remark he made during the darkness of the civil war: "There is no longer a virtuous nation and the best of us live by candle light."[11] To come at Yeats correctly we must keep in mind that politically he was always in a position of defeat; but also that his celebration of defeat as an opportunity for heroism served his poetry, if not his politics, wonderfully well. Political despair, strong enough to make the whole of the past seem waste, was the occasion for "Parnell's Funeral." The fascist lunge fell apart in early 1934; later that year came the poem.

Against defeat Yeats summons gaiety or rage. The former sometimes strains, but the blaze of the latter is straight from the heart. In Parnell's funeral poem, rage is compressed into perfect iambics. If the Chief's downfall calls for a curse, this is its saying:

> All that was sung,
> All that was said in Ireland is a lie
> Bred out of the contagion of the throng,
> Saving the rhyme rats hear before they die.

Yeats is making strong charges, but also a singular claim. Irish politics has been false, so has Irish poetry, everything said or sung except this— "the rhyme rats hear before they die." But what sort of rhyming is that? The usual gloss is from *As You Like It* (III, ii) where Rosalind mocks: "I was never so berhymed since Pythagoras' time, that I was an Irish rat." For Shakespeare the allusion is no more than a stitch in a patchwork of humor. For Yeats it would be something more, as it was for Ben Jonson, who had his pretentious peers in mind when he threatened to

> Rime 'hem to death, as they doe *Irish* rats,
> In drumming tunes.

Doubtless they existed, the "rat-rhymers," and perhaps exactly as the loose ends of legend record—wandering poets trading off the status of their bardic betters, going about the countryside chanting poems in front of infested hovels and barns, working charms and incantations, earning a living by cursing. The notion of rat-rhyming is remarkably apt for what Yeats has in mind; it is also, I think, an accurate emblem for poetry confronting politics. In English literature there are a few further allusions to poetry's business with rats. Sir William Temple connected runic incantation (the kind "to cause Terror in . . . Enemies") with "the proverb of rhyming rats to death." Alexander Pope had it that "Songs no longer move, / Nor Rat is rhym'd to death, nor Maid to love," mocking the notion that once they might have. And at the conclusion of his *Apologie for Poetrie*, Sidney bids his reader a wry farewell: "I would not wish unto you . . . to be rimed to death, as is said to be done in *Ireland*." Sir Philip ought to know, as one whose father had been Lord Deputy in Ireland during the period of Tudor campaigns to savage the Irish.

These allusions to rat-rhyming suggest a tradition or field of practice specific to earlier Irish ages, centering on "the supposed potency of the verses pronounced by the professional rhymers,"[12] a power sometimes reputed to reach further than rats. As late as the 1820's it was said among Ireland's peasantry that "many a man, who would kindle into rage at the sight of an armed foe, will be found to tremble at the thought of offending a rhymer."[13] Irish bards were often more famous for their cursing than for their more constructive powers, their duties and privileges as ministers to the tribe. In 1912 Osborn Bergin, an Irish scholar and translator of Gaelic manuscripts, sketched the following picture of the bard as he existed in Ireland from prehistoric times until the end of the sixteenth century, a portrait that with minor retouching would fit and, I do not doubt, have flattered Yeats:[14]

> He was, in fact, a professor of literature and a man of letters, highly trained in the use of a polished literary medium, belonging to a hereditary caste in an aristocratic society, holding an official position therein by virtue of his training, his learning, his knowledge of the history and traditions of his country and

his clan. . . . He was often a public official, a chronicler, a political essayist, a keen and satirical observer of his fellow-countrymen. At an earlier period he had been regarded as a dealer in magic, a weaver of spells and incantations, who could blast his enemies by the venom of his verse, and there are traces down to the most recent times of a lingering belief, which was not, of course, confined to Ireland, in the efficacy of a well-tuned malediction.

In common discourse the bardic notion of the poet is honored for its antiquity. But at the same time, we have reasoned away the magical properties of language, and nowadays to talk of "bards" seems frivolous or old-fashioned. In current criticism it no longer occurs to us that a keeper of bardic powers is what a poet—any poet—is. But Yeats did not think as we do. He avowed that magic and the supernatural were real, and saw himself as the receptacle of tribal wisdom, a mystical lore he called the *anima mundi*. His relation to bardic practice is thus of more than passing interest. Most poets are atavistic in degree, but in Yeats the tendency was nearly total, so much that his politics as well as his poetics could be summed up in this once-and-future way: What Ireland had been it should be.

The rat-rhymers were a minor but colorful part of a tradition that, among the Irish, goes back very far indeed. Ireland has been the home of distinctive peoples since at least 6000 B.C. A grand civilization—its jewelled brooches, its golden torques and war gear are on view in Dublin's National Museum—flourished between 3700 and 1800 B.C. Irish mythology contains numerous references to occupation of Ireland before the coming of the Celts themselves, who began arriving around 1200 B.C. in successive waves from the continent. Ireland's heroic sagas grew out of the exploits of these early Celtic tribes, a period that lasted into the fourth century A.D. Among these are the stories of the "Ulster" or "Red Branch" cycle, the best-known of which is *The Cattle Raid of Cooley*, a battle saga dominated by the figure of Cuchulain. In this epic poem, moreover, bards appear as characters in the plot, and their power to curse is a serious part of the action.

The magical-religious functions of the bards went unquestioned until Patrick began the Christianization of Ireland in 432. With the new breed of Irish saints—themselves renowned for cursing—the bards found their authority challenged and sometimes usurped. But also, it was during this early Christian period that clerical scribes began to record, in bulk and pell-mell, the countless stories of the earlier oral tradition. (*The Cattle Raid of Cooley*, for example, began to be recorded in the seventh and eighth centuries but was fully written down only around 1150 in the *Book of Leinster*.) The bards added the Christian art of writing to their repertoire of skills, and went on to regroup themselves into a literary caste with specific duties, schools, and ranks. The bardic schools were a great success and flourished from about 1200 into the 1600's—until the British were able to destroy the old Gaelic order supporting the bardic system. During the time of the schools, Irish verse reached its highest level of perfection and stands today as the oldest, most finely wrought vernacular of medieval Europe. By the end of the seventeenth century, however, the complicated craft of the schools was dying. The bards found themselves adrift, lacking patronage and courtly function. Now came the turning point, the great divide in bardic practice. Accentual meter replaced syllabics, and vowel rhyme gave way to consonantal chiming as the base of Irish poetry. Bards turned from court to countryside, and this "stepping down," as it was called, meant that poets had to take up the popular and usually penniless ways of the wandering rhymer.[15]

With rebellion crushed and England in control, poets sang of local events and the trials of neighborhood peasantry at the hands of alien overlords. In the bardic poetry of dispossession, lament and rage combined, and now the *aisling* appeared, the vision poem that catches a glimpse of Ireland's once and future glory in the form of a grieving young woman. The development of bardic craft was thus toward democratic forms. For the first time the figure of the bard emerges as the voice of "the Irishry." The paradox is that while Ireland's misery—its failed rebellions, its poverty and cultural deprivations enforced by the English—all but annihilated the earlier bardic order, there remained a distinct spirit of "bardic ambition," as I would call it, ready to serve the nation's need. Imagination had been transformed by political circumstance into a nationalistic force with enormous potential. The bardic past, with its capacity to empower, lay repressed but alive.

The ruin of Gaelic society was complete with Cromwell's invasion (1649–50) and the Williamite wars at the close of the seventeenth century. Even then, bards were remembered with respect. Writing in 1760, Oliver Goldsmith praised Thurlough O'Carolan, who died in 1738, as the last famous bard. Goldsmith also mentions, however, that among the Irish of his own day "their bards, in particular, are still held in great veneration."[16] For Yeats, writing in 1906, the last bard was "blind Raftery," who died in 1835 and whose grave, in 1900, Lady Gregory and Yeats honored with a headstone. Yeats gives Raftery an honored place in two poems, and makes him the example of oral artistry in his important essay "Literature and the Living Voice." Lady Gregory wrote twice about Raftery's life and art, essays that T. R. Henn edited with the following comment: "He [Raftery] was a remarkable man, and perhaps the last of the satirists of power, whose verses and epigrams were feared and admired by all. We may remember that satirists were regular members of the battle staff of ancient Irish kings, their business being to make poems against the enemy that might 'rot the flesh from their bones,' or, in lighter moments, destroy rats."[17]

When Yeats refers to "the rhyme rats hear before they die," he calls up an old and potent tradition, a fabric of practice and belief that can be recognized on decent evidence and pointed to concretely. As far back as documents reach (and not in Ireland alone), poets are famed and feared for their power to curse. The universal name for verse of this kind is *satire*, and the target—the person satirized—could expect terrible things to result: one might "lose face," or break out in a blistering rash, or die outright. Whether or not these effects stemmed from the force of a poet's words, whether they occurred at all, is not the point. The remarkable fact is that such anxious beliefs were so widespread and ingrained. Remarkable, too, is that neither in ancient times nor more recently has the Irish tradition admitted a distinction between the primitive *magical curse* and more sophisticated notions of *literary satire*. Fred Norris Robinson has taken up this point in detail; "Satirists and Enchanters in Early Irish Literature," his 1912 essay, remains the classic study of Irish bards at their malefic best:[18]

It seems like an unjustifiable looseness in language to use the same word [satire] for such dissimilar things. But as soon as one begins to examine the so-called satirical material in Irish literature, one finds difficulties in dispensing with the name. In the first place, the Irish language itself employs the same words (most commonly *aer* and its derivatives) for the rat-spells of Senchan and for the stricter satire of a later age. Furthermore, the persons described as pronouncing satires, even of the old destructive sort, were by no means always merely enchanters, but in many cases poets of high station, either in history or in sage. And finally, the subjects of their maleficent verse—often, for example, the inhospitality or other vices of chieftains—are such as might form suitable themes of genuine satire; and the purpose of the poets is frequently described as being to produce ridicule and shame. In short, it seems impossible in old Celtic literature to draw a line between what is strictly satire and what is not; and one ends by realizing that, for the ancient Celts themselves, the distinction did not exist. Just as their poets were not clearly separable from druids and medicine-men, but often combined in one person the functions of all three, so they freely mingled natural and supernatural processes in the practices of their arts. Destructive spells and poems of slander or abuse were all thought of together as the work, and it sometimes seems almost the chief work, of the tribal man of letters.

Robinson observes that "the association of mockery, invective, and magical injury" was "usual" in Gaelic practice. Ireland's ancient Brehon laws list many kinds of satiric abuse, with gradations as fine as these— "the blemish of a nickname, satirizing a man after his death, and satire of exceptional power [?]." This last kind isn't described; quite possibly it was connected with the dangerous skills of "hard attackers," as one class of bards was called. But with such powers assigned, we see why abuses of bardic privilege were classified as "crimes of the tongue."[19] As late as the seventeenth century a famous bard (Teig, son of Daire) challenged his own patrons (the O'Briens) by threatening to "nail a name" on them with his "blister-raising ranns."[20] The power implied here draws its force from values that anthropologists ascribe to "shame" cultures, although "fame" or "prestige" might better describe a culture of this kind. To "nail a name on a man" could ruin his tribal standing, destroy his reputation and the honor on which his personal worth depended. Pride, we recall, was chief among virtues for Yeats. Also interesting is that in Gaelic the same word stands for "face" and for "honor." In tribal Ireland, one's good name was one's pride and source of power. We get some idea of this from Frayes Moryson, an Elizabethan traveller who saw Irish chieftains "assume their old barbarous names whensoever they will have the power to lead the people to any rebellious action. For in those barbarous names and nicknames, the Irish are proud to have the rebellious acts of their forefathers sung by their bards and poets at their feasts and public meetings."[21]

For many centuries bardic practice was indigenous to the whole of the Indo-European world. In one regard, however, Ireland is special; its bardic tradition is more abundantly documented, and its practices survived a great deal longer than elsewhere in Europe. Because Ireland was never invaded by the Romans, the vernacular remained the language of learning and power. The spirit of the Renaissance, moreover, never crossed the Irish Sea; while other nations were pursuing the disenchantment of the world, Ireland was fighting for *its* world against the Tudors. The Normans had arrived in 1169, but made no attempt to stamp out native customs. But with the Reformation, and the decision of Henry VIII to centralize England's empire, Ireland found itself in a renegade posture, a defensiveness that was cultural as well as military.

Thanks to the hazards of history, the Irish held to a system of practice and belief that was common to the Indo-European past but that had vanished or been demoted to folklore and superstition on the continent. In *The Power of Satire*, Robert C. Elliott broadens this view by suggesting that the archaic reputation of poetry owed its prestige not only to the centrality of memorialization in oral cultures, but likewise to the authority of the curse as a formal or legal device—"Cursed be he who does (or does not do) this or that"—a patriarchal echo, perhaps, of "the father's curse." Elliott speculates, and I would agree, that cursing's magical rites are the spring from which bardic forms derive, and that the hegemony of poetry in antiquity had as much to do with fear—in other words, with power—as with the more obvious services that Plato had in mind when he advised poets to hymn the gods and praise famous men.[22] To suggest that Ireland's bardic tradition empowered Yeats to write as he did is not so wild a claim. If his confrontation with politics derives authority from bardic practice, this is only to say that an Irish poet took to heart an Irish option, a native and highly developed disposition that has often played its part in Irish art.

Sir John Davies called Ireland "the land of Ire." Edmund Campion, another Englishman observing the Irish, said in 1571 that "greedy of praise they be, and fearful of dishonor."[23] The English conviction that poets were responsible for Ireland's outlaw spirit provides the perspective from which to view Edmund Spenser's famous hostile remarks against Ireland's poets. Spenser was fascinated but also alarmed, and felt he should censure bardic behavior as he observed it from his castle in Cork. In *A view of the present state of Irelande*, written in 1596, he reports that the Irish "feare to runne into [bardic] reproach" because to be satirized is to "be made infamous in the mouthes of all men"—infamy of a sort that, to an Englishman, might be amusing. Not so the honor got from praise; in this case, Spenser judged, the rhymers were dangerous:[24]

> But these Irishe Bardes are for the moste parte of another minde and so farre from instructinge yonge men in morrall discipline that they themselues doe more deserue to be sharpe-lye discipled for they seldome vse to Chose out themselues the doinges of good men for the argumentes of theire poems but whom soeuer they finde to be moste Licentious of life moste bolde and lawles in his doinges most daungerous and desperate in all partes of disobedience and rebellious disposicion him they set vp and glorifye in theire Rymes him the praise to the people and to yonge men make an example to follow.

Spenser, of course, wrote the longest praise-poem in English. He would know that one policy dignified by *The Faerie Queene* was the Tudor attempt to quell the Irish by killing them off. What is interesting in Spenser's critique is how perfectly, by observing the Irish rhymers of his day, the Elizabethan poet foresaw Yeatsian preferences. In poem after poem Yeats celebrates figures who in orthodox terms can only be called "moste bolde and lawles" as well as "desperate in all partes of disobedience and rebellious disposicion." Maude Gonne is a capital instance, she who would

> Have taught to ignorant men most violent ways,
> Or hurled the little streets upon the great,
> Had they but courage equal to desire.

To praise is to recommend, to present an image for respect and emulation. It is also to endorse communal identity by lifting heroes into everyone's sight. This Yeats does, be it with Parnell and early martyrs like Robert Emmet and Wolfe Tone or, in "Beautiful Lofty Things," his father's "mischievous head thrown back" in answer to Abbey rioters. There is no question but that Yeatsian heroes are politically licentious;

no question but that Yeats was attentive to violence and embattled situations. But his delight in contention has the backing of bardic tradition. Irish bards have always cursed and called to battle. That has been their job, and in "Parnell's Funeral" the call to fight is direct:

> Come, fix upon me that accusing eye.
> I thirst for accusation.

It has been suggested that Yeats is calling Parnell's spirit to come and accuse him, but these lines are in the imperative mood and can be read as a command as much as a challenge. Of course there *is* a challenge here, but further on in stanza four we come to another command, this time overtly imperative: "Leave nothing but the nothings that belong / To this bare soul," and then yet another: "let all men judge that can." These charges summon a tribe and at the same time indict a collective antagonist. Those who destroyed Parnell, or made his kind of leadership impossible, are called by the poet to confront him face to face. When he says, "Come, fix upon me that accusing eye," Yeats spurns the *evil eye* of his opponents. Against their power he has powers of his own. He *thirsts* for confrontation, knowing Parnell and Swift will be with him. In this small but superlative instance Yeats sets himself up for a fight. He enacts the stance of the bard upon a field of war, then proceeds to do that which, in time of battle, bards do: hex and chant down the enemy.

That Yeats knew bardic tradition is certain. In an early letter he remarks that he has "found a wonderful account of the old bardic colleges" in *Memoirs of the Marquis of Clanricarde* (1722), a standard description of an actual bardic school (Yeats particularly liked the fact that fledgling poets were required to compose in the dark).[25] In his polemics of the 1890's he makes repeated use of the words *bard* and *bardic*, sometimes to designate a general type, at other times with meanings more historically exact. From early on, he took delight in "the power of the bards," as he calls it, including their satiric prowess:[26]

> The bards were the most powerful influence in the land and all manner of superstitious reverence environed them round. . . . Their rule was one of fear as much as love. A poem and an incantation were the same. A satire could fill a whole country-side with famine. Something of the same feeling still

survives, perhaps, in the extreme dread of being "rhymed up"
by some local maker of unkind verses.

For Yeats and his generation, the recovery of Ireland's heroic literature, and therefore of bardic tradition, began with Standish O'Grady's
History of Ireland, published in two volumes in 1878–80, along with
his *Early Bardic Literature*, published in 1879. His aim was to inspire
the Irish with their own heritage, and this, for Yeats, was "the start of
us all."[27] O'Grady argues in a fanciful but vigorous way that the heroes
of bardic literature owe their origin to historical figures, and that thanks
to the bards this important past has not been lost. He leaves the impres-
sion that the early bards were as grand, as large, as crucial to the nation
as the legendary heroes themselves.

If O'Grady was the catalyst and prophet to bardic recovery, Douglas
Hyde was its conduit and active oracle. Even today Hyde's books on
Celtic literature are worth reading. His *A Literary History of Ireland*
appeared in 1899 and is a work of real sweep and inspiration. A smaller
study, *The Story of Early Gaelic Literature*, came out in 1895, in which
the kernel of Hyde's larger argument first appeared. Perhaps the best
summary of his *History*, especially about bardic practices, is his *Irish
Poetry*, an essay in Gaelic with English translation for the little volume
of 1902. Finally, the whole of this tradition was wedged into an entry
called "Bards (Irish)" that Hyde wrote for Hastings' *Encyclopaedia of
Religion and Ethics*, including the following passage:[28]

We know, in the first place, that the poet was regarded as
possessed of powers sufficiently supernatural to make even
princes tremble; for with a well-aimed satire he could raise
boils and disfiguring blotches upon the countenance of his
opponents, or even do them to death by it. This belief continued until the later Middle Ages; and, even down to the days
of Dean Swift, the Irish poet was credited with the power of
being able to rhyme at least rats and vermin to death. Again,
the early Irish poet was, by virtue of his office, a judge in all
cases of tribal disputes and in other matters. He was also, if
not a Druid himself, probably closely allied with the Druidic
order.

Hyde was an open advocate of Irish culture as it encouraged national identity. In his work there is a steady mix of research and excited speculation. These ideas were available to Yeats at the peak of his own concern for literary nationalism, and at a time when Hyde's scholarship was (as we would now say) state of the art. That Yeats and Hyde were often together is clear from Yeats's early letters. They also ran into each other at Coole Park as frequent guests of Lady Gregory. When later Hyde allowed political programs to use him as a figurehead, Yeats took a dim view. But in the beginning he had nothing but respect; in his *Memoirs* he calls Hyde "the man most important to the future."[29] He went so far as to have one of his *Hanrahan* stories translated into Gaelic by Hyde, hoping that in this way it "might pass into legend as though he [Hanrahan] were an historical character."[30]

The "Stories of Red Hanrahan" were written in 1897 and revised, with Lady Gregory's help, in 1907. There is little doubt that Yeats put into his creation of Hanrahan much of the bardic lore that he and Lady Gregory gathered on their excursions among the peasantry in Ireland's western counties. Hanrahan begins as "the hedge schoolmaster," and spends most of his time wandering "among the villages," the village of Ballylee included, "finding a welcome in every place for the sake of the old times and of his poetry and his learning." During his lifetime Hanrahan has visions, encounters the Sidhe, and cannot be asked to leave any house he visits because "he is a poet of the Gael, and you know well if you would put a poet of the Gael out of the house, he would put a curse on you." In the story entitled "Red Hanrahan's Curse," the poet blasts the neighborhood's old men and has the children sing it about. The curse makes an interesting poem, but more to the point is that Hanrahan's rite of composition mimics the method practiced in the bardic schools: "he went and lay down on the bed to make a poem or a praise or a curse. And it was not long he was in making it this time, for the power of the curse-making bards was upon him."[31]

The Hanrahan stories show the slant of Yeats's concern, and it seems fair to suppose that he invested some part of himself in these tales. [It has been suggested, in a psychoanalytic sort of way, that the development of the character of Red Hanrahan is the poet's hidden script for his own aspirations, and possibly it is.[32]] I would also guess that the figure of the outcast poet, as it emerged in Irish history from the seventeenth into the nineteenth century, was the historical ground for Yeats's praise of beggars and visionary fools, "blind Raftery" in particular, the Gaelic poet famous among the farms and villages of Galway.

Hanrahan and Raftery make their appearance together in "The Tower," one of Yeats's central poems about his career as a poet. At age sixty, Yeats laments physical debility and is troubled by how to conduct himself. Section two opens with the poet pacing "upon the battlements," a defensive position in need of support—and thus the motive for the next twelve stanzas: he will summon, as he often did, powers of assistance. Chief among them are Hanrahan and Raftery. Yeats refers to Raftery's poem in praise of a young woman's beauty; certain men were "maddened by those rhymes," and in a later stanza Yeats says that "if I triumph I must make men mad." Next comes the story of Hanrahan turning a hand of cards into a pack of hounds. With these fabulous images in mind, Yeats goes on to ask a question of those he has summoned: Did they "rage / As I do against old age?" But of Hanrahan he asks a further question—Does imagination dwell most on defeat or victory?—and it is, finally, the figure of the bard that Yeats wants for assistance through the "labyrinth" of self-doubt. He bids farewell to the tribe he has summoned on these terms:

> Go therefore; but leave Hanrahan,
> For I need all his mighty memories.

Possibly these "mighty memories" include the whole of Ireland's past, the heroes of bardic remembrance among them. At this point Yeats is ready for the poem's finale, where he wills his "faith and pride" to Ireland's poetic posterity. There is more to "The Tower" than my attention to symbolic action discloses; but by making the poem's resolution depend on help from Hanrahan and Raftery, consanguinity is established between Yeats's poetic identity and his notion of Ireland's bardic heritage.

This is what Yeats knew himself to be, an inheritor of powers very old and very Irish. In confrontation with politics he relied on bardic practices, centrally on praise and blame, blessing and cursing, and then on lament and celebration, remembrance and instruction, complaint, consolation, and the keeping of wisdom. All poets make use of bardic resources in degree, but Yeats deployed them openly, in full force, and was most effective with these poetic tools—and weapons—in hand. They justified his calling and grounded his identity. They gave him the authority of a tradition that was undeniably grand and specifically Irish; and this ready tradition, in turn, was the source of his unusual confidence. Thus equipped, he could meet the world and know his audience. He could speak *to* and *for* and *against*. Moreover, as politics and the bardic stance emerge, the oppositional structure of Yeats's verse becomes more apparent: myth versus history; tragedy versus comedy; the crowd versus the lonely hero. He could assume poetry's importance in spite of politics—and then again because of politics.

Bardic practice does not restrict the poet's themes nor limit it to public occasions. Praise and blame are elementary or even elemental dispositions, and under their hegemony much else takes place. The bardic foundation of Yeats's poetry hinders neither the complexity of his art nor the range of private energies—thematic, symbolic—that Yeats sets going in his poems. In "Parnell's Funeral" moments of lament and blame are surpassed, in the end, by praise. These choices anchor the poet in relation to the world he speaks for and against, and also the world he speaks to. Once sure of his points of departure, he goes forward with a liberty the greater for the stability he enjoyed in setting forth. There might be several veins of concern, multiple beds of meaning, and much that transpires will be difficult to fathom.

Why, for example, does Yeats play out the drama of Parnell's downfall at this point in time, so many years after the event? The poem enacts a purgation of political sin, a cleansing that is national and private at once, but still—Why now? Possibly because lament for a dead leader is the occasion Yeats picks to broadcast his own quitting of politics. The poem is an elaborate rite of death and resurrection (Parnell's), a venting of despair (Yeats's), as well as a forum for bardic announcement. What Yeats declares is that from now on he will refuse the hospitality of any tribe—any party or ideological group—involved in Irish politics. Possibly, too, he feels that by identifying with the poem's hero (a symbolic action in any elegy) he partakes of the poem's regenerative blessings. His own "bare soul" having passed through Swift's dark grove is enriched by a bitter wisdom. We might even guess, as Auden once suggested, that in the end it's Yeats who eats of Parnell's heart.

Poetry of this kind is public and private at once. Threads of personal meaning can be traced so far and no further. For public issues, however, the use of bardic practices ought to include clear signals of social function—signs that an audience is part of the poem's occasion. In some final way, of course, the audience is anyone who takes delight and nourishment from what the poet has to say. More immediately, however, we can expect evidence of an auditor or addressee, named or implied. And this is, in fact, how Yeats proceeds. With poems of strict praise, the one spoken *of* is the one spoken *to*—for example, Maude Gonne in "Her Praise," which begins: "She is foremost of those that I would hear praised." The same can be said—speaking *of* as a means of speaking *to* —in poems that strictly blame or curse. "On Those That Hated 'The Playboy of the Western World,' 1907" is a poem aimed at the riotous defamers of Synge's play, and the delight in insult is plain to see:

> Once, when midnight smote the air,
> Eunuchs ran through Hell and met
> On every crowded street to stare
> Upon great Juan riding by:
> Even like these to rail and sweat
> Staring upon his sinewy thigh.

Yeats calls his enemies envious and vulgar, tells them to go to hell, and says they are lacking manly parts. As with much of bardic blaming, the poem attacks unworthy patronage, in this case the Abbey Theatre audience. In these instances the poet speaks to and about members of his own personal-professional world. Overall, Yeats's bardic "court" includes the following: persons he has known (the Gregorys, Maude Gonne); and then people he has known about (Parnell, Raftery); then the heroic figures of the Irish nationalist tradition (Tone, Fitzgerald et al.); then names from literature and legend (Blake or Swift on the one hand, Fergus and Cuchulain on the other); and finally fictional characters (Hanrahan, Crazy Jane) of his own imagining. Oddly interesting are moments when Yeats seems to be speaking *with* those whom he is speaking about. In "All Souls' Night" he praises dead friends as a way of evoking their presence—for thus, one by one, he would "call" them.

About Yeats's bardic ambition there is, however, a pressing question. In the twentieth century, a time of artistic as well as political alienation, how can someone like Yeats set up as a bard? He can choose any persona he likes, of course, and with it an appropriate manner. More to the point, Yeats had the good (if troubled) fortune to live in Ireland, where the century's tumult had been enacted small-scale, amid allegiances still distressingly tribal, with the added excitement of a recently recovered

"Celtic" tradition. And then—like any post-traditional poet—he simply had to rally what he needed to fulfill the requirements of his art. A poem like "The Fisherman," written in 1914, may seem an odd choice to follow "Parnell's Funeral," but in one way they are similar. The process of lifting Parnell into Swift's high company took Yeats many years, and this same process is the theme of "The Fisherman." In both poems the heroic image evolves from its unheroic opposite, and is praised against a background of blame. Here are the first lines:

> Although I can see him still,
> The freckled man who goes
> To a grey place on a hill
> In grey Connemara clothes
> At dawn to cast his flies,
> It's long since I began
> To call up to the eyes
> This wise and simple man.

Yeats might have had someone particular in mind, but the figure here is all archetype, a dawn-light hero to be praised for his solitude and patient skill, virtues that confer (or so Yeats would have it) wisdom and simplicity. These are virtues against the grain of modern personality, elements of an image antithetical to the real, and thus the poem continues:

> All day I'd looked in the face
> What I had hoped 'twould be
> To write for my own race
> And the reality.

What is looked in the face is both the reality and what the poet "hoped 'twould be," the magical word being *'twould* with its half-hidden *it*. Out of this mirror-like gap the fisherman begins to emerge, apart from the blameworthy crowd:

> The living men that I hate,
> The dead man that I loved,
> The craven man in his seat,
> The insolent unreproved,

> And no knave brought to book
> Who has won a drunken cheer.

"In scorn of this audience," Yeats summons an ideal recipient, someone fit to praise, and also someone glad for the gift of a poem:

> A man who does not exist,
> A man who is but a dream.

Yeats's concern for audience is constant, and much of his art depends on a bardic reciprocity whereby the poet summons a tribe even as the tribe has need of its poet. But how can an imaginary auditor suffice? The question of audience is crucial for poets in our century, especially for those who profess or attempt to take up bardic duties. In Yeats's case we should remember that, as a voice allied with the nationalist movement in politics and the arts, he had from early on a large and enthusiastic readership; at the turn of the century Ireland's literary consciousness was higher, more alert, than it would ever be again and Yeats often addressed the public—and expected to have an impact—by publishing his work in newspapers and popular magazines. Then too, he always had his friends; no modern poet has written more often or finely of loved ones and compatriots. Yeats, that is to say, was luckier than most; his tribe was never merely imaginary.

At the same time, however, he had a sort of genius for setting himself against prevailing opinion, especially in politics, and as a member of the Protestant Ascendancy he would always be apart from the Catholic majority in Ireland. These differences were pronounced to the degree that Yeats took seriously his role as bard to the Irishry; and here he did prefer to project an ideal audience, based on his embattled faith in what was possible to Ireland. In this latter sense, the lone figure in "The Fisherman" is the first member of a visionary company. Ten years later, in "The Tower," the poet begins by cursing his life, then goes on to praise his life, and ends by greeting—through naming—his once-and-future tribe:

> It is time that I wrote my will;
> I choose upstanding men
> That climb the streams until
> The fountain leap, and at dawn

> Drop their cast at the side
> Of dripping stone; I declare
> They shall inherit my pride,
> The pride of people that were
> Bound neither to Cause nor to State,
> Neither to slaves that were spat on,
> Nor to the tyrants that spat,
> The people of Burke and of Grattan.

The solitary fisherman has multiplied and formed alliance with a community of intellect beyond the shame of politics. This is Yeats's Anglo-Irish band of heroes that, in "The Seven Sages" especially, he liked to think of as his "tradition." Critics have been skeptical of a lineage so selective, but we might suppose that Yeats also had in mind an imagined court or tribe of the kind that any bard would value. (It's an interesting jolt to recognize that the last stanza of "Sailing to Byzantium," with its golden bird and drowsy Emperor, celebrates bardic practice—the court poet at work—in visionary terms.) Yeats's ideal audience becomes more elite as his political values become more aristocratic. And in this latter sense, Yeats's "tradition" begins with "The Fisherman," gathers head in "The Tower," and comes to resolution in "Under Ben Bulben," where the poet's will is a set of instructions passed on to those the poem evokes:

> Irish poets, learn your trade,
> Sing whatever is well made,
> Scorn the sort now growing up
> All out of shape from toe to top. . . .
> Cast your mind on other days
> That we in coming days may be
> Still the indomitable Irishry.

In sum, Yeats's audience finds itself named, or otherwise signified, in the rhetorical strategies of poem after poem. The poems I have mentioned carry with them their own scenes of reception, and they depend for their success on a rhetoric of address that creates its addressee or receiver. Yeats goes out of his way to let us know that he has an audience in mind, or that he wishes to include us in the tribal court he constructs for himself. And once his audience is right, praise follows.

Very rarely, however, did Yeats have the actual audience he wanted. Only in special circumstances does his embattled voice transcend the call to confrontation and address an audience from which no one is excluded—or at least no person Irish. One audience of this special kind was created by the Easter uprising. To that event Yeats responded with "Easter 1916," a poem often cited for its excellence. This famous example of poetry in the political vein is also a poem in the bardic mode. Much of its power derives from the bardic formalities Yeats used to speak for all of Ireland on this exceptional occasion.

The Easter revolt of 1916 had not been foreseen by Yeats, a circumstance that must have challenged his bardic prowess. He was in England and "fretted somewhat that he had not been consulted, had been left in ignorance of what was afoot."[33] Three years earlier he had thought the extravagances of romantic nationalism were dead, and in "September 1913" announced that the time of heroes was over:

> Romantic Ireland's dead and gone,
> It's with O'Leary in the grave.

Yeats had been expecting less and less from his compatriots at large. But from at large the uprising came; from men and women who had grown up on Yeats's own celebrations of heroic Ireland, especially his early and wildly popular political drama, *Cathleen ni Houlihan*, a play that insinuates the need for sacrificial blood ("They that have red cheeks will have pale cheeks for my sake") in Ireland's cause. A number of the rebellion's members Yeats knew personally, among them Thomas MacDonagh and Padraic Pearse. To Yeats MacDonagh dedicated his first book of poems; he also wrote a "rebel" play that was produced by The Abbey Theatre in 1908. Yeats's association with Pearse was closer and more profound. At St. Edna's School, Pearse taught Gaelic and the legends of heroic Ireland. Over the school's entrance he painted Cuchulain's motto: "I care not though I were to live but one day and one night, if only my fame and my deeds live after me." Later Yeats would say, in a letter, that "the young men who got themselves [killed] in 1916 had the Irish legendary hero Cuchullain [sic] so much in their minds that the Government has celebrated the event with a bad statue,"[34] the monument now in the Dublin Post Office. Pearse had a play staged at the Abbey and several times Yeats loaned the theater to St. Edna's students for benefit performances. There is no doubt that Pearse revered Yeats; and from Pearse came the call to rebellion. As Yeats put it without quite seeing the point: "There is going to be trouble—Pearse is going through Ireland preaching the blood sacrifice."[35] These men—along with John MacBride, the estranged husband of Maude Gonne, and the labor leader James Connolly—were among the heroes-to-be, the small souls grown magnificent under siege in the Dublin Post Office, and afterward shot by the British.

In stanza one of "Easter 1916" Yeats presents the leaders of the uprising as "them," a group of Dubliners such as the poet knew and moved among daily:

> I have met them at close of day
> Coming with vivid faces
> From counter or desk among grey
> Eighteenth-century houses.

Their lives conspire with the "casual comedy," or seem to; yet from this place "where [only] motley is worn" the uprising came. And it hit Yeats with greater impact than at first he could handle. In a letter to Lady Gregory, he described his initial reaction: "I had no idea that any public event could so deeply move me—and I am very despondent about the future."[36] That was in May 1916, when Yeats feared involving his art in issues directly political. But politics had intruded profoundly; he was unable to forswear his own deep feeling and the poem was finished in September.

In stanza two, the heroes of the uprising are individualized, but only as they appeared *before* the event—Constance Gore-Booth, who in her youth "rode to harriers"; Padraic Pearse, who "kept a school / And rode our winged horse"; Thomas MacDonagh just "coming into his force"; and John McBride, who "had done most bitter wrong." In stanzas one and two Yeats does the bardic work of announcing the heroes he intends to praise, but without naming them, and so far the verse—except for the visionary codas—has been descriptive only. But then an abrupt change occurs. Stanza three is wholly metaphorical, suggesting that the poem's formal movement is from "comic" scenes of desk and street to the "tragic" dais of sacrifice, from historic to prophetic envisionment. The poem likewise moves from blame to highly dignified praise. Much of the matter in stanzas one and two would be, in other poems, solely occasion for blame. To call someone a "drunken, vainglorious lout" is exactly what the bards meant by "nail[ing] a name on a man." In normal times, this kind of blame (and praise) would be enough. But in this poem the point is that normal times are suspended. Something extraordinary has burst upon the scene, transforming everything. Yeats brings up, and then overrides, his job of casting blame and gradually rises to praise purely. The condition of acceptance becomes so thorough that even the English—who "may keep faith"—are given the benefit of doubt. This generous stateliness of mood is possible because on this occasion the poet addresses his perfect audience. For once Yeats isn't counting his enemies. He leaves off bitterness and is reconciled with everyone, seeing instantly that in this the whole of Ireland shares:

> Now and in time to be,
> Wherever green is worn.

A condition of atonement informs "Easter 1916," and perhaps the sudden release from factiousness is reason enough to speak of astonishing change. But of the poem's four stanzas, three end in versions of the famous refrain, and it is clearly the transformation itself that is being praised as well as underscored by prophetic announcement:

> All changed, changed utterly:
> A terrible beauty is born.

Yeats had a habit of using "all" as a quick way to universalize his themes, but here the "all" is strictly meant. Every aspect of Irish life had been altered in the wake of the uprising, for good and for ill; and while critics like to stress the latter, playing on the reservations Yeats voiced in letters, there are no lines or sets of lines that stand up to, or against, the "terrible beauty" of the poem's refrain. What, then, does Yeats mean by this insistent chant? Very possibly, that the heroic dream has been reborn, compounded of honor for blood sacrifice and faith in the power of martyrdom. These energies are terrible (the violence) and beautiful (the poetic idea of heroism Yeats consistently praises). What saves this event, in Yeats's view, is that the resolve of sacrifice remained wholly ideal. The uprising was not undertaken in a spirit of practical politics. Knowing they were outflanked and outgunned, the rebels could not hope for an actual seizing of power. They were there as O'Rahilly was there:

> "Because I helped to wind the clock
> I come to hear it strike."

We might therefore ask, as Yeats does, what else besides death is there to announce? Or in that death, what spirit? What other triumph was at stake in a rebellion where defeat was foreknown? Might was not on their side; but the rebels had, instead, the tradition of romantic nationalism. They possessed the compelling authority of long-praised examples, the empowerment of figures like Cuchulain first of all. And if so, the uprising was invested with bardic energies. Yeats says as much in one of his last poems:

> When Pearse summoned Cuchulain to his side,
> What stalked through the Post Office?

If we conceive of poetry in postmodernist terms or in the fashion of practical criticism, we shall conclude that it can have no bearing upon life or action's deeper passions. But if we come at poetry from the bardic point of view, and assume a social-political situation in which the poet stands to his audience as the bard once stood to his tribe, then it begins to be possible that a connection exists between poetry and action *on occasion*. Yeats's "Easter 1916" is a praise-poem and its deeper theme is the splendor of the poetic idea as it transforms political action. About the "poetic idea" itself, furthermore, there is no shade of doubt; to look back upon the long torment of Irish history is to know that in Ireland one idea prevails, or so Yeats believed. In "The Literary Movement in Ireland," an important early essay, he wrote: "The popular poetry of England celebrates her victories, but the popular poetry of Ireland remembers only defeats and defeated persons. A ballad that is in every little threepenny and sixpenny ballad book asks if Ireland has no pride in her Lawrences and Wellingtons, and answers that they belong to the Empire and not to Ireland, whose 'heart beats high' for men who died in exile or in prison; and this ballad is the type of all."[37]

It was certainly the "type" for Yeats, the kind of heroism that stirred his imagination most and, during Easter week of 1916, the spirit that inspired not only "Easter 1916," but also "Sixteen Dead Men," "On A

Political Prisoner," and "The Rose Tree." The last of these ends with the resolve of sacrifice that informed the uprising:

> O plain as plain can be
> There's nothing but our own red blood
> Can make a right Rose Tree.

But actions of armed rebellion—especially those in which the rebels are at strategic disadvantage—do not reach the stage of no-return without imagination, broadly alive and fiercely focused, to carry them. Such actions will be bloody and Yeats's principal care, expressed in "Parnell's Funeral" and lodged at the heart of "Easter 1916," is to have violence informed by the poetic idea of sacrifice, and by the heroic resolve that sacrifice entails. This alone makes violence acceptable in Yeats's view. Quite possibly, therefore, the "terrible beauty" celebrated in this poem is a highly peculiar union of politics and poetry. It bears repeating, however, that for Yeats the only case in which a poetic idea informs a political action without the latter betraying the former is when the resolve of sacrifice is embraced as its own end. There will be no poems of praise for the victors but only for those on the losing side—or rather, the side that in the immediate event goes down.

This attitude toward sacrifice is a part of Yeats too often played down or denied, as if by going on and on about "heroic death" he could not mean real blood. But he did; he also believed that defeat is the condition for heroism and becomes thereby a prophetic force. That this was his conviction is plain in his praise for Robert Emmet: "Emmet had hoped to give Ireland the gift of a victorious life, an accomplished purpose. He failed in that, but he gave her what was almost as good—his heroic death. . . . And out of his grave his ideal has risen incorruptible. His martyrdom has changed the whole temper of the Irish nation. England celebrates her successes. . . . In Ireland we sing the men who fell nobly and thereby made an idea mighty."[38] In our time good poets won't be praising winners. Yeats makes this plain in "A Model for the Laureate":

> The Muse is mute when public men
> Applaud a modern throne.

I stress the centrality of defeat because beauty cannot be terrible, nor can terror call forth an exalted response, unless the beholder stands against the power that directly does the destroying. And it's exactly here that Yeats develops his notion of the sublime. Power is in every case the ground of exaltation, but there is vast difference between acceptance of external power (identification with the aggressor) and the kind of counterpower arising from within in the moment of terror. This crucial difference suggests that "terrible beauty" is Yeats's version of the *political sublime*, something as fitly Anglo-Irish as Edmund Burke saying "I know of nothing sublime which is not some modification of power,"[39] and as penetrating as Kant's notion of sublimity in which fear and grandeur meet to quiet the will and purge the self of pettiness. Speaking of boundless forces like the ocean in storm (Yeats's "murderous innocence of the sea"), Kant described sublime encounters this way: "we readily call these objects sublime, because they raise the forces of the soul above the height of vulgar commonplace, and discover within us a power of resistance of quite another kind, which gives us courage to be able to measure ourselves against the seeming omnipotence of nature."[40]

This "violence within," pushing back against "violence without," is a victory got from the knowledge of possible ruin, and the feeling that arises is not fear but sudden elevation. If one faces and stands up to terror, one discovers resources of one's own, "a power of resistance of quite another kind"; and it's this interior potency, in Kant's view, that gives us the courage to confront forces capable of extinguishing us. This isn't always possible, of course; but it is, all the same, the crucial point. The sublime moment is the key to human dignity because, in terms Yeats would approve, it provokes a necessary pride. As Kant says, it "saves humanity in our own person from humiliation, even though as mortal men we have to submit to external violence."[41]

In "Easter 1916" Yeats twice announces the advent of "terrible beauty," then turns to praise the agent of transformation. Stanza three is the singular section of the poem, the only sustained metaphorical part, the point where the poetic idea of sacrifice is introduced in its image of the stone and then connected to the power or agency of spirit that during the uprising showed itself equal to the forces of empire. Stanza three begins:

> Hearts with one purpose alone
> Through summer and winter seem
> Enchanted to a stone
> To trouble the living stream.

By the end of the stanza we know that "the stone's in the midst of all," and also that it stands in relation to "hearts with one purpose." Like the stone, this purpose and the hearts that hold it do not change with the seasons or the eroding motions of time. Everything else—horse and rider, cloud, stream, the moorcocks and hens—signifies life going on, ordinary and unheroic, the humdrum stream of Heraclitean flux. But just here, "in the midst of all," stands the stone. In moments of near-miracle it instigates another kind of change, the kind that transforms the human world by altering our sense of destiny. We might conclude that heroic potential always exists, at least in its poetic idea, and that no one knows when next it will break forth. We might also conclude, in Yeats's more metaphysical vein, that beyond the multitudinous surface of daily living the great historical gyres continually turn.

At first glance "Easter 1916" asserts that fundamental changes in our sense of destiny are owed more to events than to ideas; but *political* events are informed by ideas of their own. Yeats might scorn political beliefs in the abstract, but he saw instantly that the idea behind the Easter uprising was the poetic distillation of long experience, and that when it found its occasion, things did in fact change drastically. But if the poetic idea sometimes works wonders, its costly side effect is a hardness of heart in those who embrace it and a depleting impatience in those who love its promise. Thus stanza four begins:

> Too long a sacrifice
> Can make a stone of the heart.
> O when may it suffice?

The poem's last stanza is where critics find evidence to set Yeats at a distance from the violent action and obvious blood the poem commends. But Yeats is not at a distance. The objections usually cited—that sacrifice is "excessive," that "dreaming" can get you killed, that the British might be trustworthy and heroism "needless"—are raised to be transformed. The terms "needless" and "excess," as they appear in the poem, are not liabilities; within the framework of heroic striving they are virtues, and if needless excess allowed the uprising to embrace the poetic idea, then to "know they dreamed and are dead" is redemptive. To quiet doubts that might edge toward blame, Yeats fastens on hard fact ("No, no, not night but death") and makes it the unqualified ground for final praise—

precisely the tactic he used to insure challenged praise in "Sixteen Dead Men":

> You say that we should still the land
> Till Germany's overcome;
> But who can talk of give and take,
> Now Pearse is deaf and dumb?
> And is their logic to outweigh
> MacDonagh's bony thumb?

"Sixteen Dead Men" is an angry poem as "Easter 1916" is not. There Yeats addressed an opposition to the action he praised. "Easter 1916" envisions no opposing element. To everyone on this occasion the poet says that "our part [is to] murmur name upon name, / As a mother names her child" in sleep. The heroic names, once the poet gives them public life, will nourish from the cradle Ireland's dreams. Like the stone at the center, the poetic idea is everywhere on this occasion, shared by the dead, by the living, by the living with the dead. In the last lines the present is projected into the future ("Now and in time to be"); the implication is that the dream will be known and shared *because* the poet sets it forth in verse.

In "Easter 1916," Yeats was aware of his own bardic dignity more than he was in most of his poems. The roles of poet and audience are assigned; "we" is used twice, the "I" seven times and twice in an overtly bardic manner. In stanza two the poet says, "I number him in the song." Then in the great last lines of the poem, he shifts from his reckoning of communal responsibility ("our part," "We know") to an obligation solely his own as bard to the Irishry. With these distinctions in place, the formality of bardic utterance becomes the certification for what is announced in the poem's last lines. Yeats names the heroes in a way that celebrates community, and in a mood of muted exaltation offers a prophecy to the nation:

> I write it out in a verse—
> MacDonagh and MacBride
> And Connolly and Pearse
> Now and in time to be,
> Wherever green is worn,

> Are changed, changed utterly:
> A terrible beauty is born.

The formal progress of "Easter 1916" makes clear Yeats's strategy to heighten an expectation that shall then be fulfilled. He begins with "them," as if they were unnamed Dubliners merely. Then individual lives are cited, but without names. In stanza three they are elevated and set apart by the emblematic grandeur of the stone, but still unnamed. Finally, in the fourth and last stanza, the audience is told "to murmur name upon name," an instruction that anticipates the public success of the bardic naming in progress. Only *then*, after having foreseen this ceremonial moment through the whole of the poem, does Yeats write "it" out in a verse—as if these names were everything, which in the poem they are; as if a sacred rite were brought to conclusion, which in the poem it is.

Like many poems in response to political events, this one does not indicate or establish in the poem itself what its occasion is. The title sets the scene and sounds the theme of resurrection, but historical context must be found elsewhere—if, that is, the reader is not a member of the poet's tribe. No one ignorant of Ireland's torment could surmise, from the information in the poem, what the poet celebrates, although one might, as I suggested, determine the intended audience. This kind of obliquity is not unusual, not in Yeats nor in political poetry more generally. But here the omission works to enforce the poet's closeness with his tribe—those who know. This rapport accounts for the poem's compromise in response to an event so momentous. And the mood of atonement, in turn, allows for the simplicity of the poem's formal arrangements. The three- and four-beat lines are modest and exact; the rhyming is hushed, hardly noticed—not an easy feat for the shortness of line—and the rhyme scheme quietly stitches a pattern of quatrains into the larger stanzas. These minor traits of line and rhyme call attention to the fact that "Easter 1916" is a political ballad, a joining of praise and lament that, in Ireland, has been the bardic way.

·IV·

Yeats and *Hysterica Passio*

> With their vehement reaction against the despotism
> of fact, with their sensuous nature, their manifold striv-
> ing, their adverse destiny, their immense calamities,
> the Celts are the prime authors of this vein of piercing
> regret and passion. . . .
>
> —Matthew Arnold, 1867

The Easter uprising of 1916 was the only time Yeats saw his notion of the poetic idea—what I have called the resolve of sacrifice or the heroism of defeat—enter history directly, and with an integrity unshaken by circumstance. Soon the memory of that event would merge with a theology of bloodletting that haunts the Irish even now. Yeats went on to publish "Easter 1916," along with "The Rose Tree" and "Sixteen Dead Men," in 1920, in the middle of the Anglo-Irish war—a bold political maneuver that did not stop short of praising blood. To revive the mystique of the rebellion and turn it to account against the British was his aim. But if the poetic idea had worked for colonial conflict, it was of little use to what came next. Once Ireland's civil war got under way, Yeats saw his vision of "terrible beauty" become a shameless horror. As he said in 1922, "Perhaps there is nothing so dangerous to a modern state, when politics take [sic] the place of theology, as a bunch of martyrs. A bunch of martyrs (1916) were the bomb and we are living in the explosion."[1]

In later years Yeats questioned his role in Ireland's violent rise to nationhood. He knew "whatever flames upon the night / Man's own resinous heart has fed," and knew his work had helped inflame that heart:

> Did that play of mine send out
> Certain men the English shot?
> Did words of mine put too great strain
> On that woman's reeling brain?

From "The Man and the Echo," these are questions a poet sensible to bardic obligation would ask. They are also examples of Yeats's preference for rhetorical questioning, a much-used strategy allowing him to put forth his convictions in suspended form and goad the tribe to agreement. The rest of the poem suggests that they are night-thoughts as well ("I lie awake night after night"), the kind of what-ifs at three in the morning that make the dark seem darker. The power of language is at issue, and that Yeats troubles himself suggests his care for the ongoing way his words would be "modified," as Auden put it, "in the guts of the living."

Bardic responsibility is therefore part of it; but when *this* poet examines his relation to the tribe he has something more in mind, something deeper and more darkly shared. In Yeats's case, despite love of country and a steady will to bless, there's no doubting that his deepest disposition was his proneness to rage. Like Thersites among the Greeks at Troy, Yeats thrived on execration. This might have blighted his art but did not; one of the foremost things about Yeats is that he is splendid to the degree he holds his daemon in check. I have already mentioned the exceptional calm of "Easter 1916," a tranquillity unusual for Yeats in that so much of his work enacts a drama of opposites, keeping the poems impassioned and the poet in a fervor. The remarkable thing is the degree to which Yeats and much of his Irish audience were given to seizures of political hate:

> popular rage,
> *Hysterico passio* dragged this quarry down.

Public passion of this kind isn't special to Ireland, but is the outcome of extremity anywhere. Even so, to take Yeats seriously is to come away with a feeling for the poet and the Ireland of his time that is thick with political wrath. He suggests that dreaming too often defeated can be terrible—as the civil war was terrible—in its outcome:

> We had fed the heart on fantasies,
> The heart's grown brutal from the fare;

More substance in our enmities
Than in our love.

Yeats is speaking for the nation and himself, as well he might, knowing his daemon with almost fearsome candor. In "Remorse for Intemperate Speech," dated August 28, 1931, he blames himself in a keen determined sort of way, but the sound is closer to praise than to blame or remorse. I quote all three stanzas, the better to appreciate the way the end-lines speak obsession:

I ranted to the knave and fool,
But outgrew that school,
Would transform the part,
Fit audience found, but cannot rule
My fanatic heart.

I sought my betters: though in each
Fine manners, liberal speech,
Turned hatred into sport,
Nothing said or done can reach
My fanatic heart.

Out of Ireland have we come.
Great hatred, little room,
Maimed us at the start.
I carry from my mother's womb
A fanatic heart.

The poem is part confession, part curse, its hardness made the harder by the line "my fanatic heart" having (as Yeats says in a page note) only two beats. The poet unburdens himself by placing the onus of his curse on Ireland as a whole, moving from "I" to "we" and from "my" heart to "a" heart. The result seems almost prideful. Or is it despair? If the latter, then it's of the kind that Kierkegaard called "demonic despair," the kind that vaunts in its own damnation as, for example, Satan does in *Paradise Lost*. Is the poem a plaint or a boast—or both together? Nothing, the poet tells us, can rule or reach a core of brazen anger at the heart of him. That, I believe, is the stark unlovely truth about Yeats. But at the same time I take the hint from "mother's womb" to suggest that although Yeats was a large and inveterate hater, his portion of "Celtic ferocity" was also his mother-wit, the dark strain in his vision that was his motive, often, for metaphor.

Perhaps I overstate. In a poet whose capacity to bless was also great, hatred may be muted or transmuted by the interplay of praise and blame. And Yeats did often "bless." The word and its variants appears some fifty times in his poetry. In "A Prayer On Going into My House," for example, the poem begins:

> God grant a blessing on this tower and cottage
> And on my heirs.

The occasion is a happy one, the Norman tower Yeats purchased in June 1917 being now, in October 1918, ready to inhabit. The poem ends with a playful curse:

> . . . and should some limb of the devil
> Destroy the view by cutting down an ash
> That shades the road, or setting up a cottage
> Planned in a government office, shorten his life,
> Manacle his soul upon the Red Sea bottom.

Ten years later, in "Blood and the Moon," the blessing and the curse are more serious—and harder to sort out:

> Blessed be this place,
> More blessed still this tower;
> A bloody, arrogant power
> Rose out of the race
> Uttering, mastering it,
> Rose like these walls from these
> Storm-beaten cottages—
> In mockery I have set
> A powerful emblem up,
> And sing it rhyme upon rhyme
> In mockery of a time
> Half dead at the top.

What had intervened, amid much else, was the terror of the civil war, and it's in "Meditations in Time of Civil War" (1923) that Yeats makes one of his most extreme curses. Here he does his best to bless his house, his table, his descendants; yet with his visionary sense of "Coming Emptiness" he fears his children may betray the place and tradition his work of a lifetime would give them. Should that come to pass,

> May this laborious stair and this stark tower
> Become a roofless ruin that the owl
> May build in the cracked masonry and cry
> Her desolation to the desolate sky.

Only in "Nineteen Hundred and Nineteen," in the section on mockery, does Yeats elsewhere utter a curse so severe. His daemon was often provoked, sometimes beyond the help of blessing. And then the hard sayings came. To think otherwise is to mistake Yeats and not to know his art, or its kind, or the dark fount from which its famous power sprang.

As critics like to point out, Yeats had at least two views on every issue, the outcome of his attraction to antinomies. His attitude toward hatred was true to that form. Sometimes he praised it, sometimes he condemned it. In "Poetry and Tradition," an early essay, he takes a surprisingly splendid view. Criticizing Maude Gonne for too much engagement in "little" enmities, he goes on to say: "All movements are held together more by what they hate than by what they love, for love separates and individualises and quiets, but the nobler movements, the only movements on which literature can found itself, hate great and lasting things."[2] We get some idea of what Yeats means by "great and lasting things" in "A General Introduction for My Work," one of his later essays, where he argues that the historical conflict between Ireland and England, so replete with misery and failure, is the ground of the hatred he finds in himself: "No people hate as we do in whom that past is always alive; there are moments when hatred poisons my life and I accuse myself of effeminacy because I have not given it adequate expression. . . . I am like the Tibetan monk who dreams at his initiation that he is eaten by a wild beast and learns on waking that he himself is eater and eaten. This is Irish hatred and solitude, the hatred of human life that made

Swift write *Gulliver* and the epitaph upon his tomb, that can still make us wag between extremes and doubt our sanity."[3]

Yeats praises Parnell by saying "through Jonathan Swift's dark grove he passed," and the affiliation of hatred with eating or being devoured might also suggest why the author of "A Modest Proposal" was chief among Yeats's Anglo-Irish heroes. "Swift's Epitaph" is Yeats's homage to a species of rage that in his view is exemplary, a version of political *virtu*:

> Swift has sailed into his rest;
> Savage indignation there
> Cannot lacerate his breast.
> Imitate him if you dare,
> World-besotten traveller; he
> Served human liberty.

If Yeats's capacity for anger is understood in the wider context of Irish history, and if to that is added his horror of impotence in any form, another perspective opens on his readiness to arm his poems with rage. In the "Introduction" to his edition of *The Oxford Book of Modern Verse*, Yeats said he did not include "poems written in the midst of the great war"—work by Wilfred Owen, for example—because these poets felt bound "to plead the suffering of their men [and] passive suffering is not a theme for poetry."[4] There is very little depiction of suffering in Yeats's poetry, although much pain is taken for granted. More to the point, the Christian exhortation to accept suffering and bear it with humility is an abnegation, for Yeats, of necessary pride. Ireland loves its martyrs, but the pagan or tragic sense of life Yeats celebrates permits no cult of the victim. (In this he is very unmodern, and at odds with more recent Irish poets, Seamus Heaney in particular.) The substantial irony is that while Yeats's heroic ethic rejects the pathos of suffering and defeat, his atavistic politics compels him always into no-win situations. His solution, his way out, has everything to do with the active attitude he takes in his art. Rather than be cowed or wear blood on his sleeve, he chooses instead to praise the heroism of defeat on the one hand, and on the other to rail, blame, curse, accuse, and generally thrive on rage. He will *not* be passive, he will *not* feel powerless. Rather, he takes up an honored stance and performs an honored office. He exercises his bardic right, long blessed by Irish example, to savage indignation.

The numerical instance of angry poems, of hate songs plain and simple, is as manifest as other voices in Yeats's work, often within poems that register blame and praise by turns or as one amid several voices in discordant chorus—lines, for example, in "Under Ben Bulben," Yeats's bardic farewell:

> Know that when all words are said
> And a man is fighting mad,
> Something drops from eyes long blind,
> He completes his partial mind,
> For an instant stands at ease,
> Laughs aloud, his heart at peace.

Yeats liked to be "fighting mad." At the same time, however, he was often of a mind to condemn this kind of passion. Perhaps the lines best known, and most often used by critics to defend Yeats from himself, come from "A Prayer for My Daughter." Here he says, "to be choked with hate / May well be of all evil chances chief," and he concludes by affirming that "hatred driven hence, / The soul recovers radical innocence." Certainly Yeats knew the effects of political rancor, but rather than blame himself, his habit was to put the burden on women who had entered politics. Maude Gonne is called "an old bellows full of angry wind." The mind of Constance Gore-Booth becomes "a bitter, an abstract thing." Yeats projects his own opinionated mind upon women whom he would rather see, in the old Pre-Raphaelite way, as icons of mysterious beauty. His constant instruction is to avoid contention. His constant promise is a ceremonious grace to be gained. These are blessings he would like to have, but cannot manage, for himself.

Yeats had plenty of reason to know that political wrath is dangerous energy. What saves him is the responsibility—and even more, the formality—that comes with his bardic obligation to cast blame. When he curses in a fit of rage he condemns abuses worth the curse. When he blames women for indulging in public anger, he produces a critique of habits harmful to himself or anyone. Either way the poetry gains. A hatred so primal, however, argues more than thematic vigor, more than bardic authority. There is also, as Conor Cruise O'Brien has suggested, hatred's sheer prophetic power in Yeats's case.[5] O'Brien argues that Yeats's extraordinary talent for hate put the poet in touch with the monstrous capacity for hatred emerging all across Europe—the national self-hatred of Russia under Stalin, of Germany under Hitler, or the way lesser nations, France, Italy, the Balkans, allowed the "growing murderousness of the world"[6] a stranglehold upon their own abysmal destinies. O'Brien quotes the passage I cited earlier from Yeats's "A General Introduction to My Work," and goes on to quote these further remarks from the same essay:[7]

> When I stand upon O'Connell Bridge in the half-light and notice that discordant architecture, all those electric signs, where modern heterogeneity has taken physical form, a vague hatred comes up out of my own dark and I am certain that wherever in Europe there are minds strong enough to lead others the same vague hatred arises; in four or five or in less generations this hatred will have issued in violence and imposed some kind of rule of kindred. I cannot know the nature of that rule, for its opposite fills the light; all I can do to bring it nearer is to intensify my hatred.

Yeats's view of Dublin in 1937 expresses the despair of national destiny he announced in "Parnell's Funeral"—a revealing, or even damning, moment of horror at the modern world's gross discord. Yet one appreciates these remarks for their honesty. Yeats's candor is the more valuable for the connection he makes between his own political nihilism, born of defeat, and the furious nihilism, born of political vacuum, that would soon flatten Europe and change the world utterly. Yeats, who died in January 1939, was right more deeply than he had the time to know. His great prophetic poem "The Second Coming" is remarkable for the force of its forecast, and also for the precision of Yeats's instinct for political catastrophe:

> Things fall apart; the centre cannot hold;
> Mere anarchy is loosed upon the world,
> The blood-dimmed tide is loosed, and everywhere
> The ceremony of innocence is drowned;
> The best lack all conviction, while the worst
> Are full of passionate intensity.

O'Brien concludes that his capacity for rage gave Yeats, more than other poets of the time (except perhaps Brecht, also a hater), the visionary means to grasp the political character of the century he lived in—which is largely, I believe, why the poetry of Yeats continues to strike us as news that stays news. O'Brien sums it up this way:[8]

> The 'fanatic heart', an unusual capacity for hatred and an unusual experience of it, probably made him more sensitive and more responsive to the 'telepathic waves' coming from Europe than other writers in English seem to have been. The forces in him that responded to the hatred, cruelty and violence welling up in Europe produced the prophetic images of 'The Second Coming' and the last part of 'Nineteen Hundred and Nineteen.'

The demonic element in Yeats cannot be ignored, in particular his share in the political passion he named, with mingled fascination and disgust, *hysterica passio*. Yeats took the phrase from *King Lear* (II, iv, 57), where the old king first detects the madness welling up within him. Lear has lost his kingdom and his kingly powers. He has exiled Cordelia and Kent, and now sits open to disasters that are greater than human agency but are still, in no small part, of his own instigation. Foretelling the whole of his mad rage on the heath, Lear says:

> O how this mother swells up toward my heart.
> *Hysterica passio!* Down, thou climbing sorrow!

Shakespeare got his terms from Harsnet's treatise on demonic possession, a source that Yeats might have appreciated. But the surest gloss is the spectacle of *Lear* itself—the crazed wedding of storm and madness on the heath; the ruling metaphors of blindness and monstrosity; the indissoluble mix of personal and political emotion; and not least, in this darkest of tragedies, the ubiquitous rhetoric of cursing. Such are the symptoms of politics gone mad with rage. The peculiar horror of *hysterica passio* is that it engulfs its cause; it consumes everything it embraces and feeds upon itself but, like the world before creation, remains without form and void. To think of historical examples—Robespierre's Terror or the Stalinist purges—is to behold the underside of apocalypse.

Yeats uses this peculiar phrase to deepen the view we take, presuming immunity, toward political fanaticism generally. Rarely have victims of rabid politics survived, or recovered sufficiently to testify to symptoms that arise from hysteria of this collective kind. In his last poem about Maude Gonne, he imagines her eternalized by art, her soul forever facing the "*hysterica passio* of its own emptiness." That Yeats himself was subject to this affliction means that he was daemon-driven but more exactly that a principal problem for his art was how to handle it, how to seize to art's advantage "the uncontrollable mystery on the bestial floor." No poet, after all, can hope for clarity of vision while caught up in frenzy. Possibly this explains why so many poets in our century prefer to believe that political passions cannot matter. To decide otherwise is to risk confronting a *hysterica passio* destructive to art and life both. Yeats, to his credit, did confront it. He took the risk, and through it turned his art into its great maturity.

The commonplace about Yeats is that he started a dreamer in the languid ornate style of Pre-Raphaelite aestheticism, but that he then revised himself—*Responsibilities*, the volume of 1914, is the turning point usually cited—and thereafter became tougher and more direct, as if speaking *to* someone. As he himself put it, his early style was "dream-laden," but by 1902 he was starting to change: "My work has got more masculine. It has more salt in it."[9] Critics who prefer Yeats's occult speculations point to the emergence of an "anti-self" as the circumstance that changed his style. Critics who think poets only respond to the goings-on of other poets attribute the change to Ezra Pound, who, from around 1912 to about 1916, was often in Yeats's company. Doubtless Pound helped; but Yeats had embarked upon a major revision of his earlier poems in 1908, and the mature style of his later poetry is plainly visible in such pre-Poundian work as "The Fascination of What's Difficult," written no later than March 1910:

> My curse on plays
> That have to be set up in fifty ways,
> On the day's war with every knave and dolt,
> Theatre business, management of men.

The endless ordeal of "theatre business" brings us closer to the truth where, to begin with, the writing of plays—the requirements of speech responsive to situation; the need for language alive with the force of its occasion—accounts for part of the change in Yeats's style. He and his friends founded the Irish National Theatre Society in 1902, followed by The Abbey Theatre two years later, and by 1908 Yeats had a dozen plays to his credit. That writing for the stage accounts in part for Yeats's stylistic shift seems certain. But there would also be the social and political "business" of Dublin theater, the "day's war with every knave and dolt." The Irish had never had a theater, and Yeats expected drama to do great things for the nation. The author of *Cathleen ni Houlihan* was pleased, moreover, to produce drama involving politics. But he was besieged by people insisting that a play was not "political" unless its value as propaganda was declared outright, nor would the strident sectors of the Dublin audience—the press and the burgeoning middle class—tolerate portraits of Irish character not cast in saintly light.

The history of Yeats's disillusionment involved more than I can recount here. The point to keep in mind is that once Yeats came into his own as poet and playwright and then director of The Abbey Theatre, he possessed real power but ran into nonstop resistance from every side. And gradually his rage kindled. He saw Maude Gonne hissed off the stage for daring to separate from her husband. He saw Synge's *Playboy of the Western World* answered by riots and Synge dead, in 1909, at the age of forty-five. Other of Yeats's cherished friends, Lady Gregory included, were reviled by the press. The audience Yeats hoped to inspire with heroic ideals was showing instead a penchant for bigotry and spite. During this same period, further cause for bitterness came with Hugh Lane's attempt to build an art gallery and donate his valuable private collection to the nation, an act of largesse defeated by rancor and rebuff in a sequence of shameful events lasting into 1913. About the Lane affair Yeats wrote some of his finest early political verse. In "To a Shade" he calls to Parnell and, ringing praise against blame, curses the "pack" for once more dragging down a benefactor:

> A man
> Of your own passionate serving kind who had brought
> In his full hands what, had they only known,
> Had given their children's children loftier thought,
> Sweeter emotion, working in their veins
> Like gentle blood, has been driven from the place,
> And insult heaped upon him for his pains,
> And for his open-handedness, disgrace. . . .

The poem is dated September 19, 1913, just when the design for Lane's Dublin museum was rejected, causing Yeats to say: "I had not thought I could feel so bitterly over any public event."[10] Decidedly, his dream of a nation insuring its "children's children loftier thought" was foundering. Approaching his fiftieth year, Yeats saw Ireland's heroic tradition abandoned, the public import of his own work cancelled. Now it was he wrote "September 1913," one of the poems of "bitter wisdom" that makes *Responsibilities* his first important book:

> Was it for this the wild geese spread
> The grey wing upon every tide;
> For this that all that blood was shed,
> For this Edward Fitzgerald died,
> And Robert Emmet and Wolfe Tone,
> All that delirium of the brave?

"The wild geese" is Ireland's name for a military elite that held out against the British after the Gaelic chieftains fled in 1607, but that finally departed for courtly service in Europe. Yeats, too, felt forced to abandon home ground. And because he was proud and quick-tempered, because he loved the fight but found himself outflanked, years of anger swelled into a rage that set him contending with attacks of *hysterica passio*. That this was his own especial daemon is not the least in doubt. Here is how he describes it: "The feeling is always the same: a consciousness of energy, of certainty, and of transforming power stopped by a wall, by something one must either submit to or rage against helplessly. It often alarms me; is it the root of madness?"[11] Yeats is describing a profoundly political emotion. When he speaks of *hysterica passio*, he knows what he means. And he knew it would destroy him if the one weapon always his, his great gift for language, did not provide rescue.

Rage controlled is the circumstance of power as we feel it in Yeats's language. He said in his memoirs, "I had to subdue a kind of Jacobin rage. I escaped from it all as a writer through my sense of style."[12] And in a letter to Dorothy Wellesley, speaking of the power in his art, he said: "[it] comes from the fact that the speakers are holding down violence or madness—'down Hysterica passio'. All depends on the completeness of the holding down, on the stirring of the beast underneath."[13] This is the deep and final dynamic of the stylistic change so often remarked as the factor that turned Yeats to greatness. Fundamental to everything else about Yeats is the intimate degree to which political experience is integral to his genius. His confrontation with politics precipitated a crisis that, by resorting to his art to save him, saved his art and brought his bardic powers to full exercise. He always insisted that heroism is born of self-struggle and self-overcoming. This was his struggle, and in his art we see the overcoming.

Yeats's strengthened art is first evident in the fistful of political poems in *Responsibilities*. Here he curses the *Playboy* rioters, curses likewise "the obscure spite / Of our old Paudeen in his shop," and mocks the dolls that deride the living child. Here, too, he warns Maude Gonne's daughter, Iseult, against "the monstrous crying of the wind" and counsels Lady Gregory to "be secret and exult" when attacked by the press. And here, finally, he praises Hugh Lane by comparing him to the figure of a Renaissance prince "upon Urbino's windy hill." In a fury over Dublin's refusal to appoint Lane curator of the Municipal Gallery, Yeats wrote "An Appointment," a poem that may appear slight or merely playful but that addresses a bitter occasion and is a good example—in fact this is its theme—of rage reined in and transformed by style:

> Being out of heart with government
> I took a broken root to fling
> Where the proud, wayward squirrel went,
> Taking delight that he could spring;
> And he, with that low whinnying sound
> That is like laughter, sprang again
> And so to the other tree at a bound.
> Nor the tame will, nor timid brain,
> Nor heavy knitting of the brow
> Bred that fierce tooth and cleanly limb
> And threw him up to laugh on the bough;
> No government appointed him.

The poem begins in angry impotence, but then goes on to praise a style the poet would salvage from his rage, a style neither tame nor timid, with "fierce tooth and cleanly limb," and with a voice, agile as a squirrel, that leads its occasion. In this light, the poem reads like a small manifesto. Right style is equated with the investment of rage in a stance that is "wayward" and lean. In *Responsibilities* Yeats masters political hatred. At this point in his work the bardic voice, speaking to and for and against, begins to be his mainstay.

In his later poetry, Yeats confronted the climate of atrocity that prevailed in Ireland as the Irish Free State was coming into being, a terror of the kind that typifies violence in our century, terror blank and unredeemed, with nothing heroic about it and no poetic idea to absorb the blood or dignify the loss of life. As times grew darker, Yeats's sense of political violence hardened as well. In its more disastrous enactments, politics seemed something impersonal, demonic, a force like the "levelling wind." And in its aftermath came bitterness. The word *bitter* carries an aura of political meaning in Yeats's later poems, signalling the spiritual outcome of long wounding that is very like scar tissue—except that to "be bitter" implies an active state, a "holding down" of ruinous passions. And while bitterness is not without its cost, it also has its uses. In 1928 Yeats wrote to Olivia Shakespear: "Re-reading *The Tower* I was astonished at its bitterness, and long to live out of Ireland that I may find some new vintage. Yet that bitterness gave the book its power and it is the best book I have written. Perhaps if I was in better health I should be content to be bitter."[14]

When Parnell passes through "Jonathan Swift's dark grove," he is blessed by "bitter wisdom"; he moves, that is, from fallenness to redemption. The fall is into time and politics, and when it happens, innocence is lost; so is sweetness of soul. Life is inescapably tragic because we take "our greatness with our bitterness"; everyone falls, but few gain understanding. Ireland is a "blind bitter land," and Dublin a "blind bitter town." Wisdom is the highest prize Yeats knows, a bardic gift he labors to conserve and pass on to others of his tribe. But they "turn dull-eyed away" when (in "The Results of Thought") he tries to "summon back" their "wholesome strength":

> The best-endowed, the elect,
> All by their youth undone,
> All, all by that inhuman
> Bitter glory wrecked.

What kind of bitter glory might be anybody's guess—except that this is Ireland and the poet is Yeats. We know, that is, that politics has played its part in the wreckage. We might also guess that these—the elect, the best-endowed—succumbed to the sort of hysterical passion that Yeats most dreaded, having barely survived it himself. The power of politics is "inhuman" in its exercise, but also in the way it possesses mind and soul, and makes of the self "a bitter, an abstract thing." When it takes hold of a nation, it is like the rough beast arriving—or the ruinous brunt of a mainforce wind.

In 1903 came a devastating storm that impressed Yeats for the damage it did to Lady Gregory's woodlands at Coole Park. That was also the year of Maude Gonne's marriage to MacBride, another sort of disaster. And 1903 was when *In the Seven Woods* appeared, the volume that included "Adam's Curse" and "Red Hanrahan's Song About Ireland," to which Yeats added a note about "the big wind of nineteen hundred and three [that] blew down so many trees, & troubled the wild creatures, & changed the look of things."[15] As early as 1899, in *The Wind Among the Reeds*, Yeats imagined the wind in mythical terms. In a note to "The Hosting of the Sidhe" he speaks of transhuman powers, and in a reference to Herodias he anticipated by twenty years the nightmarish ending of "Nineteen Hundred and Nineteen":[16]

The gods of ancient Ireland . . . still ride the country as of old. Sidhe is also Gaelic for wind, and certainly the Sidhe have much to do with the wind. They journey in whirling wind, the winds that were called the dance of the daughters of Herodias in the Middle Ages, Herodias doubtless taking the place of some old goddess. When old countrypeople see the leaves whirling on the road they bless themselves, because they believe the Sidhe to be passing by.

In Yeats's imagery of wind there is an expanding significance, from early associations with the inhuman Sidhe to later usage in the poems about political terror, where again it signals a calamitous power. Like so much of Yeats's work, this kind of imagery includes vein upon vein of reference, until finally the hope of mapping it becomes impossible. Yeats's usage of what he called "the symbol" or "the poetic image" exploits the fact that figural language carries meaning in excess of that which, in any controlled thematic sense, particular contexts can account for. This is true of words generally, a condition of language that the poets of the Symbolist Movement explored with great excitement in the 1890's. Their lesson was not lost on Yeats. He delighted in ending poems with grandly overdetermined images—the beast of "The Second Coming," the great horse-chestnut in "Among School Children" are proof of his genius for turning doubtful theories (in this case the symbolist mystique) to potent account. A poem like "Easter 1916," with its abrupt shift to the image of "the stone" in stanza three, and the last part of "Nineteen Hundred and Nineteen," with its elaborate image of the wind as cause of demonic compulsion, suggest that the symbolist manner and prophetic announcement work well together in bardic practice, increasing Yeats's capacity to deal with political violence.

At the close of his elegy on the death of Robert Gregory, Yeats says the poem was prompted by "seeing how bitter is that wind / That shakes the shutter." In "To a Child Dancing in the Wind," he worries at a young girl's ignorance, but praises the charm of such intrepid disregard:

> What need have you to dread
> The monstrous crying of the wind?

In "A Prayer for My Daughter" he answers that question. He foresees the worst, then counters his vision of the tree-wracking wind with praise for innocence rooted in the wisdom of the laurel. Yeats dated this bardic invocation June 1919, as the war with England was edging toward horror, when like any parent anywhere he feared for the life and mind of a child born into dark times:

> I have walked and prayed for this young child an hour
> And heard the sea-wind scream upon the tower,
> And under the arches of the bridge, and scream
> In the elms above the flooded stream;
> Imagining in excited reverie
> That the future years had come,
> Dancing to a frenzied drum,
> Out of the murderous innocence of the sea.

Images of howling storm and "roof-levelling wind" announce the disturbance approaching. The storm of 1903 comes to mind, but this one screams like a voice out of the whirlwind. It is a sign of the times, and Yeats is certain he knows what it means. In "excited reverie" he beholds the coming of calamity, disasters already under way. The world begins its "dancing to a frenzied drum," driven by the political distraction of elemental energies.

The sea is innocent, a realm of primal energy; but when the waves are wind-swept, innocence turns murderous. The union of these images suggests that the world's increasing violence is political (the open meshing of human actions), but also metaphysical (necessary cycles in historical time). These contraries mark the ultimate antinomy in Yeats's poetry. When he rails against politics he blames and curses, looking upon the world of action as a mass of events created by men and women acting freely. But when he takes up the bardic office of prophecy, he gains a vantage from which all things are brought to pass by forces at once transhuman and inexorable. In this visionary perspective, the world of action is blameless; no one rails against the wind, and history viewed under the aspect of eternity suggests that the world isn't what it seems. Up close one sees politics as a field of bitterness and rage. But at a distance the design comes into view, and one beholds the great relentless gyres that inspire wise acceptance.

This duality—violence as freedom, violence as necessity—is the heart of politics as tragedy. What Sophocles said in *Antigone*, Yeats repeats in his poem on civil war: we "take our greatness with our violence." In the prayer for his daughter, what therefore can the poet do, once he hears "the sea-wind scream," except bless his child, bless her repeatedly and in the old conventional ways: "May she be granted beauty . . . O may she live like some green laurel." He curses political hatred, makes an example of Maude Gonne, then offers this assurance:

> If there's no hatred in a mind
> Assault and battery of the wind
> Can never tear the linnet from the leaf.

If these lines are not received for what they are—a bardic blessing—an apparent conflict arises between the premonition of violence so convincingly announced in stanzas one and two, and the gracious certitudes Yeats seems to utter thereafter, as if "in custom and in ceremony" his daughter might somehow find real safety. But there is, Yeats knows, no safety. What, then, can be the point of setting the polite laurel against the tree-wracking wind? If this were a poem in the high Romantic manner, wherein poetic imagination is sufficient to transform that which threatens it, we might accept an image of the world in which "ceremony's

a name for the rich horn, / And custom for the spreading laurel tree"—
accept it and take it for a victory. But not here. The poem is replete
with warning and instructs us to take the vision of political violence—
the catastrophic bodings of "excited reverie"—as the poem's occasion.
The most the poet can do for loved ones is bless them. As he tells
us, the poem is a *prayer*, a bulwark of words against misfortune.

In both "A Prayer for My Daughter" and "Easter 1916" the immediate
(political) office of the bard invites the wider (visionary) authority of
the prophet. That this doubleness of vision is proper to Yeats's blessing
seems certain from "A Meditation in Time of War," the brief poem that
follows the prayer for his daughter:

> For one throb of the artery,
> While on that old grey stone I sat
> Under the old wind-broken tree,
> I knew that One is animate,
> Mankind inanimate phantasy.

The One compels the Many; the strife of worldly affairs gives way to
invisible order. In his finest poems Yeats is alert to politics as the field
of action but also, and equally, to history as mankind's transhuman
ground. From this perspective the two sides of bardic inclination—
political scrutiny and prophetic announcement—act to enhance and certify each other.

In "A Prayer for My Daughter" and even more in the later poems of
political violence, the terror Yeats faces is no longer on a human scale.
He is forced to admit that he has no resources—no triumphant powers
to fall back on—except the bardic capacity for naming. But the power
of naming can be a formidable weapon, especially when impelled by
rage, by energetic "hate of what's to come." Without question Yeats is
at the height of his powers when excited by the turbulence of events.
Readers are sometimes troubled by his apparent intimacy with the violence he envisions. But his "emblems of adversity," as he called his
prophetic images, owe nothing to a psychology of identification, and
we would be mistaken to assume that Yeats approved or took a hidden
share in the violence of his time. On the contrary, worldly rage provoked
in Yeats his own defiant frenzy, a fearless agitation enabling him to face,
and name, the terror he beheld.

In Yeats's later visionary poems he confronts the powers of the world with powers of his own, a state of "excited reverie" that depends on a vigorous or even violent act of imagining. Pitched to extremes, the poet's prophetic energies develop an interior intensity in response to the press of the real—precisely a "violence within" pushing back at the "violence without," as Stevens would say; or as Kant put it in his notion of sublime encounter, "a power of resistance of quite another kind." That the source of creative vigor is rage, rather than pleasure, is a measure of the poet's task in dark times. Another measure is the peculiar use Yeats makes of *reverie*. The easeful dreaming of an earlier time (his own early poems, for example) has become a lost luxury. To "repose in the well-being of an image," as Bachelard put it in *The Poetics of Reverie*, is no longer possible.[17] There is no repose, no well-being, but only the embattled excitement that comes of confrontation.

Yeats stood up to terror by naming it; that was his pride and his valor. He knew that when a thing or occasion is named, when its principle is either *found out* or *assigned* by force of acute description, power is gained over (or granted to) that which is named. In bardic practice, moreover, a name can be mimetic or visionary; it can represent appearance or, through the force of metaphor, penetrate to essence. In his prophetic work, Yeats relies on visionary naming, the assignment of images to capture energies not otherwise describable. For any poet, the problem is how to face political violence and reveal its *hysterica passio*, its demonic spirit in times of extremity. From the prophetic section of "Meditations in Time of Civil War," this is how Yeats does it:

> 'Vengeance upon the murderers,' the cry goes up,
> 'Vengeance for Jacques Molay.' In cloud-pale rags, or in lace,
> The rage-driven, rage-tormented, and rage-hungry troop,
> Trooper belabouring trooper, biting at arm or at face,
> Plunges towards nothing, arms and fingers spreading wide
> For the embrace of nothing; and I, my wits astray
> Because of all that senseless tumult, all but cried
> For vengeance on the murderers of Jacques Molay.

What Yeats sees in prophetic vision, and knows from neighborhood news, is mutilation of the human image as the means and end of politics in extremity—precisely the madness of Creon's decree. The New Leviathan, as we might call it, is a self-devouring mass impelled by a rage wholly innocent, wholly murderous—and exceedingly contagious. It is the kind of evil that befouls life's sweetness and mocks faith in politics as an art of the possible, an evil so blindly terrible that finally just to stand and face it, to pace the battlements and *see* the undelivered world destroying itself, compels a furious, wildly creative distress. As the poet says in lines introducing the passage above:

> Frenzies bewilder, reveries perturb the mind;
> Monstrous familiar images swim to the mind's eye.

In the same poem Yeats compares his tower, with its winding stair and "chamber arched with stone," to the place of Milton's visionary poet:

> *Il Penseroso's* Platonist toiled on
> In some like chamber, shadowing forth
> How the daemonic rage
> Imagined everything.

When poets like Yeats, or Milton, confront the political sublime, they depend on a "daemonic rage" that is provoked by, and then that pushes back against, the monstrous rage of the world. From this violent meeting comes a nobility of diction equal to the darkness upon us.

"Nineteen Hundred and Nineteen" is the great poem of Yeats's political-prophetic maturity, to which "Prayer for my Daughter" and "Meditations in Time of Civil War" stand as sister poems with "The Second Coming" for a preface. "Nineteen Hundred and Nineteen" takes for granted that politics is given to violent extremes and that against the levelling wind there's nothing that will stand. Rage is palpable and we see, moreover, that the inclination to curse takes its justification from events.

In December 1918 the party of revolt, Sinn Fein, won the vote in Ireland and on January 21, 1919, a republic was declared. The Irish Republican Army attacked police stations and British troop trucks, and the war with England began. Soon the Black and Tans arrived, a freelance soldiery very like the proto-fascist *Freikorp* in Germany (organized at the same time), given to random atrocity and terrorizing the countryside. Elsewhere in 1919, a British unit opened fire on a political rally in the Punjab, killing four hundred and wounding more than one thousand. The Amritsar Massacre, as it came to be known, started a politics of revolt that would finally break the British hold on India. In Paris, meanwhile, the Versailles Treaty humiliated Germany enough to insure another war, and gave the victor nations permission to recarve the colonial map of Africa. Perhaps the most obvious sign of the times, in 1919, was the Russian Revolution, which was just then reaching its peak of madness in the war between Whites and Reds. In Moscow the Communist International was established, and for a few weeks of 1919 Marxist forces took control of cities like Munich and Berlin. It was at this point, with the murder of Rosa Luxemburg for a symbol, that roving bands of German veterans methodized violence and set a model for fascist order in Germany. And now, finally, a small anti-Semitic group calling itself Deutsche Arbeiterpartie, The German Workers Party, arrived on the scene. Hitler was its spokesman and then its leader, and by the end of 1919 he had done two things: hammered out his twenty-five-point platform and found out—in a backroom of the Hofbrauhaus, in the hall on Dachaustrasse—the power of his voice.

All told, 1919 was not as lethal as the years directly preceding, but in Ireland, in Europe, and in the new-born Soviet Union, it was sufficient to inspire dark foreboding. Originally entitled "Thoughts upon the Present State of the World," Yeats's "Nineteen Hundred and Nineteen" announces the new disorder, and designates 1919 as the moment when the downward slide of the West began to feel certain. The poem is therefore "a lamentation," as Yeats said in a letter, "over lost peace and lost hope,"[18] and the first lines of the opening stanza strike that note and toll that bell:

> Many ingenious lovely things are gone
> That seemed sheer miracle to the multitude,
> Protected from the circle of the moon
> That pitches common things about. . . .

That the poem surveys more than the war in Ireland is made clear by beginning not with Irish matters—there is little in the poem that is specific to Ireland alone—but with Periclean Greece, the fountainhead of Western splendor, and just at the moment when Athenian empire was at the peak of its grandeur and about to be sacked. Here again Yeats takes up the heroism of defeat, but gives it a new turn in his reference to "Phidias' famous ivories." He who built the colossal gold and ivory Athena for the Parthenon, he whose Zeus was one of the world's Seven

Wonders, is known in terms of loss. There is great pathos in the fact that no work of his remains, that Phidias is heroic by reputation only. To fame of this kind Yeats pays homage. He sees, however, that reputation comes to nothing; that immortality conferred by fame is doubtful at best. Hellas is gone, and gone as well our older faith in art as the one thing transcending time and politics.

Phidias' heroic works, moreover, are not stressed so much as his ornamental "grasshoppers and bees," suggesting that for an empire in its prime, indulgence and display certify illusions of permanence. But for the British as for the Athenian empire, peace at home was purchased by continuous "little wars" elsewhere. To those well away from frontiers, the claims of progress might seem genuine, and in "Nineteen Hundred and Nineteen" Yeats blames his generation for having accepted power's fraud. Even in Ireland the myth of moral advancement thrived:

> habits that made old wrong
> Melt down, as it were wax in the sun's rays;
> Public opinion ripening for so long
> We thought it would outlive all future days.
> O what fine thought we had because we thought
> That the worst rogues and rascals had died out.

Contempt for "fine thought" now turns, in stanza three, to the way empire promotes itself through spectacle—the irony of power pretending innocence:

> All teeth were drawn, all ancient tricks unlearned,
> And a great army but a showy thing;
> What matter that no cannon had been turned
> Into a ploughshare?

The political charade was, for a time, a promise that Yeats and the friends of his youth had wanted to believe, an illusion that for the Irish began to crack in 1916 and in 1919 collapsed outright. Hence the sudden leap into the violent imagery of stanza four, the only part of the poem in which atrocity is directly depicted. The specific reference is to the killing of Ellen Quinn by the Black and Tans, an incident that happened in Yeats's own neighborhood, and that he takes as *the* sign of political intrusion:

> Now days are dragon-ridden, the nightmare
> Rides upon sleep; a drunken soldiery
> Can leave the mother, murdered at her door,
> To crawl in her own blood, and go scot-free;
> The night can sweat with terror as before
> We pieced out thoughts into philosophy,
> And planned to bring the world under a rule,
> Who are but weasels fighting in a hole.

For the first time, visionary diction (lines one and part of two) announces the theme of demonic possession that will gradually take over the poem. The effect is to magnify local atrocity and the terror that random killing inspires. Visionary and mimetic dictions now proceed in counterpoint, and the metaphorical last line, the "weasels fighting in a hole," increases the sense of nonhuman forces at work. Most important, the stanza as a whole enacts the moment of political intrusion—the way an event breaks in to break up the dreams and abstract designs we use to keep ugliness distant.

Three kinds of disturbance intrude: there are demonic energies on the loose; there is the news of killing; there is the spectacle of high-mindedness reverting to rodent frenzy. These are "the signs" referred to at the start of the next two stanzas, which complete part one of the poem by turning back to the unbelievable but de facto ruin (or ruin in progress) of all things good and beautiful. For those who can see, the lesson is that nothing stands, no monument or masterwork, nor is there comfort to be had:

> He who can read the signs nor sink unmanned
> Into the half-deceit of some intoxicant
> From shallow wits; who knows no work can stand,
> Whether health, wealth or peace of mind were spent
> On master-work of intellect or hand,
> No honor leave its mighty monument,
> Has but one comfort left: all triumph would
> But break upon his ghostly solitude.

> But is there any comfort to be found?
> Man is in love and loves what vanishes,
> What more is there to say? That country round

None dared admit, if such a thought were his,
Incendiary or bigot could be found
To burn that stump on the Acropolis,
Or break in bits the famous ivories
Or traffic in the grasshoppers and bees.

Yeats reads the signs and knows no work will stand, his own included. He would therefore retreat, as he did at the end of "Meditation in Time of Civil War," into the comfort of a "ghostly solitude." But now the well-used strategy fails, and at *this* point the caldron of the poem—its torment of political intrusion—begins to boil. Hemmed in by animal terror on the one hand, by demonic intimations on the other, is real escape possible? To say that "man is in love and loves what vanishes" ought to suffice; it ought to be the last word, but it isn't. There is more to be said even if "none dare admit." For while comfort is not to be "found," incendiary and bigot are "found" in every direction. In this extremity, consoling truths are neither sweet nor consoling.

Despite his ideas of historical necessity, Yeats is unable to accept neighborhood horrors with visionary calm. At the end of the poem's first section, he is back where he started, pressed by a knowledge of political intrusion worse than his own fine thoughts had prepared him to subdue. A greater effort is called for, and the poem reformulates itself (section two) in visionary terms that bring the demonic element visibly to the fore:

When Loie Fuller's Chinese dancers enwound
A shining web, a floating ribbon of cloth,
It seemed that a dragon of air
Had fallen among dancers, had whirled them round
Or hurried them off on its furious path;
So the Platonic Year
Whirls out new right and wrong,
Whirls in the old instead;
All men are dancers and their tread
Goes to the barbarous clangour of a gong.

The earlier vision of "dragon-ridden" days now summons an image from the art of Yeats's own time, a prophetic emblem that lends familiar substance to the second half of the stanza. The "new right and wrong" of the Christian era is driven out by a feral "dragon of air." The forces now at work are demonic and beyond mere human will; but what counts most, in this stanza, is the way visionary and mimetic dictions begin to work together. By the last line Yeats has achieved a harder diction, has called on a "violence within" to equal the "violence without."

The progress of "Nineteen Hundred and Nineteen" begins to be clear if we compare earlier formulations of the poem's theme with the one at the end of part two:

> Many ingenious lovely things are gone
> That seemed sheer miracle to the multitude.

*   *   *

> Man is in love and loves what vanishes,
> What more is there to say?

*   *   *

> All men are dancers and their tread
> Goes to the barbarous clangour of a gong.

The change is from a generalized lilt to the harder music of uncompromising metaphor. This turn suggests the direction the rest of the poem will take and offers an answer to the question Yeats put in a letter to Olivia Shakespear: "I wonder will literature be much changed by that most momentous of events, the return of evil?"[19] The message of "Nineteen Hundred and Nineteen" is that some part of poetry will be changed if the political climate continues to worsen. And in fact the change takes place before our eyes as progressive shifts in rhythm, diction, and stance alter the character of the poem as a whole.

"Nineteen Hundred and Nineteen" announces the return of evil, and its immediate occasion is the experience of political intrusion. This occasion provokes the poet's most bitter curse upon his time, and gives rise, finally, to a vision of the demonic nature of politics in our century. Yeats discovers that when one is caught up and terrorized by violence in one's own backyard, protective strategies that should work don't— not the consolations of philosophy, not the distance gained through myth, not retreat into solitude. In part three of the poem, Yeats tests

these options by comparing "the solitary soul to a swan." He aligns the
public confession of part one ("we") with a more private confession of
his own ("I"), and will be satisfied if for a moment he can see, as in "a
troubled mirror," his soul as he hopes it might be—as the image of a
swan in free and confident flight:

> The wings half spread for flight,
> The breast thrust out in pride
> Whether to play, or to ride
> Those winds that clamour of approaching night.

Two things discourage a vision so masterful. The soul becomes "lost"
in its own defenses; then it finds that having preserved itself through
art it cannot, even in death, shake off what its art has engaged. This is
a startling admission for Yeats, that he cannot get free of his work. The
discontent of poems confronting politics—the outcome of living one's
time in one's art—becomes part of his soul's last condition:

> A man in his own secret meditation
> Is lost amid the labryinth that he has made
> In art or politics;
> Some Platonist affirms that in the station
> Where we should cast off body and trade
> The ancient habit sticks,
> And that if our works could
> But vanish with our breath
> That were a lucky death,
> For triumph can but mar our solitude.

Instead of solitude there is only desolation. This sudden insight triggers a burst of self-destructive rage that is reflected in the leap (or is it
the fall?) of the swan; and with it a renewal of the experience of political
intrusion—from dreaming of goodness to facing evil's return—that Yeats
had hoped to escape:

> The swan has leaped into the desolate heaven:
> That image can bring wildness, bring a rage
> To end all things, to end

What my laborious life imagined, even
The half-imagined, the half-written page;
O but we dreamed to mend
Whatever mischief seemed
To afflict mankind, but now
That winds of winter blow
Learn that we were crack-pated when we dreamed.

The recognition that ends part three is final—so final that in a further burst of rage Yeats insists on the spite of naming it again, jamming the entire experience of hope and despair into a single bardic rann that is the whole of section four:

We, who seven years ago
Talked of honour and of truth,
Shriek with pleasure if we show
The weasel's twist, the weasel's tooth.

In this intensely bitter mood Yeats goes on, with part five, to utter the most sustained curse in his poetry. The madness of *hysterica passio* is barely contained, and the curse is directed as much against himself as any of the great, the wise, or the good:

Come let us mock at the great
That had such burdens on the mind
And toiled so hard and late
To leave some monument behind,
Nor thought of the levelling wind.

Come let us mock at the wise;
With all those calendars whereon
They fixed old aching eyes,
They never saw how seasons run,
And now but gape at the sun.

Come let us mock at the good
That fancied goodness might be gay,
And sick of solitude

> Might proclaim a holiday:
> Wind shrieked—and where are they?
>
> Mock mockers after that
> That would not lift a hand maybe
> To help good, wise or great
> To bar that foul storm out, for we
> Traffic in mockery.

Yeats does not usually blame defeat, but here he seems to side with the levelling wind, as if for once the stirring beast beneath were not held wholly down. Here Swift's savage indignation is complete, provoking the poet to speak *in the voice of* what he hates. Despite precision of the verse, rage is so total in its irony that it become indistinguishable from what it attacks. He calls his tribe to curse its elders, and we are invited—"Come let us mock"—to join in, to make of the curse a choric counterpoint to the tragedy in progress.

The answer to "What more is there to say?" might be to curse the darkness and die. But that kind of defeat Yeats could never abide. No matter the infernal depths, he goes on, as Milton did, to body forth the "darkness visible." This he does in the great last section of "Nineteen Hundred and Nineteen." Throughout the poem, images of the wind have gathered force and mass—a dragon of air, a wind of winter and approaching night, the storm's foul shriek. Now these energies regroup into an image arising directly from the violence of the Irish countryside. In language at first mimetic but almost at once visionary, the levelling wind shows forth the horror at the heart the poem:

> Violence upon the roads: violence of horses;
> Some few have handsome riders, are garlanded
> On delicate sensitive ear or tossing mane,
> But wearied running round and round in their courses
> All break and vanish, and evil gathers head:
> Herodias' daughters have returned again,
> A sudden blast of dusty wind and after
> Thunder of feet, tumult of images,
> Their purpose in the labyrinth of the wind;

> And should some crazy hand dare touch a daughter
> All turn with amorous cries, or angry cries,
> According to the wind, for all are blind.

In its grim magnificence, this is one of poetry's great images of politics out of control, power devoid of reason or self-interest, *hysterica passio* with no aim but glee in destruction. None knows what nor why nor whither, but only the blind excitement that comes from desecration. Here Yeats says what "none dared admit"; not just that incendiary and bigot arrive in multitudes, but that the spectacle of ruin fascinates—that delight in destruction is part of power's enchantment.

How might this obscene seductiveness be named? If twenty centuries of stony sleep are vexed to nightmare, what vexing shape comes now to pass? Yeats says in his note to the poem that "these horsemen, now that the times worsen, give way to worse"; and also that the culminating image is "an evil spirit much run after in Kilkenny at the start of the fourteenth century," an incubus whose victims consorted with demons.[20] This, then, is Yeats's emblem of evil returning:

> But now wind drops, dust settles; thereupon
> There lurches past, his great eyes without thought
> Under the shadow of stupid straw-pale locks,
> That insolent fiend Robert Artisson
> To whom the love-lorn Lady Kyteler brought
> Bronzed peacock feathers, red combs of her cocks.

In the end, even Eros is suborned, the sea's innocence again made murderous by the wind. The gloss on these lines comes from "Dove and Swan," the section of *A Vision* in which Yeats surveys the playing out of Western hegemony. He says that "a civilization is a struggle to keep self-control," and that as control is lost and things fall apart there is "first a sinking in upon the moral being, then the last surrender, the irrational cry, revelation—the scream of Juno's peacock."[21] I take it that the scream of the peacock is one with the shriek of the wind, the sound of calamity in a time when brazen undraped power is the welcomed god, and politics is destiny. Other poets have had intimations of monstrosity, but none has been as bold as Yeats with outright prophecy of this kind. If we wonder why poets sometimes write in a manner so appalled and seemingly hopeless, we have an excellent reply in Yeats's example. He wrote this poem to confront the political sublime and not be cowed by what his vision forced him to behold.

There is a small late poem entitled simply "Politics." The poem has been dismissed by critics as a "little lyric," as "happy-thoughted," or as "an old man's gay goodnight,"[22] and readers of Yeats know that in the official *Collected Poems* the closing poem is "Under Ben Bulben," with "Politics" fifth from the end. In Richard Finneran's 1983 edition of Yeats's complete poetry, however, "Politics" rightly stands last, an order we have known since Curtis Bradford established the correct sequence for the last poems in 1966.[23] Throughout his career, Yeats arrayed his poems for publication with meticulous care, and now that we are certain he intended "Politics" as his end-piece, we might ask why. The further question is whether or not Yeats's bardic ambition had any bearing on the final arrangement of his poetry; and if so, what sort of hindsight he himself provided for his work as a whole. Here, then, is "Politics":

> How can I, that girl standing there,
> My attention fix
> On Roman or on Russian
> Or on Spanish politics,
> Yet here's a travelled man that knows
> What he talks about,
> And there's a politician
> That has both read and thought,
> And maybe what they say is true
> Of war and war's alarms,
> But O that I were young again
> And held her in my arms.

The poem was written in late May 1938, less than a year before Yeats died. Much of the quarrel about its meaning—does it dismiss or accept the importance of politics?—hinges on how the poem answers the epigraph that announces it, a remark attributed to Thomas Mann:

In our time the destiny of man presents itself in political terms.

Yeats did not take these words from Mann, but from an essay by Archibald MacLeish, and his account of the poem's inception is given in letters to Dorothy Wellesley, dated 24 May and 10 June 1938. The following remarks are from the first letter:[24]

> There has been an article upon my work in the *Yale Review*, which is the only article on the subject which has not bored me for years. It commends me above other modern poets because my language is 'public'. That word which I had not thought of myself is a word I want. Your language in 'Fire' is 'public', so is that of every good ballad. (I may send you the article because the criticism is important to us all.) It goes on to say that, owing to my age and my relation to Ireland, I was unable to use this 'public' language on what is evidently considered the right public material, politics. The enclosed little poem is my reply.

Against the charge that he is "unable" to manage a public style in cases of political import, Yeats counters with the poem. Then as an afterthought he says: "No artesian well of the intellect can find the poetic theme."[25] What theme? Yeats might be arguing that his art can *evade* politics successfully; that politics is not a worthy theme. Or, he might be saying that his work does *confront* politics in a suitably public language. What is certain is that he thought a public style essential, and that the poem is some kind of answer to the notion of politics as destiny.

In "Politics" the scene is a public place in which the speaker goes about his business. The woman is *there* while the poet, caught up in the day's news, is *here*. Between them—between the first and last lines—comes the body of the poem, most of it about politics with special reference to Mussolini, Stalin, and Franco. The poem is also, of course, about the despair of desire. An old man admires a young woman's beauty. That is ordinary enough. What makes it dramatic and of consequence is the way politics intrudes to make the moment unusual—insofar, that is, as "war's alarms" are out of the ordinary.

But then, it might be that war and war's alarms have become the normal state of affairs, the expected thing in our time, so that now it's the moment of erotic longing, seldom unharried, that is rare. And if politics intervenes from without, it is also integral to the poet's (the speaker's) position in life. Either way, politics is part of the poem's occasion. We might say that the intense yearning expressed in the last lines has been present from the beginning and that desire undercuts political response. But it's also the case that public issues are frustrating private desire, that erotic reverie is upset by bad news. The romantic theme undermines the political theme, but the political theme disrupts the romantic theme, displacing it for nine of the poem's twelve lines. The two themes twine about each other and cannot be kept separate.

The specific references to Roman, Russian, and Spanish politics are signs of the time, a time from which anyone might wish to withdraw. It's not, therefore, only alarm and consternation that compose this example of political experience, but also the hapless yearning for escape that melds with another yearning, also escapist, for youthful unconcerned delight. The urge to escape is what makes "that girl standing there" so very present to the poet. Were he undisturbed by history, he would lack the sounding board that makes his emotion dramatic. Private desire becomes significant when complicated by public impediment, a situation as elementary as *Antigone*. That is one sense in which destiny finds its meaning in political terms. Moreover, because he is old the poet is only fit for politics and must, against his will, forego erotic dreams; politics is *his* destiny, like it or not. The themes of age, desire, and political intrusion play upon each other; but also, as I've suggested, a poet committed to heroic themes will know that private destiny becomes heroic in terms of—and in conflict with—public forces.

"Politics" supports a political reading of Yeats's poetry. It can be taken, moreover, as a specific genre in bardic tradition—the kind of vision poem called the *aisling*—and viewed this way it makes a fitting conclusion for the poetry of an Irish poet in love with his nation as well as with his art. As a bardic form, the *aisling* arose when the Irish chiefs were driven into exile; it became widespread after James, the last of the Stuarts, was defeated in 1690 by William of Orange at the Battle of the Boyne. From then on, a principal kind of bardic lament framed itself as the fleeting glimpse of a wonderful young woman who represented Ireland's one day being free. The *aisling* became a way of preserving hope against the reality of political defeat. The vision of nationhood still lives, as Hanrahan says in his song, "hidden in our hearts." Did Yeats know this tradition? At the close of *Cathleen ni Houlihan*, after the old woman leaves with the son who will die for Ireland, a returning brother is asked: "Did you see an old woman going down the path?"

He answers in the play's last line: "I did not, but I saw a young girl, and she had the walk of a queen."

In dreams begins responsibility, and so it was with Yeats at the end of his life. Mired in loss and alarm, he stamped his career with a backward look to "all that delirium of the brave," long since betrayed and played out. There is no nationality without great literature, John O'Leary had told the young poet, and no great literature without nationality. Bringing the two together was a lifetime's labor and, as Yeats came finally to feel, a lifetime's defeat. Yet the dream was exceedingly fair. It was like the glimpse of a goddess or, with her queenly unconcern, "that girl standing there," impossible to reach.

·THREE·

ATTACK
&
MALEDICTION

·V·

Bertolt Brecht, Germany

A Brechtian maxim: do not build on the good old days,
but on the bad new ones.

—Walter Benjamin[1]

No poet has done more to advance the prestige of political art
than Bertolt Brecht. He is one of the prime figures in European
literature and has influenced writers of every kind in many countries.
Most of us in America, however, know him better for his plays than for
his poems despite the fact that Brecht owes his dramatic excellence
directly to his language—to his powers as a poet. The two careers ran
broadly parallel, and in view of Brecht's poetry, his later poems especially,
the famous cynicism of his plays looks less savage, less brazenly tough.
Not that Brecht can be praised for his tenderness; like Yeats, he was
chiefly a hater, a poet whose foremost gift was for cursing. His hard-
boiled hauteur was part of an unwillingness to be kind when kindness
flatters established order. It was his proof against his enemies, the Nazis
in particular. As he put it in "To Those Born Later": "Anger, even
against injustice / Makes the voice hoarse."

Brecht's theater overrides his poetry because his fame as a playwright
came early and lasted; but also because he published a mere fraction of
poetry during his lifetime. Events kept upsetting plans for printings,
and what did appear came out in a confusion of ways, from poems stuck
in the plays to those in the small gray chapbooks, the *Versuche*, that
Brecht issued over the years. Of substantial volumes there were only
three: the early *Hauspostille* or *Devotions for the Home* of 1927; the *Svendborg Poems* published in exile in 1938; and finally, five years before his
death in 1956, *A Hundred Poems*. Around this last book a situation

developed that made its occasion an example of politics and art in collision.

John Heartfield designed the book's cover, which featured the picture of a Chinese tea-root carved in the shape of a lion. Brecht liked it but his East German (Soviet) publishers did not. They argued that the design would brand the poetry as "formalism" and be condemned by party-line critics. The situation was typical for Brecht, and so was the solution. *A Hundred Poems* appeared in an initial edition of ten thousand copies, half with the lion, half in plain cover. To the hacks went the latter, while booksellers preferred (because it sold better) copies with the design. As a final touch Brecht put the following poem on the cover with the lion:

> The bad fear your claws.
> The good enjoy your elegance.
> This
> I would like to hear said
> Of my verse.

The aggressive element in Brecht's work is well known, and the little poem about the lion, so simple and direct, is Brecht at his elegant best. But to value the whole of his poetry for its "elegance" is surely odd. In the German the last word of line two is *Grazie*, denoting "grace" or "charm" or a kind of "suppleness." Graceful and charming Brecht's work isn't. He detested decorum and evident polish, any sort of visible refinement, preferring instead the vigor of the street and lowbrow forms like ballads, pop songs, tunes of the music hall and the street. Brecht's preference was for a language down to earth, and his turn toward the rude and unmannerly was less "a protest against the smoothness and harmony of conventional poetry," as he says of his early poetry, than "an attempt to show human dealings as contradictory, fiercely fought over, full of violence."[2]

A lion might be supple, but hardly charming, certainly not the bristly creature of Heartfield's design; and this points to one of the problems reading Brecht. His poetry does not charm, invite, or tease out thought. It would be heard, not overheard, and does not bank on its status as Art. Its import is in its occasion and it does not, therefore, claim to be transcendent or self-contained; it insists, rather, on its place in history, its provisional nature as utterance in situ. Poets, Brecht believed, ought to say something; and what they say ought to be worth hearing even in a world where frightful forces attack and erode our self-possession. History is too much with us, and if we would believe Max Frisch, looking upon the ruins of Europe after World War Two, Brecht's poetry is of the kind most worth having: the kind that "can stand up against the world in which it is spoken."[3]

Brecht was born in 1898 and came of age as a poet and playwright during the ugly years after World War One, when Germany was ruled by defeat and the vengeance of Versailles, by upheaval and paramilitary violence, by resentment, poverty, and rampant profiteering. He witnessed the rise of fascism and when Hitler assumed power in 1933, Brecht began a life in exile that lasted sixteen years. From the time of his return, in 1948, until his death in 1956, he lived in East Berlin under a Stalinist regime and amid the hysteria of the Cold War. When Brecht speaks of "dark times" he knows what he is talking about:

> Truly, I live in dark times!
> The guileless word is folly. A smooth forehead
> Suggests insensitivity. The man who laughs
> Has simply not yet had
> The terrible news.

Written in 1938, those are the first lines of "To Those Born Later," a poem sometimes translated as "To Posterity." The phrase "dark times" occurs often in Brecht's poetry. It refers to half a century during which, by conservative estimate, more than one hundred million men, women, and children died in wars, in concentration camps, by bombings and firing squads. Millions more lived out their lives in harrowing dread. To say that civilization collapsed is not to exaggerate, and the great questions—how to stay human, or, as Adorno put it, how to have poetry after Auschwitz—are still with us. In "To Those Born Later" Brecht goes on:

> I would also like to be wise.
> In the old books it says what wisdom is:
> To shun the strife of the world and to live out
> Your brief time without fear
> Also to get along without violence
> To return good for evil
> Not to fulfill your desires but to forget them

> Is accounted wise.
> All this I cannot do:
> Truly, I live in dark times.

In an age of enormity the old wisdom fails, drifts out of reach, becomes a luxury. How, for example, return good for evil when genocide or the threat of nuclear wipeout confronts us? How remain sane amid madness or bring up children without the desire for a decent peace? We are embedded in the world's strife and cannot shun it even if we would. Everything has become political and "dark times" prevail. And this condition affects not only how we view the world morally, but also how we see it in aesthetic terms:

> What kind of times are they, when
> A talk about trees is almost a crime
> Because it implies silence about so many horrors?

That was the question Brecht faced, and it remains a question for poets today. Can poetry keep its innocence? Do any of us have the right to ignore *what we know*? Nature is either a false retreat or is so politicized that images of earth no longer uphold our need for nature's "counterpoise." Poems that celebrate self-sufficient nature hint at a class-bound or elitist poetic not valid for the state of affairs that is in fact the world. Is poetry a universal human gift or is it the exclusive province of those who, by birth, money, and education, can afford to see the earth and world as they please? In one of his "notational poems," as I would call this form, Brecht takes up the problem and has—as usual—his answer, severe though it may be. "Reading Without Innocence" was written in 1944, in response to an entry in Gide's journal of July 3, 1940, immediately after France gave in to the Nazis, while Gide vacationed in the Pyrenees:

> In his wartime journals
> The writer Gide mentions a gigantic plane tree
> He's been admiring—quite a while—for its enormous trunk
> Its mighty branching and its equilibrium
> Effected by the gravity of its preponderant boughs.

In far-off California
Shaking my head, I read this entry.
The nations are bleeding to death. No natural plan
Provides for a happy equilibrium.

A classic example of casting blame, this poem; its title is meant as a description of Brecht's position, but clearly the idea of "reading without innocence" applies in a multitude of ways, literary, political, plain human, to the texts of our time. At the same time, of course, we need contact with earth's quiet powers, need it the more desperately as the world pushes to cancel nature's solace. Surely none of us would want Gide's wondrous tree expunged from the face of the earth. We behold the tree of life, are uplifted by its strength. We know, however, that even as we seek renewal the spectacle of life in torment goes on. We know, that is, that deep images are loaded with desire, in this case the desire to get away from it all, to think that in the end things balance out.

In Brecht's art there is little care for nature in itself. This is consistent with his later Marxism, a perspective from which nature is the realm of necessity that humankind struggles to transcend, a field of force opposed to freedom until it is humanized. When nature appears in Brecht's poetry, a human element usually intrudes. The abundant cherry tree has a thief in it, the spectacular Finnish countryside is viewed by a refugee, or this:

                    Fog envelops
                    The road
                    The poplars
                    The farms and
                    The artillery.

Brecht sometimes uses nature symbolically, the purity of the empty godless sky, for example, or water's constant flow. But his preference is for earth in its humanized aspect. By disposition Brecht prefers the imagery of human acts and agencies—tools and utensils, houses, people doing things—and poetry informed by an alertness to politics commits itself to the human sphere in any case. Brecht was appalled by Gide's journal entry because while nations and peoples are being wiped out a famous writer pursues a private consolation. Gide was seeking, maybe, no more than a moment's relief, but for Brecht something further is at stake. By ending with "No natural plan / Provides for a happy equilibrium," he means that no natural design or governing Providence, but solely the concerted efforts of men and women, will bring about a peaceful world. He suggests that Gide's aestheticism, with its mystical tinge, induces blindness to history and allows a feeling of well-being where no well-being is.

When Brecht refers to "dark times" he has in mind the Hitler years in Europe first of all, and then the Stalinist period in Russia, with—in all cases—the afflictions of capital causing disaster in the background. These forces compose the world his art would "stand up against." For the poet in exile, it is a world that feels this way: "When I listen to the news on the radio in the morning, at the same time reading Boswell's *Life of Johnson* and glancing out at the landscape of birch trees in the mist by the river, then the unnatural day begins not on a discordant note but on no note at all."[4] We know what he means, listening to "news on the radio"—the way it enters the mind to grate on the soul. In its ambiance "unnatural" days begin. The press of the real subverts existence and shoves life askew—as in this cottage on an island:

> An oar lies on the roof. A moderate wind
> Will not carry away the thatch.
> In the yard posts are set for
> The children's swing.
> The mail comes twice a day
> Where letters would be welcome.
> Down the Sound come the ferries.
> The house has four doors to escape by.

Entitled "Place of Refuge," the poem might almost be read as a portrait of summer bliss. The place is quaint, the kids are set, the postal service works. If neighbors become bothersome, one can slip out the back and maybe, in a better world, the poem *would* be that. But that kind of innocence, as Brecht put it in another context, is "like having a cloud of dust blow into one's face. Can you imagine that sort of thing ever coming to mean anything again?"[5] The poem describes exile and its range of reference includes a *complex of circumstance* not fully manifest in the poem but that functions as part of the poem nonetheless. Context, in this case, includes knowledge of the historical situation and of the poet's life.

Brecht left Germany in 1933. His name, although he did not know it then, was number five on one of the Nazi death lists. In "Place of Refuge" the time is 1937, the site is a fisherman's cottage outside the Danish city of Svendborg. Hitler would soon invade Denmark, forcing him to use one of the "four doors to escape by." (From there he went to Sweden, then Finland, then on across Russia to the Pacific, and finally to America until the end of the war.) Poetry like Brecht's brings history with it—restores to art, even to a poem so slight, a dignity and amplitude not otherwise obtainable. Brecht's early poetry invents its imagery as it goes; but gradually his images come more and more from historic situations of which the poems are a part. No doubt a paint-peeled oar lay on the picturesque roof. But oar-on-thatch is an image of disorder, of things out of place, and we understand that destructive winds might come. Boats also come, and in the poem's context these images of things approaching take on sinister tones. The children play, but not safely. Mail brings pain more than gladness, and business as usual—ferries crossing the water—is not to be trusted.

Like many of Brecht's poems, "Place of Refuge" is based on personal circumstances, but it is not really personal. Of his work Brecht once said: "maybe the poems in question describe me, but that was not what they were written for. It's not a matter of 'getting acquainted with the poet' but of getting acquainted with the world, and with the people in whose company he is trying to enjoy it and change it."[6] To be acquainted with the world is to discover that no place is safe, no refuge secure. This is the experience of political intrusion, one example among many in Brecht's work. History requires evasions that, like the poet's retreat, cannot be counted on, neither in life nor in art. Brecht takes this sense of intrusion further with a poem in which the old death-and-rebirth theme stands for a very tenuous and shaky hope, hope edged by hostile facts and brute foreboding, which is to say hope in its modern, political form. Here is the first stanza of "Spring 1938":

To-day, Easter Sunday morning
A sudden snowstorm swept over the island.
Between the greening hedges lay snow. My young son
Drew me to a little apricot tree by the house wall
Away from a verse in which I pointed the finger at those

Who were preparing a war which
Could wipe out the continent, this island, my people, my family,
And myself. In silence
We put a sack
Over the freezing tree.

We might consider which of his fingers Brecht was pointing, and how he pointed it.

Brecht's Easter Poem would be a sentimental rerun of the theme of rebirth, were it not for the political references. For now rebirth cannot be counted on; our defenses, our stock of old themes, no longer keep us intact as once they did. Yet there are only the old themes. Brecht gives them new life by allowing politics its place, and in consequence a mythic experience, beset by history, regains its authority. Anyone with children, watching for signs of war, knows how poignant that silence is, when with nothing but a miserable sack, son and father go out to save a dying tree. Slight in itself, the poem is like a stone at the neck.

Political exile is as old as its ancient Greek and Roman examples. In our time it becomes ordinary, a condition bereft of basic trust, homelessness as a way of life and of knowledge, and with a terror all its own. The fifth section of a poem called "1940" goes this way:

I am now living on the small island of Lidingo.
But one night recently
I had heavy dreams and I dreamed I was in a city
And discovered that its street signs
Were in German. I awoke
Bathed in sweat, saw the fir tree
Black as night before my window, and realized with relief;
I was in a foreign land.

To fear one's home is a mutilating reversal of the normal. So is the tree "black as night," ordinarily frightening but here a comfort. And so, above all, is the poet terrified of his own language. Brecht portrays a situation that is surreal but actual, a plight that goes to the heart of a time during which life uprooted by politics—the century's deportations, displacements, and forced migrations—has been the fate of millions.

· · ·

Brecht declared himself a Marxist in 1929, and critics often speak of his "conversion" as if there are two Brechts, the strident satirist and then the faithful ideologue. Over time, of course, his poetry shows change. Early expansiveness gives way to later concentration; more poems are rooted in fact as time goes on, and Brecht's didacticism moves from ironic depiction to straightforward statement as its central vehicle. What stays unchanged is his basic disposition, his rapport with outcasts and his militant stance toward the world. The early poetry is as hostile to the prevailing order as the later work of his Marxist years; but between early and late came the abyss, the shock of moral and political vacuum in the wake of the First World War. Brecht's work assumes that the defeat suffered by Germany was a defeat for the whole of Western Europe insofar as Christian traditions and humanistic codes had been discredited by violent events. With inflation and unemployment rampant, the walking wounded, meanwhile, the million crippled veterans from the war were seen in their silent parade on any street in any town or city. The upper bourgeoisie, with no thought for the dehumanizing plight of the masses except to keep it, the misery, quiet at any cost, including violent repression, insisted on business as usual, seeing nothing of its own social cost. Brecht later described the world of his early work this way: "The bulk of the poems deal with decline, and the poems follow our crumbling society all the way down. Beauty founded on wrecks, rags becoming a delicacy. Nobility wallows in the dust, meaninglessness is welcomed as a means of liberation. The poet no longer has any sense of solidarity, not even with himself."[7]

The poems in *Devotions* are a sustained attack against Weimar decadence, a round-robin hymn to disorder insofar as the virtues of anarchy—authenticity and vitality, life free and intense and one's own—are preferred to the cant and dreadful pieties in the "carrion land" of postwar Germany. His attack on religion, as well as his attack on middle-class claims, suggests that both are infected with a nihilism that neither would acknowledge. Brecht acknowledged it; he took pride in brute candor and turned his sense of emptiness into a weapon:

> I admit it: I
> Have no hope.
> The blind talk of a way out. I
> See.

His "Hitler Chorales," for example, were to be sung to the melodies of traditional Lutheran hymns, the first of which begins, "Now thank we all our God / For sending Hitler to us," and ends:

> He'll paint the filth and rot
> Until it's spick and span
> So thank we all our God
> For sending us this man.

Parody of liturgical forms is one of Brecht's favorite devices; implemented by the ironies of cliché and doggerel, the result can be clawlike indeed.

His arrogance allowed him his sarcastic cheer, and vitality—the intensity of life in itself—was the only virtue he would recognize. His ballads in praise of life in the gutter, the vigor of his poems about outlaws and lost souls, mock a culture unwilling to face its own decline. Against moral duplicity Brecht pits the appalling innocence of his antiheroes. He speaks up for "sullen souls, fed up with their own crying," and permits all manner of outcasts their say—as if their every word were glorious, "the cursing included." He mocks the anomie of his own situation: "You smoke. You shit. You turn out some verse." And in general he refuses to make judgments: "Off we went then, friend and foe." Or again, preaching against preaching:

> In the house of the hanged man it is not
> Proper to talk about the noose.

The saint shall lie down with the shark and life be what it is—crude and unmediated, to be praised in passing or blessed with gleeful spite toward those who object. In "Ballad of the Secrets of Any Man at All," the spat-upon hero crams bread in his mouth and with a "shark-look" laughs. If he is killed, "it's no great loss." Brecht offers a blessing anyhow, and would have us join in:

> But laugh with him! And wish him luck!
> And let him live! Even help him, too!
> Oh, he isn't good—you can count on that—
> But you don't know yet what will be done to you.

Brecht salutes the debris of society, the outcasts and pariahs whose existence questions the official pretense of well-being. Against a destructive milieu he takes up a destructive position, until what is ironic and what is not is hard to say. Even so, Brecht says it repeatedly, in the following instance with an aggressive nonchalance that is clearly satirical, but also, in a dim time, plain sense:

> One shouldn't be too critical
> Between yes and no
> There's not such a great difference.
> Writing on white paper
> Is a good thing, so are
> Sleeping and having one's evening meal.
> Water fresh on the skin, the wind
> Pleasant clothes
> The ABC
> Opening the bowels.

Brecht had *Devotions for the Home* printed in the format of a prayer-book. He offers his blasphemous poems under the headings of homily and spiritual exercise, and concludes with "Do Not Let Them Fool You!" in which we are asked to see that after death there is nothing, that life is all there is. Brecht is unyielding toward bourgeois notions of exalted selfhood and private destiny. His animus against self-aggrandizement becomes a part of his own stand as a poet, an aspect of self-judgment that Hannah Arendt, herself no stranger to dark times, has valued this way:[8]

> What set him apart was that he realized how deadly ridiculous it would be to measure the flood of events with the yardstick of individual aspirations—to meet, for instance, the international catastrophe of unemployment with a desire to make a career and with reflections on one's own success and failure, or to confront the catastrophe of war with the ideal of a well-rounded personality, or to go into exile, as so many of his colleagues did, with complaints about lost fame or broken-up life. There is not a shred of sentimentality left in Brecht's beautiful and beautifully precise definition of a refugee: *"Ein Bote des Unglücks."*

A bringer of bad news—that was Brecht's position long before he went into exile, and this poetic disposition makes sense of his turn to politics. To be acquainted with the night, as he was, was to have a choice; he could take courage in the candor of nothingness, or he could stem the tide of nihilism in his art by taking a political stand. And once Hitler arrived on the scene, taking a stand was imperative. The wonder is that Brecht made so much of his early art, that he could extract beauty, as he puts it, "founded on wrecks." But certainly he did, and by way of a last example here is "Grand Chorale of Thanksgiving," a poem attacking the ego's claim to a significant private fate by summoning Pascal's terror of infinite spaces. In terms that are very nearly sublime, Brecht parodies a seventeenth-century hymn ("Praise ye the Lord"/"Praise ye the night"), and by sanctifying the void his praise-poem is also a curse. In the rendering of H. R. Hays, here is the whole of "Grand Chorale":

Praise ye the night and the darkness which surround you!
Gather in crowds,
Look into the heavens above you,
Already the day fleeth from you.

Praise ye the grass and the beast which neighbor you, living and dying.

Behold, like to yours
Is the life of the grass and the beast,
Like to yours must be their dying.

Praise ye the tree which groweth exultant from carrion to heaven!

Praise ye carrion,
Praise ye the tree that ate of it
But praise ye the heavens likewise.

Praise ye from your hearts the unmindfulness of heaven!
Since it knoweth not
Either your name or your face,
No one knoweth if you are still here.

Praise ye the cold, the darkness and corruption!
Look beyond:

It heedeth you not one jot.
Unmoved, you may do your dying.

How earnest it sounds, how sternly funny. But perhaps for Brecht it *was* a blessing, an honest encounter with nothingness that became the condition for rebirth. Brecht's early art, I would say, anticipates the existentialism of the generation that would come of age in the Second World War. His turn to politics exhibits a route that was later to be mapped out by others, by Albert Camus in particular, who answered *The Stranger* with *The Plague* and put off estrangement in favor of collective commitment. In dark times, how to be and what to do become ultimate questions. Coming out of the war, Camus had the benefit of hindsight. Going in, Brecht had the risk implicit in the stand he took.

Early and late, what never changed was Brecht's bedrock loyalty to victims—to losers and outcasts, the underclasses doomed to misery from birth. His choice, moreover, can't be laid to sentimentality; no poet is less given to wearing his heart on his sleeve. To honor the wretched of the earth is to be on earth's side and to call upon earth's powers, as Antigone does, against a world brazenly unjust and therefore inhuman. And the virtue of this perspective is simply its honesty, its unwillingness to be fooled by worldly vanities. Many of Brecht's early poems, furthermore, are political in a nascent sense; they take a plural point of view and address collective experience. Images of mass death occur often. And Brecht's dominant early form, the narrative, is handled with the dedication proper to a poet whose concern would always be with the ways men and women determine, or have forced upon them, the basic conditions of their life.

For example, while the war was still on (1918) and he was serving in a military hospital, Brecht wrote his famous "Legend of the Dead Soldier." In the fifth springtime of the war, as the poem begins, the soldier dies a hero's death, but—

> Because the war was not quite done
> It made the Kaiser blue
> To think the soldier lay there dead
> Before his time came due.

So the dead man is dug up, revived with schnapps and declared fit for service. Soon the corpse is goose-stepping off to a second death, blessed by churchmen and cheered on by patriotic crowds. The ballad, with its cynical clichés, its jaunty rhythms and grotesque imagery, is typical. Rimbaud, Villon, and Kipling sound in the background, as does other antiwar poetry written in Germany at that time. The poem rides on the nihilism it mimes, and depicts the horror of perpetual war in terms impossible to stomach (the Nazis *hated* this poem). Brecht always preferred satire to invective; evil is best exposed, and its authority deflated, by letting it display its own disfiguration—a process of naming informed by the curse. And repeatedly, by using emphatic rhyme and barroom rhythms, by exaggeration and blunt refrains, Brecht condemns the voice through which the poem seems to speak. This corresponds to his theory of theater, to the way he wanted actors to carry their parts. They were not to identify with, but rather to "quote," the role they played, and in such a way as to show moral judgment.

The following poem, "The Ballad of Paragraph 218," was written in 1930 during the distress of the Great Depression. The number 218 refers to the section of the criminal code outlawing abortion, and the situation of the poem, as the first line indicates, is that of a pregnant woman begging a doctor to help her:

> Please, doctor, I've missed my monthly . . .
> Why, this is simply great.
> If I may put it bluntly
> You're raising our birthrate.

The three dots are part of the poem; they occur each time the woman begins to give her reasons—her husband is out of work, they have no home, no money—but she never gets far before the doctor cuts her off with this refrain:

> You'll make a simply splendid little mummy
> Producing cannon-fodder from your tummy
> That's what your body's for, and you know it, what's more
> And it's laid down by law
> And now get this straight:
> You'll soon be a mother, just wait.

The lines are very cruel, and Brecht intends them to be. Whether a doctor would use such cynical terms is not the point. From the vantage of the state this is the expedient function of motherhood; the poor are there to be used and used up, and their dehumanized plight is expressed in the doctor's brute command. Brecht tears away the mystique surrounding the notion of "motherhood," revealing woman's role as mere producer. And here also he makes a connection still not understood by many of us. Very few people who oppose abortion on principle are also opposed to war on principle. The pro-lifers, one is tempted to suspect, are gearing up for death on a grand scale and won't feel secure until a surplus of manpower is at the state's disposal.

Brecht sets forth the doctor's position in a manner he came to call *gestisch* or "gestic" writing, a technique for exposing the interior logic of a situation in terms of a gesture or action at the level of language. The basic unit in Brecht's poetry is not the image or the musical phrase, as in so much of modern poetry, but rather the line. Like a Bauhaus beam, each line contributes to some larger structure but at the same time declares its own shape and strength. To read Brecht correctly is to halt with subtle emphasis at line breaks. Even enjambment works this way, and in Brecht's management of line, moreover, the end of the German phrase or sentence is usually a substantial word, not the *ab* or *auf* we might expect. The rapid pileup of pointed lines can be very forceful, especially when stressed by rhyme. These techniques, in turn, are compounded still further by Brecht's use of paratactic syntax ("*And* it's laid down by law / *And* now get this straight"), which makes of the poem the inventory of a subjective state revealing, through its specific gesture, the political situation.

Brecht's bald and deliberate application of the gestic principle is remarkably suited for jamming pathos and violence together. Below is a last example from the early poetry, "Of the Infanticide Marie Farrar," written in 1922. Like many of Brecht's poems, this one was inspired by an event, in this case a young woman (a servant) who without assistance gave birth to her child in the servants' outdoor latrine and then, senseless with pain and desperation, killed it. The poem pretends to be an itemized record of the girl's own testimony, a police report rather than the tragedy it is. Praise and blame are intimately tangled, but not so tightly that we can't sort them out. Of the poem's nine stanzas, the following is the eighth:

> Between the servants' privy and her bed (she says
> That nothing happened until then), the child
> Began to cry, which vexed her so, she says
> She beat it with her fists, hammering blind and wild
> Without a pause until the child was quiet, she says.
> She took the baby's body into bed
> And held it for the rest of the night, she says
> Then in the morning hid it in the laundry shed.
> > But you I beg, make not your anger manifest
> > For all that lives needs help from all the rest.

Paratactic sequence (one thing after another) plus the jabbing repetition of "she says" suggests a torment verging on hypnosis. The rest of the poem makes clear that the child's death is the outcome of a life brutalized beyond endurance, the grim last act of a woman whose existence had been unbearably grim from the start. The irony of "nothing happened until then" is overwhelming but also instructive. Marie Farrar truly does not know what brought her to this awful pass, nor does her ordeal—giving birth alone, in the winter dark of a cesspool—seem to her unusual in its degradation. The story is horrible, but also matter-of-fact. Brecht's sympathy is with the servant. But that the poem does have a political thrust, and is not merely social criticism, depends on how we read the final couplet.

On the face of it, the last lines address those who judge the crime, and then anyone who, upon hearing the story, would be appalled by something so "unnatural" and "inhuman." Part of the irony, therefore, lies in reversal: Brecht aims for us to see that the child's death follows "naturally" from a life that start to finish could only be called inhuman and unnatural. And further, that those to whom the couplet addresses itself—those whom servants serve—are not as natural and humane as they themselves like to suppose. By repeating the couplet after each stanza, it gradually takes on the character of a formula, a plea uttered by rote, a useless gesture. And so it is. The plea is genuine but empty. The real message of the last lines is that such an appeal—a Christian appeal made to a Christian society—falls on deaf ears. Those for whom the message is meant are victims like Marie Farrar, who suddenly see their fate in hers and see also that to beg help from the class that keeps them down will get them nowhere.

The last lines do not ask forgiveness but state a great truth—"all that lives needs help from all the rest"—which is, or ought to be, the guiding principle for any sound political order. That the appeal is made in earnest but also in vain creates the dialectical perception that gives the poem its political character. As always, Brecht speaks *of* the exploiters and *to* those exploited, exposing infamy and instructing the oppressed. What "Marie Farrar" says finally is said again and again in Brecht's poetry, right up to one of the last poems ("And I Always Thought") he wrote:

> That you'll go down if you don't stand up for yourself
> Surely you see that.

When cursing is wholly absent, praise becomes suspect. Almost against its will, poetry promotes acceptance of the world, lyrically through celebration, tragically by leaving us with the feeling that, yes, that's how things *are*. Homer's *Iliad* is great and uplifting, but its subject is horrendous. We admire the grandeur of *King Lear*, but who would wish Lear's wheel of fire upon him? When a poem would neither praise nor blame, it ends up praising; its figural language heightens any subject and gives it, in capable hands, nobility. This is what Nietzsche had in mind when he said that history is bearable only from an aesthetic point of view. Brecht, however, would not put up with that result, which is, after all, the option of a leisured elite. This would be, in his vocabulary, art of the "culinary" kind. But if poetry's capacity to praise becomes suspect, if a purely aesthetic point of view is ruled out, how might art's cosmetic power be used against itself? And at what cost?

One solution, for Brecht, is satire as brutal as history itself. Another is reliance on didactic forms, which draw their strength from the conviction that life can be changed. A third strategy is to avoid metaphor, especially insofar as metaphor creates the illusion of transcendence—of being "above" X by seeing it in terms of Y. Of his *Svendborg Poems* Brecht said: "From the bourgeois point of view there has been a staggering impoverishment. Isn't it all a great deal more one-sided, less 'organic,' cooler, more self-conscious (in a bad sense)?"[9] One-sided like an ax, cool like metal at night, and thus a poetry that is sometimes disrespectful of the reader's sensibilities, at other times insisting on a distance between reader and poem, a sort of thoughtful estrangement. Brecht's notion of *Verfremdungseffekt* or "alienation effect" applies not only to his theory of theater, but to his poetry as well. There is no emotional solace, no catharsis, no tidy resolution. The appeal, in Brecht's poems (the didactic works most especially), is to the mind rather than the heart. We are not to indulge but to *see*, and to see we must not feel too much at home. In bardic terms, Brecht's willful disruption of the reader's expectations is the summoning of a special audience—a warrior tribe, so to say; a group committed to the general war on injustice.

In 1934, in a poem that takes its title from the first line, Brecht set forth his definition of poetry, and not as a theory only, but as the decision any poet trapped in dark times might make:

> Solely because of the increasing disorder
> In our cities of class struggle
> Some of us have now decided
> To speak no more of cities by the sea, snow on roofs, women
> The smell of ripe apples in cellars, the senses of the flesh, all
> That makes a man round and human
> But to speak in future only about the disorder
> And so become one-sided, reduced, enmeshed in the business
> Of politics and the dry, indecorous vocabulary
> Of dialectical economics
> So that this awful cramped coexistence
> Of snowfalls (they're not merely cold, we know)
> Exploitation, the lured flesh, class justice, should not engender
> Approval of a world so many-sided; delight in
> The contradictions of so bloodstained a life
> You understand.

No semicolon occurs in the German original; the poem is one headlong sentence, a "gestic" enactment of the clarity and conviction with which the poet intends to proceed. In line nine the word here translated as "indecorous" is *unwürdige*, which carries the sense of being unworthy, undeserving or, in sum, not respectable. And in the German version of the poem, Brecht slams the issue home by putting *unwürdige* in quotation marks, thereby transforming the word into its opposite. The concluding irony of "You understand" challenges, or perhaps insults, the "decorous" reader. We see, too, why Brecht brings the indecorous diction of politics into his poems; it allows him *not* to approve of the world as it is, to write poetry that does not inadvertently take "delight in / The contradictions of so bloodstained a life."

Outright political vocabulary seldom appears in Brecht's poems. When it does it bears a dignity entirely free of jargon. The following example, "A Bed for the Night," was written in 1931 in the depths of the Great Depression when the streets of Europe and America were thick with jobless men:

> I hear that in New York
> At the corner of 26th Street and Broadway
> A man stands every evening during the winter months
> And gets beds for the homeless there
> By appealing to passers-by
>
> It won't change the world
> It won't improve relations among men
> It will not shorten the age of exploitation
> But a few men have a bed for the night
> For a night the wind is kept from them
> The snow meant for them falls on the roadway.
>
> Don't put down the book on reading this, man.
>
> A few people have a bed for the night
> For a night the wind is kept from them
> The snow meant for them falls on the roadway
> But it won't change the world
> It won't improve relations among men
> It will not shorten the age of exploitation.

The poem is a good instance of Brecht's dialectical vision. Irony is static, a form of despair, at most a form of subversion that comforts the ironist but does not expect to get very far. Dialectic, on the other hand, offers a form of hope. Two conflicting views are not merely juxtaposed and left to mock each other. The older ethic (stanza two) is turned inside out and made to yield its opposite (stanza four), while the latter is seen to emerge from that which it goes beyond through contradiction. Helping people at the local level was sufficient once, in the era of rural and small-town neighborliness, maybe; but in times of great suffering and whole families homeless, the appeal to individual charity—the street-corner approach—cannot hope to meet mass needs. The Christian ethic, based on the good deed, now defeats itself; the behavior it promotes is decent, but inadequate and finally sentimental. Also harmful; for as long as we accept face-to-face help (and the good will of passersby) as the limit of human obligation, we shall not see the magnitude of the problem nor move toward organized solutions. But of course, those who profit from the status quo can hide behind strategic charity; they may even persuade those whom they exploit that real care exists—the self-advertised munificence of corporate kingdoms, for example, promoting token programs.

By using a didactic voice and the dialectical viewpoint within a political framework, Brecht restores in a minimal, no-nonsense way poetry's visionary element, its capacity to reach beyond the actual. This is all the more astonishing in his case, for no poet has had a better grasp of the actual. Yet in just this way poetry reclaims its integrity, its power to *be* in the daytime world of public forces. And the simplicity with which Brecht makes this work is remarkable. Who would think that hope for the future resides in present despair? Who would guess that to repeat, word for word, lines in reverse order could provide the literary means for a historical-political vision that might otherwise require volumes of argument? The poet renames, in this case, not by naming anew but by turning the old name downside up.

The dialectical process, or rather its poetic enactment, is a good example of poetry and politics working together. The poetic aim is to capture a serious part of the world—a social-political complex—in an instant of time. The political aim is to cut through false pieties and reverse accepted attitudes. Here is another example:

> The peasant's concern is with his field
> He looks after his cattle, pays taxes
> Produces children, to save on labourers, and
> Depends on the price of milk.
> The townspeople speak of love for the soil
> Of healthy peasant stock and
> Call peasants the backbone of the nation.
>
> The townspeople speak of love for the soil
> Of healthy peasant stock
> And call peasants the backbone of the nation.
> The peasant's concern is with his field
> He looks after his cattle, pays taxes

Produces children, to save on labourers, and
Depends on the price of milk.

Translated as "concern," the German *Kummer* loses its sense of grief and constant worry, just as *Knechte*, rendered as "labourers," no longer hints of slavery. Meanings of this kind slip away in translation, but Brecht's major meanings are carried by formal gestures sturdy enough to survive. The poem above depends entirely on gesture, in particular the collision of romantic generalities with grim facts, as when "healthy peasant stock" becomes "children, to save on labourers." And the political point is obvious: as in Hegel's master-slave dialectic, the peasants serve the townspeople while the townspeople depend on the peasants, and this the laborers should see. The peasants depend on the price of milk, which is fixed in town, but the town needs the milk. The situation is dialectical, hence the form of the poem, the way stanza two inverts stanza one. How the dual act of reversal and repetition contributes to the poem's success is puzzling. Either stanza contains all the *visible* information, yet either stanza alone would be trite compared to the power of the two faced off against each other. It's as if the poem's contradiction, in the instant of enlightenment, arrives at a truth beyond the reach of irony merely—a fine example of announcing against.

The didactic element is constant in Brecht. He thought of himself as a teacher, a guide, a keeper of practical wisdom. The point of his work, as he often said, is to make people see. There have of course been great didactic poets, Virgil and Lucretius among them, but for formal inventiveness and aesthetic effects as powerful as any "pure" poet might hope to create, the poetry of Brecht is the outstanding example of successful didactic art in our time. The didactic mode served as Brecht's most durable device for bringing poetry and politics into fruitful union, and if, as Walter Benjamin has argued, the important artist not only uses a mode but also transforms and extends it, then Brecht's importance is obvious. Satire of the modern kind is inherently didactic, but the lyric is not; that Brecht could be didactic *and* lyrical enlarges our idea of poetry itself. He cleared the way for new options and also used the didactic stance to solve perhaps his biggest problem; for in sharp contrast to the Soviet brand of Marxism, which would speak *for* oppressed peoples, Brecht goes no further than speaking *to* them, propounding no authorities or programs but only insisting that victims everywhere should see themselves in the full sadness of their plight and see also that if politics is part of the human condition, a great deal of the human condition is political.

And yet there is something else, subtler, more delicate, about Brecht's use of didactic form. It allows him to remain impersonal, it rules out small talk and self-pity, and where deep emotion arises the didactic stance becomes a technique for restraint, for expression of feeling about world events without splashing the event or its corresponding emotion all over the page. If his role as teacher demands discipline, it also gives Brecht moments of happy freedom. Consider the following poem, quoted complete:

> Refresh yourself, sister
> With the water from the copper bowl with bits of ice in it—
> Open your eyes under water, wash them—
> Dry yourself with the rough towel and cast
> A glance at a book you love.
> In this way begin
> A lovely and useful day.

A love poem, of course; it is addressed to the actress Carola Neher, one of the women Brecht loved. That she later died in a Soviet concentration camp suggests the retrograde impact of future events on Brecht's kind of poetry—or perhaps any art that dares a political content. But in the little love poem, the poet's aim is not politics or advice. He wants to preserve a moment of beauty "so that painters could make pictures of it," as once he said.[10] The tenderness, in this case, is heightened rather than curbed by the rigor of its expression, and this leads to a general observation about Brecht's style: his severity, his militant push, his sometimes savage irony, these are formal strategies through which, in dark times, care and humanness remain active.

When Brecht started out, in the aftermath of World War One, he, along with Rilke and Gottfried Benn, represented the ways open to poetry in dark times. Rilke retreated into an exalted mysticism that glorified death and said, in effect, that the world is not as it seems. Benn, on the other hand, embraced the abyss, the primacy of slime, and took cold comfort in precise delineation of physical decay as the emblem of the human world. On the one side, praise and blessing, on the other a level cursing. Brecht was determined to do both, to blame the world before him and praise its possibilities. He was surely aware of decay, but never seduced by easeful death. Rather, he attacked the nihilism of his age head-on, through satire, and worked toward a political position that would give him the strength, purpose, and also the scope, necessary to confront history without loss of hope or compassion. But to speak in terms of options is misleading. With very little choice, any poet is always committed to his or her vision; or rather, is obliged to honor the relation between self and world that provokes poetic creation. In Brecht's case there is no doubt what this relation was:

> The great boats and the dancing sails on the Sound
> Go unseen. Of it all
> I see only the torn nets of the fishermen.

Those lines are from "Bad Time for Poetry," written in 1939. Brecht's favorite way of cursing Hitler was to name him "the house-painter"; here are the last lines from "Bad Time for Poetry":

> Inside me contend
> Delight at the apple tree in blossom
> And horror at the house-painter's speeches
> But only the second
> Drives me to my desk.

For Brecht the curse would always come first. Praise was a privilege he valued but could seldom afford. Not joy or celebration, but rather the need to take a stand and announce against informs his art. But if poetry arises from the soul's need to sing, how does song survive the world's horror? Brecht offered an answer in a little poem, "Motto," that he used for an epigraph in the *Svendborg Poems*:

> In the dark times
> Will there also be singing?
> Yes, there will also be singing
> About the dark times.

In German the last two lines go this way:

> *Da wird auch gesungen werden.*
> *Von den finsteren Zeiten.*

He does not say yes; that would be too easy, too thoughtless. He restates the question as its own answer, a crucial reversal that is again an example of dialectical form. His placement of a period after the second-to-last line not only makes the line stronger and more final, it also calls for a halt and a silence before going on to the last line, a halt and a silence that, in a cliché I think Brecht would appreciate, speaks volumes. *There will also be singing.* How? What kind? *About and against the dark times.* And the cost will be large. The range of vision will narrow, and worse, will focus on unhappy and often terrible things. This entails an obligation that will not, once accepted, be lightly cast off. And the poetry itself will be of a kind that some among us might dismiss as too spartan, too seldom an occasion for delight and happy grace.

Brecht measured these costs and took them for granted. But two things he did not anticipate. The logic of his politics *and* the logic of his poetry would come to dominate his personal fate, leading him—a German, a Marxist, a man returning to his country—to end up in East Berlin. His early travel back and forth, his Austrian passport, his Swiss bank account, all this confirms, as I see it, Brecht's decision against grave personal doubts to stay in the struggle, despite Stalin, despite the shabby and sometimes grim conditions of life in East Germany. Hannah Arendt missed the main point when she condemned Brecht for his choice; it was the outcome (not the betrayal) of his whole life as a poet. If living in the Soviet sector did damage to his poetic capacity, that too was part of the cost for one who would sing about and against the dark times.

But the worst cost could not be seen coming until too late. Brecht's poetry embraces a political vision, inspiring in its ideals, which did not survive its totalitarian perversion. The historical failure of Marxism has had enormous consequences for all of us, but for people directly involved the outcome was shattering. Recurring anti-Soviet sentiment and outbreaks of bitterness in Brecht's late poetry reveal the suffering of a man coming to see—as a generation of decent men and women came painfully to see—that the great moment had passed, that the magnificent dream of liberty would go unrealized. But if defeat is the likely outcome in actual politics, in poetry the case is strangely otherwise. Brecht's vision was betrayed by history but his poetry does not therefore suffer forfeit or become irrelevant. Defeat, on the contrary, becomes the proof of its power. It gains in retrospective depth, taking on dignity and an import that did not exist when the poems were written but which exists now because of the way things turned out.

After the war Brecht returned from exile in America and arrived in East Berlin on October 22, 1948. He lived there six and a half years before he died in 1956 at the age of fifty-eight. That is a short time for any artist—especially amid political unrest on all sides—to begin a new life, to set up a theater company and see to its success. He had been refused entry to the American sector of Berlin, but he would have gone to the Eastern zone in any case. He was a Marxist and this would be Marxism on German soil, his own tribe's chance to rebuild from the rubble on socialist principles. Germany, we might recall, was not yet two countries and Brecht had enormous hope for a unified nation. With a national theater in mind, and knowing the urgency of gathering the best of German talent before it dispersed across Europe, Brecht urged his friend Picastor to join him: "It is a good moment, one should not put it off much longer, everything is still in a state of flux and the direction things take will be determined by the forces at hand."[12]

Despite gossip to the contrary, it is now certain that Brecht was not bribed, not promised a theater of his own, to settle in East Berlin. His recent German biographer, Klaus Volker, is emphatic on this point. There was no "official invitation." Volker thinks, on the contrary, that in his usual style Brecht "forced his way in."[13] His idea for a theater first met with indifference and then with much difficulty before it was realized officially, more than two years after Brecht's departure from America, and the Berliner Ensemble would not have its own building until March of 1954. Only six productions were staged before, in 1951, a new round of Soviet purges and the vicious atmosphere of the Cold War destroyed, once and for all, Brecht's hopes for a national theater that would contribute to the creation of a united Germany. It was at *this* point that Brecht observed: "Time will show if pessimism is to be rated negatively."[14]

He nonetheless pushed on with his task, building up a first-rate acting company and adapting plays to fit his own ideas of dramatic art. He began new plays, and he was also writing poetry. His last poems are spare and swift and might appear slight on first reading, but many are excellent, the "Buckow Elegies" in particular. What chiefly characterizes his art during these last years is the frequency and bitterness of poems bearing anti-Soviet sentiment, such as "Still at It," the theme of which—everything changed but nothing changed—was strong in Brecht's work at the time:

> The plates are slammed down so hard
> The soup slops over.
> In shrill tones
> Resounds the order: Now eat!
>
> The Prussian eagle
> Jabbing food down
> The gullets of its young.

Some of his late poems are sarcastic in the fiery early style, for example "The Solution." After the East German regime crushed the workers' uprising of June 17, 1953, Brecht wrote that perhaps the best course for government would be to "dissolve the people / And elect another." Many of the late poems are muted and subtle, as if these were the last, half-uttered words of a man talking only to himself, a man, say, whose entire life had taught him that "as always the lovely and sensitive / Are no longer," and who steps into the ragged shade of an abandoned greenhouse to see "the remains of the rare flowers."

A final and perhaps stronger criticism is that Brecht's basic disposition—to attack and to curse—was relentless against Hitler, but that he deployed no similar assault against Stalin, despite the death of dear friends in the Soviet Union. It's true that Brecht was in Russia only briefly, but he followed the Soviet scene with keen interest. When Walter Benjamin asked him, in 1938, if his support for the Russian program might need changing he answered that "unfortunately or God be praised, whichever you prefer,"[15] available news had not yet coalesced into certainty. Meanwhile, as a realist, as an especially strong dreamer, he would take his courage from setbacks and put up with a great deal of adverse evidence before quitting. As in any long fight, victory would require sacrifice. That there would be no victory is a point too easily made by those who make it in hindsight. For Brecht there was only a wall of urgent wrong against which any decent person might make the choice to stand and fight. And there was also this: Brecht's tribe at large was composed of men and women who embraced a Marxist vision and, anywhere in the world, fought for radical change. But his more intimate audience was the tribe of his mother tongue, the German nation that he attacked, blessed, defended, and called to like a prophet. He *knew* Hitler, knew him by his language early on, which suggests that his poetry is focused less on international politics than on the political condition of his own disbanded homeland.

It is the fate of all poetry to be overtaken by time, and after death it reads differently—after, that is, the world it addressed and drew life from no longer exists. For art that addresses history directly, in any case, and especially for poetry that fathoms the human interaction with time itself, the outcome is often melancholy, the more so when the poet has been in love with a cause that like all causes fails. About the way poetry has of surviving itself, this much needs keeping in mind. Political art—the kind attached to a cause—possesses a destiny, and when its destiny ends in defeat, the result is not failure but tragedy. When we read it now, Brecht's poetry bears within it a tragic sense of life that the poet himself could not have detected. Or no, in his late years Brecht began to feel it deeply, and in the following poem, one of the last he wrote, the destiny of his art—which is the tragedy of hope in dark times—is fully recognized:

> At the time when their fall was certain—
> On the ramparts the lament for the dead had begun—
> The Trojans adjusted small pieces, small pieces
> In the triple wooden gates, small pieces.
> And began to take courage, to hope.
>
> The Trojans too then.

In 1947, with Europe still flat and the Cold War order already conscripting the world, Max Frisch observed: "Most of what goes by the name of poetry looks like irony of the crassest sort when I compare it for even only a single day with my own life."[16] One knows exactly what he means. One knows the distractions of art that is blind to the world. Poetry that confronts its time, on the contrary, can't claim innocence of any sort. Like Frisch, I find Brecht sustaining, even beautiful, for the way his poems stand up to the world in which they were written. He took the risks and kept his art open, allowing history its maiming intrusions, making the best of bad prospects. In "To Those Born Later," Brecht says of himself:

> All roads led into the mire in my time.
> My tongue betrayed me to the butchers.
> There was little I could do. But those in power
> Sat safer without me: that was my hope.
> So passed my time
> Which had been given to me on earth.

His hope was betrayed, as hope usually is. And no doubt there was little he could do. All honest vision leads into the mire—as Yeats noted—and not just the familiar squalor of selfhood but the bloody, man-created sorrow that darkens the world, from which no one is exempt, about which no one can claim not to know. In a recent poem, half horror, half surreal play, Charles Simic inserts some lines to suggest how politics grips those swept up, but also the rest of us—those who only behold:

> The act of torture consists of various strategies
> meant to increase
> the imagination of the homo sapiens.

Coleridge never thought of that one. Neither did Emerson. For the Romantics and their offspring, imagination was its own sweet prod, a passage to worlds elsewhere. For those born later, imagination faces and defends, and the irony of Simic's lines makes terrible sense. Brecht, at least, would think so.

·VI·

Breyten Breytenbach, South Africa

> But what does one do if you are White, if in fact you
> are part of the privileged minority in power? When
> you come in revolt against such a system, how do you
> oppose it effectively?
>
> —Breyten Breytenbach[1]

In the harrowing light of his prison memoir—*The True Confessions of an Albino Terrorist*—Breyten Breytenbach's poetry comes at us differently than when it began to appear (in English translation) during the 1970's. What started out with extravagant purpose ends up reduced, doubtful, almost melancholy. Militant high spirits gave way to pessimism, and with Breytenbach's career in view, the prison years especially, poems that once seemed distinctive for their wildness now appear commendable for their candor and patience. One looks back to the early surreal work, full of blood and rot, and thinks: "So he meant it after all." One wonders at the vehemence of his attack on apartheid politics and then sees—thanks to the news and photojournalism—a world-class tragedy in progress. South Africa is going down and this poet, with his Afrikaner rootedness, had known it all along. "I fear," Breytenbach said in 1983, "that the price to be paid—in the cruel game directed and enforced by those now in power—will be exorbitant; the suffering will rip the country asunder and create generations of blindness, bitterness and hate. Are we not heading for an ungovernable Lebanon-type situation where killing will be the only form of communication?"[2] That is the view from *Confessions*. It is also the view from most of Breytenbach's poetry, with its imagery of dismemberment, its bitter twistings of sense, its brave but cramped attempt to envision life clearly, beyond the veil of *hysterica passio*.

Not that seven years in South African jails was Breytenbach's choice. Still less that it takes extremity to certify one's art; but rather that for poetry confronting politics, context is fate. He bears witness in a very off-beat manner, disdainful and urgent at once, but it's clear that the experience of political intrusion has always been Breytenbach's sounding board. In a poem that would later amaze his Afrikaner prosecutors, a poem called "breyten prays for himself," humor mutes but does not tune out the bitterness. It begins:

> There is no need of Pain Lord
> We could live well without it
> A flower has no teeth [.]

Breytenbach goes on, in his mock-Christian way, to implore that while "we are only fulfilled in death . . . let our flesh stay fresh as cabbage." He calls for "mercy on our mouths our bowels our brains," so that "we" may decay in peace. Then the poem swings around, turning the plea to a grievance:

> And gradually we will decompose like old ships or trees
> But keep Pain far from Me o Lord
> That others may bear it
> Be taken into custody, Shattered
> > Stoned
> > Suspended
> > Lashed
> > Used
> > Tortured
> > Crucified
> > Cross-examined
> > Placed under house arrest
> > Given hard labour
> Banished to obscure islands till the end of their days
> Wasting in damp pits down to slimy green imploring bones
> Worms in their stomachs heads full of nails
> But not *Me*
> But we never give Pain or complain

The list, although it gives way to metaphor toward the end, is a straight catalogue of the misery inflicted on South African blacks by their Afrikaner bosses, including the "damp pits" of the mines and banishment to the notorious obscurity of Robbins Island, where black dissidents, Nelson Mandela among them, were being held in Breytenbach's time. Much of this he would endure or witness in his own person while inside Maximum Security. The poem from which I've quoted was written prior to 1964, when it was published in an early collection. Breytenbach knew, with precision even then, what his country was coming to.

But there is more, of course, than context merely. The poem is a curse made sharper by pretending to bless. But if the poet is "Me," who is "we"? Breytenbach is parodying a well-known poem, "St. Ignatious prays for his order," published in 1956 by H. P. van Wyk Louw, an established Afrikaner poet. One of Breytenbach's constant enemies is Afrikaner piety, the huge hypocrisy of a nation pledged to apartheid in Christian terms. This is the more loathsome in that he has himself absorbed a good deal of the Christian ethic, and in a better world would have been glad to follow Christ's way. As things stand, Breytenbach deploys his heritage against itself, sometimes bitterly, sometimes with delight, as in the following lines from a poem that plays with the Lord's Prayer:

> Give us this day the chance to earn our daily bread
> and the butter, the jam, the wine, the silence,
> The silence of wine,
> And lead us into temptation of various kinds
> So that love may jump from body to body
> Like the flames of being—being from mountain to mountain
>
> Brambles of fire brought to the whitest moon
>
> But let us deliver ourselves from evil
> So that we may reckon with the trespass of centuries
> Of stored up exploitation, of plunder, of swindling[. . . .]

His attack, here, is against the overbearing presence of the fathers in Afrikaner tradition, and Breytenbach's maledictions are most often levelled directly at patriarchal power. There might be a genuine religious element in his work as well, in which case his liturgical or scriptural references (of which there are many) will be ambivalent to a radical degree, a blessing and a curse together.

In South Africa, religion and politics join forces, a condition that allows Afrikaner political culture, like most political cultures, including your own, to subscribe to the myth of exceptionalism. This rugged tribe with its errand in the wilderness was assigned by God a privileged role in world affairs, a role that might require the suppression or even extermination of alien peoples along the way, but that assures the master race immunity from wrongdoing because the Lord himself is guiding them to glory. And hence, in Afrikaner consciousness, the right to exemption from suffering such as "others may bear," and hence their righteousness: "we never give Pain or complain." Breytenbach would like to defeat these notions or, as he would later declare, to see them destroyed outright. But here, in "breyten prays for himself," and long before he fell into the hands of the state, his duty is to curse the world that Afrikaner piety upholds. This he does by mocking the Afrikaner heritage. He deploys a lively irreverence and uses irony to speak *for* the tribe that in fact he is speaking *against*.

Devices of this kind cut deeper than their technical use might suggest. As a poet whose native tongue is Afrikaans, Breytenbach *must* speak for the tribe he rails against, and the poet's "prayer," in this case, is a curse upon himself as well as the tribe he attacks. His accusation is as much against himself as the Afrikaner poet he mocks, and in consequence his art finds itself at odds with itself. Praising or blaming, Breytenbach must go forward in a language preempted by the state—a situation very like Antigone's. As he says in *Confessions*, "Afrikaans is the language of oppression and of humiliation, of the Boer. Official Afrikaans is the tool of the racist."[3] The jugular rending of language in Breytenbach's poetry is disturbing on any account, and its destructive force derives from this circumstance: here is a man without a nation, and a poet without a language, of his own. Breytenbach says of his condition: "nothing can ever bridge the gap between the authorities of the Afrikaner tribe and myself."[4] And also, as recently as 1983: "I do not consider myself to be an Afrikaner."[5] Like the work of other poets who confront political experience, Breytenbach's art thrives on situations that permit the poem's occasion to bring poet and tribe together. But unlike the other poets studied in this book, he has rejected the audience his language naturally summons. This misfortune defines the character of his art. Quite consciously, he is a bard without a tribe.

• • •

Breytenbach's poetic reputation is inseparable from his role as exile, as political prisoner, as outspoken enemy of one of the ugliest states on earth. Among South Africans, as André Brink has observed, his renegade fame insures that "every line of poetry he writes—even if it is the purest lyrical verse—acquires *political* implications."[6] Born in 1939, Breytenbach is of solid Afrikaner lineage. Part of his good fortune was to grow up in the southern part of South Africa, within the more relaxed hegemony of Cape Town rather than the narrow rectitude of Pretoria— a difference comparable to the split between Leningrad, with its cosmopolitan spirit, and Moscow's phobic dark. He left home in 1959, wandered Europe for several years, then settled in Paris to paint (first exhibit, 1962) and write poems (first book, 1964). Because his wife is Vietnamese, his marriage to Hoang Lien Yolande was an "immoral" act according to South African statute, and in this way Breytenbach cut himself off from the freedom of homecoming. He has done almost all his work in exile, and the exile's plight is a recurrent theme in his work. In 1973 he and his wife were allowed a ninety-day return to South Africa, out of which came *A Season in Paradise*, a visionary prose work that is part memoir, part political tract, and part exuberant poem. Then in 1975 Breytenbach reentered South Africa illegally, in disguise and bearing a false passport. After three weeks—the police were tracking him the whole time—he was arrested, then convicted of terrorism and sentenced to nine years in prison. He served seven, two in solitary, and was released in 1982. Since then Breytenbach and his wife have lived in Paris.

At the time of his arrest, and for most of his imprisonment, it wasn't possible to get dependable information about Breytenbach's condition or the circumstances that led to the charge of terrorism. But in 1983 *True Confessions of an Albino Terrorist* came out, and Breytenbach acquits himself rather well, I think, not least for the candor with which he admits his shortcomings—in particular the sort of naivete and unpreparedness for action that one might expect of a visionary embracing politics. While living in Paris, Breytenbach helped start a clandestine group called Okhela (the Zulu word for "spark"); then he returned to South Africa with a copy of the group's manifesto in his pocket (with language like "armed struggle" and "offensive direct action"). The aim of Okhela, as I understand it, was to gather disaffected South African whites into a network in order to assist the general struggle under, ultimately, the black leadership of the African National Council (ANC). Okhela also hoped to foster a socialist alternative to the Soviet brand. Breytenbach's mission was to make contacts, to seek out leaders and test the political climate. But he was fingered by someone inside the European group—South African surveillance is *that* well organized—and Okhela's plan of action was dead before it got started.

Breytenbach's art has thrived and now falters in the nightsoil of politics. In his case, moreover, poetry and politics don't just collide; they are violently yoking, historically, culturally, to a condition of language. English and Afrikaans, in South Africa, are both authorized languages, but Afrikaans comes first politically. The British won the Boer War, but that has mattered little in the disposition of power, which since 1948 has been in the hands of the intensely tribal Afrikaners. Apartheid is their rule and likewise their word. It means, in Afrikaans, *apartness*. It means 87 percent of the land given over to whites exclusively, with mass deportation of blacks, mass arrests, and, more recently, mass killings as the conditions for civil war increase. Under provision of the Terrorism Act, apartheid means a state security apparatus that detains whom it pleases, tortures whom it pleases, conducts interrogations in such a way that black men fall to their deaths from high windows. It means a system of domination rooted in a local tongue evolved from Dutch, a language little more than two centuries old, largely empty of tradition, its historical function to keep a small people, the Boers, the Afrikaners, united and on top. Like other colonial languages, Afrikaans isn't innocent, and this is bound to cause trouble for poets, especially a poet like Breytenbach who has stationed himself against his own identity as a native Afrikaner.

In a poem called "(lotus)," the poet enters a world where a "horse of air" comes charging across the sky, the sky "a blue tent," the sun "a banner." We might suppose the horse to be Pegasus in an airy world of poesy. But the voice of the poet, on the contrary, rises out of the muck to curse his poetic destiny:

> the Great Task is
> to turn dog turds
> into stars
> and to trample down the Great Void[.]

To evoke the world's waste, even by way of cursing, is to be on earth's side, and this is Breytenbach's habit. He does not inherit the sun, as he might like, but a solid plate of night that he must somehow face and transform. The problem is words themselves:

> all words are only phantoms
> galloping like horses of breath
> through the emptiness[.]

The poet goes on to identify his "tongue" with his "shadow," and addressing the lotus (a tree of life?) he concedes a defeat:

> for I must shake that shadow
> from the night-mouth
> and with that shadow as a knife
> bareback and astride that tongue
> I must be able to unfold all your leaves
>
> to here where you turn to a pearl,
> to the blind, self-fulfilling pearl
>
> don't you smell the stars now?
> everything comes up out of experience
> and sinks back into it again:
> the horses eat pearls[.]

Breytenbach pits tongue against horse, and the horses, we see, are words—language itself devouring the results of the poet's "Great Task," permitting the Void to prevail. It's not language per se that's the villain, but language politically suborned and in service to an antihuman order. No poet with solid tribal connection would feel as Breytenbach does about words—words that in the volume *Death White as Words* are delimited by "death" and by "white." Among so much else, words are social realities, powers that take their specific substance from the history of the tribe that gives them their life. Surely the relation of language to its political base is not so arcane, or not, at least, in Breytenbach's example. Language is informed by power, and then against by power's lack. The enemy is the state, and the way the state exploits language to uphold its authority. Of course, governmental powers everywhere attempted to control and empty out words. But few poets have had the problem facing Breytenbach and his South African colleagues.

There was, of course, a scattering of poetry already available in Afrikaans, but early stirrings of an Afrikaner voice stayed within the pale and at a time when apartheid was not yet the official order. For the poets of Breytenbach's generation, there has been no counterculture, no alternate or adversary tradition to fall back on, unlike, say, the Russian language with its tradition of revolt against tzarist imposition. When the Soviets appropriated Russian culture there was an earlier legacy— the gift of Pushkin, Gogol, and Chekhov among others—in place to depend on. In English we have the subversive powers of Swift in his savage indignation, of Milton in his darker moods, of mad saints like Blake and Smart, and then the renegade stance of American English in the hands of poets aiming to improve on the "belched words" of Whitman's speech, the "crotch and vine" of his expandable syntax. The situation nearest to Breytenbach's today is in poetry of the women's movement. But even here, as in Adrienne Rich's steady summoning of a feminist past, there *is* a past, a Dickinson to bless the new beginning.

No similar resources are available to the poet who must pursue his or her art in the language of state power, although, as I'll suggest later, Afrikaans is not a lost cause by necessity, if only because those who find themselves officially damned are beginning to use their linguistic inheritance in drastically unofficial ways, much as Breytenbach himself has used it—this "tongue" that shows up everywhere in his poetry as an image of dismemberment, a tongue with no body, no worthy tribe to empower it. But overall, as political conditions deteriorate it would seem that the situation in South Africa weds Afrikaans ever more closely to the violence of the state. This is Breytenbach's view in "The Struggle of the Taal," a poem written in 1976 about the struggle to keep "the Taal" (the official version of Afrikaans) alive and, in Miroslav Holub's phrase, as "clear as the conscience of a gun." The poem was smuggled out of prison, and has appeared in several places. I quote from the translation in *Confessions*, where the poet takes up a righteous wrathful voice against those who have "yet to master the Taal," those for whom the Taal has been so good and done so much:

> From the structures of our conscience
> from the stores of our charity
> we had black constructions built for you, you bastards—
> schools, clinics, post offices, police stations—

> and now the plumes of black smoke blow
> throbbing and flowing like a heart.

Since then the "plumes of black smoke" have grown longer, thicker, more numerous, and we behold in the voice of the Taal (which speaks for the Afrikaner's tribal "we") how language and violence are yoked:

> For we are Christ's executioners.
> We are on the walls around the locations
> gun in one hand
> and machine gun in the other:
> we, the missionaries of Civilization.
>
> We bring you the grammar of violence
> and the syntax of destruction—
> from the tradition of our firearms
> you will hear the verbs of retribution
> stuttering.

Those beneath the lashing of the Taal are given "new mouths for free," and each mouth is a bullet hole—"where each lead-nosed word flies / a speech organ will be torn open." And therefore: "you will please learn to use the Taal." This is Breytenbach's most direct use of the voice of the oppressor. He turns the enemy's position against itself, as Brecht often did, but with the added irony that he is satirizing a voice and a culture inescapably his own. Brecht went back to Luther, among others, but Breytenbach goes back to none but himself. Were it not for the restraint his art allows him, his vehemence would be frantic, out of control. At moments he falls into the kind of "demonic" despair we saw Yeats enthralled by. This is a dangerous position because it depends on the tactics of the enemy, and as the level of political violence escalates the problems of poetry also escalate. At what point does a language informed by the berserk power of a dying state become too terrible for native sons and daughters to digest? At what point can the poet only "vomit," as Breytenbach often puts it?

In 1983, shortly after his release from prison, Breytenbach told Donald Wood that he would write no more in Afrikaans: "I've long felt there was hope for it only if it were used in resistance to apartheid, but I think it is now too late."[7] In an after-note to his *Confessions*, Breytenbach is more detached yet: "To me it is of little importance whether the language dies of shame or is preserved and strengthened by its potentially revolutionary impact."[8] I don't know that Breytenbach has produced any poetry since the poems written or published while he was a political prisoner. If he abandons his native tongue for good, how likely is it that he will go on writing poetry? Novelists have been successful at making the switch to a new language, Conrad and Nabokov for example, but few poets even try. The mother tongue is an absolute source, impossible to replace. Poets like Joseph Brodsky or Czeslaw Milosz will sometimes do their own translating after a poem is alive in its first language. But to take up another tongue—that's as intimate as having one's actual tongue cut out and another stitched over the wound. The only prominent example is that of Paul Celan, whose success is admittedly astonishing. Celan was Romanian and, after the death of his family in the Second World War, wrote in a shattered sort of German. But his language seems alienated even from itself, and in the end, perhaps for many reasons, Celan committed suicide.

Breytenbach, meanwhile, has declared himself still committed to the struggle for liberty in South Africa, and his political position is bound to affect his poetic options in ways that cannot, perhaps, be judged by anyone, not even Breytenbach himself. Two of his collections, *Death White as Words* and *In Africa even the flies are happy*, are available in English translation, enough to convey an art and a spirit. The poetry is characterized by a surrealist tenor that from poem to poem is more or less distraught and ill-tempered, more or less the cry of *hysterica passio*. There is little calm or tenderness, although some of his poems to his wife are wholly gentle and bright with blessing. Everywhere the problem of language shows up, a radical ambivalence magnified by feelings of guilt and self-doubt. There are moments when he is able to identify with the black condition, or when he manages to become one with the land apart from those who defile it. But in the main, Breytenbach's poetry is notable for its surreal dismemberment of biological forms; for a comic spirit that is playful and raucous but that darkens quickly; and for a sense of woundedness, sometimes muted, sometimes grimly festering. These signs of maiming are the cost of close proximity to politics, the faithful record of a nation's political experience. And how else, except by close proximity, could a testament of this kind come into existence?

A nation that keeps its flies happy is a place, as Hamlet would say, far gone with rot. And more than a little, Breytenbach recalls Hamlet,

vexed and melancholic, darkly playful and given to antic fits. In "Good-
bye, Cape Town," the poet is on his way into exile; this is his leave-
taking, addressed to the city.

if someone would grant it me I'd search beyond your walls
for a Jonah tree
if you were a woman I'd elaborate on the smells
of your pocked skin and gurgling glands
lovely arch-whore
slut flirt hell-cat bitch
but you're not even a mother
you're an abortive suicide
gushing wounds of water between the quay and the flanks of this boat
my cape, man's cape, capelove, heart's cape
I wanted to breathe you into a full blown rose
but you stayed just a mouth and a tongue[.]

Mere name-calling, you might say, and offensive as well for its sexism.
But the calling of names is any poet's job. And what sex can a city be,
a prolific city at one with climate and terrain, but female, as the land
itself is female beneath its patriarchal burden? Still, in the lines above
the rapid renaming seems frantic or obsessive. While there is no denying
Breytenbach's metamorphic vigor, his surge of naming seems stuck, as
if for all its steady inventiveness the poem were unable to surmount its
occasion. Breytenbach's ambivalence, in this case, is rooted in outright
love and hate. We are with a poet for whom peace, if it comes at all, is
momentary in the image of an isolated tree; with their small zones of
saving shade, trees appear often in his poems. The reference to Jonah
suggests further that Breytenbach is unsure of his prophetic appointment. His mission is urgent but its success is in doubt—here the poet's
capacity to breathe life into a language that, as he receives it, is no more
than a mouth.

Much of Breytenbach's harshness, his fitful intensity, is the result of
his fight with Afrikaans. The Taal must be subverted, its authority broken. But in what manner and at what cost? The task is formidable; it
provokes distrust toward poetry itself, and there are times when writing
in Afrikaans feels like going over to the enemy. But in that case what
is poetry? In a poem called "Constipation," Breytenbach offers one of
his several answers:

Not that Coleridge doesn't belong to the school of damned poets
    he says
the outcasts capable of ejecting at a given moment
a waxy fart of hideous pain
through the tunnel and turnstile of blood
    and there I agree
for what is a poem
other than a black wind?

Again Breytenbach allies himself with the muck, and seems to agree with Artaud that "all true poetry is cruel." But cruel to whom? The poem's epigraph is from Artaud's commentary on van Gogh: "No one has ever written or painted, sculpted, modelled, built, invented except to get out of hell."[9] Hell, for Breytenbach, is the moral torment of being white in South Africa. And hell is language itself. This poet writes, then, to escape the infernal predicament that his poetry keeps him locked into. What are his options? There are the Fathers, whom he rejects. And then there are the Brothers, with whom he knows he is not one. Describing his first night in Maximum Security, Breytenbach writes: "And in the background all around me in this weird place, I heard male voices; it sounded like scores of voices singing in unison very rhythmically, very strongly, what sounded like tribal music and sometimes like religious hymns."[10] He would later learn that when a black man walks to the gallows, the entire population of the prison—the *black* population— chants its strength to the man about to die. Such intense communion can be admired, even envied, but tribal rapport of this kind is not, Breytenbach knows, a poetic resource in his case.

"Reality," he says in one poem, is "just a boundary, a rumour." But having conferred that sort of potency upon his art, he goes on, elsewhere, to take it back: "poems are just day trips." Seeking solid ground, Breytenbach's imagery settles at the biological level; and while there is much stench and rot, there is also life's sweetness, a mothering plenitude that blesses and protects. In "Fiesta for an eye" he defines his place of reprieve:

> you know no other fig tree which stands
> as this one stands cleaved by the butchering sun
> bleeding over its litter of coolness
> stuffing its figs full of palates so that later it can
>   taunt the sun

> no tree rivals this mother of coolness
> where wedlock is celebrated
> where the firm root is fitted
> to the red-mouthed orifice in the ground
> flesh rouses flesh
> and the figs are full of milk[.]

That is life under the aspect of the Mother, fruitful, erotic, a good unto itself; and here is a female power, moreover, with male capabilities, as when its "firm root" penetrates the "red-mouthed" earth. But these images of fecundity are countered by another imagery, sterile and cold-blooded. This is the domain of the Father, where life is empty, caged, at best a shabby affair or even a kind of death. The following lines are from a poem called "I will die and go to my father":

> friends, fellow mortals
> don't tremble; life still hangs
> like flesh from our bodies
> but death has no shame—
>   we come and we go
> like water from a tap
> like sounds from the mouth
> like our comings and goings:
> it's our bones which will know freedom
> come with me
>   bound in my death, to my father
> in Wellington where the angels
> use worms to fish fat stars from heaven;
> let us die and decompose and be merry:
> my father has a large boarding-house[.]

As we have seen, blasphemy and biblical parody are constants in Breytenbach's work. His easy reference to both the Old and the New Testaments suggests a rich religious upbringing. He presumes, in any case, that Afrikaners take their Christian National Education seriously, and he attacks state religion as an especially repugnant hypocrisy. The poet's assaults are sometimes dancing, sometimes heavyhanded. His saving grace is humor, humor as an irreverent aside that keeps him safely to the side. It also turns grimness to whimsy, and Breytenbach's zaniness is among his best strengths. Often, however, he lets his sense of urgency hobble what might otherwise impress us as true wit. We are left to guess how much is laughter, how much grimace. In a poem called "icon" he surveys the gory world depicted in a Bosch-like painting, then concludes:

> above all this a spiky jesus stands out on a cross
> with no more hope of decomposing
> than a butcher bird's prey on a barbed wire fence,
> with a sneer along his beard;
>
> further behind for ever out of reach (like marilyn monroe)
> rises an empty cool grave[.]

Too often Breytenbach seems fierce in his focus yet reckless in his connections. But on closer inspection, the passage holds much that is his hallmark. Of the six lines above, each in turn surprises; none could be predicted, yet they add up to a complex image. Who is this sneering Jesus if not the poet himself, a savior who cannot save or remove himself from the horror he beholds? And seen through the barbed wire of apartheid, who is Monroe but the White Goddess promising a bliss not to be had, neither in life nor in death nor in art, certainly not in South Africa. We might wonder at the exact balance of humor and distress, but the passage itself is a convincing emblem of impotence, of anger venting itself in bitter play. The religious reference counts as well. In this land, the poet says, there is no redemption in sight.

There is no denying Breytenbach's hyperbolic tendency, his deliberate unpleasantness, his penchant for insult. But these tactics are applied at various temperatures, with the barometer sometimes dropping toward storm, sometimes rising to a wispy sky. And he does not always write in a black wind of rage and disgust. We might even guess that Breytenbach's poetic disposition favors praise and blessing, but that in his circumstances, his exile and status as a poet without a tribe, there is little he can celebrate. On occasion, however, he reaches altogether beyond these entrapments. The small poem below comes to us quietly, with kindness and unusual lyricism. It is called "First prayer for the hottentotsgod," and we need to know three items of background information: first, that *hottentot*, like *kaffir*, is an Afrikaner term of derision for blacks; next, that *hottentotsgot* means "praying mantis" in Afrikaans;

and then that in Bushman myth, this small insect is thought to be a god. Here is Breytenbach's prayer:

they say, little beast, little creator, the elders say
that the fields of stars, the earth-dwellers and all things
that turn and rise up and sigh and crumble
were brought forth by you, that you planted an ostrich feather
in the darkness and behold!   the moon!
o most ancient one,
                              you who fired by love
consume your lover, what led you to forsake
the children of those—the human stuff—
remember?   summoned by you
from the mud?
there are fires in the sky, mother, and the moon
cold as a shoe, and a black cry like smoke
mixed with dust—for your black people, people maker, work
like the dust of knives in the earth that the money
might pile up elsewhere
for others—
grassyyellow lady of prayer,
                              hear our smoke and our dust—
chastise those who debased your people to slavery[.]

Empowered by prayer and a myth not his own, Breytenbach transforms an Afrikaner saying ("plant a feather and a chicken will sprout up"), goes on with humor to make serious use of rhetorical stuttering, then moves from myth into history, from the high sorrow of the Human Condition to a particular plight, in the course of which a second diction intrudes, to end where a poem of this kind must end, not with the consolations of *lacrimae rerum*, but with the black cry rising from its definite pain. Breytenbach's surrealist tilt, in this instance, rests lightly in his appeal for an insect's intervention in human affairs, a joke not altogether joke when we consider the likely efficacy of any black appeal to any South African deity, be it God or god or little beast. In this poem Breytenbach identifies successfully with the voice of the victims. When he does, the interdictions of the white fathers give way to the wisdom of the black elders. And as befits a creation myth in Breytenbach's erotic cosmology, we are again within the governance of the Mother, she who in her ardor devours the Father. In every way but one—the prayer won't be answered—the poem works to appease and absolve the poet's political torment. He does not expect peace, but guilt dissolves and rage no longer consumes him.

Especially effective is Breytenbach's use of repetition. Midway the poem starts renaming itself. The first half culminates in the stammer of its big question, and then the poem goes on in a way that demystifies myth and allows history to show through—a Fall, in this case from eternity into the specific anguish of time. The little creator becomes a people-maker, the starry fields turn to fire. The moon, now a cold shoe, loses its consoling splendor. Life rising, sighing, falling, becomes a particular people being worked, as we might say, to death, ground down like the blade of a knife. Humankind's muddy genesis thus ends up concretely with blacks enslaved. Here a second diction intrudes upon the first, clashes, takes over. The result is a minor infraction of poetic statute, not unlike the marriage of white and "non-white," which, in some places, isn't lawful.

My analogy may seem out of place, but I use it to suggest the way this poem, by permitting the language of politics to intervene, becomes an allegory of political intrusion—life debased by injustice politically imposed. The poem's subject is not only the spectacle of Creation and the Fall, but also the reality *behind* the myth, in this case the plight of millions of human beings enslaved and brutalized, working *in* the diamond mines, the asbestos mines, working *for* the more than one thousand international corporations that, until their profit line began to quiver, used these people and used them up. And plainly, through labor of this kind money does pile up elsewhere, for example in the endowments of American universities. Nothing is gained, I realize, by citing our government's support for the regime in South Africa; but we might at least recognize our connection to Breytenbach's world. More than a little, my remarks are like the poem's last lines—these do not, it might be argued, belong to poetry or proper criticism. But the test of the poem's last lines is not received taste or purity of diction. The test is how false and trivial the poem would be without these lines. If the political references were absent, or veiled in metaphor, the poem might be more pleasant, but it would also be inconsequent, an assurance got by habitual retreat into myth. History would then appear as we prefer it to appear, under the aspect of eternity—in other words *necessary*, as if slavery were in the nature of things, which it isn't.

• • •

Breytenbach's debt to surrealism is fundamental. It defines his art as much as his problematic relation to Afrikaans. The psychic rending his language forced upon him may have predisposed him to surrealist solutions, but timing is also an important factor. The young poet-painter arrived in Paris in 1961, just as the upsurge of the sixties was getting under way—a time of zany politics and tactics quite bizarre. Surrealism itself, as the brainchild of Breton and his friends, was still much in evidence, in fact established and respectable, even a tradition. Exhibitions and journals devoted to surrealist art had become part of the cultural environment, and the movement's basic techniques—summed up by Picasso as "a horde of destructions"—had become a resource for poets anywhere. The principle of radical freedom in the arts is now commonplace and any poet might use surrealist techniques on occasion, if not centrally then as one resource among many.

But for Breytenbach surrealism meant more than taking easy liberties. The movement's originating impulse—insurrectionary and bent on cultural demolition—is very much alive in Breytenbach's need to dismantle official versions of reality. No doubt the weapons of ridicule and dark humor appealed to a poet whose job was to curse. Humor is essential to the surrealist spirit; but surrealism's lighthearted delight in havoc should not obscure its more ferocious intent. To *fire a pistol randomly into a crowd* was the movement's emblem. The surrealist game of chaotic sentence construction, in its first and most famous session, came up with *le cadavre exquis boira le vin nouveau*—new wine to be sipped by an exquisite corpse. And the image of the slashed eye in *Un chien andalou* suggests more now than it did in 1928 when Buñuel haphazardly made the film. In retrospect the surrealist assault on the human image seems clear, and in his memoirs Buñuel says of himself and the band of exterminating angels to which he belonged: "we all felt a certain destructive impulse, a feeling that for me has been even stronger than the creative urge."[11] Much of this can be written off as *épater les bourgeois*, but not all. And the logic of assault, once let loose, can't be recalled. The distance between the pen and the gun is less than once it seemed. This doesn't mean that artists should be timid, but that context generates consequence and no poet, today, can pretend to innocence. In our time, as Camus put it, to create is to create dangerously.

It may be that all art harbors delight in destruction; that the motive for metaphor is as much transgression as transformation; or that visionary faith in a new world is fuelled by a fury of disgust for what is. The patron saint of surrealist assault is Rimbaud, from whom, along with Lautréamont, the surrealists in France took their lead. They were the first poets and painters of our century to proceed as a group, with manifestos and programs and tribal rites, eager to tap the soul's darker energies. These they hoped to put at art's disposal—and in some cases, notably for Éluard and Aragon, at the disposal of the Communist Party. Breytenbach himself has not been a doctrinaire Marxist. But the revolutionary spirit of surreal attack must surely have spoken to the youthful poet's need.

That Breytenbach has seen his own identity in this fracturing light is apparent from his private myth of Rimbaud. *A Season in Paradise* is his re-envisionment of Rimbaud's *Season in Hell*, and in it Breytenbach locates Rimbaud as his special precursor. The French poet, in this telling, dies several deaths and then, after the loss of his leg, returns again to Africa. "What is clear," Breytenbach says, "is that the track of his single foot was later noticed in the desert. He vanished without trace, gloriously, like a white line on a sheet of white paper. Africa is reality. And in Africa you cannot die."[12] The renovated Rimbaud begins "to migrate southward." He turns up in Namibia, in the mines of Kimberley, is a hunter, a bartender, a mercenary. In one of these appearances Rimbaud causes the death of Eugène Marais, the poet often called the father of serious poetry in Afrikaans. And if, as Breytenbach concludes, "there's arms smuggling again these days off the Skeleton Coast,"[13] that too is Rimbaud's doing. The point of this sketch of Rimbaud, as I read it, is that the history of the surrealist spirit began in France and then passed to the African continent, where now, with Breytenbach in the vanguard, it continues in the land of the Boers.

Every writer constructs his or her own prehistory, but for an Afrikaner the task is especially difficult. With no illustrious tradition to take in and cast out, the bearers of Afrikaans must go elsewhere to escape from parochial constraint. Breytenbach went to Paris, received the confirmation of Rimbaud, created a voice never heard before. This has been his strength, and also the cause, maybe, of his downfall. For like the mythical Rimbaud, Breytenbach returned from France to Africa with revolutionary objectives. "Everyone," he wrote in *Season*, "should be an arms-smuggler at least once in his life."[14] So it was that in 1975 Breytenbach came back. He arrived, made some contacts, and the Bureau of State Security—known as the BOSS—swept him up like a fly.

A conceit became grimly real, and paradise passed into hell. Breytenbach's example provides a glimpse of the *literary* secret agent. I do not mean the writer who puts forth revolutionary ideas in his work only, but one who like Byron begins to take his literary identity seriously and comes to believe that what he is in his poems he must also be in the world. From the *Confessions* it would appear that some of Breytenbach's European friends were more eager than he was to view the poet and the revolutionary as one. In any case his misreading of Rimbaud's life—the abandonment of poetry for African gun-running—suggests the logic of what came next. Except that whereas the French surrealists had been satisfied to barge into halls and theaters to cause scandal and break up cultural events, Breytenbach aimed to crack the BOSS, one of the world's most efficient organs of terror. At best, we can say that he took poetry seriously. But then, we might say as well that he did not take it seriously enough.

The situation suggests that Breytenbach had grown dissatisfied with the kind of power to be had from words alone. He was sick of his impotence as *mere* writer, and wanted literary commitment to be more, or different, than it can be. During his 1973 return he joined a symposium at the University of Cape Town and there delivered what can only be called a diatribe, aimed point-blank at himself and his South African colleagues. His remarks, and even more the tone of his address, throw light on his poetry and reveal the state of mind that would shortly land him in prison. He began by saying that "all talk in this bitter motley-funeral-land is politics—whether it is whispered talk, talking shit, spitting into the wind or speaking in his master's voice."[15] Breytenbach's categories are revealing, especially the agony implicit in "speaking in his master's voice." Presumably, his own category would be "spitting into the wind." He went on to ask: "Are we nothing, then, as writers, but the shock-absorbers of this white establishment, its watchdogs?" He attacked not only *apartheid* but also American policy in Vietnam, and advocated "taking a stand." In conclusion he put the problem of his art this way: "I want to come as close as I can in my work to the temporal—not the infinite; that has always been around. And infinity says nothing. What hurts is the ephemeral, the local."

Breytenbach's Cape Town manifesto is not without point, but it brims with *hysterica passio* and what it tells us, finally, is that his burden had become more than he could bear. Art and life crossed, and the larger truth of his predicament is that politics drags eternity down into time. The temporal *is* what hurts—conditions that do not have to exist but that do, to the detriment of many and the benefit of some few, so long as men and women support or do not seek to change the status quo. Breytenbach's response also suggests that apartheid devastates not only bodies but the soul as well. For those who think that poetry's proper realm is the human condition minus its political torment, Breytenbach's run-in with politics might seem to prove their point. But for those in search of a poetry that would confront rather than evade, Breytenbach deserves honor for the chances he took and the mistakes he made.

Impossible to say what might come next. Almost by accident Breytenbach has created, in his native tongue, the precedent he needed but could not find when he began. In his *Confessions*, moreover, he notes a hopeful development: "already," he says, "the language which is spoken in township and prison and in the army, on fishing-boats and in factories, has escaped entirely from the control of the Afrikaners. In that shape it is a virile medium, ever being renewed, which so far finds but little reflection in the writing."[16] Perhaps, then, despair is premature. There may be, surely there will be, young poets for whom Breytenbach opened a way. He was the first, he was there, his example stands.

CODA: Afrikaans is a small language made smaller by its almost total lack, at present, of moral appeal. To volunteer as students of the Taal is not a likely choice for most of us. At the same time, however, few are avid to know—as perhaps we *need* to know—the spiritual temper and moral quality of events now taking place in South Africa. Because of censorship and the news blackout, we get only the poorest sense of things from the usual media sources. In this respect our situation recalls conditions during the First World War, when propaganda and tight censorship cut off the reality of the trenches from the rest of the world so that the awful truth, when it came, was carried entirely by poets. Still today, we know the spiritual climate of Flanders and the Marne through the poetry of Owen, Sassoon, Graves, and their peers. And even when other information is available, the life of poetry cuts deeper, reaches further, is more accessible to imagination.

The Dutch set foot on the Cape of Good Hope in 1652. During the next two centuries the interaction of native Africans with Dutch colonialists generated a new tongue, a historical process described by André Brink: "the Afrikaans language emerged from the efforts of non-Dutch speakers to speak Dutch in an African environment. Hence the very development of the language implied a dimension of the exploration of the African experience, a process intrinsic to the language itself."[17] While patriotic Afrikaners sometimes still insist on its Teutonic pedigree, discerning scholars are convinced that it is a creole language, a local patois that by chance and circumstance arrived at its present incarnation. Moreover, after 1806 the British attempt to impose English meant that Afrikaans was under siege, and something of a siege mentality informs the posture of Afrikaans even now. After the Boer War the Afrikaners were de facto rulers in local affairs, and in 1948 the whole of this embattled history came to a head with the emergence of the South African state on an apartheid base, with Afrikaans the language of power. That Afrikaans is also the first language of many blacks has always been overlooked; today, in South Africa, more blacks than whites speak Afrikaans. Hein Willemse describes (in 1987) the situation for black writers in these terms:[18]

> Given the generally high level of bilingualism in South Africa, some black Afrikaans writers may expediently opt out and write in English, in the process avoiding the suspicion of being less committed and literarily in cahoots with Afrikaner rule. Personally, however, this would have meant the premature death of my creative endeavors, and the beginning of an unbearable language schizophrenia. The task now is to continue writing in Afrikaans and to be constantly aware of this dichotomy: the oppressed writing in the language of the oppressor.

It's not unlikely, therefore, that Afrikaans as Breytenbach has used it, along with the politicization of black usage, will play its part in big changes, changes that will reverberate throughout the African continent, and that Americans, with their government's long-time loyalty to Afrikaner tyranny, shall want to understand. But we do not, of course, have Afrikaans at our disposal; and if we attend to political experience in that crucial part of the world, getting the feel of history as its victims and dissidents know it, we shall have to turn to translation. That's clear enough, and it seems possible that what goes for South Africa goes finally for political experience in all the earth's reaches. The moral drama of our time is most distinctly played out in totalitarian states and third-world nations; we shall have little sense of our own being-in-the-world without imagining the torment of others through, first of all, their poets.

Traditionally, the American commitment to other languages has been limited to French and German, perhaps Spanish and Italian also. But few among us know any second language finely enough to penetrate its poetry, and even fewer of us know a third or fourth language—in which case, what becomes of the rest? The multitude of urgent tongues around us? What, for example, of the great Russians, Akhmatova and Mandelshtam, Pasternak and Tsvetayeva? Or of Polish poets like Milosz and Herbert? Of Seferis and Ritsos in Greek? Or, without Spanish, of our great neighbors Neruda, Vallejo, and Para to the south? What, in other words, can be the fate of global consciousness deprived of the means to consciousness that languages provide? Are we at the mercy of official pronouncements and partial news reports? Is the soul, the sharing of resistance to indignity, to be both blind and nine-tenths mute?

Translation's new authority is abundantly visible. The poets cited above are available to us in many renderings, and the recent surge in translation corresponds to awareness of the world at large, an alertness heightened by multiple catastrophes and nuclear threat, a consciousness whose blooming has been specific to this century. When higher education crystalized in the nineteenth century it took its inspiration from the German model with an emphasis on philology; in practice this meant that any educated person—almost always white, male, and upper class—would master Greek and Latin as well as languages endorsed by European powers. Hence the equation of "civilization as we know it" with proficiency in languages that constitute "Western culture." And hence the duplicity of a privilege that was quick to condemn anyone who did not, say, read Dante in Italian, but that had no such reservations when, early in the century, the astonishments of Russian fiction burst—in translation, of course—on Western sensibility.

The world is bigger than we are, larger than the superpowers that battle for control. Earth juts back, and its affirming undervoice arises in tongues and traditions not a part of elite education. Perhaps we were never meant, by the logic of cultural hegemony, to know the power of voices beyond our own self-interest. But with the planet itself in view, imagination either loses contact with the travail and resilience of our time, or it pays tribute to poets from linguistic tribes not our own. Translation is no longer an exotic indulgence; it is an act of solidarity, a political choice.

·FOUR·

WITNESS
&
BLESSING

·VII·

Thomas McGrath,
North America West

"America is too terrible a subject for an American."

"Then we can forget the West."

"No, no. We cannot forget the West. There is no
American outside the West, and there never will be.
It is the dream, and that dream is the only hope. No,
we cannot forget the West. Where all the races meet
in a place of beauty, not in a place of blood. The land
cannot grant amnesty."
                              —from *McGrath on McGrath*[1]

Sweetened with a harvest song, the work goes well.
                              —Christopher Caudwell[2]

Thomas McGrath has been writing remarkable poems of every size
and form for nearly fifty years. In American poetry he is as close
to Whitman as anyone since Whitman himself. McGrath is master of
the long wide line (wide in diction, long in meter), the inclusive six-
beat measure of America at large. The scene of his work is the whole
of the continent east to west, with its midpoint in the high-plains rim
of the heartland. His diction, with its vast word stock and multitude of
language layers, is demotic to the core yet spiced with learned terms in
Whitman's manner, a voice as richly American as any in our literature.
But for all that, McGrath is little known. He has been championed by
one no less worldly than E. P. Thompson, as well as other poets, Kenneth
Rexroth and Donald Hall among them, devoted to his work. In the
main, though, McGrath hasn't had the attention that a whole flotilla of

our lesser poets enjoy, a situation out of joint with the facts of the matter
and a scandal to those who know McGrath's four-part epic, *Letter to an
Imaginary Friend*, a poem of witness to the radical spirit—"the generous
wish," as McGrath calls it—of American populist tradition.[3]

If McGrath remains an outsider, his humor might be part of the
reason. Apart from Stevens' wispy playfulness and some of Auden's wit,
we don't expect an important poet to be broadly comic, especially when
the same voice rails in earnest against the time's worst abuses. McGrath
holds high expectations for poetry—he wants to see it change the world
by calling us to recovery of our finest dreams—yet he delights in excess
and in punning and is, seemingly, hyperbolic by conviction. Humor of
this kind supports irreverent freedom and a desire to pull things back
"down to earth." In his will to dislodge prevailing pieties, McGrath
aligns himself as Twain did in *Huckleberry Finn*, with oddity and
outcasts:

> —I'm here to bring you
> Into the light of speech, the insurrectionary powwow
> Of the dynamite men and the doomsday spielers, to sing you
> Home from the night.

McGrath's diction is more expansive than the sort now in fashion.
Some of us will probably be shaken by his vigorous vocabulary, and
jolted still further by a bawdy argot of physical frankness informing the
whole. McGrath's language is an amalgam of field-hand grit and Ox-
bridge nicety seasoned by working-class dialect from the 1930's and
40's. These choices give him an almost fabulous voice, at least on occasion, and a range of lyrical textures uniquely his own. Finally, there
is the singular way he manages materialism (Marxist) and sacramentalism
(Roman Catholic) side by side as if they composed a doctrinal continuum
that surely they don't—except in McGrath's special usage.

McGrath identifies himself mainly with the western side of the country
and sets much of his best work in the place and rural spirit of the Dakotas,
a region by definition graceless and provincial to the dominant urban-
eastern sensibility, a place and spirit that to many among us is noplace
and thus a sort of utopian badlands politely forgot. On top of that comes
McGrath's politics—an insurrectionary stance that in its Marxist emphasis might have been international but which, nourished by the grain-

land countryside west of Fargo, is decidedly homegrown, a radicalism that McGrath calls "unaffiliated far Left."

When McGrath says in *Letter* that "North Dakota is everywhere," one can fairly hear the strain upon an urbane sensibility that isn't easily able, and may in fact be unwilling, to imagine that the West (outside of California) exists. McGrath says that his own family had to deal with "Indian scare[s]"; that "the past out here was bloody, and full of injustice, though hopeful and heroic."[4] What, after all, is *American* about America if not the frontier experience and how the fate of the Indians questions ours:

> From Indians we learned a toughness and a strength; and we gained
> A freedom: by taking theirs: but a real freedom; born
> From the wild and open land our grandfathers heroically stole.
> But we took a wound at Indian hands: a part of our soul scabbed
> over[.]

As a boy McGrath saw "the Indian graves / Alive and flickering with the gopher light." In his art the landscape is weighted with the human world. Even when abandoned, the land is not empty. Nature is peopled, strife-ridden and—"where the Dakotas bell and nuzzle at the north coast"—of surpassing beauty. For most of us, however, these early defeats and distant splendors are of little consequence. Most of us pretend freedom from history and would go weightless into tomorrow like leaves in a wind, whereas McGrath summons the past of his own time and place, the essential history of personal, and then of national, experience insofar as each—the private and the public testaments—bears witness to the other. Like any bard, he preserves the memory of events in danger of being repressed or forgotten. This is not an easy job, given that much worth recalling is gone for good. It is important to remember that McGrath's grandparents homesteaded the farmland his family worked and his own generation was forced to leave; here (from *Echoes Inside the Labyrinth*) is "The Old McGrath Place":[5]

> The tractor crossed the lawn and disappeared
> Into the last century—
> An old well filled up with forgotten faces.
> So many gone down (bucketsful) to the living, dark
> Water . . .

> I would like to plant a willow
> There—waterborne tree to discountenance earth . . .
>
> But then I remember my grandmother:
> Reeling her morning face out of that rainy night.

McGrath plants the poem instead, and his attention turns from cursing to blessing. The outcome is a praise-poem in the manner of elegy, its nostalgia nipped in the bud by "bucketsful." The scene is the dead site of a family farm—of which, in America, there are still sights countless. The aim of the poem is to regenerate the past through memory's witness; or rather, to claim that task as the poet's mission. The "faces" won't be forgotten. The farmyard well is still there, still alive, and becomes an entrance to ancestral sources, a complex emblem of death and rebirth. In its dark water abide the mothering powers of farm and family that McGrath grew up with and from which, as a poet, he draws his strength.

Thomas McGrath was born in 1916 on a farm near Sheldon, North Dakota, of Irish Catholic parents. Every aspect of this heritage—the place, the hard times, the religious and political culture—informs his art. His religious upbringing figures centrally in Part Three—"the Christmas section"—of *Letter*, and in his poetry at large there is a steady preference for the ritualistic forms and sacramental language of the Church. Being Irish also worked in his favor when, in 1941, he entered the maritime world of seamen and longshoremen—the Irish community that worked Manhattan's West Side docks—where the fight for reform went forward on the piers and in the bars and walk-ups of Chelsea. There McGrath worked as a labor organizer and, briefly, as a shipyard welder. His politics led him into a world of experience that, in turn, backed up his political beliefs in concrete ways. To be a Red on the waterfront was to be the natural prey of goon squads patrolling the docks for the bosses and the racketeers. It was also to see the world of industrial work at first hand. In Part Two of *Letter* McGrath recalls his job as a welder at Federal Drydock & Shipyard:

> "After the war we'll get them," Packy says.
>   He dives
> Into the iron bosque to bring me another knickknack.
> The other helpers swarm into it. Pipes are swinging

As the chain-falls move on their rails in.
                              Moment of peace.

The welders stand and stretch, their masks lifted, palefaced.
Then the iron comes onto the stands; the helpers turn to the wheels;
The welders, like horses in flytime, jerk their heads and the masks
Drop. Now demon-dark they sit at the wheeled turntables,
Striking their arcs and light spurts out of their hands.

                                              "After
The war we'll shake the bosses' tree till the money rains
Like crab-apples. Faith, we'll put them under the ground."
After the war.
            Faith.
                    Left wing of the IRA
That one.
            Still dreaming of dynamite.
                                    I nod my head,
The mask falls.
            Our little smokes rise into roaring heaven.

These lines are alive of commotion and wordplay, for example the double meanings of "faith" and "war" and the "nod" at the end. The scene itself suggests McGrath's larger figure of the "round-dance," his emblem of communal action wherein his double vision—materialist and sacramentalist at once—is reconciled with itself. In the passage above, the rites of work become an act of prayer, a moment of *working together* beneath the hegemony of a "faith" now defeated. After the war the bosses had won and it was Packy O'Sullivan gone, him with his curse on capital. McGrath returned to Chelsea to find everything changed, his friends dead or departed, the vigorous radicalism of the National Maritime Union bought off and a new breed of "labor-fakers" running the show:

And the talking walls had forgotten our names, down at the Front,
Where the seamen fought and the longshoremen struck the great ships
In the War of the Poor.
                    And the NMU had moved to the deep south
(Below Fourteenth) and built them a kind of Moorish whorehouse

For a union hall. And the lads who built that union are gone.
Dead. Deep sixed. Read out of the books. Expelled.

McGrath's family emigrated from Ireland, and the Sheas (his mother's side) were Gaelic-speaking. Some arrived by way of Ellis Island, others through Canada. Both grandfathers worked their way west as immigrant laborers on the railroad. They got as far as the Dakota frontier and settled as homesteaders, living at first in the ubiquitous dirt-built "soddies." For young McGrath, the specific gifts of family and place included the liturgical richness of Catholicism to fill up frontier emptiness, but also the political richness of farming in a part of the country and at a time when the broad-based Farmers Alliance was strong enough (during the 1880's and early 90's) to pursue the first and only nationwide attempt at a national third party, the People's Party, thereby awakening radical consciousness and endorsing a spirit of grass-roots insurgency. From Texas up through Kansas and into the great Northwest, the Farmers Alliance gave rural populations their first taste of dignity. For the first time power was more than a courthouse coterie. Decent life for a while looked possible. And from early on, this unique addition to American political culture, now called Populism, was strong in the Dakotas.[6]

Neighborhood, for McGrath growing up, was part of an adversary culture, an order against the mainstream economy, with collective traditions of self-help and sharing. This state-within-a-state gave countless small farmers a defense against the unchecked plundering of grain companies, banks, and the baronial railroads. When McGrath curses wealth and the money system, we should keep in mind that his family was working to get a foothold in America during the depths of the Gilded Age, our most ruthless era of capital accumulation. Boom and bust were the signs of the time, when economic depression and political helplessness ruined "plain folks" by hundreds of thousands and, an important point, made every year's harvest—each autumn's race with nature and the money supply—a time of national crisis.

The glory days of the Farmers Alliance were over by McGrath's time, but the political imagination of the populist tradition was ingrained and open to new forms of expression each time economic disaster shredded the nation. Until the First World War, members of the Industrial Workers of the World—the Wobblies—were a strong and often strong-armed force in key sectors of labor (lumber and mining most firmly), carrying forward the tradition of agrarian revolt. After the war the Non-Partisan

League (started in 1916, the year of McGrath's birth) organized the vote and worked toward the public ownership of vital facilities. In North Dakota the League came to control the state legislature and established a public granary system. The populist spirit thrived on these successes; it also counted on a tradition of communal work that rural peoples have known since the dawn, maybe, of independent yeomanry. This broader background, as McGrath suggests in an interview, underwrites his own kind of visionary populism:[7]

> The primary experience out in these states, originally, anyway, was an experience of loneliness, because the people were so far away from everything. They had come out here and left behind whatever was familiar, and you find this again and again in letters that women wrote out here. The other side of that loneliness was a sense of community, which was much more developed—even as late as thirty or forty years ago—than it is now. The community of swapped labor. This was a standard thing on the frontier; everybody got together and helped put up a house or put up a soddy when a new family came along. You helped with this, that or the other, and you swapped labor back and forth all the time and that community was never defined. It wasn't a geographical thing; it was a sort of commune of people who got along well together, and right in the same actual neighborhood there might be two or three of these. . . . This sense of solidarity . . . is one of the richest experiences that people can have. It's the only true shield against alienation and deracination and it was much more developed in the past than it is now.

In McGrath's poetry this "community of swapped labor," and the populist sentiment rising from it, cannot be overestimated. This was the political milieu, or simply the spirit of place, that he inherited. Parts One and Two of *Letter to an Imaginary Friend*, in which McGrath evokes his roots, are devoted to moments of compact drama recalling the populist legacy as it spun itself out and into his soul. The Great Depression was the definitive learning experience for McGrath's generation, the testing ground for political belief of any kind and, as it seemed to McGrath from his own encounters, the historical proof of populism's capacity to endure as a force. Drifters of every sort filled the land, men from different backgrounds, some of them schooled, others not, all of them angry and talking politics nonstop. Companionship with laborers like these provided the forum for McGrath's education—working, for example, with a logging team:

All that winter in the black cold, the buzz-saw screamed and whistled,
And the rhyming hills complained. In the noontime stillness,
Thawing our frozen beans at the raw face of a fire,
We heard the frost-bound tree-boles booming like cannon,
A wooden thunder, snapping the chains of the frost.

Those were the last years of the Agrarian City
City of swapped labor
Communitas
Circle of warmth and work
Frontier's end and last wood-chopping bee
The last collectivity stamping its feet in the cold. [. . .]

The weedy sons of midnight enterprise:
Stump-jumpers and hog-callers from the downwind counties
The noonday mopus and the coffee guzzling Swedes
Prairie mules
Moonfaced Irish from up-country farms
Sand-hill cranes
And lonesome deadbeats from a buck brush parish.

So, worked together.

Diction shoves and bristles within a theme of solidarity, affording McGrath's figuration of harmony-in-conflict another lively example. The object of praise is again a community united through work, and again the world it comes from is gone. Some hundred lines later McGrath's mood turns elegiac as he remembers the collective rapport of a time when people of all sorts came together in common need to help out; and then how they lost and disappeared:

The talk flickered like fires.
The gist of it was, it was a bad world and we were the boys to
                                                    change it.

And it *was* a bad world; and we might have.

In that round song, Marx lifted his ruddy
Flag; and Bakunin danced (And the Technocrats
Were hatching their ergs . . .)
                                        A mile east, in the dark,
The hunger marchers slept in the court house lobby
After its capture: where Webster and Boudreaux

Bricklayer, watchmaker, Communists, hoped they were building
The new society, inside the shell of the old—
Where the cops came in in the dark and we fought down the
                                                            stairs.

That was the talk of the states those years, that winter.
Conversations of east and west, palaver
Borne coast-to-coast on the midnight freights where Cal was
                                                        riding
The icy red-balls.
                        Music under the dogged-down
Dead lights of the beached caboose.
Wild talk, and easy enough now to laugh.
That's not the point and never was the point.
What was real was the generosity, expectant hope,
The open and true desire to create the good.

Passages of this kind epitomize McGrath's poetic enterprise, and I
quote at length to mark the tonal shifts, the conjunction of blessing and
cursing, and then the reach of language establishing historical complexity. No mere catalogue, this is a kind of lyrical documentation at which
McGrath excels, and through which he preserves his firsthand sense of
the nation at odds with itself. He bears witness to "the generous wish,"
and curses the McCarthy years ("the hunting" conducted by HUAC)
for ending that hope:

Now, in another autumn, in our new dispensation
Of an ancient, man-chilling dark, the frost drops over
My garden's starry wreckage.
                              Over my hope:
                                          Over
The generous dead of my years.
                              Now, in the chill streets
I hear the hunting, the long thunder of money.
A queer parade goes past: Informers, shit-eaters, fetishists,
Punkin-faced cretins, and the little deformed traders
In lunar nutmegs and submarine bibles.
And the parlor anarchist comes by, to hang in my ear
His tiny diseased pearls like the guano of meat-eating birds.
But *then* was a different country, though the children of light,
                                                    gone out
To the dark people in the villages, did not come back . . .
But what was real, in all that unreal talk
Of ergs and of middle peasants (perhaps someone born
Between the Mississippi and the Rocky Mountains, the unmapped
                                                    country)
Was the generous wish.
                              To talk of the People
Is to be a fool. But they were the *sign* of the People,
Those talkers.

The parts of *Letter* I've been quoting mark episodes of personal importance to McGrath's political development. They are also—the em-
passioned talk of the Depression years, the welders on night shift during
the war—representative moments in the life of the nation. McGrath has
deliberately stationed himself to document the populist spirit *in action*
from the 1930's on through the 40's and 50's, and then beyond into
our own time. He is on the lookout for evidence of political promise,
and a witness to communal possibilities. His care is for people working
and living together—the productive spirit of *Communitas*. Without question, this is McGrath's grand theme, based on his poetry's recollection
of his own experience as a boy, as a young man, and then active poet.
His art is motivated by a visionary care for the future, but also by "grief

for a lost world: that round song and commune / When work was a handclasp."[8]

When McGrath began publishing in the early 1940's, his work was shaped by the strain and agitation of the 30's. For political visionaries it had been a painful but exciting time to come of age. On the disheartening evidence of events, the future was bound to be a glory. After the lament, the exaltation. This doubling—first the bad news, then the good—is the form of the American jeremiad, a type of political-visionary stance that thrives on unfulfillment.[9] Each failure to fulfill our destiny as a people becomes a period of probation and then revival along the way to triumphant conclusion. This view of the country's course and prospects owes everything to our nation's founding fathers and nothing to Marx, but it yields an enlarged notion of consensus when recast in Marxist terms. For McGrath, in any case, the jeremiad is a natural vehicle for enduring failure and keeping faith in "the generous wish"; it allows him to rail and reconfirm, to deplore the backsliding and lean years of his tribe, without flagging or abandoning hope.

In the poems of the 1940's, McGrath announces and proclaims. His language is abstract and mythical, a style distinct from the kind of line and language in *Letter*. Repeatedly, in these early poems, the poet calls to his tribe and predicts redemptive apocalypse. In "Blues for Warren," a poem of 197 lines with the inscription "killed spring 1942, north sea," the dead man is praised as one "who descended into hell for our sakes; awakener / Of the hanging man, the Man of the Third Millennium."[10] A radical prophecy is informed by traditional archetypes; Marx and the Church are made to join in common cause, while the hero, a "Scapegoat and Savior," is united—in spirit and in body—with the dispossessed multitudes his death will help redeem:

> Those summers he rode the freights between Boston and Frisco
> With the cargo of derelicts, garlands of misery,
> The human surplus, the interest on dishonor,
> And the raw recruits of a new century.

Much of McGrath's work in his early style—collected in *The Movie at the End of the World*—declares belief, addresses action and actors in the political arena, blesses and blames. Many of these poems are informed by a sense of humor that is tough and playful at once, a manner that reaches a comic highpoint and takes on a broad, easygoing confidence with a little volume of poems printed by International Publishers in 1949. Entitled *Longshot O'Leary's Garland of Practical Poesie*, the book is dedicated to the friends of McGrath's waterfront days in New York. Most of these poems express the spirit enacted by the title. The center-piece is a ballad of nineteen stanzas, "He's a Real Gone Guy: A Short Requiem for Percival Angleman,"[11] celebrating the death of a local gangster. Like Brecht, from whom he learned a great deal, McGrath often praises renegades and losers, figures that rebuke the prevailing order as part of capital's bad conscience. "Short Requiem" is an exercise, so to say, in jocular realism, a satire that goes to the tune of "As I walked out in the streets of Laredo." The violence of the West comes east and this is stanza one:

> As I walked out in the streets of Chicago,
> As I stopped in a bar in Manhattan one day,
> I saw a poor weedhead dressed up like a sharpie,
> Dressed up like a sharpie all muggled and fey.

The poem portrays a man who was a worker getting nowhere and who turned, therefore, to the profits of crime. Here is the core of dialogue between the poet and the crook:

> "Oh I once was a worker and had to keep scuffling;
> I fought for my scoff with the wolf at the door.
> But I made the connection and got in the racket,
> Stopped being a business man's charity whore.

> "You'll never get yours if you work for a living,
> But you may make a million for somebody else.
> You buy him his women, his trips to Miami,
> And all he expects is the loan of yourself."

> "I'm with you," I said, "but here's what you've forgotten:
> A working stiff's helpless to fight on his own,
> But united with others he's stronger than numbers.
> We can win when we learn that we can't win alone."

In the uproar and aftermath of the Depression, a poem like this would find its grateful audience. But by the time it appeared in 1949, labor was damping down and in the schools the New Criticism was setting narrower, more cautious standards of literary judgment. McGrath, with his Brechtian huff, was out in the cold, although any reader nursed on Eliot might still appreciate the poem's hollow-man ending:

> He turned and went out to the darkness inside him
> To the Hollywood world where believers die rich,
> Where free enterprise and the lies of his childhood
> Were preparing his kingdom in some midnight ditch.

The poem surpasses its Marxist scene (the world as classes in conflict) with a vision of community (the workers of the world united), and translates a political predicament into spiritual terms. In *Longshot O'Leary*, McGrath's style is at once streetwise and jubilant. Slang and local patois invigorate his diction, and a distinctly "Irish" note (nearly always at play in the later poetry) is struck in namings, allusions, and parody. Humor becomes a leavening element, and the comedy of word-play keeps the spirit agile in hard situations. And now McGrath can imagine his audience, lost though it might be. His model derives from the men and women he worked with in New York before the war, tough-minded socialists devoted day by day to the cause, a working commune worthy of tribal regard. To call this tribe back into action, to witness its past and praise its future, becomes McGrath's poetic task.

In 1954 McGrath took a job at Los Angeles State College, a teaching position that did not last long. The spirit of McCarthy was closing down "the generous wish," and McGrath, after declaring to a HUAC subcommittee that he would "prefer to take [his] stand with Marvell, Blake, Shelley and Garcia Lorca,"[12] found himself jobless and without recourse. Being blacklisted was an honor of sorts, but money and prospects were in short supply. So was the hope for a better world. It was then that McGrath began his thirty-years' work on *Letter*. It was then, too, that the earlier, more formal style gave way to the lyrical expansiveness that marks McGrath's best poetry. As a friendly critic puts it, "We can at least make an honest guess that McGrath's direct experience of repression in the early fifties threw him back into touch with his earlier experiences."[13] Counting his losses, it must have seemed that praise and blame were not enough; that the defense of his art would require enlargement of resources as a witness—some way, that is, of speaking for the nation as well as for himself, a song of self made valid for all.

What McGrath discovered is that each of us lives twice: not only that we are first in the world and then make of it what we can through the word; but also that each of us bears a representative (political) as well as an individual (private) life. The representative parts occur when history and the path of personal life intersect, and to make this distinction is to suggest one way that politics and poetry converge. By the time he came to write *Letter*, McGrath saw that "In the beginning was the *world*!"[14] and that he would have to locate himself exactly at the crossroads where self and world meet:[15]

> All of us live twice at the same time—once uniquely and once representatively. I am interested in those moments when my unique personal life intersects with something bigger, when my small brief moment has a part in "fabricating the legend."

By way of "fabricating the legend," *Letter* begins: "—From here it is necessary to ship all bodies east." McGrath has said the line was given to him by poet and friend Don Gordon during the blacklisting 1950's when, out of work and uncertain in spirit, McGrath was living "in Los Angeles at 2714 Marsh Street, / Writing, rolling east with the earth." The opening sequence of *Letter* continues with a shift in voice: "They came through the passes, / they crossed the dark mountains in a month of snow, [. . .] Hunters of the hornless deer in the high plateaus of that country." Then the two voices join as McGrath goes on to declare his relation to the grandest of our native themes—America's heroical westering:

Aye, long ago. A long journey ago,
Most of it lost in the dark, in a ruck of tourists,
In the night of the compass, companioned by tame wolves, plagued
By theories, flies, visions, by the anthropophagi . . .

I do not know what end that journey was toward.
—But I am its end. I am where I have been and where
I am going. The journeying destination—at least that. . . [.]

At the onset of *Letter*, the poet stations himself at land's end, but he does not yearn in the way of Whitman or Jeffers for further passage, some intenser rapport of solitary Self with the Universe at large. Rather he turns, faces back to consider where he's been and what he's learned and how, in some added stretch of time, this northern continent might become the great thing it has always symbolized. America, having fulfilled its claim to manifest destiny, having defined itself through westward migration, finds itself in some way finished. This terminus is either a dead end or a new beginning, and simply put it comes to this: the vision of ourselves that Whitman strained to realize, McGrath aims to recover. *Letter* is a poem of remembrance and what it celebrates is the American Dream in its first freshness, countless times exploited, countless times betrayed, but still alive in memory and actual terrain; the covenant and the promise, not of a city on a hill like a fortress, but of a loose-knit neighborhood upon a spacious plain. He will approach this mighty task by summoning—out of a farmyard well, maybe—the voices of family, companions, co-workers; the chorus, in short, of what he calls his "generous dead."

McGrath's distinction between "personal" and "representative" kinds of experience suggests that the voices in *Letter* address events larger than the person or persons speaking, events in which private and political destinies intersect or collide. These points of conjunction are generally shared by more than one voice, and from them comes an enlarged view— an "expanded consciousness," in McGrath's terms—of the nation's gains, losses, and wrong turns, together with the seeds of possible redress and renewal. In Part Two, for example, McGrath confronts the historical irony of "the Dakota experience": how, that is, a land of pioneer farms was bled and broken to make way for the ranges of missile sites (the ICBM's) that now infest the landscape. The poet looks out upon "the abandoned farmhouses, like burnt-out suns, and around them / The planetary out-buildings dead for the lack of warmth," and asks: "where / Have *they* gone? Those ghosts that warmed these buildings once?" The missiles hum in their silos, but "the people?" In answer comes this voice:

"First they broke land that should not ha' been broke

                                              and they *died*

Broke. Most of 'em. And after the tractor ate the horse—
It ate *them*. And now, a few lean years,

And the banks will have it again. Most of it. Why, hellfar,
Once a family could live on a quarter and now a hull section won't do!"

Disastrous economic policy has cleared the land for a weaponry of global destruction. As E. P. Thompson has put it: "if Dakota were to secede from the United States it would be, with its battery of Minutemen, the third most powerful nuclear state in the world."[16] He isn't joking. As recently as 1985, the nuclear count in McGrath's part of the country stood this way:[17]

> North Dakota ranks 3d with 1510 nuclear warheads deployed
> and 10th with 19 facilities in the nuclear infrastructure. It
> houses two main SAC bases, Grand Forks AFB and Minot AFB,
> both housing a B-52 bomber wing as well as a Minuteman
> missile wing, two of only three such bases in the world.

That North Dakota, one of the first and firmest of our populist states, one of the few places in America where democracy has been tried in earnest—that North Dakota should now bear the brunt of our nuclear arsenal is an irony replete with American consequence. McGrath's sense of Indian genocide as the nation's first "wound" suggests that our triumphalist culture pushes us to reenact the country's primal scenes; that the killing of native Americans now stands as an Original Sin of the Republic permitting more recent evils like Hiroshima or death-squad governance in our Latin vassal states. The battle of Wounded Knee, which eliminated the Sioux nation and ended our "Indian Wars," was replayed in whiteface with the defeat of rural populism, and then replayed again, this time in the noface of nuclear weaponry taking control of the land. These are events of national magnitude, but *in the same place*? Three stages of destiny inflicted one on top of another in McGrath's own neighborhood? Searching throughout *Letter* for examples of "the wrong turn," moments when the American Dream went bad, McGrath has good reasons for saying "Dakota is everywhere."

But he is even more concerned with moments when the nation's dream was decently realized. At the heart of *Letter to an Imaginary Friend* beats the rhythm of work in the rural countryside of McGrath's youth, reminding us how narrow our habitual poetics has been. The theme of work has been indispensable to the nation's sense of itself, but in our poetry it has seldom appeared. One can go back to Whitman, in a vague sort of way, and Gary Snyder's celebration of work has been exemplary. Some of Frost's New England pieces, and Philip Levine's vision of Detroit, have taken work seriously. More recently our feminist poets, Adrienne Rich among them, have insisted on the theme of work, in particular the thankless labors necessary to the life of the body. Apart from these, however, McGrath is alone in his insistence on the primacy of work to American experience.

He is most concerned with the community-creating aspect of work— the "erotics of labor," if I might put it so, having in mind the notion of Eros as the binding energy shaping social units into larger and larger productive wholes. There were, for example, the work teams that assembled haphazard every fall for harvest, matter on the face of it unpromising, but from which McGrath takes moments of real and mythical beauty. In Part Two, Section IV, there are a number of episodes from the earth-bound world of that time, starting with a barnyard version of *in principio*. Note the active character of McGrath's wordplay, and then the multiple destinies within a common fate:

Morning stirring in the haymow must: sour blankets,
Worn bindles and half-pitched soogans of working bundle-stiffs
Stir:
    Morning in the swamp!
                I kick myself awake
And dress while around me the men curse for the end of the world.

And it *is* ending (half-past-'29) but we don't know it
And wake without light.
                Twenty-odd of us—and very odd,
Some.
    One of the last of the migrant worker crews
On one of the last steam threshing rigs.
                    Antediluvian
Monsters, all.
        Rouse to the new day in the fragrant
Barnloft soft hay-beds: wise heads, grey;
And gay cheechakos from Chicago town; and cranky Wobblies;
Scissorbills and homeguards and grassgreen wizards from the
                              playing fields
Of the Big Ten: and decompressed bankclerks and bounty jumpers

Jew and Gentile; and the odd Communist now and then
To season the host.

                    Stick your head through the haymow door—
Ah!
        A soft and backing wind: the Orient red
East. And a dull sky for the first faint light and no sun yet.

4:30. Time to be moving.

The scene is the last of America's unfallen moments, before the Flood,
as McGrath suggests, but with the Crash of '29 on its way. The men
don't see what's arriving and yet they do not seem lost; "without light"
they may be, but with the wind for "backing" and the "new day" coming
at them out of the "red / East." And it's no accident that the Crash comes
now, at *this* time of the year. When McGrath says Dakota is everywhere
let us not forget that the Great Depression allowed Hitler to come to
power and World War Two to transpire and the nuclear order to rise
from those ashes. And let us recall how every autumn, during the early
years of the century, the economy fell into financial crisis as western
banks put too much strain on eastern banks for loans to process the
buying, shipping, selling, and profit taking for the year's harvest.

But here the Fall has not yet occurred, and McGrath goes on to depict
his boyhood's descent into a "green" world of purely animal existence,
a prelapsarian realm recalling Whitman's praise for dumb and placid
beasts. Here is the still unfallen earth—world of animals as McGrath
recalls it from his youth:

                    Into the barnfloor dark
I drop down the dusty Jacob's ladder, feeling by foot,
The fathomless fusty deep and the sleepy animal night
Where the horses fart, doze, stomp: teams of the early
Crewmen: strawmonkey, watermonkey (myself) and the grain haulers
They snort and shift, asleep on their feet.
                            I go, carefully,
Down the dung-steamy ammonia-sharp eye-smarting aisle
Deadcenter: wary of kickers, light sleepers and vengeful wakers.

A sleep of animals!
                    Almost I can enter:
                              where all is green[. . . .]

  The barn with its "aisle" becomes a holy place. But to enter the green
world's hush, and then to sense its otherness, is directly to recoil at
humankind's intrusion, as the imperatives of work tie man to beast and
beast to man. And thus the moment of the green world's fall:

                              But, in the world
Of work and need that sacred image fails.
                                   Here,
Fallen, they feed and fast and harrow the man-marred small acres
Dull; and dulled.
                         Alas, wild hearts, we have you now:
—Old plugs
              hayburners
                        crowbait
                                   bonesack
                                        —Hail!

  At once slangy, sacral, traditional, and nonce, McGrath's diction welds
the universality of ancient pastoral images with grass-roots patois that
only a namer could know—having grown up, as McGrath did, on the
strength in names like *crowbait, bonesack, hayburner*, ambivalent terms
that curse and bless at once, thick with echoes of pathos and fate.
  There are many passages in *Letter* devoted to scenes of physical labor
and to the theme of communal order that work inspires. The finest of
these occurs early in the poem—the whole of Section III in Part One.
Section III opens out of childhood's sleep, with the call of the steam-
driven thresher usurping the mother's call—no soothing voices of nurse
and stream, as in Wordsworth, but the blast and clamor of a vast machine. On this day, during the harvest season of McGrath's ninth year,
the bitter knowledge of work and politics begins:

Out of the whirring lamp-hung dusk my mother calls.
From the lank pastures of my sleep I turn and climb,
From the leathery dark where the bats work, from the coasting
High all-winter all-weather christmas hills of my sleep.

> And there is my grandfather chewing his goatee,
> Prancing about like a horse. And the drone and whir from
> > the fields
> Where the thresher mourns and showers on the morning stillness
> A bright fistful of whistles.

The field teams are short a man and the boy must take his place. There is, moreover, greater urgency in this moment than might at first appear. Harvest is each year's season of crisis, the time of time running out with all life governed by the twin gods of machinery and the sky:

> The machine is whistling its brass-tongued rage and the jack-booted
> > weathers of autumn
> Hiss and sing in the North.
> The rains are coming, the end of the world
> Is coming.

If the rains come, if the harvest fails, the end of *this* world is certain; the banks will foreclose and the farm will be lost. Thus a child steps into a man's job "too soon, too young," with no allowance for playful rites of passage:

> > > Aloft on the shaking deck,
> Half blind and deafened in the roaring dust,
> On the heaving back of the thresher,
> My neck blistered by sun and the flying chaff, my clothes
> Shot full of thistles and beards, a gospel itch,
> Like a small St. Steven, I turned the wheel of the blower
> Loading the straw-rack.
> The whistle snapped at my heels: in a keening blizzard
> Of sand-burrs, barley-beards and beggars-lice, in a red thunder
> Where the wheat rust bellowed up in a stormy cloud
> From the knife-flashing feeder,
> I turned the wheel.

This is the harvest of savage work and ruthless circumstance described by Christopher Caudwell, a thoughtful Marxist critic during the 1930's whose book *Illusion and Reality* McGrath has praised and often cites. Harvest is Caudwell's primary example of our collective struggle with nature, the historical contest that defines reality and social relations. Poetry was born of this struggle, or so Caudwell believes. Around actions essential to survival—chiefly war and harvest—the tribe builds festivals of dance and song to generate the energy, enthusiasm, and communal focus necessary to the hard days ahead. Caudwell puts it this way:[18]

> In the collective festival, where poetry is born, the phantastic world of poetry anticipates the harvest and, by doing so, makes possible the real harvest. But the illusion of this collective phantasy is not a mere drab copy of the harvest yet to be: it is a reflection of the emotional complex involved in the fact that man must stand in a certain relation to others and to the harvest, that his instincts must be adapted in a certain way to Nature and other men, to make the harvest possible.

Caudwell argues that ancient harvest was poetry's first occasion; that art mediates, collectively, the ceaseless struggle between need and reality. His stress is on *need*, not on *desire* merely. And no need is stronger or more often in jeopardy than feeding the tribe—true even now, as famine sweeps the sub-Sahara or, during the Reagan Era, as the American family farm goes down the drain, some 3,000 lost per month in the last year. Caudwell claims that poetry in a festival setting gives—or did once give—humankind the heart and communal will to work in common and accomplish urgent tasks.

McGrath's boyhood experience of harvest was both traumatic and exalting. From that past he summons a superlative image, festive in mood and gritty in detail, with the threshing rig at its center:

> Feathered in steam like a great tormented beast
> The engine roared and laughed, dreamed and complained,
> And the pet-cocks dripped and sizzled; and under its fiery gut
> Stalactites formed from the hand-hold's rheumy slobbers.
> —Mane of sparks, metallic spike of its voice,
> The mile-long bacony crackle of burning grease!
> There the engineer sat, on the high drivers,
> Aloof as a God. Filthy. A hunk of waste
> Clutched in one gauntleted hand, in the other the oil can
> Beaked and long-necked as some exotic bird;
> Wreathed in smoke, in the clatter of loose eccentrics.

And the water-monkey, back from the green quiet of the river
With a full tank, was rolling a brown quirrly
(A high school boy) hunkered in the dripping shade
Of the water-tender, in the tall talk and acrid sweat
Of the circle of spitting stiffs whose cloud-topped bundle-racks
Waited their turns at the feeder.
And the fireman: goggled, shirtless, a flashing three-tined fork,
Its handle charred, stuck through the shiny metallic
Lip of the engine, into the flaming, smoky
Fire-box of its heart.
Myself: straw-monkey. Jester at court.

The threshing machine with its steam engine is at the heart of the scene, or rather *is* the scene. And what a vast thing it is. In the 1950's, when McGrath began *Letter*, there were still threshing machines to be seen, belt-driven by combustion engines. Even these were mammoth, but the earlier steam-driven threshers were by all accounts awesome— and dangerous too, as Willa Cather reminds us in *My Ántonia*. In McGrath's rendering, however, the dread machine possesses festive features; it laughs and dreams and complains. It slobbers like a monstrous animal with sparks for a mane. Its voice is a steam whistle, always described in metallic images, signalings a boy might take to heart. Clearly McGrath *likes* machines, the threshing rig first of all. Machines are the primary site for the world of work, and this one stands in union with the land like a blessed and blessing monster—"its whistling brass commandments" amid "the barb-tongued golden barley and the tents of the biblical wheat."

Those who work the rig take from it even identity—names like water-monkey, straw-monkey, spike-pitcher—festival figures ranged from mock-God to mock-devil, in this case a dirty engineer and a fireman armed with a pitchfork. Using the harvest machine as his anchor, McGrath goes on to create a monstrosity of a world, brimming with abundance and unruly beauty, full of ambivalent names and exaggerated figures, set forth in language that brings "down to earth" all that would otherwise be fearful or official, a communal world seething with energy. And over all of it, the straw-monkey poet as "Jester at court."

Once the boy begins his job in the fields, even dreaming is occupied by the threshing rig: "the whistle biting my ears, / The night vibrating, /

In the fog of the red rust, steam, the rattle of concaves"—all a permanent part of McGrath's imaginative world:

> So, dawn to dusk, dark to dark, hurried
> From the booming furious brume of the thresher's back
> To the antipodean panting engine. Caught in the first
> Circle.

Hell's first circle, of course, one of *Letter's* many echoes of Dante. But also the circle to be transformed into commune and round-dance. The boy's overriding desire is to work his way into manhood, to go as an equal in the circle of men who run the rig and move the grain. Impossible, of course, for a child of nine years; he can be a "man to the engine's hunger, to the lash of the whistle," but not to the young toughs, the old-timers, or to his uncle, who is "boss of the rig." His luck is to have a mentor: "Cal, one of the bundle teamsters, / My sun-blackened Virgil," who would teach him to take his time, not grow too fast, a field hand whom McGrath calls a "good teacher, a brother." The figure of Cal becomes one of the tutelary spirits of *Letter*, a quiet man aged about thirty, with a "brick-topped mulish face," who reads *The Industrial Worker* and is one of "the last of the real Wobs." Initiation into the world of work will thus be compounded by a bitter first taste of politics. When Cal leads the men against McGrath's uncle, any notion of rural romanticism—the spacious skies and amber grain of our collective pastoral fantasy—is dispelled from McGrath's view of the heartland:

We were threshing flax I remember, toward the end of the run—
After quarter-time I think—the slant light falling
Into the blackened stubble that shut like a fan toward the headland—
The strike started then.

Cal speaks for the men, is cursed by McGrath's uncle; a fight starts between them and the boy is appalled:

> I heard their gruntings and strainings
> Like love at night or men working hard together,
> And heard the meaty thumpings, like beating a grain sack
> As my uncle punched his body—I remember the dust
> Jumped from his shirt.

This is Eden invaded by real-world conflict, a forceful instance of political intrusion. What happens next is remarkable and signals the coming together of two voices, McGrath's and the metallic blast of the rig. Shaken by the violence, the boy runs in anger to the idling machine and tries to throw it into gear:

> And the fireman came on a run and grabbed me and held me
> Sobbing and screaming and fighting, my hand clenched
> On the whistle rope while it screamed down all our noises—
> Stampeding a couple of empties into the field—
> A long, long blast, hoarse, with the falling, brazen
> Melancholy of engines when the pressure's falling.

Here, it seems to me, McGrath allies himself *with* the voice of the machine. Then directly after the drama of the fight comes a long lyrical expanse of the poem (nearly three pages) in which the boy goes off toward the river, alone in the gathering dusk:

Green permission . . .

            Dusk of the brass whistle . . .

Gooseberry dark.
Green moonlight of willow.
Ironwood, basswood and the horny elm.
June berry; box-elder; thick in the thorny brake
The black choke cherry, the high broken ash and the slick
White bark of poplar.

           I called the king of the woods,
The wind-sprung oak.

           I called the queen of ivy,
Maharani to his rut-barked duchies;
Summoned the foxgrape, the lank woodbine,
And the small flowers; the woodviolets, the cold
Spears of the iris, the spikes of the ghostflower—
It was before the alphabet of trees
Or later.

           Runeless I stood in the green rain
Of the leaves.
      Waiting.

He enters the "green world," hoping for contact with a peace at life's heart. Instead, "under the hush and whisper of the wood, / I heard the echoes of the little war" as hawk and mink go about their separate hunts. Later he goes for a swim and "under the river the silence was humming, singing." Finally his grief breaks into weeping and he encounters for the first time the burden of the mystery, the gore amid grandeur of life's rapacious innocence. He hears "the night hawk circling," but also the "comfort of crickets and a thrum of frogs." For the first time, the horror and the glory exist together:

> The crickets sang.   The frogs
> Were weaving their tweeds in the river shallows.
>
> Hawk swoop.
>
>   Silence.
>
>   Singing.
> The formal calls of a round-dance.
> This riddling of the river-mystery I could not read.

This is, I think, the primal figuration in McGrath's poetry, this coming together of violence and harmony in ways that serve to keep his knowledge of class conflict and his vision of communal oneness united. American pastoral is ersatz without its historical disruptions; at the same time, political violence cannot be redeemed—or perhaps even borne—without the festive dream of pastoral solidarity. When, finally, the boy returns to the farmyard his father is kneeling in the dust, fixing a harness by lantern light outside the barn—his gesture of atonement to Cal lying hurt inside:

> "Hard lines, Tom," he said. "Hard lines, Old Timer."
> I sat in the lantern's circle, the world of men,
> And heard Cal breathe in his stall.
>   An army of crickets
> Rasped in my ear.
>
>   "Don't hate anybody."
> My father said.

All unexpected, this has been the boy's passage into manhood; that same night the men leave in "a rattle of Fords." The harvest is ended, far from the spirit of festival that for a moment emerged. Referring to the strike in the fields, McGrath concludes by letting the momentum of his narrative carry him forward in time, in jumps of quick transition that anchor other of the poem's episodes and voices in this one strong incident—as if what had just happened were opening remembrance into the future:

> They had left Cal there
> In the bloody dust that day but they wouldn't work after that.
> "The folded arms of the workers" I heard Warren saying,
> Sometime in the future where Mister Peets lies dreaming
> Of a universal voting-machine.
> And Showboat
> Quinn goes by (New York, later) "The fuckin' proletariat
> Is in love with its fuckin' chains. How do you put this fuckin'
> Strike on a cost-plus basis?"

The condition of the workers—their will to join ranks, their fear and hesitation—is seen both in the episode of the strike and again in the voices at the end of Section III, a raucous outburst cut short by a tone growing somber and quieting out. What happens, in these last fading lines, links the pioneer dream (populist) to the newer vision of justice (socialist). Both are tangled in violence, both rooted in the meaning of the West and with the lofty, meat-eating hawk for an emblem:

> "The folded arms of the workers."
> I see Sodaberg
> Organizing the tow boats.
> I see him on Brooklyn Bridge,
> The fizzing dynamite fuse as it drops on the barges.
> Then Mac with his mournful face comes round the corner
> (New York) up from the blazing waterfront, preaching
> His strikes.
> And my neighbors are striking on Marsh Street.
> (L.A., and later)
> And the hawk falls.

A dream-borne singing troubles my still boy's sleep
In the high night where Cal had gone:

         They came through
The high passes, they crossed the dark mountains
In a month of snow.
Finding the plain, the bitter water, the iron
Rivers of the black north . . .

Hunters

        in the high plateaus of that country . . .
Climbing toward sleep . . .

But far

      from the laughter.

And there, no doubt, McGrath stood: far from the laughter but in sight of the mystery—a burden to be shouldered and, somehow, made light of. And finally that is what happens: McGrath goes on to make light of the sorrowing world by a laughter that brings it down to earth. This notion of making-light-of, moreover, is not an easy pun but the key to McGrath's remarkable combination of contrary states, Marxist materialism and Catholic sacramentalism on the one hand, historical necessity and frontier freedom on the other, and then his serious recovery of the American Dream to be carried out, more and more as works progress, by comic means.

Into his art McGrath introduces, gradually, a jocular spirit composed of praises and curses together. He envisions the human predicament as an extended Feast of Fools and himself as the "Jester at court." Drawing on Old World traditions, he turns to the rites of festival and feast day, and takes up a carnival style. And always his choices have political as well as poetic implications. Here is a humor no hierarchy can digest or tolerate. Nor can any imposition stamp it out. When this sort of laughing takes effect, "the great night and its canting monsters turn[s] holy around [us]. / Laughably holy." McGrath possesses a comic charity that precludes *hysterica passio*, but also a grotesque, expansive laughter that pushes back (like the "violence within," in Stevens' notion) against the intrusive world. This is the comic spirit in its most rampant, freely ruthless mood, a humor that is raucous, earth-bound, carnivalesque.[19]

In *Letter*, the first sign of carnival comes early, in Section I of Part One, where McGrath turns to the matter of his family. At age five he ran away from home, as children will. He says he has never been back; but says also he "never left." Running from family, he took them along and "had the pleasure of their company":

> Took them? They came—
> Past the Horn, Cape Wrath, Oxford and Fifth and Main
> Laughing and mourning, snug in the two seater buggy,
> Jouncing and bouncing on the gumbo roads
> Or slogging loblolly in the bottom lands—
> My seven tongued family.[. . .]
> Conched in cowcatchers, they rambled at my side.
> The seat of the buggy was wider than Texas
> And slung to the axles were my rowdy cousins;
> Riding the whippletrees: aunts, uncles, brothers,
> Second cousins, great aunts, friends and neighbors
> All holus-bolus, piss-proud, all sugar-and-shit
> A goddamned gallimaufry of ancestors.
> The high passes?
> Hunter of the hornless deer?

Excess and exaggeration are primary signs of carnival style. As a diction the lines above might be called the magnified colloquial, a colorful popular idiom found almost anywhere (at one time) in rural America, certainly in the middle south and heartland plains, where people slog over the gumbo roads even now. Some of McGrath's diction appears literary, like "gallimaufry," and some, like "loblolly," might be archaic; but who's to say these very words didn't come off the boat with McGrath's grandparents. The point about obscurity is that most *spoken* language, the local speech of a place and its spirit, goes unrecorded. When found in literature it tends to be discounted as regionalism and remains "unofficial." For McGrath, however, the unofficial forces in language are best suited for utopian attack against the press of the established world. Terms for bodily functions—the primary four-letter words—remain off the record despite the fact that they have been the argot of all times and places, the core of nonconsensus (but universal) speech. These are the anchor-words of carnival style, and one or more of them will be operative, setting the earthward pitch in McGrath's later poetry. Often, as in the example above, an entire batch comes at us holus-bolus, at once in a lump. Language like this is in league with the tall tale (the buggy "wider than Texas") and is decidedly *of the people*, even of the *folk* in the American sense of "just plain folks."

The primary "curse words," as they are often called, can be relied on to upset prevailing taste and established decorum, while at the same time they can *also* convey covert alliance and express goodwill or solidarity. This is an idiom that can be used both to curse and to bless, to reduce and magnify, to pull down and elevate. It is, furthermore, a language independent of scene, wording in no way tied to a specific place or time or class or subject matter, language as available and packed with loamy energies as earth itself. When McGrath calls his family "sugar-and-shit" and "piss-proud," he casts blame while expansively showering praise. This part of McGrath's idiom is, so to say, the spittin' image of Mark Twain, the first master of American vernacular. Whitman had this goal as well, but only as a goal; and Twain, of course, had to contend with censorship. With McGrath an American vulgate comes into its own, a *basso continuo* of the populace at large.

To judge from the likes of Whitman, Twain, and McGrath, to be an American poet is to speak the language of the hard-pressed but irrepressibly optimistic masses. It's at this linguistic gut level that the "violence within" pushes back at the "violence without." To *speak American* is to combine one's regional idiom with the vernacular at large. It's also to appropriate any other language that seems apt, be it learned, technical, foreign, or just the day's jargon. And to speak American is to exaggerate routinely, to talk in a larger-than-life voice megaphoned by the continent itself. In an interview McGrath has said that "one of the modes of this poem is exaggeration." He is referring to *Letter*, and goes on to say: "exaggeration in terms of language, the exaggeration of certain kinds of actions to the point where they become surreal, fantastic—yes."[20] The surreal element in his earlier style becomes, in the later poetry, the distortive aspect of carnival excess—as in McGrath's bardic image of himself:

And now, out of the fog, comes our genealogizer
And keeper of begats. A little wizened-up wisp of a man:
Hair like an out-of-style bird's nest and eyes as wild as a wolf's!
Gorbellied, bent out of shape, short and scant of breath—
A walking chronicle: the very image of the modern poet!

McGrath's combination of excess and vulgarity might puzzle or offend some readers, and we see the excuse it affords to deny him his seriousness. But then we see as well that McGrath's language has earnest, even valiant, purposes. *In the beginning is the word, the curse word; the new world starts by get down to earth*. That is the logic of carnival. Certainly it's the order that governs McGrath's epic poem, a logic writ large in the following example. Out of the depth of the Second World War (McGrath was in the air force, stationed on a snow-blind island in the Aleutians) he extracts "a hero" who is destroyer and builder, who gets rid of and creates, a figure most lowly and therefore most high. I quote at length because the following lines (from Book X of Part One) make a typical unit in the rhythm and expanse of *Letter*:

> —From those days it's Cassidy I remember:
> Who worked on the high steel in blue Manhattan
> And built the top-most towers.
> Now on our island [Amchitka],
> He was the shit-burner. He closed the slit-trench latrines
> With a fiery oath.
> When they had built permanent structures
> And underlaid them with the halves of gasoline drums,
> He took the drums out on the tundra in the full sight of God
> And burned them clean.
> Stinking, blackened, smelling
> Like Ajax Ajakes, he brought home every night
> (Into the swamped prymidal, where, over two feet of water,
> Drifting like Noah on the shifting Apocalypse
> Of the speech of Preacher Noone, I read by the ginko light)
> Brought home mortality, its small quotidian smell.
>
> There was a hero come home! (The bombers swinging
> Around his neck, the gunners blessing his craft
> From dropping their load in comfort!) Him who on the high and windy
> Sky of Manhattan had written his name in steel, sing now,
> Oh poets!
>
> But that's a hard man to get a line on.
> Simple as a knife, with no more pretension than bread,
> He worked his war like a bad job in hard times

When you couldn't afford to quit. He'd had bad jobs before
And had outwon them.

                       Now in a howl of sleet,
Or under the constant rain and the stinking flag of his guild,
He stood in his fire and burned the iron pots clean.

  Meanwhile: "Into the gun-colored urine-smelling day, heroic / The
bombers go," and when the crews returned in their shot-up planes "we
ran like rabbits down the dead flat road of their light / To snatch them
home to the cold from the fiery cities of air." The war, for McGrath,
was just such a city of air, a sky in need of clearing and renovation.
Between the dead and unborn worlds comes Cassidy, construction-
worker, shit-burner, time's hero—except that he too is gone. Hit by an
off-track aircraft, he never came back:

                       Nowhere, now, on the high
   Steel will he mark on the sky that umber scratch
   Where the arcing rivet ends.

  An "umber scratch," the color of rust, feces, and fertilization, scrapes
the sky and maps the next reach of creation. It is the hero's signature
blazing the heavens—an image not without its grotesque majesty. This
is, moreover, a primary case of earth asserting its claims against the
worldly cities of air; life and the sources of life must be free and kept
uncowed, particularly in bad times like war, when the official world
demands complete submission. Then especially the earth pushes back.
And as we saw in *Antigone*, there can be no overestimating the degree
to which the human body is the foremost location of the earth-world
antagonism. The body is earth's domain in creatural terms but equally
the world's insofar as social-political order inscribes itself in bodily functions through sexual mores, eating habits, and excretory rites of the kind
over which McGrath's Cassidy presides.

  The point of carnival—its symbolic action—is to turn the world upside
down; to pull down ranks, privileges, pretensions; to suspend official
hierarchy in favor of a radical equality, wherein everything is laughed
at and anything can be said. No power setting itself above the community
can escape ridicule, and the lower forms of humor prevail—jokes, puns,
parody, slapstick, and clowning. In this festive manner contact with
earth is renewed at the gross level all men and women share. Con-

sciousness is anchored in the physical foundation of life, most often in the belly and the genitals. If this is "obscene" it is also the key to festive, and communal, affirmation.[21]

In America, affirmation of community is mandatory in public but not, in private, an article of serious faith. We are, most of us, torn between our genuine populist impulse and an economically rewarding self-interest that cannot serve itself and protect its privileges while at the same time taking in earnest the dream of a country held in common. To point to "the people," moreover, is to summon something that hardly exists apart from the rhetoric of its summoning, especially if what's meant is some kind of inclusive, like-minded group organized to act on its own behalf toward emancipation and enlarged consensus. Even so, "the people" is a valuable and very American idea. The early successes of populism in the West suggest that those who are exploited and powerless will eventually reach a collective sense of themselves. As they do, they discover a courage not available in isolation, a resilience reflected in festive forms. The interesting point is that victory over fear, and the purging of self-pity, are registered in speech officially proscribed. Not only *what* but also *how* we praise and blame positions us in the world. What this comes down to, finally, is enlistment of the powers of earth against whatever world is pressing to extradite its earthly foundation.

McGrath's language makes no sense apart from the double-edged freedom of unsanctioned speech. The essence of any creatural idiom is its deep ambivalence. The case with carnival language is not praise *or* blame but *both together*. Cassidy, in *Letter*, flies "the stinking flag of his guild" and works "in the full sight of God." When earth pushes back against world, the forces of riddance and creation set in motion the utopian thrust of McGrath's poetics. In addition to "curse words," his fusion of praise and blame magnifies the contrary thrust of other key words—"stiff," for example, which is McGrath's routine name for nameless field hands and laborers. The working man is a "stiff," a "bundle-stiff," part of "the circle of spitting stiffs." At first it sounds demeaning, slang for "corpse"; "to stiff" or "be stiffed," moreover, suggests victimization, in particular the plight of workers under capital. But the plain "working stiff" can be reborn, can rise again, in the manner of the male sexual member; in which case "stiff" also signifies erection and generative power. The word is multivalent and perfectly suited to a Marxist perspective. Through work the matter of earth is transformed into shapes of world. At the heart of this miracle is the worker, the lowly "stiff," and one day the last shall rise up and be first.

The extraordinary energy of "curse words" in familiar talk, their explosive power in formal situations, their vigor (and valor) in poetic usage—all this is obvious from daily observation. In McGrath's case this multivalent energy is the key to his diction. In *Letter* there are *no neutral words*. That must be true for poetry in general, but in McGrath's work especially. He is always praising or blaming, often both together. Benediction is his final goal, but first comes the need for descent, the poet blazing a path into song with a curse:

> Listen:
> Under the skin of dark, do I hear the singing of water?
> The trees tick and talk in the almost windless calm
> And the stream is spinning a skein of an old and lonesome song
> In the cold heart of the winter
> constant still.
> One crow
> Slowly goes over me
> —a hoarse coarse curse
> —a shrill
> Jeer: last of the past year or first of the new,
> He stones me in appalling tongues and tones, in his tried
> And two black lingoes.
> A dirty word in the shine,
> A flying tombstone and fleering smudge on the winter-white page
> Of the sky, my heart lightens and leaps high: to hear
> Him.
> And the silence.
> That sings now: out of the hills
> And cold trees.
> Song I remember.

The entirety of *Letter to an Imaginary Friend*, in two volumes, adds up to a total of 329 pages, a very large work. The first two parts, published in 1970, are under the sign of Easter, inside the carnival time of Shrovetide festival. The third and fourth parts of *Letter*, published together in 1985, are under the sign of Christmas, within the time of feasting and glad tidings. In the Middle Ages, moreover, Eastertide and Christmas differed from other modes of carnival; during these two seasons sacred dogma and liturgical forms could be openly mocked, and there was a definite name for this license: *risus paschalis* or "paschal laughter." Formal unity of *Letter*, therefore, encompasses as points of departure the popular-festive form of carnival, the occasion of paschal laughter in particular; then the underlying rites of death and resurrection; and last the spectacle of earth in endless becoming with, always, a new world verging into view.

The change, in tone and style, the first to the second half of *Letter*, is decisive. In all ways extravagant, this latter part is the collective belly laugh of high feasting on ancestral holy days, a comic mode from which nothing is spared. In remarks on the poem, McGrath has said that the two halves share a common content, but that in the second half "the method will be wilder."[22] Certainly it is. Language in *Letter*'s first half is mimetic in principle, intent upon the work of witnessing. Parts Three and Four, on the contrary, are joyously antithetical or antimimetic; here language is destructively excessive, hostile to any image of the status quo, determined to push into a further world. I have, however, concentrated mainly on the poetry of Parts One and Two. *Letter*'s first half, I think, reveals McGrath at his finest in terms of witnessing and his art of lyrical documentation. However, the language of One and Two cannot be wholly appreciated without a sense of its final purpose (its symbolic action in broadest terms), which comes to view only in Parts Three and Four, where McGrath subsumes and *goes beyond* the historical world, arriving at the edge of apocalypse.

For an epigraph to *Letter*'s last part, McGrath cites Caudwell and includes this remark:[23]

> . . . the instincts must be harnessed to the needs of the harvest by a social mechanism. An important part of this mechanism is the group festival, the matrix of poetry, which frees the stores of emotion and canalises them in a collective channel. The real object, the tangible aim—a harvest—becomes in the festival a fantastic object. The real object is not here now. The fantastic object is here now—in fantasy. . . . That world [of fantasy] becomes more real, and even when the music dies away the ungrown harvest has a greater reality for him, spurring him on to the labours necessary for its accomplishment.

Poetry creates images of renovation so real and compelling to the mind that we are spurred onward "to the labours necessary." This kind of incitement is, I take it, the political justification for carnival poetry in a visionary mode. It also reminds us of the main point in *Letter*: that at the back of McGrath's epic we find the harvest festival. And at the ritual's center stands a godlike machine that together with the weather determined the pace and shape of life in rural Dakota when McGrath was coming of age. The powerful earth image of the threshing rig holds the poem in place and gives readers an anchor for a text that is otherwise wildly informal. And who shall receive this "letter"? McGrath's "generous dead" to begin with, the ancestral part of his tribe; and then any of us called by the poem as McGrath was called by the blast of a monstrous machine in the remembered fields of his youth.

The "imaginary friend" is you, me, the whole of the disbelieving world. McGrath calls us "friend" and I take him at his word. For all his cursing and "hard lines," his public stance is genial, outgoing, utopian by nature as well as conviction. In a "Note" on *Letter* McGrath says: "Work, for example, is not something which most poets write about. Also communality and solidarity—feelings which perhaps are more important to us than romantic love—never appear in our poetry."[24] When McGrath speaks of "communality and solidarity," he is talking about Eros in its political, all-embracing form. Love of this kind—call it charity, *caritas*, communal husbandry—is at the heart of his poetic enterprise. Generosity and hopefulness go together in his work, fields of blessing empowered by laughter. With these ideas in mind I conclude by citing "The End of the World," published in 1982 in *Passages Toward the Dark*:[25]

The end of the world: it was given to me to see it.
Came in the black dark, a bulge in the starless sky,
A trembling at the heart of the night, a twitching of the webby flesh of
the earth.
And out of the bowels of the street one beastly, ungovernable cry.

Came and I recognized it: the end of the world.
And waited for the lightless plunge, the fury splitting the rock.
And waited: a kissing of leaves; a whisper of man-killing ancestral
night—

Then a tinkle of music, laughter from the next block.

Yet waited still: for the awful traditional fire,
Hearing mute thunder, the long collapse of sky.
It falls forever. But no one noticed. The end of the world provoked
Out of the dark a single and melancholy sigh

From my neighbor who sat on his porch drinking beer in the dark.
No: I was not God's prophet. Armageddon was never
And always: this night in a poor street where a careless irreverent
                                                              laughter
Postpones the end of the world; in which we live forever.

The poem might be read in a number of ways, but in one way principally if McGrath's homage to Eros is as steady as I think. The onset of "traditional fire" would be the final Biblical Wrath that even today (or especially today) the Fundamentalists among us forecast. But while men of God call for brimstone, McGrath does not. The only end of the world is the one we all feel daily, life's senseless silent wasting, its sad predictable blundering that seems, often, too beastly to go on. But on it goes, and while much is dying much else is coming to birth. The world feels open and closed, final and full of possibility. That, as I take it, is the point of the poem: that once we admit the perpetual burden upon us, we might then begin to reach out, make an effort, work on ways of making light of it and sharing it about. Meanwhile what keeps this life-in-death from death itself is "a tinkle of music, laughter from the next block." Against the old ultimatum, not thunder and the fall of sky, but the street's careless laughter and the sigh of a neighbor next door.

·VIII·

Adrienne Rich, North America East

> We write for ourselves and each other—an ever-expanding sense of whom is part of our imagining.
>
> —Adrienne Rich[1]

The poetry of Adrienne Rich presents the clear-eyed instance of a poet whose work began in a formal self-regarding mode devoid of politics; but a poet who has gone on, by virtue of attention to experience, to establish a major voice in forms overtly political. Nor is there any uncertainty about the meaning of politics in Rich's view. When the "way of grief / is shared, unnecessary," we can discern forces—forces as unnecessary as Creon's decree—preempting the fate of private being. That *the personal is political* has been a feminist notion much challenged; but for the experience of women in a patriarchal order I do not see that it can be denied or even declared a special case. Women are Antigone's sisters by virtue of their status as women. In this light the play by Sophocles takes on added relevance, suggesting that the conflict of the individual with the state finds its broadest example in the struggle of women for self-determination.

Rich's poetry is political from the moment she confronts her own condition as a woman, with variations on the primal theme of intrusion that accrue from her roles as wife and mother and daughter-in-law. It is the law, the legalization of power relations, that keeps the daughter a daughter, indentured first to the father and then to the husband's family. There is no moment of day or night, in Rich's view, when women are fully at liberty to define and live their own destiny. Intrusion is public and private together, often extremely intimate, and in ways that the history of accommodation has not been able to transcend. As with Antigone, a woman's fate is hers but not her own.

As Alicia Ostriker has pointed out, Whitman could "celebrate myself" and take for granted "What I assume you shall assume," while Emily Dickinson had to fight her more difficult battle alone, without models or encouragement, on the bleak assumption that "I'm nobody."[2] Together these two compose the fountainhead of our poetry. Both poets start with evidence of self. But thereafter they go separate ways. Dickinson admits, as Whitman does not, that there are powers beyond the self, impersonal arrangements curtailing the healthy expansion of self in the world. Whitman cast his lot with the national experience; he could enjoy the bonhomie of the open road and grow up with the country. He could afford to loaf. Dickinson, meanwhile, had to give birth to herself with no help outside her own willfulness and the natural midwifery of her art—a predicament that Rich knows well:

> your mother dead and you unborn
> your two hands grasping your head
> drawing it down against the blade of life
> your nerves the nerves of a midwife
> learning her trade [.]

That is an image of terrible will and terrible birth, but at least it *is* birth and not the paralysis implied by Arnold's nineteenth-century use of the two-world image. He might complain that the old world was dead with a new one "powerless" to be born, but that kind of flagging comes from writing at the center of empire, a malady now widespread in American letters but not, significantly, among poets who are women.

The politician intrusion that is integral to Antigone's political experience also defines Adrienne Rich's home ground, "the light / that soaks in from the world of pain / even when I sleep." The primary metaphor— and concrete case—of political intrusion is rape, and actual or feared rape is also a primary experience of women. When Rich imagines it in her poetry she sees its agent as an upholder of prevailing order, a policeman for example. When she theorizes, on the other hand, she equates rape with military violence; rape as the prerogative of invaders in all times and places, "the great unpunished war crime in every culture."[3] Those who thrive in the shadow of the fathers will prefer to ignore the severity of Rich's claims. But her critique of patriarchy—male reliance on force relations, male pride in not feeling, male disregard for pain in others—isn't meant to console. The personal-historical symmetry of her feminist vision aligns political experience generally with women's condition in particular, and compels this central point: "woman's body is the terrain on which patriarchy is erected."⁴ In *Antigone*, Creon controls the state by controlling the rights of the body; and if we allow for Rich's association of female with earth and male with world, her position incorporates the earth-world antagonism as well.

For Rich and women like her, the first outcome of political alertness is anger—anger as a generator of the will to change, as a prerequisite to the revival of hope. Anger endorses the primacy of the curse, and the examples of Yeats and Brecht or Breytenbach suggest that rage toward public situations can be, and often has been, turned to creative account. To be in a fury at the order of things is to be possessed of oneself through the last emotion still one's own. For poets, indignation is a further "violence within" to be directed against the "violence without." Anger, with its sustaining fearless energy, becomes the dark unspoken side of joy. But for a creative flame to ignite, it has to reach beyond mere sweetness of destruction:

> Each day during the heat-wave
> they took the temperature of the haymow.
> I huddled fugitive
> in the warm sweet simmer of the hay
>
> muttering: *Come*.

Those lines are from "The Phenomenology of Anger." The American ravagement of Vietnam is equated with male domination at home, a compound of experience and insight that, having become conscious, becomes combustible. Like fire, anger is destructive when left to itself; but contained in the service of creation it becomes a source of power.

In one of her recent "tracking poems" (1983–86), Rich says of her work: there is "no art to this but anger."⁵ No doubt this element—the pressure of combat—is what readers are offended by in much of Rich. And yes, her art is often *offensive*, in the several meanings of that word, with as much cursing as blessing (although Rich's regular use of lament and consoling intimacy is a mode of muted praise). Her poems, moreover, seldom flatter the reader; they do not seduce or cajole but rather challenge. One feels that agreed-upon laws of decorum are being ignored, the ad hominem rule in particular. Not that Rich attacks people by name; she does, however, often attack the patriarchal goings-on of males-in-power, a violation of etiquette that makes her poetry harsh on occasion but that exposes the ad hominem rule for what it is—an agreement among club members not to criticize colleagues, the better to defend the privileges of the club.

In her critical prose, Rich returns repeatedly to the value of anger as a political/poetical resource. In "When We Dead Awaken," an essay written in 1971 with the subtitle "Writing as Re-Vision," Rich offers these remarks:[6]

> In re-reading Virginia Woolf's *A Room of One's Own* . . . I was astonished at . . . the tone of that essay. It is the tone of a woman almost in touch with her anger, who is determined not to appear angry, who is *willing* herself to be calm, detached, and even charming in a roomful of men where things have been said which are attacks on her very integrity.

> Both the victimization and the anger experienced by women are real, and have real sources, everywhere in the environment, built into society. They must go on being tapped and explored by poets, among others. We can neither deny them, nor can we rest there. They are our birth-pains, and we are bearing ourselves.

There is a direct link between anger and creation, and in "Three Conversations" Rich makes the connection explicit:[7]

> . . . for women to dissemble anger has been a means of survival, and therefore we turn our anger inward. . . . I almost think that we have a history of centuries of women in depression: really angry women, who could have been using their anger creatively, as men have used their anger creatively.

She concludes that "an enormous amount of male art is anger converted into creation," and while anger isn't art's sole source, it plays a cardinal role. Rich connects anger to victimization on the one hand, to creative transformation on the other. Women reach political *and* poetic maturity when they resolve not to be victims merely. The value of anger in poetry is its push for survival. Useful rage turns outward into the world; turned inward, it becomes a tide of destruction and in severe cases contributes to tragedies like those of Virginia Woolf and Sylvia Plath. Anger's value to survival, on the other hand, is apparent in the careers of poets like Rich or Margaret Atwood or, first of all, Emily Dickinson:

> you, woman, masculine
> in single-mindedness,
> for whom the word was more
> than a symptom—
>
> a condition of being.
> Till the air buzzing with spoiled language
> sang in your ears
> of Perjury
>
> and in your half-cracked way you chose
> silence for entertainment,
> chose to have it out at last
> on your own premises.

By repeating the word "chose," Rich isolates the act of will in poetic achievement. That Dickinson was willful in creative ways is plain from her refusal to accept the domestic, religious, or social slots held out to women of her time. Her alternative was poetry, and through it she took a place in the world. In "Vesuvius at Home" Rich says of Dickinson:[8]

> It was a life deliberately organized on her terms. The terms she had been handed by society—Calvinist Protestantism, Romanticism, the nineteenth-century corseting of women's bodies, choices, and sexuality—could spell insanity to a woman of genius. What this one had to do was retranslate her own unorthodox, subversive, sometimes volcanic propensities into a dialect called metaphor: her native language "Tell all the truth—but tell it Slant—." It is always what is under pressure in us, especially under pressure of concealment—that explodes in poetry.

Dickinson is no longer patronized as a "fragile poetess in white," but has become, as Rich says, "a source and a foremother." She confronted the world on her own terms and allowed her art to be her defense. Through language "nobody" became "somebody," though not without social cost. Thomas Higginson could still belittle Dickinson by calling her "my partially cracked poetess at Amherst." But she would answer back, and put her case this way: "You think my gait 'spasmodic'—I am in danger—Sir—You think me 'uncontrolled'—I have no Tribunal."[9]

From that exchange Rich takes the title for her praise-poem: "I am in danger—Sir." The danger, I take it, is anger with no outlet. The danger is not to realize one's gift, to live with "spoilt language." The danger is also, as Rich puts it, that the woman-as-poet will be "split between a publicly acceptable persona, and a part of yourself that you perceive as the essential, the creative and powerful self, yet also as possibly unacceptable, perhaps even monstrous."[10] Dickinson created her own ground and took her place in the world regardless of her image— uncontrolled, spasmodic, cracked—in the eyes of the fathers.

To those upholding the status quo, any person in revolt appears "revolting." A woman not in a woman's place will be a freak, a witch, a monster. Official order demonizes the powers it suppresses; and when, for example, a woman refuses her social role as mother merely, she may expect to seem monstrous—even to herself. In "Night-Pieces: For a Child," the poet-mother beholds herself this way:

> You blurt a cry. Your eyes
> spring open, still filmed in dream.
> Wider, they fix me—
> —death's head, sphinx, medusa? [. . .]
> Mother I no more am,
> but woman, and nightmare.

The image of woman as monster is central to Rich's work. The lines just quoted are fretted with guilt, here the poet is inside the patriarchal point of view, and the image of woman as monster is wholly negative. Women with aspirations that deny or contradict motherhood will be seen as "unnatural." At the core of this curse swirls a dark cloud of misogyny, the male fear of women who don't stay put in places men assign. If archetypes exist, this is surely one, the composite image of loathing and terror that governs male paranoia toward self-possessed women:

> A man is asleep in the next room
>   We are his dreams
>   We have the heads and breasts of women
>   the bodies of birds of prey
>   Sometimes we turn into silver serpents
> While we sit up smoking and talking of how to live
> he turns on the bed and murmurs [.]

On the one hand, a man dreaming; on the other, two women "talking of how to live." That is the great divide in Rich's poetry. Men often think of women as unnatural and distorted if they stray from expected roles. Just as often, women accept such mutilating definitions. In the passage above, monstrous dreaming is countered by talk of "how to live." What these women are working out is how to live with—and then beyond—the obsessional images imposed upon them.

Caroline Herschel, "sister of William," is one among the heroic women Rich praises for not keeping her assigned place. She was an astronomer like her brother, a woman who discovered eight comets, "she whom the moon rules / like us." When she looked up into the night she saw what we see:

> A woman in the shape of a monster
> a monster in the shape of a woman
> the skies are full of them [.]

Those are the opening lines of "Planetarium," and as the poem goes on it becomes clear that the image of woman as monster is no longer negative. The "galaxies of women" are a grand and awesome spectacle. Caroline Herschel is the match of Tycho Brahe and shares with him this wish: "Let me not seem to have lived in vain." In the poem's last part, the images of woman as constellation and as astronomer are called upon to bless the poet who, empowered by Caroline Herschel's example, can claim her self-assigned task:

> I am an instrument in the shape
> of a woman trying to translate pulsations

> into images for the relief of the body
> and the reconstruction of the mind.

The image of woman as monster might be a vehicle of censure, but not necessarily. It can, in fact, be the badge of heroism. Rich's usage suggests that myths imposed on women can be revised and made to function in ways nourishing to the woman who feels that she, too, is out of place and susceptible to attack as unnatural. This strategy is central to Rich's own mythology. But the image of woman as monster isn't Rich's alone; as a number of feminist critics have pointed out, it is common to a wide spectrum of poets who are women, sometimes used with ambivalence, as much a curse as a blessing, but often too with straight praise. The image of the monster-woman, in Western mythology, goes back as far as mythic memory reaches, to Lilith and the Sphinx, to the Medusa and sometimes, as Yeats reminds us, to Helen. The figure is always powerful, often dangerous, and when viewed from male perspective, rudely unbecoming.

In "Necessities of Life," one of Rich's early manifestos celebrating her identity as a poet who is specifically a woman, Rich constructs an extended image of her poetic self that is grotesque in a modest but resolute way. From out the mouths of monsters, other monsters come:

> Jonah! I was Wittgenstein,
> Mary Wollstonecraft, the soul
>
> of Louis Jouvet, dead
> in a blown-up photograph.
>
> Till, wolfed almost to shreds,
> I learned to make myself
>
> unappetizing. Scaly as a dry bulb
> thrown into a cellar
>
> I used myself, let nothing use me.
> Like being on a private dole,
>
> sometimes more like kneading bricks in Egypt.
> What life was there, was mine,

now and again to lay
one hand on a warm brick

and touch the sun's ghost
with economical joy,

now and against to name
over the bare necessities.

Rich describes herself as an ugly outcast, but she ties herself to earth by distinctly female images of the bulb and warm bricks. The program that goes with the description—to be "unappetizing," to "let nothing use me"—is the kind of behavior that men call unnatural when they find it in women. The role of monster is embraced, used as a fulcrum of strength. And among the multitude "kneading bricks in Egypt," might not a prophet appear? A female Moses with a bardic voice? Armed with this identify, Rich "dare[s] to inhabit the world / trenchant in motion as an eel, solid / as a cabbage-head." The poem ends with a blessing from "old women knitting, breathless / to tell their tales," tales the poet will absorb, and praise, and transmit.

Adrienne Rich didn't start a leader. Her early work, praised by Auden and Randall Jarrell among others, shows her the dutiful daughter of the fathers, Auden and Jarrell among them. Not until *Snapshots of a Daughter-in-Law*, published in 1963, twelve years after her first book, does Rich begin to speak *as a woman* and allow that kind of content to underwrite her vision. Of this turning point Rich says: "Over two years I wrote a ten-part poem called 'Snapshots of a Daughter-in-Law' [1958–1960] in a longer looser mode than I'd trusted myself with before. It was an extraordinary relief to write that poem."[11] A relief and also, I want to suggest, a breakthrough.

Part one begins with an older woman as mother, her mind "moldering like a wedding cake." Part two depicts the sullen daughter who bangs the coffee pot into the sink as she hears "the angels chiding." They tell her to have no patience, to be insatiable, to save herself; but stuck in her anger, she "let[s] the tapstream scald her arm." Part three presents the dangers of taking anger seriously; when women turn it upon themselves they become "like Furies," distorted and possessed:

A thinking woman sleeps with monsters.
The beak that grips her, she becomes.

Part four summons Emily Dickinson, "iron-eyed and beaked and pur-
posed as a bird," her life a loaded gun. Part five recalls woman in her
standard role as ornament, she who pleases men *dulce*, sweetly, grooming
her legs to gleam "like petrified mammoth-tusk." Parts six through nine
explore the consequences of enforced shallowness, including the judgments of Diderot ("You all die at fifteen") and Dr. Johnson ("that it is
done at all") upon "time's precious chronic invalid." Here too, Mary
Wollstonecraft is named with praise and thereby defended against the
curse—"labeled harpy, shrew and whore"—of men who took her for a
monster. At the end of part nine Rich confronts the consequence of
following precursors like Dickinson and Wollstonecraft; for women who
"cast too bold a shadow / or smash the mold straight off," the curse to
be borne will be as painful as "tear gas, attrition shelling." Then, as if
in result and repudiation at once, part ten concludes by casting a shadow
fierce enough to smash all the molds listed in the poem. Here, in imagery
she has not used before, Rich summons the new woman:

> Well,
> she's long about her coming, who must be
> more merciless to herself than history.
> Her mind full to the wind, I see her plunge
> breasted and glancing through the currents,
> taking the light upon her
> at least as beautiful as any boy
> or helicopter,
> poised, still coming,
> her fine blades making the air wince
>
> but her cargo
> no promise then:
> delivered
> palpable
> ours.

The meaning of the poem is governed by this composite image of
woman-as-deliverer, a ship plunging through the currents with her

cargo. As she cuts "breasted and glancing" through the wind, she is also the foremost part of the ship, and I do not see that the image of the *figurehead* (the carved bust on a ship's prow) can be avoided here. She who arrives "more merciless to herself than history" is a monster to the imaginative eye—a ship and its prow, but also a beautiful boy, and then, too, a purposeful airborne machine, the helicopter, cutting the air with sharp pounding blades. To see these images together is to behold a monstrosity that is, nonetheless, the bearer of a cargo long-promised and now at last delivered.

Through the first nine parts of the poem, Rich speaks *to* and *about* ("you bird," "the beak that grips her," "handsome women, gripped") the women who compose the group portrait. In the tenth part a new relation between poet and audience emerges, active rather than passive, in motion rather than stuck. The poet concludes with "ours," a word not used before, suggesting that the isolated earlier parts of the poem have been transformed and regathered into a union decidedly tribal. The tribe, in this case, is made of those who in the poem represent the daughter-in-law in multiple aspect, the many kinds of women confined by patriarchal law. The main point is that Rich begins, in "Snapshots," to speak to and for a definite group. The poem is prophetic, announcing the coming of the tribe's new figurehead and leader. That tribe and leader are consubstantial is marked throughout the poem by a consistent use of imagery associated with monstrosity, climaxing with the "coming"—repeated twice—of this poised and merciless woman, who arrives in an act of maternal/erotic/political delivery. The composite figure of the last stanzas is midwife, lover, and potent monster, vastly female but with male aspects as well. A new totem emerges to "smash straight off" the old taboos. The result is a liberation for the poet and her tribe.

"Snapshots of a Daughter-in-Law" is a curse upon the condition of women, a malediction that turns at the end into a poem of praise and atonement. What is celebrated is the image of a new woman, but also the community of women that the poet is able at last—and with "extraordinary relief"—to feel one with. For the first time Rich assumes, when she speaks, a tribal intimacy. Where once she wrote polite poems for her father to approve while "unspeakable fairy tales ebb[ed] like blood through [her] head," now she writes with a monster's outlaw freedom, addressing the many women to whom the ubiquitous "you" of her work refers in poem after poem. Communal pronouns—"we," "us," "our"—provide the frame for exchanges between "I" and "you."

And now the poet's identity takes its feminist form as midwife, combining creative and procreative powers:

> like a midwife who at dawn
> has all in order; bloodstains
> washed up, teapot on the stove,
> and starts her five miles home
> walking, the birthyell still
> exploding.

How women give birth and who helps them, Rich says in *Of Woman Born*, "are political questions." Charting the history of midwifery, Rich points to "the centuries of witchcraft trials, during which midwives were a particular target."[12] In America, the first person executed for witchcraft was Margaret Jones, a midwife. Ann Hutchinson was also a midwife. The practical wisdom of midwifery (seen by men as magical and demonic) is ancient; but by reviving a tradition of healing that men have condemned as monstrous, Rich is able to combine in one image the notions of woman as monster and woman as poet with long practice of female power—specifically, women helping women.

In "When We Dead Awaken," her account of development from a poet as dutiful daughter to the poet as monster and midwife, Rich observes that "to be a female human being trying to fulfill traditional female functions in a traditional way *is* in direct conflict with the subversive function of the imagination."[13] For a woman to claim male powers goes against the grain of patriarchal order. More, to take up the role of the bard is to violate a wholly male tradition. Women might be permitted to speak of private themes and in a quiet voice, *dulce ridens, dulce loquens;* but to speak out and take place and assume a public voice has been, until recently, unheard of. Lest we forget, men who cast blame are honored as prophets, while sharp-tongued women are in league with the devil and at one time paid with their lives.

In the poem "Orion," written five years after "Snapshots," Rich reclaims a part of herself that in traditional terms is thought to be masculine only. The poem's imagery of kinship and blood suggests the completeness with which Rich possesses the powers of her male double:

> my fierce half-brother, staring
> down from that simplified west

your breast open, your belt dragged down
by an oldfashioned thing, a sword
the last bravado you won't give over
though it weighs you down as you stride

and the stars in it are dim
and maybe have stopped burning.
But you burn, and I know it;
as I throw back my head to take you in
an old transfusion happens again:
divine astronomy is nothing to it.

As Rich says in her essay, Orion possesses "the active principle, the energetic imagination,"[14] a strength she reclaims for herself while careful to distinguish it from phallic power merely; male posturing has devolved into a "last bravado," and even now the sign of the sword is burning out. We might also recall that Orion was a hunter slain by Diana, goddess of chastity. In this poem, moreover, poetic power is defined as "cold and egotistical," as if loss of love and empathy were the cost of creative assertion. Rich sees that the division of human potential into male and female zones is a mutilation of our humanness made worse by traditional claims that such division is natural and the way things should remain. She is also aware that one definition of monstrosity, in traditional terms, is the merging of gender differences within a single self. She is not, however, going to assume male prerogatives at the expense of female resources. What she does instead is "put on" a suit of "body-armor" such as a merman "in his armored body" wears, and go down into the wreck.

"Diving into the Wreck" takes the theme of woman-as-monster as far as it goes, all the way to "the thing itself and not the myth," an androgynous condition of being that is "she" and "he" together but impossible to visualize. By reading "the book of myths" (in which "our names do not appear") she is able to locate the site of the wreck. And going down, she learns power of a wholly different kind: "I have to learn alone / to turn my body without force / in the deep element." And once at the wreck she finds herself "among so many who have always / lived here." The remarkable thing about this poem is how solid it seems with its paraphernalia of diving, its wrecked ship and quest for treasure; yet at no point does it yield a comprehensible image of that which the poet encounters. As with the composite image at the close of "Snapshots," here too the thing being praised cannot be seen except as a quilting of images. Nevertheless, it's here that the "I" becomes "we," here that the poet arrives at the goal of her quest:

> This is the place.
> And I am here, the mermaid whose dark hair
> streams black, the merman in his armored body
> We circle silently
> about the wreck
> we dive into the hold.
> I am she: I am he
>
> whose drowned face sleeps with open eyes
> whose breasts still bear the stress
> whose silver, copper, vermeil cargo lies
> obscurely inside barrels
> half-wedged and left to rot[. . . .]

The principle of form evident above is characteristic of Rich's mature poetry and, with "Diving" for proof, depends on a kind of wovenness or netting of images held in loose communion—an overlapping of disparate elements from many directions together. What unifies this kind of poem is its *threshold image,* if I may call it that, a larger composite of imagery that almost but not quite reveals its oneness in diversity, as if it were on the point of crossing into visibility, an emerging image in and through the poem's parts, but nowhere dominant in itself. Images of this kind carry Rich's sense of female possibility, her vision of the new woman in the moment of "her coming." This holds for poems like "Snapshots" and "Orion," and for much of the later poetry as well. Rich's important images possess threshold presence and have, as well, the character of a matrix. They are matrices out of which, and back into which, the disparate imagery of the poetry moves—as if the actual poem were a door, or rather a door frame where, in its crossing, the image resides.

With "Diving into the Wreck," Rich completes her re-vision of woman as monster. It becomes a source of poetic/political identity extracted from the wreckage of self and society under patriarchal rule. The old dispensation is displaced and a new "book of myths" can be written.

But as a matrix or threshold image, woman as monster remains useful. In "Turning the Wheel," written in 1981, Rich travels to "the female core" of the American continent, where she calls back from our native past "the desert witch, the shamaness." She aims to recover from history's normalized mythology the abnormality of a pueblo sorceress, a woman "slightly wall-eyed or with a streak / of topaz lightning in the blackness / of one eye." The figure of the shamaness is then recognized in Mary Colter, our earliest architect to use native American principles of design. Rich suggests that "history" has been largely a male province and that the powers of women have been apart from history, man/ world/clock-time on the one hand, woman/earth/tidal-time on the other.

The summoning of strong women is a constant occasion in Rich's poetry. Thereby she celebrates a feminist genealogy of heroes and martyrs from whom to take courage and direction. Among those who give the tribe its identity are Willa Cather, Marie Curie, Emily Dickinson, Elizabeth Barrett, Diane Fossey, Jane Addams, Susan B. Anthony, Mary Woll-stonecraft, Caroline Herschel, Paula Becker, and Clara Westhoff, as well as personal friends of the poet (Audre Lorde, for example), and then finally the eponymous "deviant" woman of "Heroines" and, with no remembered names, the frontier women in "From an Old House in America." The first step toward political union of any sort, as Rich knows, is the establishment of collective identity by naming and praising. This revisionist stance toward history has been a principal aim of the feminist movement, and the fact that the cause of women *is* a movement, a self-conscious effort to acquire power and take place in the world, gives Rich the urgency of her voice, a voice that assumes, as most recent poetry does not, vital relation to widespread real-world needs.

In the feminist movement there are many voices—poets, scholars, critics—addressing the community of women. No one of them can speak for women as a whole, but a striking feature of Rich's work is the intensity with which it is received by its audience, an audience that feels itself embattled and in need of a voice that each of its members can recognize, share, and take to heart. The fact that Rich has championed a separatist movement among feminists, or that she often praises erotic love exclusively female, has not narrowed her appeal nor reduced her authority. Of her work Rich says: "As long as I wrote in the hope of 'reaching' men, I was setting bounds on my own mind, holding back;

trying to make the subversive sound unthreatening, the unthinkable reassuring." And of feminist writing in general, she goes on: "when we write for women we imagine an audience which *wants* our words—which desires our courage, our anger, our verve, our active powers, instead of fearing or loathing them. We write for ourselves and each other—an ever-expanding sense of whom is part of our imagining—passionately listening and reading as we write because other women's words are vital to our own."[15] To be "part of our imagining" is the great condition for political coherence; here it signals a shared excitement in poetry's keeping.

As the voice of her tribe, Rich incites revolt and calls to battle; she combats the curse set upon her as a poet, and upon women in general, at the hands of patriarchal censure. We've seen that one way to do this is to take a principal curse, the woman-as-monster, and transform it into praise and blessing. This kind of transformation is constant in Rich's work, and can be seen as part of the "re-naming" and "re-vision" essential to the feminist program in its literary aspect. Of this revisionary struggle Rich says that "the act of looking back, of seeing with fresh eyes, of entering an old text from a new critical direction—is for women more than a chapter in cultural history: it is an act of survival."[16] She postulates a "dynamic between a political vision and the demand for a fresh vision of literature," and concludes in poetry's favor:[17]

> For a poem to coalesce, for a character or an action to take shape, there has to be an imaginative transformation of reality which is in no way passive. . . . If the imagination is to transcend and transform experience it has to question, to challenge, to conceive of alternatives, perhaps to the very life you are living at that moment. You have to be free to play around with the notion that day might be night, love might be hate; nothing can be too sacred for the imagination to turn into its opposite or to call experimentally by another name. For writing is re-naming.

What happens, say, if the common word *mother* is turned into its opposite or called by another name? How about the word *wife*? or the traditional meaning of *maternal*? What happens is that mystifications collapse and truths emerge that guardians of patriarchal order find appalling and outrageous. Reaction is swift, sometimes violent, and the contest between Antigone and Creon replays itself yet again.

The path of poetic fate in our century suggests that repressive regimes do not tolerate, are in fact afraid of, the subversive powers of language, most especially poetry in the hands of those whom the political order aims to keep powerless. To an important degree, the very different careers of Brecht and Breytenbach reveal the same predicament that Rich and her feminist colleagues find themselves in, a fate and a predicament for which Osip Mandelshtam is perhaps the saintly patron. Viewed from a feminist perspective, established order is not on any poet's side. The hostile impact of Creon's decree, moreover, is for women extremely intimate. When men in the seats of power manipulate women by inscribing laws on the wall of the womb, when self-determination is withheld and women do not have control of their own bodies, we are back to the situation in *Antigone*, where carnal desecration is the sign of spiritual rape. For reasons of this kind, Rich is adamant about the moral centrality of physical existence. In her view, mind and body are one agency; poetic knowledge is a "thinking through the body," and the truths of the flesh are never trivial. Rich might even say, as I would, that physical recoil is our first response to evil, the initial (and initiating) stage of revolt that makes us human:

> The will to change begins in the body not in the mind
> My politics is in my body, accruing and expanding with every
>   act of resistance and each of my failures
> Locked in the closet at 4 years old I beat the wall with my body
> that act is in me still[.]

Maturity of vision arrived, for Rich, when she began to feel "that politics was not something 'out there' but something 'in here' and of the essence of my condition."[18] Thinking through the body is the bedrock of moral intelligence for much of feminist writing, a way of judging the world in direct relation to physical need and physical vulnerability, including the vulnerability of childbirth and nurturing generally. To recognize this simple concrete condition, furthermore, is to revise some very old and honored principles. The male obsession with high versus low, with spirit versus the flesh, with the cultural versus the natural, gives way in the feminist view to a mutuality of categories, a network of values that are complementary rather than opposed, and a care for earth as strong as allegiance to any world. We must, says Rich to her tribe, "view our physicality as a resource, rather than a destiny."[19] In one of her "tracking poems" she praises the body as our connection to earth, as the raft that saves us from abstract foundering:

> The best world is the body's world
> filled with creatures   filled with dread
> misshapen so   yet the best we have
> our raft among the abstract worlds
> and how I longed to live on this earth
> walking her boundaries   never counting the cost[.]

A gynocentric order would affirm "our bond with the natural order, [and] the corporeal ground of our intelligence."[20] In the contest between earth and world, Rich allies her hope for the future with the odds of the earth.

For women, self-determination begins with "repossession" of the body, including the processes of birth. The male demand for control of female destiny is spelled out in medical and legal constraints, and quite apart from the genuine problems surrounding abortion as a moral issue, nothing reveals the hypocrisy of the prevailing system so readily as proclamations of "reverence for life" or "the sacredness of life" by an order that thrives on war and prides itself on the destructive prowess of its machines. Without question we live in a world that celebrates the power of technology. Without question the glory of patriarchy is conquest. Like Simone de Beauvoir before her, Rich thinks that the masculine disregard for life and pain (the male preference for armored states of body and mind) is the product of interaction between men and their technologies. As she suggests in "The Knight," men wear armor even when the destructive momentum of machines is plain to see. Against such potent seductions, how shall the frail claims of bodily life be respected? Perhaps it *is* the spectacle of destruction that excites us most. Perhaps, as Mary Daly speculates, violence against women is the stem and prototype of all violence—against other bodies, against the earth itself. Meanwhile, abstract desires compel us. Contempt for life, contempt for pain, contempt for all that's powerless and open; that is the content of Creon's decree. It is the logic of power in a world where might is right, the product of patriarchal order like a levelling wind or rabid god of air against which, in Rich's urging, women must take a place of their own. And thus this manifesto:[21]

> One of the devastating effects of technological capitalism has been its numbing of the powers of the imagination—specifically, the power to envision new human and communal relationships. I am a feminist because I feel endangered, psychically and physically, by this society, and because I believe that the women's movement is saying we have come to an edge of history where men—insofar as they are embodiments of the patriarchal idea—have becomes dangerous to children and other living things, themselves included; and that we can no longer afford to keep the female principle enclosed within the confines of the tight, little post-industrial family, or within any male-induced notion of where the female principle is valid and where it is not.

By the time she wrote *Diving into the Wreck*, Rich had become the woman "merciless to herself" that she had envisioned the coming of in "Snapshots of a Daughter-in-Law." And she had answered her greatest question—"With whom will your lot be cast?"—in a way that settled her politics and her poetry together. She casts her lot with women, and then with the internal colonies at the mercy of superpower empires, and finally with third-world peoples in general. Rich is consistently critical of an earlier feminist position that spoke mainly to women who were white and educated, a middle-class feminism of the campus and suburbs. She has always been critical of "exceptional" women, those who abandon the cause of women to excel professionally and enjoy a male-approved margin of freedom. Feminism, as Rich sees it, does not mean that women are turning their backs to the world or to men; women are simply, and at last, turning to face each other. And power, in Rich's definition, is "not power of domination, but just access to sources."[22] Among the sources of power denied to women have been their own history of struggle and endurance, their own tradition of heroes and role models, and perhaps most of all in Rich's view, the access of women to each other.

Speaking of how "Snapshots" came to be written, and of the change in direction that the poem represents, Rich says that she "had been taught that poetry should be 'universal,' which meant, of course, nonfemale."[23] Language seems open to everyone, of course, and insofar as inclusive experiences (oppression, endurance, revolt) can happen to any group or class, poems about particular experience will speak to anyone in general. But poets do not speak with a "universal" or disembodied voice. Particular voices arise from particular occasions; the poem becomes valid generally when its values are shared. Significant form is shared form. Language is timeless but also of the moment; or rather, because language is timeless it is available to the moment, and the moment's impact can't be discounted. Poetry begins where we begin, in a concrete time and place, in the body of a man or woman alert to concrete problems, the difficulties of power and gender especially. General wisdom might be offered, but always to a definite tribe, in relation to which the voice of the poet is always in situ. In "North American Time," Rich says it this way:

> Try sitting at a typewriter
> one calm summer evening
> at a table by a window
> in the country, try pretending
> your time does not exist
> that you are simply you
> that the imagination simply strays
> like a great moth, unintentional
> try telling yourself
> you are not accountable
> to the life of your tribe
> the breath of your planet.

"Poetry," as Rich says in the same poem, "never stood a chance / of standing outside history." One of the more successful illusions of high culture has been the usage of the humanistic "we" in reference, supposedly, to all of us or "man" in general. But this "we" has always been the property of an educated elite, male, white, and eurocentric. Rich escapes this illusion by relying on the forms of "you." If "you" refers to a man the rhetorical slant of the poem might be to blame or curse. If "you" refers to a woman the poem will be informed, most of the time, by praise and blessing. But at all times, in her mature poetry, Rich speaks in her own voice. She has no liking for the ploys of persona. Her voice is responsible to its time and place, and accepts what humanists would rather escape: that even poetry (or especially poetry) is positioned for and against, that the political problem of us-and-them is the poet's limit as well. The poetry of utopia might someday transcend these divisions; here and today, meanwhile, divisions continue in force, and Rich will not be fooled by "humanity" or "the human condition" when such terms are used to mask discord. She stands against an order that is male-governed and that keeps women alien to themselves and each other. She distrusts "revolution" in the old style because after much violence the old patriarchy is replaced by a new patriarchy and women are no better off than they were. Rich sums up this position in an interview:[24]

I do see saving the lives of women as a priority. The "humanity" trip—not women's liberation, but human liberation—tends to feel too easy to me. Women have always supported every "human" liberation movement, every movement for social change; there have always been women womaning the barricades, but it's never been for us, or about us. I think that women ought to be putting women first now. Which is not to say that we're against the other half of humanity, but just to say that if we don't put ourselves first, we're never going to make it to full humanity.

The political identity that does not limit itself, the movement that goes forward in the name of everyone, can expect to be at odds with itself and exploited by covert interests. Simply to use the term *woman* or *women* is perilously wide, and in fact Rich usually has in mind a more specific tribe, one overtly feminist and antipatriarchal. One might expect, then, that a majority of Rich's readers will be offended to some degree when, in fact, some are and some are not. One doesn't have to be a woman to see the decency of feminist concerns. Men enjoying a measure of male privilege can see the damage done by patriarchal claims. Being female is not in itself the criterion for valuing Rich's poems against males, like "Trying to Talk with a Man," for example, which integrates nuclear and patriarchal orders, or the merciless "Ghost of a Chance," with men like beached fish, or—to my mind one of the best—the pained and somber "August," in which the poet's curse is pitted against what might be called the primal curse of the fathers. The poem develops mythical time, beginning with the collapse of Eden in the first four stanzas:

> Two horses in yellow light
> eating windfall apples under a tree
>
> as summer tears apart   milkweeds stagger
> and grasses grow more ragged
>
> They say there are ions in the sun
> neutralizing magnetic fields on earth
>
> Some way to explain
> what this week has been, and the one before it!

To "explain" the sullen days of late summer, we can point to electromagnetic goings-on in the heavens. And if it were only the "yellow light" of dog-day afternoons, the scientists might be right. But for Rich the seasons correspond to spiritual conditions, with oppressive heat signalling the pain of political intrusion. In "Burning Oneself In," written along with "August" in 1972, the summer "heat-wave" lifts at last but awful news from the war in Vietnam "has settled in" and "a dull heat permeates the ground / of the mind." In "August," something similar is tearing things apart and "neutralizing" the earth's "magnetic" powers, a force that throws eros (the binding power of life itself) into ragged confusion. And "it," whatever it is, goes on and on; this week was bad, but "the one before it!"—the one before was worse. As we enter the rest of the poem we see the poet torn by, and struggling to confront, her own recognitions:

> If I am flesh sunning on rock
> if I am brain burning in fluorescent light
>
> if I am dream like a wire with fire
> throbbing along it
>
> if I am death to a man
> I have to know it

His mind is too simple, I cannot go on
sharing his nightmares

My own are becoming clearer, they open
into prehistory

which looks like a village lit with blood
where all the fathers are crying: *My son is mine!*

A merciless poem, hard-edged and honed to its purpose—which is to confront the curse of the fathers—and a poem that cuts to the quick of its painful occasion. As the summer devolves toward its ruin, so the poet begins to see how men imagine women, a recognition that forces a further terrible knowledge, impossible now to avoid or rationalize further. She beholds, that is, the curse of the fathers in its blood-lit origin, while off in the background Mister Kurtz is whispering "the horror, the horror."

"August" and "Diving into the Wreck" were written at about the same time. Both are poems of confrontation. Having seen through the book of myths, the poet is face to face with the thing itself. What to *do* has become a question of what to *be*. The "I am" of the middle stanzas asserts self-possession by confronting the monster in male nightmare, which is to say that the poem makes little sense until we grasp its threshold image, in this case a reptilian thing that suns itself on a rock and that, like the Medusa, is believed by men to be death to him who beholds it. We are back to the sleeping man of "Incipience," dreaming of female monsters while women talk of "how to live." In "August," the mind of the dreaming man is "too simple" because as victor and beneficiary he can be satisfied with myths. He does not *need* to contemplate complexity, nor does he *wish* to acknowledge the ancient cry of the fathers. Meanwhile, the patriarchal curse resounds through the poem, and once heard it opens on awful truth: the male child is separated from the life-serving body-world of women and inducted into the warrior cult of men, the moment when mother-right is defeated. That is the horror implicit in "My son is mine!" The fathers claim the son for themselves. They raise him to scorn life and women. They ready him— *Pro patria!*—for the wars they will declare. Women are "given" in marriage, men in battle.

But how is it that someone like myself, or any man, reads Rich's work with care and benefit? The question isn't only how men enter into and enjoy poems by women who are feminists, but how any of us, male or female, enter into the world of any poet who is actively for and against; how we come to value Brecht blasting the Nazis, or Breytenbach cursing his native tongue while blessing the cause of blacks in South Africa. I am not of the tribe to whom these poets speak, yet I join in and feel involved. In the presence of the poet's voice I willingly suspend disbelief in my own exclusion. How is that?

The problem of belonging is extended by recalling the age-old obligation of poetry to give, with so much else, pleasure; and then to consider what pleasure can be found in poems as filed and tuned to pain, or as merciless, as those by Rich when she is least lyrical, least reconciled. If the politics of her work can be off-putting, so can the splintlike diction and edgy imagery that give her art its feel, and then the unrelieved attention to torment that keeps this poet from solace and joy. If, for example, we have been trained to take delight in language, its music and its elegance, what are we to make of Rich's poem called "A Woman Dead in Her Forties," which begins with this stanza:

> —Your breasts/ sliced off The scars
> dimmed as they would have to be
> years later[.]

No lyricism or lifting rhythm sustains that language; phrasing is bland or even banal except for the startling intimacy of its occasion. Yet the poem with its ungainly lines and fractured stanzas turns out to be an elegy intense with female travail, a declaration of love complete with the scars and wounds that, in Rich's art generally, attend her praises of women's selves. The lines above, moreover, help suggest why Rich is not like other poets cited in this study. Working with her art does not yield the same enjoyment got from working with Yeats or Brecht or McGrath. Only with Breytenbach has the case been similar. He, like Rich, is wild with the burden of injustice, is often angry and feels besides that his art must go forward, *if* it goes forward, against a language that is grossly patriarchal. But he is not as resolute as Rich, not as starkly willful, nor does he pass up small consolations, humor among them. Rich stands alone. And her poetry takes its tribe into poetic-political terrain so unknown and newly entered that we might speak, as Rich does, of "a whole new poetry beginning here."[25]

Rich stands up to the world. She takes place as a poet and a woman, with poetic conduct and the conduct of life informing each other. Language is held accountable to history, to women's collective experience first of all. And insofar as her poetry and her politics share a common vision, her example has about it a "nobility" such as Stevens might point to, a moral symmetry that is cause in itself for delight. In the following section from "Natural Resources," poetry becomes a *vita activa* and the way itself a communal continuum:

> There are words I cannot choose again:
> *humanism   androgyny*
>
> Such words have no shame in them, no diffidence
> before the raging stoic grandmothers:
>
> their glint is too shallow, like a dye
> that does not permeate
>
> the fibers of actual life
> as we live it, now;
>
> this fraying blanket with its ancient stains
> we pull across the sick child's shoulder
>
> or wrap around the senseless legs
> of the hero trained to kill
>
> this weaving, ragged because incomplete
> we turn our hands to, interrupted
>
> over and over, handed down
> unfinished, found in the drawer
>
> of an old dresser in the barn,
> her vanished pride and care
>
> still urging us, urging on
> our works, to close the gap

> in the Great Nebula,
> to help the earth deliver.

Rich's art arises immediately out of history, out of life's embattled moments day by day, and with the added sense that where "I" am there also "we" are. This tribal construct has a firm grip on the actual, but it also extends the poem's occasion to include readers outside the tribal exclusivity at issue, and allows any one of us, finally, to join in and "help the earth deliver." That something like this occurs I cannot doubt, given my own attention to, and pleasure in, the poetry of a feminist like Rich. Her work offers an alternative vision, one that curses the sins of patriarchal order and goes on to praise strengths and virtues basic to everyone, precisely the life-reclaiming strengths and virtues of women through the ages.

For all the radicalness of Rich's feminism, her work has about it a radicalism that goes even deeper, a way of life that men can no longer scorn or despise, a *vita activa* that anyone might find worth having in this, the twilight era of nuclear politics. The poet, therefore, summons a tribe, and we—men and women—respond to the call. The situation is startling, perhaps, but only at first. For if poets in times of political upheaval tend to revive bardic practices, might not the case be likewise that we, as readers in a time of political strain, tend to fall back on the older relation to poetry and take up our role in the bardic situation? In adversity the bard emerges. So, it would seem, does the tribe.

The feminist poetics that Rich has worked to realize depends on capacities essential to women, including alertness to the pain of others, a fierce attention to relationships of all kinds and, along with these, a sense of self with boundaries less rigid and guarded, more flexible and embracing, than most men's. Women do not wear armor, do not go panoplied with weapons, do not automatically see people as challengers and, in consequence, do not reify the world of selves into a wall of otherness. This, in part, is Rich's sense of female powers, a view she praises in the following lines:

> And I think of those lives we tried to live
> in our globed helmets, self-enclosed

> bodies self-illumined gliding
> safe from the turbulence
>
> and how, miraculously, we failed[.]

The failure of the self to shut down and close off, the refusal of poetry to turn in contempt from the earth—these "failings" are part of women's strength in Rich's view, and they provide her feminist poetics with a crucial element. For her the virtues of reception and response are primary. She wants to mobilize empathy, compassion, the imaginative capacity for suffering with—a seeing *beyond* the self *into* the world; or, a seeing *through* the self, an entrance into the experience of others via one's own self-knowledge. In "Hunger," Rich responds to the spectacle of African famine in terms that are more actual than metaphoric:

> I know I'm partly somewhere else—
> huts strung across a drought-stretched land
> not mine, dried breasts, mine and not mine, a mother
> watching my children shrink with hunger.
> I live in my Western skin,
> my Western vision, torn
> and flung to what I can't control or even fathom.

To reduce these lines to a poetics of guilt is to forget the power of anger to override indulgence. It would also be to ignore Rich's consistent melding of self and world, private grief and public pain, insisting that between the two no demarcation exists except, of course, the false division of experience into separate categories as a stratagem of evasion. The following lines are often quoted, but not always with sufficient care for the actualization of metaphor that takes place:

> In the bed the pieces fly together
> and the rifts fill   or else
> my body is a list of   wounds
> symmetrically placed
> a village
> blown open by planes
> that did not finish   the job[.]

The reference is to Vietnam, and the poem in which these lines occur is "Nightbreak," written in 1968 at the peak of the war when the horror has reached such a pitch that the poet, so to say, is cracking up. The poem goes on to encircle napalm with anger, then devolves into the following characteristic (for Rich) stanza:

> Time is quiet   doesn't break things
> or even wound   Things are in danger
> from people   The frail clay lamps
> of Mesopotamia
> row on row under glass
> in the ethnological section
> little hollows of dried-
> up oil   The refugees
> with their identical
> tales of escape   I don't
> collect what I can't use   I need
> what can be broken.

The "dried- / up oil" of the ancient lamps, which once afforded sacred light, is played against the "oildrum" of napalm that balls into fire over an Asian village. The clay lamps, now useless, are preserved with great care when, meanwhile, the breaking of vessels elsewhere goes without notice. In the last stanza of "Nightbreak," the night itself seems to shatter, and the pieces, which are also the bits of the shattered self, at dawn "move / dumbly back / toward each other." The theme of this poem is the shattering impact of political intrusion on a self that feels shockingly continuous with the suffering of children in a distant place. The poem's threshold image is the earthen vessel (signalled by the clay lamps) that Rich links to the creative powers of women. Rich argues, in *Of Woman Born*, that "the woman potter molded, not simply vessels, but images of herself, the vessel of life, the transformer of blood into life and milk." She goes on to say that "the pot, vessel, urn, pitcher, was not an ornament or a casual container; it made possible the long-term storage of oils and grains, the transforming of raw food into cooked; it was also sometimes used to store the bones or ashes of the dead." The earthen vessel, then, "is anything but a 'passive' receptacle; it is *transformative*—active, powerful."[26]

"Nightbreak" is an angry probe into the experience of political intrusion. The poet's openness to the world makes her vulnerable to the world's horror, especially the violence her own nation visits upon helpless children elsewhere, a violence Rich apprehends as a citizen and as a woman acquainted with the pain of motherhood. The outcome is devastating. Even sleep is "cracked and flaking," and the dawn feels like a "white / scar splitting / over the east." If we follow "the woman/vessel association," as Rich calls it, we see that the poem is about the breakup of self, including the self's poetic capacity, under the ruinous press of the real. This sounds extreme, but the crisis portrayed in "Nightbreak" is not, I think, overdone. To an open imagination the Vietnam war was everywhere. Its atrocities and ravaged faces—chiefly of women and children—filled the news and haunted the places of sleep. We in America were always safe, unless of an age and a class to be drafted, but not, after a certain point of horror's surfeit, immune.

What happens in the world happens over in the heart, not in an exact equivalent way, of course, but as suffering transformed by imagination; pain is pain however we know it, and can be called the ground (and cost) of alertness to life. Speaking of feminism and the "connection between inner and outer," Rich says:[27]

> We are attempting, in fact, to break down that fragmentation of inner and outer in every possible realm. The psyche and the world out there are being acted on and interacting intensely all the time. There is no such thing as the private psyche, whether you're a woman—or a man, for that matter.

Rich praises acts of extended awareness. Unfortunately, this opening outward of self, and the vulnerability that must follow, are often criticized as a fault which men avoid and women fall prey to. Rich thinks of it as a "source of power" and therefore a hopeful gift. She says: "the so-called 'weak ego boundaries' of women . . . might be a negative way of describing the fact that women have tremendous powers of intuitive identification and sympathy with other people."[28] That is the point, of course; and if it should be considered a fault—if empathetic imagination is thought unmanly, or if care for life beyond one's own is discounted as "feminine" and therefore weak—then masculine preference for detachment and "objectivity" is more vicious than we usually admit. In patriarchal culture, transcendence has meant "rising above it all"; in Rich's feminist ethos, on the other hand, transcendence means reaching beyond oneself in sympathy with the plight of others. Male transcendence negates and masters; female transcendence moves to acknowledge and interact. There are easy formulations, of course, but even so one sees the benefit to a poetics incorporating female *virtu* of this kind. A truly *political* imagination moves beyond the self and into the world. The kind of political experience I've called political intrusion becomes, in Rich's poetry, more than historical torment. It becomes her art's occasion.

Adrienne Rich bears witness to pain that is shared and unnecessary. She curses those who ignore the suffering they create and sustain. She praises those who absorb the impact and survive. In "Hunger," the closing image stares back at us indelibly:

> Swathed in exhaustion, on the trampled newsprint,
> a woman shields a dead child from the camera.
> The passion to be inscribes her body.

An image of African famine got from a photograph, its import resides in its political dimension. "The decision to feed the world," Rich says earlier in the poem, "is the real decision. No revolution / has chosen it." That, I take it, is the plain shocking truth of the matter. And at its heart is the victim's lack of public existence—a "passion to be" that fails to be acknowledged. Those who suffer have neither a name nor a voice, a condition that makes their lives easy to ignore and dispose of, and reminds us that worldly power controls people by controlling names. If she could, Rich would praise the mothers and children in "Hunger" by lamenting their lives and cruel lot. She would, that is, restore them to their name. To create a public existence, however, requires a revelation of private being. In extremity private being is often inaccessible to anyone outside the circle of suffering. It's here, too often, that "political" poetry gives way to propaganda and falls back on ideology.

In "Hunger" Rich returns repeatedly to the image of mothers and children; as a woman and a mother, she trusts maternal anger to guide her art. In "Integrity" she praises "anger and tenderness: my selves," and in "From an Old House in America" rage and compassion are united with the will to bear witness:

· · ·

Who is here. The Erinyes.
One to sit in judgment.

One to speak tenderness.
One to inscribe the verdict on the canyon wall.

These lines announce a feminist poetics. Rich's defense of poetry rests on the moral and imaginative power of maternal anger and female care. Not everyone, however, can or would wish to invoke the Furies. There are several ways to stand *in relation* to suffering not directly our own— the kind of disturbance that photojournalism is capable of causing, for example. In representations of suffering it's the experience of relation— the submerged connectedness of self to other selves—that poets like Rich explore. We might even define poetic imagination, in this case, as willing suspension of disbelief in other people's pain. Rich has spelled out the relation of poetry to political distress this way:[29]

> No true political poetry can be written with propaganda as an aim to persuade others "out there" of some atrocity or injustice (hence the failure, as poetry, of so much anti-Vietnam poetry of the sixties). *As poetry*, it can come only from the poet's need to identify her relationship to atrocities and injustice, the sources of her pain, fear, and anger, the meaning of her resistance.

In "Hunger," Rich explores her relationship to disaster. She faces the experience of political intrusion, in this case the impact of catastrophe abroad upon moral awareness at home. But here also she envisions the solidarity of all women whose pain is shared and unnecessary:

Is death by famine worse than death by suicide,
than a life of famine and suicide, if a black lesbian dies,
if a white prostitute dies, if a woman of genius
starves herself to feed others,
self-hatred battening on her body?
Something that kills us or leaves us half-alive
is raging under the name of an "act of god"
in Chad, in Niger, in the Upper Volta—
yes, that male god that acts on us and on our children,

that male State that acts on us and on our children
till our brains are blunted by malnutrition,
yet sharpened by the passion for survival,
our powers expended daily on the struggle
to hand a kind of life on to our children,
to change reality for our lovers
even in a single trembling drop of water.

Rich offers a global summary of suffering anchored in famine, then curses its political cause, and then with small praises goes on to the ordeal of women surviving. What this poem blesses, grim though it may be, is a state of mind generous enough to grasp the underlying oneness of victims. What it curses is the claim that some kinds of suffering are less (or more) terrible than others. Rich abhors the notion that "pain belongs to some order." She would bless all cases with equal urgency, as if victimization were the basis of tribal union. But if the solidarity of political victims exists de facto it remains to be recognized and acted upon. Hence the poem's end: "Until we find each other, we are alone."

The "true nature of poetry," Rich says elsewhere, is "the drive to connect." The chief means in Rich's possession is her own experience of erotic rapport. In this regard, "Twenty-One Love Poems" is one of her finest works so far, a poem of steadfast blessing, in which a lesbian relationship is praised and offered as a testament. This is also Rich's longest poem, too lengthy to examine in detail, but with salient points that can't be overlooked. And finally, "Twenty-One Love Poems" names and honors—allows to take place with dignity—an experience that is profoundly challenging to patriarchal norms. The poem was composed through 1974–76. It is set in Manhattan, and section one maps the hard terrain through which "two lovers of one gender" make their way:

Wherever in this city, screens flicker
with pornography, with science-fiction vampires,
victimized hirelings bending to the lash,
we also have to walk . . . if simply as we walk
through the rainsoaked garbage, the tabloid cruelties
of our own neighborhood.
We need to grasp our lives inseparable
from those rancid dreams, that blurt of metal, those disgraces,
and the red begonia perilously flashing

from a tenement sill six stories high,
or the long-legged young girls playing ball
in the junior highschool playground.
No one has imagined us. We want to live like trees,
sycamores blazing through sulfuric air,
dappled with scars, still exuberantly budding,
our animal passion rooted in the city.

From the ugly dreams surrounding them they need to take back their lives, grasp them in a way that makes the two inseparably one, and then go on to comprehend the broader fact that life together is embedded in the reality of the streets through which they must walk. Public and private realms intersect from the start, and the poem's *raison d'être* is announced by saying simply: "No one has imagined us." Many names have and will be given them, including those on the street's obscene marquees. Against these the poet creates a different name that is, in sum, the poem. But none of it, neither the poem nor the relationship from which it springs, will be easy or encouraged. Beauty, whether the red begonia or the young girls at play, shows itself "perilously." Every sort of life is "dappled with scars," yet still, like the trees, things persist:

> *Tristan and Isolde* is scarcely the story,
> women at least should know the difference
> between love and death.

And in the end, "the story of our lives becomes our lives." This one won't have a happy ending, but it's not a tragedy either, no *Liebestod* to distract from survival. The main thing is not "to make a career of pain," and on this point Rich is resolute: "The woman who cherished her / suffering is dead. I am her descendant."

"Twenty-One Love Poems" includes an unnumbered "floating" poem replete with erotic detail. This poem serves as threshold image for the whole, an emblem of physical love to uphold—as earth upholds the airy world—the more meditative poems. Modern love poetry speaks in a small voice, nowadays, off somewhere to the side amid the passions of our century, recalling lines from Shakespeare's sonnet: "How with this rage shall beauty hold a plea / Whose action is no stronger than a flower." Rich answers by making politics love's occasion, not only as love's embattled backdrop but also the fight to extend love's meaning in feminist terms. In this way very personal poetry takes on dignity and historical weight.

Rich is firmly of the belief that love alone, love apart from the world (like poetry lost in the isolated self) can never be an answer to life, contrary to its representations in Western art. In "Splittings" Rich announces against "abnegating power for love," announces against "splitting / between love and action." Even when love's fulfillment is real and privately wondrous, as it is at the end of "The Origin and History of Consciousness," it does not suffice:

> Trusting, untrusting,
> we lowered ourselves into this, let ourselves
> downward hand over hand as on a rope that quivered
> over the unsearched. . . . We did this. Conceived
> of each other, conceived each other in a darkness
> which I remember as drenched in light.
>   I want to call this life.
>
> But I can't call it life until we start to move
> beyond this secret circle of fire
> where our bodies are giant shadows flung on a wall
> where the night becomes our inner darkness, and sleeps
> like a dumb beast, head on her paws, in the corner.

Plato's cave, perhaps—or any beneficent place where life is but a shadow and night appears the image of one's own unwakeful self. Within this circle, restful and apart, comfort is real but (for the poet) a danger to courage:

> When my dreams showed signs
> of becoming
> politically correct
> no unruly images
> escaping beyond borders
> when walking in the street I found my
> themes cut out for me
> knew what I would not report
> for fear of enemies' usage
> then I began to wonder[.]

Most of us would back off from such hard demands, even seeing their need politically—or poetically, for that matter. Rich does not back off. She confronts, and then again confronts. If there is a line where battle is joined, she scouts that line without respite. In her example we see great bravery, and understand the urgency that gives her art its willfulness. We can also appreciate her puritan strain, disconsolate and sometimes grimly dogged, despite her care for earth and bodily life. These are some of the costs a woman who is a poet will assume in the kingdom of the fathers.

Adrienne Rich is nothing if not a survivor, and so long as she keeps faith with earth against the world's oppressiveness, she draws on strengths that run very deep. Every peak a crater, she says; "no height without depth, without a burning core." Now and again, in "Transcendental Etude" most securely, height and depth connect; then the earth is sound beyond doubt. Willfulness abates and the "immense fragility" of life seems, briefly, enough:

> Still, it persists. Turning off onto a dirt road
> from the raw cuts bulldozed through a quiet village
> for the tourist run to Canada,
> I've sat on a stone fence above a great, soft, sloping field
> of musing heifers, a farmstead
> slanting its planes calmly in the calm light,
> a dead elm raising bleached arms
> above a green so dense with life,
> minute, momentary life—slugs, moles, pheasants, gnats,
> spiders, moths, hummingbirds, groundhogs, butterflies—
> a lifetime is too narrow
> to understand it all, beginning with the huge
> rockshelves that underlie all that life.

A rare poetic confidence has kept Rich sane and creative through a lifetime of combat. At the end of "Transcendental Etude," she presents us with an emblem of womanly art as she discovers it—the woman "turning in her lap" the scraps and rags of her life—then goes on to close the poem with a poetics that reaches beyond will or anger merely, to a clemency or gentleness without which "the passion to be" could not take place:

Such a composition has nothing to do with eternity,
the striving for greatness, brilliance—
only with the musing of a mind
one with her body, experienced fingers quietly pushing
dark against bright, silk against roughness,
pulling the tenets of a life together
with no mere will to mastery,
only care for the many-lived, unending
forms in which she finds herself,
becoming now the sherd of broken glass
slicing light in a corner, dangerous
to flesh, now the plentiful, soft leaf
that wrapped round the throbbing finger, soothes the wound:
and now the stone foundation, rockshelf further
forming underneath everything that grows.

"Transcendental Etude" is the closing poem in *The Dream of a Common Language*, and the book's last section, in turn, is called "Not Somewhere Else, But Here." Exactly what "dream of a common language" means has provoked much critical debate. Usually the several meanings of "common" are stressed—plain and ordinary on the one hand, accessible and shared on the other—but the sense of "dream" is also important, suggesting a goal, the visionary state of poetic thinking, maybe also a *second* language, preconscious and unbroken, like a rockshelf of linguistic resource underlying poetry in general. For a feminist poet, in any case, the condition of language as she finds it will be a vexing problem, "a knot of lies / eating at itself to get undone." How shall the integrity of female experience be kept intact once "rendered into the oppressor's language"?

Rich's solution is implicit in her sense that "Only where there is language is there world." This notion has been formulated most succinctly by Wittgenstein in his *Philosophical Investigations*, where he says, for example, that "to imagine a language means to imagine a form of life."[30] To imagine a language befitting a feminist form of life is, I take it, Rich's "dream." Wittgenstein also says that "the *speaking* of language is part of an activity," a specific way of taking place in the world. He adds that "only those hope who can talk." That the basic scene in a Rich poem is two women talking—the poet speaking to and with a woman like herself—suggests the kind of language, and the form of life, Rich works to imagine. Language and world together make up "the weave of our life," as Wittgenstein puts it. And when, finally, he observes that the totality of our linguistic milieu consists "of language and the actions into which it is woven," he endorses Rich's fundamental belief as an activist-poet: "Poetry never stood a chance / of standing outside history."

This, finally, is where Rich stands: inside her own body's sorrow and deeply settled into time—"not somewhere else, but here." Her language is time's stark vernacular, the idiom of being-in-the-world where "being" is female and "the world," as ever, is still a kingdom of the fathers. Against the patriarchal order she sets her art and her life because, as things now stand, it's an order given to conquest and illusions of mastery, hostile to earth and the flesh. In the tradition of bardic practice, her poetry announces communal identity, calls for courage and fortitude in battle, keeps a language (and a lore) by which members of the tribe can stand up, take place, and together realize their collective "passion to be." In Rich's case, moreover, it's not difficult to say when she took up her political station. It began when she "was finished with the idea of a poem as a single, encapsulated event, a work of art complete in itself."[31] It began, that is, when she started appending dates to her poems, beginning with those that make up *Snapshots of a Daughter-in-Law*, her volume of 1963 in which she breaks free to imagine herself as "long about her coming, who must be / more merciless to herself than history." To herself she has been merciless, and often to her enemies as well, but with tenderness to temper her anger, and always with "care for the many-lived, unending / forms in which she finds herself."

Conclusion:
Toward a Changed Poetics

Living in the Age of the Bomb, it's not hard to see that between them the superpowers have recolonized the globe; that they have carved the planet into spheres of influence, forcing smaller nations to toe the new alignment, and that now they proceed with the standoff they've locked themselves into. This means that most of the fighting gets done by proxy, by pitting groups or nations against each other to no end, of course, except *this* end—the demise of cities and countrysides as, over and over, populations get caught in the cross fire. About these cross-fire situations, furthermore, there is a redundant pathos, a familiar sorrow, reminding me that life for all of us, today, depends on two empires not unlike Athens and Sparta, dividing their version of the world between them, preparing for war and surmising it must come because one seems to be gaining an edge on the other. As Thucydides puts it, "Finally the point was reached when Athenian strength attained a peak plain for all to see." And thus the Spartan vote for war; because—as Thucydides says—"because they were afraid." It's an old story, except for the nuclear angle. For Thucydides it was Hellas going down. Now it's life on earth. None of this is news, of course; but being caught in the cross fire provokes interesting questions, in particular what we might still expect from fiction and poetry—enlightened feeling? finer sensibilities?—amid the *hysterico passio* of nuclear Cold War politics.

I've always thought of literature as a fierce vote for the future, but now that's not so certain. Recently Günter Grass has reminded us how much good writing depends on a hearing at some point forward in time. Sometimes a new style or vision will not find its audience for decades; and often, too, writers must outlive, through their work, the censorship and silence that governments have a habit of imposing. Literature's "superior staying power" is what Grass has in mind when he says: "Sure of its aftereffect, it could count on time even if the echo to word and sentence, poem and thesis might take decades or even centuries to make itself heard. This advance payment, this provision of time, made the poorest writers rich." But now the promise of delayed reception can't be counted on, nor the hope of immortality through fame. Thinking on his own career, Grass concludes: "I know that the book I am planning to write can no longer pretend to certainty of the future. It will have to include a farewell to the damaged world, to wounded creatures, to us and our minds, which have thought of everything and of the end as well."

Writers must, it seems to me, vote to see the world keep going. Creating an idea or image is like planting a tree: its fullest foliage will be well beyond one's time. But if history has often shown us the long-term victory of truth, it also reveals the catastrophic outcome, both short-term and long, of power-politics. I mean to say that while notions of fate and historical necessity don't convince me, the sameness in political behavior, especially the way powers contend and empires fall, is hard to ignore. The past, in any case, seems most real to me as parable, the way Cavafy used Hellenic anecdote, or the way Zbigniew Herbert does now, to get a handle on chaos and better comprehend the odd way personal experience has begun to feel collective. Recasting big events as old tales restores, at least, a sense of scale. I can even suppose that in a post-nuclear era the pretensions of a civilization built from debris will include, among its inheritance of hearsay and junk, legends of the Bomb.

I'm trying not to fool myself, although lately I find myself thinking a good deal about the hereafter—not some thirty-minute shoot-out that brings on nuclear winter, but beyond that, in quick flashes forward, the shapes the maiming will finally settle into. For the first time, always having loathed science fiction, I discover substance in imaginings of the future. Maybe that's dangerous, implying as it does that the world I love is lost already. I am encouraged, however, by what Elaine Scarry says in *The Body in Pain*, especially her idea of personal language as counterforce to political injury, and also by this remark: "Beyond the expansive ground of ordinary, naturally occurring objects is the narrow extra ground of imagined objects, and beyond this ground, there is no other. Imagining is, in effect, the ground of last resort."

Why does that way of saying it seem so accurate? The ground of ordinary, naturally occurring objects now includes the Bomb, "Star

Wars," feelings of doom. Beyond that lies whatever imagination can construct. And beyond that there's nothing. Between ourselves and nothing, then, nothing intervenes except the small creations we ourselves put forth for use, among them images of the world going on in some post-nuclear way, or, harder and more urgent, images of ourselves surviving intact despite current forecasts. Elaine Scarry can speak of imagination as a *last resort* and Czeslaw Milosz speaks of poetry as a *last rampart*. Scarry came to part of her conclusion from studying Amnesty International's reports on torture. Milosz came to his after surviving the German and then the Russian savaging of Poland. Are we ready to receive such notions and take them at face value? If we profess the value of creative language, are we ready to grant that poetry can be important? And if so, can't we go on from our limited experience to say when poems are most *wanted*?

I think we can, and by calling on nothing that I have not myself felt or witnessed, I recommend (quietly, always amazed) this example—the intense degree to which men and women live by and sometimes die for words, sheer words upheld by nothing but the strength in saying, wording that seems weightless until uttered in the force of deep feeling. Robert Hass, for example, writes of himself as a young man desperate to engage his destiny, walking the streets repeating Lowell's lines:

> And blue-lung'd combers lumbered to the kill.
> The Lord survives the rainbow of His will.

Or in Warsaw during the Nazi occupation, as Milosz tells us, "an entire community is struck by misfortune" and "poetry becomes as essential as bread." Or this, Akhmatova's image of Mandelshtam as she saw him in Voronezh near the end:

> But in the room of the banished poet
> Fear and the Muse stand watch by turn,
> and the night comes on,
> which has no hope of dawn.

At times like these, perhaps because there's nothing else, poetry becomes the one thing needful. Or maybe it's because in moments that seem ultimate, nothing else is *good* enough, shared enough, of a precision equal to our joy or suffering. What's wanted to celebrate a marriage or a birth, what we ask to get us through pain, what we need by the side of the grave isn't solemn claims nor silence either, but rather the simple saying of right words. Literature, as Kenneth Burke puts it, is "equipment for living." I take Burke seriously when he talks this way, and his ideas about "symbolic action" and "disburdening" are worth remembering. When through language we confront the worst, or discover ourselves in ways that convince us we matter, we partake of available blessings. "As essential as bread" is what Milosz says, and I think yes, the gain in strength and nourishment is real.

Between the self and the terrible world comes poetry with its minute redemptions, its lyrical insurgencies, its willing suspension of disbelief in tomorrow. These ministrations, I take it, compose our chances. I don't mean that poems can have a say in nuclear matters, or that through poetry we may expect a general change of heart. Power listens to none but itself; and the myth of progress through enlightenment, in my view, died in 1914. What I mean to say is that right language can help us, as it always helps in hard moments, with our private struggles to keep whole, can be a stay against confusion, can start the healing fountains. And whatever helps us repossess our humanity, able again to take place and speak forth, frees us for work in the world. This is imagination's special task, as Wallace Stevens would say, because this contrary force, by pitching itself against external pressures, pushes back and makes space for liberty of spirit. Confronted by negation, imagination automatically starts asserting itself. We cannot *not* imagine, in which case the question becomes a matter of strategy. Shall imagination confront, or shall it evade? I think that it must confront—that poetry can no longer turn away from political torment, and for the following reason. Nuclear threat touches everyone everywhere, but unlike private kinds of death, collective wipeout has no mystery, no myth to temper its terror except the crudities of cold-war propaganda. The Bomb is a reality so pressing and so naked that it cannot be ignored. One day we *see* the enormity of it, and then also we see that between the self and the cold-war world there is no interceding champion, no worldly power on our side, but only, as Elaine Scarry puts it, imagination as last resort.

I've been speaking of imagination as the great good thing, but those who control our external fate, the handful of men in Washington and Moscow, are deep into war-games and nuclear scenarios, so it's clear that imaginative energies also serve destruction and are not always, by definition, on the side of care. This duality of function is summed up in a single hard remark by Octavio Paz: "Facing death the spirit is life, and facing the latter, death." Imagination, Paz is suggesting, pushes back *that* fiercely against the urgencies that threaten it. Politics, having always to face unruly life, in crisis ends up serving death. And if, finally, we wish to identify the kind of demonic imagination now on the loose in high places, it has been rendered with jolly grit by Thomas Pynchon in *Gravity's Rainbow,* a Zone, as he calls it, under the rule of rampant paranoia, automatic systems, and idolatry of global weapons.

Imagination can be dangerous, no doubt about that; and even to be firmly on the side of life is no guarantee. The problem with facing death in order to defend life is that death begins to cast its shadow everywhere. A sort of vertigo sets in, as if the hysteria of the world were infectious, which it is. Sometimes, in my own experience, the nuclear issue becomes so pressing—this is one of the Bomb's worst consequences, simply as threat—that it turns me from life, makes me blind to the needs of my neighbors. But living in the age of atrocity is no excuse for dismissing lesser claims because they are local or private. By way of correcting myself, I think of a woman I recently met, writing a book about sexual abuse as a child, about years of rape by Dad and brothers, the whole town knowing but crusted with silence, a Christian community deep in the heartland, letting some of its children be ruined. For this woman, the act of writing becomes a settlement of memory, a recovery of self by dreaming back through nightmare. These are very personal matters, but no, not altogether; for this awful story is precisely of the kind that, so long as it goes untold, sealed in silence, supports the larger cover-up of violences (for example, the way the superpowers keep the international arms market, on which small wars depend, stocked to overflowing). Power isn't only hierarchical, as Foucault reminded us. It accumulates in multitudes of small enactments, forcings of any sort, including those within the closed-up family. So yes, the world hangs by a thread, but no case counts less than another.

What makes our experience valuable to others is of course the way we word it. This is always a lonely task, and well might we wonder, inside the solitude of writing, where empowerment comes from. That all language assumes relation to power is visible in the fact that simply to verbalize, to use words at all, is instantly to be *with* or *against*. To the extent that this is so, writers choose their base, and not all powers are alike. Some pay off in dollars and nonsense, or in safety, more handsomely than others. The structure of political-institutional powers is vast, a kingdom with many mansions. Some writers, however, will seek a different potency, poets especially; but if so, what power can there be besides the big ones that run the warring world? What power was it, exactly, that tribal bards possessed when they went about their office of blessing and cursing, of praising and casting blame? Or the Irish rat-rhymers, what did they think they had that allowed them to clear infested places with chants? Wallace Stevens spoke of a "pressure within" that pushes back against the "pressures without." By external pressure he meant the political horror of World War Two, and by the inward kind he meant imagination, which he identified with "the sounds of words."

The self that cannot speak, as the man or woman being tortured cannot, or the self that cannot find words to make its own, has not the means to join or withdraw from the world. As poets and politicians know, *right words count that much*. And language is right when its fictive status makes no claims, serves no program or outside power, but only when, by taking place, it inspires us likewise to behold and take our place. The power base of poetry is poetry itself, the one kind of discourse that stands on its own, empowered by ceaseless imaginative motion and the vigor of its own interior music. Other discourse gains authority by indenturing itself to political orders of one stripe or another. Only poetical language, I'd like to repeat, is capable of authorizing its own generation.

This freedom is poetry's special strength, and, today more than ever, chief among its benefits. For now that we are cornered by the force of cold-war politics, we must consider in the plainest ways our access to reality, our confidence in fact, our capacity to cut through information overload. Here, from an article by John Newhouse (the *New Yorker*, July 22, 1985) is the problem we get when knowledge bends to power:

> Reality in the nuclear age tends to become what people whose voices carry say it is. Competent technicians are available to shore up any side of any argument. A given point of view may be vulnerable to ridicule but not to being disproved by facts; these are obscured by unknowns and abstractions arising from the nature, the role, the destructive potential, and the reliability of nuclear weapons.

Is that how it is? I think most certainly yes, and not with nuclear issues only, for how we respond to matters of ultimate import circumscribes our thinking in general. It's worth noting, furthermore, that what Newhouse says is written by a journalist. The experts disagree with each other, but they won't be discrediting themselves (and their institutions, and their careers) by stating the larger predicament. So there it is: when it comes to the hard questions, smart people with impeccable credentials can certify any side of any issue. Where does that leave the rest of us? Is sensible knowledge now beyond us? Does reality depend on power's endorsement? Will wars be fought, as Lyotard suggests, over information?

Truth too near to power is very like light enduring the gravity of large bodies—both, in their passage, get bent from their course. Our situation in the Nuclear Age isn't so different from Winston Smith's in *1984;* he agrees, finally, that reality is what O'Brien and the Inner Party say it is. The distinction between ourselves and Smith is small, but in one particular, at least, we have a tool, and therefore a weapon, not available in Orwell's nightmare world. We still have poetry and fiction, the language of concrete perception, and the office of art isn't located in a government bunker but in the obligation to behold and witness, praise, denounce. Just here, it seems to me, the importance of poetry has never been greater. As the age of information spills over us, as ships of state drift and list in the nuclear night, the old anchor holds. A solidly imagined story, a fiercely felt poem, still tells us where and who we are, discovers the world and us in it, gives us a sanity the "competent technicians" don't lay claim to.

Poetry won't change the nuclear order. But I want to stress that a poem can make something happen. It allows me to know what I fear, to understand (by standing under) the burden of my humanness. It also makes possible the essential decency of compassion, of suffering with— a symbolic action, to be sure, but one without which the spirit withers, the self shuts down.

Notes

Prolog

1. Kenneth Burke, "Literature As Equipment for Living," *The Philosophy of Literary Form* (Berkeley: University of California Press, 1973), pp. 293–304. First edition, 1941.
2. Czeslaw Milosz, "The Poor Poet," tr. by author, *Selected Poems* (New York: Seabury Press, 1973), p. 53.
3. *Ibid.*, "Elegy for N.N.," tr. Lawrence Davis, p. 96.
4. André Brink, *Writing in a State of Siege* (New York: Summit Books, 1983), p. 48.
5. Henry James, "Preface to Portrait of a Lady," *The Portrait of a Lady* (New York: Penguin Books, 1986).
6. Charles Simic, "Notes on Poetry and History," *The Uncertain Certainty* (Ann Arbor: University of Michigan Press, 1985), p. 124–125.
7. Edmund Spenser, *Spenser's Prose Works*, Variorum Edition, ed. Rudolf Gottfried (Baltimore: Johns Hopkins Press, 1949), p. 124.
8. Kenneth Burke, *Attitudes Toward History* (Boston: Beacon Press, 1959), p. 57. First edition, 1937.

I. Creon's Decree

1. James Joyce, *A Portrait of the Artist as a Young Man* (New York: Viking Press, 1982), p. 204.
2. Sophocles, *The Three Theban Plays*, tr. Robert Fagles (New York: Viking Press, 1982), p. 50.
3. Giambattista Vico, *The New Science*, tr. Thomas Goddard Bergin & Max Harold Fisch (Ithaca & London: Cornell University Press, 1975), p. 53.
4. *Ibid.*, p. 55.
5. G. W. F. Hegel, *The Phenomenology of Mind*, tr. J. B. Baillie (New

York: Harper & Row, 1967), p. 472. For Hegel's discussion of *Antigone*, see pages 466–482.

6. *Ibid.*, p. 472.
7. *Ibid.*, p. 472.
8. *Ibid.*, p. 470.
9. George Steiner, *Antigones* (New York: Oxford University Press, 1984), p. 11.
10. Erich Auerbach, *Mimesis: The Representation of Reality in Western Literature*, tr. Ralph Manheim (Princeton: Princeton University Press, 1974). p. 457.
11. *Ibid.*, p. 459.
12. Milan Kundera, "Conversation with Milan Kundera on the Art of The Novel," with Christian Salmon, *Salmagundi*, No. 73, Winter 1987, p. 123.
13. Martin Heidegger, "The Origin of the Work of Art," *Poetry, Language, Thought*, tr. Albert Hofstadter (New York: Harper & Row, 1975), pp. 48–49.
14. *Ibid.*, p. 49.
15. A more familiar description of "world" and "earth" is given by Jonathan Schell in *The Fate of the Earth* (New York: Knopf, 1982): "The destruction of human civilization, even without the biological destruction of the human species, may perhaps be called the end of the world, since it would be the end of that sum of cultural achievements and human relationships which constitutes what many people mean when they speak of 'the world.' The biological destruction of mankind would, of course, be the end of the world in a stricter sense. As for the destruction of all life on the planet, it would be not merely a human but a planetary end—the death of the earth. . . . We not only live on the earth but also are of the earth, and the thought of its death, or even of its mutilation, touches a deep chord in our nature" (p. 7). From a nuclear standpoint, "the world" is informed by, and responsive to, the nuclear cold-war order. The superpowers coerce a single world; and should a nuclear exchange occur, it would be the ultimate act of power on behalf of a world destroying itself in the moment when its apocalyptic logic is fulfilled.

II. The Press of the Real

1. Wallace Stevens, "Credences of Summer," *The Collected Poems* (New York: Vintage Books, 1982), p. 376.
2. Wallace Stevens, "The Noble Rider and the Sound of Words," *The Necessary Angel: Essays on Reality and the Imagination* (London: Faber

and Faber, 1951), pp. 3–36. All prose citations are from this essay in this edition.

3. C. P. Cavafy, "Dareios," *Collected Poems*, tr. Edmund Keely & Philip Sherrard, ed. George Savidis (London: Chatto & Windus, 1978), pp. 78–79.

4. John Pilling, *Fifty Modern European Poets* (London & Sydney: Pan Books, 1982), p. 57.

5. Stevens, "An Ordinary Evening in New Haven," *Collected Poems*, p. 473.

III. Yeats and the Rat-Rhymers

1. Edmund Spenser, "A vewe of the present state of Irelande," *Spenser's Prose Works*, Variorum Edition, ed. Rudolf Gottfried (Baltimore: Johns Hopkins Press, 1949), p. 124.

2. Yeats, "Easter 1916."

3. T. S. Eliot, "Yeats," *On Poetry and Poets* (New York: Farrar, Straus & Company, 1961), p. 308.

4. Yeats, *The Oxford Book of Modern Verse* (New York: Oxford University Press, 1937), p. xxxiv.

5. A. Norman Jeffares, *A Commentary on the Collected Poems of W. B. Yeats* (Stanford: Stanford University Press, 1968), p. 399.

6. Ulick O'Connor, *A Terrible Beauty Is Born* (London: Granada Publishing Limited, 1981), p. 17.

7. Yeats, "Modern Ireland: An Address to American Audiences, 1932–33," *The Massachusetts Review* (Winter, 1964), p. 258.

8. On the primacy of voice in Yeats's poetic, see Yeats, "Literature and the Living Voice," *Explorations* (New York: Collier Books, 1962); and Walter J. Ong, *Orality and Literacy* (New York: Methuen & Co., 1982), pp. 44–70.

9. Yeats, *The Letters of W. B. Yeats*, ed. Allan Wade (London: Rupert Hart-Davis, 1954), p. 811–812.

10. Yeats, *Letters*, p. 851.

11. Yeats, *Letters*, p. 691.

12. T. F. Thiselton Dyer, *Folk-lore of Shakespeare* (New York: Harper & Brothers, 1884), p. 197.

13. Robert C. Elliott, *The Power of Satire* (Princeton, Princeton University Press, 1960), p. 36.

14. Osborn Bergin, *Irish Bardic Poetry*, ed. David Greene & Fergus Kelly (Dublin, The Dublin Institute for Advanced Studies, 1970), p. 4.

15. Daniel Corkery, *The Hidden Ireland* (London: Gill and Macmillan, 1967), p. 96.

16. Oliver Goldsmith, *Collected Works*, Volume III, ed. Arthur Friedman (Oxford: The Clarendon Press, 1966), p. 118.

17. T. R. Henn, *Poets and Dreamers: Studies and Translations From the Irish By Lady Gregory* (New York: Oxford University Press, 1974), p. 5.

18. Fred Norris Robinson, "Satirists and Enchanters in Early Irish Literature," *Studies in the History of Religions*, ed. David Gordon Lyon and George Foot Moore (New York: Macmillan, 1912), pp. 98–99.

19. Robinson, *Ibid.*, pp. 105–106.

20. Douglas Hyde, *A Literary History of Ireland* (London & Leipzig: T. Fisher Unwin, 1910), pp. 518–519.

21. Fynes Moryson, "An Itinerary," *Elizabethan Ireland*, ed. James P. Myers, Jr. (Hamden: Archon Books, 1983), pp. 199–202.

22. Elliott, *The Power of Satire*, pp. 3–48, 285–292.

23. James P. Myers, *Elizabethan Ireland*, Davies p. 179, Campion, p. 24.

24. Edmund Spenser, *Spenser's Prose Works*, p. 125.

25. Yeats, *The Collected Letters of W. B. Yeats*, Volume I, ed. John Kelly and Eric Domville (Oxford: The Clarendon Press, 1986), p. 133.

26. Yeats, *Uncollected Prose of W. B. Yeats*, Volume I, ed. John P. Frayne (New York: Columbia University Press, 1970), pp. 163–164.

27. Yeats, *Memoirs*, ed. Denis Donoghue (New York: Macmillan Publishing Company, 1972), p. 59.

28. Douglas Hyde, "Bards (Irish)," *Encyclopaedia of Religion and Ethics*, Volume II, ed. James Hastings (New York: Charles Scribner's Sons, 1913), pp. 414–416.

29. Yeats, *Memoirs*, p. 54.

30. Yeats, *The Autobiography of W. B. Yeats* (New York, Macmillan Company, 1964), p. 266.

31. Yeats, *Mythologies* (New York: Collier Books, 1969), pp. 213–261.

32. David Lynch, *Yeats: The Poetics of the Self* (Chicago: University of Chicago Press, 1979), pp. 17–28.

33. Elizabeth Cullingford, *Yeats, Ireland and Fascism* (New York: New York University Press, 1981), p. 95.

34. Cullingford, *Ibid.*, p. 100.

35. Cullingford, *Ibid.*, p. 94.

36. Yeats, *Letters*, p. 613.

37. Yeats, *Uncollected Prose*, Volume II, ed. John P. Frayne and Colton Johnson (New York: Columbia University Press, 1975), p. 196.

38. Yeats, *Ibid.*, 319.

39. Edmund Burke, *A Philosophical Enquiry into the Origin of our Ideas of the Sublime and the Beautiful*, ed. James T. Boulton (Notre Dame: University of Notre Dame Press, 1968), p. 64.

40. Immanuel Kant, *The Critique of Judgment*, tr. James Creed Meredith (Oxford: The Clarendon Press, 1969), p. 111.
41. Kant, *Ibid.*, p. 111.

IV. Yeats and *Hysterica Passio*

1. Yeats, *The Letters of W. B. Yeats*, ed. Allan Wade (London: Rupert Hart-Davis, 1954), p. 690.
2. Yeats, *Essays and Introductions* (New York: Macmillan, 1961), pp. 249–250.
3. Yeats, *Ibid.*, p. 519.
4. Yeats, *The Oxford Book of Modern Verse* (New York: Oxford University Press, 1937), p. xxxiv.
5. Conor Cruise O'Brien, "Passion and Cunning: The Politics of W. B. Yeats," *In Excited Reverie*, ed. A. N. Jeffares, (New York: Macmillan, 1965).
6. Yeats, *The Autobiography of William Butler Yeats* (New York: Macmillan, 1953), p. 118.
7. Yeats, *Essays and Introductions*, p. 526.
8. O'Brien, "Passion and Cunning."
9. Richard Ellmann, *Yeats: The Man and the Masks*, rev. ed. (New York: Norton, 1978).
10. Elizabeth Cullingford, *Yeats, Ireland and Fascism* (New York: New York University Press, 1981), p. 79.
11. Yeats, *Memoirs*, ed. Denis Donoghue (New York: Macmillan, 1972), p. 157.
12. Yeats, *Ibid.*, p. 157.
13. Yeats, *Letters on Poetry from W. B. Yeats to Dorothy Wellesley* (London: Oxford University Press, 1964), p. 86.
14. Yeats, *Letters*, p. 742.
15. A. Norman Jeffares, *A Commentary on the Collected Poems of W. B. Yeats* (Stanford: Stanford University Press, 1968), p. 86.
16. Yeats, *The Collected Poems* (New York: Macmillan, 1956), p. 524.
17. Gaston Bachelard, *The Poetics of Reverie*, tr. Daniel Russell (Boston: Beacon Press, 1971), p. 193.
18. Yeats, *Letters*, p. 668.
19. Yeats, *Ibid.*, p. 680.
20. Yeats, *The Collected Poems*, p. 455.
21. Yeats, *A Vision* (London: Macmillan, 1981), p. 268.
22. Respectively: John Unterecker, *A Reader's Guide to W. B. Yeats* (New York: Farrar, Straus & Giroux, 1977), p. 289; Joseph Hone, *W. B.*

Yeats (New York: Macmillan, 1943), p. 502; Curtis Bradford, "Yeats's *Last Poems* Again," *The Dolman Press Yeats Centenary Papers MCMLXV*, ed. Liam Miller (Dublin: The Dolman Press, 1968), p. 275.

23. Bradford, *op. cit.*; Richard J. Finneran, *The Poems of W. B. Yeats, A New Edition* (New York: Macmillan, 1983).
24. Yeats, *Letters on Poetry*, pp. 179–181.
25. Yeats, *Ibid.*, p. 180.

V. Bertolt Brecht, Germany

1. Walter Benjamin, "Conversations with Brecht," *Reflections*, tr. Edmund Jephcott (New York: Harcourt Brace Jovanovich, 1978), p. 219.
2. Bertolt Brecht, *Poems 1913–1956*, ed. John Willett and Ralph Manheim (New York & London: Methuen, 1976), p. 465.
3. Max Frisch, *Sketchbook 1946–1949*, tr. Geoffrey Skelton (New York & London: Harcourt Brace Jovanovich, 1977), p. 151.
4. Brecht, *Poems 1913–1956*, p. 460.
5. *Ibid.*, p. 460.
6. *Ibid.*, p. 463.
7. *Ibid.*, p. 458.
8. Hannah Arendt, "Bertolt Brecht," *Men in Dark Times* (New York: Harcourt, Brace & World, Inc., 1968), p. 225–226.
9. Brecht, *Poems 1913–1956*, p. 458.
10. Klaus Volker, *Brecht: A Biography*, tr. John Nowell (New York: Seabury Press, 1978), p. 129.
11. Bertolt Brecht, *Gedichte* (Frankfurt am Main: Surkamp Verlag, 1960), Vol. 4, p. 19.
12. Klaus Volker, *Brecht*, pp. 333–334.
13. *Ibid.*, p. 333.
14. *Ibid.*, p. 338.
15. Walter Benjamin, *Reflections*, p. 215.
16. Max Frisch, *Sketchbook 1946–49*, p. 152.

VI. Breyten Breytenbach, South Africa

1. Breyten Breytenbach, *The True Confessions of an Albino Terrorist* (New York: Farrar Straus & Giroux, 1985), p. 73.
2. *Ibid.*, p. 359.
3. *Ibid.*, p. 354.
4. *Ibid.*, p. 280.
5. *Ibid.*, p. 280.

6. André Brink, *Writing in a State of Siege* (New York: Summit Books, 1983), p. 86.
7. Donald Woods, "A South African Poet on His Imprisonment," *The New York Times Book Review*, May 1, 1983.
8. Breytenbach, *Confessions*, p. 354.
9. *Ibid.*, p. 31.
10. Breytenbach, *Confessions*, p. 31.
11. Luis Buñuel, *My Last Sigh*, tr. Abigail Israel (New York: Knopf, 1984), p. 107.
12. Breytenbach, *A Season in Paradise*, tr. Rike Vaughan (New York: Persea Books, 1980), p. 144.
13. *Ibid.*, p. 145.
14. *Ibid.*, p. 142.
15. *Ibid.*, p. 152.
16. Breytenbach, *Confessions*, p. 354.
17. Brink, *Writing in a State of Siege*, p. 106.
18. Hein Willemse, "The Black Afrikaans Writer: A Continuing Dichotomy," *Triquarterly 69*, Spring/Summer 1987, p. 238.

VII. Thomas McGrath, North America West

1. "McGrath on McGrath," *North Dakota Quarterly*, Fall 1982 (Volume 50, Number 4), p. 22. McGrath attributes these remarks to William Eastlake, "from Arizona."
2. Christopher Caudwell, *Illusion and Reality: A Study of the Sources of Poetry* (London: Lawrence & Wishart, 1977), p. 38. First published 1937.
3. McGrath, *Letter to an Imaginary Friend*, Parts I & II (Chicago: The Swallow Press, 1970); Parts Three & Four (Port Townsend: Copper Canyon Press, 1985). Unless otherwise noted, all citations are from Parts I & II.
4. McGrath, *North Dakota Quarterly*, p. 23.
5. McGrath, *Echoes Inside the Labyrinth*, (New York & Chicago: Thunder's Mouth Press, 1983), p. 33
6. For a history of the populist movement in relation to our political culture more generally, see Lawrence Goodwyn, *Democratic Promise: The Populist Moment in America*. (New York: Oxford University Press, 1976).
7. Mark Vinz, "Poetry and Place: An Interview with Thomas McGrath" (July 25, 1972), *Voyages to the Inland Sea, 3*, ed. John Judson (Center for Contemporary Poetry, Murphy Library, University of Wisconsin–LaCrosse, LaCrosse, 1973), pp. 39, 41.

8. McGrath, "Trinc: Praises II," in *Echoes*, p. 14.
9. See especially Sacvan Bercovitch, *The American Jeremiad* (Madison: The University of Wisconsin Press, 1978).
10. McGrath, *The Movie at the End of the World: Collected Poems* (Chicago: The Swallow Press, 1972), p. 47.
11. McGrath, *Longshot O'Leary's Garland of Practical Poesie* (New York: International Publishers, 1949), p. 14.
12. McGrath, "Statement to the House Committee on Un-American Activities," *North Dakota Quarterly*, p. 9.
13. Rory Holscher, "Receiving Thomas McGrath's *Letter*," *North Dakota Quarterly*, p. 116.
14. "McGrath on McGrath," *North Dakota Quarterly*, p. 19.
15. "McGrath on McGrath," *North Dakota Quarterly*, p. 25.
16. E. P. Thompson, "Homage to Thomas McGrath," *The Heavy Dancers* (London: Merlin Press, 1985), p. 324. Reprinted in *Triquarterly*, No. 70 (Fall 1987), p. 106.
17. William M. Arkin & Richard M. Fieldhouse, *Nuclear Battlefields: Global Links in the Arms Race* (Cambridge, Mass.: Ballinger Publishing Company, 1985), p. 203. The scale of comparison is global.
18. Caudwell, *Illusion and Reality*, p. 81.
19. Mikhail Bakhtin, *Rabelais and His World*, tr. by Helene Iswolsky (Bloomington: Indiana University Press, 1984). This book was written in the late 1930's, but not published in the Soviet Union until 1965. First published in English 1968.
20. Mark Vinz, *Voyages to the Inland Sea*, p. 47.
21. Bakhtin, *Ibid.*, p. 19.
22. McGrath, *Passages Toward the Dark* (Port Townsend: Copper Canyon Press, 1982), p. 94.
23. Caudwell, *Illusion and Reality*, p. 34.
24. McGrath, *Passages*, p. 93.
25. McGrath, *Passages*, p 22.

VIII. Adrienne Rich, North America East

1. Adrienne Rich, *On Lies, Secrets, and Silence: Selected Prose 1966–1978* (New York: W. W. Norton, 1979), p. 108.
2. Alicia Ostriker, *Writing Like a Woman* (Ann Arbor: University of Michigan Press, 1983), p. 1.
3. Adrienne Rich, *Of Woman Born* (New York: W. W. Norton, 1986), p. 74.
4. *Ibid.*, p. 55.

5. Adrienne Rich, *Your Native Land, Your Life* (New York: W. W. Norton, 1986), p. 98.

6. Adrienne Rich, "When We Dead Awaken: Writing as Re-Vision," *On Lies, Secrets, and Silence*, pp. 37, 49. The last sentence does not occur in this edition, but is retained in Gelpi & Gelpi, p. 98, cited below.

7. Barbara Charlesworth Gelpi & Albert Gelpi, *Adrienne Rich's Poetry*, Norton Critical Edition (New York: W. W. Norton, 1975), p. 111.

8. Rich, *On Lies, Secrets, and Silence*, pp. 161–162.

9. Gelpi & Gelpi, *Adrienne Rich's Poetry*, p. 30.

10. Rich, *On Lies, Secrets, and Silence*, p. 175.

11. *Ibid.*, pp. 44–45.

12. Rich, *Of Woman Born*, pp. 128, 149.

13. Rich, *On Lies, Secrets, and Silence*, p. 43.

14. *Ibid.*, p. 45.

15. *Ibid.*, p. 108.

16. *Ibid.*, p. 35.

17. *Ibid.*, p. 34, 43.

18. *Ibid.*, p. 44.

19. Rich, *Of Woman Born*, p. 40.

20. *Ibid.*, p. 40.

21. Gelpi & Gelpi, *Adrienne Rich's Poetry*, p. 104.

22. *Ibid.*, p. 119.

23. Rich, *On Lies, Secrets, and Silence*, p. 44.

24. Gelpi & Gelpi, *Adrienne Rich's Poetry*, pp. 120–121.

25. Rich, "Transcendental Etude," *The Dream of a Common Language* (New York: W. W. Norton, 1978), p. 76.

26. Rich, *Of Woman Born*, pp. 97–98.

27. Gelpi & Gelpi, *Adrienne Rich's Poetry*, p. 114.

28. *Ibid.*, p. 115.

29. Rich, *On Lies, Secrets, and Silence*, p. 251.

30. Ludwig Wittgenstein, *Philosophical Investigations*, tr. G. E. M. Anscombe (New York: The Macmillan Company, 1969), pp. 8^e, 11^e, 174^e.

31. Adrienne Rich, *Blood, Bread, and Poetry: Selected Prose 1979–1985* (New York: W. W. Norton, 1986), p. 180.

Select Bibliography

Brecht, Bertolt. *Bertolt Brecht: Poems 1913–1956*, eds. John Willet and Ralph Manheim (New York & London: Methuen, 1976).

Breytenbach, Breyten. *And Death White as Words*, ed. A. J. Coetzee (London: Rex Collings Ltd., 1978).

——————. *In Africa Even the Flies Are Happy: Selected Poems and Prose, 1964–1977.* (London: John Calder Ltd., 1978).

——————. *A Season in Paradise*, trans. Rike Vaughan (New York: Persea Books, Inc., 1980).

——————. *The True Confessions of an Albino Terrorist* (New York: Farrar Straus & Giroux, 1985).

McGrath, Thomas. *Echoes Inside the Labyrinth* (New York: Thunder's Mouth Press, 1983).

——————. *Letter to an Imaginary Friend, Parts 1 & 2* (Chicago: The Swallow Press, 1970).

——————. *Letter to an Imaginary Friend, Parts 3 & 4* (Port Townsend, WA: Copper Canyon Press, 1985).

——————. *Longshot O'Leary's Garland of Practical Poesie* (New York: International Publishers, 1949).

——————. *The Movie at the End of the World: Collected Poems* (Chicago: The Swallow Press, 1972).

——————————— . *Selected Poems 1938–1988*, ed. Sam Hamill (Port Townsend, WA: Copper Canyon Press, 1988).

Rich, Adrienne. *Adrienne Rich's Poetry*, eds. Barbara Gelpi and Albert Gelpi (New York: W. W. Norton & Company, 1975).

——————————— . *Blood, Bread and Poetry: Selected Prose 1979–1985* (New York: W. W. Norton & Company, 1986).

——————————— . *Diving into the Wreck: Poems 1971–1972* (New York: W. W. Norton & Company, 1973).

——————————— . *The Dream of a Common Language: Poems 1974–1977* (New York: W. W. Norton & Company, 1978).

——————————— . *Of Woman Born* (New York: W. W. Norton & Company, 1986).

——————————— . *On Lies, Secrets, and Silence: Selected Prose 1966–1978* (New York: W. W. Norton & Company, 1979).

——————————— . *Your Native Land, Your Life: Poems* (New York: W. W. Norton & Company, 1986).

Yeats, William Butler. *The Autobiography of William Butler Yeats* (New York: Macmillan, 1964).

——————————— . *The Letters of W. B. Yeats*, ed. Allan Wade (London: Rupert Hart-Davis, 1954).

——————————— . *The Collected Poems* (New York: Macmillan, 1956).

——————————— . *Memoirs*, ed. Denis Donoghue (New York: Macmillan, 1972).

——————————— . *A Vision* (New York: Macmillan, 1961).

Acknowledgments

Chapters I and II of *Praises & Dispraises* first appeared in *The American Poetry Review*, July-August 1988; Chapter VII in *TriQuarterly 70*; and "Toward A Changed Poetics" as "Equipment for Living" in *TriQuarterly 65*.

Grateful acknowledgment is made for permission to reprint the following copyrighted works:

Excerpt from "From the Canton of Expectation" from *The Haw Lantern* by Seamus Heaney. Copyright © 1987 by Seamus Heaney. Reprinted by permission of Farrar, Straus & Giroux, Inc.

Excerpts from "The Poor Poet" and "Elegy for N. N." from *The Collected Poems 1931–1987* by Czeslaw Milosz. Copyright © 1988 by Czeslaw Milosz Royalties Inc. Published by The Ecco Press in 1988. Reprinted by permission.

Excerpt from *A Portrait of the Artist as a Young Man* by James Joyce. Copyright 1916 by B.W. Huebsch. Copyright renewed 1944 by Nora Joyce. Copyright © 1964 by the Estate of James Joyce. By permission of Viking Penguin Inc. and The Society of Authors as the literary representative of the Estate of James Joyce.

Excerpts from "Credences of Summer" and "An Ordinary Evening in New Haven" from *The Collected Poems of Wallace Stevens*. Copyright 1947, 1950 by Wallace Stevens. By permission of Alfred A. Knopf, Inc.

"Dareios" from *Collected Poems* by C.P. Cavafy. Copyright © 1978 by C.P. Cavafy. Published by Chatto & Windus. Used by permission.

Selections from *The Poems: A New Edition* by W.B. Yeats, edited by Richard J. Finneran. Copyright 1916, 1919, 1924, 1928, 1933, 1934 by Macmillan Publishing Company, renewed 1944, 1947, 1952, 1956, 1961, 1962 by Bertha Georgie Yeats. Copyright 1940 by Georgie Yeats, renewed 1968 by Bertha Georgie Yeats, Michael Butler Yeats and Anne Yeats. Reprinted with permission of Macmillan Publishing Company. Published in Great Britain as *The Collected Poems of W.B. Yeats*. By permission of A.P. Watt Ltd. on behalf of Michael B. Yeats and Macmillan London Ltd.

Excerpt from "Conversations with Brecht" from *Reflections* by Walter Benjamin. By permission of Harcourt Brace Jovanovich, Inc.

Selections from *Bertolt Brecht: Poems 1913–1956*, edited by John Willett and Ralph Manheim. By permission of the publisher Routledge, Chapman and Hall by arrangement with Suhrkamp Verlag and Methuen London. All rights reserved.

Excerpts from "The Struggle for the TAAL" and other material from *The True Confessions of an Albino Terrorist* by Breyten Breytenbach. Copyright © 1983 by Breyten Breytenbach. Reprinted by permission of Farrar, Straus & Giroux, Inc.

Selections from *And Death White as Words: An Anthology of the Poetry of Breyten Breytenbach*, selected, edited and introduced by A.J. Coetzee. Published by Rex Collings Ltd., 1978.

Selections from *In Africa Even the Flies are Happy* by Breyten Breytenbach, translated by Denis Hirson. Published by John Calder (Publishers) Ltd., London and Riverrun Press Inc., New York. Copyright © 1976, 1977 by Yolande Breytenbach and Meulenhoff Nederland, Amsterdam. English translation copyright © 1978 by John Calder (Publishers) Limited, London.

Excerpt from *Illusion and Reality: A Study of the Sources of Poetry* by Christopher Caudwell. By permission of Lawrence & Wishart Ltd.

Excerpts from "Blues for Warren" from *The Movie at the End of the World: Collected Poems* and excerpts from *Letter to an Imaginary Friend, Parts I and II* by Thomas McGrath, Swallow Press, 1970. Reprinted with the permission of Ohio University Press/Swallow Press.

Excerpts from "He's a Real Gone Guy" from *Longshot O'Leary's Garland of Practical Poesie* by Thomas McGrath. By permission of the author.

Excerpt from "The End of the World" from *Passages Toward the Dark* by Thomas McGrath. By permission of Copper Canyon Press.

Selections from *Snapshots of a Daughter-in-Law*; *Diving into the Wreck: Poems 1971–1972*; *The Dream of a Common Language: Poems 1974–1977*; *On Lies, Secrets and Silences: Selected Prose 1966–1978*; *Of Woman Born: Motherhood as Experience and Institution*; and *Blood, Bread and Poetry: Selected Prose 1979–1985* by Adrienne Rich. Reprinted by permission of the author and W. W. Norton and Company.

FOR THE BEST IN PAPERBACKS, LOOK FOR THE

In every corner of the world, on every subject under the sun, Penguin represents quality and variety—the very best in publishing today.

For complete information about books available from Penguin—including Pelicans, Puffins, Peregrines, and Penguin Classics—and how to order them, write to us at the appropriate address below. Please note that for copyright reasons the selection of books varies from country to country.

In the United Kingdom: For a complete list of books available from Penguin in the U.K., please write to *Dept E.P., Penguin Books Ltd, Harmondsworth, Middlesex, UB7 0DA*.

In the United States: For a complete list of books available from Penguin in the U.S., please write to *Dept BA, Penguin, Box 120, Bergenfield, New Jersey 07621-0120*.

In Canada: For a complete list of books available from Penguin in Canada, please write to *Penguin Books Ltd, 2801 John Street, Markham, Ontario L3R 1B4*.

In Australia: For a complete list of books available from Penguin in Australia, please write to the *Marketing Department, Penguin Books Ltd, P.O. Box 257, Ringwood, Victoria 3134*.

In New Zealand: For a complete list of books available from Penguin in New Zealand, please write to the *Marketing Department, Penguin Books (NZ) Ltd, Private Bag, Takapuna, Auckland 9*.

In India: For a complete list of books available from Penguin, please write to *Penguin Overseas Ltd, 706 Eros Apartments, 56 Nehru Place, New Delhi, 110019*.

In Holland: For a complete list of books available from Penguin in Holland, please write to *Penguin Books Nederland B.V., Postbus 195, NL-1380AD Weesp, Netherlands*.

In Germany: For a complete list of books available from Penguin, please write to *Penguin Books Ltd, Friedrichstrasse 10-12, D-6000 Frankfurt Main I, Federal Republic of Germany*.

In Spain: For a complete list of books available from Penguin in Spain, please write to *Longman, Penguin España, Calle San Nicolas 15, E-28013 Madrid, Spain*.

In Japan: For a complete list of books available from Penguin in Japan, please write to *Longman Penguin Japan Co Ltd, Yamaguchi Building, 2-12-9 Kanda Jimbocho, Chiyoda-Ku, Tokyo 101, Japan*.

FOR THE BEST IN LITERARY CRITICISM, LOOK FOR THE

FOR THE BEST POETRY, LOOK FOR THE

FOR THE BEST LITERATURE, LOOK FOR THE

☐ THE BOOK AND THE BROTHERHOOD
Iris Murdoch

Many years ago Gerard Hernshaw and his friends banded together to finance a political and philosophical book by a monomaniacal Marxist genius. Now opinions have changed, and support for the book comes at the price of moral indignation; the resulting disagreements lead to passion, hatred, a duel, murder, and a suicide pact.   *602 pages   ISBN: 0-14-010470-4*   **$8.95**

☐ GRAVITY'S RAINBOW
Thomas Pynchon

Thomas Pynchon's classic antihero is Tyrone Slothrop, an American lieutenant in London whose body anticipates German rocket launchings. Surely one of the most important works of fiction produced in the twentieth century, *Gravity's Rainbow* is a complex and awesome novel in the great tradition of James Joyce's *Ulysses*.   *768 pages   ISBN: 0-14-010661-8*   **$10.95**

☐ FIFTH BUSINESS
Robertson Davies

The first novel in the celebrated "Deptford Trilogy," which also includes *The Manticore* and *World of Wonders*, *Fifth Business* stands alone as the story of a rational man who discovers that the marvelous is only another aspect of the real.   *266 pages   ISBN: 0-14-004387-X*   **$4.95**

☐ WHITE NOISE
Don DeLillo

Jack Gladney, a professor of Hitler Studies in Middle America, and his fourth wife, Babette, navigate the usual rocky passages of family life in the television age. Then, their lives are threatened by an "airborne toxic event"—a more urgent and menacing version of the "white noise" of transmissions that typically engulfs them.   *326 pages   ISBN: 0-14-007702-2*   **$7.95**

FOR THE BEST LITERATURE, LOOK FOR THE

☐ **A SPORT OF NATURE**
Nadine Gordimer

Hillela, Nadine Gordimer's "sport of nature," is seductive and intuitively gifted at life. Casting herself adrift from her family at seventeen, she lives among political exiles on an East African beach, marries a black revolutionary, and ultimately plays a heroic role in the overthrow of apartheid.

354 pages   ISBN: 0-14-008470-3   **$7.95**

☐ **THE COUNTERLIFE**
Philip Roth

By far Philip Roth's most radical work of fiction, *The Counterlife* is a book of conflicting perspectives and points of view about people living out dreams of renewal and escape. Illuminating these lives is the skeptical, enveloping intelligence of the novelist Nathan Zuckerman, who calculates the price and examines the results of his characters' struggles for a change of personal fortune.

372 pages   ISBN: 0-14-009769-4   **$4.95**

☐ **THE MONKEY'S WRENCH**
Primo Levi

Through the mesmerizing tales told by two characters—one, a construction worker/philosopher who has built towers and bridges in India and Alaska; the other, a writer/chemist, rigger of words and molecules—Primo Levi celebrates the joys of work and the art of storytelling.

174 pages   ISBN: 0-14-010357-0   **$6.95**

☐ **IRONWEED**
William Kennedy

"Riding up the winding road of Saint Agnes Cemetery in the back of the rattling old truck, Francis Phelan became aware that the dead, even more than the living, settled down in neighborhoods." So begins William Kennedy's Pulitzer-Prize winning novel about an ex-ballplayer, part-time gravedigger, and full-time drunk, whose return to the haunts of his youth arouses the ghosts of his past and present.

228 pages   ISBN: 0-14-007020-6   **$6.95**

☐ **THE COMEDIANS**
Graham Greene

Set in Haiti under Duvalier's dictatorship, *The Comedians* is a story about the committed and the uncommitted. Actors with no control over their destiny, they play their parts in the foreground; experience love affairs rather than love; have enthusiasms but not faith; and if they die, they die like Mr. Jones, by accident.

288 pages   ISBN: 0-14-002766-1   **$4.95**